D0882312

Westmoreland

Also by Samuel Zaffiri:

HAMBURGER HILL

WESTMORELAND

A BIOGRAPHY OF

General William C. Westmoreland

Samuel Zaffiri

William Morrow and Company, Inc. • New York

It is the policy of William Morrow and Company, Inc., and its imprints and affiliates, recognizing the importance of preserving what has been written, to print the books we publish on acid-free paper, and we exert our best efforts to that end.

Library of Congress Cataloging-in-Publication Data
Zaffiri, Samuel, 1945–
   Westmoreland : a biography of General William C. Westmoreland / by Samuel Zaffiri.
      p.   cm.
   ISBN 0-688-11179-3
   1. Westmoreland, William C. (William Childs), 1914–   .
2. Generals—United States—Biography.   3. United States.   Army—
Biography.   I. Title.
E840.5.W4Z34   1994
959.70434'092—dc20
[B]   93-23305
                                                                       CIP

Printed in the United States of America

First Edition

1   2   3   4   5   6   7   8   9   10

BOOK DESIGN BY LINEY LI

For my father

Contents

Westmoreland

PROLOGUE: April 28, 1967

At exactly 12:31 P.M., April 28, 1967, the doorkeeper of the House of Representatives, William "Fishbait" Miller, swept down the aisle and announced in his sharp, resonant voice, *"Mr. Speaker, General William C. Westmoreland."* At the words, the entire audience leaped to its feet and began a thunderous applause that would continue for the next three minutes. Flanked by seventeen prominent members of the House and Senate, the general walked swiftly up the aisle, mounted the podium, and awaited their attention.

As always, he was impressive-looking, the paragon of the professional soldier—tall, square-jawed, thick-browed, his hair slashed with gray at the side, his chest forward and his shoulders squared. Just as impressive were the six rows of ribbons, commemorating service in three wars, that bedecked his chest. He had worn them all for the occasion—the Presidential Unit Citation his battalion had earned for making a 789-mile forced march through the snow-covered Atlas Mountains in order to stop General Rommel's breakthrough at the Kasserine Pass; the Legion of Merit he had been awarded for risking his life to personally reconnoiter enemy positions in both North Africa and Sicily; the Air Medal he had been presented for calling in the counterbattery fire against a murderous German railway gun in Tunisia; the Bronze Star General Louis A. Craig had pinned on him in Germany for first organizing the expansion of the Remagen Bridgehead and then directing the defense of it against furious German counterattacks; and a half dozen others.

As the applause went on, he grabbed the sides of the podium and looked out over the sea of faces, just a hint of a smile etched in his cheeks. This, the first speech by a battlefield commander in the midst of a war, was a historic first. This fact was not lost on him, or on those awaiting his speech. There had been other eminent military men who had preceded him up this aisle, ten others in fact, and that fact was not lost on him either. Was he thinking of them now? How could he not. Who could forget the iron-willed John J. "Black Jack" Pershing stepping up here in September of 1918 to be honored for leading the American Expeditionary Force to victory in Europe; or the Everyman Dwight Eisenhower nearly twenty-eight years later standing in this very spot to thank Congress and the American people for providing him with the resources to crush Hitler's Nazi menace, then nearly breaking into tears as he praised the courage and fighting ability of the average GI; or the imperial Douglas MacArthur ending his career here in April of 1951 with his haunting refrain, "old soldiers never die . . ."

But they, unlike Westmoreland, had come here as victors, come at the end of long, impressive careers to receive the accolades of a nation and Congress united and grateful. He stood here now as a commander who had not yet fought his last battle, coming to deliver a report on a war that had left his country more divided than it had been since the darkest days of the Civil War.

When the hall finally quieted, Speaker of the House John McCormack announced: "Members of Congress, I have the great pleasure and high privilege of presenting to you General William C. Westmoreland, United States Army, Commander of the United States Military Assistance Command, Vietnam."

When applause broke out yet again, it was punctuated with shouts and hurrahs. During it, Westmoreland turned and nodded to McCormack, then to Vice President Hubert Humphrey standing to the Speaker's left. A minute or so later, he finally got a chance to speak. His words, as one commentator would say later, "were strong, but not strident, emphatic without becoming emotional."

"I stand in the shadow of the military men who came before me," he began, "but none of them can have had more pride than is mine representing the gallant fighting men in Vietnam today . . ." Before he could finish his sentence, Congress broke in again and applauded him, as they would fifteen more times during his twenty-five-minute speech.

His message to them was a simple one, his thesis pure Westmoreland: The South Vietnamese were a small, valiant people fighting for survival against a totalitarian force "organized, directed, and supported from without . . ." He began by disputing the contention held by critics of the war that the conflict was simply an "internal insurrection." To the contrary, he told them, in his three years as commander in Vietnam, he had concluded that North Vietnam was the sole source of the conflict. Rather than being a civil war, the Vietnam conflict instead represented an invasion of one sovereign country by another.

To support this contention, he asked them to simply look at the facts. And the facts showed conclusively, he pointed out, that for the last two years North Vietnam had been infiltrating large numbers of troops into the South. They had infiltrated so many troops, in fact, that North Vietnamese units made up more than half the Communist forces there. He assured them, however, that his own forces had blunted the North Vietnamese attempt to take over South Vietnam, and in the process had destroyed numerous "main force units." This they were continuing to do with spoiling attacks and swift, deadly, and overwhelming applications of firepower.

But, unfortunately, he also told them, the North Vietnamese main force battalions were not the only threat to South Vietnam. Just as deadly were the Vietcong and their secret war of terror against innocent men, women, and children. And by terror, he specified "murder, mutilation, abduction, and deliberate shelling" of noncombatant villages. To bolster his point further, he read a litany of all such terrorist acts committed in just the preceding week, then wondered out loud why the media continued to report in grim detail all the civilian casualties resulting from our bombing of North Vietnam, but ignored the "brutality" the Communists committed against equally innocent civilians in South Vietnam.

He left the question dangling, left it for them to decide for themselves. But at the same time he assured them that he and his men were not about to be deterred by anything the Communists did. While the enemy was still a strong, formidable force, "and far from quitting,

there are signs that his morale and his military structure are deteriorating. The rate of decline will be in proportion to the pressure
directed against him."

He meant these last words as a challenge to them. He did not
mean them as the proverbial light at the end of the tunnel that his
critics would later claim, but merely as a simple statement of fact:
The length of the war would depend on their commitment to it.

It would also depend, he further emphasized, on the enemy's
perception of that commitment. Evaluating the enemy's long-term
strategy, he had concluded that "he believes our Achilles' heel is our
resolve. Your continued support is vital to the success of our mission."

These last words brought a roar of applause. A few in the chamber,
thinking the speech was over, leaped to their feet. Determined to
finish, Westmoreland continued speaking, unwilling to be denied his
ending:

"Our soldiers, sailors, airmen, marines, and coastguardsmen in
Vietnam are the finest ever fielded by our nation. And in this assessment I include Americans of all ages, creeds, and colors. Your
servicemen in Vietnam are intelligent, skilled, dedicated, and cou-
rageous. In these qualities no unit, no service, no ethnic group and
no national origin can claim priority.

"These men understand the conflict and their complex role as
fighters and builders. They believe in what they are doing. They are
determined to provide the shield of security behind which the Republic of Vietnam can develop and prosper for its own sake and for
the future and freedom of Southeast Asia.

"Backed at home by resolve, confidence, determination and continued support, we will prevail in Vietnam over communist aggression."

He had started with a paean to the American fighting man and
ended with one. It brought the intended response, which was every
man and woman in the hall on their feet and an applause that jumped
several decibels over everything that had preceded it. Westmoreland
smiled and for a moment just stood there and enjoyed it, let it wash
over him. Then as if on impulse, he turned suddenly and shook hands
with both McCormack and Humphrey, and then stepped back and
saluted them. Facing front, he saluted four more times, first to the
front, then to the left and right sides of the chambers and finally to
front once more. This last gesture, which one commentator would
call "blatantly patriotic" and another "politically astute," sent the
assembly into a new paroxysm.

It was reported later that one senator from the South let out a rebel yell at the sight of Westmoreland saluting; that Senator Russell Long of Louisiana got so excited he began hopping up and down; and that L. Mendel Rivers, a congressman from South Carolina, shouted to two colleagues, "This separates the men from the boys!"

Westmoreland stepped down off the podium into pandemonium. Legislators on both sides of the aisle surged forward to shake his hand or pat him on the back. Others shouted out their approval—"That was great!" "Wonderful!" "Congratulations!" And over it all, the applause continued. It would go on, in fact, even when he exited the chamber and was moving down the hallway to a waiting limousine. But when it finally died, it died for good. Less than nine months later, many of those same cheering congressmen, stunned by the savagery of the enemy's Tet Offensive, would suddenly sour on both Westmoreland and his war and begin calling for a change of command in Vietnam.

CHAPTER ONE

Lost Causes

Like two predators waiting for the right moment to strike, the two armies had been circling each other for days. King Charles had at first considered making a direct attack on the Parliamentarian forces but, seeing himself badly outnumbered, had turned his forces north and headed for the Royalist stronghold at Newark. Smelling a kill, Sir Thomas Fairfax and Oliver Cromwell hurriedly gave chase. The king continued his flight for a time, but when sudden rumors hinted that the Scots might be moving down on him from the South, closing one side of a giant pincer, he finally decided that he had no choice but to stand and fight.

The clash took place on June 14, 1645, near the town of Naseby. Outnumbered almost two to one, the king's cavalry commander, Prince Rupert, thought to rely on boldness as a substitute for numbers. He opened the battle with a reckless, thunderous charge into the left flank of Fairfax's formation. Although the charge broke the flank, it was not decisive. Fairfax in response unleashed his hardened and perfectly disciplined infantry into the king's center, then ordered Cromwell and his cavalry to launch a countercharge against the king's left flank. The struggle was uncertain for about an hour, but slowly the Royalist infantry began giving way. Soon it was a rout, with foot soldiers and cavalry fleeing frantically north to avoid death or capture. While the bulk of the king's cavalry managed to escape, the victory of the Parliamentarian forces was nonetheless complete. Other victories would follow in quick succession, forcing the king finally to flee England for a Spanish exile.

In complete ascendancy now, the Parliament began to wreak an awful vengeance upon anyone who supported the king. Many large estates were seized outright and many others were taxed so heavily that their owners were forced to sell them for nominal fees. Worse, many of the younger sons of these families, who had not only supported the king financially but had actually taken up arms with him, were forced to flee England.

One such man was Robert Westmoreland, the son of the eighth earl of Westmoreland, a county where over half the gentry had sided with the king. Although the evidence is fragmentary, one Westmoreland family history claims that this Robert had ridden with the king's cavalry at Naseby. He is reported further to have fled England four years later with "Cromwell's dogs snapping at his heels."

Robert arrived in Virginia sometime in the late 1640s, and his name appears in court documents in early 1650. That is the last record we have of him until his death in 1706. It seems that he had many children and they in turn had many more, for at the time of his death, the name Westmoreland could be found in the records of three Virginia counties and in parts of Pennsylvania. By the time of the Civil War, in fact, there were Westmorelands in the Confederate Army from every southern state except Florida.

The South Carolinian branch of the family claim as their first ancestor a man named Thomas Westmoreland, who makes his first appearance in family accounts during the hard winter of 1732. Those accounts tell of him leaving—or possibly fleeing—Virginia with his wife Tina Hamby during the hard, bitterly cold winter of that year. According to these reports, because of the deep snow they traveled by sled down mountain trail—and through the heart of hostile Indian territory—the entire four hundred miles to the Piedmont of South Carolina.

They liked what they saw. It was a beautiful country of gently rolling hills, large grassy meadows, endless tracks of timber, and swift clear streams and rivers. It was beside one of those rivers, the Enoree, in present-day Laurens County, that Thomas and Tina finally stopped.

With a hatchet they marked off six hundred acres of land, then secured a grant for it from King George.

Getting the grant was not difficult at the time. Along the coast, English settlement had only pushed inland seventy or eighty miles, for the upcountry was considered too wild and inhospitable for any but the most desperate or adventuresome. Whether this described Thomas and Tina is unknown, but they certainly must have been brave, for they had staked out their farm right in the heart of Cherokee country. Fierce warriors, the Cherokee had been curious when the whites first arrived in the upcountry, but as more and more whites began trickling in, taking over former Indian farmland in order to grow tobacco and cotton or graze cattle, the Indians struck and struck hard. Their faces painted black and red, festooned in feathers and breastplates, they formed raiding parties and roamed throughout the Piedmont wiping out isolated homesteaders and forcing others to flee back to their families in Virginia or Pennsylvania or down to the safety of Charleston.

Thomas and Tina stayed. Not only stayed, but raised five sons, while each year clearing a little more land and planting ever larger tobacco and cotton crops. To protect themselves against the Cherokee, Thomas, like all able-bodied men in the Piedmont, joined a militia. He also joined with others to petition the Colonial government in Charleston to put an end to the Indian problem. After years of ignoring the plight of the upcountry people, the Colonial government finally moved against the Indians. Through the threat of force, they pressured them to cede Laurens and nine other counties to the crown. The Indians, in turn, got to keep what is present-day Cherokee County. For the Indians, who had once roamed freely throughout the entire upcountry, the division of their land was a humiliation that they could not long bear. A year later, they broke the treaty and once again painted their faces and with hatchet and scalping knife descended on the Piedmont farmers.

The Colonial government responded this time with a brigade of hardened British infantry and cavalry. Once in the upcountry, they went on a rampage of their own, attacking Cherokee villages, burning their lodges and trampling their crops in the field. The Cherokee who survived limped back into Cherokee County, where they would spend the next decade waiting for another chance at revenge. It would finally come with the Revolution, when they would ally themselves with the British and once again wreak havoc throughout the Piedmont.

*   *   *

For now though, their threat had waned, and new settlers, hungry for land, flooded into the upcountry from Pennsylvania and Virginia. While they were mostly decent men and women, following on their heels were bands of outlaws and desperadoes. Their arrival set off a fresh cycle of robbery and pillaging. In response, men like Thomas Westmoreland organized the Regulators, a vigilante group that hunted down outlaws and either hanged or shot them on the spot. Between 1765 and 1770, hundreds more died on both sides of these sudden violent encounters, until finally a semblance of law and order prevailed.

In this interim between the time of the Regulators and the American Revolution, another Westmoreland arrived in Laurens County. His name was Robert, and he arrived carrying a king's grant for two hundred acres of land on the side of the Enoree opposite from Thomas's land. This Robert is also somewhat of a mystery man. Some think he was a son of Thomas, but that does not seem likely given the new man's ignominious end. It seems more likely that he was a distant Virginia relative, though blood would turn out to be the only thing the two men shared.

Regardless of his lineage, Robert could not have received the deed to his land at a more inauspicious time, for less than two months later a provincial congress met in Charleston, ordered all the king's officers out of the province, and authorized a million pounds for the defense of South Carolina. A year later many of these same men signed the Declaration of Independence, setting off the first fighting of the Revolution.

The fighting was to be particularly bloody in South Carolina—and for good reason. There were so many Tories in South Carolina at the time that the fighting took on the tenor of a civil war, with all its fury and madness. Of the battles and skirmishes fought in the state, 107 were between South Carolinians themselves, many times between close neighbors and former friends. By 1780, numerous bands of brigands—usually Tory in sympathy, and now cloaked with an ideology—were once again roaming the Piedmont robbing and murdering.

One of the worst of those brigands was the Tory firebrand "Bloody" Bill Cunningham. A member of one of the leading families of Laurens County, his name would eventually become synonymous with wanton cruelty. In November of 1781, Cunningham and about three hundred armed men left Charleston and started northeast on an expedition that according to local history would "leave the upcountry in tears."

Cunningham was adept at launching sudden raids on the homes of either officers or supporters of the Continental Army. During those raids, his enemies were either dragged or smoked from their homes and then either hanged, shot, or hacked to death, while the women of the family looked on in horror.

Two of Cunningham's victims were Thomas Westmoreland, now an old man, and his young son, Thomas junior. Thomas and his boy were working in their fields one day when they suddenly found themselves surrounded by Cunningham and fifty of his followers. Asked to reveal the hiding place of his money and crops, both man and boy defiantly refused. Infuriated, Cunningham beat the old man until he died and the boy until he was unconscious.

Apparently the act left no desire for revenge in Thomas's widow, Tina Hamby. The next morning, there was a sharp battle on the other side of the river between Tory and Continental units. Exploring the battlefield later, she found a young Tory officer who had been left for dead. With three of her sons (one of whom, Thomas junior, would spend the last year of the war as a soldier), she carried the officer back to her house and nursed him back to health.

Most Continentals were not to be as kind to the upcountry Tories as Tina. Shortly after the British abandoned South Carolina, the state general assembly convened and passed laws calling for the punishment of all Tories. The punishments varied.

The most prominent Tories were imprisoned or forced to flee to places like Canada or the West Indies. Lesser Tories merely had their property seized.

One of the many imprisoned was the same Robert Westmoreland who had gotten a king's grant only five years before. His exact connection to the king's cause is unknown, but it was obviously serious enough to warrant a prison sentence. (Robert would end up being a thorn in the family's side, and an embarrassment especially to one of his direct descendants in Texas who, when applying for admission to the Daughters of the American Revolution, would discover that she was the direct descendant of a Tory.)

While Robert sat in prison, the Westmorelands on the other side of the Enoree began to rebuild their lives. The eldest son, Thomas, took over the land and married a local girl, Hannah House. Together they had thirteen children, and passed the land on, in turn, to their eldest son, Andy.

Andy abandoned the original family home on the edge of the river and built a larger one a short distance away on a small rise. The house, which still stands, is a huge three-story structure with forty-foot walls, two imposing gables, and a full basement. He would fill it with thirteen children, two of whom, John and Tett, he sent to medical school. Upon their return, he built them an office attached to the house. A lighthearted man, Andy also built each of his children a fiddle. Many evenings, he gathered them all together around their massive fireplace and in unison they fiddled away into the night.

One of the better fiddlers was Andy's oldest boy, Squire Jim. A strong-willed boy, he would eventually take over the land and gain a reputation in the area as scrupulously honest in his business dealings, morally above reproach, with a strong attachment to ideals, traits that would get passed down like an heirloom through three more generations of Westmoreland men.

One ideal that Squire Jim was particularly and passionately attached to was the Southern cause. Shortly after the fall of Fort Sumter, he and his two sons, John and James White, rode into Woodruff and enlisted. All three had to falsify their ages, for at thirty-eight Squire Jim was too old and at sixteen and fifteen, John and James White too young. Like so many who answered the call, they came buoyed by a certainty that they represented a righteous cause and a morally superior civilization, an undefeatable combination. The day they marched off to war, a colonel gave a speech ensuring them that the war would soon be over "because we can whip those Yankees with pop guns." The comment brought loud cheers from the assembled men—the Westmorelands included—and then they marched off to war, certain that in just a few months they would be marching back victorious.

From Woodruff the three moved off in two separate directions. The father joined Holcombe Legion as a lieutenant, and a short time later was wounded at Winchester, Virginia. After recovering from his wounds, he resigned his commission and joined the Knight's Cavalry of Wade Hampton's Legion. Under Hampton, he participated in dozens of raids, skirmishes, and pitched battles. Eventually, he got the trusted job of a courier and while carrying a message to Stonewall Jackson was captured by a Union cavalry detachment. They came upon him suddenly but not before he could swallow the message. For this action, a Union officer had him beaten, then stripped of his coat and shoes. Cold and barefoot, he joined a long POW column slowly heading north. Two weeks later, he arrived at the Federal prison at Hart Island, New York, so crippled that he could barely stand. There the treatment was just as bad, and he was made to stand outside in the cold winter wind coatless and barefoot from noon till midnight. In desperation he flashed a Mason's sign with his hand at every soldier who looked his way. He finally caught the eye of a young Union officer, a Mason himself, and was soon issued winter clothes and blankets. He would later say that only his faith in God had allowed him to forgive his treatment by the Yankees. It was an erroneous statement, for he, in fact, would never forgive them.

Although the sons would not suffer as grievously as their father, they nevertheless would both face a trying ordeal. As part of General Robert E. Lee's legendary Army of Northern Virginia, the 14th South Carolina Regiment would soon see hard fighting in the Seven Day Battles around Richmond, at the Second Battle of Bull Run, at Fredericksburg and Chancellorsville, and at a dozen fights with lesser names. In these first fights, most of which were victories, both would join their comrades in developing an absolute trust in and an almost religious reverence for Lee. Both feelings were so strong that when Lee finally turned the army north toward its eventual destination at Gettysburg, the men of the 14th marched forward with buoyed steps, certain that they were about to deliver the hammer blow that would end the war.

They kept that confidence until the first day at Gettysburg when their brigade suffered nearly 80 percent casualties during a bayonet charge. The next day, standing in reserve, they watched in horror as Pickett's Division was shot to pieces in the wheat field below Cemetery Ridge. Gettysburg was the beginning of the end for the Confederacy. Following defeats at the Wilderness, Spotsylvania Courthouse, and a number of smaller battles, Lee was forced to withdraw his now tattered and starving army back into the trenches around Richmond and Petersburg.

There, with defeat looming over them like a dark cloud, an incident took place that James White would never tire of talking about. Out of nowhere, Lee himself rode up and inspected the men of the 14th as they stood at attention before their trenches. Then he gathered them around him and praised them for their neat appearance and for the fact that their regiment had never had a single desertion.

Dedicated units like the 14th, however, could not stop Grant's huge army, which was pummeling the Confederate trenches with a torrent of artillery fire followed by massed infantry assaults. On April 2, 1865, a massive assault finally broke Lee's lines around Petersburg.

In desperation, he led his hungry army in a breakout west into open country, looking for food and some way to keep his army fighting. He didn't find either, only hordes of federal cavalry that nipped at his flanks. Starving, wounded, or hobbled, many of the men dropped out along the route of march. One of them was John Westmoreland. Captured, he was shipped to Hart Island, New York, to join his father in prison. James White marched on.

It was over seven days later. The 14th got the word as they were preparing for an attack near Appomattox Courthouse. They were arranging their equipment when Union Brigadier General George Armstrong Custer rode up waving a white flag. At first they thought the blond-haired boy-general had been taken prisoner. But seeing how arrogantly he bore himself, they knew something was wrong, terribly wrong. When a Confederate officer rode up a moment later and told them to form up in ranks, the implication struck them all like a volley of rifle fire. One of James White's officers asked the horseman if it was indeed over. Yes, he answered, bowing his head in shame. As the news spread through the ranks of the 14th, some men cried out in agony, others broke into tears, but most just stood there numbly, cursing to themselves. Soon, however, as an officer from the 14th would write later, they were consoling themselves, reminding each other that they had done all they could and "bore no share in the national disgrace." They had not been defeated through any fault of their own but by a "government unable and a people unwilling to sustain them."

What followed was another incident that James White would also never cease talking about. While standing in ranks near Appomattox Courthouse, he watched in silent reverence as Lee—resplendent in new uniform with red-silk sash, jeweled sword, and red-stitched boots—rode up on his famous horse, Traveler, and surrendered to Grant.

Three days later, his stomach full of Union rations, James White started the long walk home. Released from prison a short time later, his father and brother soon followed. In fifteen days, they all limped back into Laurens County. Although the area had not been directly touched by the war, it had still suffered grievous losses. One quarter of the white men in the county had marched off to war and a quarter of them had been killed, including eight Westmorelands, all of them cousins of either Squire Jim or his boys.

These personal losses, coupled with the humiliation of the defeat, left in all three men a rancor against the North that they would carry to their graves. Once when a former Union soldier living in Woodruff said to James White in jest that since they had both been at Gettysburg, "maybe it was you that shot me in the hip," James White responded, "If it was, I wish to God I'd killed you." To show his own eternal contempt for the North, Squire Jim named his third son, born shortly after the war, John Wilkes Booth.

To assuage their bitterness, all three men regularly attended reunions of their former units and marched in the many United Confederate Veterans' parades held yearly all over South Carolina and the South. At these gatherings, they were cheered and fussed over by an adoring populace and treated to speeches by either former high-ranking Confederate officers or politicians. Always the message was the same: They had nothing to be ashamed of. They had fought hard and bravely and had only succumbed because of the overwhelming weight of Yankee numbers and materiel. Theirs may have been a "lost cause," but it was a noble one.

CHAPTER TWO

Rip's Son

For small yeoman farmers like Squire Jim and his boys, the times were particularly hard after the war. Although his wife and daughters had managed to run the farm during the war, the lack of hard cash finally forced Jim to sell off his land in the early 1870s and move his entire family into Woodruff. With the proceeds from the sale, he sent his boy John to medical school, then started and successfully ran a number of small businesses, all staffed by his ever-growing family. One of Jim's partners once described him as a man he trusted so completely that he never bothered checking the books during the twenty years they were in business together. Apparently Jim could have grown very rich, but he gave so freely to the town poor and helped out so many relatives that he ended up only financially comfortable.

His son John was apparently cut from the same cloth. Although he could have commanded large salaries at any number of hospitals in South Carolina, he chose instead to buy a small farm near Fountain Springs in Laurens County and take up the hard life of a country doctor, just like his uncles before him. It was a life that would prove too hard. While still only a young man, John, exhausted after making calls to isolated farmhouses during a cold, wet winter, died of pneumonia. He left behind his widow, three daughters, and two sons. His death forced the family to sell the farm and move into Woodruff and for a time live off the charity of Squire Jim. The death also forced the youngest son, James Ripley, to quit school for four years and not only help support the family but help his older brother, Fred Stroble, to get through medical school.

When Rip, as he was called, finally got a chance to start college himself he was already twenty and apparently broke, for he was accepted at the Citadel, South Carolina's famous military school, on a proprietary scholarship, which was reserved for promising students without money.

Whether or not his family's sudden plunge into poverty and his own struggle to help them were shaping forces in his life is unknown. But Rip—described by a cousin at the time as a very thin man, with black bushy eyebrows, a stern look on his face, and a critical temperament—spent his days at the Citadel with very definite ideas about what he wanted to do with his life once he graduated. His stated ambition in his senior yearbook is simply "to be rich." In another section of the same yearbook that asks for each cadet's favorite quote, we find his reading, "Get money, boy, no matter by what means." It seems that Rip's classmates knew him as well as he knew himself, for the class prophecy after the usual stories of great explorers, scientists, and soldiers, has him on Wall Street making fortunes in speculation.

His desire for success and money, however, was balanced by an equally passionate commitment to ideals such as personal honor and a contempt for laziness, immorality, and dishonesty. During his sophomore year when another cadet committed an act that Rip and a number of fellow cadets thought had brought dishonor on the school, they formed a committee and demanded that the boy leave school. When he refused, they marched on his room with the intention of physically evicting him. They were stopped at the last moment by the superintendent of the Citadel. Infuriated by what he considered a mob action, the superintendent ordered everyone to pack their bags and be off campus in two hours. Later in more formal deliberations, they were all expelled. While Rip and a number of underclassmen were allowed to reapply the following year and were subsequently readmitted, the upperclassmen were denied their diplomas. Apparently the incident did not leave any bad feeling either with the school or Rip, for he eventually became chairman of the Citadel's Board of Visitors and a lifelong school booster. The incident did show that Rip was willing to sacrifice a great deal for a principle, including a college diploma.

Rip graduated from the Citadel in 1900. For years he had dreamed of going on to law school once he graduated, but because of financial problems he had to forget the idea. Instead he returned home and accepted a job as the cashier of the new Bank of Woodruff. It was a small first step but a wise one. The bank was owned by Augustus W. Smith, Jr., the scion of former wealthy landowners from Abbeville County, but more importantly part of a new class of entrepreneurs in the region and the state who saw that the real key to wealth was not through growing cotton (which some bankers thought had brought nothing but poverty to the state) but in the massive expansion of the banking and textile industries.

In the banking business, Rip was known as a thrifty man with a head for figures. They are attributes that apparently impressed Smith, for when he opened a textile mill in Union, South Carolina, in 1906, he sent Rip there as his office manager. Then when he opened an even larger mill in nearby Saxon two years later, he made him the manager of the entire mill.

It was while at Saxon in 1913 that Rip, now thirty-seven, wed Eugenia Talley Childs, a small, handsome, vivacious, quick-witted woman of twenty-eight from Columbia. Her father, Colonel W. G. Childs, was the builder of the Columbia, Newberry and Laurens Railroad, and the founder of the Bank of Columbia, and a man with considerable political clout in the state capital.

Rip and Mimi, as she was soon called, brought to the marriage a strong commonality of heritage and background, which would serve their marriage well. Like her husband, Mimi could trace her lineage all the way to the Revolution and, like him also, she had lost relatives in the Civil War, most prominently her father's younger brother, who was killed at Chickamauga at the tender age of sixteen. Because of her lineage, she had grown up immersed in the stories and myths of the war. Much of it had apparently taken root, for she refused to refer to the conflict as the Civil War, which was a Yankee term. To her, it was simply the War Between the States, thereby giving the Confederacy a geographical and political legitimacy not accorded by the former name.

While living in Saxon, Mimi gave birth to her first child, a boy, who was duly christened William Childs Westmoreland. The date was March 26, 1914. Some of Westmoreland's contemporaries would later joke that the delivering doctor that day had presented their new baby to Rip and Mimi with the words, "Mr. and Mrs. Westmoreland, I'd like you to meet your son—General Westmoreland." Though meant as obvious sarcasm, the joke expressed an undeniable truth, for those of his contemporaries who knew of his youth and had watched his rapid rise up the Army ladder realized that there was nothing random or accidental about it.

Soon after his son's birth, Rip accepted a higher-paying job as manager of the Pacolet Mill, a large cotton-processing plant about twelve miles southeast of Spartanburg. The mill, like five others in the area, was owned in part by Victor Montgomery, one of the foremost cotton manufacturers in the state. He was supposed to have hired Rip because of the latter's hardheaded business sense, but their relationship was deeper than monetary. Montgomery was married to the daughter of H. P. Griffith, a man with deep ties to the Westmoreland family. Griffith was presently the president of Limestone College but during the war he had been James White and John Westmoreland's company commander, and for a time afterward James's partner in a company that manufactured buggies. It is difficult to gauge exactly how important this connection was, but it counted for something. Soon after taking up his new position at the mill, Rip, with the help and encouragement of Montgomery and a number of other prominent men from the Spartanburg area, started the Employees Savings Bank of Pacolet. The bank was an immediate success, and Rip deftly plowed his profits into a stock-and-bond portfolio that would eventually be worth well over a million dollars.

To go with their ever-rising status, Rip and Mimi moved into a new house in Victor Park, an exclusive hillside suburb for officials at the Pacolet Mill. The house was a ponderous, gambrel-roofed structure with wood-shingle siding and a long front porch supported by square pillars and girded with railing and lattice. The porch looked down on the Pacolet Mill in the valley below, a number of long, dark brick buildings, flanked by the muddy, sluggish Pacolet River on one side and a rail line on the other. The mill was connected to the opposite side of the river by a narrow steel bridge. Beyond the bridge were the small clapboard duplexes of the millworkers, strung out in neat rows up and down the small hills, each with its own outhouse and small garden.

It was only a few hundred yards from the Westmoreland home

to those of the millworkers, but in reality their worlds were miles apart. They represented distinct social classes, both of which had grown rapidly following the end of the war and the demise of the plantation oligarchy. Though they were dependent on each other economically, that was the only level where they interacted. They were called simply the "town people" and the "mill people," the former being the business and professional classes and the latter the huge numbers of propertyless impoverished white "crackers" who came in a steady stream out of the southern hills and mountains looking for work in the mills springing up all over the Piedmont of South Carolina.

The "mill people" literally lived in a world of their own. Fiercely proud of their Anglo-Saxon heritage, they considered independence their birthright. Although eager to get the wages the mills offered, they did not like being "bossed" or having their lives rigidly organized. They worked for wages only because they had to to survive. Clannish and deeply suspicious of outsiders, they were easily stirred to anger and quick to violence. At the time, the hero of most millworkers was Coleman Blease, a wild-eyed demagogue who had been the governor from 1911 to 1915. During his tumultuous term, Blease had opposed all social legislation such as child-labor and compulsory-school-attendance laws and had stirred up frenzies of class hatred against both middle-class whites and poor blacks. In 1913, Cole, as he is still referred to by old-timers in Pacolet, had refused to send in the state militia when a mob of "cotton mill boys" terrorized Spartanburg trying to lynch a black man. Later he even tried to get a bill passed legalizing lynching.

Although the young Westmoreland attended an elementary school in Pacolet with mill children and was occasionally allowed to invite a few mill children over to his house to play, his sister Margaret, who was three years younger, was not allowed to associate with them. Any other contact the boy had with them—in keeping with the rigid caste system of the time—was minimal. As one family member said, "Mimi wasn't about to let Childs run wild with a bunch of mill kids."

On the contrary, according to Margaret, from day one they kept a tight rein on him and began inculcating him with the idea that he was something very special. Early family albums are filled with photos of the boy in various uniforms, which his parents loved dressing him up in and he loved wearing. One in particular shows him at three years old in the baggy uniform of a World War I American "dough-boy," his head dwarfed by a huge overseas cap. In another he is a little sailor, his hat tilted jauntily to the right, his right hand mimicking a perfect salute.

His love of uniforms led him eventually to the Boy Scouts, which he joined at the age of twelve. He liked everything about scouting, but especially the self-discipline it demanded, the challenge of learning new skills, the excitement of going on long hikes and campouts, and, of course, the new uniform. He especially loved the uniform. As Mimi would tell it later, he would hover over her as she sewed his insignias and merit badges on it in order to make sure she kept them perfectly straight and properly spaced.

He took everything else about scouting as seriously as he took his uniform, and demanded, in turn, that everyone under his charge did also. Once on a camping trip when a young Cub Scout refused to pay attention during a lecture he was giving, Westmoreland picked the boy up bodily and threw him into a nearby creek. The boy started moaning pathetically, "Oh, my grandfather's watch—it's ruined!"

"You'd think the boy would have resented my boy for that," said Mimi in a 1966 interview, "but instead he adored him and my boy never had any more trouble with him." Apparently, the boy's feeling for Westmoreland was universally shared, for Mimi went on to say that "younger boys just naturally looked up to him and followed him."

He was a natural leader. He knew it as early as the age of twelve, knew that he had the skill and personal magnetism to get men to follow him. Years later during a speech at West Point, he told the assembled cadets that most men wanted to be led and looked up to the natural leader. And he was that leader. He could see his own talents almost from the beginning. And he seemed to accept them with little hesitation; seemed to know himself and what he was capable of.

Watching him develop at this early age was a bit unnerving for his sister Margaret, however.

"He was so committed to everything he did and so good at it that it made me feel terrible about myself and very insecure, for I just didn't have that passion for mastering things and being the best at them that he had. My parents, of course, loved it. They were so ambitious for him and he took great pleasure in pleasing them."

Rip, of course, was the most ambitious for him. He liked sitting down with his son and giving him long lectures and pep talks during which he encouraged him to read widely and develop an interest in politics, history, and world affairs. At the same time, he pushed him to develop a Renaissance man's mastery of a wide variety of activities, everything from boxing and baseball to playing the flute. Behind the encouragement was Rip's ambition for the boy. Now on the Citadel's Board of Visitors, he hoped someday for his son to take his undergraduate degree there, then go on to Yale Law School. He felt that a career in law offered a man an aura of status and nobility not accorded a businessman. To bolster his wish, he loved reciting for his son's benefit Robert E. Lee's famous quote that "duty is the sublimest word in the English language."

His mother, on the other hand, wanted her boy to become a doctor, following in the solid footsteps of three generations of Westmoreland men, including Rip's brother, Fred Stroble, then a renowned surgeon in Spartanburg. For the present, however, the boy had no particular ambition other than finishing up his studies at Pacolet Elementary and transferring to Spartanburg High School, which he did in 1928.

There he proved himself to be a good but not brilliant student and a fair athlete. In his freshman year, he played on the basketball and gymnastics teams, but failed to go out for either during his sophomore year. Scouting was still his first love and it was into it that he poured much of his free time. Older now, he and his two best friends, Conrad Cleveland and Wardlaw Hammond, began accumulating the more difficult merit badges on their drive toward their ultimate goal of becoming Eagle Scouts. To satisfy the requirement for one merit badge, they all made a grueling fourteen-mile hike that left them footsore for days. For another, they bicycled twenty-six miles to Union, South Carolina, and returned hobbled and cramped. Both Hammond and Cleveland would eventually tire of the Eagle Scout quest, but Westmoreland stuck with it and by the end of his sophomore year had accumulated the twenty-one required badges.

To celebrate the event, he asked his parents' permission to attend an international Scout jamboree being held in June of 1929 in Birkenhead, England, to be combined hopefully with an old-fashioned, leisurely "grand tour" of Europe. The cost of both was $395, a princely sum at the time. Seeing the trip as an opportunity for their son to have a broadening experience, both parents readily agreed to let him go.

With a group of Scouts from Georgia, Westmoreland sailed aboard the steamer *Belgenland* from New York in late June, and arrived in Cherbourg, France, a week later. From there he started on a leisurely forty-five day jaunt through France, Germany, and Belgium. Among the hundreds of sights he took in, he was particularly impressed by the Arch of Triumph and Tomb of the Unknown Soldier in Paris and the battlefield at Belleau Wood. He also found time to go hiking in the Alps and boating down the Rhine. While visiting Heidelberg, Germany, he got his first glimpse of the dark side of the German soul. A group of German students fawned over him because they thought a scar on his cheek, which he had gotten in a car accident, was the result of a duel. He did not tell them anything different.

The boy found Europe exhilarating and discovered that he loved travel, but not in the sense of a casual tourist who quickly took in a kaleidoscope of sights then rushed back home again. He liked it instead in a more cosmopolitan sense, as a man who could easily and comfortably have lived in any of the countries he passed through. By the time he arrived in England for the jamboree, he found a number of profound changes beginning to take place in himself. He was not quite sure what they were at first, or what they signaled, but he was slowly coming to the decision that however he decided to eventually lead his life, it was not likely to be in the Piedmont or anywhere else in South Carolina, for that matter. He would narrow his feeling a little later when he met a group of midshipmen from Annapolis, who like himself were touring Europe. He was deeply impressed with the confident way in which they carried themselves and enthralled by their tales of academy life. They were equally impressed with him, and before they parted ways a member of the midshipmen was encouraging him to apply to Annapolis. Listening to them, he suddenly found his vague feeling of discontent becoming somewhat more definite, coalescing into various images of himself as a naval officer, images that he found very appealing.

He also found appealing the attention he received upon his return home from Europe in August. As if he were some nineteenth-century explorer returning to London after two years of exploring the Amazon or the Nile River, the *Spartanburg Journal* devoted a half page to a detailed description of his trip, capped with the heading SPARTAN-BURG'S OWN. In the center of the piece is a photo of the young Westmoreland in his summer uniform of shorts, knee socks, kerchief, and wide-brimmed campaign hat, all accentuated by a full merit-badge sash and a chest full of medals. The pose is deliberate and exaggerated, almost a parody. Like a colonel preparing to dress down his battalion, the boy's legs are spread slightly apart, his clenched fists are planted firmly against his hips, his eyes are narrowed, and his lips tight with determination.

The pose seems arrogant, but back at Spartanburg High School,

Westmoreland's classmates saw him as a genuine hero, man of the world, who had a right to be proud of his accomplishment. If anything, to them he was the exact opposite of arrogant. Those who knew him well say that he was one of the most well-mannered boys in the school, a person who refused to spread vicious gossip and treated everyone old and young alike with deference and a polished equanimity. And he did so according to a number of classmates not to put on an act but because he genuinely liked people.

And the reverse was also true. Most of his classmates genuinely liked him in turn. They liked him so much, in fact, that they elected him class president without bothering to hold an election. They just all got together one day in the gym and decided that he was the only one worthy of the job.

Westmoreland's last two years in high school were an easy, light-hearted time. Although the stock market crashed soon after his return from Europe, his family was only slightly stung by the national calamity that followed. Of the dozens of banks in the Spartanburg area, Rip's was one of the few that did not fail. And according to Leo Kirby and Herbert Jones, two former employees of the Pacolet Mills, it did not fail because Rip, whom they both described as "all business," had been cautious in whom he loaned money to and conservative in how he invested the bank's profits. Although the state records do show that Rip had to eventually devalue the bank's stock by 50 percent, it was only a temporary setback, and in three years he had the stock back up to its precrash value.

His solvency allowed Rip to buy his son a new green Chevrolet, to be used primarily to haul him and his sister back and forth to school every day. Although it was rare for teenagers in Spartanburg to own their own cars during this time, a number of Westmoreland's more affluent classmates either had their own or had access to their parents'. And then, as now, much of teen socializing in the town revolved around cars. One of the evening pastimes for teenagers was to cruise the downtown area, making endless trips around and around Morgan Square, in the center of which stood a statue of General Daniel Morgan, a Revolutionary War hero. Some of the more daring boys waited until the police were not around and then in a squeal of burning rubber drag-raced up and down Main Street. Others loaded up their cars with pairs of girls and boys, bought some moonshine or beer, then drove out to a nearby lake to drink and neck. According to one of his classmates, Westmoreland "was a little too proper to be a participant in these diversions." One of the drag racers at the time was Joe Moore, who owned a souped-up Model-T Ford. He would eventually end up as Westmoreland's air commander in Vietnam from 1964 to 1966. At the time, though, they ran in completely different circles.

Westmoreland instead ran around with a group of six boys and six girls who arrogantly referred to themselves as the Big Twelve. Except for him they were all from Spartanburg, and like him came from families permanently entrenched in the area's upper-middle class. Though they finished high school at the height of the Great Depression, the survivors of the group today describe their activities in scenes that seem right out of Thornton Wilder's classic portrait of small-town life, *Our Town.*

On Friday, they might all gather at Virginia Barwell's spacious house in the exclusive Converse Heights section of town to spin records on her wind-up record player and dance. They loved to sit around and listen to the records of Tommy Dorsey and Guy Lombardo, and their favorite dances were the Charleston and the shag, a dance still popular in South Carolina. The members of the group seldom showed up in pairs, but instead socialized as just one big group, everyone continually changing dance partners. When not dancing or standing around "gabbing," they all played a game that seemed on the surface a kind of mating ritual, although the girl who organized it would certainly not have admitted it. The rules of the game required each girl to drop her name in a hat, then for the boys to each draw a name. The couples were then required to leave the house at comfortable intervals and walk slowly around the block, making conversation the entire way. When everyone returned, they held the drawing again and new pairs started out.

On other Friday nights, the group would pile into three or four cars and drive down to the Beacon, the town movie theater on Main Street, and take in a movie or two. Afterward they drifted down the street to LaPetits, an ornate, chrome-covered ice cream parlor for a hot-fudge sundae or banana split. Or better yet, they piled back into the cars and drove farther down Main Street to LaMott's Drive-In for a barbecue sandwich and cherry Coke and to take in the sight of dozens of teenagers like themselves driving around and around the parking lot.

On Saturday morning or early afternoon, the group would often gather again to pack a picnic lunch and take a long bicycle ride out to some nearby lake. If they did not feel too ambitious, they might just all walk the two miles out to the Spartanburg country club and spend the day playing tennis or swimming. A favorite pastime also was to gather at the homes of either Elizabeth Lyles or Elizabeth Jennings and spend a leisurely day roller-skating in the street or sitting around the front porch eating cookies and drinking lemonade.

Of course, there were times when members of the group actually paired up and went on dates, but the rest of the group usually tagged along or followed close behind. Westmoreland dated Elizabeth Lyles for a time, but she says that they were not really formal dates, just two friends going places together. His steady date during his last two years of high school, if she can be called that, was Elizabeth Jennings, a charter member of the Big Twelve. Even today, she admits to having had a crush on him in high school, though she quickly realized the feeling would never be reciprocated. At the time, she says, Westmoreland was extremely bashful around girls, which she attributed partly to his personality and partly to his having been brought up in a mill town, "where people's social skills were not as developed." "He had no particular interest in dating," she also says, "and if it hadn't been for me I don't think we would ever have gone out." To make a date with him, she would typically contact Boykin Lyles, one of Westmoreland's best friends. She would ask Lyles, in turn, to contact Westmoreland and see if he wanted to go to a particular athletic event or dance. Westmoreland, she says, would never call her back to confirm anything but would pass on his okay to Boykin. Most of the time, she and Westmoreland double-dated with Boykin.

Even given his lack of interest, Jennings admits that she still enjoyed dating him. He was fun to be with, a good conversationalist, a great dancer, and always well-dressed and perfectly groomed. He was not, however, always as thoughtful as he could have been. When he arrived to pick her up for the prom during their junior year, she was shocked to discover that he had forgotten to bring her flowers. "I really was not that offended, however," she says, "because I knew that he always had his mind on something else."

Unperturbed, Jennings went to the prom with Westmoreland again the following year. This time he remembered to bring flowers, but still showed a less than total commitment. As had become the custom for a number of years, on the day following the prom the senior class, accompanied by chaperones, piled into cars and drove down to Myrtle Beach in order to celebrate. There, the girls rented a number of houses and the boys an equal number, they then all spent the next two days and nights swimming, sunbathing, and dancing at a nearby pavilion. Jennings says she asked Westmoreland to come down but he bowed out, saying he had to spend the time studying for an upcoming exam. Jennings says she was not offended. By now, like most of her classmates, she had come to accept the fact that Westmoreland had his mind locked on some lofty goal far in the future.

She had no idea what that goal might be, though she, like everyone in the senior class that knew him well, theorized that it would be something very important and completely out of the ordinary. After consulting a number of classmates, Elizabeth Lyles hazarded a guess when she wrote the senior class prophecy for the yearbook. In it, she cast Westmoreland as a world-renowned explorer returning to Spartanburg in 1945 after a thrilling trip around the world. It was a fanciful, highly romantic prediction, but it was not for Westmoreland. Given his increasing attraction to the structured life, he would not have enjoyed the unstructured, chaotic, and unpredictable one of an explorer. And while he enjoyed knowing that his classmates thought so highly of him, when he graduated on June 5, 1931, he was as undecided about what he wanted to do with the rest of his life as any number of his classmates were. Although he had been feeling the stirrings of greatness in himself ever since his jaunt through Europe, he was still unable to codify them. Given the state of indecision he found himself in, he decided to temporarily accede to his father's wishes and enroll at the Citadel. Maybe while in a holding pattern there, he thought, he would finally be able to make up his mind.

CHAPTER THREE

Cadet Westmoreland

It sits on a gentle spine of land
only a few miles from the spot where the Ashley and Cooper rivers
merge into the Atlantic Ocean. With its battlements, turrets, towers,
crenellated parapets, and spacious courtyards, the cluster of buildings
look from a distance like a Moorish fortress, a kind of mini-Alhambra
mysteriously transported through space and time to this spot overlooking the marshy tidal basin of the Ashley River. It is neither. In
reality, it is the Military College of South Carolina, popularly referred
to as the Citadel; and if it can be called a fortress at all, it stands not
as a defense against some invading army or alien horde, but as a
bulwark thrown up for the protection of southern manhood and traditions and the memories of a faded age.

The school's original purpose, however, was not so magnanimous,
so imbued with high purpose. It came into being as little more than
a frantic response to a dark chain of events set in motion by an
embittered charismatic slave named Denmark Vesey. In June of 1822,
according to a very biased contemporary account, this Vesey gathered
around him a group of followers and with their help hatched a "ne-

farious" plot to slaughter all the whites in Charleston, loot the town, and gain their freedom. Thanks to "faithful slaves," who warned their masters of the impending slaughter, the uprising was quashed and "disaster averted."

In the vengeful fury that followed, Vesey and thirty-four of his followers were hanged and a large number of other slaves connected to the plot were sold off to plantations far from the Charleston area. Vesey's quick end did not, however, alleviate the anxieties of many Charlestonians, who were now convinced that there were others just like him, lurking in the deep shadows, waiting for a chance to slaughter them in their sleep. To calm those fears, the state legislature met and in a hurried session appropriated the money to establish a municipal guard of 150 cadets to protect Charleston.

Those cadets soon took up residence in an old tobacco inspection station in Charleston and quickly converted it into a guardhouse and arsenal. There they sat hunkered down for the next twenty years waiting for another slave revolt that never came. What came instead was a group of prominent South Carolinians who in 1842 eyed their makeshift arsenal and guardhouse and decided it would be an excellent spot on which to build a military school. Classes for a small group of potential officers began that same year, while at the same time workers began constructing the buildings for the new school.

It had taken twenty years for the school to evolve, and it would take nearly another twenty before it got its first taste of glory. On that day—January 9, 1861—a group of Citadel cadets manning an artillery battery on nearby Morris Island fired the first shots of the Civil War at a Federal gunboat trying to reinforce Fort Sumter in Charleston Harbor. Those cadets were the first from the Citadel to rush to the South's defense, but within a year two hundred more followed them. Of those, thirty-five were killed in battle and twice that number were wounded. All fell as officers, and many as brigade, division, and corps commanders. When the survivors of the group returned to South Carolina after the war, they did so determined to fashion their alma mater into an exclusively southern school, deeply imbued with southern hubris and openly defiant of any outsiders who did not share its values. One observer would call what they fashioned "a philosophical city-state playing Sparta to the outside world's Athens."

In the early afternoon on a warm day in September 1931, Westmoreland, his father, and Wardlaw Hammond arrived at this city-state Sparta after a four-hour drive in the family car from Pacolet. Hammond, who had likewise been accepted at the school, says that he arrived with considerable doubts as to whether he actually had mettle enough to face the ordeal that lay ahead. Westmoreland, on the other hand, Hammond says, showed up, as always, emanating supreme confidence and buoyed by a strong personal conviction that he could not only endure what lay ahead but also enjoy the challenge of doing so.

And what lay ahead for the two men and the other 260 freshman in their class was nine months of the toughest discipline, the most rigorous training, and most intense "hazing" of any military school in the country. What lay ahead of them, in fact, was social Darwinism in its most naked form, an ordeal designed to break them physically and mentally and drive out the weak from their ranks. Once broken, they would then all be reconstructed as proud Citadel men.

From the moment he arrived, the new cadet faced a plethora of rules and regulations designed to control his every waking moment. They were listed in a sixty-page pocket-sized booklet that he was expected to quickly commit to memory. Along with a hundred other strictures, the booklet told him how to clean his rifle and how to display it, how to press his clothes and in what order to arrange them in his closet, how to make his bed and the exact time he had to be out of it in the morning. It even told him the proper procedures he was to follow when using the latrine.

Listed with the rules and regulations were the corresponding punishments for anyone caught violating them. Cadets charged with minor violations were given demerits. If they accumulated enough demerits, they were punished with long hours of walking guard, the loss of all privileges, and even dismissal. Serious violations such as getting drunk, lying, cheating, or any type of immoral behavior usually warranted instant dismissal, and in many cases, public disgrace, for the world of the Citadel then, as now, was intimately inbred with South Carolina's social, business, and political world.

Unfortunately for the "rats" as freshmen at the Citadel were called, there was something that was far worse than the regulations, and that was the hundreds of methods of harassment that the upperclassmen employed against them. Although hazing was strictly forbidden, it was the one regulation the authorities conveniently overlooked. For the "rat," hazing meant doing push-ups until his arms cramped, running up and down stairs until his legs turned to jelly, standing at rigid attention shouldering a heavy rifle until he either collapsed from exhaustion or fainted, doing deep knee bends over piles of jagged glass, or being forced to eat rotten food or to drink strange nauseating concoctions until he vomited or begged for mercy.

It was a horrible, merciless ordeal he faced for those first nine months, and if he wanted to remain at the Citadel he had no choice but to endure it stoically. If he openly resisted, or even questioned what he was ordered to do, he would find the full fury of the upper-classmen turned against him. For him, that fury might translate into anything from being spanked with the flat end of a sword to being taken out behind the barracks and beaten up.

Few resisted, but before the new year was a month old, a dozen men had decided that they could not take any more and dropped out. That number would grow steadily as the school year progressed, so that by June more than a third of the class, ninety-two cadets, had either dropped out or been kicked out. It was an attrition rate more than double that of West Point that year. Supporters of the Citadel system like to brag that compared with their freshman year, West Point's was almost effete.

Westmoreland, however, was not particularly bothered by the hazing he faced, or anything else for that matter. He arrived fortified with the idea that he was going to be the best in his class, and, as many of his former classmates have attested, he soon was. Luther Marchant, who was himself an exemplary cadet at the Citadel, said that after two or three times of watching Westmoreland on the parade field, it was obvious he had the makings of an exceptional soldier. From the beginning, he projected an air of professionalism. It was there in the way he stood at attention, the way he snapped a salute, the way he marched and drilled and barked back the answers to commands. "He was a ramrod, pure and simple," Marchant concluded. Others were also taking notice, and before the year was half over, a number of freshmen had concluded that besides being skilled in the military arts, Westmoreland also possessed that rare combination of personal qualities that military men refer to as "command presence." Some of his instructors, men who over the years had seen hundreds of cadets pass through the school, even began referring to him as "the prototype military man."

Also taking notice of him was the Citadel's president and former Army Chief of Staff, General Charles Pelot Summerall. As the year drew to a close, he and his staff officers met and drew up a list of the ninety-six freshmen they deemed worthy of being promoted to corporal. Westmoreland was number one on the promotion list. It was a unique honor, for it did not take into consideration academic achievements (Westmoreland ranked a respectable thirty-third in that category) but was based strictly on a cadet's mastery of the basics of artillery and precision drill, and on such personal qualities as comportment, character, and command presence.

Westmoreland was surprised at being chosen first on the corporal list. He had always felt he would do well at the school, but he had never imagined he would do that well. He was also surprised to discover that he really enjoyed military life. This discovery set him to thinking about his trip to Europe once again and especially about the pleasant time he had spent with the Annapolis midshipmen. A short time later, he got in touch with his father and asked him to contact Jimmy Byrnes, a South Carolina senator and family friend, to see if Byrnes could get him an appointment to the naval academy. Rip had once roomed in the same Woodruff boardinghouse with the senator back when Byrnes was a young district attorney and he a bank cashier. They had remained friends since that time and now attended the same church in Spartanburg, the Episcopal Church of the Advent. A year before when Westmoreland had expressed an interest in Annapolis, Byrnes had said, "Just let me know when you want that appointment, young man."

After an exchange of letters, Westmoreland drove up to the senator's office in Spartanburg one day in early spring. A number of recommendations from officers at the Citadel had preceded him, and Byrnes told him that if he wanted the Annapolis appointment, it was his. Byrnes gave him pause, however, when he also told him that he personally thought the boy should also give some consideration to West Point and a career in the Army, which he felt offered a much broader education and just as much opportunity for travel and adventure.

West Point? Strangely, Westmoreland had become so fixated on Annapolis that he had not given much thought to an Army career before. Now that he did, he could see that it might indeed offer him more, and he told Byrnes to put his name on the waiting list. Later, when the main selection and the first alternative failed to gain entrance, Byrnes officially gave him the appointment.

The appointment did not make Rip particularly happy, at least not for the moment. When the two discussed the appointment, Rip had defended his alma mater, saying that it "offered everything but the numbers." By "numbers" he meant that West Point graduates had an automatic priority on each year's list of new lieutenants. He felt this priority was only an artificial barrier, which his son could easily overcome through perseverance and hard work.

These "numbers," however, were not the whole story, a fact that Westmoreland could appreciate, even if his father could not. At the most fundamental level the schools were different, and that difference to someone trying to build a successful Army career was critical. The Citadel was a state school tasked with the dual purpose of turning out both military men and prominent state leaders. Since the school's beginning, the latter had far outnumbered the former. West Point, on the other had, had only one purpose, which was to produce the next Lee, Grant, or Sherman. Or their senior lieutenants. While the Citadel could look with pride at the number of its men who had made their mark on American military history, those numbers paled in comparison with West Point's. If he stayed at the Citadel as his father wished, he might have eventually built himself a successful Army career, but the odds were just as likely that he would have ended up a prominent South Carolinian lawyer, banker, manufacturer, or politician. If he wanted a better guarantee of success, he had to take the surer road there, and that road started at the gates of West Point.

They arrived at the banks of the Hudson from every part of the country and by every conceivable means of transportation—by bus and automobile, by train and ferry, even a few by chauffeured limousine. They were a cross section of the great republic they would soon swear to defend—laborers and schoolteachers; farmboys and sons of millionaires; soldiers and prep school students; Catholics, Protestants, and Jews. Almost to a man they all wore suits and ties and carried a small suitcase, although scattered through their ranks were a few resplendent in colorful sweaters and sport coats, cowboy boots and hats, and rakish fedoras.

However they dressed, all did much the same thing upon arrival: They set their suitcases down and for a long moment or two stood by the edge of the river and looked up in awe at the towering, ponderous cliffs about them. Accompanying this feeling of awe for many was another of panic, a panic growing out of the grave personal doubts most arrived with, doubts about themselves and the commitment they were about to make. It was almost a universal feeling, and there were few new cadets who did not experience it. On the train trip to West Point, Ulysses S. Grant admitted, he prayed the train would have an accident, injuring him sufficiently that he would not have to enter the academy. Even the self-composed Eisenhower would admit in his later years to arriving at West Point in such consternation that he found himself wishing he had instead enrolled at the University of Michigan with his brother.

Not all, of course, brought with them such grave doubts. One who did not was Douglas MacArthur, who made his first appearance filled to bursting with arrogance, bravado, and the absolute certainty that he was about to lay the foundation for a glorious military career. Patton was another. He walked into West Point convinced that he, unlike his classmates, belonged to a higher class of soldier, a class that included men like Alexander the Great and Hannibal.

A third was a nineteen-year-old from Pacolet, South Carolina, William C. Westmoreland. Unlike his famous predecessors though, arrogance and bravado were simply not a part of his character. He arrived instead with only his usual self-confidence, plus the knowledge that he had already faced and proven himself superior to an ordeal more rigorous than the one he was about to face.

If that fact brought him considerable consolation, it also caused him to be singled out by a number of upperclassmen for unduly harsh hazing. If he was indeed the best the Citadel had to offer, then they were determined to discover why. If they were looking for a weak spot in the young man, they found instead the hardened resolve of an extremely self-disciplined individual who was not going to break under any amount of torment. Added to that, he exhibited such composure and dignity during the worst of the hazing that even the most insensitive of his tormentors could not help but be impressed. Before long, they, like their counterparts at the Citadel, tagged him as one of the most outstanding, if not *the* outstanding cadet in the class.

Being outstanding in the class of 1936 was not easy. It is said that there are certain classes that the stars shine on—and this was one of them. From its ranks would come three Army Chiefs of Staff and one Air Force Chief, two West Point superintendents, the commander of the Strategic Air Command, one NATO and eight Army commanders in Korea, two commanders of the American forces in Vietnam, and the first black general officer in Army history. Behind these eminent men would line up another two dozen of their classmates destined to command battalions, regiments, divisions, and air wings in three wars. Only Eisenhower's class of 1915 would tally a more impressive record. Yet according to numerous graduates of the class of 1936, even in the midst of all this talent Westmoreland stood out, and stood out prominently. Johnny Heintges, who would later be a deputy commander of United States forces in Vietnam, said that after watching his new classmate, he became convinced that Westmoreland "would be the next first captain. And I wasn't the only one who thought that. A lot of others did too."

Part of the good impression Westmoreland made was based on what Heintges called "his perfect posture, his command voice and his ability to shout out commands." But he cautioned that those qualities were only part of the picture. Just as impressive were the qualities that made up his character, qualities like integrity, fairness, and maturity beyond his years. But what really impressed him about Westmoreland, he said, was the fact that, given the high regard everyone at the academy had for him, he "wasn't conceited and didn't pop off about what he was going to do."

Heintge's view of Westmoreland, however, was only partially true. While he certainly did not flaunt his ambitions publicly, he did so freely in private. A friend and former roommate, Chester Clifton, a man who would himself achieve a modicum of fame as President John F. Kennedy's military adviser, said that the two of them frequently sat around their room in the evening and discussed their future Army careers. During those discussions, Westmoreland unabashedly told him that his ultimate goal was to become the Army's Chief of Staff. To achieve that goal, he wanted to make sure he made all the right career moves, and conversely, none of the wrong ones. Should he get married right after graduation, he asked his friend? Or would it be better if he waited ten years, accumulated enough rank, and then got married? Clifton claimed that neither of them knew much about the duties of an Army Chief of Staff, but they both agreed that since it was the top job in the Army, Westmoreland was a natural for it. A natural. Clifton believed so strongly in the qualities of his friend that he even began referring to him as Chief. When upperclassmen or staff officers questioned him about the meaning of the nickname, he told them he had coined it because Westmoreland had a trace of Indian blood.

Though he obviously did not have any Indian blood, Westmoreland's standing at the end of his plebe year was impressive enough that his lofty ambitions for himself did not seem out of line. As always, he did well, if not spectacularly, in his studies, finishing in the upper quarter of the class. His purely military skills, however, got him an appointment as company commander of one of the six companies preparing to go to summer camp.

Before he left for this, his first command in the United States Army, he was able to draw some inspiration for the job ahead from a commencement speech General Douglas MacArthur gave at the academy in early June. Presently the Army Chief of Staff at only fifty-two, a fact that likewise inspired Westmoreland, MacArthur spoke on a theme that would be the core of most of his major speeches for the next three years: the state of unpreparedness the United States military was in. He blamed it on "pacifism and politically inspired economy" and warned that it threatened the nation's vital security. In counterpoint to this pacifism and political hackery, MacArthur held up the ideal of West Point, which he described as "the soul of the Army," and representative of a military code that "has come down to us even before the age of knighthood and chivalry." Westmoreland thrilled to these last words. If he was looking for a rationale, a *raison d'être*, for his love of military service, he found it here. He also found a man he would continue to admire for the rest of his life, even though it would become evident later in Westmoreland's career that they were completely different kinds of men, with different philosophies, characters, and temperaments.

A few weeks later, Westmoreland encountered another Army officer he would have much more in common with when he marched his company to the nearby yearling summer camp. That man was Major Omar Bradley. Although Bradley would later go on to command both the First and Ninth armies in World War II and become known affectionately as the GI General, at the time he was little more than a West Point tactical officer. At the moment of their encounter, Westmoreland was commanding a battalion of cadets and preparing to move out of a defensive position they had constructed the day before and go into a march to contact. Westmoreland was riding a horse and his troops were marching on foot beside him. After they had advanced a few hundred yards, Bradley suddenly rode up and said, "Mr. Westmoreland, turn your horse around and let's look back at that hill that you were to defend. Do you see the mistake that you made?" After turning around, Westmoreland said, "I do indeed, Major. I see it very clearly." "The lesson to be learned here and now," Bradley continued, "is that when you have a mission, whether it is offensive or defensive, always consider it from the vantage point of the enemy. Now we are standing where the enemy was deployed, and you see the natural routes of approach to that hill which were not evident to you from your vantage point on top of that hill."

Westmoreland took away from that first encounter with Bradley a valuable tactical lesson, which would serve him well in both World War II and Korea. But in the days ahead, as he observed Bradley more carefully, he was to learn a much more fundamental and infinitely more important lesson from him. He would gain that lesson not so much with listening to Bradley as watching him, watching the way he taught and commanded and motivated the men under him. Westmoreland had always believed command presence was an essential ingredient in the makeup of a good commander, and had worked hard at developing his own. But in Bradley—a gangling, bespectacled, homely-looking man, who spoke with a slow Missouri drawl—he found little of it. Yet in spite of that fact, the major still possessed an uncommon ability to teach and motivate men, and to do so without screaming or yelling or using any other personal pyrotechnics. Bradley instead was always the gentlemen, always polite, always well-spoken, and of course, strictly business. Years later when he reminisced about his encounters with Bradley, Westmoreland claimed that watching him had made him realize that there was more than one way to command. There might be a huge difference between the loud, inflammatory Patton and the quiet, dignified Bradley, but they both got results. It was in the territory between the Pattons and the Bradleys that he would stake out his own style of command. Although, like a Patton, he would always project the strongest command presence, he would seldom use profanity or rely on what he called "desk pounding" or "razzle-dazzle" in dealing with subordinates. Instead, like Bradley, he would always try to project the image of the gentleman—polite, even-tempered, fair-minded, and morally above reproach.

When Westmoreland returned with the rest of the yearlings from summer camp in early August, he brought with him an even more enhanced reputation. That enhancement was due in part to Bradley, who had watched Westmoreland carefully all summer and had come away impressed by the professional way the cadet had handled his company. It was one thing to deliver a crisp salute or to master precision drill, and quite another to successfully maneuver troops in the field.

Westmoreland's success in summer camp filled him with a new enthusiasm, and at the start of the new year he threw himself into a wide variety of activities. He made the basketball team, tried unsuccessfully to qualify for the pentathlon, taught Sunday school, and helped put on the One Hundredth Night Show, an annual satirical production that lampooned various aspects of West Point and Army life. Although he would later be typecast by critics as a dour humorless man, he was known at West Point for having a good sense of humor. It was, however, a private humor, reserved for close friends and based on shared experiences. He would never be very good at public humor.

Instead of attending another summer camp between their sophomore and junior years, Westmoreland's class was instead furloughed.

In early June, Westmoreland boarded a train and traveled back to Pacolet to spend the summer with his parents. It was the last extended time he would ever see either of them. From that point on, he would only catch quick glimpses of them when he stopped by in between assignments and wars.

It was also the last time that Westmoreland would see much of any of his high school friends, most of whom, like himself, were home from college for the summer. In a last fling, the Big Twelve reunited for a few dances, parties, movies, picnics, and bicycle rides. Elizabeth Jennings described it as one of those golden summers, much like those they had spent together in high school, during which all of them were so full of themselves and of all the possibilities open to them.

And no one was more sure than Westmoreland. He had left home a Boy Scout, unsure of his goals, and now returned a rising star at West Point. Rather than vague goals, he now had a single one: to be the best officer in the United States Army. To show his continued dedication to that goal, during breaks from a part-time job he had as a camp counselor, he and a close friend would take a canoe and paddle to the desolate corner of a nearby lake. There, while the friend acted as a judge, Westmoreland stood near the edge of the water and practiced shouting out parade ground commands. "About face!" "Forward march!" "Eyes left!" "Forward, double-time, march!" "Company, halt! Left face!" If a particular command was not loud enough, or if it lacked the proper emphasis or modulation, the friend would tell Westmoreland and he would then repeat it until he had it right.

Before Westmoreland returned to West Point that summer, he borrowed his father's car and drove the fifteen miles to Woodruff to pay what he knew would be his last visit to his uncle, James White. Westmoreland found his uncle, now eighty-eight, living in the back two rooms of a family store in downtown Woodruff. A recently broken hip had confined him to a wheelchair, and there he would spend the rest of his days playing the part of the unrepentant rebel, reliving his glory days for whoever dropped by with endless accounts of battles and anecdotes about his numerous encounters with men like Robert E. Lee, Stonewall Jackson, and Jeb Stuart.

Westmoreland approached the white-bearded, tobacco-chewing patriarch with what he described as "trepidation," uncertain how the old man would accept the fact that he was attending West Point.

"What are you doing for yourself?" James White asked.

"I'm going to that same school Grant and Sherman went to, the Military Academy at West Point, New York."

The old man took pause for a long moment and sat there as if stunned. Finally he said, "That's all right, son. Robert E. Lee and Stonewall Jackson went there, too."

With his uncle's less-than-enthusiastic approval, Westmoreland returned to West Point in late August of 1934 for the start of his junior year. Awaiting him was the rank of first sergeant and command of Company C. The rank was his thanks to strong recommendations from the tactical officers, with Bradley's being one of the strongest.

Through attention to detail, hard work, and stubbornness, he groomed his company into one of the most polished in the corps. Yet in spite of all the hard work he put into his new position, he still found time to once again land a spot on the basketball team, to improve his horsemanship enough that he finally made the pentathlon team, to help with the production of the coming year's One Hundredth Night Show, and to keep his academic standing in the upper quarter of the class.

In late May, Westmoreland gathered with the rest of the corps to hear the long-awaited commencement address of President Franklin D. Roosevelt. During the last year, the entire corps had watched with mounting anxiety as Hitler seized power in Germany, Japan resigned from the League of Nations, and Italy prepared to invade Ethiopia. And as they had watched, they tried to balance those ominous events with the equally anxious fact that the Army most of them would soon be joining—an army equipped with antiquated World War I tanks and trench mortars, worn-out French 75-millimeters, and 1903 Springfield rifles—was woefully unprepared for another war. As soldiers, their instincts told them that the events unfolding in Germany, Japan, and Africa by their very nature demanded that the United States begin rearming, and rearming in a big way. They discovered, however, that their perceptions, no matter how firmly they seemed rooted in logic, were not shared by the Congress or the American people, both deeply isolationist. Their sentiments were not even shared, they also discovered, by the President himself. Although once considered a strong interventionist like his uncle Theodore, Roosevelt in the past year—albeit under extreme pressure from both Congress and his Bureau of the Budget—not only had refused to raise the Army's budget but had cut it by thirty million dollars. His budget director had wanted to cut the Army's funding by 51 percent, but General Douglas MacArthur, the Army Chief of Staff, had threatened to resign if they did. Of course, that had been the previous year. It was everyone's hope at the corps that during the last nine months, Roosevelt had become as anxious over world events as they were.

Although in his speech he admitted deep concern over the world situation, Roosevelt was a number of years away from being concerned enough to call for either full or partial mobilization. He did announce that he was ordering a "partial restoration of Army enlisted strength and the increased enrollment of cadets in the United States Military Academy." Although the increases Roosevelt was offering were minimal, they were an important first step, and the cadets responded with applause and cheers, which the *New York Post* described as "loud and long."

Having a chance to see the President was a memorable experience for Westmoreland, but one even more memorable awaited him that evening in the dining hall right before dinner. There, while the entire corps sat anxiously, the commandant of cadets, Lieutenant Colonel Simon Buckner, a man who would die leading the Tenth Army against the fanatical Japanese forces on Okinawa, read the names of the cadets who had impressed him and his staff officers enough during the past year to warrant rank increases. At the top of Buckner's list was Westmoreland's name, and beside it his new rank of first captain, the highest rank a cadet could attain at West Point. The rank was his in part for having shown himself superior at all the requisite military skills, but it was his primarily because he had shown through his personal actions and character to be the cadet who best exemplified the ideals of West Point.

In his first official duties as first captain, Westmoreland led his classmates on a whirlwind summer tour of four East Coast military installations. The tour was the brainchild of MacArthur, who saw it as a chance for the cadets to become familiar with the new weapons and tactics being developed and to be exposed to several different branches of the Army. His hope was that once exposed, they would have an easier time deciding which branch they preferred. The trip included several weeks at Fort Benning, Georgia, an infantry training center, and several more at Fort Monroe, Virginia, a center for coast artillery and antiaircraft study and development. The tour ended at Mitchell Field, Long Island, where the cadets were initiated into the mysteries of flying. Until he arrived at Mitchell, Westmoreland had been leaning strongly toward both infantry and artillery. But after Mitchell, where he got a chance to watch a P-36 fighter work out and to personally "take the stick" of an O-45 observation plane, he found his heart permanently gripped by the romance of flying. Although there were another nine months before he had to finalize his decision, he was now certain that he wanted to spend his Army career as an Army aviator.

Following the summer tour, Westmoreland and his classmates

returned to the academy to start their senior year. As first captain, Westmoreland took on a lot of new responsibilities, which included overseeing a small staff and being the chairman of the Honor Committee. This last position put him, and the twelve other cadets on the committee, in the unenviable position of having to decide the fate of any cadet who had either reported himself or been reported by someone else for an honor violation. Those violations usually involved cheating and lying, and the penalties were severe. If a cadet was wise enough to report himself for a violation, he faced a heavy penalty of demerits, a drastic restriction of his personal freedoms, and a heavy load of extra duty. A cadet unlucky enough to be caught violating the honor code by someone else faced dismissal. Although no records were kept of these Honor Committee meetings, Westmoreland, according to one account, was "more than once called on to recommend the expulsion of a fellow cadet." Making decisions that determined other cadets' careers weighed heavily on Westmoreland, but he was unflinching in his duty. And according to numerous men who served with him over the years, he was unflinching for good reason: He believed totally in the West Point motto of Duty, honor, and country, and he expected that anyone who desired to wear the uniform of a United States Army officer should also. His associates also say that over the years, he never deviated from his strict adherence to this motto, and likewise would tolerate no deviation from the men, and especially the officers, who served under him. To him it was an absolute standard, and as such demanded absolute adherence. In other areas of conduct, he was considerably more tolerant. He would, in fact, gain somewhat of a reputation as a commander who was very forgiving of men who committed well-intentioned errors, no matter how disastrous the consequences were. But when it came to immoral or unethical behavior, his heart turned to stone, and he allowed no room for compassion or compromise. Many an officer who served under Westmoreland would discover this fact the hard way, would discover that casual adultery or excessive drinking that some other commander had conveniently overlooked would get them banished from Westmoreland's command; and that lying or other forms of dishonesty would get them kicked out of the Army. Or, in the case of the cadets who came before his Honor Committee, kicked out of West Point.

As graduation drew near, Westmoreland put in his application for the Army Air Corps. Unfortunately, he flunked his physical because of less-than-perfect eyesight. He settled instead for his second choice, artillery. He was disappointed over not getting into the air corps, but his disappointment was considerably offset by the fact that as first captain, he had the distinct honor of leading his class through June week, a week-long celebration that doubled as a kind of final rite of passage for first classmen and a passionate reaffirmation by the academy of its ideals.

To help him and his class celebrate, hundreds of alumni, young women, proud parents, and dignitaries descended on the academy from June 4 until the formal graduation ceremonies six days later. To entertain them, the academy had scheduled a daily extravaganza of reunions, dances, hops, receptions, garden parties, luncheons, formal dinners, award ceremonies, horse shows, and parades. As first captain, Westmoreland, resplendent in his summer dress uniform and high shako, led his regiment snappily through all the parades; and as first captain also, he made the round of many of the other events. Many of the alumni wanted to get a look at him, to shake his hand, size him up, and take a quick reading of his character. To most it was a good reading, and even before he had formally left the academy, word about him was already circulating through the Army grapevine.

Saturday morning, June 11, was reserved for the final act, graduation day. It was held in a new outdoor theater built into the hillside north of the plain. There while his parents and sister, Margaret, sat proudly in the bleachers, he marched the regiment in. Once seated, they listened in rapt silence as General of the Army John J. Pershing, the man who had led the American Expeditionary Force to victory in World War I, delivered the commencement address for the class of 1936. Although he was a man who wore a presence as large as the history he had made, Pershing's message was a deceptively simple one. Maintain your own morals at a high level, he told them, and you will wind up seeing them reflected in the morals of your men. Without that solid moral center, however, an officer could not lead or be effective.

When Pershing finished, the first classmen were called up to the stage one by one to receive their diplomas and commissions. Awaiting Westmoreland also when it came his turn was the Pershing Sword, named in honor of the speaker and presented each year to the cadet who had surpassed all others in military proficiency. Westmoreland received the sword from General Charles Gates, then shook hands with Pershing himself and stepped down off the stage. With those steps, he officially entered the Long Gray Line, that long solemn procession of academy graduates that had begun with the first class, of 1802, and stretched on into the future.

CHAPTER FOUR

"Sir, that man's going to be Chief of Staff someday."

The Army that Westmoreland joined on graduation day was understrength, underfunded, and outdated. With 13,512 officers and 154,304 enlisted men on its active duty roster, it ranked only eighteenth among the world's armies, right behind Portugal and slightly ahead of Bulgaria. On paper, these 167,816 men were supposed to make up nine infantry divisions, but in reality only three of the nine even had the framework of a division in place, and not a single one of these was prepared to immediately go into battle. The other six divisions were little more than glorified brigades, with their component battalions scattered to posts around the country. To aggravate matters, the training for the skeletonized units the Army did have was inadequate and antiquated. Because of severe budget restraints, maneuvers were held only once a year for a two-week period, and of that time a mere five days were actually devoted to intensive field work. In contrast, the Germans now had a field army of over three million men and the Japanese one of one million.

As disquieting as the Army's physical condition was its psycho-

logical one. Going hand in hand with the American society's neglect
of the Army's physical needs had been an indifference toward, and
at times outright contempt for, it as an institution. Both had had a
terrible effect on the morale of officers and enlisted men. Mirroring
the attitudes of Americans at large, many in the Army—and this was
especially true of officers and senior NCOs—had long ago lost any
sense of urgency, and become lackadaisical and indifferent. Others,
angry over being stuck in the same rank for years and with seniority
as the only means of promotion, had turned despondent and cynical.
In place of this sense of urgency, many instead filled their time, and
the time of the men under them, with athletics, recreation, and
various forms of entertainment. Observing the Army on the eve of
World War II, General Eisenhower concluded that complacency was
its most prevailing attitude, and that that complacency was so widespread and so deeply ingrained that it more than lack of money was
the greatest obstacle the Army faced.

Westmoreland would get a quick taste of this complacency himself
when he received his first assignment in early September of 1936.
That assignment sent him to the 18th Regiment of the Field Artillery
School at Fort Sill, Oklahoma. The 18th was supposedly an elite unit.
It had won the Croix de Guerre in World War I after its gunners
helped stop a massive German ground assault threatening Paris. Since
then it had become both a school for student officers and a place
where new artillery doctrines and different firing methods were
tested. When Westmoreland arrived, the unit was still training with
horse-drawn French 75s, guns that would end up in mothballs a few
years later with the introduction of 105s and 155s. Regardless of the
guns' eventual destination, he was able to gain from them a solid
grounding in the basics of artillery, and was soon, as battery officer,
instructing other student officers and helping to run the battery.

In both areas, he thought he had done an exemplary job and was
certain his efficiency rating would reflect it. He was wrong. He instead
got the shock of his young career when the battery commanders
handed him the report and he discovered that he had been given a
bad rating. Seeing the perplexity on Westmoreland's face, the battery
commander—a middle-aged captain, who as much as anyone represented in the flesh the complacency that so worried Eisenhower—
said, "Lieutenant, I think you deserve a better report, but when I
was a second lieutenant this was as good as I received, and so that's
as good as I intend to give."

At first Westmoreland was barely able to comprehend what he

had just heard. Eventually when the idiocy of the words sank in, he snapped back, "Captain, if this is the basis of your making out my efficiency report, I officially request that you make out no report at all. Since you have to use this type of fallacious objectivity, I'm going to see the battalion commander about this."

Later, still angry, Westmoreland did file his protest, but it was a futile gesture. The battalion commander was not about to go against a middle-aged captain, no matter how obviously wrong the man was, for the sake of a twenty-three-year-old second lieutenant, be he a former West Point first captain or not. What made the situation particularly upsetting for Westmoreland was his later discovery that this same captain was so dumb that he had flunked the basic course at Fort Sill's own Field Artillery School. How he had come to command an artillery battery himself was not so much a mystery as a reflection on the state of the Army. As war became more and more imminent, thousands of officers like the captain would be swept aside by Army Chief of Staff George Marshall's draconian reforms. The captain would not be one of them, though, as he retired a brigadier general.

If Westmoreland had his confidence temporarily shaken by the report, he soon got it back. Not long after the incident, Leonard Shea, a former Westmoreland roommate at West Point who was also presently serving with the 18th Regiment, claimed that Westmoreland came to him and announced matter-of-factly that he didn't think he would ever make a very good platoon leader, but he was certain he would "make an excellent regimental commander." Whether Westmoreland's battalion commander thought so also is unknown. But he did think highly enough of the young man to soon promote him to battery executive officer, then a little later to battery communications officer. While he was not willing to reverse the efficiency rating, he apparently did not take it that seriously either.

Either way, the incident was soon forgotten. Most of the memories Westmoreland took away from Fort Sill were much more pleasant. And they were meant to be. The lack of a sense of urgency that permeated Army life during this period was nowhere more evident than at Fort Sill. Since it was so remote, much of the social life for officers revolved around the post itself. It was a social life, Westmoreland quickly discovered, that was as demanding as his military duties. Much of it was also very formal and seemed deliberately modeled on that of the British aristocracy of this period. As part of this formality, officers were required to dress for dinner each evening in either a white tuxedo or dinner jacket and were encouraged to make appearances at a steady stream of dances, parties, and amateur theatricals. The latter were so popular that Colonel Augustine McIntyre, the school commandant, was nicknamed the Villain after a part he had had in a play.

The most important and popular events, however, centered around the horse. Westmoreland fortunately had learned to ride well at West Point and soon found a spot on Fort Sill's polo team and with a group of riders that got together every Sunday morning for an old-fashioned fox hunt. The group was led by General Arch Arnold, the camp commander, who was also Master of the Hounds. Arnold was sufficiently impressed with Westmoreland's riding ability that he named him Whipper-In of the Hunt. As such, he spent many delightful Sunday mornings attired like everyone else in the group in a traditional pink coat and knee-high black boots riding at breakneck speed through the open country around Fort Sill. The hunts were exhilarating, and afterward all the participants gathered together for a kind of Sunday brunch, where the food and beer were plentiful and everyone had a great time singing hunt songs and ballads. A contemporary of Westmoreland's at Fort Sill during this period remembered the hunts as "high living" and concluded that "outside civilian life one would had to have a lot of money to ride to the hounds as we did."

During one particularly hard ride, Westmoreland was shocked to see a young girl suddenly flash by him, her pigtails trailing behind her, and move to the head of the pack. She rode, he said later, "as if the horse were a part of her." He discovered later than she was nine-year-old Katherine "Kitsy" Van Deusen, the daughter of Colonel Edwin R. Van Deusen, the post executive officer, and his wife, Kay. Since the Van Deusens lived only a few doors down from the bachelor officers quarters, he saw her several times after that. She was a precocious kid, with a sharp mind and a ready wit, who was determined to always get in the last word.

About two years later, Westmoreland got orders assigning him to the 8th Field Artillery Regiment at Schofield Barracks, Hawaii. As he prepared to leave, Molly Hatch, the girl he had been dating, suddenly married someone else. According to Westmoreland, these sudden events brought him "considerable sympathy from the ladies of the post," and from the now eleven-year-old Kitsy. One day while he was sitting despondently in the officers club, Kitsy suddenly walked in and leaped up on the arm of his chair. "Cheer up, Westy," she said. "Don't worry. I'll be a big girl soon. I'll wait for you."

The bickerings of insect authority, the conflicting orders from Washington, the jealousies, the late hours of social life, the white uniforms in the moonlight, the gold braid, the romantic women, the caressing climate are all part of an existence to lull our men into threadbare security.

That was Billy Mitchell's description of Hawaii in 1936, a little over ten years after his 1925 court-martial and just a few months before his death. Ironically, all the sound and fury he had unleashed against the military for its state of unpreparedness had brought little change, and the Hawaii Westmoreland arrived at in 1938 was not all that different from Mitchell's sardonic description. Nor all that different from the Fort Sill he had just left. While there were certainly a great number of officers in the United States military who were genuinely frightened by what was happening in the rest of the world, the great majority of the officer corps, according to the military historian Colonel R. Ernest Dupuy, were not that alarmed.

Westmoreland was one of those who were not. Although he was somewhat disturbed by "Hitler's posturing in Europe," and even more so by his seizure of Czechoslovakia's Sudetenland, he found it difficult conceiving of war "in the idyllic setting of Hawaii." If life for an officer had been pleasant at Fort Sill, it was wonderful at Schofield Barracks, a place that would later become immortalized as the home of Robert E. Lee Prewitt, the rebellious bugler in *From Here to Eternity*.

Life there was also slow and deliberate, moving at a pace and with an ambience that had been firmly established three decades before. As it had for years, the training schedule ran from 8:00 to 11:30 A.M., and Westmoreland's unit, the 8th, like all units, adhered to it religiously. They were armed with towed British three-inch guns, and every morning they towed them out from Schofield to a nearby firing range. There the gun crews unlimbered the small howitzers, then drilled for three and a half hours. Then the guns were towed back to Schofield in time for lunch, and the men spent the rest of the day in various other activities. For most enlisted men, that meant assignment to various fatigue details or working on close-order drill in preparation for the numerous parades and ceremonies that were an integral part of life at Schofield; for those with athletic ability, however, it meant spending the rest of the day instead playing baseball, football, or boxing in preparation for the many interservice rivalries that were also an integral part of life there. Since officers did not fraternize with enlisted men even on the playing field, they spent the rest of their day, and a good part of their weekend, playing golf, tennis, or polo or riding in horse shows, hunts, or steeplechases.

On top of the athletics was piled an equally demanding social schedule. Much of this social life took place at the officers club, where a daily fare of bridge parties, horse shows, retirement dinners, and banquets occupied every leisure moment of the officer and his wife and family. The high point of each week was usually the regimental dinner dance held every Saturday night at the club's outdoor pavilion. It was a lavish affair, where Chinese waiters in white coats scurried about serving drinks and officers and their ladies danced under the moonlight to the music of a full orchestra or chatted and mingled with friends.

As he had at Fort Sill, Westmoreland led an active social life at Schofield, playing golf and tennis and once again riding with a polo team. He also began dating again. His steady for a time was a slim brunette named Jimmie Herron, the daughter of Major General Charles E. Herron, commander of the Hawaiian Department. He and Jimmie frequently went to dances at the pavilion, and spent many lazy Saturday and Sunday afternoons touring Oahu in his car or swimming, surfing, and picnicking on the beaches at Waimanalo, Waikiki, Waimea, and Haleiwa. Whether Miss Herron perceived Westmoreland as too difficult a challenge or whether she simply lost interest in him is unknown, but she eventually broke off the relationship and later married one of his friends. Fortunately for Westmoreland, they parted friends, for while dating her Westmoreland had also gotten to know her father well. The general was very impressed with the young captain and on a number of occasions invited him to go for rides in the country. While their horses trotted along, the general gave Westmoreland advice about his career or tried to fill him in on the many intricacies of Army life.

While at Schofield, Westmoreland also got reacquainted with the Van Deusens when Colonel Van Deusen took over command of the 12th Field Artillery, the 8th's sister regiment. Kitsy was now two years older and at thirteen already an accomplished horsewoman. Westmoreland by now had developed somewhat of a passion for horses and had come to think of himself as an accomplished rider. He was shocked, therefore, when Kitsy beat him in several horse-show events.

In spite of all the time Westmoreland spent on the sporting field or attending the many social events at Schofield, he never lost sight of his career. He balanced his social hours with an equal amount of time spent cloistered in his quarters poring over books on artillery. Although not a brilliant math student, his study of artillery convinced him that there had to be a faster and more accurate way of computing firing data. After weeks of experimenting with various methods, he finally came up with a new way of computing data using logarithms. Certain that it was superior to the old method, he presented his finding to his battalion commander, a cantankerous colonel who had earlier admitted to Westmoreland that he did not like West Point graduates. Pressured by Westmoreland, the colonel begrudgingly let him test the method during the morning training hours. When it did indeed prove superior to the old one, the colonel suggested that Westmoreland write up his finding in the form of an article and send it to the *Field Artillery Journal.* To Westmoreland's dismay, he discovered that he had come very close to getting the credit for developing a new way of computing artillery fire. Unfortunately, researchers at Fort Sill, using a slightly different kind of computation, had developed a similar technique a few months before.

Westmoreland did, though, get the satisfaction of knowing that he knew as much about artillery as some of the best Army experts. Indirectly, his hard work also got him promoted to second lieutenant in June of 1939 and then to captain about a year later.

In the time between his earning the last two ranks, the world, like the rough beast in Yeats's poem "The Second Coming," had continued inching its way slowly toward the precipice of total war. In September of 1939, Germany's army invaded Poland and then in quick succession rallied against Belgium, Holland, Luxembourg, Denmark, Norway, and France. It was lightning war and the American military could do little but stand by slack-jawed and watch.

Almost a year from the day that Westmoreland was promoted to captain, he received further orders transferring him to the 9th Infantry Division at Fort Bragg, North Carolina. Upon arriving, he was assigned to be the operations officer (S-3) for the division's 34th Artillery Battalion. The 9th could trace its lineage back to World War I, where its three infantry regiments—the 39th, 47th, and 60th—had fought with distinction at Aisne-Marne, St. Mihiel, and Meuse-Argonne. But its glory days were a thing of the past. Rather than the crack force it had been when it overran the German trenches at Meuse-Argonne, it was now a hollow shell, a paper division, without the proper equipment or weapons or the trained men to use them. Its ranks instead were filled with the product of the first peacetime draft in United States history, which Congress had passed by only one vote a few months before. These raw recruits, according to one observer at the time, "were inept, indifferent, and just going through the motions."

But fortunately, things were beginning to change, and to change ever more rapidly. Prodded by men like the new Army Chief of Staff, George Marshall, Congress was grudgingly beginning to pump up defense spending. Although the money it was allocating was far short of the spectacular amount that would be reached just a year later, it was enough to allow new weapons and equipment to soon begin trickling in. With them also came a sense of urgency that the Army had not collectively felt since World War I. And according to one 9th Division historian, it could not have come too soon, for "war was now knocking on America's door and it was knocking with loud thumps."

The loudest and hardest thump came on December 7, 1941, with the Japanese attack on Pearl Harbor. The attack shocked America's sensibilities like no other event in the country's history. It also galvanized and united the nation like no other event.

Like most Army posts, Fort Bragg exploded. Almost overnight, it and the nearby town of Fayetteville were overrun by a horde of carpenters, plumbers, painters, and laborers all looking for a piece of the instant prosperity the war brought. On their heels were busloads and trainloads of more draftees and the corps of professional officers and noncommissioned officers needed to train them. Although the latter group had spent almost three decades now in the comparative bliss of a peacetime Army, it still had within its ranks the skills and knowhow necessary to transform these masses of civilians into an army skilled and tough enough to face the hardened legions of Hitler and Tojo. To compensate for its lack of numbers, this professional corps had to divide and subdivide itself over and over again. Staff sergeants who had been leading platoons suddenly found themselves first sergeants commanding companies. Majors who had been commanding battalions now found themselves doing the same with regiments, only now as colonels. And brigadier generals who only a few months before had thought that their careers had peaked with a divisional command, were happily shocked to find themselves leading corps. But not all were so lucky. In counterpoint to this upward ripple was a downward one. There were also a large number of majors, colonels, and even generals who were either forced to resign their commissions or shuffled off to dead-end desk jobs or noncritical training commands.

The upward ripple got Westmoreland an instant promotion to major, a rank that might have taken him fifteen years to achieve in peacetime, and command of the 34th Artillery Battalion. After taking the reins of the 34th, he moved to put his stamp on the outfit. Gathering all his officers together, he lectured them on how important it was for everyone in the unit to look sharp and dress sharp. He changed his uniform every day, and he wanted everyone in his command—and especially officers—to do the same. He reminded them that sloppy dress was indicative of a sloppy attitude, and said that neither would be tolerated in his battalion. As officers, he told them further, they had many duties, but one of the most important was to set a good example for the enlisted men, and to set it not only by dressing sharply, but also by acting positively and projecting an aggressive can-do attitude. It was obvious to everyone present that Westmoreland really meant business, and two hapless second lieutenants would soon discover how much.

George I. Connolly, Jr., was the first. A recent ROTC graduate from Harvard, George arrived at Fort Bragg in early 1942, wearing a brand-new set of gold bars and carrying orders officially making him an officer in the United States Army and assigning him to the 9th Division's artillery. He guessed he should have been filled with pride at the sight of the bars on his shoulder, but he found himself instead filled with uncertainty as to whether he had made a wise decision in accepting a commission. He was certain only that he was, thanks to Harvard, a bit too sophisticated to get overly enthused about the Army. He thought he would be able to keep his lack of enthusiasm hidden, but Westmoreland spotted it immediately when Connolly reported to him in his office.

"Where do you want to be assigned?" Westmoreland asked. "Do you want to be on the guns or with a service battery?"

"I don't have any preference, sir. Anything's okay."

Westmoreland paused for a moment and looked up from his desk incredulously. "Frankly, Lieutenant, I'm surprised you didn't ask for service with a firing battery. I would think that any officer worth his salt would want to be on the guns, right in the thick of things." Connolly squirmed, uncertain how to respond. He didn't need to. Westmoreland responded for him, writing out an order putting him in a service battery, then dismissing him without another word.

Connolly eventually did request and get service with a firing battery and was able to redeem himself in Westmoreland's eyes. His close association with Westmoreland—a man he would come to admire more than any other he had ever met—also gave him a sense of pride in himself he had never had, and convinced him ultimately to make a career in the Army. It was a career he enjoyed, but also found frustrating at times because he was never able to "find another commander who measured up to Westmoreland."

The next officer to endure Westmoreland's wrath was Leon Birum. Leon was likewise a newly minted second lieutenant, though unlike Connolly he did not arrive carrying a degree from Harvard or the sense of self-importance that came with it. He was instead a farmboy only a few weeks out of Officer Candidate School (OCS), and so frightened and unsure of himself that his hands were shaking when he reported to Westmoreland. This lack of aggressiveness and obvious hesitancy prompted Westmoreland to get up out of his chair. "Lieutenant," he said matter-of-factly, "in this battalion officers conduct themselves in a military manner at all times. Now I want you to go back out there and then come back in and report in the manner befitting an officer in the United States Army." Birum said that he was likewise able to redeem himself. During the invasion of Sicily, Westmoreland gave him command of A Battery and a promotion to captain.

After letting his officers know what he expected of them, Westmoreland moved on to the much more difficult task of trying to shape up the 34th. It was not going to be an easy job. According to Connolly, the battalion was a rookie outfit, loaded to the hilt with confused draftees and green officers right out of OCS and ROTC programs. Westmoreland began by completely revising the battalion's training schedule. The change was so radical, according to one man in the unit, that the only things Westmoreland left unchanged were "reveille and retreat." Westmoreland always kept himself in perfect physical condition, and he was determined to make every man in the battalion into a physical image of himself. To do so, he filled the battalion's days with two-mile runs, long rugged hikes, calisthenics, and rigorous training exercises, backed by equally rigorous classroom work. According to Birum, during the runs and hikes, Westmoreland would jog back and forth up and down the battalion column, praising those who were moving along sharply and trying to prod and motivate those who were straggling.

During one particularly long and exhausting hike, Connolly received the benefit of Westmoreland's wrath yet again. During a simulation of an actual combat situation, Westmoreland ordered Connolly, at the moment filling in as a company commander, to march his men on the side of the road rather than down the center to avoid both mines and the possibility of ambush. When he forgot to keep them off the road, Westmoreland rushed up and called the lieutenant off to the side, out of hearing of the men.

"Repeat the battalion order, Lieutenant?" Connolly did sheepishly, and Westmoreland, without raising his voice, said, "Now get those men off that road."

Connolly ran back to the company and was preparing to bark out the new instructions when Westmoreland's voice caught him with his mouth open. "Lieutenant, get back over here."

"Yes, sir."

"Lieutenant, it's the job of the first sergeant to give that order—not an officer. That's something you should know."

"Yes, sir. Sorry, sir."

If Connolly thought he was being picked on, he soon discovered that Westmoreland could be just as hard on the enlisted men. When during another combat simulation the men from one of the batteries failed to dig their slit trenches deep enough, he kept the battery out until after dark digging by flashlight. When he was convinced they knew how to dig in properly, he finally marched them back to the barracks. Westmoreland also made a point of telling the men the reason for the punishment, which was that he had the ultimate responsibility for their welfare. And while he realized there would inevitably be casualties in the battles ahead, he did not want a single one of them to be a result of laziness or carelessness.

Westmoreland balanced the demands he made on the men under him with an equal concern for their welfare. A number of veterans from the 34th recalled that he was constantly mingling with the enlisted men in the battalion and asking them questions about themselves and their families. He had an incredible ability to match names and faces, and very quickly not only knew the name of every man in the battalion, but also something about each man's personal background. During breaks in training, Westmoreland made a habit of walking around among the enlisted men and asking them things like, "How's your father's grocery store doing, Corporal?" Or, "How's your mother doing, Sergeant? Is she out of the hospital yet?" According to a former battalion chaplain, this personal concern on Westmoreland's part for the humanity of each man under him had a miraculous effect on the battalion's morale.

All the work Westmoreland put into his battalion eventually paid dividends. At the Carolina Maneuvers in late February, the 34th

Artillery earned the highest point total of any of the artillery batteries competing. It also earned him a reputation among senior officers at Fort Bragg as someone to keep an eye on, someone who was going places in the Army and was going there in a hurry. Years later in retirement, Westmoreland would say that he never politicked or schemed to get ahead in the Army, that he just did his job to the best of his ability and trusted in the system to reward him. The statement was essentially true, but not completely. While it is true that he never made a conscious effort to influence his superiors by having powerful friends or people with political connections intercede on his behalf—something MacArthur did on a number of occasions— he was not above consciously trying to manipulate his career so that he could speed it up. Like any officer with big ambitions, he was an opportunist, and he was quick to take advantage of any opportunity that would jack his career up one more notch.

At Fort Bragg, he thought he had found that opportunity in an airborne command that had recently been set up at the post to study and develop America's brand-new airborne capability. After watching a number of jumps and training exercises, Westmoreland became convinced that airborne units were going to play an important, if not critical, role in the war, and for an aggressive ambitious officer like himself it seemed like the place to be. A short time after he came to this conclusion, he drove over to the airborne compound for a talk with Colonel James Gavin, a man who was helping to develop the new 82nd Airborne Division at nearby Fort Benning, Georgia. Gavin and Westmoreland already knew each other. They had met briefly a few months before during a training exercise. In fact, after that first meeting, a fellow officer had walked up to Gavin and in reference to Westmoreland said, "Sir, that man's going to be Chief of Staff some-day." It is not known whether Gavin also thought so highly of the young major, but after talking with Westmoreland a second time, he was impressed enough to want him in the 82nd. The decision to add him to the division, unfortunately, was not Gavin's to make. It rested instead with Brigadier General S. LeRoy Irwin, the commanding officer of the 9th Division Artillery, and Irwin was not willing to give up his hotshot subordinate.

CHAPTER FIVE

Hotshot

Westmoreland was disappointed over not being allowed to hook up with the 82nd, but he was consoled considerably by his promotion to lieutenant. In September, the 9th Division got orders to ship out as part of the American force earmarked to invade North Africa. According to the orders, the 9th's three infantry regiments were to sail first, but during the invasion were to fight separately as regimental combat teams. Westmoreland's battalion was not needed in the initial invasion, but was to join with the rest of the division when it was reunited in late 1942.

The invasion of North Africa was code-named Operation Torch. Its purpose was to destroy Field Marshal Erwin Rommel's much vaunted Afrika Corps and his Italian allies. Rommel had already been dealt a major defeat by Field Marshal Sir Bernard Montgomery's Eighth Army at El Alamein in October of 1942, and the Allies now felt it was time to deliver the knockout blow. To deliver that blow, Operation Torch called for landings by American forces under Major General George S. Patton at Casablanca in Morocco and Major General Lloyd Frendenhall at Oran in Algeria and a combined landing of British and American forces under British Major General William Ryder at Algiers, also in Algeria. Once ashore, the first two forces were to attack east and Ryder's forces southeast, while Montgomery's Eighth made a simultaneous advance north from Egypt. In the end, it was hoped, the Germans and Italians would be caught in Tunisia by a giant pincer and destroyed. The landings went well. Although the French Vichy forces defending Morocco and Algeria put up some fierce initial resistance, they quickly surrendered, and all three forces secured their beachheads and began pushing inland.

After a twelve-day voyage from New York, Westmoreland and his battalion arrived in Casablanca on Christmas Eve, 1942. There they unloaded their howitzers and equipment, packed it aboard trucks, and started inland. Eighty miles later, they finally caught up with the rest of the division at their bivouac near Port Lyautey, French Morocco. The 9th had already been blooded fighting the French, and Westmoreland hurried to prepare his battalion for the harder fighting he knew lay ahead when they eventually met Rommel's Afrika Corps. As soon as his men had settled their personal gear at the bivouac, he called them out for a long hike through the surrounding hills and desert. Halfway through the hike, he called a break on a small hill facing a partially destroyed French tank, then gathered the men in a semicircle around him. Pointing to the tank, he told them that it was important for them to keep in mind that many times in the fighting ahead they would not have infantry to protect their gun positions and so it was important that each of them learned to fire both the bazooka and rifle-grenade. After demonstrating both, he then took up a position about two hundred yards from the tank and proceeded to hit it over and over again with grenades and bazooka rounds. According to Connolly, it really calmed the men knowing that they were going into battle with an officer who could not only demonstrate how to use a weapon, but could actually use it himself.

The battalion would soon need the extra bit of confidence it gained that day. For while the Allies were still planning their next move in Algeria and Tunisia, Rommel made one of his own. Realizing that his forces could, in fact, become trapped between Montgomery's Eighth Army pushing north and the three new Allied forces moving east, he decided to do the unexpected, to strike the Allied forces moving into Tunisia first, in the hope that a powerful decisive blow might drive them completely out of North Africa. Once they were eliminated, he could then turn the full fury of his panzers against Montgomery.

Rommel's armored forces struck first at Faïd, seriously damaged the United States 1st Armored Division, then pushed on to the Kasserine Pass. There, with frightening ease, they methodically smashed the American infantry division, and battered a British armored brigade trying to come to their rescue. For the Americans at Kasserine, it was their first fight against a first-class foe, and they proved themselves unworthy of the encounter. The defeat there was total. Three thousand Americans were killed or wounded, and another four thousand taken prisoner. The roads for miles through the pass were littered with the grim sight of hundreds of burned and smashed American tanks, trucks, halftracks, and jeeps. A British officer taken prisoner during the battle, when asked by his German captors to describe the American soldier, bitterly remarked, "They're our Italians."

Furious over the defeat, Eisenhower took direct command of the battle himself. His first priority was his only one: He had to stop the Germans from advancing any farther or face having his forces ignominiously expelled from North Africa. To help stop them, he ordered the 9th Division's artillery commander, General Irwin, to rush three battalions and two companies of guns up to Kasserine. Irwin, in turn, ordered Westmoreland and his 34th to lead the column.

After getting his orders, Westmoreland called all the officers in the battalion into his command post and had them gather around him. "When you fellows came into the service," he told them, "we took you from civilians and made soldiers of you, then when we came overseas we separated the men from the boys, and now we're moving out and we're going to make artillerymen out of you."

A short time later, they boarded their trucks and started off on a 789-mile journey through the heart of the Atlas Mountains. The column started out in a drizzling rain, which quickly turned to a light snow, then to a freezing rain. In places, the narrow, snaking road was a sheet of ice; in others, a quagmire of gooey mud, forcing the truck drivers to drive for miles in low gear, with their engines whining under the hard pull. The weather was hard on the men, but its effect was compounded by the fact that few had any winter clothing, which was still in a warehouse at the rear.

Instead of the heavy wool coats they needed, they men sat in the back of the trucks shivering in light field-jackets, their heads and ears covered with towels and blankets. As if immune to the cold, Westmoreland moved up and down the column. When a truck got mired in the mud, he was there to help get it moving again. When a howitzer went into a ditch, he was there to help pull it back out. To make better time, the trucks were never turned off. To avoid attracting roaming Messerschmitts, the drivers drove at night with their blackout lights on. When they got so tired that they could no longer see the road through the rain and snow, others took their place, making the change while the truck was still moving.

In spite of the weather, the column covered 210 miles the first day, 234 the second, and the final 345 miles on a third and fourth day. It finally halted on the outskirts of Tebessa, a small Arab village that had been blasted into ruin by shell fire. There, the battalion was greeted by the demoralizing sight of hundreds of American soldiers and Arab civilians fleeing in panic before Rommel's juggernaut.

Westmoreland left his battalion at Tebessa and drove a jeep up to Thala, where he met with some British officers from the 5th Leicesters, a British infantry brigade. After the American debacle at Kasserine, the Leicesters, along with an additional brigade of tanks under Brigadier Charles A. L. Dunphie, had moved forward to stop any further German advance out of the pass. For four days, they had been fighting tenaciously to contain the German advance, but were finally breaking under the incessant attacks. When they finally did give way, Rommel would have an open road north. After a hurried conference, it was agreed that the best way to meet the German attack was for the 9th's artillery to set up their guns along a trail that ran parallel to the road out of the Kassserine Pass. By placing their guns there, they could hit the German tank formations with enfilading fire.

While he was still talking with the British, Westmoreland began snapping out orders. He sent a runner back to his battalion with the message "Move the guns up here immediately. Leave behind everything that's nonessential." He then ordered his forward observers to string wire out to forward observation posts, so that they could better call in fire on any German attack. Within a few hours, all forty-eight guns arrived on the ridge and Westmoreland helped position them. In the dark, gun crews began preparing stacks of rounds, organizing their fuses and powder bags, and digging bunkers. They slept around their guns that night, curled up in blankets and sleeping bags against the freezing night air and drizzling rain.

Fortunately for the gun crews, the rain stopped during the night, and the fog cleared. They awoke to a brilliant sun and a gray desert visible for miles in all directions. At 7:00 A.M., Rommel's panzers rolled out of the Kasserine Pass and started forward toward their immediate goal, Thala, completely unaware that the forty-eight guns on the ridge were zeroing in on them. The first volley caught them by complete surprise. When Rommel received word of the fire, he realized that reinforcements had arrived. He hesitated for a moment, unsure if he should continue the attack, then finally decided to go ahead with it. His tanks kept rolling. Three or four of his tanks took hits and caught fire, then two or three more. Rommel's ground commanders spotted the guns on the ridge and brought counterbattery fire against them, which soon knocked out two of them. German Messerschmitts, braving American antiaircraft fire, strafed the United States gun positions, wounding and killing a number of men. Still the guns kept firing. When a dozen German tanks turned from the road and got on line to attack the gun position head-on, the artillerymen lowered the barrels of their 105s and 155s, rammed home armor-piercing rounds, then bore-sighted the guns and opened up. A direct hit on a panzer resulted, and then another. The rest of the panzers pulled back.

For the rest of the morning, the Germans continued mounting new attacks, and the 9th's guns responded by smashing them. By late morning, Rommel, now in despair, called off the attack. Like the Americans who had fought in the Kasserine Pass a week before, the Germans left behind a trail of smashed burning tanks, halftracks, and trucks.

Although the Americans had no way of knowing it, Rommel's retreat meant that the Battle of Kasserine Pass was over, and with it any chance of an Axis victory in North Africa. In his detailed analysis of the battle, *Kasserine,* the historian Martin Blumenson concluded that the 9th Infantry Division's timely arrival and deadly accurate fire had been the deciding factor. Since the 34th had played such a crucial role in the victory, it was awarded a Presidential Unit Citation. The citation applauded the battalion for its "incredible forced march which contributed in great measure to the defeat of the enemy's attempt to break through the Thala defile."

The citation given the 34th was well received by the men in the battalion. They knew they had done an excellent job, and there was no doubt in their minds that they deserved it. Not many other American units who fought at Kasserine could say the same, however. Rather than being exemplary, most of the performances turned in by other United States units there were disgraceful, a black mark on the American Army that would be hard to erase.

To guarantee that there never occurred another Kasserine, Eisenhower telephoned Patton on March 4 and ordered him to meet him in Algiers the next day. During that meeting, Eisenhower officially turned over II Corps to Patton, and with it a set of impassioned instructions: He was to get II Corps back on its feet, restore the pride and self-respect of its fighting men, and convince them that they could and must defeat the Germans. When necessary, Patton had the power to relieve any commander.

After Thala, Westmoreland's job was secure, but a number of senior officers were shaken by the news that Patton was on the way to take over II Corps. Patton arrived on fire, his face locked in a permanent frown, his now legendary pearl-handled .38s strapped arrogantly to his hips. During a whirlwind tour of every unit in II Corps, he was everywhere at once, shouting, cursing, prodding, and threatening. During the uproar, he instituted instant and drastic changes. In his belief that discipline was the essential ingredient in a fighting army, he made the wearing of neckties, leggings, and helmets mandatory, demanded that military courtesy and saluting be observed at all times, and began wholesale firings of officers who had proven themselves unworthy at Kasserine or who he did not think were aggressive enough. During one speech to a battalion of infantry, he urged them to be vicious to the Germans and to kill rather than die for freedom. "We must utterly defeat the enemy. . . . I know you will be worthy."

Eleven days after taking over II Corps, Patton went on the attack. On the night of March 16, he sent a rejuvenated 1st Infantry Division against Gafsa, then the complete 9th Infantry Division, with all their artillery, against El Guettar. The 9th was tasked specifically with clearing a mountain pass near El Guettar of its German defenders so that an armored force could get through and into the open plains beyond. To soften up the German positions at El Guettar, the 9th's artillery blasted them for hours with a torrent of shells from over one hundred guns, guns that according to one historian were "lined up hub to hub." Behind the barrage, the 9th's infantry surged forward and attacked the German positions, was thrown back, then attacked again. As the infantry gained ground, the artillery followed close behind, always getting as close as possible in order to bring more accurate fire on the enemy positions. During the attack, Westmoreland made his presence felt everywhere, checking on the gun crews, making sure an adequate supply of rounds was being moved forward from rear depots, helping to plot firemissions, talking with the aerial observer. When a German 170mm howitzer took one of his batteries under fire from a distance way beyond the range of his 155s, he personally helped the battery to move forward under continuous fire until they were close enough to duel the 170. When one of the division's infantry regiments requested assistance coordinating their night defensive fire, he ordered his jeep driver to take him up to the position. On the way up, they drove through a gauntlet of shell fire so heavy that the driver later likened the experience to walking the plank. One round did, in fact, glance off the jeep's rear fender, fortunately exploding to the rear.

In spite of the overwhelming firepower the 9th brought against the enemy positions at El Guettar, and in spite of repeated tenacious infantry assaults, it still took six days to clear the pass of Germans. Once it was clear, the 1st Armored Division, also the beneficiary of a Patton rejuvenation, rolled through and headed for the coast. A short time later, elements of II Corps and Montgomery's Eighth Army linked up, a moment that signaled death for the remaining Axis units in North Africa. Now all along the coast, German and Italian units— cut off, out of food and water, low on ammunition, demoralized by incessant bombardment and shelling—began surrendering. When the final mop-up was complete, over 275,000 Axis prisoners, more even than at Stalingrad, had surrendered. By May 13, 1943, all of North Africa was under Allied control. The victory in North Africa was a monumental achievement for the Allies. Just as Thala had been a turning point at Kasserine, North Africa, viewed through a wider lens, was a turning point in the war. The initiative the Germans had held exclusively since their blitzkrieg rolled over Europe in 1939 had now been seized by the Allies, and seized for good.

North Africa was also a turning point for the careers of many officers. Those who had proven themselves there under fire got instant promotions and better commands; those who had not, those who had failed under fire, were shuffled off to Army backwaters, to training commands or meaningless desk jobs. Westmoreland joined the former group. Although it would be stretching the point to say that North Africa made his career, it certainly gave it a giant boost forward. During the four months he had spent pushing the 34th across Morocco, Algeria, and Tunisia, he had proven himself an able, innovative, and aggressive commander, and proven it over and over again. During that same period, Westmoreland had also gradually developed what one historian called a "subsurface reputation" among senior commanders in North Africa. "That Westmoreland is a real hotshot," they said of him. "Sharp commander! Really knows how to move a unit."

But Westmoreland was not content with the accolades he took away with him from North Africa. While the Allies were completing the final mopping up in North Africa and begining preparations for the invasion of Sicily, he was making plans of his own, plans that he hoped would get him into an airborne unit.

The invasion of Sicily, code-named Husky, officially kicked off on

July 10, 1943, with the landing of portions of the Seventh Army, now under Patton, against the southwest corner of the island and a landing by Montgomery's Eighth Army against the southeast corner. In all, 180,000 Allied troops took part in the invasion; opposing them were 315,000 Italian and 90,000 German troops. Leading the assault in the American sector were the paratroopers of the 82nd Airborne Division, who had been orderd by Patton to parachute into the hills above Gela in order to protect the landing there the next morning. The airdrop was a disaster. Winds and pilot confusion scattered the four battalions of troops sixty miles up and down the coast. In spite of that fact, Major General Mathew Ridgway, the commander of the 82nd, was able to round up enough paratroopers and enough bazookas to hold back the crack Hermann Goering Division, which came racing from the west in an attempt to erase the Seventh Army's beachheads. Thanks to the 82nd, the Seventh Army got ashore with barely a fight. As part of that uneventful landing, Westmoreland and his 34th went in at the port of Licata in support of the 39th Infantry Regiment, then pushed forward to set up a perimeter and await further orders.

During the brief pause before his unit was committed to action again, Westmoreland got a jeep and drove up into the hills above Gela. After a hurried search, he parked in front of Ridgway's command post, then boldly strode inside. Ridgway at the moment was briefing a group of his officers. The moment he finished, Westmoreland stepped up and introduced himself, then said that he had heard the 82nd would be one of the units spearheading the attack across Sicily and he was here to offer him "the best artillery support you have ever had." If Westmoreland had been expecting a hard sell, he was wrong. Ridgway had been looking to add some punch to his artillery component, which carried the 75mm howitzers standard for all airborne units, and that punch had just walked in his door. Without hesitation, he rang up Bradley, who had taken over II Corps from Patton, requested a loan of the 34th, and got it.

To make sure that Westmoreland and his battalion could hack it with an airborne unit, Ridgway sent his artillery commander, Brigadier General Maxwell D. Taylor, down to Licata to inspect them. Taylor admitted later that he went down to make the inspection thinking that as an old artilleryman he pretty much knew all the "tricks" in handling 155s, but in Westmoreland he found "somebody who knew them all, too." Taylor came away so impressed with Westmoreland and his unit that he invited him to join him for dinner that evening. For Westmoreland, it would turn out to be the most important dinner of his career. Although he could hardly have foreseen it, the man sitting across from him that evening was destined to become the most prominent American military man since Douglas MacArthur. During dinner, Westmoreland and Taylor forged the beginning of what would be a long friendship and professional relationship. For Westmoreland, one benefit of that relationship would be his 1964 assignment to Vietnam. Critics of Westmoreland would say later that what also happened that night over dinner was Westmoreland's introduction to what they would sarcastically call "the airborne mafia," a kind of private club headed by Taylor and Gavin "with lines of succession and intertwining careers that reached from World War II to Vietnam and included Westmoreland, most of Westmoreland's commanders in Vietnam and a host of others in key Army positions throughout the 1960s and early 1970s."

The next morning, Ridgway assigned the 34th to support Gavin's 505th Regiment. For Westmoreland it was a fortunate assignment. He had previously developed a method of moving artillery rapidly during a fast-paced attack, a method he had aptly named "the blitz formation," but he had been unable to use it in North Africa because of the slow pace of the advance. Using this new "blitz formation," he was able to keep his artillery pieces right behind Gavin's paratroopers as they and the rest of the 82nd took off on an eight-day, 120-mile lightning campaign across Sicily's west coast, an attack that smashed and scattered three different Italian divisions along the way and took over twenty-three thousand prisoners. During those eight days, the 34th changed firing positions five different times and helped to soften up enemy positions at Ribera, Santa Margherita, Sciacca, and finally Trapani. During the final stages of that fight, again while out scouting ahead of his battalion, Westmoreland was blown from his jeep when it ran over a German land mine. Although he was not wounded by the mine, this incident, combined with his aggressive command work at Thala and El Guettar, earned him a Legion of Merit. The accompanying citation specifically lauded his "supreme courage and devotion to duty."

Following the presentation of the Legion of Merit, Westmoreland led his battalion to a rest and recuperation camp on the Tyrrhenian coast, where they were soon joined by the rest of the division. For the next ten weeks, the men of the 9th Infantry Division had a chance to catch up on their sleep, repair damaged equipment, watch USO shows, and eat their fill from chow lines heaped with piles of meat, fresh vegetables, and fruit. Westmoreland felt the rest, especially for his battalion, was well deserved. He was shocked, however, when orders came down from division headquarters ordering the 34th to stay behind and clean up the bivouac site while the rest of the division was trucked to Palermo, where transports awaited to move them to England. Westmoreland, according to one of his officers, Leon Birum, bristled at the thought of his men—men who had fought so bravely at Thala and El Guettar and all across Sicily, and exhibited a degree of professionalism few units could match—picking up the cigarette butts and garbage or filling in the latrines of other units. "It is simply unthinkable," Westmoreland is reported to have told his staff. After the pronouncement, Westmoreland marched off to division head-quarters and there told Lieutenant General Manton S. Eddy's staff that the 34th was a crack unit, one of the best in II Corps, and that it would destroy the morale of his men and their sense of unit pride to be forced to do police duty after other units. Westmoreland ap-parently made his point, for the next day division headquarters re-scinded the order. According to Birum, the fact that Westmoreland had stood up for them only increased the respect they already had for him.

Their pride intact, the 34th Artillery Battalion rode on to Palermo, then boarded a transport ship for the long trip to England. They joined the rest of the division in Barton Stacey, a quaint country town about sixty miles southwest of London, where a camp consisting of rows of barracks was set up. Like the nearly one million Americans already bivouacked all over southern England, the 9th Infantry Di-vision went back into training for what everyone knew was coming, the massive Allied invasion of Europe sometime in mid-1944.

One of the units earmarked to lead that invasion was the 101st Airborne Division, which Maxwell Taylor, now a major general, took command of on March 18. The moment he did, Taylor set about putting together the kind of staff he wanted. For Taylor that process began with a drive to Barton Stacey and a visit with Westmoreland, whom he tried to entice to join the 101st by offering him a position on his staff as the division's artillery executive officer and an immediate promotion to colonel. Although Westmoreland had grown quite fond of the 9th Infantry Division, he realized he likely had a greater future with an airborne unit, and told Taylor he would be happy to join the 101st. Unfortunately for Westmoreland yet again he could not approve his own transfer. It rested instead in the hands of General Eddy and he was not about to cut loose such a valuable young commander. To assuage Westmoreland's feelings, however, Eddy offered him a deal equivalent to Taylor's: an immediate promotion to colonel and the position of division artillery executive officer.

The promotion came on April 13, 1944. Twenty-one days later,

Eddy got an alert order telling him to prepare the 9th for action. That action finally came on the evening of June 9, when the entire division, now under the operational control of General Lawton Collins's VII Corps, was ordered aboard transport, which promptly sailed for France. In the early morning hours of June 10, those transports docked just outside Utah Beach, one of the five beaches assaulted during the initial invasion three days before. There the men of the 9th boarded landing craft and started ashore to join the battle for France.

The 9th went into the line for the first time on June 14 when they replaced the 90th Infantry Division, a green outfit that had become demoralized after their first hard contact. Along with the 4th Infantry Division and 82nd Airborne Division, they were ordered to attack and seal off the Cherbourg Peninsula, where four German divisions were menacing the right flank of the Allied beachheads. The 9th was now a veteran outfit, and they performed like one. Attacking to the southwest, they quickly smashed and overran the German positions at Ste.-Colombe, Reigneville, Hautteville-Bocage, Orglandes, and Quineville. Their advance was so rapid that by July 16 they were closing in on the German defenses along the Douve River. There, after a particularly fierce fight, the 9th's artillery smashed the German 91st Division and sent its survivors reeling toward the sea. By July 17, the 9th and its two sister divisions had completely cut off the Cherbourg Peninsula.

With four divisions now penned inside the Allied cordon, the commander of the German Seventh Army inexplicably ordered his 77th Infantry Division to attempt a breakout south toward La Haye-du-Puits. There it was to join with the German forces southeast of the cordon and then join with the German forces southeast of the cordon and then join a massive attack on the Allied beachheads. In order to make the breakout as strong as possible, the commander of the 77th, Generalmajor Rudolf Stegmann, massed a large number of tanks at the front of his column, which he hoped to use as a giant fist to punch a hole in the 9th's lines. Before Stegmann could deliver his punch, however, Westmoreland delivered one of his own. Marshaling the forty-eight guns at his disposal, he massed their fire against the front of the enemy column and with barrage after barrage smashed the lead tanks and sent the accompanying infantry running for cover. Then, according to the official account of the battle, he "methodically destroyed" the rest of the three-mile-long column of tanks, artillery pieces, and trucks. When infantrymen came upon the scene a short time later, they found the road was so clogged with burning, smashed vehicles that it had become impassable. In the rubble, they counted over five hundred German dead, including Stegmann. Only one battalion from the 77th managed to get through the 9th's line, and it without any of its equipment. Those few survivors would soon count themselves lucky. After flying in from Berchtesgaden, Hitler personally charged the commandant of the Cherbourg garrison "to defend it to the last bunker and leave the enemy not a harbor but a field of ruins."

The American leaders were quick to oblige Hitler. After a hurried meeting with General Bradley, General Collins instructed his division commanders to "advance directly on Cherbourg as rapidly as possible." Like the attack to seal off the peninsula, the attack to reduce it was executed with speed and daring. The 9th Infantry Division led the way on the right flank. Supported by Westmoreland's artillery, they quickly overran, or in many cases bypassed, German positions at Rauville-la-Bigot, St.-Germain-le-Gaillard, Rocheville, Couville, St.-Christophe-du Foc, and a dozen others. Two days after the start of their attack up the peninsula, the 9th finally stopped just short of Cherbourg itself, a thick-walled port city that the Germans had adroitly turned into a fortress. To reduce it, hundreds of fighter-bombers and heavy bombers attacked the enemy bunkers and shelters with high explosives and napalm. When German antiaircraft batteries shot down twenty-four of the planes on the first day, Westmoreland and the two other division artillery commanders coordinated their fire and systematically knocked out nearly every enemy battery. The next day, the bombers went at Cherbourg through a sky nearly clear of flak.

Finally, in the late afternoon of June 22, backed by a rolling artillery barrage, the 9th and its sister divisions started their ground attack. Although the Germans put up some initial resistance, it quickly collapsed. An intercepted message from the Cherbourg commander, General Karl Schlieben, to Rommel told the reason for the collapse. "Artillery fire," he stammered, "had completely crushed all resistance." Schlieben surrendered the next day.

After taking part in the mop-up of Cherbourg, the 9th Infantry Division wheeled south once again and quickly secured the Cap de la Hague Peninsula on June 29. After beating back an armored counterattack near Le Desert, the division then pushed on and helped take St.-Lô. Finally in late July, it went on line once again with the rest of VII Corps and prepared for what would later be called the Normandy breakout, a massive attempt by the Allies to blast their way out of their beachheads and into the open country beyond. To smash a hole in the German lines opposite VII Corps, General Bradley unleashed Operation Cobra on July 25, which translated into an attack by over twenty-five hundred heavy bombers and fighter-bombers, carrying forty-two hundred tons of high explosives, against the German lines. Although two of the main bomb runs accidentally hit the American lines, causing nearly five hundred casualties, many of which were from one of the 9th's battalions, most landed on target with deadly accuracy. During one ninety-minute bomb run, an entire panzer division was wiped out, and a number of other units were so crippled and dazed that they had to be pulled out of the line. In all, the two days of bomb runs blasted a five-square-mile hole in the German line and through it poured VII Corps's armor and infantry at full throttle. After penetrating deeply through the German lines, the units of VII Corps then hooked in behind those same lines, shooting up the enemy units in retreat from the shock of the air attack. The Germans managed to shake off the shock momentarily at Mortain, where they mounted a fierce but disorganized counterattack, but these units too were eventually ravaged by air attacks and massed artillery fire and put in full retreat.

With Mortain cleared, VII Corps crossed the Seine and rolled into Belgium, where it was finally stopped dead in its tracks at the Siegfried Line, a three-mile-deep labyrinth of deep bunkers, pillboxes, and fighting trenches, all with interlocking fields of fire. Tied in with the fortifications were miles of pyramidal concrete projections called dragon teeth, which had been designed to stop tanks. It was a formidable obstacle, which Hitler had once boasted was impregnable.

To knock out the bunkers and pillboxes in the 9th Infantry Division's sector, a number of artillery pieces were moved to the front lines. There, working with the infantry, the artillery gunners used their guns as they had at Thala. Bore-sighting them, they opened fire at point-blank range with armor-piercing rounds, which turned the bunkers and pillboxes into jagged piles of concrete and steel-reinforcing rods. In one day, the 9th's gunners took out twenty-five German emplacements and on another day twenty. Within a week, the 9th was through the Siegfried Line and gearing up for further attacks north toward Germany.

At this time, the 9th Infantry Division got a new commander, Major General Lewis A. Craig, to replace Eddy who was moving up to take over VII Corps. For Westmoreland it was a fortuitous change, for Craig arrived from the United States without a staff. Since Eddy took his entire staff with him, Craig had to pick a new staff from the ranks of the 9th's officers. After hearing wonderful things about West-moreland, he made the colonel his chief of staff on October 13, 1944. Ironically, one of Westmoreland's best recommendations came from the artillery commander, Brigadier General Reese M. Howell, a man who was more than happy to be rid of his subordinate. The two had argued earlier after Howell had accused Westmoreland of trying to subtly usurp his authority by taking over too many jobs that were within the rightful purview of the commander. Angry, in turn, at the charge, Westmoreland had asked to be transferred back to the 34th Artillery Battalion. To Howell's credit, he had not let the disagree-ment cloud his overall view of Westmoreland, whom he considered an officer of the highest integrity and character.

Westmoreland's new position put him at the center of power in the 9th Infantry Division. But if he reveled at all in his good luck, it was short-lived. Almost immediately afterward, the 9th was ordered to begin an attack through the Huertgen Forest, an attack that he as chief of staff had to coordinate. The Huertgen was a three-mile-deep forest of towering trees and thick gnarled underbrush, which the Germans had festooned with thousands of bunkers, pillboxes, and fighting trenches. The thousands of men who fought there would forever remember the name Huertgen as synonymous with dread.

The men of the 9th Infantry Division would certainly be among them. Attacking down narrow trails clogged with fallen timber and heavily seeded with mines, they were savaged by machine-gun fire coming from deep bunkers so carefully camouflaged with leaves and tree branches as to be almost invisible. As they tried to manuever against the bunkers, snipers pecked at them from treetops and fighting holes. When pinned down, enemy mortarmen put air bursts in the trees above them, peppering them with hot shrapnel and jagged tree splinters. The first day's advance was a mere hundred yards, the second only a few more. Casualties mounted with each yard gained. One company from the 39th Infantry Regiment lost two thirds of its men killed or wounded in a single day, another 50 per cent. One week after the start of the attack, the 9th, having suffered three thousand casualties, had to be pulled out of the line and sent to the rear. They left the job of taking the Huertgen to the two other di-visions in VII Corps. According to the official Army history of the battle, one of those division, the 4th, was "reduced to near impotence" by its losses there. The forest was, however, finally cleared of Ger-mans, though at such a frightful cost that everyone wished the ordeal forgotten.

When the 9th Infantry Division went back into the line again, they were facing the Roer River and tasked with taking the city of Düren in close coordination with the 3rd Armored Division. Their attack had hardly gotten under way, however, when on December 16, 1944, the Germans suddenly and inexplicably launched one of their own against the weakly defended American lines in the Ardennes Forest. The attack was massive. Behind a thundering artillery barrage, the spearhead of three full German armies—backed by two thousand tanks and nearly two thousand planes—smashed a hole in the American lines forty-five miles wide. Through that hole, the armored columns poured and started a mad dash for the Allied supply dumps on the Meuse River and at the port city of Antwerp. Hitler, who had been planning the attack for three months, hoped that its boldness and ferocity would split the Allied forces, cut them off from their supply depots, and suddenly turn the tide of the war in his favor.

A number of American units, including the ill-fated 106th Infantry Division, were crushed by the initial assault and a number of others were ignominiously put on the run. The 9th Infantry Division was not one of them. After getting word of the attack, Westmoreland helped pull the division out of their attack against Düren and headed south. After containing enemy tank assaults at Mariaweiler and Guerzenich, the 9th made a twenty-four-mile forced march down icy, snow-covered roads to the Allied lines between the towns of Monschau and Elsenborn. There they relieved the badly bloodied and shaken United States 2nd and 99th infantry divisions. After digging in in the frozen fields, they beat back repeated attempts by the Germans to expand their salient north. Their defense helped channel the force of the German attack down a narrow corridor, where it eventually collided with the 101st Airborne Division at Bastogne. Held at bay by the 101st's ferocious defense, the German juggernaut ground to a halt, and was soon easy pickings for some five thousand Allied aircraft and a relief column of tanks under Patton.

The Battle of the Bulge ended on January 1, 1945, with the Germans in full retreat. Thirty days later, the Allies went back on the offensive. For the 9th Infantry Division that meant regenerating their attack against Düren, which they overran after two days of street fighting on February 25, 1945. Then just as quickly they cleared a German battalion from Stockheim and captured Binsfield. Finally, attacking behind armor from the 3rd Armored Division, it took the heavily defended town of Moedrath, smashing an enemy armored division in the process. From Moedrath, the 9th joined a number of other United States divisions in a mad rush to the Rhine River, the last major barrier barring the Allies from the heart of Germany. The broad, meandering river had not been crossed by an invader since Napoleonic times. To make certain the Allies did not cross it now, Hitler ordered all the bridges over the river destroyed. At that point, according to the historian Robert Leckie, "one of the great mischances of history" took place.

Arriving at the town of Remagen, the 9th Armored Division discovered that the bridge across the Rhine at this point had inexplicably not been blown. They did not know the truth, that the Germans had detonated charges under the bridge but they had not been strong enough to drop it.

Regardless, the 9th Armored pushed across the bridge, then radioed back to corps headquarters for further instructions. Those instructions eventually came down from Eisenhower himself. Build up the bridgehead, he ordered. Eisenhower's general order was eventually translated into a more specific order from the First Army commander, Lieutenant General Courtney Hodges, to the 9th Infantry Division commander, General Craig. "We got a bridge at Remagen; I need a regiment."

Since Craig wanted to stay with the main body of the 9th Infantry Division, he ordered Westmoreland to take the 47th Regiment and make a forced march to Remagen. There he was to take over command of the bridgehead and begin expanding it as new units arrived. After an all-night march of twenty-five-miles through constant rain and over a road that had been turned into a swirling sea of mud, Westmoreland brought the 47th to the bridge in the early morning hours of March 8. Because of a blackout, he walked the last two miles out in the front of the lead jeep, guiding the driver with voice commands as he slogged through knee-deep mud. Groping in the darkness, they then crossed the bridge, as German artillery crashed all around them. By the light of flashlights, they set up a command post about seven hundred yards north of the bridge.

They got set up just in time. The next morning swarms of German Stukas came out of the north and, their sirens wailing, dove at the bridge with 500- and 750-pound bombs. A number of the bombs hit the structure, but failed to bring it down. Undeterred, the Germans next turned their artillery against it, and for hours a rain of high-explosive shells smashed into the steel spans and cratered the bridge's concrete roadway.

Still it stood. Almost simultaneously with their attack on the bridge, the Germans moved to smash the bridgehead. Employing two armored divisions, led by Afrika Corps veteran General Fritz

Bayerlein, the Germans moved against the bridgehead late in the afternoon of March 9. They aimed most of the force of that attack at the 47th Regiment, which Westmoreland had placed in the center of the bridgehead. Bayerlein's plan was to smash the 47th, split the bridgehead in half, and then roll up its flanks. He and his panzers did none of these. Their backs literally to the wall, the 47th put up what the official history called "one of the most tenacious defenses in U.S. Army history." Day and night for two weeks, the men of the 47th braved continuous shell fire to throw back repeated assaults by the 2nd and 9th panzer divisions, both of which had been ordered by Hitler himself to erase the bridgehead or perish in the process. Through all the fighting, Westmoreland was right there behind the 47th, directing new units into the line as they arrived, organizing convoys of trucks to haul supplies forward and to haul back the hundreds of wounded, and most important, keeping III Corps and First Army headquarters continually apprised of the situation inside the bridgehead.

He did his job well, as the Bronze Star he received from his actions inside the bridgehead attested. But not everyone in the chain of command could claim as much. As the fight for the bridgehead got hotter, it became apparent to both Westmoreland and General Craig that their corps commander, Major General John Millikin, was hampering the operation with orders that were so confused and indecisive that both men actually feared for the safety of the bridgehead. They both also agreed that Millikin needed to go. But Craig, being what Westmoreland called excessively "loyal" to Millikin, refused to say anything to Lieutenant General Hodges, the First Army commander. Westmoreland did not suffer from the same qualms. When Hodges visted the bridgehead around March 14 or 15, Westmoreland immediately sought out Hodges's aide, Captain Billy Sylvan. Sylvan had been a boyhood friend back in South Carolina and Westmoreland told him pointedly what he and Craig had concluded. As Westmoreland had hoped, Sylvan carried the news directly to Hodges, who it turned out was already angry with the slow way Millikin was building up the bridgehead. It is unknown if Westmoreland's revelation was the deciding factor, but the next day Hodges called Millikin into his command post and announced, "I have some bad news for you. I'm relieving you." To which Millikin replied, "And I have some bad news for you. The bridge just collapsed."

The collapse might have doomed the bridgehead a week before, but the 47th Regiment's tenacious defense had brought the Americans the time they needed to get three more bridges across the river, over which now were pouring the reinforcements needed to expand the bridgehead. Historians would later cite the defense of the Remagen bridge as one of the decisive moments of the war. The bulge it created in the German lines provided an ideal springboard for the coming offensive east of the Rhine. As it expanded, the bulge also became the southern end of a giant pincer that trapped over three hundred thousand German troops in the Ruhr Valley, a fact that appreciably shortened the war.

The 9th Infantry Division, just as they had at the Remagen Bridgehead, played a crucial role in closing the Ruhr pocket. After another one of their now-patented forced marches, they repulsed a massive German attempt to break out of the pocket near the town of Sauerland. Then once the Germans in the pocket had surrendered, the 9th wheeled north again and took part in the brutal fighting to clear the Harz Mountains of some diehard SS units.

A short time later on May 7, 1945, the war in Europe ended. The end found the 9th Division dug in on the edge of the Elbe River, opposite a Russian division. It should have been a moment of joyous celebration, but for most men in the division, and that certainly included Westmoreland, the celebration was low-key, muted by the horrible experiences they had faced during the two and a half years the division had been in combat. During that time, the division had lost 4,504 men killed and 17,416 wounded in action, for a total casualty figure that was twice as high as the number of troops the division had gone into North Africa with.

If the men of the 9th Infantry Division had anything to be joyous over it was the news that they had been earmarked as occupation troops and would not have to face the horrors of an invasion of the Japanese home island, an invasion many military men were predicting would cost a million American casualties. And so while other divisions were packing their equipment and preparing for shipment to the Far East, the 9th moved to the Bavarian town of Ingolstadt and went back to their prewar regimen of sports and drill.

Corresponding with the move to Ingolstadt, General Craig received an order transferring him to XX Corps, of which he would assume command. Before his departure, he summoned Westmoreland to his command post and, during a fatherly chat, gave the colonel some of the best advice he would ever receive—which was that he should switch to the infantry. It was from the infantry, not the artillery, Craig told him, that the future leaders of the Army were going to come, and if he wanted to be one of those leaders, he should make the switch as soon as possible. Although Westmoreland did not immediately change his military specialty, a move he felt would be too blatantly opportunistic, he did accept the command of the 60th Infantry Regiment when it became available.

Shortly after he took over that command, he got a visit from General George S. Patton, a man he had had frequent contacts with during the fight for North Africa, when Patton was commanding the Third Army and he the 34th Artillery Battalion. Although there had been a huge gap between their respective positions in the Army hierarchy, Patton had taken notice of Westmoreland's potential and on occasion had made him the beneficiary of his hard-bitten advice. Advice, in fact, was what he brought with him today, that and a tale of woe, which was the reason for the advice. Patton, who had spent a good part of World War II in hot water with Eisenhower because of his many ill-advised statements and actions, had finally committed the ultimate gaffe during a recent visit to the States. During that visit he had referred to the Nazis as a political party "like Republicans or Democrats." Patton's statement and the subsequent firestorm it caused in the press had enraged the ardent anti-Nazi Eisenhower, a man already sufficiently angry at Patton for openly fraternizing with ex-Nazi officials at his Third Army headquarters. While Patton did not understand the reason for all the hubbub, and never would, he had come to caution Westmoreland not to make a similar mistake. "Westy," Patton said solemnly, while they ate lunch, "don't forget when you return to the States to be careful what you say. No matter what, they'll put it in the newspapers."

Westmoreland would write later that he took Patton's advice to heart, but it seems unlikely that he needed to. He had always been known as a closemouthed cautious person and would continue to be known as one. It was simply not in his character to make outrageous statements, nor to openly question the decisions of his political and military superiors.

One of his duties as regimental commander was administering a half-dozen camps around the Ingolstadt area for displaced persons. These DPs, as they were more commonly called, were former slave laborers whom the Nazis had forcibly conscripted to work in their armament factories. Starving and dressed in rags, hundreds of thousands of them were now wandering aimlessly around Germany like living ghosts, or huddled in ramshackle camps waiting for shipment home.

When Westmoreland visited the DP camps under his control and saw how shabbily dressed everyone there was, he immediately had notices posted all over Ingolstadt asking for voluntary contributions of clothing. Instead of clothing he got defiance. During the night, either former Nazis or Nazi sympathizers defaced all the notices with huge black swastikas.

Westmoreland had no idea what sort of response the people who drew the swastikas intended to get from him, but they likely got one they were not expecting. The next morning, according to his own account, he ordered "previously arrested Nazi officials rounded up and confined, imposed a strict night curfew in the city and posted American guards to enforce it." And finally, he "sent teams of Americans and Germans into the homes of former members of the Nazi party to take from their wardrobes the clothes that were needed."

If Westmoreland was hard on the Germans in Ingolstadt, he was equally hard on the men doing occupation duty under him, especially the officers, from whom he expected the same adherence to high standards that he had always demanded. In the turbulent, chaotic period in Germany following its surrender, with corruption epidemic and with black-marketeering a part of the daily life of many units it was difficult maintaining standards, but Westmoreland made it clear the moment he took over the 60th Infantry Regiment that he would not tolerate any corruption in the unit. To make his edict stick he soon relieved two battalion commanders for "improper conduct," and brought charges against a captain for stealing furs.

It is difficult to tell just how long Westmoreland intended to maintain his feelings about fraternization, but it ultimately did not matter. About the same time he was bringing charges against the captain for stealing furs, a silvery Superfortress named the *Enola Gay* lifted off from the airstrip on the tiny Pacific island of Tinian and with a roar of its engines headed west for a deadly rendezvous with the Japanese city of Hiroshima. The Japanese surrendered nine days later, closing the curtains on World War II. That surrender also accelerated the already heated clamor by the soldiers in Germany and their loved ones in the States to "bring the boys home." By late 1945, with that clamor having grown to a howl, the government began putting division after division on the inactive list, and shipping home their men en masse. One division picked for early shipment home was the 77th Infantry Division, and its new commander, Colonel Westmoreland.

Westmoreland did not get the rank of a brigadier general to go with his new position, for it was only temporary, but he did get the honor of having it noted in his personnel records that he had commanded an infantry division at the age of thirty-one, albeit for only a few days. After escorting the division back to the United States, where it was disbanded, he headed home on leave to South Carolina.

CHAPTER SIX

The Rocket List

Home was now on Waccamaw Avenue in Columbia, the state capital. Rip and Mimi had moved into the house the year before, right after Rip, after nearly thirty years of running it, had closed his Employees Savings Bank in Pacolet. Now in semiretirement, Rip spent much of his time playing the commodities and stock markets, and, as he had been since his son landed in North Africa, bragging to his close friends about his son's exploits in the war. Needless to say, both were overjoyed at Westmoreland's return, and, with their daughter Margaret, who was now married to a lawyer in town, they were soon driving him all around introducing him to their friends and business associates so that he could show off his medals and Rip could brag about him further.

Westmoreland enjoyed all the attention, but it was short-lived. After only about a week at home, he received a call one morning from Major General James M. Gavin, the commander of the 82nd Airborne Division, the division Gavin had led to glory during the Normandy invasion. Gavin had not forgotten the hotshot lieutenant colonel whose artillery battalion had provided him with such excellent support during the 101st Airborne Division's blitzkrieg strike across Sicily, and now he was finally able to reward him with something commensurate with his abilities.

"How would you like to take over the 504th?" Gavin asked, referring to one of the three parachute regiments in his division.

There are two versions of what happened next. According to Gavin's version, Westmoreland told him he would love taking over the 504th, but thought it would be "wishy-washy" on his part to accept a better assignment after he had already made a commitment to the Operations and Plans Division (OPD). Then, Gavin says, he used his clout to get Westmoreland's orders changed, a change that Westmoreland reluctantly accepted after working at OPD for two or three weeks.

General Robert J. Wood, at the time a colonel of the OPD staff, tells a different story, however. According to Wood, General Abe Lincoln, the commander of OPD and a man, having been General Marshall's chief strategic planner during World War II, with considerable clout of his own, refused to release Westmoreland from his assignment at OPD. As Wood tells it, Westmoreland did not accept this refusal graciously, but made it known through his attitude and through his work, that he was "quite unhappy" and "didn't want to do staff work." Westmoreland's attitude apparently angered Lincoln, but Wood interceded before the two could bump heads. "This fellow is basically a field soldier," he claims to have told Lincoln. "He's not going to be happy here. He commanded a regiment in World War II, and I think it would be best for everybody if we let him back with the troops." Lincoln relented and agreed to the transfer, but he was not very happy doing so.

Regardless of his feeling, in May of 1946, Westmoreland packed his bags and headed for Fort Bragg, North Carolina. If there was indeed such a thing as the "airborne mafia," as his critics claim, he was now an official member of it. Ironically, Westmoreland had come to command an airborne unit even though he had never jumped out of a plane himself. To remedy that problem, he stopped off at Fort Benning on his way to Bragg and went through their six-week jump school, a man ten years older and ten grades higher than the average student there. Once airborne qualified, it was on to Fort Bragg, where in late July he officially took command of the 504th Airborne Regiment. He did so with a certain unease. Not having jumped in combat himself, he now found himself in command of what were considered the toughest men in the army. Almost every man in the unit had already had dozens of jumps, and for many of the officers and NCOs those jumps had been under fire in Sicily, France, and Belgium. Westmoreland realized these men were not going to be easily impressed, so he did not try to. Instead he let his officers and NCOs know that when it came to things airborne he realized they were all considerably more qualified than himself and that he welcomed any suggestion they might have to make the unit better and to help him do a better job. Westmoreland's lack of arrogance, according to one of his staff officers at the time, won the men in the unit over, and convinced them that he was not "trying to play God."

His lack of arrogance also likely saved him from being terribly embarrassed a short time later when he made his second jump with the unit. During that jump, he tripped on exiting the plane and the metal link that connected the risers to the suspension line hit him in the back of the head and knocked him out. He landed on the ground unconscious, then groggily staggered to his feet and mumbled to the first officer that approached him, "Are we fighting the Russians?" A lot of officers would have been embarrassed by such an incident, feeling that they had made themselves look foolish in front of their men, but Westmoreland was not. He, in fact, enjoyed retelling the incident later, not minding the fact that he was the butt of his own joke.

Of course, one of the reasons he did not mind was that his position in the Army as one of its rising stars was now so secure that there was little that could dislodge it, short of some act of madness on his part. Although Westmoreland claims not to have been aware of it at the time, Lieutenant General Phillip B. Davidson, who was his intelligence chief in Vietnam, writes that around that time Westmoreland had come to the attention of Eisenhower himself. According to Davidson's scenario, sometime in August 1946,

> Eisenhower, then Army Chief of Staff, ordered his personnel chief to prepare a list of ten (some say twelve, others fifteen) young officers who had shown extraordinary promise during, and immediately after World War II. The careers of these officers, the future leaders of the army, were to be specially molded and monitored. There was no formal selection board. The list was compiled through the "old boy" method, with each senior general sending in his list of candidates.

Apparently, those in Eisenhower's inner circle privy to this "rocket list," as it came to be called, claimed that Westmoreland's name was one of the first to go on it. Whether he knew it or not, he was now on what Davidson calls "a special track."

One track he was not on at this time, however, was the one that led to marriage. Strangely, the age of thirty-two, an age at which most officers were already well on their way to raising a family, found Westmoreland not only single, but apparently content that way. Although it had become almost a routine for the senior officers' wives at Fort Bragg to act as a matchmaker on his behalf, none of their choices so far had interested him enough to make him consider marriage. All that was changed on a day in the early fall of 1946 by a single phone call.

"This is Kitsy. Do you remember me?"

"Of course I do. Are you a big girl now?"

"Why don't you come and see for yourself?"

Since he was scheduled to go to dinner at the Gavins' that evening, he called Mrs. Gavin and asked her if it would be all right if he brought a date. Being one of those on post who had just about given up on Westmoreland ever getting married, Mrs. Gavin was delighted.

That evening when he picked up Kitsy, he discovered that she had indeed grown up since he had last seen her six years before back in Hawaii. At the time, she had been a pigtailed quick-witted little girl riding horses with a reckless abandon, now she was a grown woman, an attractive nineteen-year-old college student with a lively sense of humor and an engaging personality. Westmoreland was smitten, and was soon regularly making the ninety-mile drive from Fort Bragg to Greensboro, where Kitsy had enrolled at the Women's College of The University of North Carolina following her father's transfer to Fort Bragg. After a seven-month courtship, they were married on May 3, 1947, at St. John's Episcopal Church in Fayetteville.

According to an old Army adage, "An officer's success depends on his ability, his conduct, and his wife." While the ill-mannnered or ill-bred wife does not guarantee the destruction of an officer's career, nor a well-mannered, gracious one guarantee its success, the wise and ambitious officer knows that his choice of a wife might very well be a deciding factor in his career. For Westmoreland, Kitsy was a wise choice, but not necessarily for the most obvious reason, which was that being an "Army brat" she already knew the system and how to get along and prosper in it. Her real value to him was the personal qualities she brought to the marriage and by extension to his career. Those who knew them most intimately during this time say she had a tempering influence on him, that her sense of humor, her very

Southern graciousness and social skills tended to offset his aloofness and bluntness and to smooth over the other rough edges of his personality.

Shortly after his marriage, owing to an Army-wide cutback in rank, Westmoreland had to endure having his rank reduced one grade to lieutenant colonel. The pain of this small indignity was eased somewhat a few months later when Gavin made him his chief of staff, then again in December 1948 when his first child, Katherine Stevens, was born. About the time of her birth, the pace of his career began to pick up momentum once again. In early 1949, Gavin was transferred to Champaign, Illinois to become the chief of staff of the Fifth Army. Arriving to take his place was Major General Williston Palmer, whom Westmoreland would later describe as a "crusty bachelor" completely wedded to his military career. Although he and Westmoreland butted heads on a number of occasions, Palmer came away from their association in the 82nd Airborne Division a Westmoreland backer. Like Gavin and Taylor, he was a dyed-in-the-wool airborne man, and like them also he would have an influence on Westmoreland's career.

He began exerting that influence in June 1950. Sometime during that month, Westmoreland received a letter from the personnel director at the Pentagon suggesting that he might want to consider attending the Command and General Staff School at Fort Leavenworth, Kansas. It was a plum assignment, and one just about any officer his age would have jumped at without a second thought. But he was not just any officer, and instead of being overjoyed, he was livid with anger at the thought that he, with all his combat experience, was being asked to take a course in basic tactics with a bunch of captains a few years out of West Point or OCS. He thought he was above all that by now, years beyond it, and when he expressed his outrage to Palmer, he found a sympathetic ear. Palmer agreed with him. It was an outrage, but it was not anything to get excited about. It was obviously a mistake. "Don't worry, Westy," he told him. "Your career is being guided on a different level, one that that personnel officer obviously knows nothing about." Palmer was so sure it was a mistake that he advised Westmoreland not even to bother responding to the letter. It is unknown if Palmer personally called the Pentagon and interceded for him, but it seems a good possibility. Regardless, a few weeks later Westmoreland got another letter from the same personnel officer, notifying him that he was still being assigned to Leavenworth, only now as an instructor, not as a student.

Westmoreland was very happy with the assignment. It meant that the Army had more or less officially recognized him as one of a very small group of Army officers who had gained such a solid grasp of military science through various command and staff positions that they did not have to bother taking any formal schooling. He would find it ironic later when his critics and detractors presented him as David Halberstam does in his book *The Best and the Brightest* as an example of the rigid, hidebound officer who does everything "by the book." As General Phillip Davidson points out, the truth was that "Westmoreland had never read the book." Outside of West Point, the only formal Army school he had attended was the two-week-long mess-management class at Fort Sill. To show how seriously he took the course of instruction in the class, he titled his final paper, "The Uses of Mother's Milk in the Field."

At Leavenworth, Westmoreland taught a course in airborne warfare. The length of a teaching assignment there was typically a year, but after only two months of holding classes, Westmoreland found himself transferred once again, this time to the recently reactivated Army War College, also at Leavenworth. The transfer was another enormous plus for his career. At the Command and General Staff School, he had been instructing captains and majors in battalion-level tactics. At the AWC, his students were a very select group of lieutenant colonels and colonels being groomed to be commanders and staff officers in the highest positions in the Army. Being picked to instruct these men was a unique honor, but for Westmoreland that honor was soon not enough to satisfy him. In June 1950, portions of the North Korean Army invaded South Korea, and by the early part of July the first American troops were killed near Osan trying vainly to stop that invasion. In the blink of an eye, America once again found itself in a major war, and Westmoreland found himself stuck in a classroom at Fort Leavenworth.

Almost from the moment he realized that America was irrevocably committed to the war, Westmoreland began badgering the Pentagon for a release from his teaching job and an assignment to one of the many units heading for South Korea. In late 1951, he nearly landed a spot with X Corps when "crusty" Williston Palmer requested him as his chief of staff. But the Pentagon nixed the assignment, citing as their reason Westmoreland's lack of rank. Undaunted, Westmoreland kept up his badgering, but it was not until nearly a year later in July 1952 that he finally got the Pentagon to respond. They did, with orders making him the commander of the 187th Regimental Combat Team. A few days later, he was on a plane heading for Korea.

Catching up with the 187th at Taegu, where they were resting and refitting, Westmoreland led them into the lines at Changnim-ni. The war of maneuver was over in Korea. It had ended a year before with the beginning of the peace talks at Kaesŏng. If Westmoreland had been expecting to take part in the mobile lightning war he had learned so well in North Africa, Sicily, France, and Germany, he was soon disappointed. The 187th was tasked with the very unspectacular job of guarding a valley that led toward Seoul, the South Korean capital, from the Chinese divisions dug in in the hills to the north. It would turn out not to be too difficult an assignment. Tired of having their troops slaughtered in the open by massed artillery-fire and na-palm, the Chinese commander had ordered them instead to hunker down in their deep bunkers and wait out the negotiations. And so instead of maneuvering companies, battalions, and regiments as he had done in World War II, Westmoreland found himself organizing and directing small patrols, raids, and ambushes, many of which resulted in sharp, bloody encounters with small groups of Chinese venturing out from their lines on similar missions. It was a frustrating business, for it meant Westmoreland had to accept casualties without having anything to show for them. If it was any consolation to him, the situation was short-lived. In late August, the 187th was suddenly ordered out of the line and was flown to Beppu, Japan, to become a part of the theater reserve. Awaiting the men of the 187th in Japan was a long-needed rest; awaiting Westmoreland was Kitsy, quarters in a beautiful old home, and a promotion to brigadier general. At thirty-eight, he was one of the youngest generals in the Army.

Westmoreland expected that the 187th Regimental Combat Team might eventually find their way back to Korea, but as the static warfare and the negotiations continued, that began to look less and less likely. That changed in the summer of 1953. With the end of hostilities at long last in sight, the enemy was faced with its final opportunity to give the world a convincing display of Communist military might and to improve their bargaining position in the process. In mid-June, after maneuvering elements of five Chinese armies into position across the central front, the Communists struck. The main force of the attack fell on three Republic of Korea (ROK) divisions, many of whose troops fled in disorder. Rather than advancing swiftly through the massive hole in the Allied lines, however, the Chinese consolidated their position and seized the hills vacated by the ROKs. Fearful that they were preparing for an even bigger attack, General Maxwell Taylor, the 8th Army commander, ordered the 187th to Korea immediately.

On July 14, the day they arrived, he ordered them further to hustle forward to Kumwha, where they were put under the operational control of the 2nd Infantry Division.

The 2nd was commanded by Major General William L. Barriger. According to the division G-3 at the time, Lieutenant Colonel James D. Bartholomees, Barriger was a hardheaded, rigid man who demanded unquestioning obedience from his officers. Since Barriger had not commanded troops in the field since 1938 and then only a horse cavalry squadron in Texas, Bartholomees says, he, like most senior officers in the division, did not think Barriger deserved such obedience. This lack of command experience had been evident repeatedly during battles when it was obvious that Barriger simply did not know how to properly maneuver his units. As could be expected, the decisions he made had led to a number of disagreements with his regimental commanders and staff officers. None of those disagreements, however, had ever motivated Barriger to change his mind once he had made a decision or given an order. That was simply something he refused to do, no matter how convincing the logic of his officers.

As can be imagined, given Barriger's intransigence, he and Westmoreland soon found themselves in sharp disagreement over a number of issues. When the Chinese launched what would turn out to be their last attack of the war in late July, that disagreement turned into open conflict. Those attacks, which began around midnight on a pitch-dark rainy night, drove a salient into the lines of an adjacent ROK unit. In the process, it also left a battalion emplaced on Hill 624 holding a critical shoulder of that salient. Just how "critical" that shoulder was soon became a matter of sharp disagreement. When he heard of the attack, Barriger ordered Westmoreland to pull his battalion off Hill 624 before they were flanked and cut off. As politely as possible, Westmoreland told Barriger, in turn, that he was not worried about the battalion being flanked and cut off. He, in fact, did not think they were in any danger. They were wired in tight, they had great fields of fire and plenty of ammunition, and he was convinced they could stop anything the Chinese threw at them. And besides, he did not think it wise to try to withdraw a battalion and all its equipment across steep rocky terrain in the middle of a dark rainy night and under fire. That to him was a greater risk than just staying put. Barriger listened and then repeated the command: Withdraw the battalion immediately. Westmoreland instead went over his argument one more time, and one more time was ordered to make the withdrawal. When Westmoreland continued arguing, Barriger got angry and shouted over the phone that if Westmoreland did not move those men and move them immediately, he was going to find himself standing in front of a court-martial.

It was a sobering thought, but it apparently did not sober Westmoreland. He told Barriger he would make the move. But he wanted to make clear before he did that he was making it under protest, and as such he wanted a written order from him stating specifically that the move was Barriger's idea, not his. Westmoreland got his written order, and his battalion executed the withdrawal, which went without incident. After a few insignificant gains, the Chinese attack ran out of steam, and seven days later the armistice was signed, formally ending the Korean War. A short time later, Westmoreland pulled his regiment out of the line and said good-bye to Korea.

When he left, however, he took with him the eternal enmity of General Barriger who, according to one of his staff officers, "was so pissed I thought he was going to come unglued. He would have loved to bring Westy up on charges, but he knew he couldn't. Not with Taylor running 8th Army, anyway."

As the Barriger incident makes clear, Westmoreland came out of the Korean War with his status as an officer on his way to the top even more solidified. One of the youngest brigadier generals in the Army, on Eisenhower's "rocket list," with the backing of Gavin and Taylor, two of the most powerful men in the Army, it was obvious he was now a man to be reckoned with. And he was also, according to one of his contemporaries, a man to stay clear of, as Barriger might have wished he had. "Westmoreland had a lot of power and clout," he says, "and he wasn't hesitant about using it. He was definitely an outstanding officer, one of the finest I've ever served with, but you didn't want to get in his way or do something to cross him. I felt sorry for anyone who did."

CHAPTER SEVEN

Protégé

Although Westmoreland had successfully avoided duty at the Pentagon after World War II, with the end of the Korean War, he finally had to accept the inevitable. The inevitable in his case was assignment in November 1953 as the Army's deputy chief of staff for manpower control, or assistant G-1 as it was more commonly called. This lengthy title translated into very unspectacular duty testifying in front of various congressional committees about Army manpower needs. In spite of the mundane nature of the job, Phillip Davidson writes, Westmoreland proved himself as eminently qualified "to impress congressmen and stroke their egos" as he was at commanding troops at the Remagen bridgehead. During his various testimonies, two men he particularly impressed were Congressmen Gerald Ford of Michigan and Lyndon B. Johnson of Texas.

Although not a congressman, another man impressed with Westmoreland's committee work was the new Army Chief of Staff, General Mathew Ridgway, the same Ridgway he had served under briefly in Sicily. Although Westmoreland was not in any way close to the critical decision making that took place in Ridgway's office, he met with him frequently to discuss various issues and problems and was privy to much of the information that came out of high-level discussions there and in the rest of the Pentagon.

Around the end of February, many of those discussions began to deal with the increasingly desperate situation at Dien Bien Phu, the powerful fort the French had constructed in the mountainous country of northern Vietnam. There a force of ten thousand French troops was now surrounded and under siege by five times that number of Communist Vietminh. As different French outposts around Dien Bien Phu began falling to the Vietminh in March, those discussions became more and more intense.

What was to be done about Dien Bien Phu? Could it be saved? Or was it doomed to fall to the Communists? Those were the questions Eisenhower asked his service chiefs in early March. Those questions set off a flurry of activity as each service staff grappled with one of the most difficult problems it would ever face. In anticipation of a time when the U.S. Army might be sent into Indochina to bail out the French, Ridgway had sent an Army survey team there two months earlier to determine the requirements for fighting a ground war. The report they brought back was grim and pessimistic. To get even more input, Ridgway also held a series of briefings for his staff on the types of difficulties the Army would face in the Indochina jungles.

Westmoreland attended one of those briefings in late March. It dealt with the medical difficulties of fighting a war in a jungle, and was delivered by the Army's surgeon general. His message, Westmoreland would say later, was "pure doom-and-gloom." Having studied the health and disease problems of the French in Indochina, the surgeon general had concluded that Americans simply could not survive there very well. Westmoreland says that he did not buy the surgeon general's contentions, but he claims it had a big influence on Ridgway's thinking. Just how big is unknown.

Regardless, a few days later, with the situation inside Dien Bien Phu now desperate, Ridgway went to the White House to deliver his report to Eisenhower. He came in right on the heels of his boss, Admiral Arthur Radford, the Chairman of the Joint Chiefs of Staff, who had told Eisenhower that massive United States air strikes might break the Vietminh siege and save the French garrison. Not so, said Ridgway bluntly, reminding Eisenhower of what they had both learned the hard way in Korea, which was that neither air nor naval power alone could win a war. It simply could not be done that easily.

In using air power at Dien Bien Phu, the United States had to be prepared to use troops also. There was simply no other way. And if the United States committed troops, it had to commit them with the idea of winning. And to win—to decisively defeat the Vietminh—would take as many as a million troops. To get those troops would require the drafting of one hundred thousand men a month. The reserves would also have to be mobilized, and the United States would have to be prepared to use them. To support all those troops, a massive logistical structure—at the cost of billions of dollars—would have to be built in Vietnam from scratch. Finally, the American people had to be ready to accept a war that promised to be longer and bloodier than Korea. Dien Bien Phu was doomed, he concluded, the outcome of the siege a foregone conclusion. It could end in but one way—death and capture of its defenders.

A cautious man always, Eisenhower agreed with Ridgway. As one historian put it, "There would be no U.S. Cavalry sent to rescue the French." After a massive Vietminh ground assault, Dien Bien Phu fell on May 7. A short time later, a large French armored and mechanized force—Group Mobile 100—was ambushed and destroyed piecemeal as it attempted to run a gauntlet of Vietminh fire down Highway 19 in the Central Highlands. The destruction of Group Mobile 100 was the final act in the long war. Without American support, France had no choice but to sign an armistice and depart.

A peace conference at Geneva followed. Out of it came a Vietnam divided at the 17th Parallel into two separate statelets. In the North, with their capital at Hanoi, the Vietminh ruled; in the South, with their capital at Saigon, a Vietnamese government created by the French before they departed ruled. Part of the agreement signed at Geneva called for an election to be held in Vietnam in 1956, but the new prime minister in the South, Ngo Dinh Diem, refused to go along with it.

When his tour at G-1 ended in August, Westmoreland was able to maneuver for himself a truly unique assignment—a three-month course in advanced management at Harvard's Graduate School of Business. Owing to the birth of a son, James Ripley II, Kitsy stayed at their quarters in Washington and Westmoreland moved into a Harvard dormitory with the other 115 men taking the course, the majority of whom were the presidents and vice presidents of some of the largest corporations in the United States. Westmoreland enjoyed the class. He had taken it, according to General Phillip Davidson, because of his "distrust and disdain for the Army's conventional wisdom and its educational institutions," and was eager to explore the many unique ways of managing men and materiel that had gained currency in the business world since the war. Like so many aspects of his career, this simple intent was skewered by his critics. To them his taking the class and his admission later to having an interest in the science of management proved that he was essentially a bureaucrat, a paper pusher and a master organizer, not a fighting general like Patton, Bradley, or Clark. Or, as one historian put it, it proved that he was moving "away from the ethos of combat" toward "textbooks, toward organization charts and toward bureaucratic advancement." Most of this criticism simply ignored the most basic fact of Westmoreland's career, which is that he had built his reputation in the Army as a field commander, not as a staff officer, as men like Eisenhower and Marshall had. Both those men were, in fact, great bureaucrats, yet neither has ever been accused by historians of lacking legitimacy.

After Harvard, Westmoreland took up his old job at G-1 once again. But after only six months there, he got another lucky break, the result of a nasty disagreement over the defense budget between President Eisenhower and General Ridgway, the Army Chief of Staff. When Ridgway resigned as a result of the disagreement, Taylor was brought in to take over as Chief. As could be expected, he immediately brought in Westmoreland to be his secretary of the general staff. Since Taylor had worked in the secretary's office under General Marshall when Marshall was Army Chief, it was felt by many that Taylor, long a supporter of Westmoreland, had now officially crowned him as his protégé and was grooming him to be Army Chief himself someday. To add to the honor of the new position, Kitsy gave birth to a second daughter, Margaret, in December 1956.

As SGS, Westmoreland performed what can only be described as high-level secretarial work for Taylor. But it was secretarial work with a tremendous amount of power and clout. From his desk outside Taylor's office, he was able to decide what staff work was forwarded to Taylor and who among the many people who wanted access to the Chief actually got a chance to see him. Because of the respect Taylor had for him, Westmoreland also had the power to influence the Chief's views on the numerous problems and issues the Army faced on a daily basis.

Of course, one of the biggest issues facing the Army when Westmoreland took over as SGS was the one it had always faced in times of peace—manpower and money. Historian John M. Taylor, General Taylor's biographer, notes that Taylor took over as Army Chief during a difficult time for the institution, one of the most difficult it would ever face: "The 1.4 million-man Army that he inherited was to be cut by 300,000 in 1954 and by an additional 80,000 the following year. At the same time its sixteen divisions were deployed from South Korea to West Germany and could be required to deal with threats growing out of more than forty mutual assistance pacts." Given all these possible threats, Taylor did not think such severe cutbacks were justified.

Eisenhower did, however, even though he recognized the threats. Since becoming President in 1953, he had had to wrestle with a frightening problem for which he could find no easy solution: what to do if the Soviet Union, with its huge land army, decided to launch an all-out invasion of Western Europe. He reasoned that to stop such an invasion he would need at least ninety infantry divisions and over eight thousand combat aircraft, and he did not have even a third of that. He likewise had no desire to go to the American taxpayer and ask for the money to raise such a force. He had stated early in his presidency that he did not intend to turn the United States into a "garrison state," and he intended to stick by that statement. On paper the problem facing Eisenhower seemed irreconcilable, but Eisenhower and his secretary of state, John Foster Dulles, did finally manage to come up with a solution, which they called "massive retaliation." They made it the cornerstone of their foreign policy. Dulles defined "massive retaliation" as the capacity of the United States to "retaliate instantly" against any enemy threat "by means and at places of our choosing." For the Russians these words were meant to be nothing less than a warning, which told them in very specific terms that if their huge land army invaded Western Europe, the United States would not hesistate to use nuclear weapons against it. Knowing that the United States was prepared to use nuclear weapons, Eisenhower and Dulles reasoned, the Soviets would now never contemplate starting a war. A group of public relations experts in the Pentagon eventually changed "massive retailiation" into the New Look, a term not as blatantly aggressive. Eisenhower now thought he had a way of protecting American interests while holding down the defense budget.

On the basis of his new strategy, Eisenhower proceeded to cut the military budget by 25 per cent and to put much of the redistribution of the remaining budget into the hands of Admiral Arthur Radford, the Chairman of the Joint Chiefs of Staff, and Charles Wilson, the secretary of defense. Both men believed categorically in the New Look and sought to fashion a budget that would reflect it. If nuclear deterrence was to be the backbone of our defense posture, they reasoned, then the Navy and the Air Force, the two branches of the service that were to provide that deterrence, should get the lion's share of the defense budget. Since the Army was to play only a marginal role in this new strategy, Radford, a man already noted for his hatred of the Army, wanted it reduced to little more than a constabulary force. Or as another admiral sarcastically put it during a speech in Washington, "Just enough troops to guard the Tomb of the Unknown Soldier."

As could be expected, the Army was shocked and angered by the views of both men, and especially so when Eisenhower accepted their recommendations that the Army's budget be reduced to 50 per cent of what it had been during the Korean War. No one in the Army was more shocked and angry than Ridgway. He not only disagreed with the new budget, but was appalled by the strategy that backed it up. He thought the New Look was not only shortsighted but dangerous, and he told Eisenhower so with logic that seemed difficult to refute. While he agreed with the New Look contention that, faced with nuclear destruction, the Soviets would never launch an attack against Western Europe, that was only one of many threats they posed to the West. Instead of a massive confrontation on the plains of Europe, he told the President, the Soviets were more likely to fight wars on "the periphery," in areas where we would have difficulty deploying and supporting a conventional force and where we would be unable or unwilling to use nuclear weapons. To contest the Communists in those areas, he argued, the United States needed a strong Army, not the huge numbers of nuclear missiles and B-52 bombers that Radford and Wilson wanted.

Eisenhower accepted Ridgway's criticism begrudgingly, but reminded him of something he had already made clear to the service chiefs: He did not want him going public with any disagreements he had with the defense budget. He could disagree in private, but in public he wanted a consensus from his chiefs.

Ridgway went public nonetheless. In late 1954, during an appearance before a congressional appropriations hearing, he told Congress that in the event of another war, with his "tiny army" he could not be held responsible for the security of American troops. Ridgway's comments made the front pages of the nation's newspapers and infuriated Eisenhower. They also put the two men on a collision course, which ended with Ridgway's forced resignation.

As one historian makes evident, Ridgway's "departure was a clear signal to his successor, Maxwell D. Taylor and the other chiefs. Indeed before he was appointed he had to promise Wilson that he would not cause trouble." The promise was unnecessary. Although Taylor also hated the New Look, he would not go public with his feelings until he retired. He did not do so out of loyalty to Eisenhower, but because he was a man who totally subscribed to the tenet that the military must always subordinate itself to the civil government. Although he agreed with all of Ridgway's views, he thought the general had been amiss in speaking out and embarrassing the President. One of the reasons he brought in Westmoreland as his secretary—over and above their airborne connections—was the fact that he saw in him a kindred spirit, someone who likewise completely accepted the sanctity of civilian rule and would not challenge it.

There were others on Taylor's staff still willing to make that challenge, however. Those others were a group of intellectually sharp young colonels in the Army's Secretariat, which was a think tank set up to study what the Army's needs were and what its budget should be to meet those needs. Shortly after Taylor took over as Chief, one account has it, the leader of the Secretariat, a bright young colonel named Donovan Yeuell, approached him and urged him to take advantage of the controversy Ridgway's resignation had created. Yeuell wanted Taylor to work with him in putting together a campaign to attack and discredit the New Look before Air Force and Navy positions became too entrenched on Capitol Hill. Taylor was very interested in Yeuell's ideas but "had a determined reluctance to make a public break with Wilson and Eisenhower unless he was assured that such a campaign could not be traced to the Army staff." In other words, he was willing to attack the New Look, but only surreptitiously. He was not willing, as Ridgway had been, to openly challenge the President. As a military man he not only didn't think he had a right to make such a challenge, but knew that it would have finished off his career. And so "without Taylor's supervision, but with his knowledge, the colonels prepared to distribute anti-New Look papers to Washington reporters and legislatures."

As the colonels had hoped, distillations of these position papers soon found their way into the headlines. A DECADE OF INSECURITY THROUGH GLOBAL AIR POWER, read one in an early-May edition of *The New York Times*. INTER-SERVICE RIVALRY FLASHED, read another a week later.

Both articles set off a firestorm of controversy in the press, and alerted the American public to the disquieting fact that its military was deeply divided over how to properly defend the country. Furious at the leaks and embarrassed by the furor in the press, Charles Wilson was reported to have shouted at one of his assistants at some point during the controversy, "There's a bunch of eager beavers down there in the

Army staff, and if they stick their heads out again, I'll chop them off."

Wilson was lying. He did not intend to give the men in the Secretariat a second chance. Accounts differ as to what happened next. One has it that Wilson made it clear to Taylor that he wanted the Secretariat broken up and the seven colonels there "scattered to the wind." Taylor, in turn, is reported to have delegated this onerous task to Westmoreland even though he knew his secretary "had one foot in the cabal and one foot out." In spite of his own complicity in the revolt, Westmoreland is reported to have told Taylor "that he would take care of the colonels for him and clean it all out." The colonels were then ordered, by whom it is not clear, not to come to their offices any longer. Yeuell's files were cleaned out and burned, and all seven men were reassigned to "meaningless posts" and assignments around the country.

Westmoreland's account of the Revolt of the Colonels is considerably different from the one above, placing him and Taylor in a better light. In his account, the colonels are portrayed as "working on their own." As a "matter of principle," he says, they did not tell either him or Taylor. He says further that while he agreed with the content of the position papers the colonels put together, he did not agree with their decision to go public with them. That he considered a blatant "political act," something neither he nor Taylor would have endorsed.

The revolt did manage to bring the Army's case before the public, in spite of the controversy that followed. One who took particular notice of that controversy was a young Massachusetts senator on the powerful Senate Armed Services Committee—John F. Kennedy. One of the most vocal congressional critics of Eisenhower's New Look, Kennedy had long believed, like Ridgeway and Taylor, that the United States needed to embark on a serious conventional arms buildup, coupled, in turn, with a more innovative response to Soviet-backed Third World insurgencies in areas like Indochina. In the Revolt of the Colonels, he saw for the first time just how much discontent there was in the Army over Eisenhower's defense policy, and he moved quickly to touch base with that discontent. Although it is difficult to specifically date, one account of this period mentions that around the time of the revolt, Kennedy began "initiating firm, if brief, contacts" with Taylor whenever the general testified before the Senate Armed Services Committee. While those contacts were certainly not something Eisenhower would have approved of, they laid the groundwork for what would be a long professional and personal relationship between Kennedy and Taylor. One benefit of that relationship for Taylor would be the chairmanship of the Joint Chiefs of Staff; one for

Westmoreland would be command of the U.S. Military Assistance Command in Vietnam.

For the present, however, things did not look so bright for Taylor. Like Ridgway, he had hoped he might be able to change Eisenhower's mind on the New Look, but like him also had finally given up in desperation. Unlike Ridgway, though, Taylor did not make a public statement attacking Eisenhower, but instead retired from the Army quietly. Once safely in retirement, Taylor hurriedly wrote and published a detailed and scathing attack on Eisenhower's defense policies aptly titled *The Uncertain Trumpet*. The book's main thesis took on the New Look's basic premise, contending that "massive retaliation" was completely bankrupt as a strategy now that the Soviet Union, like the United States, was armed to the teeth with nuclear weapons. In place of the New Look, the book called for a massive buildup of conventional forces. To counter a Soviet Army of two and a half million men, Taylor wanted an American military force of two and a half million. And to go with the numbers, he also called for a new, more aggressive national leadership willing to commit those men whenever and wherever needed. That aggressiveness was needed, Taylor argued, in order to prove to our allies that "the United States was willing to share with them the hazards of living under communists guns."

On the surface, *The Uncertain Trumpet* appeared to be little more than a lengthy elaboration of Ridgway's ideas. But that similarity existed only at the most superficial level. In the meat of the book, Taylor was positing an anticommunism that was much more rugged and confrontational than Ridgway's. As one example of that "ruggedness," Taylor intimated in the book that if he had been Army Chief during the Battle of Dien Bien Phu, he would have committed United States troops to the rescue of the French, an act Ridgway was vehemently opposed to.

As Taylor had hoped, his book was widely read in government circles and even more widely discussed, especially among those who had long held Eisenhower's defense strategy in disrepute. In November 1960, fresh from his victory over Richard Nixon, the new President, John F. Kennedy, hailed the book and decided to make it the bible for his new, more creative strategic philosophy. He also hailed Taylor as a truly unique thinker and one deserving of a better hearing than Eisenhower had given him. To make sure that he got that hearing, he made Taylor his military adviser a year and a half after assuming the presidency.

CHAPTER EIGHT

The Job of a Lifetime

Taylor was now at the center of power in the Kennedy administration, and Westmoreland, it seemed, was headed there. Before Taylor retired, he gave his protégé's career two more giant boosts forward. In late 1956, Taylor promoted him to major general, and then a little over a year later gave him command of the elite 101st Airborne Division at Fort Campbell, Kentucky. Although he could have given Westmoreland any number of plum assignments, he sent him to the 101st primarily because he believed Westmoreland would exhibit the same hands-on, hyperaggressive style of leadership that had been the trademark of the great World War II airborne commanders like Gavin and Ridgway and, of course, himself.

Events quickly proved him right, for shortly after Westmoreland took command his leadership qualities received a severe test during an airborne exercise called White Cloud. The exercise called for a mass parachute drop onto a large drop zone only a few miles from the center of the post. As planned, the first planeloads of paratroopers landed on the ground without incident. But just as the second load was bailing out of their C-130 transports, a sudden violent wind gushed up out of nowhere and began raking the field. As the men from the second load touched down, this wind began funneling them toward two gullies at the south side of the field where the trees and debris bulldozed off the drop zone had been deposited. The rest of the story, according to one paratrooper there that day, can only be described as "a nightmare." Nearly a hundred men were dragged helplessly over the jagged pile of twisted and splintered trees. Many were impaled; others suffered severe concussions and a multitude of broken bones and fractures, and some others were strangled by their suspension lines. When rescuers finally reached the gullies, they found five men dead and dozens injured.

Overhead, Westmoreland and his command group were just coming over the drop zone in their own C-130 when the accident happened. Apprised of the situation on the ground by radio, he was suddenly forced to make one of the most difficult decisions of his life. If he decided not to jump, which was seemingly the most logical thing to do at that point, he could avoid any further injuries, but as his G-3, Colonel John Singlaub wrote later, such a decision would make it appear "as if were willing to risk others in a dangerous situation that he himself refused to face." Westmoreland decided to jump. On hitting the ground, he was dragged over a hundred yards across the hard, rocky drop zone and would have met the same fate as the men in the gullies if some paratroopers already on the ground had not rushed forward to collapse his chute.

Although there was some criticism of Westmoreland's decision to needlessly risk his life (one former paratrooper called it an extreme case of "hotdogging"), his jump was, in fact, the very sort of action Taylor would have wanted him to take. It showed that he had the requisite bravado, bravery, and reckless daring of an airborne commander. As someone who had made a reputation in World War II putting himself in harm's way, Taylor prized those qualities in a commander infinitely more than the methodical cautiousness that had been the forte of so many ground commanders during the last two wars.

Someone else who prized those qualities in a commander was John F. Kennedy. As Kennedy's former secretary of the Army Cyrus Vance, attests, as soon as Kennedy became President, he and the key men in his administration quickly earmarked the airborne commanders like Westmoreland to provide the future leadership of the Army. "People in the airborne had style, zeal and motivation," says Vance. "They knew it and knew where they wanted to go. They were strong, highly motivated and walked into a power vacuum in 1960. The Army needed people to give it thrust and it was a damn good thing we had the airborne types there."

It did not matter to Kennedy and his men, as Ward Just makes clear in his *Military Men*, that the "airborne concept had only barely proven itself in World War Two." It did not matter that "the 82nd's jump behind the lines at Normandy was a near disaster, and that the operation at Sicily was scarcely better." Nor did it matter to them that jumping out of airplanes during a battle was extremely "dangerous and very wasteful of lives." What mattered to them was that just being a paratrooper was "prima facie evidence of energy, initiative, and bravery," which were the exact qualities they wanted in the men leading the Army. In Westmoreland, Kennedy would find these qualities in abundance.

Westmoreland finished up his two-year tour with the 101st Airborne Division in June 1960 at the height of the presidential campaign. Although Taylor was still in retirement at the time and on the outs with the Eisenhower administration because of *The Uncertain Trumpet*, he still had tremendous influence inside the Army. In early June, he used that influence to convince one of his good friends, General Lyman L. Lemnitzer, the Army Chief of Staff, to appoint Westmoreland as the superintendent of West Point.

According to a history of West Point, the appointment of Westmoreland, "a soldier's soldier," was "widely viewed as an effort by the Army hierarchy to steer the academy back to military fundamentals" following the tenure of the reform-minded General Gar Davidson. It is an interesting conjecture, but not true, for it ignores the most obvious fact that Taylor, who had been superintendent himself for four years right after World War II, had been so reform-minded himself that he was widely characterized as a "liberal." Given Taylor's reputation, Lemnitzer had no reason to think Westmoreland would be any different. Westmoreland got the superintendent's job for the most obvious reason—it was the most prestigious one available and Taylor wanted him to have it.

Westmoreland did make changes at West Point, but unlike past reformers, he did not focus those changes on either the curriculum or the elaborate system of rules and regulations that governed a cadet's personal behavior. His reform had to do with changing the way the academy focused on the most basic questions of preparing cadets to fight in the next war. That war, he had been convinced since 1954, was going to be in South Vietnam. There nearly a thousand United

States military advisers (that number would be seventeen thousand by 1963) were in a desperate struggle to keep the South Vietnamese Army from being overwhelmed by the Communist Vietcong, and Westmoreland was convinced things were only going to grow worse. When they did, he was equally convinced that he and most of his cadets were going to end up right in the middle of it.

To prepare his cadets for this inevitability, he instituted a program of counterinsurgency warfare training at West Point and demanded that all his cadets enroll in it. At the time, counterinsurgency was roughly defined as the strategy and tactics for winning a revolutionary guerrilla war, but in Washington the Kennedy administration had made the term a rallying cry for their determination to stop Communist expansion into the Third World, and most especially Southeast Asia. Although Westmoreland had long had a deep interest in the study of guerrilla warfare, now he could pursue that interest with the stamp of approval of the Kennedy administration, something the Eisenhower administration would not have given.

Besides the cadet training, Westmoreland also organized a series of lectures on counterinsurgency warfare, and as a high note to his program even put on a large counterinsurgency warfare conference at the academy. The seminar attracted scholars from all over the country. Most were knowledgeable about particular aspects of low-intensity and insurgency warfare, and a number had devoted their entire careers to their study.

Walt W. Rostow, a member of President Kennedy's brain trust, was the featured speaker at one conference. A hard-line anti-Communist, Rostow had been urging Kennedy since the election to commit the United States to an all-out effort in Vietnam. Now with Kennedy's approval, he was going around the country speaking on counterinsurgency to select audiences. His speech, like his personality, was combative. "To defeat the insurgents, you must take the offensive. If you wait passively, he will cut you to ribbons." Westmoreland wrote later that he was so impressed with Rostow's message that he committed parts of the speech to memory.

Rostow's speech was notable, but he was only one of several speakers who came to West Point during Westmoreland's tenure and spoke on the need for the United States to be prepared to decisively meet and defeat the threat of communism. In 1961, Vice President Lyndon Johnson spoke to that need during his commencement address, only with words that were far more earthy and colorful than Rostow's. "The Communist will find," he said in his best Texanese, "that a nation which produced Davy Crockett and Daniel Boone and Jim

Bowie is afraid of no forest or no swamp and no game of fighting, however toughly it is played." A year later, at West Point to receive the Sylvanus Thayer Award, General Douglas MacArthur also spoke on the need for United States readiness. "Your mission remains fixed, determined, inviolable," he charged the cadets. "It is to win our wars. Everything else in your professional careers is but corollary to this vital dedication."

By far the most important speaker during Westmoreland's tenure was President Kennedy, who came to address the graduating class of 1962. Kennedy, accompanied by General Taylor, arrived for the speech by helicopter, a flamboyant gesture that he knew the cadets would appreciate. His speech, however, was deadly serious. Like his inauguration address ("Ask not what your country can do for you but what you can do for your country"), it was a call to action.

"I know," he told the 589 cadets assembled, "that many of you feel, and many of our citizens may feel, that in these days of the nuclear age, when war may last in its final form a day or two or three days before much of the world is burned up, your service to your country will be only standing and waiting. Nothing, of course, could be further from the truth." Instead of Armageddon, a new type of war threatened freedom lovers, he told them, a conflict "new in its intensity, ancient in its origin—war by guerillas, subversives, insurgents, assassins, war by ambush instead of by combat, by infiltration instead of by aggression, seeking victory by eroding and exhausting the enemy instead of engaging him. . . . These are the kinds of challenges that will be before us in the next decade. If freedom is to be saved, we need a whole new kind of strategy, a wholly different kind of force, and a wholly different kind of training and commitment."

It was a moving speech, and no one was more moved than Westmoreland. He wrote later that listening to Kennedy made him recall the "stirring words the president had uttered at his inauguration, words that the American military around the world had taken to heart as expressing the national objective for which the military was to strive." The speech also reminded him, as it should have, of Taylor's message in *The Uncertain Trumpet.*

Whether Westmoreland attempted to convey the depth of his feeling to the President is unknown. He denies, as some claim, that he very calculatingly arranged the schedule for Kennedy's two-day visit to West Point so that the President spent the majority of that time with him. He denies also that he spent the majority of that time trying to impress the President. Whatever the truth, it is a fact that Kennedy did come away from their first meeting deeply impressed with him. In Westmoreland, these accounts claim, Kennedy found all the qualities he wanted in a man to lead the Army. Westmoreland was young, he was handsome, he was self-confident, he was aggressive, he was intelligent, he was a war hero, he had been an airborne commander, and most important, like Taylor and himself, he embraced the need for a new, more innovative military strategy. Kennedy is reported to have been so impressed with Westmoreland, in fact, that shortly after arriving back in Washington he proposed making him Army Chief of Staff—that is, once the present Chief, General George Decker, a man who had not been enthusiastic enough about counterinsurgency for Kennedy's taste, retired in October. Taylor, however, nixed the idea, telling the President that while he likewise wanted to see Westmoreland Chief someday, he wanted him to get there at the proper time. At present, he was much too young and too far down on the senority list. Making him Chief now would not only be ill-advised but very bad for Army morale. Kennedy took Taylor's advice for the moment, but still continued looking for a way to advance Westmoreland's career. A little over a year later, in the weeks before his assassination, he had pushed him as a replacement for General Paul Harkins, the Command of the U.S. Military Assistance Command in Vietnam, who had likewise fallen out of favor with Kennedy. But Taylor again nixed the idea, telling the President that such a move "was entirely too unorthodox."

Not getting either job was but a minor setback for Westmoreland, for he now had something nearly as valuable, and that was Kennedy's personal stamp of approval, something no other general but Taylor could claim. When that was added to Taylor's continued patronage, he knew he was still firmly positioned on the track to the top. If he had any doubts about that fact, he did not evidence them by any of his actions. Shortly after Kennedy's visit, Westmoreland did something that no other officer in the Army would have done at the time. He turned down a promotion to major general so that he could stay at West Point and finish some projects he had started. (One of those projects was to convince Kennedy to double the size of the cadet corps to 4,417, which Kennedy eventually did.) Westmoreland's refusal of his third star sent a minor tremor through the Army because, as Phillip Davidson points out, "a military careerist rejects promotion about as often as the Pope says mass at the Shiloh Baptist Church. For a major general to refuse promotion to three-star rank bespeaks extraordinary selflessness or sublime self-confidence, and probably both."

Whatever Westmoreland's reason for the refusal, it certainly did not hurt his career. For in July 1963, he won the promotion nonetheless and with it command of the XVIII Corps at Fort Bragg, North Carolina. The XVIII had operational control over the 82nd and 101st airborne divisions, and with Vietnam looming more and more over the Army's horizon, Westmoreland began upgrading the training of both divisions with heavy doses of counterinsurgency training. To head some of that training, he brought in Green Beret instructors from the nearby Special Warfare School, which had been Kennedy's personal creation.

In Vietnam itself, the situation continued to deteriorate. The Vietcong were now waging large-scale guerrilla war, initiating over seven hundred incidents each month and exercising various degrees of control over nearly 60 per cent of the countryside. Diem, the man Kennedy had once believed could save Vietnam from Communist domination, no longer seemed up to the job. After nearly six years in power, he had accomplished little except doubling South Vietnam's rice production. Although he frequently talked about political reform, he had yet to initiate any. Instead of the broad democratic government Kennedy had hoped he would install, Diem instead presided over an autocratic government, with his personal friends and family members controlling all the important cabinet positions. The power that Diem and his family did not hold was parceled out to prominent members of the two-million-strong Catholic minority in the country, of which Diem was the most prominent member. Diem had deliberately excluded members of South Vietnam's ten million Buddhist majority from any but the most insignificant positions of authority. Although the Buddhists had long smarted under Diem's autocratic rule, they had been unable to get him to broaden the base of his government and share power with them. And neither could President Kennedy, who since his election had been pressuring Diem to initiate a wide spectrum of reforms, all to no avail.

While Diem stonewalled, the Vietcong continued striking. In late 1962, in one of their most spectacular acts of the war so far, a Vietcong force of fifteen hundred captured a provincial capital, Phuoc Vinh, only fifty-five miles north of Saigon, then publicly tried and decapitated the province chief in the public market before hundreds of onlookers. Following their bold victory at Phuoc Vinh, they launched another regimental-size attack, this time in Darlac Province, and in three days of sharp fighting wiped out two ARVN infantry companies. By mid-1962, the Vietcong, once merely a small indigenous terrorist organization, had grown to an estimated strength of nearly twenty thousand. Many were equipped with modern weapons and superbly trained and motivated. Facing this hardened guerrilla army was Diem's own, an army riddled with corruption, nepotism, and incompetence.

As if to compound Diem's problems, in the early spring of 1962 the Buddhists rose up en masse and began staging protests against his government in nearly every major city in South Vietnam. When government troops, on Diem's orders, fired into a crowd gathered in Hue to protest an order forbidding the display of flags on Buddha's birthday, the countrywide demonstrations grew more unruly and violent. In the days that followed, Buddhist leaders accused Diem of religious persecution, and he accused them, in turn, of being dupes of the Communists. When a monk immolated himself in front of a large mob in Saigon, the protests gained added notoriety and caused consternation in Washington.

Kennedy responded by condemning Diem's suppression of the Buddhists and telling him pointedly that he doubted the war could be won unless he made a greater effort to gain popular support. When Diem once again did not make that effort, Kennedy grudgingly gave his approval to Henry Cabot Lodge, the American ambassador to South Vietnam, to initiate a change of government in South Vietnam. Lodge was instructed to tell a group of discontented army officers— men who had been secretly plotting against Diem for some time— that although the United States did not "wish to stimulate a coup," it would not thwart a change of government. The United States likewise promised to support any new government if it initiated reforms and promised to prosecute the war against the Vietcong with vigor. Making the decision to change governments in Vietnam was one of the most difficult Kennedy ever made. It would also turn out to be one he would wish he had not made.

Kennedy had expected some type of peaceful change of governments, with a scenario that had Diem being gently eased out of power and sent into blissful retirement. He got instead a bloody coup, during which Diem and his brother were brutally murdered in the back of an armored personnel carrier, then hauled off like refuse. The murder stunned Kennedy. In his memoirs, Taylor, who was now Chairman of the Joint Chiefs of Staff, recalls that when the President received news of the assassination, he "leaped to his feet and rushed from the room with a look of shock and dismay on his face." His defenders say that the shock and dismay were there because he realized that Vietnam had been his greatest failure in foreign policy.

We will never know Kennedy's true feelings, for just three weeks later he himself was assassinated in Dallas, and Lyndon B. Johnson assumed the presidency. Some Kennedy defenders, many of whom became active critics of the war in later years, contend that had he lived, he would have pulled the United States out of Vietnam. It is an interesting conjecture, but not based on much solid evidence. It is, in fact, based on little but Senator Mike Mansfield's report that in 1963 Kennedy told him that he was having serious doubts about the war and had decided to pull out of Vietnam once he was safely reelected. While Mansfield is certainly a credible source, a number of men much closer to Kennedy report otherwise. Ted Sorensen, Kennedy's special counsel and speechwriter, is one of them. To the contrary, he writes that while Kennedy was certainly "skeptical of the extent of our involvement, he was unwilling to abandon his predecessor's pledge or permit a Communist conquest." Sorensen also recorded in November 1963 that as far as Vietnam went, "Kennedy was simply going to weather it out, a nasty, untidy mess to which there was no other acceptable solution." Robert Kennedy, who would later heap a lot of blame on himself for his own early enthusiasm for counterinsurgency warfare, completely supports Sorensen's claim. This, of course, does not imply that Kennedy would have fought the Vietnam War the same way Johnson did, but as the historians Lawrence J. Basset and Stephen E. Pelz point out in a lengthy essay on Kennedy's Vietnam policy, to imagine that Kennedy would have abandoned Vietnam simply ignores the degree to which he had committed both himself and the country to "supporting a non-Communist Vietnam." To do so he would have had to publicly admit the "failure of his counterinsurgency effort," which he had specifically designed to have no other purpose than stopping "national liberation wars everywhere." In the end, it is simply inconceivable that Kennedy would have made such a total financial and philosophical commitment to counterinsurgency only to abandon it before it could face its first real threat.

Following the assassination of Diem, a junta took power in South Vietnam. It was led by General Duong Van Minh, who proved to be even more ineffective than Diem, and the military decline and political chaos only continued. While the South Vietnamese military and political leadership squabbled and grappled for power, the Vietcong launched another major military offensive in late 1963, overrunning a number of government outposts and forcing many others to be abandoned. With incredible boldness and confidence, a Vietcong company even shot their way into a U.S. Special Forces training camp and captured four Americans.

In an attempt to get a firsthand assessment of the situation there,

Secretary of Defense Robert S. McNamara flew to Saigon on December 19, 1963. He returned very depressed, and told President Johnson that the situation there was "very disturbing" and that unless it was quickly reversed South Vietnam would soon be a Communist-ruled state. One "major weakness" was the official American team in Saigon, which was hopelessly divided and unable to formulate a common plan. By "team" he meant the United States ambassador, Henry Cabot Lodge, and General Paul Harkins, commander of USMACV. The two were in such profound disagreement about the proper way to fight the war that they never spoke to each other except when absolutely necessary. McNamara told Johnson further that he was particularly upset with Harkins, who he was convinced had been systematically sending him false information and misleading accounts, all meant to make it appear that the ARVN was winning battles and making progress, when in fact the opposite was the case. After two years of Harkins's duplicity, McNamara was now convinced that in order to get South Vietnam back on track, Harkins had to be replaced. Johnson agreed. To let Harkins save face, however, they agreed to let him down slowly. Instead of replacing him immediately, which both men wanted to do, they decided to assign him a deputy commander, who could then take over when Harkins retired in September. According to Lieutenant General Barksdale Hamlett, Harkins was actually being relieved, though it was arranged to appear as a retirement. In a remarkable use of duplicity himself, McNamara cabled Harkins and instructed him to make it appear as if the deputy was merely there to help with the heavy workload and not as a replacement. The press did not fall for McNamara's ploy.

Once the decision to replace Harkins was made, Johnson, McNamara, Taylor, and General Earle Wheeler, the Army Chief of Staff, met to pick a deputy. One account claims they checked the records of forty of the most qualified generals in the Army, then after a long deliberation narrowed that down to four. Those four were supposedly the *crème de la crème* of the Army.

The senior man on the list was Lieutenant General Harold K. Johnson, the Army's deputy chief of staff for military operations. Johnson was a dour man who had survived the Bataan death march and spent all of the war in a Japanese prison camp. Both experiences had left him a deeply religious man, who did not approve of either vulgarity or profanity in the men who served under him. His great drawback, according to one account, was his "lack of political tact or grace."

The youngest on the list was Major General David Palmer, at the moment Harold Johnson's assistant for plans and operations. A classmate of Westmoreland's at West Point, Palmer had graduated sixth in his class and gained a reputation as both a thinker and a ramrod. Like Westmoreland, he had been the chief of staff of an infantry division during World War II. With that division, the 6th, he fought all through the war in the Pacific. Since the war, Palmer had gained a deserved reputation as one of the brightest men in the Army, if not the brightest. Many in the Army hierarchy felt that, at least intellectually, he was the best qualified to deal with the complicated situation in Vietnam.

And then there was Westmoreland; and finally Lieutenant General Creighton W. Abrams, also a member of the class of 1936. At the academy, Abrams had been a rowdy mischievous cadet who graduated near the bottom of his class. There also he had gained some notoriety as a hard-playing, hard-hitting, second-string guard on the football team. Because of his aggressive, daring tank maneuvers in World War II, he gained even more notoriety as Patton's favorite tank commander. While serving under Patton, Abrams's regiment had helped lead the Normandy breakout, and during the Battle of the Bulge, he had commanded the force that broke the German siege of Bastogne and relieved the beleaguered garrison. According to Davidson, Abrams had one of the best combat records of any young officer in World War II, winning two Distiguished Service Crosses, two Silver Stars, and two Legions of Merit. Abrams would later say that there were two kinds of officers, "the intellectuals and the cannon fodder." He put himself in the latter group. His main deficiency was his open dislike of paratroopers. He felt they were unduly glamorized and received too much attention and notoriety. (He also hated the Special Forces for much the same reason.) His dislike of paratroopers likewise extended to their hierarchy, to the so called "airborne clique." Abrams claimed that this "clique" had been running the Army since World War II and vowed that if he ever had the power, he intended to break it up. Needless to say, with Taylor as Chairman of the JCS, Abrams had little chance of becoming Harkins's deputy.

There has been much conjecture as to what criteria President Johnson, McNamara, Taylor, and Wheeler used in picking Westmorland to be Harkins's deputy. The historian Ernest Furgurson contends that both Johnson and McNamara believed he was a good choice "because his experience as a West Point superintendent showed he could take a scholarly rather than a dogmatic approach" to the problems he would be facing in Vietnam. Supposedly, Johnson liked him because of Westmoreland's "lingering Southern accent," which made him "feel comfortable with the general." In the same account, Taylor is portrayed as recommending him "because of his familiarity with Westy's character and record," and additionally because he considered an airborne background valuable "for someone fighting guerrillas." According to Mark Perry, another historian, the deciding factor in the choice of Westmoreland was the fact that he had been "handpicked for the job by the martyred Kennedy," and that Johnson was merely fulfilling Kennedy's wish.

There is, of course, an element of truth in both accounts. But only an element, for both ignore the more fundamental issues behind the decision. As Morris Janowitz shows in his classic *The Professional Soldier,* that decision rested on much more than the fact that Westmoreland had airborne training and a southern accent. While those issues were certainly taken into consideration, they were overshadowed by the political and ideological concerns of the four men, and especially by the concerns of Johnson and Taylor. To Janowitz, there are basically two types of military men—the absolutist and the pragmatist. In the first group, he puts men like MacArthur, men who, he says, think "in terms of conventional definitions of victory." (Though Janowitz doesn't mention them, Patton and Lemay also come to mind.) In the second, he puts men like Marshall, Ridgway, and Taylor, men "more concerned with the measured application of violence and its political consequences." Janowitz claims, in fact, that there was a direct line of descent in the pragmatist school from Marshall to Ridgway and Taylor and finally to Westmoreland. According to Janowitz, Westmoreland was chosen to take over in Vietnam because he was a man willing to subjugate his personal feelings to political realities. When President Johnson early in the war cautioned Westmoreland, "I hope you don't pull a MacArthur on me," he already knew the answer. He already knew that Westmoreland would never openly challenge and embarrass him the way MacArthur had challenged and embarrassed Truman during the Korean War. Taylor knew it as well. Taylor had thought MacArthur dangerously out of line to question Truman's authority and even more dangerously out of line to push for an invasion of China, an invasion he was certain would have ended in a debacle for the American Army.

In late January 1964, Westmoreland got the phone call he had been anticipating for some time. It was from General Wheeler, the Army Chief of Staff, ordering him to fly up to Washington in the morning.

When he entered Wheeler's office the next morning, the Chief asked matter-of-factly, "Do you know why you're here?"

"No, but I have a suspicion."

"You're going to Vietnam."

"That's fine with me, but could I have a week to get my family settled?"

"That's reasonable enough because McNamara wants you to go as soon as possible."

From Wheeler, Westmoreland also got word that MacArthur wanted him to come down to New York City and pay him a short visit. Since Westmoreland had always admired MacArthur, it was not a request he would have refused, even as busy as he was at the moment. He made the trip down two days later. Sitting in a high-backed easy chair, MacArthur received him in the living room of his Waldorf-Astoria apartment. The general seemed a smaller man physically than Westmoreland remembered him, but he reasoned that that probably had more to do with his age—eighty-four—and his failing health.

"I see, Westmoreland, that you have a new assignment," MacArthur said once they had exchanged greetings and Westmoreland was seated across from him. "I'm sure you realize that this job is full of opportunities but fraught with dangers." According to Westmoreland, after his opening, MacArthur proceeded to talk without interruption for an hour and a half. A master of the English language, his speech was precise and deliberate. He spoke in complete sentences and many of the verbs and adjectives he used were colorful and well chosen, making Westmoreland suspect that he had rehearsed his presentation, a common MacArthur practice. And since it was rehearsed, MacArthur would not tolerate any interruption. When Westmoreland occasionally during the hour and a half tried to get a word in, to comment on something or to note a point of agreement, even to show he was still attentive, he discovered that nothing he said interrupted MacArthur's line of thought, that he simply continued his presentation as if Westmoreland had not said anything.

MacArthur began by emphasizing what he termed "the complexity of the situation" in Vietnam and the problem Westmoreland was going to face trying to deal with the South Vietnamese military. He suggested that he deal with them the same way he dealt with his cadets at West Point, that is with courtesy, fatherly understanding, and of course, firmness. He told him further that he did not have a lot of confidence in Ambassador Lodge, but that he should do his best to get along with the elder statesman, in spite of the man's shortcomings.

Then he turned to the war itself. The oriental, he claimed, was terrified of artillery, and if properly used, it was the best way to break his morale. But he should not conclude from that fact that he was going to be facing an easy war, for it was not going to be. It was going to be hard and bloody, and Westmoreland had to be prepared to do whatever it took to win, no matter how draconian, and that included instituting a "scorched-earth policy" if necessary.

Westmoreland was not sure what he exactly meant by these last words, and strangely did not ask for a clarification. Had he meant that Westmoreland should merely advise the President if he thought his policies were hampering the war effort? Or did he mean for Westmoreland to take more drastic actions, to resign in protest, even to do what he himself had done in Korea, which was to go public with his views and challenge the President in the political arena? If he meant the latter, and had he lived, he would have been sadly disappointed, for Westmoreland, unlike himself, was not a political general, and was unwilling to use his prestige as a soldier to influence diplomatic and political objectives, or worse, to challenge the doctrine of civilian supremacy.

Following his meeting with MacArthur, Westmoreland headed north again, this time to West Point to deliver a speech to the class of 1964, the same class he had arrived with at the academy in 1961. For Westmoreland it was a sentimental occasion, and he used it to reveal his true feelings more than he had ever done before.

He told the cadets that he was taking on his new job in Vietnam "with a great deal of pleasure and anticipation" and with a sense of mission unlike any he had ever had. What made that mission easier to take on was the fact that he, like them, was a West Pointer. West Pointers were a special breed and, as such, answered to a higher calling, which was to serve and protect the nation and to do so with honesty and integrity.

He warned them, however, that when they graduated, they would discover that not all people shared the values that had been instilled in them at the academy. In the outside world, he warned, "you're going to be dealing with ordinary people . . . all people aren't honest. Many have low, if any, sense of duty . . . many citizens go to extremes to avoid any type of military service or any type of service to their country for that matter. I feel that West Pointers must be different, and that is why as a group they have been universally and uniquely successful throughout history."

In that outside world, they would also find many temptations, the biggest of which would be the lure of higher-paying jobs. He hoped they would not be lured away from the service by strictly financial concerns, hoped they would make a "commitment to the service for better or for worse." If they did, he was "confident that in the long run" they would be happier. "It's been my observation over the years that the unhappy and discontented man is the man who's undecided and undedicated. He's the man who's restless. He's the man who's looking across the hill to contemplate greener pastures."

In counterpoint to the indecisive man, he put before them his own ideal—the man of action—an ideal he hoped they would all strive to imitate. "Men welcome leadership. They like action and they relish accomplishment. . . . Speculation, knowledge, is not the chief aim of man—it is action. . . . All mankind feels themselves weak, beset with infirmities, and surrounded by danger. The acutest minds are the most conscious of difficulties and dangers. They want above all a leader with boldness, decision and energy that, with shame, they do not find in themselves. He, then, who will command among his fellows must tell them more in energy of will than in power of intellect. He has to have both . . . but energy of will is more important."

And finally he warned them that as commander, they had to "be aware of snow jobs." And as an example of one of the worst "snow jobs" in history he told them the tale of how Catherine the Great had been so mislead by the false progress reports of Potemkin. "You will find many Potemkin demonstrations in the service and in any other walk of life, for people will try to deceive you as to their standards, their qualities, their accomplishments. . . . In connection with my own forthcoming assignment, that is one of the real problem areas— to get the facts from the Vietnamese as to what is going on in their strife-torn country. Because the Vietnamese, as soldiers under your command, are inclined to tell you what you want to hear, and not what the actual facts are."

There are some who think that this last bit of advice was really a not very subtle attack on Harkins. It is, in fact, difficult to read it any other way, especially when you take into consideration the fact that before coming to West Point Westmoreland is reported to have gone around recommending "books to friends which were highly critical of Harkins and his reporting method." Whether Harkins knew of this is unknown. If he did, he never told anyone. He may have found it ironic later, however, when Westmoreland was likewise criticized for his optimistic reporting, reporting that, many of his critics claim, like the reporting of Harkins, had no basis in reality.

CHAPTER NINE

Decisions

M
ore than any other period during the Vietnam War, 1964 was a time of bewildering confusion. Diem's overthrow, which the United States government had first thought would be a harbinger of stability, had brought instead increased instability, added confusion, and in the minds of American government leaders more doubt as to how to proceed with the situation in Vietnam. Suffering similar doubts were the men who ran the government of North Vietnam, and suffering them most intensely were the handful of men who served on the Communist party's prestigious Central Committee. They, too, had watched the assassination of Diem with bewilderment, and they, too, had been racked with doubt as they tried to fathom how the assassination was going to affect the direction and outcome of the war in the South.

In late December 1963, the Central Committee, as they had eight other times since 1959, met to discuss what part they should play in future direction of the war. Since 1959, the committe had been directly supporting and controlling the southern insurgency, but that support had consisted mainly of supplying their comrades with political, tactical and strategic directions, with training and with providing a modicum of supplies and logistical support. There were men on the committee now, however, who believed it was time for the North to change both the nature and intensity of that support.

One of those men was Le Duan, the secretary general of North Vietnam's Communist Workers party. In an impassioned plea to the committee, Duan gave his reasons. He told them that he had watched the assassination of Diem and the ensuing chaos and concluded that the South Vietnamese government was teetering on the edge of collapse and all it would take was one good hard shove to bring it about. As things stood now, he did not think the southern insurgency had the strength to mount an all-out attack. But he was certain they could if they were supplied with new arms and ammunition and their ranks were bolstered with the addition of thousands of northern cadremen. The addition of those cadremen was especially important for it would provide the insurgency with better training and more professional direction.

Duan's was a radical proposal, and the Central Committe was quickly divided down the middle on it. Coming in on Duan's side was Le Duc Tho, one of the founders of the Indochina Communist party and presently the man on the committee in direct charge of the war in the South. An old revolutionary like Duan, he likewise believed it was time to give their southern comrades the green light, time, as he was fond of saying, "to complete the revolution."

In opposition to the proposal were two equally eminent old revolutionaries, "the Tiger of Dien Bien Phu," General Vo Nguyen Giap, who was presently the commander of the North Vietnamese Army, and Truong Chinh, the leading Communist theoretician in North Vietnam. Both believed—and both stated that belief vehemently to the committee—that the southern insurgency lacked the necessary popular support at the moment, and that it was far more important to consolidate the revolution in the North before trying to topple the government in the South. In addition, both feared that a vigorous attack against South Vietnam might provoke an even more vigorous reaction from the United States. The thought of American B-52s carpet-bombing Hanoi into rubble and of U.S. Marine divisions crashing ashore at Haiphong did not appeal to either man. Giap and Chinh wanted instead to let the war proceed as it was, a protracted guerrilla struggle. It was a struggle that might conceivably take ten or twenty years to bring victory, but it did not entail the enormous risks of an aggressive move against the South, which neither felt could bring victory.

Ho Chi Minh did, however. The venerable president of North Vietnam was reported to have leaped up with joy and begun dancing around his office at the word of Diem's assassination, shouting, "Now we've won the war." Although Diem was portrayed in the American press as nothing but a hopelessly corrupt dictator, Ho knew him better as the ardent nationalist he had tried to recruit into his government before the war against the French. Instead of joining Ho, Diem had instead denounced him as a "criminal," then fled into exile in the United States. Ho, however, had not lost his respect for Diem, whom he saw as the only person who could hold the South Vietnamese Government together. For Ho, his death was a godsend, a gift from heaven, and an opportunity not to be missed. Le Duan and Le Duc Tho were correct—it was time to complete the revolution.

Soon after casting his deciding vote, Ho ordered that the Vietcong be completely rearmed with new weapons, that thousands of northern cadremen start the journey south down the Ho Chi Minh Trail, and that the southern insurgency begin escalating their attacks, especially terrorist attacks against United States personnel and installations. Designated to carry out his orders was General Giap, the man who did not believe the war could be won.

It is one of the great ironies of the Vietnam War that Westmoreland, who would be portrayed in the press as Giap's counterpart throughout the conflict, did not think the United States could achieve a military victory in Vietnam, either. Although numerous accounts of the war depict him as approaching his new assignment filled with self-confidence and gripped by the conviction that he was the man who could turn the war in Vietnam around and then win it, those portrayals are based primarily on his public persona as a rock-jawed, take-charge airborne man, and on his public pronouncements, not on his actual beliefs, which he would only express in his cable traffic to Washington or in private conversations with close friends and associates. Although it is certainly one of the least understood facts of the Vietnam War, Westmoreland was never the bubbling optimist he is so often portrayed as. On the contrary, as Blair Clark writes: "Westmoreland, in all his conventionality, never ceased being realistic, pessimistic really, about what he was doing and its possible outcome."

Contrary to the popular view of him, when Westmoreland arrived in Vietnam on January 27, 1964, he carried inside of himself not some myopic plan for a quick victory in Vietnam but instead grave doubts about the war and America's ability to win it. And those doubts, as we shall see, only continued to grow as he got a more and more comprehensive look at the situation. When he stepped off the plane at Saigon's Tan Son Nhut Airport, however, he kept those doubts to himself, kept them carefully hidden behind his classic military presence, a presence that, as one historian writes, said to those watching, that here was a man who would solve the problem of Vietnam. Here was a man who would do what Harkins had failed to do, and who would do so without "the overoptimism and the self-delusion."

As protocol demanded, waiting on the tarmac to meet him that day was Harkins himself. A photo of the sixty-year-old general at that moment shows him smiling, seemingly ebullient over Westmoreland's arrival. In this instance at least, the smile must have been false, for Harkins could not have been too happy over the events that had led to this moment, nor how those events had been interpreted by the press. Westmoreland's impending arrival had been widely heralded in all the newspapers, and most of the accompanying stories had not been kind to Harkins. None had accepted the McNamara fiction that Westmoreland was only a deputy brought in to lighten Harkins's workload. On the contrary, they portrayed Westmoreland's assignment for what it was—a relief of Harkins.

But if Harkins was embarrassed, he did not let on to Westmoreland. Instead, he graciously welcomed him to Vietnam, then helped him get settled in temporary quarters in the Rex Hotel. Two weeks later when Kitsy, Rip, and Margaret arrived (Stevie joined the family in June), he also helped Westmoreland find a villa for himself and his family. Owing to the delicate nature of their relationship, however, they did not have a lot of contact with each other. Harkins, who admitted he did not care to go to the field, delegated that job to Westmoreland, then settled back to finish out his time at the U.S. Military Assistance Command in Saigon. It was a setup Westmoreland was more than happy with. He loved being in the field and, accompanied by his aide, Captain David Palmer, was soon making daily trips all over Vietnam in an attempt to get a firsthand look at the seriousness of the problem facing him. According to one account, he let the word go out ahead of him that "he wanted to learn the full story, not only the part that conformed to the line that progress was steady and victory certain."

He got his story, though it was not a pleasant one. Just as he had imagined back in the States, South Vietnam was on the slippery slope to its own demise, only it was moving much more rapidly than he could have ever imagined. All the indices for that demise were there. The government was still in turmoil, and the ruling junta, in spite of what Westmoreland called "high-sounding declarations about estab-

lishing genuine democracy" was stymied by indecision. That indecision had led to near complete social breakdown, with thousands of
workers on strike, more thousands of students engaged in disruptive
and confrontational demonstrations, and a plethora of military men
running around Saigon plotting and scheming against the government. Westmoreland had hoped that South Vietnam's army, after
years under the tutelage of American advisers, would have provided
him with one ray of hope, but he was disappointed. The ARVN was
still poorly trained, even more poorly led, and a long way from being
ready to hold its own in a fight with the Vietcong. To compound this
already dismal situation, on January 30, only four days after his arrival,
another coup took place. This one was led by General Nguyen Khanh,
a professional plotter who, according to Stanley Karnow, had "built
his career on switching allegiance to whichever faction promised to
fulfill his limitless ambition."

A short time after he had had a chance to size up the situation in
Vietnam, Westmoreland is reported to have told a friend that he was
"amazed and depressed" by what he had seen; and to have told
another friend, that "there is no military solution to the problem of
Vietnam. Only a political one." If it was any comfort to him, he found
that Lodge not only shared his views but was even more pessimistic.
It was primarily Lodge's pessimism that had led to his split with
Harkins, who, in the words of Westmoreland, was "optimistic to the
point of fault."

In their initial conversations, Lodge told Westmoreland that he
had tried unsuccessfully to find the glue "to hold together the South
Vietnamese political patchwork," and was now so disheartened over
the situation in the country that he thought Westmoreland had better
designate a coastal haven to which, in an emergency, the Americans
and their dependents could retire "for a Dunkirk-type evacuation."
When Harkins was told of Lodge's suggestion, he laughed and said
the whole idea was ridiculous, that Lodge had blown the Vietcong
threat all out of proportion.

As had been the case so many times in the past, there was a
considerable gap between Harkins's statement and reality. A short
time after he mocked Lodge's concern, the Vietcong—armed with
new weapons, their ranks bolstered with highly professional northern
cadre—started a new offensive. On February 3, Vietcong terrorists
blew up a compound housing United States advisers in Kontum City,
seriously wounding one man. A few days later, another group of
terrorists blew up a Saigon bar, killing five Americans; and a third

exploded a bomb in a movie theater frequented only by Americans, killing three and wounding fifty.

On the battlefield, Vietcong regular forces also struck. In early February, five hundred guerrillas infiltrated into South Vietnam from their base in Cambodia and seized five strategic hamlets near Ben Cau. The five hundred then dug in around the hamlets and repulsed a government counterattack supported by dive bombers and artillery. Ninety-four South Vietnamese soldiers died in the counterattack, the most in a single engagement so far in the war. Emboldened by their success at Ben Cau, the Vietcong next employed their first frontal assault of the war during an attack on a government outpost near Long Dinh. After overrunning the outpost, they likewise dug in and drove off repeated ARVN counterattacks. Eventually, twenty-five hundred ARVN reinforcements managed to surround the enemy force, but before they could close with them, the black-pajama-clad guerrillas boldy shot their way out of the trap and escaped.

The enemy attacks brought a worried Taylor and McNamara to Saigon on March 8 for a series of high-level conferences. Of the two, McNamara was the more worried. The former "whiz kid" president of Ford Motor Company, whose keen analytical mind had revolutionized both the accounting system at Ford and the procurement system at the Pentagon, was finding he could not solve the problems of Vietnam with a calculator and an M.B.A. from Harvard. Two years ago, on the basis of reports from Harkins, he had predicted United States military commitment to Vietnam could be completed by late 1964, but during the last year those words had repeatedly come back to haunt him and make him realize just how foolish he had been to think there was an easy solution to the problem of Vietnam.

Still, in spite of his disappointments in the past, McNamara continued looking for answers, for the key or keys that would unlock the riddle. To try to find those answers, he set up an office in a vacant conference room in the United States embassy and called both Harkins and Westmoreland in. It is difficult to understand why he wanted to see Harkins, but protocol likely demanded it. Once both men were seated, he began firing questions at them. At one point he suddenly asked Harkins, "Paul, how long do you think it will take to wind up this war?"

"Mr. Secretary, I believe we can do it in six months. If I am given command of the Vietnamese, we can reverse this thing immediately."

Like McNamara, Westmoreland was incredulous. "Mr. Secretary, I will just have to disagree with General Harkins. We have a large formidable task ahead of us, and it is just inconceivable to me how anybody can forecast or even foresee the turning of the tide that quickly."

After a series of other questions, McNamara brought up Dien Bien Phu and queried both men again. "Could a similar disaster possibly happen in South Vietnam?"

"It's simply inconceivable," Harkins said.

"I don't agree with that either," Westmoreland replied. "I can easily see the enemy moving from Laos by infiltration and seizing Hue. And if they did, I would say the South Vietnamese would have a difficult time dislodging them."

Later, without Harkins present, McNamara and Westmoreland had a long private discussion. For Westmoreland, it was an opportunity to speak his mind without constantly apologizing to Harkins, and he did, bluntly and with a frankness that stunned McNamara a bit. He told him that Vietnam was a "bottomless pit" and that the task the United States faced was "herculean." "No matter how you look at the situation here, Mr. Secretary—and I've spent five weeks now travelling around and talking to hundreds of people—one can only conclude that this is going to be a long war. And it's going to be a war that will try the patience of the American people. And because of that I believe it is essential to get the American people emotionally involved with the plight of the Vietnamese people. No matter what we do, though, the American people will have to feel a sense of broad involvement."

McNamara listened quietly and then, according to Westmoreland, "rather brushed the suggestion aside." Westmoreland had been curious to get the secretary's reaction to something he considered of the utmost importance and was surprised when he showed no interest in pursuing the issue any further. Later from one of McNamara's aides, he discovered that his idea had been discussed at the White House, but that President Johnson, in order to keep the war from becoming a political liability, had decided to keep things low-key. Johnson feared that Goldwater hawks in the House and Senate would take advantage of any attempt to get the American people emotionally involved in the war by demanding such strong military action that the Chinese might be provoked into entering the war. The thought of hordes of Chinese soldiers pouring into South Vietnam was as frightening to Johnson as the thought of U.S. Marines crashing ashore at Haiphong was to Giap.

Westmoreland could take some solace from the Taylor-McNamara visit, in that it motivated McNamara to make a comprehensive reappraisal of the war. In a memo to the President, McNamara outlined in detail the deteriorating situation in South Vietnam, including the grim fact that the Vietcong now controlled 40 percent of the territory in South Vietnam and in many provinces over 50 percent. After presenting his grim litany of facts, McNamara then proposed that the United States radically change its policy toward South Vietnam. Until that time, the American policy had been to "help the South Vietnamese win their contest against the externally directed and supported Communist insurgency." McNamara wanted the new policy to state that the United States was now prepared to do whatever it took to defeat a Communist takeover in South Vietnam. He stated further that unless the United States achieved that objective, almost all of Southeast Asia would likely fall under Communist domination. Although the memo was suggesting a radical change of American policy in Southeast Asia, a change that would have seemed to necessitate a lengthy debate of the issues involved, Johnson, after only a single day of soul searching, approved the memo and had it turned into National Security Action Memorandum (NSAM) 228. NSAMs were considered official policy of the United States government.

McNamara's NSAM 228 represented a big step in our involvement in Vietnam, but as would so often be the case, as far as the Joint Chiefs were concerned, it was not big enough. They had appreciated McNamara's philosophical commitment to a free and independent South Vietnam, but they wanted that commitment backed up with heavy bombing raids against North Vietnam, which they referred to as the "source of the aggression."

Although Westmoreland was not apprised of the JCS proposal, he got a first look at it in early June when he flew to Honolulu for a high-level conference with McNamara, Secretary of State Dean Rusk, CIA Director John McCone, Lodge, and Admiral Harry Felt, the CINCPAC (Commander in Chief, Pacific). The recent events in South Vietnam had shocked Washington more deeply than he had imagined, and in his own words, the "meeting took place in an atmosphere of gloom and doom."

When asked his opinion at the meeting, Westmoreland took issue with the JCS's wish to start an immediate attack on Hanoi. While he agreed with the JCS contention that Hanoi was the source of the insurgency and that military action would eventually have to be taken against it, he did not feel the time was right for such a precipitous move. He feared that an attack against the North might provoke

Hanoi, in turn, to launch an all-out attack against the South. While he was certain that in time, and with political stability, the South Vietnamese would be able to contend with the Vietcong, he was equally certain that at the moment they would have no chance of repelling a North Vietnamese invasion. He assured McNamara, Lodge, and the rest, however, that at this point in time such a threat from the North was very remote.

He was wrong. Even as he spoke, the decision that would send North Vietnam's legions south was in its initial planning stages. In late July, the Central Committee met once again in order to try to hammer out a solution to the problem of the South. Since their last meeting—the meeting during which they had decided to upgrade their support for the southern insurgency—the situation in the South had undergone considerable change, all to their favor. But to Le Duan, Le Duc Tho, and Ho Chi Minh that change had not brought what they had expected it to bring—the fall of the South Vietnamese government. Although their southern comrades had continued to win impressive victories on the battlefield, the ultimate victory—a victory that would have seen Vietcong forces storming the presidential palace in Saigon—had not only eluded them but daily began to seem more and more beyond their grasp. Seven months before, the three had been certain the revolution in the South was in its final stages and victory within easy grasp, but now it seemed the southern insurgency was headed for what Giap and Truong Chinh had desired all along, a protracted struggle that might take a generation to resolve. To the three, this was a frightening prospect in itself, but it was made even more so when they took into consideration the fact that the United States was moving rapidly to upgrade the ARVN. If they did manage to turn them into a viable fighting force, the Vietcong might never be able to deliver the knockout blow. The three feared additionally that a protracted struggle only increased the chance that the United States would get frustrated and insert its own troops in order to quickly resolve the situation.

This final possibility was the most frightening of all, for it portended a long, bloody war against a superpower. How to avoid that war suddenly became the question on all their minds. They decided eventually—how exactly is unknown—that the key to victory in the South was to keep the United States from sending in troops, and they reasoned further that the way to do so was to present the United States with a *fait accompli,* in this case a situation in the South that the Americans would view as irreversible. To create that situation,

the three decided that the time had come to make the move Westmoreland had least feared they would make—to send their legions
into the South for a quick decisive victory there. Their hope was that
the United States, faced with a situation that was beyond repair, might
accept a political solution, as it had in Korea and Laos, or simply
withdraw, as it had in China.

Westmoreland, of course, had not the slightest inkling of the
momentous decision—a decision that marked the beginning of the
Second Indochina War—the Central Committee had made in Hanoi
in late summer. When he returned from Honolulu, he assumed the
post of COMUSMACV (Commander, U.S. Military Assistance Command, Vietnam), and Harkins headed home. He took over with little
fanfare and almost no guidance from Washington. In World War II,
Eisenhower's mission directive had read: "You will enter the conti-
nent of Europe and, in conjunction with other United Nations, un-
dertake operations aimed at the heart of Germany and destruction of
her armed forces." For Westmoreland, there not only was not a
written directive, there was not even the vaguest guidance. As Blair
Clark points out, the only thing Westmoreland knew specifically was
that he had to keep the Communists from taking over South Vietnam.

To try to accomplish that very nebulous task, he first began putting
together his staff. He wrote later that in order to avoid being accused
of "fostering a Westmoreland cult or entourage," when he started
considering candidates for his staff, he elected "to submit a list of
qualified officers from which officials in the Pentagon might choose."
While it is true that Westmoreland did not haul around an entourage
with him, the way MacArthur did, for instance, it is not true, as his
initial cable traffic to Washington makes clear, that he allowed the
Pentagon carte blanche in picking his staff. He had very definite ideas
about whom he wanted on his staff and only created the illusion in
his cables that he was interested in the input of Wheeler and
McNamara.

For the key post of deputy COMUSMACV, for instance, both
Wheeler and McNamara cabled Westmoreland in late June suggesting
Abrams for it. They gave as their reason the most obvious one: Since
Westmoreland was soon to be promoted to four stars, they wanted
his deputy to be a three-star man, and as far as they were concerned,
Abrams was the most qualified three-star man available. While it is
not clear why McNamara preferred Abrams, one source claims
Wheeler had wanted Abrams for COMUSMACV back in January but
felt it was useless to try to go against the wishes of both Taylor and

the martyred Kennedy. This same source claims further that by trying to get Abrams appointed as Westmoreland's deputy, he was hoping to be able to indirectly influence Westmoreland, whose command abilities he was not sure about.

Whatever the truth about Wheeler's ultimate intention, it is a fact that Westmoreland did not want Abrams as his deputy. In his cables to Wheeler, he cites two basic reasons: the first, he wanted someone with two-star rank in the position, though it was obviously a three-star spot; and the second, he felt that Abrams, a man with a status in the Army that equaled his own, might not be comfortable as a number-two man. Reading between the lines of the cable, it seems just as likely that Westmoreland was indirectly expressing his own very real fear of being overshadowed or upstaged by the very charismatic Abrams.

The officer Westmoreland wanted as his deputy was Major General John L. Throckmorton, and he wanted him for a reason that must have seemed blatantly simple to both Wheeler and McNamara. Throckmorton—a dyed-in-the-wool airborne man—had been Westmoreland's deputy when he ran the 101st Airborne Division, and during that time the two had developed a perfect working relationship. When Westmoreland proposed Throckmorton, however, he ran into immediate resistance from both Wheeler and McNamara, and especially from McNamara. Both felt that Throckmorton not only did not have enough rank for the post but, should Westmoreland become incapacitated, was not qualified to take over as COMUSMACV. In spite of their objections, Westmoreland maintained that he wanted Throckmorton, and Wheeler finally relented. To get his deputy, Westmoreland had to agree to Wheeler's proposal that should he become injured or fall ill, Throckmorton would not automatically become his successor. The agreement satisfied both men. Westmoreland got a trusted airborne man as his deputy, and Wheeler, it seems, was able to keep the door to COMUSMACV open for Abrams.

A year later during the big troop buildup, Westmoreland would again fight hard to get men of his choice into key staff positions and major field commands. Although General Harold Johnson as Army Chief technically had the authority to make all general officer assignments, he would approve most of Westmoreland's requests, though at times grudgingly. And those requests, as the record clearly shows, would be for men with either a strong airborne background, a West Point diploma, or both.

Westmoreland would award a number of staff positions and commands to men who had served with the 82nd Airborne Division. John Norton, who had been Gavin's operations officer during the fighting on Sicily, would get the deputy commander's job of USARV (United States Army, Vietnam) and later command of the elite 1st Cavalry Division. Stanley "Swede" Larsen, who had commanded a regiment with the 82nd during the late 1950s, would get command of the I Field Force; and Bruce Palmer, a former 82nd division commander (and a Westmoreland classmate at West Point) would serve a stint as deputy commander, USARV.

The majority of men Westmoreland would pick, however, had the stamp of the 101st Airborne Division on them. And many of these same men would likewise have strong ties to Taylor. George Forsythe, who had been chief of the 101st's planning group in the mid-fifties, would serve a tour as assistant deputy of the Civilian Operations and Revolutionary Development Agency (CORDs), which was in charge of pacification in Vietnam, and another as commander of the 1st Cavalry Division. Julian Ewell, who had commanded both a battalion and regiment for Taylor during World War II, would be rewarded with command of both the 9th Infantry Division and the II Field Force. William Desobry, who had led a combat team in the relief of Bastogne, would get command of the IV Advisory Group. Harry Kinnard, who as Taylor's chief of staff had planned the defense of Bastogne, would likewise get a shot at commanding the 1st Cavalry Division; and so, too, would John J. Tolson III, who had commanded the 503rd Parachute Regiment for Taylor during the war.

Westmoreland would also give prominent spots in his command to West Point graduates. During his four-year tenure in Vietnam, all three of his deputies at both MACV and USARV, as well as half his division and two thirds of his corps commanders, would be academy men. In fact, of his key officers at MACV, only William E. DePuy, his operations officer, would be a non-West Pointer. So while it is true that Westmoreland did not haul an entourage around with him like MacArthur, it is also true that he knew what type of men he wanted serving in his command and got them.

Westmoreland's choice of Throckmorton coincided with a widespread change of senior leadership in both Saigon and Washington. For the second time in his career, Taylor was retired from active military duty. His new assignment sent him to Saigon to replace Lodge as ambassador. Almost simultaneously, Admiral Ulysses S. Sharp replaced Admiral Felt as Commander in Chief, Pacific (CINC-PAC); General Wheeler moved up to take Taylor's job as Chairman of the Joint Chiefs of Staff; and Harold Johnson took over as Army Chief of Staff.

Westmoreland welcomed the shake-up, especially Taylor's assignment, which meant he would be reunited with his mentor. Taylor arrived in Saigon on July 7 and immediately began trying to put the American effort there on track. He brought with him a broad mandate from the President giving him "full responsibility for the effort of the U.S. government in South Vietnam," including the military effort. Although the popular perception existed then and now that Westmoreland was the supreme commander in Vietnam, he was really only Taylor's deputy for military affairs. Westmoreland, in fact, had little authority except that granted him by Taylor. Through that authority, he commanded all U.S. units and operations in South Vietnam and managed the assistance and advisory effort to the South Vietnamese military. With that, however, his authority ended. He was not a theater commander, as Eisenhower had been in World War II, for that authority rested in the hands of Admiral Sharp in Honolulu; nor did he have any control over activities in Thailand or Laos, for that authority lay in the hands of Ambassadors Graham Martin and William Sullivan respectively. Although he did control tactical air strikes inside South Vietnam and would eventually come to control them into the extended battle area across the demilitarized zone (DMZ) and the Laotian border, he had no control over B-52 bombers, which were within the purview of the Strategic Air Command, nor over air strikes against North Vietnam, which were decided upon by either Washington or CINCPAC.

Given the limits of his authority, Westmoreland was lucky to have Taylor as his superior. As Taylor's biographer points out, the ambassador's "entire philosophy was based on finding qualified people and then letting them do their job." Although Westmoreland "was expected to clear all policy cables with the embassy," Taylor had no intention of interfering in the everyday running of the war.

At the moment that war was not running very smoothly. As everyone had expected who knew General Khanh's character, he had proven himself to be an inept ruler with almost no popular mandate. As a result, workers, students, and Buddhists once again took to the streets. In the midst of this renewed turmoil, on July 19, Khanh, in what can only be described as an act of pure megalomania, gave a speech in Saigon calling for an invasion of the North.

Not only was the speech ill-advised, for it angered both Taylor and Westmoreland who saw it as an effort by Khanh to force the United States into taking drastic actions it was not prepared to take at the moment, but it was so illogical as to be laughable. For while Khanh was issuing his call, the Vietcong were acting on a similar call recently issued to all their fighters. Responding to that call, in mid-April a reinforced Vietcong battalion captured the district capital of Kien Long, killing over three hundred South Vietnamese soldiers and two hundred civilians. Then in early July, a Vietcong force of regimental size overran the Special Forces camp at Polei Krong in Pleiku Province, killing fifty members of the civilian irregulars guarding the camp. And finally, two days later, another enemy regiment partially overran the Nam Dong Special Forces camp in northern South Vietnam, killing fifty-five South Vietnamese soldiers, two members of the United States Special Forces, and an Australian adviser.

For Westmoreland, just as disquieting as the attacks was the news his intelligence staff provided him in late July, which was that North Vietnamese Army cadre were participating in Vietcong operations. He could not tell just how extensive their involvement was, but he feared the worst. To prepare, he requested and got several thousand more American advisers in order to strengthen the advisory effort at province level. He hoped eventually to expand that effort to the district level as well, but even with the reinforcement, he lacked the manpower. The advisers did not arrive a moment too soon, for the war was beginning to take on a momentum of its own, a momentum that grew in speed and intensity with each passing day.

Something that would add to that momentum was an event that began on August 2, 1964, in the Gulf of Tonkin, just off the coast of North Vietnam. On that date, the U.S.S. *Maddox*, a destroyer, was attacked by three North Vietnamese torpedo boats while in international waters. In the brief engagement that followed, the *Maddox* opened fire with her deck guns, the torpedo boats launched an undetermined number of torpedoes, and jet fighters from the aircraft carrier U.S.S. *Ticonderoga* conducted a number of strafing runs. After one torpedo boat was badly damaged, the other two broke contact and headed for shore. President Johnson was angered over the incident, but resisted the urge to immediately retaliate. To avoid the appearance that he was backing down, however, he allowed the *Maddox*, accompanied by the destroyer *C. Turner Joy*, to resume operations in the same area.

On the night of August 4—a night one seaman described as "darker than the hub of hell"—the *Maddox* and *Turner Joy* once again reported that they were under attack. These initial reports were based on sonar and radar, however, not on actual sightings, leaving considerable doubt whether this second attack actually took place. Regardless, Johnson, who himself doubted the legitimacy of the attack reports, authorized retaliatory raids against a North Vietnamese torpedo-boat base and a nearby oil-storage facility.

Johnson also used the opportunity to gain congressional support for a Tonkin Gulf Resolution, which gave him as President the power "to take all necessary measures to repel any armed attack against U.S. forces and to prevent further aggression." Critics of the war view the Tonkin Resolution as an attempt by Johnson to get a blank check from Congress to prosecute the war however he saw fit. Such criticism implies bad intentions behind Johnson's action that simply were not there. His real reason for getting the resolution passed was quite the opposite. As George Herring notes in his diplomatic and political history, *America's Longest War,* what Johnson was really trying to do was "indicate to North Vietnam that the nation was united in its determination to stand firm in Vietnam." Johnson hoped that that determination alone might be enough to deter the North Vietnamese from any further aggression in the South.

Following the Tonkin incident, on August 6 Westmoreland held a meeting with General Khanh and the key members of his military staff in order to explain the nature of the retaliatory strikes. He believed the Vietcong might retaliate, in turn, for the air strikes and wanted to alert Khanh to the necessity of putting maximum security around ports, airfields, communications facilities, and along vital roads and waterways. Khanh agreed the security was necessary, but the actions he took went far beyond Westmoreland's mandate. Instead of moving to protect the country's critical installations and vital arteries as Westmoreland wanted, Khanh used the Tonkin crisis as a smokescreen behind which he hoped to strike back at his political enemies and hopefully save his political position. Using the emergency measures as a front, Khanh ordered the arrest of numerous political dissidents and opponents, imposed severe restrictions on civil liberties and assumed dictatorial powers. He also promoted himself to the presidency. The move backfired, however, and thousands of Vietnamese took to the streets. For days anarchy reigned in both Saigon and Hue, with mobs and gangs of thugs rampaging and pillaging. During one particularly bloody riot, Khanh was surrounded and ignominiously forced to resign. In the game of political musical chairs that followed, a Harvard-educated economist, Nguyen Xuan, became prime minister for a short time, only to be quickly ousted by Khanh making another bid for power. This latest action also backfired, and rioting and looting again swept through the country's major cities. He reigned for nearly a week, which was followed by a coup attempt, which Khanh only barely managed to squash.

While Khanh and his cohorts struggled for power, the Vietcong continued their offensive. On October 11, three Vietcong battalions ambushed two ARVN battalions along Highway 1 in Tay Ninh Province and inflicted heavy casualties on them. In early November, two enemy regiments mounted a sustained attack against the heavily populated central coastal Binh Dinh Province. After a series of ground attacks and ambushes, all the government forces in the province were overrun, destroyed, or driven back into their fortified camps. By the end of November, except for the province capital itself and a few district towns, the entire province was under enemy control. The ARVN managed to score a victory of their own in late December when their 21st Infantry Division mauled three Vietcong battalions at Ba Xugen, but the victory celebration in Saigon was short-lived. A few days later at the Catholic village of Binh Gia, the Vietcong 9th Infantry Division—fighting as a division—scored the most decisive victory so far of the war. After seizing Binh Gia, the 9th ambushed and virtually destroyed the ARVN 33rd Ranger Battalion and the 4th Marine Battalion and inflicted heavy casualities on the relieving armored and mechanized forces.

Westmoreland watched the fight for Binh Gia with particular interest. He had concluded a short time before that he needed to increase the ARVN strength to 650,000, which he reasoned would "be enough to counter the growing VC strength," though not enough, of course, if the North Vietnamese decided to intervene in force. He had also reasoned that it would take him at least a year to bring the ARVN up to that strength, but after Binh Gia, he realized that the enemy did not intend on giving that year. During that battle, for the first time in the war, the Vietcong had conducted a division-size attack and had conducted it with precision and daring. At Binh Gia also for the first time, they had remained on the battlefield in sustained combat, rather than fading away into the jungle after the initial contact as they had always done in the past. For Westmoreland, the lesson to be learned was both obvious and ominous: The Vietcong were "ready to move into Mao Tse Tung's Phase Three, the big-unit war." As Westmoreland knew only too well as one well versed in the Communist doctrine of revolutionary war, it was obvious that the Vietcong now felt they were ready and able to deliver the knockout blow to the South. If he had needed this very foreboding conclusion buttressed, he got it only a week after Binh Gia, in the form of an intelligence report offering conclusive proof that one North Vietnamese regiment—the 101st—had arrived in the Central Highlands of South Vietnam and that two other regiments—the 95th and 32nd—were on their way there. As Phillip Davidson points out, the arrival of these three regiments into South Vietnam "was one of the hinge events" of the war, changing it forever "from a Viet Cong insurrection, supported more or less openly by the Communist North," to an open invasion of South Vietnam by North Vietnam. After Binh Gia, the war began gradually to change from a "guerilla-counterinsurgency war into a large-unit, conventional war of divisions, corps, air forces and naval flotillas."

Of course, while the Communists were now more than prepared to fight a big-unit war, they were hoping that war would be against ARVN battalions, regiments, and divisions, not American ones. In the hope of frustrating any American attempt to enter the war in force, at the same time they were launching their big-unit war against the ARVN, they also launched a series of sapper and terrorist attacks against United States installations. In early November, with the obvious intention of impacting on the American presidential election, they unleashed a heavy mortar attack against the American air base at Bien Hoa, killing five Americans, wounding fifty, and destroying or damaging twenty-six aircraft.

Soon after the attack, a shocked Westmoreland and Taylor arrived on the scene to inspect the damage. Since the planes had been bunched together in order to better protect them against sapper attacks, Westmoreland said later that parts of the scene reminded him of the damage at Hickam Field following Pearl Harbor. Afterward, both men cabled Washington and urged President Johnson to immediately respond to the attack by launching air strikes against selected targets in North Vietnam. Along with the raid, they recommended further that a message be sent to Hanoi warning them that more bombing would occur unless they ceased their aggression in the South. In Washington, the JCS concurred with their call for retaliation, but thought their proposal was too mild. Instead of what they call a "tit-for-tat" approach, the JCS wanted Johnson to initiate a relentless, sustained attack against North Vietnam. As the Communists had likely foreseen, Johnson, wary of doing something that might, as Stanley Karnow says, "dismay voters or offend them," instead did nothing.

Less than a month and a half after the shock of the Bien-hoa attack, Westmoreland got a greater shock with the notification that his eighty-four-year-old father, Rip, had died in Columbia, South Carolina. Later he would reveal that while Kitsy held his hand, he broke down and cried—the first time he had cried since childhood. His admission showed both how strongly he had loved his father and how carefully he had kept his emotions in check during his life.

While Kitsy remained in Saigon with their three children, he flew directly to Columbia for the funeral. In attendance were a number of South Carolina VIPs, including the present governor of South Carolina, Robert McNair, and the former governor, Jimmy Byrnes. During the ceremony, Westmoreland found his mind fluctuating back and forth from the grief he was feeling and a letter his father had written him only a few days before. The letter showed quite clearly that his father was experiencing the same confusion, irritation, and anger over Vietnam as the average American. "I hardly know what to think about the situation in Vietnam," Rip had written. "That condition there has been going on for ten or more years and it seems some solution could have been found by this time . . . If I have the public opinion sized up, this country would order all of you home and let the country go to 'that place.' "

After the funeral, Westmoreland flew back up to Washington for a conference with the JCS, and then back to Saigon. Awaiting him there was still another shock. On Christmas Eve while he and Kitsy were preparing their villa on Tran Quay Cap Street to entertain a few guests for dinner, they were jolted by the tremendous explosion of a car bomb, which Vietcong terrorists had set off directly under the Brink's Hotel, a billet for American officers. The explosion killed two Americans outright, wounded over one hundred Americans and Vietnamese, and turned the hotel into a rubble of masonry and broken glass. Both Westmoreland and Kitsy rushed immediately to the scene, he to size it up, she, as a Red Cross nurse, to help evacuate and treat the injured. The scene reminded Westmoreland of a slaughterhouse. Dozens of dazed, bleeding people, many missing arms and legs, were scattered about in the rubble like rag dolls. Others, their faces bleeding from the impact of flying glass were staggering around in confusion, looking for someone to help them. Westmoreland felt the bombing cried out for retaliation. He and Taylor rushed to the United States embassy and sent an urgent cable to Washington. Again they pleaded with Johnson to strike back at the North. But Johnson, for a number of reasons, was still not ready to act.

Instead, Johnson sent a cable to Taylor, the contents of which illustrate the confusion and indecisiveness he was experiencing as he and his country drew ever closer to war with North Vietnam. In his cable, he questioned whether Taylor and Westmoreland "were doing enough to protect our installations and whether they were communicating effectively with the various political factions in the country." He also expressed doubt that bombing the North represented "any panacea" and encouraged them instead to "think of putting some starch into the ARVN by introducing specialized American ground troops, such as Rangers and Special Forces."

Both men were "stung" by Johnson's implied criticism and appalled that Johnson thought introducing ground troops was less serious an act than bombing the North. After consulting with the deputy ambassador, Alexis Johnson, the two drafted a cable in reply. In it, they very pointedly told Johnson that they were faced "with a seriously deteriorating situation characterized by continued political turmoil, irresponsibility, division within the Armed Forces, lethargy in the pacification program, growing anti-U.S. feeling, signs of mounting terrorism by the VC directed at U.S. personnel and deepening discouragement and loss of morale throughout South Vietnam." They were careful to also let Johnson know that there were already enough advisers in the country and introducing combat troops "might result in South Vietnam letting the U.S. carry the ball." And even if they did introduce American troops, it would take seventy-five thousand of them to provide proper security everywhere, and even that figure did not guarantee that the VC could not pull off another Brink's bombing. What could be done? Neither man had any easy solution to give Johnson, and they told him so, told him that they doubted a graduated bombing campaign would convince North Vietnam's leaders to desist. But what other choice did they have at the moment? To do nothing was "to accept defeat in the fairly near future."

It was a grim assessment, and Johnson accepted it grimly. Although many accounts of the war portray Johnson as a promethean figure charging into the war filled with a sense of his own invulnerability and of his country's exceptionalism, a proud man ready to stand tall and, as the historian John Stoessinger writes, squarely face the "personal challenge of Ho Chi Minh," in reality he was a man, like Taylor and like Westmoreland, racked by grave doubts and very uncertain what to do with this war that, like it or not, was forcing itself on him. The problems facing Johnson, however, were much more complex than the ones Taylor and Westmoreland faced. While they only had to concern themselves with the situation in Vietnam, he was faced

with a wide array of complex political and social issues that tran-
scended the war and for which there were no easy answers.

Coming into the war in the shadow of Kennedy, Johnson had
wanted to put a distinct stamp on his administration, a kind of label
that was easily distinguishable from Roosevelt's New Deal, Truman's
Fair Deal, and Kennedy's New Frontier. After much staff debate, he
chose for his label, the Great Society, a phrase that would come to
symbolize his very innovative and far-reaching domestic program.
That program called for a massive war on poverty, a huge infusion of
money into education, greatly expanded health care for the elderly,
and a broad program of civil rights protections for blacks. While it is
true that Johnson resisted escalating the war out of fear that the North
Vietnamese, and possibly even the Chinese, might enter it, his greatest fear was that the war would scuttle his Great Society program and
in the process deny him a place in history as a President who had
made a monumental impact on the quality of American life.

Yet as much as he feared escalating the war and the repercussions
that would result, he feared equally what would happen if he pulled
the United States out of Vietnam. As one of the most astute politicians
of his age, he knew such a pullout would empower the far right in
the country to attack him the same way they had attacked Truman
following the Communist victory in China in 1949. Johnson dreaded
having to face a McCarthy-type witch-hunt as much as he dreaded
committing his country to war. But, as he asked his biographer Doris
Kearns in 1968, what was he to do? "If I left the woman I really
loved—the Great Society—in order to get involved with that bitch
of a war on the other side of the world, then I would lose everything
at home. All my programs. All my hopes to feed the hungry and
shelter the homeless. All my dreams to provide education and medical
care to the browns and the blacks and the lame and the poor. But if
I left the war and let the Communist take over South Vitnam, then
I would be seen as a coward and my nation would be seen as an
appeaser, and we would both find it impossible to accomplish anything
for anybody anywhere on the entire globe."

Johnson did not respond to the Taylor-Westmoreland cable. In
spite of the logic of their argument, he still could not accept the fact
that he and his country were irrevocably headed toward a major war.
Instead, he continued to agonize, continued to look for an answer to
the problem of Vietnam that simply was not there.

By the start of 1965, Lyndon Johnson was still unable to decide
whether to authorize air strikes against North Vietnam, though he

was increasingly being pushed in that direction by both his civilian and military advisers.

One who was not pushing was Westmoreland. Although he felt the President needed to do something to show that the United States was committed to saving South Vietnam, he felt the decision to bomb North Vietnam was a political one, and one, as a military man in the field, he should avoid getting entangled in. Pushed from all sides to act, Johnson in late January took a small, cautious step toward a greater commitment when he sent Westmoreland a cable granting him the authority to begin joint planning with the Vietnamese for reprisal bombing. It was a small step, but it was something. On the heels of that cable, he sent National Security Adviser McGeorge Bundy to Saigon to survey the scene so that he might assure Johnson that before we began bombing we were first sure "we were missing no real bets in the political field." After a week of traveling around South Vietnam, Bundy concluded that the political situation was really as bad as Taylor had said it was, that it was going to be worse, and it was futile to expect the emergence of a stable regime in Saigon, at least in the near future.

After completing his survey and cabling his bad news to Johnson, Bundy was preparing to depart Vietnam when the news reached Saigon that a Vietcong sapper company had penetrated the wire surrounding Camp Holloway, an American advisory camp and airfield near Pleiku in the Central Highlands. Advancing behind a mortar barrage, the sappers had then run wild inside the camp, flinging satchel charges and grenades at sleeping Americans and blowing up fighter-bombers sitting on the runway. The thirty-minute attack, conducted with lightninglike precision, left eight Americans dead, over one hundred wounded, and ten aircraft completely destroyed. At word of the attack, Bundy rushed to Westmoreland's operations room in Saigon and there joined him and Taylor. As Westmoreland described it later, Bundy arrived tense and abrupt. Watching the security adviser's overreaction, he concluded that like a lot of civilians who had smelled gunpowder for the first time, Bundy had "developed a field marshall psychosis."

After a short discussion with Taylor and Westmoreland, Bundy, still in a state of excitement, telephoned the White House and recommended to the President that a Pentagon plan titled "Punitive and Crippling Reprisal Action on Targets in North Vietnam" be put into action immediately. This time Johnson concurred and within hours Operation Flaming Dart, which called for bombing of a North Vietnamese army camp near Dong Hoi, a coastal town just above the DMZ, was under way. Participating in the attack were jet fighters from the carrier *Ranger* and South Vietnamese planes from Da Nang led by the flamboyant Air Vice Marshal Nguyen Cao Ky.

Once the decision to launch the strikes was made, Westmoreland says, both Bundy and Taylor expressed great relief and seemed to regard the air strike as some kind of great turning point in the war. Westmoreland did not get the same kind of emotional kick out of it that they did, for try as he might he simply could not share their belief that the decision to launch the retaliatory raid was anything "momentous." While he thought the bombing might help South Vietnamese morale, he did not think it would have any effect on North Vietnamese resolve.

He was right. Three days later, Vietcong terrorists blew up a hotel in the coastal city of Qui Nhon being used as an American enlisted men's billet. The explosion brought the hotel down like a house of cards, killed twenty-three men and wounded twenty-two others. Within hours, United States and South Vietnamese jets were in the air and headed for North Vietnam for the second raid of Operation Flaming Dart. This time, however, President Johnson was careful not to portray the raid as retaliatory, but instead as a generalized response to "continued acts of aggression." This new terminology represented a conscious decision by the administration to broaden the reprisal concept almost imperceptibly in order to accommodate a wider policy of sustained air attacks against North Vietnam. That policy was codified on February 13 when Johnson adopted a formal program called Operation Rolling Thunder, which called for the United States and South Vietnamese to begin "a measured and limited air action" against selected military targets in North Vietnam. Rolling Thunder, which officially began on March 2, was to last eight weeks, but continued instead all though the Johnson presidency.

As a corollary to Rolling Thunder, Johnson also ordered the evacuation of the over eighteen hundred American dependents in South Vietnam. On February 16, Westmoreland said good-by to Kitsy and his children at Tan Son Nhut Airport, surrounded by hundreds of tearful children. As sixteen-year-old Katherine Westmoreland moved up the tarmac toward the plane, one of her friends taunted her with the remark that it was her father's fault that all the children had to leave. To which, Katherine snapped back, "It is not. It's the fault of Lynda Bird's father, not mine."

The decision to embark on Rolling Thunder was a major turning point in the war, but it was one Johnson was forced to make without getting anything close to the unanimity he had hoped for from his civilian and military advisers. On the contrary, the two sides not only had not been able to agree on Rolling Thunder but had opened a vociferous and at times nasty debate that would continue throughout the war. The civilian side of the debate, led by Secretary of Defense Robert McNamara and Assistant Secretary of Defense for International Security John McNaughton, had almost without reservation supported Rolling Thunder and the strategy of "gradualism" that backed it up. That strategy was underpinned by the belief of these civilians that the key to ending the war in Vietnam was to use air power judiciously, by gradually applying pressure against North Vietnam until their will to fight weakened and they stopped their aggression in the South. Inherent in gradualism also was the belief that this moderate but firm use of force would not panic the Soviets or Chinese into entering the war, but would instead encourage them to push the North Vietnamese into a negotiated settlement.

In open opposition to these civilians was nearly the entire military establishment, led as always by the Joint Chiefs of Staff. Speaking for that establishment, the JCS made it clear that they not only did not think gradualism would work but, just the opposite, they felt it would prolong the war. General Curtis LeMay, the very hawkish Air Force Chief of Staff, even predicted before his retirement in early 1965 that gradualism would bring about the destruction of the U.S. Army. Instead of gradually applying pressure against North Vietnam, the JCS recommended a "short war" scenario. This plan called for the President to call for a national emergency, then mobilize the reserves, mine North Vietnam's major harbors, and turn the United States fleets of B-52s against her cities and military installations. Rather than carefully moderating that bombing, the JCS wanted to hit the North hard and keep hitting it hard until its leaders either got the message or faced the complete destruction of their country. In an extreme expression of the JCS position, LeMay called for "bombing North Vietnam back to the Stone Age."

Although it would be simplistic to make it appear that there were no gray areas between the civilian and military positions, it forced many well-intentioned men in the administration to take sides in the dispute. Ironically, Taylor, the hard-liner whose *The Uncertain Trumpet* had been such an anti-Communist clarion call, was a gradualist, while Westmoreland, his protégé, sided with the JCS.

CHAPTER TEN

Fire Brigade

T he bombing issue was not of prime importance to Westmoreland at the moment, however. His problems with the ground war were infinitely more critical. He would later refer to 1965 as the "fire brigade" period of the war. It was a phrase meant to conjure up the obvious image of himself putting out enemy fires whenever and wherever they erupted.

His most immediate problem at the start of 1965 was the airfield at Da Nang, from which many of the Rolling Thunder missions came. Fearful that the Vietcong might do the same thing to it that they had done to the strip at Bien Hoa, on February 22, he ordered his deputy, Major General Throckmorton, to fly up to Da Nang and inspect its security. Throckmorton returned the next day with grim news: The security was lax and the base in imminent danger of being overrun by the twelve VC battalions in the immediate area. Throckmorton recommended that a Marine expeditionary brigade of three battalions be landed there as soon as possible. Westmoreland agreed with Throckmorton's analysis but, preferring to keep American ground forces at a minimum, cabled Washington and told them he wanted to put two battalions in Da Nang and hold two more in reserve in ships just offshore.

The cable arrived in Washington on February 25, at the same time as a cable from Taylor, who in strong words objected to bringing in the Marines. Although he agreed with Westmoreland's contention that the base was vulnerable, he told Washington, he had deep reservations about reversing the "long-standing policy of avoiding the commitment of ground forces in SVN," and feared that once that policy was breached, it would be "difficult to hold the line." He also feared that the introduction of American troops would encourage commanders (and by commanders everyone knew he meant Westmoreland) to eventually seek to use them in more "mobile counter-VC operation." And the "white-faced U.S. soldier," Taylor cynically concluded, "armed, equipped and trained as he is," was simply not going to make a very good "guerrilla fighter." In an addendum, Taylor did grudgingly concede that, given Westmoreland's concern for the safety of Da Nang, it might be suitable to send in one Marine battalion to defend it, but only one.

Taylor's response was an odd one, given the fact that only six months before he had advocated landing a marine combat force at Da Nang. Odder still was his deprecating remarks about the guerrilla-fighting abilities of the American soldiers, because he had been one of the chief architects of the counterinsurgency doctrine, which took for granted that American troops could fight anywhere and under any conditions. Needless to say, these last remarks struck an odd chord in Washington, and especially so with the JCS. What was wrong with Taylor, the Chiefs asked each other? Had his experience with South Vietnamese politics, which had not been a pleasant one for the fastidious Taylor, soured him on the entire situation there? Or was he merely expressing honest sentiments? Whatever his rationale, to the military his reluctance to introduce United States troops into Vietnam was very baffling.

Yet in spite of Taylor's dire warning and his cynicism, President Johnson approved the request for troops. He was motivated to do so in part by a cable from Admiral Sharp, who urged him to send the troops "before the tragedy," while at the same time belittling Taylor's denigration of the American soldier. "The Marines have a distinguished record in counter-guerrilla warfare," he said.

It is not known if Taylor saw Sharp's cable, but he was not happy with the rapid changes taking place. He showed just how unhappy he was on February 26 when the two battalions of Marines arrogantly crashed ashore on the white sand beaches of Da Nang, along with their amtracks, tanks, and self-propelled artillery. There they were met by young Vietnamese girls waving welcoming banners and carrying garlands of flowers. It was a spectacle, and when he heard about it, Taylor bristled. Not only had he—the ambassador!—not been notified that the landings were imminent, but their high profile was contrary to specific orders he had given Westmoreland to keep it as low-key and as inconspicuous as possible. Slighted and infuriated that his orders had been so blatantly ignored, Taylor called Westmoreland to the embassy, expressed his anger over the landings, then dressed him down like an errant private. "Do you know the terms of my reference, and that I have authority over you?"

"I understand fully," Westmoreland replied, "and I appreciate it fully."

The deployment of the U.S. Marines was another crucial turning point in the war. The Pentagon Papers speculate, however, that the deployment meant something different to the principals involved in the decision, that Washington viewed it as an "isolated phenomenon rather than as part of a sequence," while Westmoreland "saw it as the first step presaging a U.S. ground force buildup in Southeast Asia."

Westmoreland has denied this, but whatever his intentions, it is obvious from the cable traffic between Westmoreland and Washington that neither saw two battalions of Marines as being something that would turn around the deteriorating situation in Vietnam. On the contrary, both saw it for what it was, a temporary stopgap measure. In fact, shortly after the Marines crashed ashore, Wheeler cabled Westmoreland and fatalistically asked him if the situation was not already so bad "that regardless of your actions, the country is going to fall apart?"

Wheeler's fatalistic question brought a grim reply from Westmoreland. He termed the enemy gains in the past year as "massive and rapid" and called the present countrywide security situation "critical." The Vietcong were not only winning and winning big, he concluded, but along the way had implanted in the minds of most South Vietnamese people "a sense of the inevitability of their success." In spite of his grim conclusion, Westmoreland refused to accept that inevitability. Even without the assets available to reverse the situation in Vietnam, he still felt that if he did everything in his power, he might be able to stop a Communist takeover.

One thing he was sure of was that a takeover was already under way, even if he was not absolutely certain he could stop it. On February 19, the Vietcong again massed their forces around the Catholic village of Binh Gia, the sight of a terrible ARVN defeat the year before. Westmoreland was not sure if they were massing to overrun the town or just to cut the roads leading into it, but it ultimately did not matter. While the VC units were still in their assault positions, he hit them with massive air strikes, delivered by wave after wave of B-24 "Canberra" bombers and rocket-firing A1-E propeller-driven Skyraiders. Following a three-hour-long rain of high-explosive bombs, napalm, and rockets, the VC units around Binh Gia retreated into the jungle, carrying hundreds of their dead and wounded with them.

Less than a week later, Westmoreland had to act again, this time to save a combined force of Vietnamese Rangers, civilian irregulars, and U.S. Special Forces troops trapped in an enemy ambush near the Mang Yang Pass on Route 19 between An Khe and Pleiku. In 1954, this same area had been the last resting place for a French armored brigade, Group Mobile 100, which the Viet Minh had systematically destroyed after trapping it in the Mang Yang. Now eleven years later, they were trying to repeat themselves. It was not 1954, however, and the Americans were not the road-bound French. Taking personal charge of the fight, Westmoreland marshaled twenty-four F-100s and an equal number of B-57s, and then sent them against the VC ambush positions. While the bombers were pummeling the enemy positions, he sent in fleets of helicopters and helicopter gunships to protect them and evacuated the entire force from the pass without the loss of a single man. The VC again suffered grievous casualties, and to escape the waves of bombers, again had to retreat from the battlefield.

The good news of Mang Yang Pass was followed by some much better news on the political front. Khanh, who had briefly taken command of the armed forces following his short premiership, was finally ousted in late February and, to the relief of everyone, was sent out of the country to be South Vietnam's "roving ambassador." Following another confusing series of coups and countercoups, a government was finally formed under the leadership of Phan Huy Quat. For a time, there was peace in Saigon, but when Quat attempted to remove some cabinet members he disliked, another crisis developed. During that crisis, it was Quat who ended up being removed.

Moving into the power vacuum created by Quat's removal were the Young Turks, a group of young, aggressive, and ambitious military men. One of those Young Turks, Nguyen Van Thieu, assumed the position of commander in chief of the armed forces, and another Turk, the flamboyant pistol-packing fighter pilot, Air Marshal Nguyen Cao Ky, took over the premiership. With a well-earned reputation as a womanizer, drinker, and gambler, Ky's sudden rise to power shocked Taylor and President Johnson and his staff. One member of Johnson's staff, Assistant Secretary of State for Far Eastern Affairs William Bundy, summed up all their feeling when he said that the Ky-Thieu combination "seemed to all of us the bottom of the barrel—absolutely the bottom of the barrel." Bundy was wrong, however, and so too were Taylor and Johnson. Their impressions of Thieu and Ky were based on superficial impressions. In spite of the numerous faults of both men, they would prove to be competent enough at running the government to stay in power during the rest of the war.

Of course, as Johnson monitored the latest power struggle in Saigon, he certainly could not have foreseen their success. To him, it was just more of what he called "that coup shit," and when he added this latest coup to the deteriorating situation on the ground in South Vietnam, it was more than the volatile Texan could bear. On March 2, in a foul mood over the war, Johnson called General Harold Johnson, the Army Chief of Staff, and his staff to the Oval Office for a conference on the war. Like the President, General Johnson was likewise in a bad mood because of the war, only as a military man he could not openly express it. A complicated man, the general had deep doubts about whether the American military even belonged in Vietnam, and because of that he had been "exasperated" by Westmoreland's recent request for troops. With great foresight, he saw that request for what it would indeed end up becoming, the first of a long series in another bloody indecisive war like Korea. Because of that fear, only a few days before he had gone to the other Chiefs and had tried to get them to join him in presenting a united front to the President. With that united front, they then had to tell the President pointedly that the United States should "either get in this thing and win it or not go on at all." But the other Chiefs had not been willing to take such a drastic step, and General Johnson had been forced to shelve the idea.

During the meeting in the Oval Office, the President queried Johnson's views on the war, and the general gave them honestly and bluntly, although he quickly wished he had not. He told the President that he disagreed with McNamara's "gradualism," and thought instead that the United States should move decisively against North Vietnam, mining all its major harbors, cutting all rail traffic from China, and launching massive air strikes against all major military and industrial installations.

The general's views were hardly something the President had not heard before, but they were apparently something he did not want to hear at the moment. Before the general could even finish his presentation, the President leaped to his feet and began shouting at Johnson and his staff officers. "All I hear from my generals is bomb, bomb, bomb. That's all you know. Well, I want to know why there's nothing else. You generals have all been educated at taxpayers' expense and you're not giving me any ideas or any solutions for this damn piss-ant country. Now I don't need ten generals to come in here ten times and tell me to bomb. I want some solutions. I want some answers. You don't have any answers, do you?" At that the President stepped forward and jabbed his finger into the general's chest. "Well, go get some then!"

Being dressed down in front of his staff was a humiliating experience for Johnson, but he swallowed his pride, and, as ordered, headed off for Vietnam to get some answers. Preceding him to Vietnam was a cable from the President to Westmoreland, giving him a blank check for anything he wanted. "Assume no limitations on funds, equipment or personnel," the cable read. For Westmoreland, if not for General Johnson, the cable was a welcome sight. Although he now felt comfortable with the security at Da Nang, he was worried about the security at a number of other bases, and especially at the U.S. Army communications facility and airfield at Phu Bai and the airstrips at Bien Hoa and Vung Tau.

When General Johnson arrived, Westmoreland told him that he needed an Army brigade for both Bien-hoa and Vung Tau and a marine battalion for Phu Bai. In addition, he told Johnson that he would like to have an international force of three divisions for an anti-infiltration role along the DMZ and a single American division to defend either Bien Hoa–Tan San Nhut complex or for the Central Highlands. Although the last two areas were both critical, he was particularly concerned about the highlands. With the start of the enemy's expected summer offensive, he feared the North Vietnamese Army (NVA) units now in the highlands intended on mounting a drive eastward toward the coast, in order, Westmoreland speculated, to cut South Vietnam in half and establish a separate government in northern South Vietnam, a government obviously meant to challenge Saigon's authority.

If General Johnson had any doubts about the seriousness of the problem in the highlands, for there were many in Washington who did, events quickly put them to rest. A short time after he departed Saigon, an NVA regiment attacked an ARVN outpost near Dak To in the Central Highlands. It was the first appearance on the battlefield of a complete NVA unit, and it sent a shock wave up through the chain of command.

While waiting for President Johnson's response to his request, Westmoreland sat down to make a detailed study of the situation facing him in order to come up with a more comprehensive plan for his troop needs. When completed, he sent it off to Washington. His study, as he made clear to the President, was based on the premise that the ARVN had simply been expanded to their limit, and that even with a crash program to upgrade their training, they were a long way from being ready or able to stand toe-to-toe with the VC and NVA on the battlefield. Unless Washington thought the bombing of the North was going to deter the North Vietnamese, or unless Washington was willing to create an international force of about five divisions to be deployed in strongpoints from the South China Sea, along the demilitarized zone and across the Laotian Panhandle, thereby cutting the Ho Chi Minh Trail and shutting off North Vietnam's infiltration of men and supplies, then the only alternative was the introduction of more American troops into the South.

For a start, Westmoreland said, he needed two divisions, one for the Central Highlands and the other for the area around Saigon. He wanted these two divisions in addition to the brigade he had already requested to defend Bien Hoa and Vung Tau and the second Marine battalion he had requested for Phu Bai. Although there was no mention in Westmoreland's proposal about using these divisions for offensive action, he claims such an assumption was "intrinsic" in the proposal.

It was not for Taylor, however. In an alternative proposal, he cautioned Washington against introducing troops for offensive action, which he claimed would encourage the South Vietnamese to "let the United States do it." He also predicted that such troops would inevitably be seen, like the French, as "alien colonizers and conquerors." But if Washington was determined to introduce troops, then he recommended that they be restricted to enclaves along the coast. Hunkered down in the comparative safety of those enclaves, the troops could both avoid costly casualties while at the same time being a symbol of United States resolve.

Just as they already had with McNamara's strategy of "gradualism" in the air war, the JCS came out in sharp opposition to Taylor's "enclave" strategy, which they viewed as not only flawed but an ignominious use of the American fighting man. To show just how flawed it was, they reminded the President of the French, who had tried their own version of the enclave strategy in their war with the Vietminh with disastrous results. While inside their coastal enclave, the Joint Chiefs told the President, the French found that they could do little to counter Vietminh moves in the interior, but instead had to sit back helplessly in their bunkers and behind their wire while the Vietminh overran the outposts of their native allies and gobbled up territory at will. The Joint Chiefs predicted just as grim a scenario for South Vietnam, one that saw the ARVN being defeated in battle after battle by the VC and NVA, all the while being driven back toward the coast, until finally, to keep from being destroyed, they too entered the enclaves. There, unable to maneuver, the JCS predicted the American and the remnants of the ARVN units would be subjected to artillery fire and massed NVA ground attacks.

Although they did not mention it in their arguments to the President, the Joint Chiefs disliked the enclave strategy for an even more fundamental reason than the French example, and that was because it went against one of the most basic principles of war, that wars are won through offensive action and only through offensive action. And the Joint Chiefs, needless to say, were irritated that Taylor, one of their own, and a man who certainly should have known better, could not see this.

For the present, however, neither apparently could the President. Still uncertain what to do, Johnson endorsed Taylor's enclave strategy as, what Westmoreland called, "an interim measure." He also approved sending two Marine battalions to Vietnam, but only the two Westmoreland had earmarked for Da Nang and Phu Bai, but not the ones for Bien Hoa and Vung Tau.

Straddling two diametrically opposed strategies was not a comfortable position for the President, and so in an attempt to resolve the dilemma and hopefully to give Westmoreland better guidance in Saigon, he scheduled a high-level conference in Honolulu for August 20. There, for a day, Westmoreland, McNamara, Taylor, and the Joint Chiefs put aside their differences and put together what can best be called a compromise strategy. Instead of the all-out attacks against the North being pushed by the JCS or Westmoreland's five-division anti-infiltration barrier, they accepted a solution being pushed by McNamara. That solution added forty thousand United States combat troops to Vietnam and three battalions from the Republic of Korea (ROK). While Westmoreland did not get the division for the Central Highlands that he wanted, McNamara did give him permission to maneuver his troops fifty miles outside their enclaves, either to conduct counterinsurgency operations or to assist ARVN units under attack. No ultimate strategic concept or plan to win the war in the classic sense was discussed at the conference, nor would such a concept ever be seriously discussed at any of the future conferences in Honolulu. Instead of some ultimate strategic goal, McNamara and Wheeler told Westmoreland that the American objective in Vietnam would instead be "to break the will of the DRV/VC by denying them victory."

John McNaughton's notes of the conference state that it would take from six months to "perhaps a year or two to demonstrate Viet Cong failure in the South," and that once that was demonstrated, once the VC realized their impotence, they would seek a political settlement.

Critics of the war claim that such words were a result of the blind optimism and arrogance that possessed the conferees and conclude that it was such optimism and arrogance that led to the Vietnam nightmare. While this view of the war certainly simplifies the matter of ascribing blame for the war, there is no hard evidence to support the assumption that the men at Honolulu accepted their optimistic prediction as an absolute article of faith. One who certainly did not was President Johnson himself. Shortly before approving the forty thousand troops requested, he anguished to his wife, "I can't get out. I can't finish it with what I've got. So that the hell can I do?" These are hardly the words of a man who believed the war was going to be over in six months.

Still, if Honolulu did not represent an exercise in arrogance and blind optimism, it did represent a major turning point in the war, a shift away from counterinsurgency to large-scale ground war in the South. It also represented a first step in a shift away from Taylor's enclave strategy toward Westmoreland's big-unit search-and-destroy strategy.

There are some who believe that this shift only took place because Westmoreland, backed by the Joint Chiefs, was simply more persuasive than Taylor. They claim, in addition, that had President Johnson heeded Taylor's advice instead and held the line at the enclave stage of the war, the United States would have never gotten itself entangled in Vietnam to the degree that it did. It is an interesting theory, portraying as it does Taylor as a man filled with a wisdom and foresight that apparently Westmoreland did not have. But the theory never examines the opposite side of its own scenario. It never asks what might have happened if indeed the President had decided to hold all American units in a few enclaves along the coast, and the North Vietnamese had then invaded the South in full force, just as they did in 1972 and 1975. Taylor's words would not have seemed so prophetic if the American people had turned on their TVs one day in late 1965 to the sight of a Dunkirk-type of evacuation of United States troops from Da Nang or Saigon, or both.

What really destroyed the enclave strategy, as the Pentagon Papers so aptly point out, was not the persuasive abilities of Westmoreland, but the enemy's long-awaited summer offensive. That offensive began on May 9 when a Vietcong mortar company shelled Bao Trai, the capital of Hau Ngia Province, killing 28 ARVN soldiers, wounding over 100 and laying a large section of the town to waste. In sharp fighting near the town the next day, the ARVN suffered another 170 casualties while barely repulsing a fierce VC ground attack. On May 11, the Vietcong struck again, this time near the Phuoc Long Province capital of Song Be. In two days of hard fighting, the attacking VC regiment overran an ARVN base on the outskirts of Song Be, routing the ARVN battalion defending it. Only the introduction of another ARVN battalion by helicopter saved the town. The VC launched their most devastating attack at Ba Gia, an outpost in Quang Ngai Province being manned by three ARVN battalions. Behind a furious mortar barrage and deadly recoilless-rifle fire, 1,000 VC, armed with the newest Chicom rifles, machine guns, and rocket-propelled grenades, stormed the outpost, killed over 100 of the ARVN defenders and routed the rest. Before they could consolidate their hold on the outpost and the nearby town, though, Westmoreland attacked them, in turn, with waves of F-100 Super Sabres and A-1E Skyraiders. After being pounded with napalm, cannon fire, and rockets for a half a day, the VC broke contact and retreated.

Following the debacle at Ba Gia, Westmoreland cabled CINCPAC and the JCS and told them pointedly that the enemy offensive was so fierce that ARVN battlions were being destroyed faster than he could replace them. He interpreted this unsettling fact to mean that the Vietcong had decided to wage a war of "attrition" against the ARVN and were willing to suffer heavy losses themselves in the process. If that was their purpose, it was working. The attacks were disintegrating ARVN morale. Desertions were high and some ARVN troops were "beginning to show signs of reluctance to assume the offensive and in some cases their steadfastness under fire is coming into doubt."

Westmoreland concluded his cable with the observation that he could only save South Vietnam from total collapse if he were given more than double the troops already in the pipeline, for a total of 180,000 men, or forty-four battalions. He wanted thirty-four of these battalions to be American and ten, South Korean.

When President Johnson questioned him as to whether the forty-four battalions would be enough, he bluntly answered, "No," then followed with a lengthy explanation. Although Westmoreland is frequently portrayed as misleading Washington with undue optimism, there was nothing vaguely optimistic about the message in his cable. To the contrary, he told the President that the forty-four battalions were merely a "stop-gap" measure to save the ARVN and "no force for victory," which, using McNamara's own definition, he defined as "convincing the DRV/VC that they could not win." As to how many troops it would take to turn the situation around and take the initiative, Westmoreland again was bluntly honest, telling the President that he simply did not know. That fact would depend on the "resources" the North Vietnamese committed to the fight, and he had no way of knowing what that might be at the moment.

He cautioned Johnson, however, to keep in mind that if we intended getting involved more deeply in the war, then it was important that we were committed "for the long pull," for it would likely be a long war that would require "increasing numbers of U.S. troops." And if we were going to commit large numbers of troops, it was essential that there be some sort of national mobilization and a public airing of the issues involved with the American people. Johnson, however, had no intention of heeding this last bit of advice. Instead, as George Herring writes, he intended on leading the United States into Vietnam just as his political idol, Roosevelt, had led it into World War II, by "indirection and dissimulation."

Westmoreland's June 7 request for troops, as noted in the Pentagon Papers, "stirred up a veritable hornet's nest in Washington." Until his request, Washington's decision makers had seen the war as a kind of low-key affair on one of the back burners of American geopolitics. Westmoreland's sudden call for massive troop increases, coupled with his stated intentions to use those troops in aggressive offensive operations, forced the Johnson administration to confront the terrifying specter of United States involvement in a major land war in Asia. And at the moment, it was a specter many in the administration simply did not want to confront.

Secretary of State Dean Rusk was one of them. While admitting the importance of Vietnam to the integrity of the American global commitment, he wondered whether Westmoreland was not exaggerating the danger. Another who questioned the need for massive numbers of troops was Taylor. Back in Washington to discuss the situation in Vietnam, he openly questioned the need for the troops, telling the President that they not only were not necessary, but even if the troops were sent they could do little but hold a few enclaves. Even the CIA, in a memo to the President that runs counter to the notion that they were eager to get the United States involved in Vietnam, concluded that a large influx of U.S. troops could do little to halt the Communists for the simple reason that the Communists believed "their staying power is inherently superior to that of the Americans and South Vietnamese."

Falling in on Westmoreland's side were the Joint Chiefs, Admiral Sharp, and McNamara. Speaking for them all, Sharp told the President pointedly that the United States would lose the war if it moved into enclaves and recommended not only that Taylor's strategy be scrapped, but that the United States take strong and immediate actions against North Vietnam, which included mining its harbors, destroying all its airfields, smashing rail and bridge systems, and wiping out every military installation of value in the country. McNamara's decision to support such a strong proposal surprised the military, but they would not be surprised for long. From that point on, the secretary would become more and more disillusioned with the war.

Was Westmoreland's assessment of the war authentic, or was it, as Rusk and Taylor believed, a bit precipitous? That was the question facing President Johnson, but as the Pentagon Papers show, he ultimately did not have to decide the issue. It was decided for him at an American Special Forces camp near Dong Xoai on the morning of June 10. On that morning, a Vietcong force of fifteen hundred, armed with new AK-47 assault rifles, grenades, recoilless rifles, and flamethrowers, attacked both the camp and the adjoining district headquarters. The 24 U.S. Seabees and 400 Montagnard civilian irregulars defending the camp momentarily stopped the attack, but were eventually overrun and forced to retreat to an area around the district headquarters building. During the retreat, half of the 424 men in the camp were killed or wounded. At the headquarters building a Second Lieutenant Charles Q. Williams took charge of the survivors and directed jets carrying napalm and phosphorous bombs against the VC assault forces. When the 42nd ARVN Ranger Battalion was choppered in as reinforcements, Williams joined it with his group of survivors and led a counterattack against the VC and drove them out of Dong Xoai.

The fight was far from over, however. Other VC battalions around Dong Xoai moved up and seized the roads around the Special Forces camp and district headquarters and took over a nearby rubber plantation. When the 7th ARVN Airborne Battalion was lifted in to break the enemy hold on the countryside, they came down right in the middle of an ambush. Of the 480 in the ARVN battalion, only 158 made it back to Dong Xoai alive. Of that 158, 50 came back wounded.

When it appeared that more VC battalions were moving up to once more attack Dong Xoai, Westmoreland decided to get involved in the fight. In an urgent cable to CINCPAC, he told Sharp that he was certain the VC intended on taking over Phuoc Long Province, and that he was thinking of committing the newly arrived 173rd Airborne Brigade to try to save the province. Did he have the authority to do so? he asked. He assumed he did, but wanted to make absolutely sure before acting. Sharp agreed that he did indeed have the authority, but cautioned him to be aware of the "grave political implications involved if sizable U.S. forces are committed for the first time and suffer a defeat."

Westmoreland was more than aware of those implications, and decided against committing the 173rd, or any other American units, until he got clearer guidelines from Washington. Fortunately, he was able to hold the enemy around Dong Xoai with just air strikes, but the casualties the ARVN sufferd there—400 killed and wounded and two battalions rendered completely ineffective—stunned the President and his advisers. Dong Xoai also pushed Johnson closer to making a decision in favor of Westmoreland's forty-four-battalion request. As a stopgap measure before he made that decision, he did give Westmoreland permission to "commit U.S. troops to combat, independent of or in conjunction with GVN forces in any situation in which the use of such troops is requested by an appropriate GVN commander and when it is COMUSMACV's judgment that their use is necessary to strengthen the relative position of GVN forces." Yet, because of worry that the American public would react adversely to widening the American role in Vietnam, Johnson decided against making a public announcement of the fact.

Though Westmoreland later wrote that he felt one of Johnson's greatest failings was his unwillingness to get the American people involved in the war, at the moment that fact did not particularly matter to him. On June 27, he initiated the first American offensive operation of the war, sending the 173rd Airborne Brigade, an Australian battalion, and four ARVN battalions on a three-day foray into War Zone D, a Vietcong base area a few miles northwest of Saigon. Although the operation, as the Pentagon Papers makes clear, was hardly a "reserve reaction" as stipulated in Johnson's guidelines for United States ground actions, the President chose to look the other way. The ground war was now under way, and as the Pentagon Papers also note, Taylor's enclave strategy was now history. It had been "overcome by events."

Now almost certain he was going to okay Westmoreland's troop request, in mid-July the President sent McNamara to Saigon with orders to find out specifically just how Westmoreland intended using the forty-four battalions if and when he got them. Upon arrival, the secretary again asked the critical question the President had himself asked Westmoreland only a month before: How many troops would he need to "convince the enemy that he couldn't win?" And Westmoreland once again had to answer that he just did not know. He did, however, lay out for McNamara a concept of his operations that, if he got more troops, he planned to execute in three major phases. In the first phase, he wanted to commit those American and Allied forces necessary "to halt the losing trend" by the end of 1965. During phase two, which he envisioned starting "during the first half of 1966," he planned to take the offensive with American and Allied forces in "high-priority areas" to destroy enemy forces and reinstate pacification programs. Finally, in phase three, if the enemy persisted, he would go after the enemy's main forces and defeat them in the field. He estimated that it would take a year to a year and half to complete this final phase. To fulfill his concept of operations, he told McNamara, to begin the "win phase" of his strategy he needed twenty-four battalions in addition to the forty-four already under consideration—for a total of 275,000 men. But, he cautioned McNamara, just as he had already cautioned the President, to keep in mind that enemy actions might well force him to increase that figure.

This three-phase campaign plan of Westmoreland's is often cited by his critics to show his excessive optimism. This claim is usually based on the Pentagon Papers, whose authors deduced from Westmoreland's concept of operations that he expected victory by 1967. Those critics unfortunately misread Westmoreland's concept for phase two. The Pentagon Papers authors interpreted Westmoreland's statement to mean that he expected to have phase two completed by the end of 1966, when, in fact, that simply is not stated, or even implied in the wording of it. Ironically, Leslie Gelb, the director of the Pentagon Papers Project, recently admitted in his book *The Irony of Vietnam* that the Pentagon Papers had misinterpreted Westmoreland's concept of operations, and that there is no evidence to show that he ever predicted how long it would take to win the Vietnam War. Gelb also is careful to point out that if Westmoreland's concept of operations, as some have claimed, was designed to deceive Washington, "it was not very inspired deception."

On July 20, McNamara returned to Washington with Westmoreland's troop request. After a quick conference with the JCS, he then not only endorsed the original forty-four-battalion request, but even added three battalions to Westmoreland's subsequent twenty-four-battalion request. He also once again recommended that the President issue a call-up for the Reserves and National Guard. Back in Saigon now, even Taylor, after a quick tour of the country, including the Dong Xoai battlefield, grudgingly told Washington that things were every bit as bad as Westmoreland said they were. He then packed his bags and headed home once again. This would be his final trip, for he had been replaced by Henry Cabot Lodge, who was returning to Vietnam for his second tour as ambassador. Taylor returned haunted by a sense of failure. There was a broad consensus that he had been a bad ambassador. A conventional soldier, he had been unable to deal with the constant political bickering and confusion of South Vietnamese politics. As far as President Johnson was concerned, Taylor's intransigence had created much unnecessary friction with South Vietnam's leaders. What had ultimately finished off Taylor, however, was his open disagreement with Westmoreland over strategy. When Johnson eventually decided to go with Westmoreland's offensive strategy, it was obvious to everyone that Taylor had outlived his usefulness. Although he would spend the next three years in Washington as a White House adviser, he would never again play a major role in the war.

Light at the End of the Tunnel

Taylor's departure was the first indication that United States policy in Vietnam was about to change and change dramatically. The second came on July 28, 1965. On that day, in the middle of the afternoon, President Johnson appeared on national television and announced that American fighting strength in Vietnam was going to be increased from 75,000 to 125,000 and that additional forces would be sent whenever Westmoreland requested them. Contrary to the advice of McNamara and the military, Johnson had decided against calling up the Reserves, seeking a congressional resolution, declaring a national emergency, or announcing fully the extent of the military buildup. Like a thief in the night, he was slipping into the Vietnam War through the back door. It was an action he would rue the rest of his life.

While the American public did not realize that their country was now locked in a major land war in Asia, Westmoreland certainly did. By midsummer the first wave of enemy atacks had died out, but they were soon followed by another wave. Those attacks were just as tenacious and hard-hitting, and by late July several district capitals had been abandoned and intelligence sources were predicting that the entire Central Highlands would fall before the onset of the winter season. Throughout the country, security, except in major cities and some province capitals, was increasingly tenuous, and in many areas the enemy had the ability to cut transportation and communication lines at will.

But now Westmoreland was ready to make his move, and as each new unit arrived from the States, he fed it right into the fight. When Vietcong units in the III Corps area cut Highway 13 north of Saigon, he ordered the 1st Infantry Division to reopen it. In a sharp fight near Bau Bang, the 2nd Battalion, 2nd Infantry, reinforced by armor and artillery, destroyed a VC battalion trying to keep the road closed. After the fight, the 2/2 and two fresh battalions, backed by armor, pushed their way north up the highway, destroying a number of enemy installations, arms caches, and an ammunition factory as they advanced. A month later in another battle, the 2/2 overran a huge VC base camp near the Michelin Rubber Plantation, killed over 300 enemy soldiers and drove the rest of the regiment north toward the Cambodian border.

It was a similar story in the II Corps area. In early August when a VC regiment, after a forty-eight-day seige, was threatening to over-run a Special Forces camp at Duc Co in the Central Highlands, Westmoreland ordered the 173rd Airborne Brigade lifted from their base camp at Bien Hoa to the outskirts of the beleaguered camp. There, by holding open against enemy counterattacks a road leading into the camp, the 173rd helped break the siege. From Duc Co, Westmoreland then moved them back down south to War Zone D, the site of his first offensive operation in June. As they had during that first operation, the 173rd conducted wide sweeps of the VC base area and uncovered a number of large arms caches. On the third day of the operation, as the paratroopers of the 1st Battalion, 503rd Infantry, were nearing a huge VC base camp, the enemy struck back. Blowing bugles, VC infantry launched a human-wave attack against the 1/503, but were beaten back in savage close-in fighting. As the VC retreated from the field, cannon-firing jets and helicopter gunships dogged their path.

For Westmoreland the successful spoiling actions of the 1st Division and 173rd Airborne Brigade were a welcome relief from the depressing news that had haunted him all during his first year in Vietnam. Yet as the summer began drawing to a close, he still had not had the satisfaction of knowing just how well his troops would do in their first big fight. He had been certain since taking over as COMUSMACV that it would take place somewhere in the forbidding double- and triple-canopy jungles of the Central Highlands, and in late August he began finalizing plans to move the 1st Cavalry Division there once it arrived in country.

He was wrong, however. The first big fight was not to take place in the highlands, but at a place Westmoreland would have least expected it, the Batangan Peninsula in northern I Corps. It was there in mid-August that Marine intelligence discovered the presence of a one-thousand-man-strong VC regiment making preparations to attack the developing Marine base at Chu Lai. Already under orders from Westmoreland to begin undertaking larger offensive operations at greater distances from their bases, Lieutenant General Lewis Walt, the commander of the III Marine Amphibious Force, quickly put together a plan of attack and had it approved by Westmoreland.

The attack itself, which was called Operation Starlite, was sudden and massive. While a flotilla of Navy destroyers and battleships pounded the enemy force with six- and eight-inch shells, eleven Marine battalions, totaling over 4000 men, backed by flame tanks, multibarreled Ontos, and artillery, hit the peninsula from three sides. With no avenue of escape except into the sea, the VC force was nearly wiped out. After the battle, the Marines claimed 573 confirmed enemy dead and another 115 estimated. They, in turn, suffered 46 deaths and 210 wounded.

It was a lopsided victory, and to Westmoreland and his senior commanders, it proved—contrary to Taylor's assertion—that American troops could fight and fight well in the inhospitable terrain of Vietnam. The only thing it did not prove, unfortunately, was how well those same American troops would match up against North Vietnamese regulars. And for Westmoreland and his senior commanders, that became the next big question. While the VC were certainly dedicated, tenacious fighters, they were hardly on a par with the better-trained, better-armed, and infinitely more professional North Vietnamese Army. That same army had beaten and beaten decisively some of the best units in the French Army, and now they were preparing to do the same to the American Army.

And those preparations, as Westmoreland discovered from a series of intelligence reports in late July and early August, were now proceeding at a fever pitch. Those reports offered conclusive proof of the fact that the 101st NVA Regiment, which had been bivouacked in the Central Highlands since January, had recently been joined by three other infantry regiments—the 32nd, 33rd, and 66th. And these last three, they also reported, numbering some six thousand men in all, were gearing up for a major offensive. Although Westmoreland did not know the particulars of that offensive, he had long suspected that when General Giap, who was in overall command of units in the highlands, made his move there it would be with the purpose of slicing South Vietnam in half along Highway 19 from Pleiku in the interior, through An Khe, and finally to Qui Nhon on the coast.

If that was indeed Giap's plan, Westmoreland intended on upsetting it. To do so, he wanted to insert the 1st Cavalry Division at An Khe, from which point they could react to threats in either direction. His plan to bring in the 1st, however, was initially criticized by Admiral Sharp at CINCPAC headquarters in Honolulu. Although Sharp had vehemently opposed Taylor's enclave strategy and strongly supported Westmoreland's to move to the offensive as quickly as possible, he was still gravely concerned that the U.S. Army at this early stage of the war was neither logistically capable nor combat-ready to face the North Vietnamese Army in open battle, and especially in a battle deep in the wild jungles of Pleiku Province. Such an operation could turn into another Dien Bien Phu, he warned Westmoreland. And at the moment, with the U.S. Army just getting unlimbered in Vietnam, the last thing it needed was to suffer a massive calamity. Such a calamity at the least might undermine South Vietnam's confidence in the ability of the Americans to defeat the VC and NVA and, at the worst, might spell the collapse of South Vietnam. Either way, he emphasized, it was simply a risk not worth taking, at least not at the moment.

Westmoreland agreed with Sharp that the risks were indeed great, so great that no sensible man could contemplate them without some trepidation. Westmoreland also believed, however, that the risk of letting the North Vietnamese seize the highlands uncontested would present the United States and South Vietnam with an equally bad situation. Such a victory would not only give North Vietnam control of the coastal plains of Binh Dinh and Phu Yet Province and other large portions of I and II Corps, but would likewise strike a devastating blow to Allied morale.

Although as CINCPAC, Sharp technically had the authority to stop Westmoreland from moving into the Highlands, it would have been inappropriate for him to use it. Like the JCS, he believed that since Westmoreland was the man on the ground, it was up to him and no one else to make tactical decisions. The decision Westmoreland made was both bold and fraught with danger. In anticipation of the 1st Cavalry Division's arrival by ship, he choppered the entire 1st Brigade of the 101st Airborne Division into the An Khe area. In conjunction with two ARVN battalions, the 1st Brigade then swept Highway 19 clean of all enemy installations all the way to the coast, killing 226 VC along the way. Then when the 1st Cavalry Division finally arrived, he ordered them to quickly get off their ship and onto a fleet of waiting helicopters and flown inland to An Khe. There, with machetes, bulldozers, and tons of plastic explosive, troops began carving a base camp out of the jungle near the village of An Khe.

They were still building that camp when the crisis Westmoreland had been anticipating finally materialized. Without warning, two newly arrived NVA regiments—the 33rd and 32nd—suddenly moved away from their base camp near the Chu Pong Mountains and began concentrating around the Plei Mei Special Forces camp, which was about twenty-five miles southeast of Pleiku. Toward the end of September, the 33rd moved up and began digging assault trenches around the camp. When the trenches were completed a few weeks later, they lay siege to the camp, blasting it with mortar and recoilless-rifle fire and barrages of 122-millimeter rockets. Captured documents would later reveal that Plei Mei was the first of three Special Forces camps in the Central Highlands that the NVA intended to reduce before capturing Pleiku. Once captured, the three regiments were going to mass their forces and launch a blitzkrieglike attack to the sea, just what Westmoreland had always expected they would do.

But before the attack could build up the necessary momentum, Westmoreland moved to crush it. While his fleets of fighter-bombers pummeled the enemy trenches around Plei Mei, he ordered a South Vietnamese armored column to push out from Pleiku down a dirt road and break the siege. In anticipation of the relief, the NVA had their second regiment in the area—the 32nd—in an ambush position right in the track of the ARVN advance. Ambushing relief columns was a favorite NVA/VC ploy, and they had used it with phenomenal success during the last three years against ARVN units. They had never used it, however, against a completely airmobile unit like the 1st Cavalry Division.

While the NVA were hunkered down in their ambush positions, Major General Harry Kinnard, the division commander, flew an entire battalion and their artillery over the enemy positions and into their rear. From there, the battalion launched an attack against the enemy positions, while the ARVN relief column, showing unusual boldness and elan shot their way into the heart of the ambush position. The maneuver represented airmobility at its best. Confused by the simultaneous attacks, while being ripped apart with air strikes and thunderous volleys of artillery, the enemy ambushers not killed or wounded fled their positions and began a retreat toward the border. In the combined American-ARVN counterattack that followed, the siege of Plei Mei was broken and the besieging enemy regiment likewise driven from their positions and forced to make a hasty retreat from the battlefield. Of the nearly 3,000 enemy soldiers who had laid siege to Plei Mei, 890 were killed and 600 wounded.

The South Vietnamese were ecstatic over the victory, but Westmoreland felt it was too early to begin celebrating. Shortly after the lifting of the siege, he received word that the two retreating enemy regiments, rather than heading for the safety of Cambodia, had instead moved into assembly areas in the valley of the Ia Drang River. There in the shadows of the Chu Pong Mountains, they were bringing in large numbers of fresh troops to replace their dead and wounded and gearing up for another shot at Plei Mei.

Westmoreland did not know this at the time. All he knew was that large enemy forces were gathering around the Ia Drang, just as they had in preparation for their first attack. This time, however, he did not intend to let them pick the time and place for the fight. The next morning in a hurried conference with Kinnard, he told him "to find, fix and defeat the enemy forces that threatened Plei Mei."

It was an order the former World War II paratrooper had been anticipating, and the next morning he had his division back in the air and headed west toward the border. In their fleets of helicopters, Kinnard's units flew back and forth over an area that was the size of Rhode Island looking for the enemy regiments. Led by Lieutenant Colonel Harold G. Moore, the 1st Battalion, 7th Cavalry was the first to make contact when they happened on an enemy hospital a short distance from the Ia Drang. After setting down at a place called LZ X-ray, Moore's men began preparation for a thorough reconnaissance of the area. Before they could move out, however, Moore discovered that a large force of NVA troops was massing in the area against him. Moore hurriedly circled the wagons, spreading the 431 men in the battalion in a circular perimeter around the landing zone. His men were hardly dug in when the NVA struck. All three battalions of the 33rd NVA Regiment surged out of the surrounding jungle and elephant grass and, with their AK-47s crackling fire, threw themselves headlong at the 1/7's perimeter. The fighting was the fiercest so far in the war. With grenades, rifles, machine guns, and many times even with bayonets and shovels, the men of the 1/7 beat back attack after attack until by nightfall the field around X-Ray was covered with enemy dead. Nightfall temporarily halted the fighting, but in the minds of Kinnard, Moore, and Westmoreland it raised the specter of another 7th Cavalry fight at a place called the Little Bighorn. Was this going to be another Little Bighorn? Another slaughter that would shock the sensibilities of the entire country? From Westmoreland's point of view especially, it was simply something he could not allow to happen.

In the morning, he threw everything he had into the X-Ray fight. Fleets of jets rose up from airstrips at Da Nang, Bien Hoa, and Pleiku and rushed to the beleaguered unit. In order to stop enemy attack, many made strafing and bombing runs within 50 yards of the 1/7's perimeter, flying through a sky filled with the enemy's blue tracer rounds. To add to their impact, Westmoreland ordered every artillery piece within firing range to lend its support. Over fifty guns joined in, sending barrage after barrage down into enemy infantry around X-Ray until by midday over thirty thousand rounds had been fired. Westmoreland even got the Air Force to commit their fleets of B-52s to the fight, in what would be their first use of the war in a tactical mission. Flying so high that they could not be seen from the ground, they inundated the enemy assembly areas, bivouacks, and other rear areas with hundred of thousands of pounds of five-hundred-pound bombs, killing or wounding hundreds of enemy soldiers before they could even join the attack. After a final unsuccessful attack against X-Ray on November 16, both NVA regiments in the area pulled out of the fight and retreated to their base camps in the Chu Pong Massif. During the three-day assault, they lost 834 men by count and Kinnard estimated that they carried away another 1,000 of their dead. The 1/7, in turn, had 79 killed and 121 wounded.

X-Ray was another lopsided victory, but even as they were being ignominiously driven from the battlefield for the second time in a month, the NVA were planning a token of revenge. On November 17, the 2nd Battalion, 7th Cavalry, one of the battalions that had helped relieve X-Ray, stumbled into a massive NVA ambush only a few miles away at a place called LZ Albany. In a matter of minutes, 155 GIs were dead and 121 wounded. Only a tenacious stand by the survivors kept the position from being completely overrun and every man on it killed. As it was, the survivors had to spend a horrifying night listening to their wounded friends out beyond the perimeter screaming as NVA moved about bayoneting the wounded.

In spite of the debacle at Albany, both Generals Westmoreland and Kinnard declared the Ia Drang battle to be a big victory, and by sheer statistics it was. During the month of fighting in the area, the NVA, according to one of their own generals, suffered over three thousand killed and an undetermined number of wounded, while the United States counted three hundred of their own KIAs and nearly one thousand wounded. They were impressive totals, and no one was more impressed than Henry Luce, the publisher of *Time* magazine. Specifically citing Westmoreland's handling of the Ia Drang campaign, he named him *Time*'s Man of the Year for 1965.

But if the Ia Drang was indeed a great victory, hindsight would show that it was also a fatal one, for as the historian-strategist retired Colonel Harry Summers, Jr., points out, the victory lulled policy-makers in Washington "into the delusion that no matter what we did we couldn't lose," convinced them, he says, that with our airmobility and firepower we could chew up enemy units at will and force their leaders to either stop the war or come to the conference table.

In hindsight, of course, both were foolish hopes, for the Communists were determined to stay the course in Vietnam, regardless of the cost. And so in spite of the fact that the U.S. Army won every major battle of the war, final victory ultimately eluded them. It would have been better in the long run, Summers maintains, if we had lost this first big battle, just as we lost the first major battle of World War II at the Kasserine Pass in North Africa. Although a disastrous defeat, the Kasserine "provided a valuable lesson, one we never learned in Vietnam. Our initial defeat in North Africa scared us with the knowledge that if we did not devise better strategies and tactics, we could lose the war." If the Ia Drang battle had instead been a defeat, United States policymakers would have been forced to take a harder look at the war, a look that might hopefully have told them that the whole nature of the war had changed, that it was now a conventional war. And because it was, the counterinsurgency doctrine, a doctrine the Army had so openly embraced, was now meaningless, and so too were "social programs such as pacification and nation building."

The source of the war lay in the North, Summers concludes. And after the Ia Drang that is where the United States should have focused its power, either through a conventional invasion of the North or by blocking the infiltration routes south. But as it was, Westmoreland's victory produced a momentary glimmer of hope in Washington and locked the United States into a war of attrition from which it would never emerge.

If the Ia Drang victory produced a glimmer of hope in Washington, it was soon dimmed by the rush of events. On November 28, only a week after the end of the fight, the ARVN 7th Regiment, while conducting a search-and-destroy operation of their own in the Michelin Rubber Plantation, walked into a VC regimental-size ambush. In the vicious fighting that followed, the ARVN unit was cut to pieces and its commander killed.

"If the Ia Drang was a milestone," wrote William P. Bundy, then the assistant secretary of state for East Asia, in an unpublished memoir, "and confirmed the importance of the search and destroy strategy," then the ARVN debacle at the Michelin Rubber Plantation proved it was only "the Americans who could make it work."

Bundy's conclusion might have been news to Washington at the time, but it was hardly news to Westmoreland. He had known since the marines landed that until the ARVN received better training, better weapons, and better leadership, American units would have to take the fight to the enemy. He had also known that when the fight came, it would be a tough one, as the Ia Drang certainly proved. But he had never been perfectly sure just how long the war might take to conclude. Although he had spent the last year continually trying to prepare Washington to accept the fact that Vietnam would be a long, bloody war, he had had no hard and fast evidence to prove conclusively that it would be. Like the policymakers in Washington, he held out some hope that the three thousand KIAs the North Vietnamese suffered at the Ia Drang would cause them to reconsider their commitment to the South, especially in manpower.

In hindsight, such a hope might seem foolish, but, in fact, right after the battle, the North Vietnamese leadership once again held a debate over strategy. As had happened during previous debates, this one again pitted Giap and Truong Chinh against Le Duan and Le Duc Tho. Awed by the firepower and mobility Westmoreland had brought to the fight and stunned by their casualty list, both Giap and Chinh argued that North Vietnam should return, and return quickly, to a protracted guerrilla struggle. Not only would such a return be less costly in manpower and materiel, but, they again warned, just as they had during the 1964 debate, a war of attrition with the United States risked a spillover that would destroy all their efforts at reconstruction since the defeat of the French.

Duan and Tho had also been stunned by the Ia Drang casualties, and did not doubt the validity of Giap and Chinh's grim prediction. But they likewise did not see how North Vietnam had any choice but to accept the American challenge and to accept it head-on. To not accept it, they argued, to retreat from the challenge, would not only abandon the southern insurgency to face the American juggernaut alone, but would destroy the revolution in the process. Once destroyed or diminished to the point of impotency, the revolution might be impossible to resurrect.

To Ho Chi Minh, as before, the arguments of Duan and Tho again appeared the more logical, and a few days later a decision was finalized to accept the American challenge and gear up for a war of attrition. Almost overnight, the entire economy was put on a war footing, and thousands of North Vietnamese regulars were added to the already large and numerous infiltration groups heading south.

The North Vietnamese decision to escalate the fight forced Westmoreland to contemplate the same. In late November, he cabled McNamara with more grim statistics. "The VC/PAVN build-up rate is predicted to be double that of U.S. Phase II forces," he wrote. "Whereas we will add an average of 7 maneuver battalions per quarter, the enemy will add 15." As far as Westmoreland was concerned, the conclusion was obvious: In addition to the 220,000 United States troops already in country or on their way, he needed 200,000 more in 1966 and possibly another 200,000 by early 1967.

Much has been written about this last troop request. The Pentagon Papers speculate that Westmoreland's decision to make his requests in increments meant either that he knew all along that it would take nearly a million men to win in Vietnam, but felt that such a huge request all at once would be politically unacceptable, or that he had not given much thought to what he would do after 1965.

The first supposition implies that Westmoreland was involved in a kind of conspiracy to dupe the President as to the seriousness of the war and what it would ultimately take in manpower to prosecute it. It is a foolish accusation. For it to be true would have meant that the President depended exclusively on Westmoreland for all his information about the war. In truth, Johnson, as mere common sense would seem to indicate, had access to information from numerous sources other than the military, which included not only his personal advisers but a number of retired military men like Taylor and General Omar Bradley. One of his main sources of hard facts about the war, however, was the CIA. Although the CIA is popularly portrayed as eagerly pushing for United States involvement in Vietnam, their reports to Johnson during the war constantly stressed the difficulties the United States would face fighting a ground war in Asia and denigrated the notion held by some members of the military that bombing could hurt North Vietnam's war effort.

To the contrary, not only was Johnson not duped by the military, but the record shows they frequently were quite frank with him. In early July 1965, for instance, when Johnson asked Wheeler, the JCS Chairman, what it would take to win in Vietnam, Wheeler was quite specific. If we wanted to drive the Communists from the field and completely pacify South Vietnam, he told the President, it would take from 700,000 to 1 million men and seven years. If, using McNamara's definition, we simply wanted to deny them victory, a lesser force would do. Given all this, it is simply ridiculous to think Westmoreland could have duped Johnson as to the seriousness of the war.

The Pentagon Papers' second supposition, namely that Westmoreland had not "given much thought to what he would do after 1965" is equally ridiculous. It is not known what the authors based this on, but it is certainly not based on the record. The record shows that in August 1964, five months before the United States committed troops, the Joint Chiefs of Staff, seeking to measure the cost of victory in Vietnam conducted a war game code-named Sigma I. The game's conclusion was that it would take, at a minimum, half a million men to fight a land war in Vietnam. So, at least a year and a half before Ia Drang Westmoreland knew quite specifically what sort of troop commitment it would take to fight a war in Vietnam. His troop requests, far from being random, were quite simply based on North Vietnam's escalations. If they had not introduced large numbers of troops into the South, then he would not have responded with equally large numbers.

The Pentagon Papers speculate further that McNamara was "shocked" by the troop request, and that that shock started him on a road that would lead to his complete disillusionment with the war. While in Saigon to discuss the request with Westmoreland, the secretary, discarding the optimism he usually displayed when discussing the war, bluntly told a group of correspondents that "it will be a long war." Back in Washington, he was also unusually blunt with the President, telling him that although he was recommending Westmoreland's troop request, it "will not guarantee success. U.S. killed-in-action can be expected to reach 1,000 a month and the odds are even that we will be faced in early 1967 with a 'no-decision' at an even higher level." A few weeks later, at a secret White House conference, McNamara again pressed his point with the President, telling him that no matter what the United States did militarily, "there is no sure victory."

There is no denying McNamara's sudden bout of cynicism, but was he really "shocked" by Westmoreland's request, as the Pentagon

Papers claim, or "shaken" or "stunned" as various other historians claim? Again the record does not support such a conclusion. If Westmoreland knew that it could take as many as a million men to fight an all-out war in Vietnam, and the Joint Chiefs knew, and the President knew, then the secretary of defense had to know also. McNamara might have been legitimately upset to discover that the North Vietnamese were massively reinforcing the battlefield in the South, but he could hardly have been shocked. As Davidson points out, for McNamara there was "no sudden revelation that the war was evil and useless, no bolt out of the blue." To the contrary, McNamara had never been comfortable with the "bloodshed and destruction of the war. He could be bold and resolute in the peaceful activities of opposing the military on force structure and weapon procurement, but a real war, with its senseless carnage and wanton destruction appalled him."

This image of McNamara reeling in shock from Westmoreland's troop request would become an enduring one in the literature of the war. And it did, because the image fits so well with the "quagmire theory," which has long been popular with so many interpreters of the war. This theory seeks to blame America's deepening involvement in the war on the fact that its main players—Westmoreland, McNamara, Johnson, and others—foolishly and arrogantly believed that each new troop levy or each new escalation of the air war would bring victory. What it brought instead, according to the theory, was America's ever deepening involvement in the Vietnam "quagmire." The theory, if true, certainly simplifies our understanding of the war, explaining as it does in such simple terms how our "best and our brightest" could have gotten the country so deeply entangled in the Vietnam War. Unfortunately, it is not true. And it is not true because it seeks to simplify the thinking of these main players, when, in fact, it was far from simple. As Gelb explains, if those men did, indeed, express optimism at each increment of the escalation, it was more than balanced with pessimism; if they expressed public confidence, they simultaneously expressed private doubt; and if they ever saw "the light at the end of the tunnel," they "never saw it for long."

CHAPTER TWELVE

Search and Destroy

I f there was a light at the end of the tunnel, President Johnson was one who never tired of looking for it. It was a search, however, that would keep him on an emotional roller coaster for the rest of his presidency. Initially buoyed by the Ia Drang victory, Johnson was gradually let down by the subsequent rush of bad news. First came the ARVN debacle at the Michelin Rubber Plantation, then McNamara's sudden pessimistic pronouncements, and finally in early December a series of intelligence reports that confirmed what he must have already suspected, that Rolling Thunder, the bombing campaign against the North, had failed to achieve its main goal, which was to stop the North Vietnamese from supporting the insurgency in the South. Not only had it failed to do that, but the North Vietnamese had now themselves entered the war in force. The five regiments they had originally sent south in early 1965 had now been joined by five others, bringing Communist troop strength in the South to 230,000. And with a fresh NVA regiment making the trip down the Ho Chi Minh Trail each month, that figure would likely grow another 70,000 by late 1966.

Like Ho Chi Minh, Johnson was also forced to reexamine his strategy. And as he did, he found himself, like Ho, being pressured by two groups with very different views of the war. The first, the military—the JCS, Sharp, and Westmoreland—as they already had in numerous memos and meetings, tried to convince the President to scrap Rolling Thunder and its "gradualist" approach to bombing the North, and to substitute a massive bombing campaign designed to deliver what the Joint Chiefs called the "knockout" blow. Delivering the argument for the opposite point of view was McNamara, who argued that the military solution simply was not working and that the United States had to begin searching for an alternative solution. Although he was not sure it would do any good, McNamara urged Johnson to stop the air strikes against the North before committing any more troops on the ground. A bombing pause would give the Communists a face-saving chance to consider a diplomatic solution, he argued further, and, just as important, would show the world that America wanted peace.

The military was horrified at the prospect of a bombing pause, for they felt that rather than telling the world how much the United States desired peace, it would instead show Hanoi just how indecisive American policymakers were. In spite of their vigorous objections, on Christmas morning, Johnson gave the orders for the bombing to cease. The pause lasted thirty-seven days and, as the military had predicted, accomplished nothing. If it did anything, the bombing pause forced Johnson to once again give consideration to Westmoreland's massive troop request. Although Johnson was now leaning strongly toward approving it, he nonetheless scheduled a high-level strategy session in Honolulu for February 6–8.

On the first day of the conference, Johnson for the first time got a chance to meet Chief of Staff Thieu and Premier Ky. In his best Texanese, Johnson told both men that he wanted the political scene cleaned up in the South and "the coonskin nailed to the wall." After their meeting, the three men issued the Declaration of Honolulu, a joint communiqué, in which both governments agreed to work together toward the defeat of the Vietcong and for peace and political and social reform in South Vietnam.

Their joint statement made the headlines, but the more important meetings were those that took place between Westmoreland and the President, whom Westmoreland found to be exhausted by the Vietnam War "and torn apart by the apparent magnitude of it." At one point during their initial discussion, Johnson's fatigue became evident when he suddenly blurted out, "General I have a lot riding on you."

Then, after alluding to Truman's problems with MacArthur during the Korean War, he cautioned, "I hope you don't pull a MacArthur on me." Since he had no intention of doing anything like that, Westmoreland did not bother responding.

Yet in spite of his weakened spirit, Johnson approved Westmoreland's troop request. To give Westmoreland guidance for the use of his new troops, Johnson also handed him a memorandum drafted by McNamara and Rusk, listing six goals for 1966. Five of them dealt with fairly mundane matters such as the percentage of villages they wanted pacified and the miles of roads they wanted opened, but the sixth goal laid out in specific terms the strategy Westmoreland was to employ in fighting the war. According to it, he was to "attrit [*sic*] by year's end, Viet Cong and North Vietnamese forces at a rate as high as their capability to put men in the field."

"Attrit," of course, was an abbreviation for attritional warfare. In more concrete terms, it meant Westmoreland was being ordered to kill enemy soldiers faster than they could be replaced. And once killed, they were to be counted, and weekly, monthly, and yearly "body counts" compiled. Westmoreland later wrote that he found the term "body count" repugnant, but in spite of that fact, his name in the minds of many Americans became permanently associated with the term, as if it were his creation and his creation alone.

This association apparently also took root in the minds of Vietnam historians, for as Davidson so adroitly points out, there is not a single book about the war which mentions this memo mandating attritional warfare. "Here was the directive which established American strategy from 1966 to 1969," he says, "and which formally made the strategy of attrition the first priority objective of the United States in South Vietnam, and yet no historian pays it the slightest attention." Perhaps it is not mentioned because it is more convenient for many to believe the common fiction that the attrition strategy was some aberration cooked up by Westmoreland, an aberration that McNamara, McNaughton, and the other civilians in the Office of the Secretary of Defense were then forced to live with. The fact that McNamara and his men drew up the mandate for attritional warfare and at least initially accepted it as a viable strategy is absent from all histories of the war, save Davidson's.

Later in the war, McNaughton and others on the OSD staff conveniently masked their association with it. None of them, however, would even question it openly, attempt to modify it, or draw up a viable alternative strategy. Neither did anyone else in authority in Washington. In fact, during Westmoreland's entire four years in Vietnam, the strategy was never subjected to a critical analysis by any of the senior policymakers in Washington.

The only one who subjected it to a critical analysis was Westmoreland himself. And that analysis told him that given the political restrictions he was forced to operate under, it was the only viable strategy available. Denied the freedom to invade North Vietnam, which he considered the source of the aggression, forbidden to attack enemy base camps and supply caches in Laos and Cambodia, lacking the necessary troops to physically defend every inch of a nine-hundred-mile border, he felt he had no choice but to wage attritional warfare, to go after individual enemy units and destroy them. He made his decision, however, without any illusions about what he could accomplish with attritional warfare, in spite of his 1967 pronouncement that he was going to bleed the Communist armies "until Hanoi wakes up to the fact that they have bled their country to the point of national disaster for generations."

Much has been made of this statement, and numerous historians have pointed to it as evidence that Westmoreland expected a clear-cut victory from his attrition strategy. It is difficult to see how they come to this conclusion, because Westmoreland is on record numerous times stating that a conventional victory in Vietnam was not possible. And he certainly was not alone in that belief. The record clearly shows that none of Johnson's senior policymakers believed in the possibility of a conventional victory, either. To the contrary, in the cables and memos Westmoreland received from Washington during the early part of the war, when victory is mentioned, it is mentioned cautiously and with the utmost circumspection. In one cable to Westmoreland Wheeler defined victory for him not as the United States winning, but as having proved to "the Communists that they cannot win." During a conference in Honolulu, the OSD defined victory as breaking "the will of the DRV/VC by denying them victory."

If Westmoreland did not think he could achieve a clear-cut victory in Vietnam, he did believe he could cripple the NVA and VC forces sufficiently to give the South Vietnamese Army the breathing space it needed to develop into a viable fighting force. If the first was unattainable, the second was a very real possibility.

And in early 1966, with the "fire brigade" period of the war successfully completed, he shifted into phase two of his three-phase campaign plan. As he had outlined for McNamara in July 1965, during this second phase he intended to gain control of certain high-priority areas.

To guide this second phase, Westmoreland planned to use three types of operations, each of which was part of a larger process. During the first operation, "search and destroy," American or Allied troops would locate, bring to battle, and then destroy or neutralize large NVA and VC units. Following their destruction, ARVN units would move in and conduct "clearing operations" designed to mop up any guerrilla forces still in the area. Finally, using "securing operations," those same ARVN units would help set up a permanent defense in the area so that pacification could take place.

Contrary to numerous myths about this search-and-destroy strategy, as it would come to be called, it was not a creation of Westmoreland's extremely bellicose operations officer, Brigadier General William E. DePuy ("The solution in Vietnam is more bombs, more shells and more napalm . . ."). The Army had developed the terminology and methodology for the three basic types of operations long before the first United States troops set foot in Vietnam, and all Westmoreland and DePuy did was utilize fixed models. Nor was search-and-destroy, as so many have claimed, merely a euphemism for mindless violence applied indiscriminately. While the promiscuous use of firepower was certainly an integral part of search-and-destroy, that had also been the case in most American wars. The axiom, "bullets are cheaper than blood," had been an important part of American military planning since World War I, and Vietnam was to be no different.

To make his search-and-destroy strategy work, Westmoreland now had two hundred thousand U.S. troops at his disposal, plus a Korean division, an Australian battalion, and some elite ARVN airborne and Ranger units. In northern I Corps, the 1st and 3rd marine divisions held a number of key areas along the coast. In II Corps, the 1st Cavalry Division, following the Ia Drang battle, had been shifted from their base camp at An Khe to Binh Dinh, a coastal province. And in III Corps, the 25th Infantry Division was positioned at Chu Chi, the 173rd Airborne Brigade at Bien-hoa, the 4th Infantry Division in the rubber plantations adjacent to the Cambodian border, the 1st Infantry Division along the northern approaches to Saigon, and a battalion of the Royal Australian Regiment at Ba Ria in Phuoc Toy Province.

Although Westmoreland would have preferred to use the two hundred thousand-plus troops at his disposal outside the major population areas, he knew that at least through most of 1966, he was going to have to direct most of his operations at areas where most of South Vietnam's people lived. Long before the United States entered the war, VC regiments had established themselves in such areas, and

Westmoreland felt those units had to be either destroyed or neutralized before he moved into the hinterlands.

For him, the area of highest priority, of course, was the area around Saigon, and especially the area to the north of the capital in the deep primordial forest of War Zones C and D. There, untouched since 1959, the VC had constructed a massive base area, well stocked with huge supplies of food and ammunition, laced with a labyrinth of underground tunnels, and protected by an intricate system of bunkers and fighting trenches. Over the years, the VC had used these zones as a staging area for so many of their attacks against the capital and the surrounding region, that the zones were now commonly referred to "as a dagger pointed at the heart of Saigon."

Another area that concerned Westmoreland was the coastal plains of Binh Dinh Province. Not only did the area's very bountiful rice harvest provide much of the food for a number of the enemy units in the South, but Westmoreland feared that the Communist forces there—a VC regiment and two NVA regiments—might try to link up with the VC forces in War Zones C and D. Such a linkage could doom the South Vietnamese government.

A third area that concerned Westmoreland was northern I Corps, and especially its two major cities, Hue and Da Nang. There the threat was both military and political. The military threat came from the nearby demilitarized zone, where two, and possibly three, NVA divisions, under the direct command of General Giap, were bivouacked, waiting for the orders that would send them streaming into I Corps. That threat was made even graver by the political situation in I Corps. Owing to the high concentration of Buddhists in the areas, and especially in Da Nang and Hue, I Corps had always shown a strong sense of regionalism, but since 1963, demonstrations, protests, and riots had become common occurrences there. Westmoreland feared that if Giap timed a military move against the region with a massive political disturbance, he might be able to capture Hue, and possibly Da Nang.

Westmoreland was particularly worried about Hue, however. As the ancient Vietnamese capital, the city had a great religious and cultural significance to the South Vietnamese, and its loss would be a profound psychological blow to the country's morale. Of all the possible enemy scenarios, he worried about this last one the most. During the Honolulu conference when President Johnson asked him what he would do if he were the enemy, Westmoreland without hesitation responded, "Capture Hue." But at the moment, Hue was on the back burner. His most immediate problem was clearing the area around Saigon and breaking the enemy's hold on War Zones C and D. In late February and early March, he ordered attacks against all three areas.

In early March, the 1st Infantry Division and First Australian Task Force launched Operation Abilene into the base area of the VC 5th Division in Phuoc Toy Province just east of Saigon. During a sweep of an abandoned bivouac, one of the 1st's battalions uncovered a huge supply of food but made only moderate contact.

With the close of Abilene, the division boarded its helicopters and wheeled inland. On April 24, in the first major Allied foray there since 1962, the division launched Operation Birmingham on the edge of War Zone C. Again they uncovered vast quantities of rice, clothing, medicine, and ammunition, but made little contact.

Shortly after Birmingham, Westmoreland replaced the 1st Infantry Division commander, Major General Jonathan O. Seaman, with Major General William E. DePuy. Westmoreland had tried to replace Seaman with DePuy five months earlier, but General Johnson had thought removing Seaman after only one month on the job was improper, and so Westmoreland had had to wait until Seaman had nearly six months in the job before making the change. To ease any pain Seaman might have felt, Westmoreland made him commander of II Field Force, a job that technically made him DePuy's superior. But it was obvious that Westmoreland made the move because he wanted the more aggressive—some say ruthless—DePuy running the 1st Infantry Division, which was one of the divisions tasked with clearing the area north of Saigon of enemy units. That fact was also obvious from Westmoreland's first order to DePuy, which was that he was "to get the 1st Division moving."

DePuy was not a man who needed to be told. A few days after taking command, he fired nearly every one of his battalion and brigade commanders, and let everyone else in the division know that the days when the 1st Infantry Division conducted small-scale sweeps in the countryside around Saigon were over. The 1st was going to start aggressively looking to make contact with the enemy every time they went out.

DePuy's wholesale firings shook the morale of the senior officers corps in Vietnam and prompted the Army Chief of Staff, General Johnson, to cable Westmoreland and express his extreme displeasure. Westmoreland chose not to act, however, preferring to let DePuy have his head, just as one might a good racehorse. Even if he had acted, it would not have done much good, for DePuy had quickly filled the vacant jobs in his command with a fresh batch of aggressive lieutenant colonels and colonels. One colonel DePuy was extremely impressed with was his new commander of the 1st Battalion, 26th Infantry—Alexander M. Haig.

With his new men in place, DePuy began moving the division around rapidly, aggressively looking to make contact. When two minor operations north of Saigon came up dry holes, he decided to plunge the division like a dagger right into the heart of War Zone C. His particular target was the elite 9th VC Division, which was bivouacked near the rubber plantation town of Loc Ninh. Intelligence suspected that the 9th was preparing for a major offensive in the coming monsoon season, and DePuy wanted to break up the attack before it even got started.

After organizing a long convoy of tanks, armored personnel carriers, and trucks, DePuy sent them boldly up Route 13 toward the heart of War Zone C. Near the village of Tau-O, the 9th Division's 272nd VC Regiment ambushed the column. Following an initial mortar barrage and a torrent of recoilless-rifle fire, VC infantry poured out of their ambush position in the tree line and charged the convoy. They got about halfway there before their ranks were shredded by tanks firing high-explosive and flachette rounds. While the VC infantry was attempting to regroup for a second charge, DePuy, flying above the fight in his command chopper, called in artillery fire against them from four different firebases. When they finished a thirty-minute barrage, he turned loose his jets and gunships. A sweep of the battlefield the next morning revealed one hundred enemy dead and numerous blood trails, indicating that hundreds more dead and wounded were dragged or carried off. Thirteen Americans also died.

Continuing his push into War Zone C the next day, the 1st Division's 2nd Battalion, 28th Infantry ran into a battalion of the 273rd VC Regiment entrenched on a hill near Loc Thien. After being ordered by DePuy to take the position, Company B charged the enemy trenches and bunkers behind a rolling artillery barrage. Stopped halfway there, they pulled back their dead and wounded and then attacked again, this time with fixed bayonets. They found success, completely overrunning the enemy position. In the rubble of collapsed bunkers and trenches, they counted another ninety-eight enemy dead and wounded. The 2nd Battalion had thirty-three killed and twenty-nine wounded.

During the next two weeks, DePuy moved his division around at will in War Zone C, uncovering one enemy cache after another while encountering only light resistance. Then on June 30, a third VC regiment, the 271st, surfaced, ambushing a United States convoy moving down "Thunder Road." It was another close-in vicious fight.

Following a mortar barrage and recoilless-rifle fire that knocked out two tanks and three armored personnel carriers (APCs) in the column, NVA infantry, four hundred strong, charged out of the tree line. They came within twenty yards of overrunning the convoy before being stopped by a hail of machine-gun fire and tank flachette rounds. The battle of Srok Dong was publicly declared a great victory, but DePuy knew that it had been less than decisive, that it had, in fact, been a near defeat, something he could not afford at this point in the war.

He felt the 1st Infantry Division needed a decisive victory to make up for Srok Dong and decided to create one. When he discovered the 272nd VC Regiment had moved into north-central Binh Duong Province, he sent the 1st Squadron, 4th Cavalry up the Minh Thanh Road as bait to draw them out.

It worked. Right in the area DePuy had predicted, the 272nd, fighting from trenches and holes, ambushed the column, not realizing that it was they who were actually being ambushed. Using the Minh Thanh Road as a fire direction line, DePuy massed his artillery and plastered the enemy positions with a two-thousand-round barrage. In the meantime, he choppered in three infantry battalions, including Haig's 1st Battalion, 26th Infantry, had them encircle the enemy regiment, then assault it behind a furious artillery barrage. A large number of enemy soldiers escaped the trap, but they left behind nearly four hundred of their dead in the smoking, shattered tree-line. The 1st Division had twenty-two dead. Following the fight, the badly battered 272nd VC Regiment retreated from the Minh Thanh area and joined the rest of the 9th VC Division in their hidden base camps along the Cambodian border. Because of the heavy losses the 9th had suffered, they had to scrap their planned monsoon offensive. It would be November before they could take the field again.

Simultaneous with his push against War Zone C, Westmoreland also unleashed a host of operations in II Corps. His biggest there, and his biggest to date in all of South Vietnam, was Operation Masher, which he had designed to drive the enemy out of the Bong Son Plains, a lush rice-growing area along the coast of Binh Dinh Province. Westmoreland knew it was not going to be an easy job. The Communists had established control over the province in 1945 and had never relinquished it. In an attempt to get a toehold in the province, in 1963 Diem had fortified three district headquarters, but a VC regiment had quickly overrun all three and forced anyone connected to the government to flee for their lives. Following their expulsion, the 2nd VC Regiment and the 18th and 22nd NVA Regiments set up elaborate base camps in four valleys west and northwest of the Bong

Son Plains. Westmoreland was convinced the three would defend the Bong Son rice bowl to the bitter end, for Communist political officers were roaming about the province telling villagers that "the sun will rise in the west before we allow the government to return."

Westmoreland gave the job of cracking the Bong Son to Major General Harry W. O. Kinnard and his 1st Cavalry Division. It was a wise choice. Recent victors at the Ia Drang, the Cav was quickly establishing a reputation as the best unit in Vietnam. Just as he had at the Ia Drang, Kinnard decided to use tactics that were bold and innovative. Reinforcing himself with an ARVN airborne brigade and the 22nd ARVN Division and the 1st Regiment of the Korean Capital Division, he set up a central base near the village of Bong Son, then put in motion a series of relentless attacks against the four main valleys. In many of his attacks, Kinnard employed a hammer-and-anvil tactic. Whenever an Allied unit received fire from a Communist position, they first plastered it with artillery fire and air strikes, then attacked on the ground. In anticipation that the enemy would flee, Kinnard already had blocking positions set up along likely enemy avenues of retreat. Many times as an enemy unit was fleeing furiously from a fight, it found itself getting fire from its rear and sides and also at time from fleets of gunships that roamed freely over the battlefields, their miniguns crackling. If the enemy unit decided not to flee but to make a fight of it, then it had to face a rain of artillery fire, bombs and napalm, and at times even B-52 strikes. Kinnard's driving attacks eventually began taking their toll on the three enemy regiments, and before the operation was thirty days old, Westmoreland received word that enemy units were abandoning their valley fortresses en masse and heading deep into the mountains.

The operation officially closed on March 5. By all accounts, Masher was a huge success. During forty-one days of combat, the 1st Cavalry Division, with the help of the ARVN and Korean brigades, had killed over twenty-one hundred enemy soldiers, destroyed five of nine enemy battalions operating in the province, along with a mortar and recoilless-rifle company, and a signal company. Just as important, Binh Dinh Province, once considered an impregnable enemy redoubt was now under government control.

The Communist leadership in the South was stunned by the ouster of their forces from Binh Dinh, but like a good boxer who has just absorbed a heavy punch, they quickly came back with a series of hard counterpunches. They delivered their hardest punch to the U.S. Special Forces camp near the village of A Shau in the A Shau Valley. There an enemy regiment, taking advantage of bad weather that hampered air strikes and made it impossible for friendly reinforcements to arrive, overran the camp after three days of savage fighting. The NVA casualties were unknown, but assumed high. Allied casualties were high. Of the 424 camp defenders, 261 were killed and 103 wounded. Five of the dead were American Green Berets, as were 12 of the wounded.

Westmoreland was as stunned by the fall of the camp at A Shau as the Communists were by the loss of Binh Dinh Province. Since the camp had represented the only Allied presence in the strategic valley, he saw the attack as a prelude to a larger, more concerted attack on all of northern I Corps, with Hue being the ultimate prize. His feelings were reinforced by a series of events that coincided with the camp's fall. In mid-March, his intelligence chief reported the existence of three enemy regiments, and possibly a fourth, in the two northern provinces, Quang Tri and Thua Thien. In addition, it reported that the North Vietnamese had moved their 324B Division from Ha Thinh 180 miles south to a staging area just above the demilitarized zone, and that troops from that division were massing near the U.S. Special Forces camp at Khe Sanh.

As for the A Shau Valley, Westmoreland placed a high priority on the strategic importance of the Khe Sanh. Only a few miles from the Laotian border, it sat on a small plateau overlooking Route 9, the only major route into Quang Tri Province from the west. Because of its location, he had originally placed the Special Forces camp there so that it could both monitor enemy infiltration and serve as a staging area for special reconnaissance operations into Laos. Eventually, if he could get President Johnson's permission, he envisioned expanding the camp so that it could be used both as a western anchor for defenses south of the DMZ and as a jumping-off point for ground operations meant to cut the Ho Chi Minh Trail.

For the moment, however, he was concerned only with holding the camp and preparing for any enemy move against I Corps. And so a few days after receiving the intelligence report, Westmoreland ordered General Lewis Walt, the commander of the III Marine Amphibious Force, to move a battalion north to Phu Bai, where it could be closer to Hue, and another up to Khe Sanh, to conduct search-and-destroy operations in the area.

Walt prepared to make the move, but he did so under mild protest. During a number of face-to-face meetings, he and his staff told Westmoreland that they had looked at the same raw intelligence data as MACV's intelligence people and had come up with an entirely different reading. While they acknowledged that there had been some enemy buildup in I Corps, they did not think it was as big as MACV claimed, nor that it was aimed at places like Hue. They thought the enemy might try to pick off another isolated Special Forces camp, even the one at Khe Sanh, but they did not believe Hanoi had formulated a grandiose scheme to seize I Corps.

And as far as Khe Sanh itself was concerned, Walt and his staff—and their feelings were strongly seconded by General Wallace M. Greene, the Marine commandant, and General Victor Krulak, the commander of all Marines in the Pacific—likewise did not see a problem. While they certainly did not want to see the camp fall to the NVA, they likewise would not have been terribly upset if Westmoreland had decided to abandon the camp and let the jungle reclaim the land it sat on. They felt running search-and-destroy operations around the camp was not only a waste of time but a waste of valuable manpower. And they felt just as strongly about running such operations in any of the mountains of northern I Corps, or even the DMZ.

They felt that the important war was in the populated and fertile lowlands, digging out guerrillas and denying the large VC and NVA units the food, taxes, intelligence, and other support they needed to survive. While the Marines, as Krulak told Admiral Sharp, did not mind taking on the big enemy units should "they sortie out of the mountains and come down to the plains," they did not see any purpose in sending "battalions thrashing about in the green hills against vanishing targets." After the war, Krulak was even more blunt, writing that "every man we put into hunting for the NVA was wasted."

They were strong words, and after the war many Westmoreland critics would point to Krulak and repeat his damning pronouncement and then bemoan the fact that Westmoreland had not heeded his advice or the advice of other Marines like him. One Westmoreland critic, Neil Sheehan, even implied in his *A Bright Shining Lie* that had Westmoreland listened to Krulak, the United States would have won the war in Vietnam. He comes to his conclusion, however, without holding the Marine strategy up to the same scrutiny he does Westmoreland's. He does not ask what would have happened if Westmoreland had indeed heeded the advice of the Marines and conceded control of the mountains and the DMZ, which represented nearly two thirds of the land in the country, to the control of the enemy. What would have happened, for instance, if the enemy had been allowed carte blanche to take over mountain towns like Kontum, Pleiku, An Kye, and Dong Ha? Or to build base camps, staging areas and various types of entrenched positions only a few miles from the coastal plains? With enemy positions so close to the heavily populated lowlands, could the Marines have reacted quickly enough to stop regimental- or divisional-size assaults? And with 15- and 20-man groups of Marines spread throughout the countryside "pacifying" the hundreds of villages in I Corps, could they even have dealt with such attacks? Or, as Westmoreland always contended, would those small groups instead have been destroyed piecemeal by large enemy units?

Those enamored of Krulak's strategy also ignore the most fundamental fact about the strategy itself: It was not a full-blown concept, but a kind of hit-and-miss affair, with massive gaps in its coverage. They also ignore, as a number of defense analysts pointed out after the war, that the Marine approach was also "slow and methodical," and as such ran the "risk of turning into an occupation, and even while being called pacification/civic action involved Americans deeply in the politics and traditions of rural Vietnam." Even McNamara, who claims that by early 1966 he had decided that the war could not be won, thought the Marine strategy would have taken too much time to make an impact, and time was one thing America lacked in Vietnam.

Westmoreland, of course, had his way, and though the Marines continued to howl in protest, by early April a Marine battalion was conducting search-and-destroy operations around Khe Sanh and another was digging in and stringing wire around a new camp at Phu Bai. Both Marine moves took place in the midst of fresh political turmoil in I Corps, turmoil that convinced Westmoreland that if the Communists did not already have plans to hit I Corps they might quickly make them in order to take advantage of the chaos.

The trouble began in mid-March when Premier Ky went back on the promise he had made earlier to retire in favor of an elected civilian government. Tri Quang, the militant Buddhist monk who had led the earlier opposition to Diem, was furious at Ky for going back on his word and quickly began mobilizing opposition to him in Hue. There he also formed an alliance with General Nguyen Chanh Thi, the I Corps commander. Thi and Ky were very much alike. Both were extremely brave, at times to the point of recklessness, and both were virulently anti-Communist. Unfortunately, Thi also had political ambitions. And those ambitions, Ky knew, were for the premiership. On March 10, Ky fired Thi and replaced him with Brigadier General Nguyen Van Chuan. Within days of Thi's removal, protests, demonstrations, and riots broke out in six cities. In Da Nang, a strike by dock workers closed the port. In Quang Ngai, students closed the school and took over the radio station. And in Saigon, gangs of youths rampaged through the streets, setting fire to autos and looting shops.

CHAPTER THIRTEEN

The Same Old Message

Three days after the turmoil began, South Vietnamese military operations stopped in the central provinces of I Corps, and hundreds of ARVN troops loyal to Thi joined the demonstrations. In Da Nang hundreds of dissident troops even threw up barricades and blocked all the roads into the city. What had started as a political disturbance now began to look frighteningly like an open revolt. The spectacle shocked members of the United States mission in Saigon, and prompted one senior American official to exclaim, "What are we doing here? We're fighting to save these people, and they're fighting each other."

Westmoreland's own response was considerably less hysterical. he was baffled by Ky's decision to fire Thi, and in a cable to the premier referred to the turmoil as "foolishness," reminding him that since the trouble started, "228 Americans in I Corps died fighting for South Vietnam." Still, while certainly upset by the disturbances, he was not surprised by them. He did not see them, as many critics of the war did, as a clear sign that democracy was not possible in South Vietnam, that the government was simply too corrupt and the people too politically immature. To the contrary, he saw the demonstrations and turmoil as merely something that all developing nations had to go through as they stumbled forward toward democracy. There just was not any simple way for a country to learn democratic principles, he felt, as America's own tumultuous history certainly proved. Westmoreland hoped, however, that the revolt could be ended without bloodshed, and he sent messages to both the mayor of Da Nang and the Buddhist leader, Tri Quang, begging them both to stop the disturbances before the Communists took advantage of them with military action.

When the chaos only worsened, Ky decided to crush the revolt, claiming that the Communists had taken it over. He was wrong. The Communists admitted after the war that they had played no part in the uprising, that they had, in fact, been surprised by it themselves. Of course, Ky did not know this at the time, and likely would not have cared if he had. After helping land a division at Da Nang, he gave command of it to Colonel Nguyen Ngoc Loan, who would gain notoriety two years later from a photograph of him executing a VC terrorist. Behind tanks and armored personnel carriers, Loan and his troops moved methodically through Da Nang street by street, slaughtering hundreds of rebel troops and more than a hundred civilians.

This show of force stunned the rebellious troops in Hue and, rather than die at their barricades also, they went back to their units. Tri Quang did manage to instigate a few more demonstrations, but by the end of June the steam had gone out of the Buddhist movement.

The turmoil had not been for naught, though. Because of Buddhist pressure, the military council added ten elected civilians to its memberships, and Ky and Thieu agreed to hold an election in September for a constituent assembly. This time Ky did not go back on his promise, and on September 16, 1966, a 117-man assembly was elected. Once seated, they, in turn, began drafting a constitution, and making plans for a presidential election the following year.

For Westmoreland the end of the political trouble in I Corps could not have come at a better time. On May 15, at the same time that Loan's troops were ruthlessly crushing the rebellion in Da Nang, night air reconnaissance pilots reported to MACV that there was considerable truck traffic moving south toward the demilitarized zone on Highways 1A and 101. The report caused a stir at MACV, and Westmoreland demanded more information from his intelligence people. He got a flood of it. A day later, South Vietnamese agents on the ground reported that elements of the NVA 324B Division were also moving into the area. More aerial observation reported small fires in the jungles and signs of large camps. Finally on May 19, Westmoreland got the hard evidence he had been waiting for. On that day, NVA units attacked two ARVN outposts, Gio Linh and Con Thien, only a few miles south of the DMZ. Following the attack on Gio Linh, an NVA soldier surrendered and told his captors that the entire 324B Division had infiltrated through the DMZ and that its commander was under orders to overrun Quang Tri City and Quang Tri Province.

In anticipation that the 324B might first attack Dong Ha as it moved south, on May 28 Westmoreland ordered General Walt to move a battalion to the Dong Ha Air Facility. As instructed, Walt moved the battalion, but he did so grudgingly. While he and his intelligence staff shared Westmoreland's concern for the enemy buildup in the DMZ, they did not feel it represented preparations for an invasion of northern I Corps. Not only did they not think the NVA had the logistical capabilities to support such an invasion, but even if they did, the Marines still did not feel they would attempt something so grandiose. To the contrary, they felt the NVA forces massing in the DMZ—and they did not believe it was the entire 324B Division—were merely there to act as bait to draw them away from their pacification duties.

Walt and his staff told Westmoreland all this in a meeting at Da Nang in mid-June, but their words predictably fell on deaf ears. Westmoreland was certain the North Vietnamese Army was preparing to invade northern I Corps, and like it or not, the Marines were going north to stop it. To ease them into the fight gradually, Westmoreland ordered Walt to start conducting large reconnaissance operations in Quang Tri Province. The Marine recon units, however, went north, as one second lieutenant said, "not optimistic about contacting the 324B." It was a bad assumption. The 324B was not only there but they were dug in and had stockpiled enough ammunition for a long fight.

Westmoreland quickly ordered Walt to reinforce the battlefield, and within two days Operation Hastings was under way. To take on the 324B, which had an estimated strength of twelve thousand men, Walt marshaled a force of eight thousand Marines and three thousand ARVN. On July 15, this combined force attacked north and west from their supply base at Dong Ha and crashed headlong into the NVA division, which was concentrated in a number of strongpoints across a quarter of the DMZ. The encounters that followed were, as one observer noted, "hard and nasty, reminiscent of the battles the U.S.

Army fought in the hedgerow country of France during World War Two." From trenches, bunkers, and fighting holes prepared weeks in advance, the 324B—armed with new heavy machine guns, large Russian mortars, long-range artillery, recoilless rifles, rockets, and AK-47 assault rifles—put up a tenacious fight, contesting one position until overrun then falling back on another. Behind thunderous barrages of naval gunfire, massed artillery-fire, and air strikes, the Marines and ARVN overwhelmed one enemy position after another, all the time advancing closer and closer to the DMZ.

After two weeks of enduring these relentless attacks, the 324B broke contact and retreated north. They left behind 800 dead and likely carried away an equal number. The Marines lost 126 killed and 448 wounded.

Hastings was a lopsided Allied victory, but it did not settle the difference between Westmoreland and the Marines over enemy intentions in I Corps. On July 22, General Krulak cabled Westmoreland and told him that he thought the 324B had retreated north across the DMZ and was no longer a threat to I Corps. In a return cable, Westmoreland replied that "just the reverse was the case and that the NVA forces were not seeking to get away," but instead were only backing off for a while to get resupplied and to replace their casualties. Furthermore, he told Krulak, recent MACV intelligence reports indicated that two more NVA divisions, the 304th and 341st, had moved into the area north of the DMZ.

This last fact did not impress either Krulak or Walt. In spite of Operation Hastings and in spite of the arrival of two more enemy divisions on the scene, they still did not think the enemy had a plan to seize I Corps. Among themselves, in fact, Marine commanders mocked terms like "massive buildup," "go for broke," "significant serious threat," and other similar expressions that originated at MACV headquarters. Where Westmoreland saw "significant serious threat," they continued to see only a wily enemy trying to bog them down in what they termed "fruitless" battles in the DMZ.

Their argument again, however, fell on deaf ears. Westmoreland was still convinced the enemy intended to attack I Corps, and he was likewise convinced that the main thrust of that attack was going to come down through the demilitarized zone. How to permanently stop the enemy from infiltrating enough troops into the DMZ for such an attack was now the main problem facing him. Because of political restraints, he had to immediately reject the idea of invading the narrow strip of land in North Vietnam just above the DMZ. Although the North Vietnamese Army used it as both a supply point and staging area, it was politically off limits. Owing to a manpower shortage, he also had to reject the idea of constructing a World War I–type trench line from the South China Sea to the Laotian border.

In an attempt to help Westmoreland solve the infiltration problem, in late July McNamara and his scientific advisers got together and came up with what they thought was a solution. Their plan called for the construction of an electronic anti-infiltration barrier across the entire length of the DMZ, to be built in stages. In the first stage, giant bulldozers were to clear a wide swath of ground through the jungle from the sea to Laos. This cleared ground was then to be liberally sown with mines, and acoustic and seismic sensors, then covered with a thick continous belt of German razor wire. Finally, to monitor the barrier, a series of outposts and observation posts were to be built.

It was a grandiose plan, but unfortunately McNamara and his advisers were the only ones who believed in it. The JCS openly scoffed at the idea, calling it an Alice in Wonderland solution; Westmoreland, in a kinder note, merely told McNamara that it would be difficult to build and even more difficult to defend.

When McNamara ordered the barrier built anyway, Westmoreland's first prophecy quickly proved true. Observing Seabees moving into position to begin construction, the NVA brought them under fire with 152-millimeter guns hidden on the north side of the demilitarized zone. At the same time, NVA snipers, hidden in the tops of trees, pecked away at the bulldozer drivers and workers. The fire from both caused numerous casualties, and forced the Marines to detail large numbers of troops to the DMZ just to protect work crews. Numerous vital air assets also had to be pulled out of combat support roles and assigned the job of hunting for hidden guns firing on the work crews. In spite of their work to find and knock out the guns, as the work progressed casualties began to mount steadily.

When McNamara visited Vietnam in October, Westmoreland took him up in his personal plane and during a flight up and down the length of the DMZ pointed out to him the enormous difficulties his construction crews were facing. McNamara agreed to let him stop construction for the moment, but said he wanted MACV to continue studying ways of making the electronic barrier work. Westmoreland agreed, but after the meeting the electronic barrier plan was never seriously considered again. The next day, Westmoreland canceled construction of the eastern portion of the barrier and diverted all his construction assets into what he had wanted to build in the first place, a series of strongpoints along the entire length of the DMZ.

When completed a few months later, he had forward strongpoints at Gio Linh and Con Thien, two former ARVN outposts, and backup positions at Camp Carrol, Cam Lo, Dong Ha, the Rockpile, and Khe Sanh. To man those strongpoints, he shifted the entire 3rd Marine Division north, putting their headquarters at Phu Bai and their forward command post at Dong Ha. To give the 3rd some added muscle, he also moved an entire Army 105mm howitzer battery north, parceling out its guns to the various strongpoints, ordered a battalion of the Army's huge 175mm guns positioned at Camp Carrol, and had an airstrip constructed at Quang Tri. Finally to ease Walt's anxiety over having to pull his 3rd Division away from pacification duties, he ordered the 173rd Airborne Brigade to move up to Da Nang and began making plans, should it become necessary, to move an entire Army division north.

In spite of the 3rd Marine Division's move north and in spite of the Amy reinforcements sent to back them up, the Marines were still stretched thin across northern I Corps. And their situation, already barely tenuous in some areas, was getting worse, for the NVA had nearly doubled their own forces in I Corps during the last four months and seemed on their way to doubling them once again.

Unfortunately for Westmoreland, the situation was much the same in all four corps. Although his big search-and-destroy operations had taken a heavy toll on the enemy manpower during the last year, their overall strength had actually increased by 42,000 during the year, and now stood at 300,575. And with MACV's intelligence staff reporting NVA infiltration south now at a rate of 8,400 a month and new VC recruits at 3,500 a month, that number was growing rapidly. When Westmoreland cabled these new statistics to Washington, he got a mixed response. Walt Rostow, the President's national security adviser, thought Westmoreland was exaggerating the enemy strength and infiltration figures in order to get more troops; some members of the CIA, on the other hand, accused him of drastically underestimating enemy strength, and especially the strength of VC irregulars.

Caught in the middle between these competing views of enemy strength, McNamara decided in mid-October to fly to Saigon for a firsthand appraisal. During Westmoreland's libel suit against CBS in 1984, McNamara testified that by the time of his October visit to Saigon, he had decided that the war could not be won. When he met Westmoreland, however, he kept those thoughts to himself. Instead it was business as usual. After discussing the enemy strength and infiltration figures, McNamara told Westmoreland to "ask for the troops you think you'll need and I'll tailor your request to availability and economic and political reality."

Westmoreland wanted to ask for the troops and permission to move into Cambodia and Laos, but realized it would be a futile gesture. The President was already under strong pressures from both the left and the right in the country, and asking for more troops and an expanded war, he realized, would only add to those pressures. He realized that the Joint Chiefs were calling for a Reserve call-up at the moment, but he personally did not think one was appropriate at the moment, either. He had acclimated himself to the fact that it was going to be a long war, and bringing in Reserves would only degrade the quality of noncommisioned and junior officers, and if they were required for any length of time, would likely lead to an outcry from the American public to bring them home. The former would lead to numerous unnecessary casualties; while the latter could hamstring the entire war effort.

Realizing that for the moment, ground operations were only going to be conducted inside the borders of South Vietnam, Westmoreland told McNamara that he would like a troop increase of approximately 30 percent, and an eventual well-balanced force of about five hundred thousand men.

Following their conference, they went on a two-day tour of the entire country, during which McNamara was briefed by senior officers at a number of division base camps and corps headquarters. The briefings were mostly upbeat, and so was McNamara when he returned to Washington to meet the press corps. He told them that progress in Vietnam "has exceeded our expectations," and provided them with the statistics to prove it. Privately, however, he was very pessimistic. In a long memo to Johnson, he told him that while "we have by and large blunted" the enemy initiative, he saw "no reasonable way to bring the war to an end soon." Though it was obvious the enemy was suffering enormous casualties, he had shown that he can "more than replace" his losses. He added that while the Saigon government was certainly more viable, the "pacification effort had if anything gone backwards," the Communists' presence still "thrives in most of the country," and "full security exists nowhere."

Something had to be done to reverse the situation in Vietnam, he told the President, and he did not believe that any further escalation of the war was the way to do it. Rejecting outright the Joint

Chiefs' recent request for 700,000 troops in Vietnam, the secretary instead recommended that Johnson hold the troop level at 469,000. He also recommended that the air war be stabilized and that the United States consider tendering a "credible peace gesture" to the Communists, such as a total bombing halt and a plan to give the Vietcong a voice in the South Vietnamese government.

After reading the memo, Johnson handed it to an aide and re-marked, "You've never seen such a lot of shit." The JCS's reaction was not as graphic, but according to the Pentagon Papers, it was "rapid and violent." In a countermemo to Johnson, they rejected outright McNamara's notion that a bombing halt might induce the Communists to negotiate. All it would really do, they said, was con-vince them that the American leadership was weak and indecisive. Rather than cutting back on the war, they urged that Johnson instead escalate it drastically. The war had reached a critical stage, they concluded, and "decisions taken over the next 60 days can determine the outcome of the war and American security interests for years to come."

Johnson was again caught in the middle between McNamara and the Joint Chiefs. While he was becoming more and more disgusted with McNamara's views, he still was not prepared to follow the advice of the Chiefs and widen the war. "I'm not gonna spit in China's face," he told an aide. Unable to decide what step to take next, on October 23, 1966, Johnson boarded a plane for Manila. There he had another summit conference planned with Thieu and Ky. And there, too, he planned to meet with Westmoreland one more time before he decided what to do about the general's recent troop request.

It is difficult to imagine what Johnson expected to come out of his meeting with Westmoreland, or whether he expected anything to come out of it at all. Two months before, he had flown the general to his ranch in Texas for private talks, but instead of the lengthy discussion of the war, which Westmoreland had been expecting, they had done little but drive around the ranch in Johnson's white Con-tinental convertible engaged in one of the President's favorite pas-times, "chasing deer." After the visit, Westmoreland was left to wonder "just why Johnson had insisted on the visit in the first place."

Westmoreland might have wondered the same about their meet-ing in Manila, for nothing was discussed there that had not been discussed or analyzed in countless memos and cables a hundred times before. Just as he had told McNamara two weeks before, Westmore-land told Johnson that he needed more troops. And just as he had told Johnson numerous times before, Westmoreland told him that he was against any type of bombing halt, that such a halt would send a clear signal to Hanoi of the lack of United States resolve, and rather than encouraging them to talk peace would encourage them instead to stay the course, in the hope that the United States would eventually weaken. And just as he had told him at Honolulu the year before, he told the President yet again that "it was going to be a long war . . . and while there was a light at the end of the tunnel, we had to be geared for the long pull." It was the same old message. It was not the one Johnson wanted to hear, but it was the only one Westmoreland had to give him.

CHAPTER FOURTEEN

Attacking the Base Areas

Under a panel of glass in his desk in Saigon, Westmoreland kept a quotation from Napoleon Bonaparte. "Any commander-in-chief who undertakes to carry out a plan which he considers defective," part of the quote reads, "is at fault; he must put forth his reason, insist on the plan being changed, and finally tender his resignation rather than be the instrument of his army's downfall." In late 1966, Westmoreland might have been wise to place beside the first quote one of Caesar's favorites: "Fame is fleeting." Certainly few military men in history would have understood the full import of those words more than he.

Yet only a year before, those words would have been personally meaningless to him. By the end of 1965, he had been able to look back on his accomplishment during the year with enormous pride. During his short tenure as COMUSMACV, he had put two hundred thousand American soldiers and Marines ashore in less time than it had taken the United States in World War II to enter the war against Nazi Germany, and by doing so had saved South Vietnam from imminent collapse. Then, with South Vietnam safely off the ropes, he had aggressively taken the war to the enemy, helping to orchestrate a Marine operation that destroyed a VC regiment in the Batangan Peninsula, then sending the 1st Cavalry Division into the heart of Kontum Province to stop an enemy attempt to cut South Vietnam in half. The fight at the Ia Drang had followed, and partly for his role in that fight, *Time* magazine made him their Man of the Year for 1965. It was a singular honor, and in receiving it, he joined an august group of men and women whose names are permanently imprinted on the twentieth century.

The award brought a plethora of media attention, and there was hardly a major American newspaper that did not send a correspondent to Vietnam to do a major story on the new MACV commander. In story after story, he was compared favorably with men like Eisenhower and Bradley. Like them, he was a decent, God-fearing man, and like them he had answered his country's call and gone off to lead an American army into battle against the forces of despotism. And just as Eisenhower and Bradley had won their war, few doubted that he would win his. And he would win—must win!—because he had right on his side. His was not just a war, but a crusade. In the enthusiasm of the moment, few in the country viewed it any differently.

Not everyone did, however. Not everyone, even at first, thought the war was just and that the United States had a moral obligation to win it. Even as the first Marines were landing at Da Nang, discontent over the war was brewing on a number of college campuses. Following that landing, a few hundred students at the University of Michigan organized a "teach-in" to discuss the war. A year later, various radical student groups organized a series of demonstrations against the war in Detroit, Chicago, Oakland, and New York, during which thousands of students marched and demanded an immediate end to the war. Those initial demonstrations became the model and catalyst for thousands that followed.

During the first two years of the war, the antiwar movement was almost exclusively student run, but by mid-1966 they were joined by a wide array of academics, politicians, journalists, and clergy. These new recruits gave it a respectability it had lacked and moved it closer to the mainstream of American life. They also emboldened the movement and gave its participants an impetus to become more and more outspoken, more and more confrontational. Soon antiwar people were openly disrupting the work of draft boards and Army recruiters, and staging "lie-ins" in front of troop trains or at the gates of munitions plants. The President was a particular target for the movement, and starting in late 1966, protesters marched daily around the White House, chanting over and over again, "Hey, hey, LBJ, how many kids have you killed today?"

Soon Westmoreland was also a target. Other than the President, to most in the antiwar movement, he quickly came to symbolize the war more than any other major player. Beginning in early 1966, he was first burned in effigy on a number of college campuses, and in radical student newspapers and antiwar literature, he was frequently referred to as a war criminal, warmonger, and murderer. Unlike the President, however, antiwar people could not attack him directly. They could attack his family, though—and did, numerous times.

One of the first to feel the fury of the antiwar movement was Kitsy. While attending a dinner party in Honolulu in mid-1966, she suddenly found herself on the receiving end of a vicious antiwar diatribe delivered by the wife of a state senator. After attacking the war, the military, and Westmoreland, the woman overturned her chair and bolted from the room in protest. Out of fear that if his family stayed in Hawaii, they were sure to be exposed to further "vitriolic attacks," Westmoreland decided to move them to quarters in the Philippines in August 1966. There they were less likely to be attacked, and there also, Kitsy, who had been working as a Red Cross nurse at military hospitals, could continue her work. Westmoreland soon discovered that he could not protect his family indefinitely, however. In September, nineteen-year-old Stevie left the Philippines to enroll at Bradford Junior College in Boston. There while attending an art class, she found herself being lectured on the immorality of the war by her art instructor.

For Westmoreland, it was a shock to find that he and his family were held in such derision by a growing number of Americans. As Davidson points out, Westmoreland was an honestly old-fashioned patriot, who believed totally in the idea that he was doing the right thing in Vietnam. Like many Americans, he had been deeply touched by President Kennedy's inaugural address, and as a military man he had taken literally Kennedy's pledge "to bear any burden, meet any hardship, support any friend and oppose any foe to insure the survival and success of liberty." He had taken those words so seriously, in fact, that he frequently quoted them in interviews and speeches. Some historians now argue that Kennedy's words were not meant to be taken literally, and that he really was not the virulent anti-Communist he portrayed himself in public to be. In Westmoreland's mind, however, there was never the slightest doubt about the depth of Kennedy's anticommunism, or the meaning of his inaugural speech. He felt he knew exactly what Kennedy stood for, knew that he was just as concerned about ensuring "the success of liberty" in Vietnam as in Germany or Austria. He was stunned, therefore, to discover that a growing minority of Americans not only did not see communism in Vietnam as an evil but, to the contrary, saw him and his army as the evil.

A number of Westmoreland's close friends and associates say that in spite of the general always bragging about being thick-skinned and oblivious to criticism, in reality he was deeply offended by all the hostility directed at him. "He just didn't understand it," says a former MACV staff officer. "The antiwar movement was alien to him, and so were the individual people in it. He did not understand it, and he did not understand them. I'm sure when he went to Vietnam, he had imagined himself as another Eisenhower. I'm sure he had it in his mind that he was going to take over there just the way Eisenhower took over in England. Then he would get the troops and supplies he needed, win the war and come back to a ticker-tape parade. Only it did not work out that way. He did not get the troops he wanted, or permission to invade Laos and North Vietnam. Instead, he found himself mired knee-deep in a nasty little war of attrition, and one of the main targets of the antiwar movement. He wanted to be a hero and instead he found himself being vilified. It was an embittering experience for Westy, but he never let on as to how much it hurt him. To the end, he kept a stiff upper lip."

Embittered or not, Westmoreland still had a war to fight and, as he had in 1965 and 1966, he knew he was going to have to fight that war within the restrictions set up by McNamara and Johnson. He still refused to willingly accept those restrictions, however. In early 1967, he sent a number of cables to Washington, all with a variation of the same message: The enemy had been badly hurt in 1966, but was still far from defeated and was continuing to send thousands of infiltrators south. And most of those infiltrators, as he pointed out in a cable to Wheeler in early February, were coming down through the Laotian Panhandle. The infiltration was so heavy there at the moment, Westmoreland told the Army Chief, that the territory "might as well be considered part of North Vietnam." Knowing this fact, he asked pointedly, why was the United States deliberately tying its hands with "self-imposed restrictions"? Why did we not instead apply the "combat power" at our disposal to the area, rather than allowing the enemy to move through there at their will?

Westmoreland, of course, was preaching to the choir. He did not have to convince Wheeler, for Wheeler had long been trying to prod McNamara and Johnson into sending three divisions into Laos to close off the Ho Chi Minh Trail. He had to convince McNamara and Johnson, and again he could not. Wheeler passed on Westmoreland's plea, and nothing more was said about it. Not only was McNamara not willing to expand the war, he was still trying to convince Johnson to order another bombing halt. Johnson himself still shuddered at the idea of invading Laos, an invasion he continued to believe would provoke the Chinese into entering the war.

Again denied the right to expand the war, Westmoreland went back to his war of attrition. It was a strategy that he knew could not win the war, but it was the only one available to him. To get the most out of that strategy, in late 1966 he sat down with the Chief of the South Vietnamese Joint General Staff, General Cao Van Vien, and drew up a Combined Campaign Plan for 1967. Much of the strategy they decided on was a carryover from 1966. As before, the United States, aided by crack ARVN Ranger and airborne units, was to fight the big-unit war against the North Vietnamese and Vietcong main-force units, while regular ARVN units would work on pacification programs, including the task of rooting out VC irregulars and political cadre from the villages. Under extreme pressure from Washington, Westmoreland agreed to also earmark some American units for pacification duties.

In the north, Westmoreland and Vien agreed to keep in place the U.S. Marine and ARVN units manning the strongpoints along the demilitarized zone, and if necessary to reinforce them. They agreed, however, to completely change the targets of their search-and-destroy operation. In 1966, they had used such operations to clear the enemy from certain high-priority areas along the coast, a job that was now nearly complete. Now they intended to launch a series of massive, wide-ranging assaults against a series of major enemy base areas, like War Zones C and D and the Iron Triangle. Although DePuy and his 1st Infantry Division had attacked both War Zone C and D in 1966, those attacks had been designed to only temporarily disrupt enemy activity there. The attacks they were designing now were to be not only massive but sustained, so as to completely destroy the enemy's logistic capabilities inside South Vietnam.

Westmoreland reasoned that unless the Communists were willing to abandon these base areas, they would have to fight for them. When they did, he intended to bring the full weight of American firepower to bear on them, thereby destroying both the base areas and the units defending them at the same time. Westmoreland picked as his first major target of 1967 the Iron Triangle, a featureless patch of double- and triple-canopy jungle, paddy land, and elephant grass that lay between War Zones C and D only thirty miles northwest of Saigon. The Communists had been using it as a bastion since their war with the French, and in the years since they had surrounded it with a formidable defense system of trenches, bunkers, tunnels, and thousands of mines and booby traps.

Westmoreland got the operation to smash the Iron Triangle under way on January 8. Called Cedar Falls, it began with an assault by ten infantry and armor battalions. Lieutenant Colonel Alexander Haig's 1st Battalion, 26th Infantry, led the way. In sixty helicopters, they launched a sudden air assault right into the center of the village of Ben Suc. After killing a number of VC sentries guarding the village, Haig and his men quickly evacuated all the villagers with their belongings, then began systematically destroying the village. While giant bulldozers leveled the village and the surrounding jungle, demolition teams seeded a massive VC tunnel system under the village with satchel charge, then pumped it full of acetylene gas and ignited it, collapsing the tunnels. Finally, engineers dug a massive hole in the center of the village, filled it with ten thousand pounds of explosives and blew it, leveling Ben Suc.

Almost simultaneously, with Haig's assault on Ben Suc, mechanized and armor battalions of the 25th Infantry Division moved into place west of the Iron Triangle and set up blocking positions, cutting off any escape in that direction. Then two miles to the north, DePuy's 1st Infantry Division, with two attached battalions from the 173rd Airborne Brigade, executed an air assault into the area between Saigon and the Cambodian border and set up another blocking position. Next, eleven artillery bases were set up around the enemy base in order to lend instant fire support. Finally, the 11th Armored Cavalry Regiment, with a mix of tanks and armored personnel carriers, started a juggernaut westward from Ben Cat. By nightfall, most of the Iron Triangle was either sealed off or in American hands.

On the following morning, all of the United States units converged on the area and began what turned into a massive treasure hunt. In the intricate system of tunnels, they found underground living facilities, hospitals, dining halls, lecture halls, printing presses, hundreds of thousands of documents, enough rice to feed a VC division for a year, and thousands of rifles.

Before the operation, Westmoreland's admonition to the ground commanders had been to think big, and they did. In a show of muscle, American soldiers dynamited miles of tunnels and using Rome plows, giant bulldozers fixed with special blades, bulldozed miles of jungle and brush into huge piles, then set the piles on fire, thereby denying the enemy much of the jungle cover he so depended on to move around safely. Although most of the large enemy units in the area managed in spite of the cordon to exfiltrate the area during the initial assault, enough stayed so that the United States units mopping up the area found themselves in a running battle with small groups of VC for the next few weeks. During those battles, seven hundred VC were killed and another seven hundred taken prisoner.

Right on the heels of Cedar Falls, Westmoreland launched its twin, Operation Junction City. It was aimed at War Zone C, where his intelligence shop told him the VC 9th Division was bivouacked guarding a treasure trove of arms and ammunition, and according to some sources, COSVN, the headquarters for North Vietnamese command of Vietcong forces in the South.

Just as he had in Cedar Falls, Westmoreland put blocking forces on three sides of War Zone C at the start of the operation, then launched an armor and track assault against it from the east. The enemy units in the area, however, once again chose not to contest the initial assault, and for the next few days American soldiers went on another massive treasure hunt.

They were preparing to turn the Rome plows loose on the area when the enemy finally struck back. On the evening of February 28 near Prek Klok, a battalion of the 272nd VC Regiment charged the perimeter of the mechanized 2nd Battalion, 2nd Infantry, which had just circled its armored personnel carriers into a "wagon train." The VC had thought the sudden charge would catch the Americans off guard. They were wrong. The United States troops had been expecting them, and the VC charged across ground ripped by machine-gun and artillery fire. Within minutes, 197 VC lay dead around the United States perimeter, and hundreds more enemy dead and wounded were carried off. The Americans suffered only three deaths.

Undaunted by the carnage at Prek Klok, on March 26 the 271st VC Regiment and the 1st Battalion of the 70th VC Guard Division launched a similar ground attack against Haig's battalion, which was dug in at a place called LZ George. There, one VC company managed to punch a hole in Haig's lines one hundred yards wide and sixty deep. Haig responded by personally moving to the area, where he led a counterattack and closed the hole. Then he hunkered down in a shell crater and directed a bevy of rocket-firing helicopters at the enemy assault troops. When the gunships expended their ordnance and went off station, Haig brought in a string of Phantom jets carrying napalm and cluster bombs and directed them against the attacking enemy. It was soon another lopsided victory. A few hours later, the VC broke contact and faded into the jungle.

In the rubble of blasted trees and shell craters, Haig's men counted 491 enemy dead, a figure that made the fight one of the most violent single actions of the war. Haig's own losses were 7 killed and 30 wounded.

Junction City continued until May 14, but by early April most of the hard fighting was over, and Westmoreland flew in to pin Bronze and Silver Stars on a number of deserving soldiers, including Haig, who won a Silver Star for his actions at LZ George. After the medal ceremony, Westmoreland had time to compute the figures for the operation. He was impressed by the totals, and announced to the press that Junction City "was a serious defeat for the enemy." Indeed it was. Over three thousand Vietcong perished in the first two months of the operation, and American troops captured over forty-five hundred tons of rice, forty tons of salt and dried fish, seventy-five hundred VC uniforms, more than one hundred crew-served weapons, fifty thousand grenades, and hundreds of thousands of rounds of small-arms ammo. In addition, COSVN and all three regiments of the VC 9th Division fled War Zone C for what would become a permanent sanctuary in Cambodia.

As Shelby Stanton points out, Junction City became a hallmark of the Vietnam War, showing as it did conclusively the shock power of a multidivision operation executed properly. Unfortunately for Westmoreland, because of demands on his forces to perform pacification duties, he would only rarely be able to mobilize the forces to launch operations similar in size and scope. Within six months, he would also come to realize that while he had cleared both base areas of main-force units, those units were now safely hunkered down in Cambodian sanctuaries, a fact that created a whole new set of problems for him and for Washington. Dealing with these sanctuaries would preoccupy both him and United States policymakers during the rest of the war.

For the moment, however, he had only to concentrate on enemy forces and their base camps inside South Vietnam. To deal with them, he had a number of operations earmarked for every corps area. Most were divisional-size operations and their names—Attleboro, Irving,

Paul Revere, Thayer, Fairfax, Sam Houston, Palm Beach, Prairie, Pershing—are long forgotten. But the fighting that took place during most of them was as fierce as the worst fighting of World War II. During them, United States and Allied units penetrated dozens of previously untouched enemy base areas and redoubts, where they often found themselves in vicious slugging matches with a brave, tenacious enemy, who was often willing to die rather than retreat or surrender. And die he did, by the hundreds and thousands in killing fields all across South Vietnam. During Operation Attleboro, 1st Infantry Division and 173rd Airborne Brigade troops counted over eleven hundred enemy dead after a vicious week-long fight with three VC regiments. During Operations Thayer and Pershing, 1st Cavalry Division troopers counted two thousand more after a running fight with the NVA 610th Division in Binh Dinh Province. And during Operation Francis Marion, the 4th Infantry Division killed over twelve hundred NVA regulars after eight battles and numerous small skirmishes with the NVA 1st Division. At any one time, Westmoreland had ten to fifteen operations under way and an equal number on the drawing board ready to go. The Communists had no shortage of hostile bastions in South Vietnam, and his intention was to smash and overrun as many of them as he could in the shortest amount of time.

The high command in Hanoi did not intend to stand by passively while Westmoreland's big search-and-destroy operations ran roughshod over base areas that had been generations in the making. And so even as some Communist forces were reeling before Westmoreland's juggernaut in the Iron Triangle, War Zone C and a half-dozen other areas were going on the attack.

In Kien Hoa Province, two VC battalions launched a juggernaut of their own in mid-January, overrunning five of nine government outposts they attacked and causing hundreds of ARVN and civilian casualties. In one particularly bloody attack, VC infantry used civilians as shields as they attacked a company of ARVN Rangers. Farther south in Binh Tuy Province, a third VC battalion, led by sappers, overran part of the province airfield; and in the Mekong Delta, a fourth battalion came perilously close to overrunning a U.S. 9th Infantry Division firebase. The greatest number of enemy attacks, however, came in northern I Corps. There, in ten different spots, NVA and VC main-force units struck with a vengeance. In late January, a U.S. Marine company suffered heavy casualties after being ambushed only a few miles west of Da Nang. A few days later, a second Marine company was ambushed at Ton Tu and then a third at Ha Mon. Both suffered heavy casualties.

As he had been doing every month since taking over as COMUSMACV, Westmoreland cabled Wheeler MACV's statistics on Large-Size Enemy-Initiated Actions for the month of January. His figures showed that there had been twenty-five such attacks for that month, a figure that was two and a half times as high as the number of large enemy attacks during January 1966. Wheeler was anguished by the figure. Having recently told the President that the "adverse military tide has been reversed," he was now confronted with a statistic that not only made a liar out of him, but one that pointed to the unnerving fact that the Vietnam War was a stalemate. In a March 9 return cable, Wheeler warned Westmoreland that "if these figures reached the public domain they would literally blow the lid off Washington."

Two days later in a lengthy cable, Wheeler expanded on the anguish Westmoreland's statistics had caused him:

> I can only interpret the new figures to mean that despite the force buildup, despite our many successful spoiling attacks and base area searches, and despite the heavy interdiction campaign in North Vietnam and Laos, VC/NVA combat and offensive activity throughout 1966 and now in 1967 has been increasing steadily, with the January 1967 level some two and one-half times above the average of the first three months of 1966.

Recognizing the severe political implications of a stalemate, Wheeler found himself on the horns of a real dilemma. "I cannot go to the president and tell him that, contrary to my reports and those of the other chiefs as to the progress of the war in which we have laid great stress upon the thesis that you have seized the initiative from the enemy, the situation is such that we are not sure who has the initiative in South Vietnam." After alerting Westmoreland yet again to the political trouble this new figure could cause in Washington, Wheeler then bluntly warned him that if he or someone on his staff was inflating these enemy-attack statistics in order to get more United States troops, he or they had better stop. Such a move, even if well intentioned, would inevitably prove to be "trouble for us all."

What was to be done about the discrepancy between the 1966 and 1967 figures? Wheeler did not know for sure, but some sort of urgent action was needed, he told Westmoreland. For now, he was sending a "team of operations and intelligence officers with PACOM representation to Saigon to sit down with you and your people and review criteria, inputs, procedures, etc."

Wheeler's cable put Westmoreland in a very difficult and uncomfortable position. A year before, he and his staff had pleaded with Wheeler to exempt MACV from involvement in any issues with political implications. Wheeler, however, had refused, and now Westmoreland could see why. Was Wheeler asking him now to juggle those statistics so that progress could be shown in the war or merely to manipulate them slightly to put the accent on the positive achievement of the United States in Vietnam? There is no ready answer to the question, for the wording of Wheeler's cable is deliberately obscure and open to a wide variety of interpretations.

Westmoreland's response was not, however. He told Wheeler that while he certainly welcomed the reviewing team, the statistics of enemy attacks were not his alone, but were the result of a recent intelligence conference in Honolulu. And "far from reflecting any inclination on the part of the Military Assistance Command to make the war seem bigger than it was, the procedures used gave results entirely consistent with the nature of the conflict."

The reviewing team arrived nonetheless. But after two days of looking at the evidence, they concluded that Westmoreland's reporting procedures were indeed accurate. In spite of their conclusion, Westmoreland did cave in slightly to Wheeler's pressure. On March 22, he cabled Admiral Sharp to let him know that he and his staff had resolved all "disputed issues by developing yet another set of definitions and formulas for assessing the enemy's combat initiatives." It was a minor concession on his part, but the die had been cast. From now on, he would not only have to fight the war but increasingly take part in helping Wheeler, McNamara, and Johnson sell it to the American people.

It was a duty Westmoreland found onerous, however. Shortly after his exchange of cables with Wheeler, he wrote in his diary:

There is an amazing lack of boldness in our approach to the future. We are so sensitive about world opinion that this stifles initiative and constantly keeps us on the defensive in our effort to portray ourselves as a benevolent power that only acts in response to an initiative by the enemy. Therefore we become victims of our own propaganda and subject to political attrition.

If Westmoreland was hoping for a sudden show of "boldness" on President Johnson's part, it was a false hope. When the general journeyed to Guam on March 20 for another high-level meeting with the President, he found the same emotionally exhausted, uncertain Johnson he had last seen in Honolulu the year before.

"Are they bringing in as many as they're losing?" Johnson asked.

"Up until now, no, sir. Their gains have exceeded their losses. However, if the present trend continues I think we might arrive at the crossover point perhaps this month, or next month. And by the crossover point, I mean where their losses are greater than their gains."

There is no record of Johnson's response to this bit of good news, but if he felt any elation over it, Westmoreland quickly deflated it. After noting a few other small indices of progress, Westmoreland reminded the President yet again that the enemy was infiltrating troops from the North at the rate of seven thousand per month and that unless military pressure caused the Vietcong to crumble and Hanoi to stop its support of the southern insurgency, the war could go on indefinitely. There is likewise no record of Johnson's response to this news. Only Walt Rostow, Johnson's national security adviser, responded. After the meeting, he penned a memo for Johnson in which he accused Westmoreland of exaggerating the enemy infiltration rate so as "to be conservative and non-promissory." Rostow felt the enemy infiltration rate was probably more like three thousand to four thousand a month.

It is not known what figure Johnson chose to believe, but the issue was soon overshadowed by the rush of events. Back in Vietnam, Westmoreland cabled the President with yet another large troop request. Expressing concern about the large enemy buildup in their sanctuaries in Laos, Cambodia, and parts of South Vietnam and the immediate threat of NVA units just north of the demilitarized zone, he told Johnson pointedly that he needed reinforcements and needed them as soon as possible.

As he always did when making a troop request, he broke it down into a minimum and a maximum request. As a minimum, he told Johnson, he needed roughly 100,000 new troops. That number would help him contain the enemy threat and maintain the "tactical initiative." For an "optimum force," he wanted 210,250 troops—a figure that would ultimately boost American forces in Vietnam to 676,616 men. The implication in the troop request was obvious: The more men he got, the quicker he could get the job done.

When the JCS received a copy of the troop request, they quickly endorsed it and made an addendum. It called for McNamara to mobilize the Reserves, extend the war into VC/NVA sanctuaries in Laos and Cambodia and possibly even into North Vietnam, and mine all of North Vietnam's ports. Without the Reserve call-up, the Chiefs told McNamara, they could only provide one and one-third of the four and two-thirds divisions that Westmoreland wanted.

The Joint Chiefs' open call for mobilization was, as the Pentagon Papers rightly claim, an open challenge to Johnson, who had long opposed the drastic measures being proposed. Johnson, however, quickly shelved the challenge. He was not interested in the shooting war at the moment, but in the political one. While Westmoreland's big search-and-destroy operations were producing higher and higher enemy body counts, they came only at the expenditure of American dead—over fifteen thousand in the last two years—and that number was growing rapidly. While the enemy casualty figure was ten to fifteen times as great, few Americans found any consolation in that fact. To the contrary, Wheeler's worst fear was coming true: The impression was slowly growing in the United States that Vietnam was a stalemate. And that impression was not held merely by civilians. In early 1967, General Fred Weyand, the head of II Field Force, bluntly remarked to a visiting Washington official: "Before I came out here a year ago, I thought we were at zero. I was wrong. We were at minus fifty. Now we're at zero."

Stalemates, as President Johnson well knew, produced war weariness, and war weariness, in turn, quickly turned into political discontent. To counter the notion that Vietnam was a stalemate, Johnson, with the help of Rostow, organized an elaborate public relations program and targeted it against various segments of United States society.

To counter congressional criticism, one of Walt Rostow's assistants monitored congressmen who gave speeches critical of the war, then bombarded them with elaborate fact-filled rebuttals, what Rostow called "correct information." Rostow himself was responsible for getting the "truth" out to the American people, which he did by feeding favorable reports to the media. Even President Johnson did his part for the PR campaign, touring military bases around the country and giving patriotic speeches.

In early 1966, realizing, as Stanley Karnow has observed, that "battle-scarred soldiers" have an "irresistible" power over the public, Johnson twice tried to get Westmoreland to give speeches in the United States to bolster prowar sentiment. In both instances, Westmoreland graciously declined the President's invitation. He gave as his reason the fact that his duties in Vietnam were simply too demanding and too vital for him to travel extensively in the United

States. But his real reason for refusal was his fear of becoming irrevocably embroiled in domestic politics.

A year later, however, that excuse was no longer acceptable to the White House. And when Johnson asked Westmoreland in February 1967 to give a speech to the Associated Press Managing Editors annual meeting in New York, he phrased his summons in such a way that it appeared more an order than a request. This time, Westmoreland had no choice but to accept. Still, as Westmoreland himself says, in spite of the fact that he would have preferred not to give the speech, since he had to, he planned on using the opportunity to keep "the American people informed" about the nature of the war, "particularly in view" of what he termed "manifold misinformation disseminated by anti-war activists."

CHAPTER FIFTEEN

Public Relations Duty

Westmoreland left Saigon on April 22. After a short stopover in the Philippines to pick up Kitsy, he flew on to West Point. There he spent part of a day visiting and reminiscing with old friends and part of the evening speaking informally to a group of cadets. During the day, Stevie drove up from Boston, and in the morning the three of them drove to New York City. For fear of worrying her father unnecessarily, Stevie did not tell him that only a few days before while walking across the Harvard campus, she had stumbled across a group of students burning him in effigy. She need not have tried to shield him from such information, however. When he arrived at the Waldorf-Astoria, where he was to deliver his speech, he was greeted by one hundred antiwar demonstrators. Marching back and forth before the front entrance to the hotel, they were chanting over and over again, "Westmoreland, war criminal!" and "Hell no, we won't go!" After about thirty minutes of marching, two members of a group called Youth Against War and Fascism soaked an effigy of Westmoreland in kerosene and set it on fire. At that the police charged in and a wild melee erupted. With the noise of the melee barely audible in the ballroom, Westmoreland began speaking.

The first part of his address was a cautious, thoughtful review of the war. He offered no simple solutions or panaceas for what he termed a complicated, difficult war. "I foresee in the months ahead, some of the bitterest fighting of the war," he warned, ". . . and I see no end of the war in sight. It's going to be a question of putting maximum pressure on the enemy anywhere and everywhere that we can. We will have to grind him down. In effect, we are fighting a war of attrition."

It was a frank admission on Westmoreland's part, but his words were soon to be obscured by the reaction to the second part of his speech. As if referring directly to the demonstrators outside, he told the assembled editors that "his troops are dismayed—and so am I— by recent unpatriotic acts here at home." Those acts, he told them, were encouraging the enemy to attempt to "win politically that which he cannot accomplish militarily." Then pointing out that North Vietnam was waging war both on the battlefield and on the propaganda front simultaneously, he said that the enemy unfortunately "does not understand that American democracy is founded on debate, for he sees every protest as evidence of crumbling morale and diminishing resolve. Thus, discouraged by repeated military defeats, but encouraged by what he believes to be popular opposition to our effort in Vietnam, he is determined to continue his aggression from the North. This inevitably will cost us lives."

This last statement caused an immediate uproar in the Congress and in the press. Democratic Senator William J. Fulbright of Arkansas, the chairman of the Senate Foreign Relations Committee, charged from the floor of the Senate that Westmoreland's speech was designed to produce a feeling of "our country right or wrong." Another democratic senator, George C. McGovern of South Dakota, agreed, then charged additionally that the Johnson administration had brought the general home to stifle criticism of the war while at the same time blaming critics for the failure of the President's Vietnam policy.

Within hours, a fresh group of protesters—these Republicans— joined the Democrats. Oregon Senator Mark Hatfield accused the administration of using "political blackmail," and likened it to the tactics of the late Senator Joe McCarthy. George Aiken of Vermont said Westmoreland's speech was "designed to suppress disapproving comments about the war." Senator Thurston R. Morton of Kentucky unleashed the sharpest rebuke, shouting from the floor of the Senate,

"Those who decry unpatriotic acts at home during a period of bloody conflict, without differentiating between flag-burners, draft-card burners, peaceful demonstrators and U.S. Senators exercising their responsible right of dissent, only add fuel to the forces of irresponsible opposition that continue to plague present administration policy."

Editorial writers joined the chorus next. One in the *Chicago Daily News* penned a heading that screamed, DISSENT IS NOT TREASON. A commentator in the *New York Post* called the speech "a forum of domestic psychological warfare." Another in the *San Francisco Chronicle* called it "a crude attempt to stifle free speech."

But Westmoreland had as many defenders as detractors. Also speaking from the floor of the Senate, Senator Mike Mansfield of Montana said that although he vehemently opposed administration policy in Vietnam, General Westmoreland had just as much right to express his views as anyone else. *The Washington Post*'s Andrew Glass added a refrain to that theme, observing that while a free government certainly had no right to stifle dissent, it was likewise under "no obligation to refrain from reply and rebuttal." Speaking directly to Westmoreland's charges, the *Denver Post* declared that the general's comments about the effects antiwar activity had on the morale of troops in the field "ought to stimulate a reappraisal by many of those who protest against the U.S. presence in Vietnam."

Westmoreland was amazed that his simple statement had managed to cause such an uproar. During a subsequent press conference, he tried to backtrack a bit, saying he had no objection to legitimate dissent. But the deed was done. The newspapers had a story they could get plenty of mileage out of, and the antiwar movement an even greater excuse to hate him.

Following his AP speech, he and Kitsy flew to Columbia, South Carolina, for a visit with his mother and to make good on a promise he had made to Governor Robert McNair to address the South Carolina General Assembly. South Carolina was a long way from New York City, both in air miles and political persuasion. When he landed at Columbia's airport, he was greeted by his mother, Mimi, his sister Margaret, her husband, Hayward Clarkson, and five hundred screaming, flag-waving, placard-carrying supporters. WIN THE WAR, one placard read. STOP COMMUNISM, read another.

It was the first time Westmoreland had seen his eighty-one-year-old mother since Rip's funeral two and one-half years before, and as he stepped off the plane he shouted, "Mimi, we're here at last!"

"You look so good," she said as he kissed her on each cheek. "It's good to have you home again."

"It's good to be home," he said, then turned and spoke to the crowd. "This is quite a contrast to New York where they attempted to burn me in effigy. I'm overwhelmed by this very warm and candid reception, I might say I've been taken by surprise. I regard this turnout, however, as support for U.S. troops in Vietnam. I speak for them when I thank you."

Westmoreland spoke to the General Assembly the next morning. In the all-white audience were a number of VIPs, including United States Senator Strom Thurmond and former secretary of state and South Carolina governor, Jimmy Byrnes—the same Jimmy Byrnes who had sponsored his appointment to West Point thirty-five years before. During the twenty-five-minute speech, Westmoreland told the assembly that "the service of the Negro servicemen in Vietnam has been particularly inspirational to me." They are "a credit to their country, loyal and efficient, and like the white soldiers over there, they have carried out their duties with a sense of responsibility." Westmoreland had worried how many in the chamber would respond to the statement, but if any were upset they kept their feeling to themselves. Even the most diehard segregationist in the chamber applauded him loudly, and many also pushed forward to shake his hand afterward.

This speech, like his last, brought an immediate response from Martin Luther King and the radical "black power" leader, Stokely Carmichael. In a sermon from the pulpit of his Ebenezer Baptist Church, King accused Westmoreland of "trying to develop a sentiment and a consensus for the further escalation of the war" and urged draft-age Negroes to refuse to fight in Vietnam for the United States, which he termed "the greatest purveyor of violence in the world today." Also speaking in Atlanta, Carmichael told a raucous rally in a park that it "was foolish for Negroes to fight 8,000 miles from home when they could not live in the neighborhood of their choice in the United States."

Some analysts speculated that Westmoreland had directed his speech at moderate civil-rights leaders like Carl Rowan, Whitney Young, Roy Wilkins, and Jackie Robinson, men who had recently openly disagreed with King's antiwar stand. Westmoreland claims this was not his intention. Regardless, none of these moderate black leaders responded to the speech, or to the criticism of King and Carmichael. The world-famous evangelist, the Reverend Billy Graham, did, however. He scolded King for what he regarded as "an affront to the thousands of loyal Negro troops who are in Vietnam." A number of editorial writers across the country also came to Westmoreland's defense and praised him for praising the Negro soldier.

In spite of the antiwar rhetoric of King and Carmichael, Vietnam was the first American war in which blacks were given an equal chance to perform in the military. In Vietnam, black men were piloting helicopters; flying jet fighters; commanding infantry companies, battalions, and brigades; and doing a hundred other jobs that would have been denied to them only a few years earlier. While most blacks had the utmost respect for Martin Luther King, many resented his statements about the Vietnam War. Many saw the military as the only equal opportunity employer in the United States and a chance for countles blacks to integrate into the mainstream of American life. Many felt it not only foolish for blacks to turn their backs on this single road of opportunity, but worried that if they did, if they followed King's advice and refused to serve in the military, they would be seen as disloyal by white America. If that happened, they feared many moderate whites would withdraw their support from the civil rights movement.

Following this second round of controversy, on April 26 Westmoreland and Kitsy boarded a plane for Washington, where he was scheduled for another high-level talk with the President. While in the air, he got a message from Wheeler telling him that Johnson had decided he also wanted him to address a joint session of Congress before departing. The President again did not ask him if he wanted to make the speech, but presented him with a *fait accompli*. When Westmoreland landed in Washington, the news of his coming speech to Congress had already been released to the press.

Westmoreland and Kitsy spent the evening as guests of the President and Mrs. Johnson in the White House. In the morning, he joined the President in the Cabinet Room for their scheduled meeting. Also in attendance were Secretaries McNamara and Rusk; Wheeler; and Rostow. Johnson had yet to act on Westmoreland's recent troop request, and he wanted to hash out the facts surrounding the request one more time before he did decide.

As the historian Larry Berman notes, Westmoreland "painted a much grimmer picture than he had the previous month" at Guam. He told Johnson that without the reinforcements he had requested "we will not be in danger of being defeated, but it will be nip and tuck to oppose the reinforcements the enemy is capable of providing. In the final analysis, we are fighting a war of attrition in Southeast Asia. . . . With the troops now in country we are not going to lose, but progress will be slowed down. This is not an encouraging outlook, but it is a realistic one."

Johnson took a moment to let Westmoreland's realistic assessment sink in, then agonized out loud. "Where does it all end? When we add divisions, can't the enemy add divisions? If so where does it all end?"

Westmoreland responded by saying that the enemy could indeed continue to reinforce the battlefield further. He had eight divisions in Vietnam at present, but had the logistical capabilities to support twelve. As far as the American battlefield position was concerned, Westmoreland again had only grim facts to offer, telling Johnson that with the 470,000 troops now either in Vietnam or earmarked for deployment there, we can do little "more than hold our own."

"How can troop increases change the overall situation?" the President asked.

"With a force level of 565,000 men, the war could well go on for three years. With the second increment of two and one-half divisions, leading to a total of 665,000 men, it could go on for two years."

At that point, McNamara entered the discussion. "Can you guarantee those predictions?" he asked. To which Westmoreland categorically answered, "No." There were simply too "many imponderables" to take into consideration.

Wheeler had his say next, announcing to the President that the Joint Chiefs thought one solution to the impasse was "an invasion of North Vietnam," coupled with a move, using mines to completely close all of North Vietnam's ports. That, Wheeler said, was one sure way of shortening the war.

Rostow agreed, telling Johnson that if additional forces were committed they should be committed in such a way as to have a spectacular effect on the battlefield. As one way to achieve such an effect, he proposed that Johnson consider an amphibious landing north of the demilitarized zone. Such a move, he said, could enable the United States to trap and destroy the large enemy units concentrated there and produce significant military results—if the President thought the political risks were worth taking, that is.

When Rostow finished, the President turned to Westmoreland. What did he think of an amphibious hook? Westmoreland agreed with Rostow that such an operation could produce significant results, but unfortunately, an adequate number of troops were not now available, and until they were, it was not feasible.

Johnson now turned to Wheeler. "What if we do not add the two and one-third divisions? What will happen?"

"Then the momentum will die," Wheeler said. "In some areas the enemy will recapture the initiative. We won't lose the war, but it will be a longer one."

According to the notes of the meeting, Johnson did not respond this time. Wheeler's projected scenario had been as grim as West-moreland's, and he decided he needed even more time to think before finalizing a decision on Westmoreland's troop request. Westmore-land, as he notes in his diary, left the meeting somewhat convinced that he and Wheeler might have finally gotten through to the Pres-ident, persuaded him, if only barely, to approve the maximum troop request, mobilize the Reserves, and possibly even give the green light to an invasion of North Vietnam. He worried, however, that McNamara would influence Johnson to hold the line on any large troop increase and caution him away from expanding the war—which is exactly what did happen.

Westmoreland delivered his speech to Congress the next day, April 28, 1967, at 12:30 P.M. As he notes in his memoirs, he "con-sciously avoided using the word 'victory' for the national goal was not to win a military victory over Vietnam." He also consciously avoided making reference again to his belief that protest against the war in the United States encouraged Hanoi and the Vietcong to continue to fight. Instead, he praised the effort of United States allies in Vietnam, with a special emphasis on the South Vietnamese armed forces. He reserved his greatest praise, however, for the American troops in Vietnam, whom he termed "the finest ever fielded in our nation's history," and that he said included "Americans of all races, creeds, and colors." "These men," he said, "understand the conflict and their complex roles as fighters and builders. They believe in what they are doing."

It was an emotionally charged speech, and Westmoreland got a similar response. Sixteen times during the speech, congressmen stopped him to cheer and applaud, and that cheering and applause went on even after he had departed the chamber. Although there was some grumbling by a few congressmen after the speech, most stood unanimous in their praise of the general. As Johnson had in-tended, a four-star general with legitimate credentials as a war hero, speaking before Congress on a purely patriotic theme, was virtually unassailable.

As was expected, the "hawks" in Congress were lavish in their praise of the general. Appearing on a CBS news special, Democratic Senator John Stennis of Mississippi said that Westmoreland "had done a truly magnificent job of telling the American people the truth about the Vietnam War." Appearing alongside him, Republican Senator John Tower of Texas said that the general "had performed a splendid service" for the American people by speaking to Congress.

Even the "doves" in the House and Senate had complimentary things to say about Westmoreland's speech. Although reiterating yet again his grave disagreement with the President over his Vietnam policy, Senator Fulbright nonetheless praised Westmoreland as a "great general." Senator Hatfield also spoke ill of Johnson's Vietnam policy, but said in spite of that policy, Westmoreland was "a genuine hero." Even Senator Robert Kennedy, now a bitter enemy of Johnson's because of their differences over the war, had good things to say about Westmoreland, calling him a "fine general" and his speech "a fine presentation."

The American people were much more enthusiastic in their support. Although the White House received hundreds of telegrams denigrating Westmoreland's appearance before Congress, it received ten times their number from those who supported the appearance. One man wrote: "I just heard General Westmoreland speak to the American people. He reaffirmed everything I thought we were in Vietnam for." Another man wrote: "Let Westmoreland speak his piece, and don't worry about the doves." A couple wrote: "We Democrats support you and your policies in Vietnam. God bless you, General Westmoreland."

Westmoreland, according to his own account, was "overwhelmed" by both his reception from the Congress, and the outpouring of support from the American people. And so too was President Johnson. He was, of course, as he always was, unhappy over the criticism he had received for bringing Westmoreland home, but the vastly greater support he was given more than offset it. It was, in fact, the most support the White House had had in the last six months. And just as Johnson had hoped, that support had both dampened criticism and vastly improved the administration's public relations campaign.

Unfortunately for Westmoreland, Johnson was the only one to benefit from the general's trip home. Westmoreland, as he would soon discover, certainly did not. To the contrary, the trip irrevocably damaged his credibility, and that credibility would stay damaged. As Colonel Winant Sidle, a former chief of MACV's information office, observed, before Westmoreland's trip home his background briefings for the Saigon press corps had been followed by a "rash of favorable news stories." Afterward, however, "all that changed. Suspecting that Westmoreland had become a tool of the Johnson administration, newsmen replaced their favorable coverage with more skeptical appraisal." In the war of political attrition, it seems, Westmoreland had unwittingly become a casualty.

CHAPTER SIXTEEN

Khe Sanh

Westmoreland finished up his duties in Washington on April 28. Early in the afternoon of that day, he and Kitsy flew to Fayetteville, North Carolina, for a brief visit with her parents; then they took off again for Palm Desert California, and a visit with former President Eisenhower and his wife, Mamie. Westmoreland made the call at the request of President Johnson, but it is difficult to see why Johnson made the request. Eisenhower was completely opposed to the gradualist-limited war Johnson was fighting in Vietnam, and had made his opinion public on a number of occasions. During the Korean War, Eisenhower had warned the Chinese that if the deadlock at Panmunjom was not broken soon he was going to use tactical nuclear weapons against their army in the field. That threat had brought the Korean War to a swift conclusion, and Eisenhower had told Johnson twice in 1966 that he should likewise do whatever it took to bring the Vietnam War to a swift conclusion. "If force is going to do the bidding, you must commit the amount of force necessary to bring the conflict to a successful conclusion."

Obviously, Johnson had not heeded his advice, and during their short talk together all Eisenhower could tell Westmoreland was that he "lamented the restrictions Washington" had placed on him. It was hardly useful advice, but it bolstered Westmoreland's morale a bit knowing that Eisenhower understood fully the kind of frustration he had to endure while fighting the war.

Westmoreland returned to Vietnam to find that the upsurge of enemy activity in I Corps that had started in mid-March had now picked up and was once again threatening Quang Tri Province. That activity had begun on March 20 when enemy gunners north of the demilitarized zone plastered the U.S. Marine position at Con Thien and the ARVN position at Gio Linh with over one thousand mortar, rocket, and artillery rounds. On the heels of the barrage, an NVA regiment shot their way into Quang Tri City, inflicted severe losses on its ARVN defenders and released over two hundred Vietcong being held in the city jail. A day after this attack, an NVA battalion ambushed a Marine ammunition supply convoy when it was only two miles from Cam Lo. The next day, this same enemy battalion attacked and badly mauled a Marine company, also near Cam Lo.

Convinced these attacks presaged an even bigger enemy move against Hue, Westmoreland decided that the 1st and 3rd Marine divisions were stretched too thin in I Corps to meet such a threat. They needed reinforcements, and to provide those reinforcements he formed a provisional Army division of three brigades called Task Force Oregon and placed it under command of Major General William B. Rosson, his former chief of staff. He then ordered Rosson to take over responsibility for Quang Ngai Province and the area around the former Marine base at Chu Lai. His deployment of Task Force Oregon allowed General Walt to move his two Marine divisions entirely into the northern three provinces, so that they could begin gearing up for the all-out enemy invasion, which Westmoreland was sure was only months away.

A few days after he ordered Oregon in motion, a five-man Marine forward observer party was ambushed while reconning Hill 861, a hill just northeast of the Marine base at Khe Sanh. That ambush was the first enemy move in what would come to be known at the Battle of Khe Sanh, one of the most controversial events of the war. Following the ambush, a regiment of the NVA 325C Division marched in from nearby Laos and occupied Hill 861 and two other hills just beyond it—881 South and 881 North. Another enemy regiment was held in reserve just north of the three hills.

Soon after getting word that the enemy had moved into the hills around Khe Sanh, Westmoreland contacted General Walt, and they hammered out a quick plan to reinforce the base and clear the enemy out of the surrounding hills. First a Marine battalion—the 3/3—was hurriedly airlifted into Khe Sanh and moved into staging position near Hill 861. The following day, a second Marine battalion, and an artillery battalion, were lifted in to provide added security to the base and added firepower for the coming attack on the three hills.

What came to be known as the Hill Fights started the next day. Advancing behind napalm and a blistering artillery barrage, the Marines of the 3/3 charged up the side of 861. Guarding the hill was the veteran NVA 18th Regiment, and according to the Marine official history, they resisted the assault "with great fury." The fighting was some of the bitterest of the war so far, and for the first two days the battle raged back and forth across three faces of the hill. Finally on the third day, with bayonets, grenades, and entrenching tools the Marines overran the last enemy bunkers and took the hill, now a blasted smoking no-man's-land of splintered trees and bloated corpses. On May 1 in fighting just as bitter, a second Marine battalion—the 3/9—assaulted and overran Hill 881 South. Then finally on May 2, two companies from the 3/3 overran and secured 881 South. During the three hill fights, the NVA lost over three hundred killed, the Marines, fifty-two.

Westmoreland was happy with the hill victories, but saw them as only the first round of what would likely be a protracted struggle for Khe Sanh. He was convinced the NVA intended to overrun the base and that they were not about to be deterred by their initial defeat. He was still convinced that holding the base was critical to his strategy both in South Vietnam as a whole and in particular in I Corps. He felt if he abandoned the position, the NVA would have a clear shot to do an end run on his DMZ strongpoints and attack Hue. Stopping an NVA attack on Hue, however, was not his only reason for wanting the base where it was. An even more important reason was his desire, if and when he got permission from the President, to use Khe Sanh as a staging area for a massive invasion of Laos. Should Johnson give his approval, Westmoreland already had three plans drawn up and ready to go. The one he favored the most called for the 1st Cavalry Division to initiate the invasion by establishing an airhead on the Bolovens Plateau. Once established there, the 1st was to drive northward toward the town of Saravane, an NVA logistics center, reduce the town, then swing north and seize Savannakhet, another NVA logistics center. Simultaneous with the 1st's move, the 3rd Marine

Division was to mount an armored drive westward from Khe Sanh along Highway 9 and sever the Ho Chi Minh Trail, which bisected the highway at numerous spots. The 3rd was also tasked with seizing Tchepone, a major NVA communications center. Also simultaneously, the 4th Infantry Division was to launch another drive from Pleiku City in the Central Highlands, and a South Vietnamese division a fourth drive from the southern end of the A Shau Valley. Those last two drives were to follow a northwestern axis, with both finally converging in the Laotian Panhandle, which was then to be sealed off.

Once Laos was sealed off as a potential infiltration route, Westmoreland felt, Hanoi would be forced to make a critical decision. They would either have to accept the fact that they could no longer ship supplies and men through Laos, thereby cutting their forces off in the South from any resupply, or they would have to challenge Westmoreland's three divisions in Laos. To do so, the North Vietnamese would have to commit a large number of regiments and divisions to the battle, and Westmoreland was convinced those regiments and divisions would then become easy targets for the massive firepower he had at his disposal. Whatever course Hanoi eventually decided to take, he was convinced that sealing off Laos was a quick way to shorten the war.

To do that sucessfully he felt he absolutely had to have Khe Sanh as a base of operations.

The Marines agreed to the necessity of the Laotian invasion. Walt, in fact, admitted on a number of occasions that he had begged and pleaded with Wallace Greene, the Marine commandant, to push Washington into approving one. To prepare for that invasion, since September of 1966, Walt's staff officers at III Marine Amphibious Force had been providing MACV with critical information on terrain features and enemy activity along Highway 9 from Dong Ha to the Laotian border and from the border along the XePone River to the town of Tchepone. But while the Marines agreed with Westmoreland on the importance of a Laotian invasion, they still did not agree with him on the importance of Khe Sanh itself, either to that invasion or as an obstacle to an enemy attack on Hue. And the original disagreement they had had over the base in 1966 was only aggravated by the Hill Fights and the high casualties the Marines suffered during them. To General Victor Krulak, the commander of all Marine forces in the Pacific, those casualties had served no purpose, and he pleaded with both Admiral Sharp and General Greene to pressure Westmoreland into dismantling Khe Sanh, or at least letting it revert to what it had originally been, a Special Forces camp. Krulak tried to convince both men of a fact that he himself was already firmly convinced of, which was that the Communists wanted "violent close-quarter combat" because "it tends to diminish the effectiveness" of American air and artillery. Therefore, he said, by fighting battles like the Ia Drang and the Hill Fights we merely played into their hands, fought the war on their terms. Staying at Khe Sanh, he concluded, was doing exactly what they wanted us to do.

Equally upset with the choice of Khe Sanh was Brigadier General Lowell English, the assistant commander of the 3rd Marine Division, whose men had been tasked with holding the base. "When you're at Khe Sanh," he told a group of his staff officers, "you're not really anywhere. You could lose it and you really haven't lost a damn thing."

While no one discounted Westmoreland's desire to invade Laos, they felt he had an equally strong reason for wanting to hold Khe Sanh, but was not telling anyone. What he also wanted, they felt, was to set up a giant killing-field at Khe Sanh and then, using the Marines as bait, to entice the North Vietnamese Army into entering it. When they did, he would turn loose his artillery, jet fighter-bombers, and B-52s and pulverize them, thereby producing the big World War II-type victory that he so badly wanted. Being used as bait did not sit well with the Marines.

CHAPTER SEVENTEEN

Abrams and Komer Arrive

Of course, the Marines had no choice in the matter. Whatever Westmoreland's ultimate motive for keeping a base at Khe Sanh, that decision was for all intents and purposes cast in stone. The Marines, like it or not, had to do his bidding. And they did. Working around the clock, a company of Navy Seabees expanded the perimeter of Khe Sanh in order to make room for the new troops, and both widened and lengthened the airstrip so that the Army's giant C-130 cargo planes could use it with greater safety. To protect the various command and communications centers either in place then or anticipated with further expansion, they also built a number of concrete-reinforced bunkers. As the Seabees labored, the staffs at both MACV and III Marine Amphibious Force continued developing plans for a Laotian invasion. They worked unaware that at the moment, a decision was being made in Washington that would deny Westmoreland the troops he needed to launch such an invasion.

As Westmoreland had suspected during his April visit to Washington, just as soon as he returned to Saigon, McNamara and his OSD staff went to work trying to convince the President not to approve the general's request for two hundred thousand additional troops. In a letter to the President, the secretary warned that the addition of two hundred thousand more men would involve a Reserve call-up, which would inevitably set off a bitter congressional debate. That debate would, in turn, unleash loud cries from the general public "to take the wraps off the men in the field." If that happened, McNamara wrote, Johnson might find himself forced into taking drastic actions, like mining North Vietnam's harbors against Soviet ships, approving ground actions into Laos and Cambodia or giving the green light for a full-scale invasion of North Vietnam. If, in fact, the United States did acquiesce to such pressure and escalate the war in the ways just mentioned, we had to accept the possibility of China entering the war. If that happened, then Johnson would find himself, like it or not, being pressured by the military into using "tactical nuclear weapons and area-denial radiological-bacteriological chemical weapons."

After laying out this grim scenario for the President, McNamara then wrote that the endless troop increases had to be stopped. Giving Westmoreland two hundred thousand more men would do little but "bog us down further and risk an even more serious escalation of the war." It could also "lead to a major national disaster; it would not win the Vietnam War, but only submerge it into a larger one." Instead of Westmoreland's massive troop increase, the secretary recommended that Johnson send only thirty thousand troops. That smaller figure would stabilize the commitment at five hundred thousand. Such an increase, he told the President, would not "win the war in a military sense," but it would avoid the danger of a "larger war."

At the sight of McNamara's memo, the Joint Chiefs again honed their knives and leaped to the attack. Turning the secretary's argument on its head, in a detailed report they argued that mobilizing the Reserves and sending Westmoreland the troops he wanted, not only would not force the United States to use tactical nuclear weapons, it was the only way the United States could avoid having to use them. What if the Chinese launched a diversionary attack in Korea, they asked, while simultaneously invading either Thailand or South Vietnam or both? Without the necessary troops, Westmoreland simply could not stop them on the ground, but would be forced "to establish a strategic defense in South Vietnam" and then use tactical nuclear weapons against bases and LOCs in South China.

As Johnson wrestled with Westmoreland's troop request, he could not have avoided seeing the grim irony of the reports of McNamara and the Joint Chiefs. The secretary had warned him that he might be forced to use tactical nuclear weapons in Southeast Asia if he okayed Westmoreland's 200,000-troop request; and the Chiefs had warned him that he might be forced to use them if he did not okay the troop request. For Johnson it was another classic damned-if-I-do, damned-if-I-don't situation, and as he had been doing since the beginning of the war, he sought refuge in a middle position. Although unwilling to face the political firestorm that a mobilization of the Reserves would cause, he nonetheless decided to give Westmoreland 45,000 to 50,000 additional troops, for a total troop strength of 525,000.

Johnson's decision on the troop request was not finalized until August, but Westmoreland got wind of it two months in advance. Shortly after the Joint Chiefs sent their report to the President, Admiral Sharp cabled Westmoreland and told him bluntly not to get his hopes up, for the 200,000 additional troops he had requested were "simply not going to be provided. The country is not going to call up the reserves and we had best accept that."

Westmoreland was not willing to accept it, however. Two months later, he again began pressuring the White House for more troops. There was one thing he would have to accept, though, and that was that Johnson had decided in late March and early April to begin deemphasizing Westmoreland's big-unit war and emphasizing pacification. That decision was triggered in part by Westmoreland's initial request in early 1967 for an additional two hundred thousand troops. Stunned by the number, Johnson decided to begin looking for alternative solutions to the war, solutions that did not require more and more troops. One alternative he decided on was to give the pacification program a giant boost; a second was to upgrade the training and equipment of the South Vietnamese Army and get them more into the ground war. To energize the pacification program, he assigned Ellsworth Bunker to Vietnam as the new United States ambassador and appointed Robert Komer, a civilian, as Westmoreland's deputy in charge of pacification. He gave the job of energizing the South Vietnamese Army to General Creighton Abrams, who became Westmoreland's deputy commander in charge of "Vietnamization."

Although Westmoreland had always picked his deputy commanders, with the arrival of Komer and Abrams that policy came to an abrupt halt. While he had some input into the choice of Komer, he had none in the decision that made Abrams his deputy. If he had, it seems unlikely Abrams would have been his choice. In June 1964, when Westmoreland took over as COMUSMACV, he resisted an attempt by General Harold Johnson, the Army Chief of Staff, to have Abrams made MACV's deputy commander. Since that time, General Johnson had continued lobbying behind the scenes trying to get Abrams sent to Vietnam in some capacity. Although General Johnson never spoke publicly about it, recent disclosures point conclusively to the fact that he was unhappy about the way Westmoreland was handling the war and was constantly looking for a way to replace him. In the end, he did not have the power to push through such a change, but he had enough to get Abrams assigned as the MACV deputy. Since all three have been so closemouthed about the issue, it is difficult to gauge the exact feelings of the President, McNamara, and Wheeler toward Westmoreland. Nonetheless, for them to approve the assignment of Abrams had to mean that they were looking for some fresh ideas on the war, some new direction.

Needless to say, Abrams's arrival in Saigon did not sit well with Westmoreland. Arriving with the general was a rash of rumors and speculation, which put an immediate strain on the relationship between the two men. One rumor, which turned out to be true, stated that Abrams did not want the new position, but had to be pressured by General Johnson into accepting it. One speculation, which also later proved to be true, was that Abrams was now the heir apparent to the MACV throne. As the head of MACV combat operations center, Brigadier General John Chaisson remembers that the only question on everyone's lips was "when he was going to take over, not if he was going to take over."

In part because of such rumors and speculation, the relationship between Westmoreland and Abrams started out strained and was never better than cool. As a result, according to Dutch Kerwin, Westmoreland's chief of staff at the time, Westmoreland seldom took Abrams into his confidence, excluded him from much high-level planning, and even denied him access to COMUSMACV back-channel messages.

Apparently, Abrams took no offense at these slights. When Lieutenant General Bruce Palmer, the deputy commanding general of the U.S. Army in Vietnam, tried to enlist Abrams's support in order to pressure Westmoreland into making some changes in the way he was running the war, Abrams categorically refused. "I'm here to help Westy," he told Palmer. "Although I agree with many things that you've said, I've got to be loyal to him and help him. He knows more about this than either you or I. We'll have to listen and learn."

Westmoreland may not have been comfortable having Abrams

around, but he still had immense respect for him as a field commander. To show just how much respect he had, during their initial
meeting, he did not bother to give his new deputy any advice, except
to tell him that getting the South Vietnamese Army in shape and
ready to fight was his job exclusively and that he should do it however
he saw fit.

The job facing Abrams was a monumental one. Most historians
agree that one reason was because Westmoreland, in his eagerness
early in the war to have American units fight the big-unit war, had
relegated the ARVN to a secondary role, that of providing static
territorial security, and had failed additionally, as the Army's own
official history points out, "to give his field and advisory effort any
sense of immediacy." As a result, the ARVN had failed to develop a
well-defined sense of itself as a fighting force.

Abrams's job was to reverse this situation, and to reverse it immediately. And he did. With the same verve and aggressiveness that
had made him Patton's favorite tank commander, he attacked the
problem of "Vietnamization" head-on. Spending most of his time in
the field, he daily visited with American advisers to ARVN units and
with ARVN commanders, listened to their problems, gave them suggestions and pep talks, then told them all pointedly that the ARVN
had to get into the fight for time was running out. Behind the scenes,
he helped to establish policies that encouraged ARVN commanders
to use battlefield promotions as the best way to get outstanding combat
leaders into positions of command and pushed them also to squash
the corruption and nepotism that was such an integral part of South
Vietnamese life. Finally, he helped to upgrade the training, logistics,
and armament of ARVN units, and to keep unit morale high, he
demanded that ARVN soldiers be paid on time and their families
properly cared for.

Working in close coordination with Abrams was Bob Komer. Until
his arrival, the pacification program had been under the control of
the United States ambassador. With his arrival, control of it was put
under Westmoreland and his MACV staff. In theory at least, pacification was now supposed to merge with Westmoreland's big-unit war
and evolve into what Ambassador Bunker called the one-war concept.
In reality, however, that never happened. While Westmoreland publicly proclaimed the need for a unified war strategy, behind the scenes
he kept them separate. Although Komer would have preferred a
unified strategy, he accepted things as they were and charged into
his duties as pacification head. He established as his first priority

providing long-term protection for the rural population of the country and, as his second, winning their hearts and minds through an extensive system of land redistribution and social programs. Before he could do anything, however, he first had to provide security for the countryside. To make sure that it was accomplished promptly and properly, he took over direct control of the training of the Popular and Regional Forces troops, increasing their numbers, upgrading their training, and providing them with modern weapons. Those forces, however, could not deal with the clandestine Vietcong infrastructure in the countryside. To root them out, he set up the Phoenix program. Using a complicated system of spies and informers, VC cadre and sympathizers were first located, then either captured or assassinated. Phoenix hit squads were composed primarily of VC defectors, nonethnic Vietnamese mercenaries, and South Vietnamese and United States Special Forces soldiers. In 1967 alone, the program claimed twenty thousand lives and spread terror through the Communist underground in South Vietnam.

With Komer focusing all his attention on pacification and Abrams on Vietnamization, Westmoreland went back to fighting his big-unit war. In I Corps, that war had a short hiatus following the Hill Fights, but on May 8 things heated up again there. The eighth was the thirteenth anniversary of the fall of Dien Bien Phu, and the North Vietnamese gunners ranged across the demilitarized zone celebrated the victory by unleashing a four-thousand-round mortar, rocket, and artillery barrage against Allied strongpoints at Gio Linh, Con Thien, Camp Carroll, and Dong Ha. At Con Thien, following a five-hundred-round barrage, two NVA battalions, led by an elite sapper company, assaulted the positions being held by the 1st Battalion, 4th Marines. After the sappers blew holes in the wire, enemy infantry charged into the Marine positions. In the wild melee that followed, the attackers killed 44 Marines and wounded over 100 before being driven out by a furious counterattack. The Marines counted 197 enemy dead around their perimeter, took 10 NVA soldiers prisoners, and captured one hundred weapons.

When Westmoreland discovered that many of the enemy positions shelling his strongpoints were located south of the DMZ in South Vietnamese territory, he issued a directive to III MAF with specific instructions for Walt to send forces into that area and destroy the enemy gun positions and troop concentrations. On May 13, under the code name of Operation Hickory, two Marine battalions—the 2/9 and 2/26—started an attack north from Con Thien. At the same time, five battalions of the 1st ARVN Division launched another attack north from their positions at Gio Linh along the axis of Route 1. Twenty minutes later, another Marine battalion—the 1/3—operating as a special landing force, made an amphibious assault into the northwest corner of the DMZ near the mouth of the Ben Hai River. Then behind massive prep fire delivered by five destroyers and two cruisers, the 1/3 began an attack westward. All three attacking groups ran into heavy resistance but smashed it with heavy doses of artillery and naval gun fire. After eight days of continual pummeling, what remained of the six enemy battalions holding the area fled north into North Vietnam. They left behind 815 dead, nearly 400 of whom were killed by the 1st ARVN Division, a fact that gladdened Westmoreland's heart.

Now that they had their momentum up, Westmoreland pushed the Marines to launch other aggressive operations in northern I Corps. They responded with a series of operations that targeted every province of northern I Corps. During Operation Union II, two battalions of the 5th Marines smashed the 3rd and 21st NVA regiments during eleven days of continual fighting in Quang Tin Province. In the bunker-to-bunker fighting, the Marines lost 73 of their own men and killed 549 NVA regulars.

In early June, the fighting shifted back to the area around Khe Sanh again. There during Operation Crockett, the 1st Battalion, 26th Marines tangled with an enemy battalion from the 324C Division, the unit that had led the massive invasion of the DMZ in 1966. This time the 324C was ensconced in a heavily fortified bunker complex just west of Hill 881 South. It was not fortified enough. After their jet fighters pummeled the enemy bunkers with five-hundred-pound bombs and napalm, the Marines attacked the complex on line and with grenades and recoilless rifles reduced the enemy bunkers still intact. After five hours of continuous fighting, the enemy battalion broke and ran, leaving 85 of their dead behind. Marine losses were 18 killed and 27 wounded.

With the arrival of July, the action swung back once again to the center of the DMZ. There in early July, the Marines kicked off Operation Buffalo, a search-and-destroy operation north of Con Thien. The operation started out as a routine sweep of Route 561 by companies A and B of the 9th Marines, but quickly turned into one of the bloodiest one-day fights of the entire war. Only four miles from Con Thien, the 90th NVA Regiment ambushed both Marine companies, then charged into their ranks with flamethrowers. The suddenness of the attack threw the Marines into turmoil and before they could get organized over two hundred of their number were either wounded or dead.

The 9th Marines quickly threw two fresh battalions into the fight. After covering the retreat of companies A and B back into Con Thien, they smashed headlong into the 90th behind a thundering barrage from the eight-inch guns of the Seventh Fleet. The NVA countered with a barrage of their own, delivered by long-range artillery hidden north of the DMZ. While their artillery was firing, the commander of the 90th massed his troops and launched a human-wave assault against the two Marine battalions. Again the enemy used flame-throwers and again their intention was to completely overrun and destroy the Marine battalions. The attack began just after nightfall and continued for the next five hours as the two sides traded blows and the battle seesawed back and forth. With help from a continual stream of jet fighters, gunships, and naval bombardments, the Marines finally stopped the attack. With daylight, the Marines pushed out from their perimeter to police the battlefield. Many were struck speechless by the horrific sight of nearly eight hundred enemy dead scattered for six hundred yards in front of their perimeter. During the all-night battle, the Marines lost forty-three men. After loading their wounded on hammocks, the 90th Regiment retreated north.

Westmoreland was particularly happy with the huge success of Operation Buffalo, but he was just as happy with the results from a half-dozen other successful operations in the other three corps areas. In II Corps, for instance, the 1st Cavalry Division had just completed Operation Thayer II, during which they had driven two NVA regiments out of Binh Dinh Province and killed over fifteen hundred NVA regulars. Likewise in II Corps, the United States 4th and 25th infantry divisions had just completed two massive border-surveillance operations named Francis Marion and Sam Houston in Pleiku and Kontum provinces, during which they had fought a running battle with the 1st and 10th NVA divisions, which were trying to cross the border in order to attack the Central Highlands. After suffering over twelve hundred killed, both enemy divisions had called off their attack on the highlands and retreated back across the border.

On July 7, with Operation Francis Marion nearing completion, McNamara arrived in Vietnam to make what would be his ninth on-the-spot assessment of the situation there. Westmoreland had looked forward to the visit, seeing in it yet another opportunity to try to convince the secretary to approve his two-hundred-thousand-troop request and, as he phrased it, to "step up the pressure against the enemy." To prepare for McNamara's arrival, he had put together a mini-public-relations campaign designed to positively influence McNamara. In one element of that campaign, he had cabled all his senior commanders in Vietnam and told them that when briefing the secretary, they "should convey a feeling for the dynamic approach which we are taking" and should further stress that "though the enemy is tough and elusive, he can and is being licked. It will just take time and resourcefulness to do it. Accent the spirit and morale of the entire command in our approach to fighting the war."

Westmoreland held his meeting with McNamara in the conference room of the MACV's new headquarters at Ton Son Nhut Airport. In his previous meeting with the secretary, he had always been guarded in his optimism, careful not to make unwarranted predictions of success. He was not this time, however. For the first time during the war, he told McNamara he was genuinely optimistic over the direction the war was taking. During 1966, he told him, Communist battle deaths had totaled about five thousand per month, But that figure had changed dramatically in early 1967 once he had gotten his big search-and-destroy operations fully unlimbered and into high gear. Since January, the month he initiated his massive operations, Cedar Falls and Junction City, Communist losses, and that included POWs and defectors, had jumped to over fifteen thousand per month. Since NVA infiltration was now running about seven thousand per month and the VC were only capable of recruiting about thirty-five hundred men per month, he was now firmly convinced that the "crossover point" had been reached—the point, that was, when Allied forces were killing or capturing enemy forces faster than the Communists could put new ones in the field.

Westmoreland concluded his briefing with a bold announcement: Contrary to news reports coming out of Vietnam, the "war is not a stalemate. We are winning slowly but steadily. North Vietnam is paying a tremendous price with nothing to show for it." Now was the time, he told the secretary, with the Communists hurting so badly, to really step up the pressure against them. Now was the time to reinforce success and go for the knockout blow.

In his diary, Westmoreland wrote that McNamara seemed impressed with his report and just as impressed by what he saw during two days of travel around the country. Both facts convinced Westmoreland that McNamara might be ready to make some drastic changes in Vietnam, not the least of which would be putting his approval on the two-hundred-thousand-troop request. Westmoreland was, of course, again wrong in his reading of McNamara, though it would be another month before he realized just how wrong.

CHAPTER EIGHTEEN

Revolt of the Generals

Back in Washington, McNamara seemed a changed man, and most of that change seemed to have been a direct result of Westmoreland's report. Exuding a very uncharacteristic optimism, shortly after his return he told a meeting of the President's principal foreign policy advisers that "there is not a military stalemate" in Vietnam. A few days later, during a meeting with the President and his Cabinet, he repeated the essence of that message, telling the assembled men that "there is no evidence of a stalemate in Vietnam."

It was exactly the kind of good news the President had been waiting for for two years, and he quickly made sure the press heard it also. During a private meeting in his office, he happily announced to Peter Lisagor of the *Chicago Daily News* that "we've begun to turn defeat into victory. I'm not distressed. There is no truth in the stalemate theory. The McNamara report this time was the best of his nine."

It was also the most blatantly dishonest of the nine, yet strangely neither Johnson nor Westmoreland saw any reason to doubt Mc-

Namara's sudden turnaround. Both seemed ready to believe that the secretary had had a sudden metamorphosis in his thinking while in Vietnam and that that metamorphosis might be permanent. But, of course, it was not. McNamara's public announcement was a lie. He still firmly believed, as his influential aide, John T. McNaughton put it, that the United States was caught in "an escalating military stalemate" in Vietnam and that there was no simple way for it to get out of it, save by cutting a political deal with the Vietcong or simply withdrawing.

Why then the sudden optimism? The optimism was quite simply a ploy on McNamara's part to put a lid on any further call for escalation. With Westmoreland's report in hand, he could now go to the President—which, in fact, he quickly did—and legitimately argue that since the United States was now making steady progress in the war, there was simply no need to expand it. There was no reason to provoke China or Russia or both and risk starting World War III, when according to Westmoreland himself, the United States was making steady progress in Vietnam. It was a message McNamara was happy to deliver, and the President happy to receive. Westmoreland in the meantime was left the odd man out. Unwittingly, he had provided McNamara with the ammunition the secretary needed to shoot down the military's plan to expand the war.

Westmoreland had a series of other meetings planned with McNamara, but on July 9 he had to cancel them when he got the news that his mother had died. After clearing up some last-minute business in Saigon, he flew to Hawaii and picked up Kitsy, Stevie, and Rip. There they all boarded a Special Mission Aircraft that had been sent from the States and flew directly to Columbia for the funeral. As with his father's funeral in 1964, a number of VIPs attended, including South Carolina's governor, Robert McNair, and U.S. Senator Strom Thurmond.

Right after the funeral, he received a message from President Johnson offering his condolences and telling him that he wanted him to stop off in Washington before returning to Vietnam. In reality, the President wanted him in Washington in order to help orchestrate another public relations effort designed to dispel persistent rumors in the press that there was grave disharmony between the White House and the military. As a key to that effort, the President held a press conference on July 13 in a sitting room of the White House. There with McNamara, Wheeler, and Westmoreland sitting on a couch behind him, Johnson mounted a podium and announced that the four of them "had reached a meeting of the minds" on how best to prosecute the war. "The troops that General Westmoreland needs and requests, as we feel it necessary, will be supplied. Is that not true, General Westmoreland?"

"Yes, sir."

"General Wheeler?"

"Yes, sir."

"Secretary McNamara?"

"Yes, sir."

The entire press conference was, of course, a complete fiction, little more than a cynical attempt on Johnson's part to create a consensus where there was not one. The four had not only not "reached a meeting of the minds," as Johnson put it, they were actually in bitter disagreement over the war. For Westmoreland and Wheeler, that disagreement could only have been aggravated by their being forced to answer yes to Johnson's question. For both men, the moment was a humiliating one.

Of the two, however, Wheeler was apparently the more humiliated—and the angrier. Having been repeatedly forced by McNamara and Johnson into situations where he had to sell the war to the American people, he was beginning to reach the end of his tether. He had been living a lie for the last three years, and he was reaching the point where he could not live it any longer. On August 25, 1967, following an appearance by McNamara before the Senate Foreign Relations Committee, Wheeler felt he could not participate in the duplicity any longer. Wheeler felt that during the appearance McNamara had distorted some fundamental truths about the war and that the American people needed to be told that McNamara was a liar and there was no consensus between the White House and the military. The notion of a consensus was a hoax.

In the late afternoon of August 25, Wheeler took an unprecedented step in the annals of the Joint Chiefs of Staff, a step that could conceivably have shaken the government to its core. Convinced that the American people neeeded to be told of the military's deep discontent over the war and equally convinced that McNamara and Johnson needed to be sent a strong message, Wheeler called a meeting of the Joint Chiefs and suggested that they resign en masse in protest against the administration's policy in Vietnam. After a short discussion of the matter, the other Chiefs agreed to go along with Wheeler. One especially eager to take such a drastic step was the Army Chief, General Harold Johnson, who felt that the military was being blamed for a war over which they had no control.

The Chiefs decided to announce their resignations the next day. After a sleepless night, however, Wheeler had a change of heart. "We can't do it," he told the other Chiefs the next morning. "It would be mutiny. We just can't do something like that." General Johnson did not have a change of heart. He still wanted to go through with the mass resignation, and argued that the four of them had become impotent, that "no one was really paying any attention" to their recommendations. "If we're going to go to war," he told his colleagues, "then we had better be honest with the American people." The war was going to be lost, and when it was the military was going to be blamed. General Johnson's was a powerful argument, but Wheeler was not about to change his mind yet again. Returning to his first argument, he again reminded them that they were contemplating "mutiny. All our lives we've been told to obey orders, we've been schooled in it. We've been told to give our lives for our country. Now we're going to throw all of that away." Eventually Wheeler's argument held the day, and the mass resignation was scrapped.

Until recently, accounts of the two meetings were carefully suppressed. General Wheeler died without telling a soul of them; so too did General John P. McConnell, the Air Force Chief of Staff. Admiral Thomas Moorer, the Chief of Naval Operations, spoke briefly of the meeting with friends, but never in specifics. In an attempt to send a warning to future generations, General Johnson, shortly before his death, told the whole story to an aide, with the proviso that eventually the story needed to be told to historians.

Although he does not say how, when, or where he learned of the two meetings, Westmoreland claims that he was aware of them, but that under no circumstances would he have ever contemplated taking such a drastic step. Such a move would have violated the very notion of civilian supremacy over the military, he says, and would have set a dangerous precedent. Even after three years of overseeing a frustrating war, during which he had repeatedly been denied the troops and strategy he wanted, he was still unwilling to "pull a MacArthur" on President Johnson. "I was not about to go to the commander in chief and say we were not up to carrying out his instructions," he told a friend in 1975, "as a matter of service pride."

Westmoreland has been criticized by the Right for not doing just that—going to the President and telling him pointedly that he was going to resign unless a winning strategy was implemented in Vietnam. Those critics say that he, like the Joint Chiefs, obviously did not feel strongly enough about his convictions to be willing to "fall on his sword" if they were not adopted.

In his own defense, he says he never imagined the possibility of a United States defeat in Vietnam and therefore never saw the necessity to resign in protest. In reference to the quote by Napoleon that he kept on his desk, a quote many saw as paradoxical, he goes on to say that "I suffered my problems in Vietnam because I believed that success eventually would be ours despite them, that they were not to be, as Napoleon put it, instruments of my army's downfall."

Does this statement release him from any responsibility for what eventually came to pass in Vietnam? Many of his critics on the right say that although he may not have foreseen the tragic end in Vietnam, he *should* have foreseen it. He is therefore as much to be blamed for that end, they claim, as the Joint Chiefs, who foresaw it, but likewise did nothing. They were both the principal military advisers to the President, says one of those critics, Colonel Harry G. Summers, Jr., in his *On Strategy,* and as his principal advisers, it was their job to "warn him of the likely consequences of his actions and to recommend alternatives. . . . In failing to press their military advice they allowed the U.S. to pursue a strategic policy that was faulty from the start."

Summers's indictment of the military is a harsh one, and especially so considering that he was a military man himself who had commanded troops in Vietnam. Whether it is a completely fair indictment, however, is open to question. Certainly the military should accept some of the blame for the failure in Vietnam, but to imply that they should accept full blame for that failure is to deny the responsibilities of the other main players in the war. Should not McNamara, who continued to oversee a war that he thought was irrevocably stalemated, accept some responsibility for what resulted? And President Johnson, who quite cynically manipulated everyone around him to paint an optimistic picture of the war for the American people, a picture that he himself did not believe? Should he likewise not accept some responsibilty? And what of Maxwell Taylor, Walt Rostow, Dean Rusk, and William Bundy? Can we legitimately fault Westmoreland for not having had the foresight to have foreseen the coming tragedy in Vietnam and not also fault those men?

Of course not. In the end, however, laying the fault on any of these men for not "throwing themselves on their swords" is a meaningless exercise. A mass resignation by Westmoreland and the Joint Chiefs would not have convinced President Johnson to expand the war, just as MacArthur's protest in Korea did not convince Truman to invade China. Johnson knew very well that Vietnam might turn out badly if he continued fighting his limited war. He had known that from the very beginning. By fighting the war the way he did, he was taking a calculated risk, but he felt that that risk and the realization that it might lead to failure was safer than the infinitely greater risk that an expanded war might bring. The idea of losing the Vietnam War did not frighten him half as much as the thought of hordes of Chinese "volunteers" pouring into Vietnam or of Russian jets strafing Da Nang.

CHAPTER NINETEEN

A Day in the Life

Westmoreland had established the routine shortly after moving into the former French wine merchant's villa in June 1964 and had adhered to it religiously ever since. He awoke every morning around six, just as the dawn was starting to pink the sky over the Saigon River. While pictures of his wife and children looked on from a bedside table, he snapped off twenty-five to thirty push-ups, then if he had the time, another twenty-five to thirty sit-ups. Fully awake now, he donned a bathrobe and moved to the classified communications center he had had installed in his room. Once connected to MACV's combat operations center at Tan Son Nhut Airport, he sat back and had a quick briefing of the night's activities. There was a generic quality about much of the news, only the units involved and places changed. Somewhere during the night, he could be sure, one or two American firebases had repulsed enemy ground attacks. In a half-dozen places, it was almost a certainty that Vietcong terrorists had struck. Along the demilitarized zone, two or three Marine or ARVN positions had most likely been shelled or probed.

After taking in as much of the situation report as he wanted, he went downstairs to breakfast, wearing his tropicals or his bathrobe to keep from staining or wrinkling his fatigues. Except for an occasional glass of orange juice, he had been eating the same breakfast for three years—one soft-boiled egg, two pieces of toast, a cup of black coffee.

Ten minutes later, he left the house fully dressed, wearing his starched fatigues, his spit-shined boots, and an olive-drab ball cap decorated with four gold stars and his jump wings. He was always an impressive sight, and he knew it—tall, rock-chinned, stolid, composed, a textbook example of command presence.

In the center of the compound, he was joined by his brief-case-toting aide, former Rhodes Scholar, Captain Larry Budge. A year before, Budge had been pushing an infantry company through the wild jungles of the Central Highlands. Now he had the safer but infinitely more complicated job of keeping the most important man in Vietnam on schedule.

If everything was going according to schedule, at seven the two got into the backseat of their black, air-conditioned sedan and were soon speeding through the teeming streets of Saigon, trailed by a jeepload of South Vietnamese bodyguards, all of whom carried .45-caliber pistols and M-16 rifles. Although he was noted for chewing out junior officers who had been ambushed bringing patrols back the same way they had gone out, Westmoreland had the chauffeur take the same route to and from Tan Son Nhut each morning, a route that took them right through the heart of Saigon, past a hundred spots where Vietcong assassins could have set off a command-detonated mine or fired a rocket grenade.

Why he chose to be so reckless was a mystery to all his subordinates, and especially so to the MACV command surgeon, Major General Spurgeon H. Neel, Jr., a man who lived in one of the rooms at Westmoreland's villa. Frequently asked by Westmoreland to ride along to MACV headquarters, Neel was convinced that sooner or later the VC were going to reduce the car, and him with it, into a pile of burning debris. He would count it a miracle that they never did.

Around seven-thirty, they arrived at Tan Son Nhut. At the main gate, South Vietnamese air police gave the sedan crisp salutes and waved it through. United States military police recognized the car with more salutes at the gate to the MACV compound, a four-acre piece of real estate dominated by MACV headquarters, a massive two-story metal building that sprawled across two thirds of those four acres. MACV had had a humble beginning in 1961 in a converted hotel on Pasteur Street, but the increasing demands of the war and security problems had forced the construction of these new facilities in 1967. Nicknamed the Pentagon East because of its seemingly endless hallways and rooms, MACV headquarters had the responsibility not only for the command of all United States forces in Vietnam but for the training and advising of all South Vietnamese forces.

At the main entrance to MACV headquarters, the chauffeur pulled the sedan over and Westmoreland and Budge hopped out. After saluting the MPs guarding the door, they entered the building and started down a long, air-conditioned hallway. Westmoreland's office lay at the end of the hallway. Seated behind a huge walnut desk, he officially began his day as COMUSMACV.

First in the door every morning was often Marine Corps Brigadier General John Chaisson, the head of MACV's combat operations center, with a detailed briefing on the preceding day's activities and an update on current operations. On Chaisson's heels came Westmoreland's executive assistant, Air Force Lieutenant Colonel William E. Whitlatch with all recent cable traffic. After reading the cables, Westmoreland dictated replies to his stenographer, Warrant Officer Charles Montgomery.

After that, there were staff conferences to attend, and following them, likely an important visitor or two to greet. In order to keep himself in condition for his rigorous schedule, Westmoreland had made it a habit the last three years to play tennis for thirty minutes during his lunch break, but when columnist Jack Anderson wrote that the general should be "at the front" rather than playing tennis, Westmoreland gave up the game. He was, however, furious that Anderson had created the perception back in the States that he was leading some type of country-club existence while his troops suffered and died.

And so now instead of tennis, he merely ate lunch, then usually sat back for another briefing from Chaisson or to deal with any fresh cables. He reserved many of his midafternoons for what were at times lengthy conferences with Bob Komer, General Abrams, Ambassador Bunker, and his counterpart, General Cao Van Vien, the Chief of the South Vietnamese Joint General Staff.

At least three times a week, the general put his administrative duties on hold and headed to the field. He felt that it was essential that he do so given the nature of the war. In the field, he felt he received a close-up look at the war from the tactical level, was able to actually see the terrain where battles were fought, and was thereby better able to understand the problems his men faced.

By preference, the general did not have either his own helicopter or jet plane, but traveled in whatever was available at Tan Son Nhut on any particular day. If the trip was to be a short one, he traveled by helicopter. On longer trips, he flew in an assortment of jets and fixed-wing aircraft.

On one particular day in April, Westmoreland covered over one hundred miles, traveling by helicopters to the headquarters of the 1st Infantry Division, to the site of a recently constructed Special Forces camp, to the command posts of the 196th and 199th infantry brigades, and to three new battalion firebases. On that day, Budge had planned all his stops in advance, but the general frequently changed his plans in order to visit a unit that had just fought a battle.

On June 10, 1966, on hearing that a squadron from the 11th Armored Cavalry Regiment had lost thirty-five men during a successful enemy ambush, Westmoreland had his chopper pilot of the day fly immediately to the scene. On arriving, he was greeted by the 11th's commander and ushered inside a circle of armored personnel carriers. A group of officers, some of whom had survived the ambush, were called forward by the 11th commander to face COMUSMACV. After locating the unit's intelligence officer, Westmoreland began firing questions at him. "Did you lose any vehicles?" "How many?" "Any back in service?" "What about the wounded?" "How many of them were hospitalized?" "You don't know? But you *will* be able to answer that question the next time I come around, won't you?"

It was a mild reproof and all the assembled officers knew it. Another officer in a similar situation—a Patton type, for instance—might have fired the intelligence officer on the spot, possibly either wrecking or damaging his career. But that was not how Westmoreland operated. He did not believe in humiliating men, in wrecking careers on a whim.

There were many in the Army, however, who thought that he should have been harder on some of the officers under him, that he should have replaced a few of them along the way and, if need be, wrecked a few careers. They point to Operation Attleboro as an example of a situation that required a strong action on Westmoreland's part, an action he was unwilling to take.

During that operation, Brigadier General Edward H. DeSaussure led his 196th Infantry Brigade into its first major battle of the war against the veteran 9th VC Division. He unfortunately made the grievous error of feeding his unit into the battle piecemeal. In the confusion that followed, he lost control of part of his command and one of his battalions was subsequently mauled.

In the midst of the battle, Westmoreland canceled all his appointments and flew directly to the scene. There, he was greeted by the fiery Major General William DePuy, whose 1st Infantry Division was at the moment moving to save the 196th. DePuy, never one to be merciful, recommended the immediate relief of DeSaussure. Westmoreland agreed to the necessity of removing him from command, but refused to relieve him in a way "that would indicate he had lost confidence in" him. DeSaussure was an artillery officer, and Westmoreland felt he himself was at least partially to blame for the debacle since it was he who had assigned the brigadier to command the 196th, a job for which DeSaussure had no qualifying experiences. So instead of relieving him outright and sending him home ignominiously, he transferred him to I Field Force as their head artillery officer. There he was later promoted to major general.

The transfer angered more than a few junior and senior officers in Vietnam. They felt that Westmoreland, even if he was operating from a basic sense of decency, was setting a bad example by not relieving DeSaussure outright. If commanders like DePuy could initiate wholesale firings of subordinates for not being aggresive enough, firings that often ruined their careers, then there was no excuse, they argued, for Westmoreland not to have relieved DeSaussure for what was really a far more grievous offense. Later many of the officers who were critical of the decision would speculate that if Abrams had been COMUSMACV at that time, DeSaussure would have retired a brigadier general. Regardless, such actions on Westmoreland's part, as Blair Clark notes, tended to make him a figure in Vietnam "more popular than feared."

During his trips to the field, Westmoreland dealt with enlisted men considerably differently than he did with officers. With officers, he was the stern but caring teacher. Around enlisted men, he became a paternal figure, someone who cared about them and understood and appreciated the terrible hardships they were enduring. Arriving at a scorched and blasted jungle clearing where a battalion from the 173rd Airborne Brigade had just soundly whipped an NVA regiment, Westmoreland moved about among the men shaking hands and congratulating them on their victory. When hot food was flown in, he moved through the chow line with everyone else then sat down on a log with a group of men to eat and talk. As he had done when running his artillery battery back at Fort Bragg before World War II, he began questioniong men around him. *Where are you from, son? What does your father do back in the States? What are you going to do when you get out of the Army?*

When the meal was over, he joined an Associated Press reporter, Hugh Mulligan, who had flown out with him to write a story. As so often happened when Westmoreland had a chance to talk with men who had been in combat, he had become openly sentimental. "This generation is going to be heard from," he told Mulligan solemnly. "They come here from all walks of life, from every possible social background, and have been exposed to problems of diplomacy and life and death and nation building that can't help but bring beneficial results to our country when they assume their position of leadership. At 20, they know more about the complexities of the world than you or I could learn in a lifetime."

While he was talking, Budge came up and told him that they were behind on their schedule. On the way to the waiting chopper, however, Westmoreland encountered seven men preparing to go out on a reconnaissance patrol and moved up to have a word with them. After going over the route the patrol was to take with a young buck sergeant holding the map, Westmoreland asked the man, "What will you do if any of your men smoke?"

"It won't happen," the sergeant said matter-of-factly. "These men have been up against old Charlie before. They know what the score is."

Westmoreland next turned his attention to a burly black soldier who was carrying an M-79 grenade launcher. "What do you think of the M-79?"

"It's hanging in there."

Westmoreland did not understand the slang and looked at the man blankly. "What did you say?"

The soldier, in turn, thought he was being reprimanded for not showing the proper military courtesty. "I said it's hanging in there— sir!" he snapped, nearly shouting the word "sir."

Westmoreland slowly smiled, then broke into a booming laugh. "You men look mean and lean," he said. "I wish you the best tonight and every night."

With that the men moved off toward the jungle and Westmoreland, Budge, and Mulligan hopped into the helicopter. As it lifted off and began pulling away, Westmoreland leaned out and kept his eyes glued to the patrol until it had completely disappeared from sight. Then he suddenly became silent, contemplative. When he spoke again the three were back in the sedan on their way to visit some wounded at the Third Field Hospital. "You know what I'm thinking about?" Westmoreland suddenly asked Mulligan. Mulligan was a bit stunned by the question. Before he could respond, Westmoreland said, "I'm thinking of that recon squad back there going off into the jungle. I've been thinking about them ever since we left there. They were really impressive, weren't they?"

If Westmoreland spent a day in the field, he usually did not get back to his desk until at least six in the evening. Awaiting him always were piles of paperwork that needed his attention. The highest pile was always the letters of condolence to the families of American dead. From day one as COMUSMACV, he had signed each of them personally, though it was always a difficult and at times a very painful task. Frequently in the pile he spotted the names of army regulars he had served with during his career, but more often it was the names of their sons, young lieutenants and captains who had fallen leading platoons and infantry companies. It was especially painful for him, however, to encounter the names of men who had been cadets during the time he had been the superintendent at West Point. Of the 565 men who had graduated from the class of 1964, the class he had arrived at the Point with, 20 were killed in Vietnam and 133 wounded. Westmoreland had known many of the KIAs by their first name.

It was often dark when Westmoreland called it a day at MACV headquarters. His work, however, was far from over. In order to maximize his office time, he often invited a mix of people to join him for dinner at the villa, which was usually at eight. His guests included congressmen, state governors, senior officers, journalists, and a wide assortment of famous entertainers. To keep the discussion rooted in reality, he frequently invited exceptional junior officers from combat units to eat with him, hoping that their presence and their personal accounts would give his guests a better sense of the reality of the war.

After dinner, he and any remaining guests usually adjourned to a small screened patio behind the villa for a drink. According to Major General Neel, when it came to drinking Westmoreland was a man of precise moderation. "He would have two gin and tonics every night," Neel says. "Never one, never three. It was always two."

Over drinks, he often held lengthy discussions of the war with senior officers. Most of those discussions dealt with specific problems the officers had encountered in their commands, but at times the discussions ranged into broader, more philosophical terrain. During one of the latter discussions, Westmoreland asked a mixed group of colonels and generals one evening how they thought the great generals of World War II would have fared in Vietnam. His guests almost unanimously agreed that the smartest generals—Eisenhower, Marshall, and Bradley, for instance—would have been successful in any war, but that the full-speed-ahead types like Patton would never be able to adjust to the tactical and strategic restrictions of Vietnam. Westmoreland agreed with their conclusion, with the implication, as one observer noted, that he did not consider himself in the latter group.

Around ten, Westmoreland usually retired to his room. Before undressing, he got on the phone one final time to MACV for a situation report. If there was a serious battle in progress, he often stayed up a little longer to monitor the situation. His aides were under orders to awaken him in the middle of the night should they feel it necessary. In bed, he finished any remaining paperwork by the light of a small bedside lamp. Finally, if he was not already too fatigued, he picked out some reading material from a small table where Bernard Fall's *Hell in a Very Small Place* and *Street Without Joy* completed for space with Jean Larteguy's *The Centurions*, an anthology of Mao Tse-tung's writings, some translations of Giap's more important musings on the art of war, a French grammar book, and a Bible.

He had already read Fall's and Larteguy's books early in the war, but he frequently read parts of them again before falling asleep. All three were sobering reading. *Hell in a Very Small Place* was Fall's lengthy account of the fall of the French garrison at Dien Bien Phu following a three-month-long Vietminh siege. *Street Without Joy* was the story of Group Mobile 100, a French armored force that in the summer of 1954 tried to make it along Highway 19 from An Khe to the safety of the coast. The Vietminh ambushed the column repeatedly along the entire sixty-mile route, then, in a deliberate act of brutality, massacred the survivors in a final ambush two weeks after the Geneva Accords were signed. Westmoreland wrote after the war that during his entire tenure in Vietnam, those two Communist victories were continually on his mind "as a reminder of communist tactics and methods."

If Westmoreland read Fall in order to periodically reinforce his belief that the Communists could not be trusted, he read *The Centurions* out of a need to remind himself that as a professional soldier he had to face not only the struggles on the battlefield but also that perennial struggle with his civilian masters. Larteguy's novel tells the story of a small group of French paratroop officers sent to fight in both Indochina and Algeria by politicians who lacked the courage to either end the wars or to mobilize the French people to win them. Caught in the middle of this cruel contradiction, like their Roman predecessors, these centurions fight with an almost fanatical dedication, only to face capture, torture, brainwashing, and the ignominy of defeat. After enduring all this, they return to France where they are condemned by the press and the intelligentsia, scorned by large portions of the general populace, and shunned by the same politicians who ordered them into battle. It is a grim scenario, and Westmoreland could only hope that he and America's centurions would not be forced to play out a similar one in Vietnam.

CHAPTER TWENTY

Border Battles

I n most popular literature of the war, General Vo Nguyen Giap, North Vietnam's defense minister, is generally referred to as Westmoreland's main adversary. In reality, he was but one of two. The other was General Nguyen Chi Thanh, the commander of the Central Office of South Vietnam (COSVN). Both men, like Westmoreland, held four-star rank, and both possessed enormous power and responsibilities. From his command post somewhere above the demilitarized zone, Giap controlled all North Vietnamese forces in I and II Corps. From his command post somewhere in the wild tracts of jungle in War Zone D, Thanh controlled all Vietcong forces in the South. Although Giap technically had more power than Thanh, during Politburo meetings and in a series of articles published in Communist theoretical journals, Thanh, a strong believer in attritional warfare, frequently criticized Giap for his desire to return the war to a protracted guerrilla struggle. In one particularly caustic article, he chastised "those who trembled" in the face of American military strength. As everyone in Hanoi knew, "those" referred primarily to Giap.

Those attacks angered Giap. If he had had the authority, he likely would have replaced Thanh with someone with views similar to his own. That authority, however, rested in the hands of Ho Chi Minh, and Ho was not only fond of Thanh but was even reported to be grooming him to be Giap's successor. Whether that was, in fact, true is questioned by some scholars, but few question the more obvious fact that Ho liked playing his two four-star commanders off against each other, thereby creating a healthy rivalry between them while at the same time keeping Giap's enormous ego in line.

Needless to say, Giap did not enjoy being pitted against Thanh. Like most senior generals in any army, he was an ambitious man who wanted as much power as he could get, and Thanh was keeping him from getting that power. For Giap it was an intolerable situation, but it did not last forever. He eventually got the power he wanted. Oddly, he got it with the help of Westmoreland. The strange course of events that led to Giap's ascendancy began on June 1965 when Westmoreland received permission from President Johnson to use his fleets of B-52 bombers in a tactical role in Vietnam. A short time later, he sat down with his air officers and drew up a list of priority targets. High on that list was COSVN.

As Lieutenant General William W. Momyer, the commander of Seventh Air Force and head MACV air officer in 1966, notes in an official history of the war, although COSVN's exact location was to remain elusive throughout the war, Westmoreland devoted a lot of time and resources to locating and destroying it. According to Momyer, Westmoreland repeatedly requested fighter strikes against suspected locations and periodically personally ordered B-52s against other suspected sites.

To this day, there is no hard evidence to indicate whether the dozens of strikes Westmoreland targeted against COSVN ever actually destroyed the place. Those strikes did, however, kill a number of high-ranking Vietcong cadre, one of whom was Thanh himself, who died sometime in early July 1967 from multiple shrapnel wounds to the chest. Whether the bombs that killed him also destroyed COSVN headquarters remains a mystery.

After being loaded on a stretcher, Thanh's body was carried overland to the airport at Phnom Penh, Cambodia, where it was, in turn, loaded onto a plane and flown directly to Hanoi. There, on July 7, it was publicly announced that Thanh had died of natural causes in a Hanoi hospital. That same day, a state funeral was held for him at the Hanoi Military Club. While Thanh lay in state, Ho Chi Minh pinned two posthumous medals on his tunic, Le Duc Tho eulogized him, and hundreds of high-ranking Communist government and military figures walked by to bid their comrade a last farewell.

Giap was one of the mourners, though it is doubtful he was as grief-stricken as many of his comrades. The death of his longtime rival had made him the supreme military commander in Vietnam with direct control over COSVN and all its activities.

He still did not control overall strategy, however. That still lay in the hands of Ho Chi Minh and his loyal lieutenants, Le Duan, Le Duc Tho, and Pham Van Dong. Seeing that Thanh's funeral had presented them with an unexpected opportunity to once again discuss that strategy, the four convened a meeting on the following day of the full Politburo.

The Hanoi regime has never published a complete record of that meeting, though bits and pieces of the proceedings have leaked out over the years. Foremost among the issues discussed during the meeting was the total failure of the Party's last two dry-season campaigns. Those failures, the leaders of the Politburo felt, necessitated a complete reevaluation of the entire war. The reevaluation was indeed thorough, too thorough for the tastes of some. Like mathematicians, these leaders added up their positives and negatives and attempted to come up with a total.

On the positive side, they could all look happily at the continuing political turmoil in South Vietnam. Buddhist protests and the rebellion of ARVN units during the unrest in Da Nang in the spring of 1966 had convinced them that the Saigon government was still wobbling on shaky legs. Equally heartening was the performance of ARVN, which, in spite of General Abrams's work, was still far from becoming a first-class fighting force. While it was true that the ARVN was bolstered by the presence of over a half-million United States troops, it was also true that only 20 percent of those troops were in combat units. And those 20 percent, as Giap noted, were "taut as a bowstring from the Delta to the DMZ." Finally, they were encouraged by the impact the war was having on the United States home front. There, the leaders of the Politburo were pleased to note the existence of a growing peace movement and a general populace becoming more and more confused and discontented over the war. With a presidential election coming up in 1968, and campaigning that would likely be divisive, they felt the American political system might likewise be stretched to its limit.

The leaders of the Politburo were not pleased, however, when they looked at the negatives. The primary negative they had to accept was that a conventional victory in Vietnam, something that seemed within their grasp in early 1965, was now completely out of reach. Thanh's conventional strategy had failed. It had failed at the battle of the Ia Drang, and it had failed in a hundred other battles, leaving thousands of Communist fighters dead and thousands more wounded. The loss of those dead and wounded had left the ranks of many local units so depleted that the Party had been forced to rebuild them with North Vietnamese regulars and with draftees forcibly conscripted from local villages. The presence of thousands of North Vietnamese regulars in formerly purely Vietcong units had transformed the war in the minds of the South Vietnamese from a legitimate civil struggle between competing South Vietnamese factions into an armed invasion from the North. The institution of a draft and the sight of hundreds of young men being led away from their villages at gunpoint also angered many South Vietnamese. Before, all the fighters in the Vietcong units had been willing volunteers. Seeing men now being forced to fight, for many southerners removed the mantle of legitimacy the VC had always claimed to be exclusively theirs.

As they compiled their negatives, the leaders of the Politburo had to look at the political situation in South Vietnam one more time. While they had certainly reveled at the sight of protesting Buddhists and rebellious ARVN units in Da Nang in 1966, they had also shuddered at the evidence of increasing political stability in South Vietnam. There had not been a coup or even a threat of one since Thieu and Ky took control of the government two years before, and the planned presidential election coming up in September would likely solidify even more the control those two men had over the country.

Just as frightening to them as the signs of growing stability in the South were the signs of growing instability and unrest in the North. War weariness, they had discovered to their dismay, was not a disease that afflicted only democracies. Recently they had had to arrest and imprison two hundred Party officials who were opposed to Hanoi's continued participation in the war. If the war dragged on inconclusively for another five years, Hanoi's leaders knew, the numbers of those dissatisfied with the war would only continue to grow.

Having analyzed all the positives and negatives facing them, these leaders finally decided that they needed to do something sudden and dramatic in order to realize a great leap forward in the revolution and possibly even win the war. Since the beginning of the war in the early 1960s, Communist strategy had been based on the idea that victory would come as a result of a combined general offensive and uprising. No one had put a specific future date on this final offensive, but it was assumed by most in the Politburo that it was far in the future, that it would come only after years of long bloody struggle. They had assumed wrong. Ho Chi Minh and his lieutenants were not willing to wait any longer. They did not feel that they could wait. The time to strike was now.

Having decided to strike, Ho and his lieutenants dusted off a plan of attack that Giap had drawn up five or six months before. His plan, officially called the Winter-Spring Offensive, had three distinct phases, to be carried out over a period of six months.

In phase one, mostly NVA units were to launch assaults against isolated border areas, with the intention of drawing United States units away from the cities and populated lowlands.

Phase two of Giap's plan called for a countrywide offensive beginning on January 31, 1968, during the height of Tet, the Vietnamese holiday commemorating the lunar new year. While the South Vietnamese were celebrating the start of the new year, the Year of the Monkey, while they were exploding firecrackers and banging drums and dancing joyously through the streets of their cities, towns, villages, and hamlets, nearly one hundred thousand Communist troops, from mostly VC units, were going to pour out of their jungle base camps and in one violent surge shoot their way into over one hundred of South Vietnam's provincial capitals, autonomous cities, district capitals, hamlets, and military installations. While the VC attacks were aimed at specific targets, Hanoi was not interested in seizing territory. The real purpose of those attacks was to so shock and demoralize the primarily ARVN units guarding these targets that they mutinied. If ARVN units started going over to the Communist side, Ho and his lieutenants reasoned, the general populace would likely follow. Both groups, they felt, were tired of the war, sick of the American presence, and disgusted with their corrupt government. All it would take to create the general uprising was the proper instigation, and one hundred thousand Vietcong armed with new AK-47 assault rifles, rocket-propelled grenades, recoilless rifles, mortars, artillery, and rockets were going to provide it.

In early February, right on the heels of Tet, the Communist planned to launch phase three of their offensive. This final phase would open and close at Khe Sanh. There with three or four infantry divisions and a division of combat support troops, Giap planned on overrunning Khe Sanh and killing or capturing every Marine on it.

A number of historians and commentators have claimed over the years that Khe Sanh, like the border battles, was a feint by Giap to draw American troops to the border prior to the Tet attacks. It was a feint, they say, and Westmoreland foolishly went for it. Few of the many who accept this theory offer any solid proof to back it up. Most simply accept Giap's contention that Khe Sanh was a feint and nothing more.

If one chooses not to accept Giap at his word, there is much more evidence to support the theory that Khe Sanh, rather than being a feint, was actually meant to be phase three of the Winter-Spring Offensive. First, there is the paper evidence. Months prior to the start of the border battles, Allied units, in different parts of the country, began capturing enemy documents that specifically referred to a "general uprising," to be followed by a final climactic battle, a battle like Dien Bien Phu. Supporting this paper evidence are the words of a number of captured NVA and VC who spoke freely of the coming "general uprising" and final battle. Most of those detainees admitted to being ignorant of the target of this final battle, but a number surprisingly said it was to be Khe Sanh.

Adding further weight to this theory are the actions of Giap himself, actions that fly in the face of his public statements. If Khe Sanh was truly a feint, then why did Giap surround the base with dozens of heavy antiaircraft batteries and more dozens of artillery pieces, mortars, and rocket launchers? If only a feint, why did he exhaust his logistics system stockpiling thousands of tons of munitions in the caves and valley around Khe Sanh? If only a feint, why did he assemble nearly forty thousand combat troops within easy striking distance of the base? As Davidson so astutely points out, "No general uses 40,000 troops to divert 6,000," and especially not forty thousand who were badly needed at Hue and Quang Tri during the Tet attacks.

If not a feint, then what were Giap's intentions at Khe Sanh? Doug Pike claims that the only "logical conclusion" that can be drawn from Giap's heavy commitment of men and materiel at Khe Sanh was that he intended on turning Khe Sanh into another Dien Bien Phu. Along with the leadership in Hanoi, Pike says, Giap reasoned that the fall of the Marine base and the loss of the six thousand Marines defending it would send a shock wave through the United States, just as the loss of Dien Bien Phu had sent a shock wave through France. France lost the war at Dien Bien Phu not because her military had been decisively defeated in Indochina, for it had not been. The garrison at Dien Bien Phu represented only a small percentage of the French forces in Indochina. France lost the war at Dien Bien Phu because after the battle, the French leaders and the French people decided that they could not win the war no matter how long they fought or how many lives they sacrificed, and a political solution was the best they could hope for. Dien Bien Phu had a profound effect on Hanoi's thinking, and played a critical role in the making of the Winter-Spring Offensive. From that battle, they had learned that a Western nation could be defeated without being defeated on the battlefield.

Giap opened phase one of his Winter-Spring Offensive at Con Thien, one of Westmoreland's six strongpoints along the demilitarized zone. Once called the Hill of Angels by missionaries before the war, the low hill was now the home of a battalion of U.S. Marines. In early September, Giap focused every artillery piece available to him in the hills and mountains north of Con Thien and began an around-the-clock bombardment of the base. His 85mm, 100mm, 122mm, 130mm, even his long-range 152mm guns focused their sights on Con Thien and began pouring rounds into it. Two hundred rounds hit the base the first day, then another two hundred the second, then over four hundred the third. September 25 was the worst. On that day, nearly twelve hundred rounds smashed into the base, collapsing bunkers and killing and wounding dozens of Marines. To add to the Marines' misery, monsoon rains arrived at the end of September, a month ahead of schedule, and the red soil of Con Thien quickly turned into a bog of knee-deep mud.

The Marine and Army gunners in the area answered the enemy bombardment with an average six thousand rounds per day, and guns from the Seventh Fleet's cruisers and destroyers added another three thousand rounds a day to the counterbattery fire. Overhead, Marine jet bombers loaded with napalm and high explosives ranged up and down the DMZ in search of enemy gun positions. The shelling, however, only continued. And so did the rain. After a week of both, Con Thien was a crazy patchwork of mud, water-filled shell craters, dud rounds, and collapsed bunkers.

While the shelling continued into the second week, North Vietnamese infantry units were detected slowly advancing on the base, digging trenches and bunkers to protect their advance. Two Marine battalions were flown in to meet them, and for the next week there were a number of sharp, bloody battles in the rolling hills around Con Thien.

Right behind the two Marine battalions came a flood of newsmen, most of whom realized that one of the biggest stories of the war was unfolding at Con Thien. In the hollow-eyed and shell-shocked Marines at Con Thien, they found great material. Within days of their arrival, young Marines were being quoted in newspapers around the country questioning the value of the base and likening themselves to cannon fodder. "President Johnson must like to see Marines get killed," one young Marine bitterly remarked. Others began making comparisons between their own predicament and the beleaguered French garrison at Dien Bien Phu. Was Con Thien to be another Dien Bien Phu, the press was soon asking in foreboding tones.

Westmoreland bristled at the quotes from the young Marines and laughed at the Dien Bien Phu comparison. Con Thien was no Dien Bien Phu and would never be, he told reporters. To prove his point, he drew up Operation Neutralize, a detailed plan to break the enemy siege of the base. Marshaling the entire spectrum of firepower at his disposal—B-52s, tactical air, artillery, and naval gunfire—he directed it at an area about the size of Manhattan. Day and night for the forty-nine days the operation lasted, the ground around Con Thien shook from thundering explosions. The B-52 was Westmoreland's most effective weapon against the besieging enemy forces. Each bomber carried sixty thousand pounds of bombs, and three flying in unison could devastate an area one kilometer by three kilometers. During September alone, his B-52 crews flew over eight hundred sorties over Con Thien and dropped nearly forty thousand tons of high explosives. Adding to the deluge was Marine artillery, which fired 12,577 rounds at enemy popsitions; the Seventh Fleet, which fired 6,148 rounds; and Marine and Air Force fighter pilots, who flew an additional five thousand close-air support missions and dropped another ten thousand tons of bombs. Stunned by the deluge, in mid-October, the North Vietnamese units around Con Thien began breaking off the siege and fleeing to safety north across the DMZ. Observers flying over Con Thien after the battle were stunned by what they saw. For miles in three directions was an apocalyptic landscape of shredded tree trunks and swimming-pool-size bomb craters. That landscape was also the graveyard for over two thousand soldiers.

Westmoreland was happy with the victory at Con Thien, but he was much happier over what he had proved during the battle: that air power alone could break an enemy siege. Unable to resist crowing over that fact, he openly mocked those who had dared compare Con Thien with Dien Bien Phu. Con Thien was indeed a Dien Bien Phu, he announced to the press, "a Dien Bien Phu in reverse."

Giap was undaunted by his losses at Con Thien. While his units there were still withdrawing back across the DMZ, he turned his attention farther south to Song Be, the capital of Phuoc Long Province. On October 27, he sent a full NVA regiment against the town and its ARVN defenders. Giap's intentions at Song Be were unclear, but the ARVN response was not. Although outnumbered four to one, they put up a tenacious defense, repulsing three separate assaults. Following the third assault, many of the ARVN defenders rushed out of their perimeter and charged the retreating NVA, shooting many of them in the back and chasing the rest deep into the jungle. The North Vietnamese left over 150 dead on the battlefield, the ARVN only 13.

Again undaunted, two days later Giap ordered yet another big ground assault against the Cambodian border town of Loc Ninh, this time by a Vietnam regiment. Awaiting the VC regiment was an ARVN battalion and two battalions from the U.S. 1st Infantry Division which had been hurriedly flown in only a few hours before. In the six major engagements that followed, the VC lost 852 men killed against 50 American and ARVN dead. In one assault, the VC lost 263 men in less than an hour. The defending United States battalion had only 1 KIA.

Westmoreland flew into Loc Ninh after the battle to savor the victory and to pass out medals. What made the victory really satisfying for him was that the ARVN had again fought well. When not a single newspaper reported the ARVN bravery at Song Be and Loc Ninh, however, he decided to hold a news conference in order to set the record straight. Unfortunately, right before the news conference, he discovered that during the Loc Ninh fight some ARVN soldiers had looted a village. Fearing that reporters would likely play up the looting and downplay the ARVN heroics, he canceled the news conference.

Song Be and Loc Ninh had been comparatively easy battles for the Allies. The next battle Giap forced on them would not be. Having fought one battle along the DMZ in I Corps and two in III Corps, Giap shifted his focus this time to the Central Highlands in II Corps. His specific target this time was the Special Forces camp at Dak To. His plan was to attack the camp with three regiments, with a fourth in reserve. When Westmoreland responded, as Giap was certain he would, by bringing in reinforcements, those reinforcements would then become the target. His orders to his senior commanders were very specific. They were to "annihilate a major U.S. element . . ."

Although Giap had been preparing for the Dak To fight for weeks, Westmoreland did not get wind of it until November 2. On that day, a North Vietnamese deserter from the 66th Regiment, one of the units earmarked to attack Dak To, turned himself in at an ARVN outpost near Dak To. Under interrogation, he revealed Giap's plan for Dak To.

There were some in MACV intelligence who did not believe the NVA deserter was telling the truth. Westmoreland did. If Giap wanted a fight at Dak To, he would give him one. To counter the three enemy regiments on their way there, he ordered sixteen thousand men from the 4th Infantry Division, the 173rd Airborne Brigade, the 1st Cavalry Division, and the ARVN Division to move to Dak To immediately.

Finding their path to Dak To blocked, the enemy regiments wheeled south and retreated into the surrounding mountains. There, in positions that had been prepared six months before, they hunkered down and awaited the Allied units. After consulting with his senior commanders at Dak To, Westmoreland ordered them to find and destroy the enemy units. They soon found them. They had taken up positions on nine different hills. They were dug in deep and they had enough ammunition, food, and water on hand for a long fight. To soften up the hills before the assaults, Westmoreland turned his B-52s loose again, then his tactical air, and finally his artillery. As at Con Thien, Westmoreland's expenditure of munitions was again staggering. The Air Force executed nearly three thousand sorties and the artillery batteries at Dak To fired over 170,000 rounds.

Right behind this massive prep fire, United States and ARVN infantry companies went on the attack. What followed was some of the toughest and bloodiest fighting of the war. With rifles, machine guns, grenades, satchel charges, and flamethrowers, Allied soldiers fought their way up the side of one hill after another. After twenty-two days of continuous fighting, the last hill—Hill 875—fell on November 23.

On paper at least, Dak To was another major defeat for Giap. Over 1,200 of his best troops lay buried in mass graves and collapsed bunkers in the hills above Dak To, and another 3,000 or 4,000 wounded had either walked or been carried to jungle hospitals in nearby Laos. In addition, all three of the regiments he had sent into battle were no longer operational and would not be available for the coming Tet attacks.

Giap was not bothered by the horrendous casualties he suffered during the border battle. "Every minute, hundreds of thousands of people die all over the world," he once told a friend. "The life or death of a hundred, a thousand, or tens of thousands of human beings, even if they are our compatriots, represents very little." He did not judge the success or failure of a battle in terms of the casualties he suffered, but only in terms of what that battle accomplished. Although he would certainly have been happy to have won the border battles, winning had not been his primary reason for initiating them. His reason for sending thousands of troops to their deaths at Con Thien, Song Be, Loc Ninh, and Dak To had been to get Westmoreland to turn his attention to the border area and commit massive numbers of additional troops there, troops who would then be unavailable when the Tet attacks began.

Although a number of histories of the war have it otherwise, Giap actually failed to get Westmoreland to commit large numbers of additional troops to the borders. While he did fly in reinforcements to meet the threats at Song Be, Loc Ninh, and Dak To, after the battles he quickly redeployed those troops back to his mobile reserve. With his border attacks, however, Giap was successful in getting Westmoreland to turn his attention to the border areas, to become permanently fixated on them, in spite of mounting evidence indicating that Giap's next major attack—an attack that would be one hundred times greater in scope and ferocity than the border battles—was aimed not at the dozens of Allied camps and strongpoints strung out along South Vietnam's northern and western borders but at South Vietnam's cities, towns, and military installations in the lowlands.

After Dak To, Westmoreland announced to the press that the enemy had "been soundly defeated." Most agreed. How soundly, however, was debatable. During the fight for Hill 875, one United States battalion had been nearly annihilated after being mousetrapped by two NVA battalions, and another American battalion had been badly shot up coming to the first's rescue. Together they had had 158 killed and over 400 wounded. When they added these figures to those of the casualties suffered taking the other eight hills—204 killed and 600 wounded—not everyone agreed with Westmoreland's assessment. One who certainly did not was Brigadier General John Chaisson, the head of Westmoreland's combat operations center. "It's been debated how great a victory it was," he said in an interview after the war. "I've even had guys in my office ask if it was a victory. 'Is it a victory when you lose 362 friendlies in three weeks and by your own spurious body count you get only 1,200?' "

While Chaisson decided not to express his misgivings about Dak

To to Westmoreland, a number of newsmen felt no such constraint. Their headlines—GIS TRAPPED ON HILLSIDE, WOUNDED PARATROOPERS SUFFER FROM EXPOSURE, TEN RESCUE HELICOPTERS SHOT DOWN, SECOND MOST COSTLY BATTLE OF WAR—were an open challenge to Westmoreland's contention that Dak To had been a decisive victory. Editorialists quickly added their own misgivings. Writing in *The Washington Post*, Lee Lescage noted that while Dak To had been an Allied victory, it was a meaningless one. Nothing of permanence had been gained, he wrote. Although the enemy had certainly suffered grievous casualties, he could easily return to his hill positions once the Allies pulled most of their forces out of the Dak To area.

Westmoreland was furious at the press response to Dak To. In a cable to Abrams, he referred to the coverage of the battle as "distorted" and said that he wanted him to make "an all-out effort to get the Saigon press to put this action at Dak To into the proper context, refuting, if refutation is appropriate, that units have been surrounded and slaughtered." On visiting Hill 875, however, Abrams discovered that it was impossible to put together the "refutation" Westmoreland wanted. Everything written about the two United States battalions there had been true. One battalion had indeed been trapped on the hill for two days, a number of paratroopers had suffered exposure from the cold, and ten helicopters had been shot down trying unsuccessfully to bring in food, water, and ammunition and to take out the wounded. Hill 875 had, in fact, been just what the press reported—an American battlefield disaster.

Westmoreland remained upset with the reports of the battle, nonetheless. Even if the stories about the hill fight were true, he believed the press should not have reported them. He felt graphic stories of United States battlefield failures exposed American weaknesses to the enemy, lowered the morale of troops in the field, and demoralized their families. Early in the war, following some graphic accounts of another battle, an incensed Westmoreland had tried to get Washington to impose some type of censorship of the press in Vietnam; but the State Department, out of fear of possible domestic and international repercussions, had recommended that the President veto the idea, which Johnson subsequently did. As a result of that veto, Westmoreland had been forced to attempt to coexist with the press, a press, that in his view, had become overly prying, contentious, and eager to dig up conflict and controversy.

According to Major General Spurgeon H. Neel, who lived at Westmoreland's villa for a year, it was not a very comfortable coexistence. The press, Neel says, represented an alien element to West-moreland, an element that he did not understand and "couldn't control." As a military man, Westmoreland by his very nature wanted absolute control over everything and everyone around him, and that included the press. If he had been commanding an army in World War II, he would have had that kind of control. But in Vietnam, the parameters, the rules governing the relationship of commanders and the press had been radically altered. Now there were very few rules governing that relationship, and reporters more or less had carte blanche to write anything they wanted provided they did not reveal military secrets to the enemy. This new relationship made West-moreland very uncomfortable. He simply could not acclimate himself to a situation where he, a highly decorated four-star general, was subject to the whim of any of the hundreds of reporters running around freely in South Vietnam.

Although he would have rather spent all his time dealing strictly with the war, as Westmoreland's tenure in Vietnam lengthened so too did the time he had to spend dealing with the press. At least once or twice a week, he and Wheeler exchanged cables attempting to figure out how to respond to a particular controversial press report. A lot of Westmoreland's cable traffic to Marine headquarters in both Vietnam and Hawaii and with his corps and divisional commanders likewise dealt with press problems. Historians can argue about whether the press had any impact on the ultimate outcome of the Vietnam War, but there is no arguing that it had a definite impact on Westmoreland's daily life as COMUSMACV.

Switching on the Light

I f Westmoreland disliked having to deal with the press in Vietnam, he hated having to face their counterparts in Washington. In spite of that fact, in early November President Johnson once again ordered him to return to Washington. Johnson publicly announced that he was bringing Westmoreland home for a high-level discussion on how to achieve maximum progress during the next six months, but it was obvious to anyone with an active interest in the war that the general was once again being forced to walk point for a massive public relations campaign.

Westmoreland again resented the order, just as he had in April the first time Johnson brought him home. Turning him into a salesman and forcing him to "court" the press, he felt, not only demeaned him and the uniform he wore, but encouraged the press to adopt a cynical, suspicious attitude. That attitude, as he had discovered following his April trip home, could quickly turn "vindictive."

Just as he had feared, at the first announcement of the trip, the press instantly responded, and the response was by far negative. In *The Washington Post*, columnist Joseph Kraft took the President to task for attempting to dupe the American people as to the real reason for Westmoreland's trip home. The general was coming home, he wrote, for one reason and one reason only, to shore up sagging support for the war. "The general would arrive with a message of great progress," Kraft wrote mockingly, "expressed in numbers of enemy dead, weapons captured and peasants recently brought under government control." Just as mocking was James Reston. Writing in *The New York Times*, he referred to Westmoreland as one of Johnson's "big guns" in the home front war to smash critics of the war. Johnson, Reston wrote, had already laid the groundwork for Westmoreland's return, with a minioffensive against doubters and critics inside the administration. "The doubters in the cabinet and sub-cabinet have shut up at dinner parties. . . . In fact, there is no longer any debate, let alone dissent, within the administration . . . only closed ranks and closed minds to any thing but the official line."

Westmoreland's planned return also gave sudden credence to a number of rumors that had been floating about Washington for the last six months. In his syndicated column, Drew Pearson claimed that McNamara was extremely unhappy with the way Westmoreland was running the war and that there was a deep fracture in their relationship. Agreeing with Pearson was Democratic Senator Stephen Young of Ohio. On the floor of the Senate, he claimed that "Westmoreland was not McNamara's golden boy anymore," and before the year was out the secretary would likely replace the general. Looking at the Westmoreland-McNamara relationship from another angle, John Angleton speculated in the *Washington Star* that Westmoreland was equally unhappy with McNamara's handling of the war, so unhappy, in fact, that Westmoreland was seriously considering running for the presidency. Giving impetus to that speculation, the South Carolina General Assembly passed a resolution "to prevail" upon Westmoreland "to enter the presidential race."

In separate news conferences, both Westmoreland and McNamara denied there was any friction between them. McNamara was the more passionate in his denial. "The allegation that there is disillusionment over Westmoreland's handling of the war is false," he told reporters. "Such false statements do a grave disservice to one of the great military commanders of this century and to all men who serve under him. Westmoreland has the absolute confidence of the president and the JCS. There is no truth to the suggestion that he may soon be relieved." McNamara's statement put Westmoreland at ease, and Westmoreland attempted to do the same for President Johnson. On hearing that a nervous Johnson wanted to know if he indeed had presidential ambitions, Westmoreland held a news conference and categorically denied having "any political ambitions." His denial stopped all Westmoreland-for-President speculation, but reports about a Westmoreland-McNamara feud continued appearing in newspapers and magazines for weeks afterward.

Westmoreland left for the United States on November 14. His first stop was the Philippines to pick up Kitsy and Margaret; next was Hawaii for a short visit with Rip, who was a student at the Hawaii Preparatory School. On the morning of November 15, his plane set down at Andrews Air Force Base, California, for a refueling stop. Westmoreland got off the plane for a moment to meet a group of Washington newsmen. "I am very, very encouraged," he told them. "I have never been more encouraged in the four years I've been in Vietnam. We are making real progress. Everyone is encouraged."

Westmoreland's optimism was met by a wall of cynicism. Did not the battles at Loc Ninh and Dak To prove that it was the enemy who "was maintaining the initiative in Vietnam?" one reporter asked him.

"That's absolutely inaccurate," he snapped. "We've beat them at every punch. We've thwarted them at every turn."

The next morning, Westmoreland briefed a closed session of the House Armed Services Committee. Asked by two committee members how long he thought the war was going to continue, he said he thought that if the present progress continued in Vietnam, the United States could begin a "phaseout of U.S. troops in two years or less." Seeing that it was a closed session, Westmoreland thought his prediction would be held in strict confidentiality. To his dismay, after the meeting, one of the committee members, Richard Icord of Missouri, held a press conference and told reporters of Westmoreland's prediction. It was the first time Westmoreland, normally the most cautious of men when it came to making predictions, had put a target date on American troop withdrawals, and to the general's great embarrassment, reporters stampeded to their phones with the news.

Four days later, Westmoreland delivered his major speech of the trip to the annual meeting of the National Press Club in Washington. All in attendance were eager to hear him elaborate on his prediction. He told them that when he had taken over as COMUSMACV, he had divided the war into four distinct phases, each to represent a stage of United States participation. In phase one, now completed, the United States had rescued the South Vietnamese government and started a buildup. In phase two, the buildup had been completed and a counterattack had begun. Now, he said, phase two was over, and it was time to move into phase three, during which the South Vietnamese were to take over more and more of the fighting, including a major share of the defense of the demilitarized zone. In phase four, the final mopping up of a defeated enemy would begin, and so also would an American troop withdrawal.

"We have reached an important point," he concluded, "when the end begins to come into view."

When asked during the question period if it was true, as he had said during his appearance before the House Armed Services Committee, that the United States could begin withdrawing troops in only two years.

"Yes, that is true," he said.

"In view of Secretary McNamara's ill-founded optimism of a couple of years ago," the questioner continued, "aren't you uncomfortable when you say we may be able to withdraw troops from Vietnam in a couple of years?"

"My statement," he responded, "is to the effect that it is conceivable to me that within two years or less, it will be possible for us to phase down our level of commitment and turn over more of the burden of the war to the South Vietnamese Armed forces. . . . Now I make the point that at the outset this may be token, but hopefully progressive, and certainly we are preparing our plans to make it progressive."

Westmoreland's comments to the National Press Club received prominent and wide display in the press. His statement "We have reached an important point when the end begins to come into view" received the most display. This single line became the focus of hundreds of newspaper and magazine articles, commentaries, and editorials around the country. As Don Oberdorfer notes in his book *Tet*, by uttering those fourteen words—fourteen words the public had been longing to hear for the last three years—"Westmoreland had switched on the light at the end of the tunnel."

Westmoreland would to his dismay discover that he had switched it on at the most inopportune moment. His prediction of an American troop withdrawal and the beginning of what would come to be called Vietnamization would prove to be uncannily true. In less than twenty months, four months sooner than he had predicted, the first United States troops would begin to depart Vietnam, and the South Vietnamese would assume the greater burden of the fighting. In the coming fury of the Tet Offensive, however, few would remember his prediction in the context it was uttered. Few, in fact, would remember anything about his National Press Club speech, except those fourteen words. Taken out of context and against the backdrop of Tet, those words would, to many, suddenly seem as foolishly optimistic as McNamara's 1963 pronouncement that the "war will be over by 1965."

Following his National Press Club speech, Westmoreland went to the White House for a family dinner. Later that evening, the President asked the general to join him in the family living room for a private conversation. Once they were seated opposite each other, Johnson suddenly became very serious. "What would my men in Vietnam think," he asked Westmoreland, "if I failed to run for re-election in 1968? Would they consider that their commander in chief had let them down?"

Westmoreland was stunned by the question. He had not been prepared for it. Catching his breath, he told Johnson that if the troops knew the reason he had made such a decision, they would surely understand.

Johnson proceeded to give that reason. The reason was his health, he said somberly. He had had a heart attack. He was tired. He had carried a heavy, heavy burden for a long time, and he did not think his body could take anymore. He talked of Roosevelt's paralysis in office and of Woodrow Wilson's incapacitating stroke and revealed that he agonized over the possibility that he might also become incapacitated while in office. Since the Constitution made no provision for an invalided President, he feared the welfare of the country would suffer if he became seriously ill. He had already discussed all this with Lady Bird and his two daughters, he said, and all three wanted him to retire.

No, Westmoreland said again, if the troops in Vietnam knew the reason, they would not be shocked or demoralized. Nor would they think their President had deserted them.

Johnson sat quietly for a moment, as if to mull over Westmoreland's reply. He was apparently satisfied with it, for he now turned the conversation in another direction. McNamara was quitting as secretary of defense, he announced, to take another job—a "big job." What did he think of Clark Clifford as McNamara's replacement? He personally thought that Clifford, "a strong man," would make a good secretary. What did he think?

Westmoreland replied that he did not know Clifford, but in any case, it was not a question that he, an Army commander, should be answering.

As Blair Clark notes: "Probably no field commander in our history had ever been presented such an opportunity to influence American politics as Westmoreland had at the moment," and proper soldier that he was he had turned it down cold. "Would it be possible," asks Clark, "to imagine Douglas MacArthur passing up a similar chance to get his hands on America's destiny?"

The conversation ended there. Before Westmoreland left, the President tactfully let him know that the subject was "sensitive," and he was not to say anything about their conversation until after it was announced publicly. Johnson, as he surely knew, need not have requested secrecy from the always closemouthed Westmoreland. Still, as Westmoreland noted later, it was not an easy secret to be a party to. "No secret I have ever kept," he told Brigadier General S. L. A. Marshall after the war, "has been a greater strain on me, if only because what I have known all along was at odds with the way history was being written."

Westmoreland returned to Vietnam on November 29. On landing at Ton Son Nhut, he was greeted by a large contingent of the Saigon press corps. They had all heard a rumor that McNamara was about to resign and wanted to know if it was true.

"All I know is what I read in the newspapers," Westmoreland said. "I gather what you're referring to is a speculative report. I have no knowledge other than that."

If it was true that McNamara had resigned, a reporter asked, "how would that affect the war effort?"

"Not in any way," Westmoreland said. "However, I will say that I will be sorry if Mr. McNamara does resign. I think he's made an outstanding Secretary of Defense. I don't believe any Defense Secretary in our history has performed with greater distinction than Mr. McNamara."

Westmoreland was, of course, being kind. Like the Joint Chiefs, he had been in sharp disagreement with McNamara's limited-war strategy since 1965, and like them also was elated to see the secretary go. He was equally elated to see him replaced by Clark Clifford. With his appointment, Westmoreland felt that the military finally had a secretary of defense who shared their views on the war, a secretary who just might be willing to make the hard decisions and take the decisive actions that McNamara had shied away from. If perchance Clifford was not willing to take some stronger actions in Vietnam, then perhaps a new administration in Washington would.

There were a number of actions Westmoreland wanted to see

taken, including an invasion of North Vietnam above the demilitarized zone, an attack on the North Vietnamese forces controlling the A Shau Valley, and an invasion of Laos designed to cut the Ho Chi Minh Trail. Of the three, however, he was most concerned with obtaining permission for the latter. The Ho Chi Minh Trail had long been a thorn in his side, and with winds of change blowing in Washington, he saw an opportunity to finally remove it. During the last three years, he had overseen work on a number of plans to invade Laos. In mid-December, he had his operations staff work up yet another. It was called Operation El Paso, and in early January he sent an outline of the operation's plan and intent to Admiral Sharp. Included was a proviso explaining his increasing concern with the Ho Chi Minh Trail. "As you know," he told the admiral, "the enemy has modernized and increased the firepower of his forces in South Vietnam and the border area. This in turn has increased his logistic requirements, which in the main have been flowing through Laos. The great increase of truck traffic during the past few months indicates his attempt to provide the munitions for present stepped up opertions." Whatever the intent of those present operations, he was convinced, he told Sharp, that it was time "to deploy forces in Laos and to cut off the enemy's access to the South."

Sharp immediately responded to Westmoreland's cable with one of his own. He began by admitting to seeing some merits in El Paso. Defeating a "major NVA force in one of their sanctuaries would provide friendly forces with a major psychological victory and demonstrate to NVA the futility of continued support of the war in the South." But he also saw some negatives in the operation, and felt he had to bring them to Westmoreland's attention. There were the political problems of invading and then occupying another country; the huge logistical problem of trying to fight deep in enemy-held territory; and the problem of casualties. Such an ambitious scheme was bound to produce "abnormally high casualties," and those casualties could and would be exploited by North Vietnam for a "major propaganda victory."

Westmoreland was unfazed by Sharp's objection. He was interested in action. He was tired of allowing the enemy sanctuaries in nearby Laos and Cambodia, and equally tired of having to sit by helplessly while that same enemy moved his troops and supplies south with almost total impunity. In his return cable, Westmoreland ignored Sharp's objections, and instead devoted six pages to a detailed outline of how he expected El Paso to unfold and what he expected it to accomplish, then requested that Sharp convince Washington to give him the go-ahead. If they did, he was convinced he could cut the Ho Chi Minh Trail.

Although he did not mention it to Sharp, he hoped the enemy would attempt to contest an Allied attempt to cut the trail. For three years, he had been anxious to get at an enemy who only stood and fought when it served his purposes, an enemy who struck and then more often than not retreated to his sanctuaries in Laos and Cambodia. While Westmoreland certainly wanted badly to cut the Ho Chi Minh Trail, he wanted just as badly to force the North Vietnamese Army, with Giap at its head, to meet him head-to-head in a huge set-piece battle, to fight him on his terms and on a battlefield of his choosing, not theirs. Unless the leadership in Hanoi was willing to give up their lifeline to the South, he reasoned, they would have to fight for the trail. And they would have to fight for it with main-force units, with regiments and divisions and with tanks and heavy weapons. When they did, when they marched out in force from their jungle base camps and bivouacs, his best divisions would be waiting for them, backed by the full weight of his military machine.

It was one of the great ironies of the war that while Westmoreland was trying to get clearance from Washington to invade Laos and provoke a World War II-type set-piece battle, the Communists were in the final stages of preparation for just such a battle; that while he was looking northwest to the Bolovens Plateau, to Saravane, Savannakhet and Tchepone—all potential spots in Laos for that showdown fight—Communist forces were already on the march south and southwest to their own showdown fight at Saigon, Hue, Ben Tre, Nha Trang, and five dozen other cities and towns.

The father, Rip Westmoreland *(back row, far right)*, with other mill officials outside Pacolet Mills, South Carolina, circa 1916

In the uniform of a World War I doughboy, three-year-old William Westmoreland snaps a salute.

Westmoreland striking a pose following his return from a summer touring Europe

William and his sister,
Margaret, in Hawaii before
World War II

MARGARET CLARKSON

The "prototype" military man at
The Citadel

MARGARET CLARKSON

Colonel Westmoreland in
England just prior to the
Normandy invasion

LEON R. BIRUM

The Westmorelands on their wedding day,
May 3, 1947

MARGARET CLARKSON

Kitsy and Westmoreland with his mentor, General Maxwell Taylor,
February 1958

Ho Chi Minh, leader of North
Vietnam

From left: Rip, Stevie, Margaret, and
Kitsy in Saigon, 1964

General Paul Harkins. Westmoreland found his excessive optimism unwarranted and embarrassing.

NATIONAL ARCHIVES

General Harold Johnson, Army Chief of Staff, and Marine Major General Bruno Mochmuth. Johnson wanted to be COMUSMACV himself. His second choice was Abrams.

NATIONAL ARCHIVES

Westmoreland meeting with Secretary of Defense Robert McNamara *(right)* and Secretary of State Dean Rusk *(center)* during their visit to Vietnam, February 6, 1966

YOICHI R. OKAMOTO/LBJ LIBRARY COLLECTION

Westmoreland and McNamara meeting with South Vietnamese officials in the spring of 1967

YOICHI R. OKAMOTO/LBJ LIBRARY COLLECTION

Westmoreland addressing Congress about the state of the Vietnam War, April 28, 1967

ARMY NEWS FEATURES

From left: Chairman of the Joint Chiefs of Staff General Earle Weaver, Westmoreland, McNamara, and Johnson meet in the White House in the summer of 1967.

KEVIN SMITH/LBJ LIBRARY COLLECTION

Two days before Christmas, 1967, Westmoreland and
President Johnson confer on the air strip at Cam Ranh Bay,
South Vietnam.

January 31, 1968, Westmoreland talks
with military personnel in the U.S.
Embassy after the unsuccessful
Vietcong sapper attack on it.

Westmoreland and Ambassador
Bunker meet General Wheeler upon
his arrival for a post-Tet inspection
tour. Westmoreland found him to be a
"tired man, seemingly near the point of
exhaustion."

Four months before assuming command of the
Vietnam forces, General Abrams meets with Johnson in
March 1968.

Westmoreland, Kitsy, President Johnson, and Lady
Bird moving across the White House lawn. The next
morning, July 3, 1968, Westmoreland was sworn in as
Army Chief of Staff.

Kitsy and
Westmoreland cele-
brating his swearing-in
as Army Chief of Staff

Westmoreland and Kitsy casting their ballots during the South Carolina Republican governor's primary, April 2, 1974

POST AND COURIER

Retired General Westmoreland carries a POW/MIA flag given to him during a parade for Vietnam veterans in Chicago. Parade organizer Tom Stack *(right)* walks behind legless Vietnam veteran Bob Wieland.

AP/WIDE WORLD PHOTOS

The fall of Westmoreland

A number of editorial cartoonists used the image of the evacuation helicopter to express their feelings about the trial's ending.

GLOBE NEWSPAPER COMPANY

Battling the Marines

After the Tet attacks, a MACV intelligence officer concluded, "If we'd gotten the whole battle plan, it wouldn't have been believed. It just wouldn't have been credible to us." His was a conclusion shared by Westmoreland. He likewise admitted afterward to not having given any serious thought to the possibility that the Communists might launch a synchronized nation-wide attack during Tet. The thought that Hanoi would order one hundred thousand of its best troops to launch frontal assaults into the teeth of Allied firepower just would not have seemed credible.

While in hindsight, his interpretation of Hanoi's intentions and capabilities appears the most grievous of errors, it was an error shared by many. MACV's intelligence staff, the Central Intelligence Agency (CIA), the Defense Intelligence Agency (DIA), the National Security Agency (NSA), and the White House all also had access to the signals of the impending Tet attacks. Like Westmoreland, all chose to ignore them, and for the same basic reason—they just did not think Hanoi would attempt something so grandiose and so seemingly doomed to failure.

The signals of the impending attack were many, however, and varied. One of the first the Allies received came in October when MACV analysts first noted an increase in truck sightings along the Ho Chi Minh Trail, an increase from a monthly average of 480 to 1,116. The number of sightings increased dramatically again in November to 3,823 and then again in December to 6,150. When apprised of the first big jump in October, Westmoreland concluded, and the CIA concurred, that the increased logistical activity demonstrated that the Communists were simply generating the materiel requirements necessary to meet increased nationwide combat activity. When MACV analysts pointed to a similar dramatic rise in the number of fresh troops moving south down the trail, Westmoreland concluded, and the CIA again concurred, that the troops were simply replacements for NVA and VC units that had suffered heavy losses during the preceding six months. When many of these replacements were tracked heading into northern I Corps, Westmoreland simply saw it as further evidence to bolster his long-held conviction that I Corps would eventually be the target of a massive enemy offensive.

Simultaneous with the truck and troop sightings, MACV analysts began accumulating a variety of paper clues, which also indicated a significant shift in enemy planning. On November 25, for instance, an element from the 1st Infantry Division captured a young enemy soldier's diary. Included in the diary were two pages devoted exclusively to an attack plan. The plan was very specific, stating that the "Central Headquarters concludes that the time has come for direct revolution and that the opportunity for a general uprising and revolution is within reach." The fighters who were to provoke that uprising and revolution were encouraged to "use very strong attacks" against the cities and towns of the lowland, and especially against Saigon. To give those attacks an extra boost, the fighters were encouraged to provoke and encourage both the populace and ARVN units to change sides and help create the general uprising.

It was all there in the soldier's diary, the entire plan of attack in a nutshell, but no one believed it to be legitimate. Westmoreland went over the diary with his intelligence people, and together they agreed that the words were only Communist propaganda. They were not alone in their belief. Although MACV released portions of the diary to the press, they likewise read it as propaganda.

By mid-December, however, so many similar items had been captured—so many attack plans and documents that referred to the general offensive and uprising—that Westmoreland was forced to conclude that something big was under way, that the enemy was preparing in earnest to launch a major attack somewhere. In spite of captured attack plans and documents, he did not think that attack would be aimed at the lowlands. He saw all the enemy documents as an elaborate smokescreen, thrown up by the Communists to hide their real intentions. If there were attacks in the lowlands, he felt, they would be small in number and strictly diversionary. To him it just did not make sense for the enemy to launch attacks against populated areas where his forces were extremely weak when he could launch attacks from Laos or the demilitarized zone, where he could quickly and easily mass large numbers of troops and massive artillery support.

And that is exactly what he told Wheeler in a cable on December 20. To support this contention, he then provided the Army Chief with what he thought was the enemy's rationale for the coming offensive. That rationale was desperation. The enemy was hurting and hurting badly, he wrote. During the last year he had taken very heavy losses, losses he could no longer replace. His coastal units had been badly mauled, his main-force units had been driven to the borders, and over a million people he had once depended on for food, taxes, and troop levies were now living in government-controlled areas. Adding to the enemy's grief was the recent election of Thieu as president and Ky as vice president. That election promised government stability, something Westmoreland felt was as damaging to Hanoi's goals as the loss of large numbers of troops.

"The enemy has decided," he went on, "that prolongation of his past policies for conducting the war will lead to his defeat, and that he will have to make a major effort to reverse this downward trend." He had concluded that the only way the Communists could reverse that trend was by winning some "significant military victory." With that victory under their belt, they would then likely seek to initiate negotiations with the Allies. He had also concluded that if the Communists failed to achieve that victory, they would not attempt to negotiate, since they "never negotiate from weakness."

He made clear finally that he hoped the Allies would not fall for any Hanoi negotiating ploy, since the Communists never negotiate in good faith and only use negotiations to attempt to gain objectives they "cannot win on the battlefield." And as far as he was concerned, he was going to do everything in his power to make certain they did not get a big battlefield victory anywhere in Vietnam.

To guarantee they did not, he wanted to strike them before they struck, to launch, at least for the moment, a series of battalion- and brigade-size raids into two enemy base areas in Laos, areas that provided the NVA forces in I Corps with many of their supplies. The raid, of course, was only a first step, a prelude to the launching of Operation El Paso against the most important target of all—the Ho Chi Minh Trail.

Wheeler attempted to get clearance from President Johnson to launch the raid into Laos, but Johnson, as he already had a dozen times before, rejected the idea. He still was not ready to take the risk necessary to expand the war.

A few days after getting Westmoreland's appraisal of enemy intentions, Wheeler gave a speech before the Detroit Economic Club and repeated the general's contention that the enemy was near desperation. Nonetheless, he told the assembled businessmen and civic leaders, "there is still some heavy fighting ahead—it is entirely possible that there may be a communist thrust similar to the desperate effort of the Germans in the Battle of the Bulge."

President Johnson apparently also liked the desperation theme. During a speech to the Australian cabinet presented four days before Christmas, he said that the North Vietnamese were under severe pressure and would soon employ "kamikaze" attacks in an attempt to gain victory. Johnson had also come to fully accept Westmoreland's contention that those desperation attacks would be aimed at I Corps.

Westmoreland might have been convinced an enemy attack was coming in I Corps, but until early January he had no solid proof to back up his belief. On January 2, he got that proof. On the morning of that day, as the mist was just beginning to burn off, six men in Marine uniforms were spotted moving around outside the Khe Sanh perimeter. When asked by guards to identify themselves, the six took off running. Rifle fire brought down five of the six. All five died, but papers in their possession identified them all as high-ranking officers of a North Vietnamese regiment.

Westmoreland was pleased when notified of the incident. It was the best evidence he had had to date on enemy intentions in I Corps. For six top commanders of an enemy regiment to do a personal reconnaissance of the Khe Sanh to him meant Hanoi had earmarked the base as a high-priority target. It also meant that the six thousand men in that regiment had to be in the vicinity.

Westmoreland got even more important evidence to support his belief during the next two weeks when agents reported that the 324th NVA Division was located inside the DMZ only fifteen miles east of

Khe Sanh, that the 320th NVA Division had been spotted east of Khe Sanh, that the 325C NVA Division was located in the mountains northwest of the base, and that the 304th NVA Division had moved into a series of base camps southwest of Khe Sanh. To many in the intelligence community, this last sighting was an ominous one. An elite home-guard unit, the 304th had fought at Dien Bien Phu and so covered itself with glory there that Giap had let the division lead the triumphal march into Hanoi after the war. Its sudden appearance in the Khe Sanh area sent a shudder through CIA headquarters in Langley, Virginia. In the rush of excitement that followed, analysts dug up aerial photographs showing the Vietminh trench system around Dien Bien Phu and had copies immediately flown to Westmoreland.

Westmoreland did not see the arrival of the 304th at Khe Sanh as ominous, but as propitious. With their arrival, he no longer had to worry about trying to get the North Vietnamese Army to meet him in a set-piece battle in Laos. Instead, they were coming to him. And they were coming to him in strength, with four divisions—forty thousand men!—and untold thousands of support troops. He could not have been happier.

During the next week, he put in motion a plan to defend Khe Sanh. After a lengthy conference with Lieutenant General Robert E. Cushman, commander of the III Marine Amphibious Force, he ordered the two Marine battalions who had been holding the Marine base during the last year reinforced. Within weeks, the base's strength rose to over six thousand. As fresh troops arrived there, they began expanding the base's perimeter and reinforcing it with multiple rows of barbed wire and German razor wire. The wire was, in turn, seeded with trip flares and claymore mines. Since the Marines had been forced to deplete their reserves to reinforce the base, Westmoreland next ordered the 1st Cavalry Division and the 2nd Brigade of the 101st Airborne Division north to Thua Thien and Quang Tri Province respectively.

While the 1st and 101st were moving north, on January 9 Westmoreland got a phone call from Lieutenant General Fred Weyand, commander of the United States field force in III Corps. Weyand told him that he needed to see him about a matter of the utmost importance. The next afternoon at MACV headquarters, Weyand told his superior that he had hard evidence that showed that large numbers of enemy troops were leaving their border sanctuaries and were moving toward the populated areas of III Corps. He had become convinced, he said, that the enemy was going to attack a number of cities in III Corps, including Saigon. Because of this conclusion, he wanted to cancel a number of planned offensive operations along the border and pull his forces back to help protect Saigon. When Lieutenant General Phillip Davidson, the head of MACV intelligence, agreed with Weyand's analysis, Westmoreland gave Weyand permission to shift fifteen United States battalions back to positions around Saigon. It was a move that possibly saved Saigon from being overrun during Tet. Unfortunately, Weyand's astute analysis did not extend to the other corps areas. Just as Westmoreland was focused on I Corps, Weyand was focused on III Corps. As a result, he failed to see that what he foresaw for Saigon was going to happen throughout South Vietnam.

After his conversation with Weyand, Westmoreland turned his attention to Khe Sanh again. In spite of what the III Corps commander had told him, he was still convinced the enemy was going to launch its major attack in I Corps, and that attack would center on Khe Sanh. Any assault against Saigon, he felt, would only be diversionary.

When that assault came against Khe Sanh, he intended to be ready for it with Operation Niagara, a mighty air bombardment that he and his air deputy General William W. Momyer were drawing up. Niagara was designed to magnify by ten, possibly twenty, times the tonnage dropped on Con Thien and Dak To. To make Niagara work properly, however, Westmoreland was convinced that operational control over all air assets in I Corps, including the 1st Marine Air Wing, needed to be put under the direct control of Momyer. He felt the Marine air control system in I Corps was too inadequate to handle the massive number of fighter-bombers and B-52s that could be in the air over Khe Sanh at any given moment.

When Westmoreland cabled Lieutenant General Robert E. Cushman, the commander of III MAF of his intention of taking over Marine air, he ran into immediate resistance. In a return cable, Cushman bluntly told him that he was "unalterably opposed to any fractionalization of the Marine air-ground team." Then in a cable to CINCPAC in Honolulu, Cushman pleaded with Admiral Sharp to use his authority to stop Westmoreland from giving Momyer control of Marine air. Although a close friend of Westmoreland, Sharp was also a Navy man whose first loyalties lay with the Marines. With those loyalties uppermost in his mind, he fired a cable to Westmoreland and requested he withdraw his request.

Westmoreland bluntly refused, and in a return cable spelled out for the CINCPAC commander his reasons why.

In view of the increasing deployment of army forces and the impending major battle it had become apparent that there needs to be an immediate major change in the control of tactical air in I CTZ. Moreover, the changing situation places a demand for greater organization and control of air resources and a premium on the need for rapid decision making.

It is no longer feasible nor prudent to restrict the employment of the total tactical air resources to given areas. I feel the utmost need for a more flexible posture to shift my air effort where it can be best used in the coming battles. Consequently, I am proposing to give my deputy for air operational control of the 1st Marine Air Wing . . .

Sharp passed this information on to Cushman, but he and his air deputy, Major General Norman Anderson, were unmoved by Westmoreland's logic. In an attempt to convince them, the next day, January 19, Westmoreland flew up to Da Nang for a personal visit with III MAF. That afternoon, he met with Cushman and Anderson and both their staffs. Historically, the Marines had always controlled their own air assets, and the idea of letting an Air Force general—an outsider!—take over that job left them cold, cold and angry. Westmoreland could feel the obvious hostility, but it did not bother him. He was not interested in preserving traditions, but in getting the most efficient use of his considerable air assets, and he simply did not believe the Marines were capable of handling those assets properly. He did not tell them he doubted their competence, but he did tell them that he felt the single-manager system was the most efficient way to manage all the air assets in I Corps. And the Air Force, he said, was much better equipped to handle that job.

When Westmoreland left Da Nang he assumed the issue was settled. It was not for the Marines. Westmoreland's jet was hardly in the air when Cushman and Anderson began firing off cables to the Marine Corps Commandant in Washington, General Leonard Chapman, pleading with him, just as they had pleaded with Sharp, to stop Westmoreland. Chapman took their case right to the JCS and for the next few hours the issue was hotly debated. As could be expected, the Chief of Naval Operations, Admiral Thomas Moorer, immediately sided with the Marines, and the Air Force Chief, General John P. McConnell, with Westmoreland, with Wheeler, the Chairman, undecided. Everyone was shocked, however, when General Harold Johnson, the Army Chief, went against Westmoreland. Johnson felt Westmoreland was setting a bad precedent. The Air Force had long sought control of the Army's fleet of light transport aircraft, and he felt Westmoreland was laying the ground work for the loss of that air fleet.

In Saigon, Westmoreland seethed with anger. He was angry that the Marines had gone behind his back and angrier still that the JCS had not automatically backed him, the commander in the field. He decided then and there that if he was reversed, he was going to resign.

Having decided to take such a drastic step, he fired off a series of cables to Wheeler, spelling out in the bluntest terms why he wanted Momyer to control the air assets in I Corps. Soon after moving the 1st Cavalry Division and the 2nd Brigade of the 101st north, he told the JCS Chairman, he had gone to see Anderson at III MAF and told him in the most specific terms that it was now his job to make sure the Army units in I Corps were given the proper tactical air support. He had assumed, he wrote, that Anderson would immediately see that his order was carried out. Upon visiting the 1st Cavalry Division a week later, however, he had discovered to his shock that they not only had not been assigned a Marine air liaison officer, but had yet to be contacted by Anderson. Already concerned about efficient management of air resources in I Corps, Westmoreland said, he was convinced by this failure that he had to move immediately. If the Marines could not properly support the 1st Cavalry Division, could they be expected, he asked Wheeler, to coordinate the B-52 fleets over Khe Sanh, the Vietnamese Air Force, and on occasion even U.S. Navy aircraft? The job was simply too complicated for the Marine system, and unless Wheeler wanted the "dog's breakfast" in I Corps to continue, Momyer had to take over.

Westmoreland did not employ such graphic language in his appeals to Sharp, who as CINCPAC was his immediate superior with the power to kill the single-manager concept. Nonetheless, he made it clear to Sharp that he felt it was his prerogative as field commander in South Vietnam to employ any resource there as he saw fit.

At this point, the Joint Chiefs decided not to issue directions on the issue, leaving that decision up to Sharp. The admiral unfortunately waffled on the issue, and did not put his stamp of approval on the single-manager concept until March 8. Fortunately for Westmoreland, Sharp likewise did not disapprove of the concept, or request that Westmoreland put it on hold until a final decision was made. And so around January 18, Westmoreland officially put Momyer in charge of all air assets in I Corps, thereby presenting the Marines with a *fait accompli*. They could still complain all they wanted to Sharp and the JCS, but until Sharp said otherwise, their fighter-bombers would go wherever Momyer directed them. For the next month and a half, Anderson and General Krulak, the commander of Fleet Marine in Honolulu, kept up a steady stream of entreaties to both Sharp and the JCS arguing for a return to the traditional Marine air doctrine. The continued actions of both men rankled Westmoreland. To his aides at MACV headquarters, he frequently denigrated them as "narrow and parochial, unable to see the big picture."

Having temporarily resolved the air problem in I Corps, Westmoreland was able to turn his full attention to Khe Sanh again. There the situation was becoming more critical by the hour. In mid-January, all intelligence sources, including key agents on the ground, confirmed that two NVA divisions, the 325C and the 304th, were now definitely converging on Khe Sanh and that two others, the 324th and 320th, were moving in closer, so, it appeared, to be close enough to support the first two.

Alarmed by these moves, on January 20, Westmoreland sent his intelligence chief, Phillip Davidson, up to Khe Sanh for a firsthand appraisal of the situation there. On arriving at the Marine base, Davidson was shocked to discover what he described later as a "general lack of preparation to withstand the artillery and mortar fire" that the NVA might bring against the base. Everywhere he looked were unprotected living quarters, command posts, and fuel and ammunitions dumps.

Davidson was equally shocked when he talked with Colonel David Lownds, the base commander. In spite of what MACV considered overwhelming evidence that two, three, or possibly even four NVA divisions were closing in on the base, Lownds refused to believe it. The colonel told Davidson that he was certain that there was an enemy regiment out there in the hills beyond the Marine wire, but that was all he was certain of. Davidson spent the next thirty minutes trying to convince Lownds of the accuracy of MACV's intelligence reports, but the colonel remained skeptical.

Around noon, Davidson flew back to Saigon and briefed Westmoreland and his deputy, General Abrams. His description of Khe Sanh and of his talk with Lownds "agitated" Westmoreland. When Davidson had completed his briefing, an angry Westmoreland turned to his deputy and said that he had lost confidence in Cushman's ability to handle the increasingly complex and dangerous situation in I Corps. "Abe," he said finally, "you're going to have to go up there and take over."

"Yeah, I guess you're right," Abrams said, though he made it clear that he was not enthusiastic about the job ahead.

That afternoon, Westmoreland officially established MACV Forward, a corps headquarters with Abrams as its commander. Abrams was officially to take command of MACV Forward on February 13, 1968. He would then have authority over not only every soldier in I Corps, but over every Marine as well. Cushman, who had once reigned supreme in I Corps, would then take all his orders from Abrams.

A few days later, Westmoreland sent a cable to Wheeler and explained his rationale for establishing MACV Forward. "The military professionalism of the Marines," he wrote, "falls far short of the standards that should be demanded of our armed forces. They are brave and proud, but their standards, tactics, and lack of command supervision throughout their ranks requires improvement in the national interest . . . many lives would be saved if their tactical professionalism were enhanced."

If the Marines were upset over having Momyer take control of their air assets, they were furious over the establishment of MACV Forward. Interviewed after the war, Brigadier General Rathvon M. Tompkins, the commander of the 3rd Marine Division and Lownds's immediate superior, called Westmoreland's move "a slap in the face. The most unpardonable thing Saigon ever did."

Although the Marines were not aware of it, they could count themselves lucky that Westmoreland was COMUSMACV and not Abrams. According to Lieutenant General Bruce Palmer, the deputy commander of the United States Army in Vietnam at the time of the furor, Abrams was even angrier than Westmoreland with the Marines and wanted to take much more drastic actions to deal with them. After returning from his own fact-finding mission to Khe Sanh, Abrams wanted to "fire Lownds on the spot and make heads roll all over I Corps." Westmoreland, says Palmer, "was more diplomatic, more conciliatory, more the Christian gentleman like Robert E. Lee."

While the Marines were smarting from this second major blow to their considerable ego and while Abrams was packing to go north, Westmoreland and Momyer put the finishing touches on the plan for Operation Niagara and prepared to put it into action. On January 20, a few days after they finished, an NVA lieutenant named Lam Than Tonc gave the plan an increased importance. On that day, Tonc, angry over getting passed over for pomotion to captain, showed up outside the Khe Sanh perimeter waving a white flag and surrendered. Tonc was a gold mine of information. With a frankness that shocked his interrogators, he revealed a detailed description of a forthcoming Communist offensive against Khe Sanh and all of I Corps. The first assault of the offensive, he said, would begin that very evening when NVA troops attacked Hill 881 South, Hill 861, and Khe Sanh itself. After wiping out the hill position and crushing Khe Sanh, the enemy divisions in the area were going to sweep south and capture all of Quang Tri and Thua Thien Province. The final target was to be Hue.

Besides the NVA battlefield plans, Tonc also brought a larger message. The campaign against Khe Sanh and I Corps was designed with the specific purpose of forcing the United States to the negotiating table. Finally Tonc reported that Giap himself was personally controlling the campaign in I Corps.

Many were skeptical of Tonc's account. Westmoreland was not. He was more than ready to believe the words of the disgruntled enemy lieutenant. That very day, he cabled Washington and told them that "the enemy will soon seek victories essential to achieving prestige and bargaining power."

Tonc, it turned out, was telling the truth. As he had predicted, that evening just after midnight, NVA gunners in the surrounding hills unleashed a furious hour-long mortar and rocket barrage against Hill 861. Behind the barrage, enemy infantry, led by sappers, charged up the side of the hill, breached the Marine wire and leaped into their trenches.

At his villa in Saigon, Westmoreland spent most of the night at his radio, monitoring the hill fight. For a few anxious hours, it seemed as if the hill might have fallen to the NVA and he continually queried III MAF for updates. Then at 5:00 A.M. he was able to breathe a sigh of relief when word came that the Marines had launched a furious counterattack, and, with grenades, rifles, bayonets, and entrenching tools, retaken their trench line. More good news followed from Hill 881 South. The NVA battalion earmarked to attack the hill had been smashed by an artillery barrage while it was still in its assault positions.

This good news was quickly overshadowed by events at the main base. At 5:30 A.M. enemy gunners hidden in the caves and rocky crevices of Hill 881 North unleashed a thirty-minute rocket barrage on the base. One rocket impacted in the center of Khe Sanh's ammunition dump, detonating fifteen hundred tons of mortar and artillery rounds. The explosions and shock waves that followed collapsed buildings and tents for a hundred meters in all directions. Helicopters were blown off their skids and sent tumbling end over end across the base like toys. Barrels of aviation fuel ignited and sent a river of flames into the ammo dump, setting off even more explosions.

While the ammunition dump was exploding, seven miles to the

southwest, an NVA infantry company attacked and overran Khe Sanh village and the nearby ARVN compound. Rather than launch a counterattack, Colonel Lownds ordered the Marine and ARVN forces there to pull back to the base.

An old saying has it that things always look better by the light of day. They did not for Westmoreland on the morning of January 21. The enemy rocket barrage against Khe Sanh had continued the rest of the evening, and leveled anything left standing after the initial barrage. The base was a disaster. Half the steel runway had been destroyed and over 90 percent of the base's ammunition supply. Daylight revealed not a combat base ready to turn back any attack the NVA threw at it, but hundreds of dirty, exhausted Marines moving about like zombies across a landscape covered with dud rounds and raging fires. After enduring a night of continuous explosions, a number of Marines had to be evacuated from the base because of "nervous exhaustion."

The night had shaken both III MAF and MACV. They both were thankful the NVA had inexplicably decided not to launch a ground assault against the base. If they had—if ten thousand NVA regulars had charged the Marine wire while the Marines had been preoccupied with the fires and explosions—there would have been no predicting the outcome. It was not a thought many at either headquarters were eager to contemplate.

If the light of day did not bring good news, it did give both the Marines and MACV a renewed sense of urgency. At Khe Sanh, Lownds, after a conference with Cushman, ordered the 1st Battalion, 9th Marines and the ARVN 37th Ranger Battalion to reinforce the position. They joined with the Marines already there in a frantic effort to rebuild the airstrip, replenish the ammunition supply, and work at hardening all their command posts and living quarters. In Saigon, Westmoreland gave the order to Momyer to unleash Niagara. The enemy had struck him a hard blow; now he would strike them back one hundred times as hard.

At MACV headquarters, Momyer had set up a special center whose sole purpose was to orchestrate the aerial operation over Khe Sanh. In that same headquarters, a half dozen of the Army's most gifted tacticians worked over a sand table of Khe Sanh, trying to figure out the most logical places for Giap to concentrate his men and supplies. Those places were then targeted by Momyer. To generate other targets, dozens of reconnaissance planes soared over the area around the base, photographing the ground below and recording the information provided by an array of acoustic and seismic sensors designed to locate enemy troop and truck movement. To coordinate all these activities, a C-130 Herky Bird was kept in the sky over Khe Sanh day and night. Using the most sophisticated electronic gear, some crewmen in the plane analyzed all the data collected by the reconnaissance planes, while others picked targets and then parceled them out to the over two thousand strategic and tactical aircraft Westmoreland had assembled for the battle.

As at Con Thien and Dak To, the B-52 was the backbone of the air assault. Flying from Strategic Air Command bases in Guam and Thailand, a group of six of the gargantuan bombers arrived over the base every three hours around the clock. Bombing in unison, six could obliterate a target "box" with 162 tons of bombs in a few seconds. Adding their firepower to the torrent were over fifteen hundred Marine, Navy, and Air Force jets. On the average of once every five seconds, at least one and often dozens were making bombing, rocket, or strafing runs around Khe Sanh. Adding even more weight were the forty-seven Marine 105- and 155-millimeter howitzers at Khe Sanh and the Army's fifteen huge 175s at nearby Camp Carroll and the Rockpile. Although individually none of these guns had the destructive power of the bombers and jets, firing in unison, they could bracket a square-mile area in seconds and kill or wound nearly every living thing in it.

Westmoreland's opening salvo at Khe Sanh was a biggie. During that first twenty-four-hour period, while the Marines were working furiously to rebuild the base, his B-52s dropped over one thousand tons of explosives, his jets two hundred tons, and his artillery fired another three hundred tons. Taken together, the tonnage was equivalent to a tactical nuclear weapon.

The NVA units maneuvering around Khe Sanh were stunned by the initial bombing. Prisoners later told interrogators that NVA soldiers died by the hundreds along the mountain trails and valleys around Khe Sanh. In spite of the casualties, however, they kept coming, closing in around the base like a medieval army preparing to lay siege to a castle.

Around the same time that Westmoreland unleashed Niagara, he had a private meeting with Ambassador Ellsworth Bunker to discuss the present situation in South Vietnam. Bunker, Westmoreland was happy to discover, had been carefully following the stream of intelligence reports on enemy movements throughout South Vietnam and had likewise concluded that the enemy might attempt a countrywide show of strength before Tet. Together they drafted a cable to the President urging him to cancel the traditional cease-fire in I Corps, which is where both men assumed the main thrust of that offensive would come. The President readily agreed. Westmoreland was not so lucky, however, when he asked President Thieu and General Vien to cancel the cease-fire for ARVN troops. Both agreed to reduce it from forty-eight hours to thirty-six, but they felt that eliminating it completely would strike a hard blow to ARVN morale and, worse, give the Communists a major propaganda victory. Under further pressure from Westmoreland, both agreed to limit leaves for ARVN troops and guarantee that a minimum of 50 percent of their troops would be at their posts during the cease-fire.

In spite of the enemy forces closing in on Khe Sanh and in spite of the countrywide reports of enemy movement, Westmoreland refused to become a defensive-minded general. As always, he wanted to go on the attack. On January 24, he cabled Washington and asked for permission to strike the enemy before he struck. With a mixed force of Marines, paratroopers, and air cavalrymen, he wanted to launch an amphibious assault above the demilitarized zone, hitting Giap's forces there from the rear, disrupting their planned offensive and destroying the huge logistical network.

Westmoreland might as well have asked for permission to invade China. At the moment, the President had his mind on Khe Sanh, and the last thing he wanted to consider was expanding the war, and especially expanding it into North Vietnam. The President had been concerned about the base since mid-December when Walt Rostow, his national security adviser, told him that a newly captured document said that the North Vietnamese intended "to reenact a new Dien Bien Phu" at Khe Sanh. As the reports of the enemy buildup around Khe Sanh came in, Johnson's interest grew. Following the attack on Hill 861 and the explosion of Khe Sanh's ammo dump, his interest turned into an obsession.

Dreams of Dien Bien Phu now haunted his sleep, and he frequently leaped out of his bed in the middle of the night and in his bathrobe rushed down to the situation room in the basement of the White House. There, surrounded by the officers on duty, he read cables, studied aerial photographs, and bombarded the officers with questions. To help satisfy his obsession, the military had constructed for him a sand table model of the Marine base, much like the one Westmoreland's staff used at MACV headquarters to pick targets. As reports came in of enemy troop movements or actions, Johnson demanded that the officers on duty pinpoint them on the sand table for him and attempt to interpret their tactical significance.

As the situation at Khe Sanh continued to intensify, Johnson began to develop serious doubts about the wisdom of holding the base. Those doubts were, in turn, fueled by his chief military adviser, General Maxwell Taylor, who thought Westmoreland had seriously erred in establishing the base. "We should not seek battle close to the cross-border sanctuaries," he told Johnson, "but rather entice him out of the sanctuaries even at the sacrifice of some terrain in order to get him into favorable killing zones."

When apprised of Johnson and Taylor's doubts about Khe Sanh, Westmoreland cabled his rationale for the base and flatly rejected the idea of withdrawal.

The area is critical to us from a tactical standpoint as a launch base for SOG teams and as flank security for the strong point obstacle system. It is even more critical from a psychological viewpoint. To relinquish this area would be a major propaganda victory for the enemy. Its loss would seriously affect Vietnamese and U.S. morale. In short, withdrawal would be a tremendous step backwards.

Westmoreland failed to mention two other reasons why he wanted to keep the base at Khe Sanh, which was to serve as bait to draw Giap into a showdown and later hopefully as a staging area for an assault on the Ho Chi Minh Trail.

Westmoreland's rationale for Khe Sanh did little to ease the President's considerable anxiety over the security of the base. As a young senator during Eisenhower's presidency, he had had an insider's view of the events leading up to the fall of Dien Bien Phu, and he shuddered at the thought that he would be the President during an American Dien Bien Phu. The ignominy would have been too much to bear.

Westmoreland was very aware of Johnson's rising anxiety over the combat base, but he thought the President was worrying needlessly. In addition, it angered him that Taylor, a man he so admired, was second-guessing him and feeding Johnson's fears. In a cable, Westmoreland tried to calm the President by explaining to him that except maybe symbolically there were few similarities between the French camp and the Marine base. Dien Bien Phu had been in a valley, he noted, and Giap's Vietminh had controlled the tops of the surrounding hills. Khe Sanh, on the other hand, was on a plateau, with the Marines controlling the surrounding hills. While it was true the French had

had twenty-eight howitzers and four heavy mortars inside the camp, they had had no artillery support from the outside. Besides the twenty-four howitzers and four heavy mortars at Khe Sanh, the Marines had the ready support of the Army's fourteen 175s at Camp Carroll and four 175s at the Rockpile. The decided difference, however, was air power. The French had only been able to marshal two hundred planes of all types for their battle, a piddling figure compared with the two thousand attack planes, three thousand helicopters, and fleet of B-52s available to support the Marines.

When the cable arrived, Johnson asked Taylor to appraise the general's argument. Taylor's appraisal was a harsh one. Contrary to what Westmoreland said, he told the President, there were many similarities between Dien Bien Phu and Khe Sanh. To start, the weather had been bad at Dien Bien Phu, making resupply always difficult and at times impossible, and the weather could cause the same problems for the Marines, denying them the supplies they would so desperately need should Giap lay siege to the base. Westmoreland, Taylor said, was essentially doing the same thing the French had done before him, which was to arrogantly believe that his superiority in machines and equipment could overcome terrain and weather. Taylor was not certain it could. Westmoreland, he felt, was also repeating another fatal French error in underestimating the North Vietnamese Army and their wily commander, Giap. The French had arrogantly believed Giap incapable of massing enough artillery in the hills around Dien Bien Phu to threaten the base, and Taylor believed Westmoreland was showing the same arrogance toward Giap now. While it was certainly true that Westmoreland had assembled an awesome array of firepower for the Khe Sanh battle, if all that firepower could not nullify Giap's artillery, Khe Sanh could quickly be in great peril. And finally, Taylor pointed out to the President an old adage of infantrymen everywhere, that a commander can take any defensive position if he is willing to pay the price in casualties. What if Giap was willing to pay that price at Khe Sanh? Given that possibility, Taylor not only did not think Khe Sanh was worth the risk, but thought a withdrawal should be immediately considered.

Johnson never revealed what he thought of Taylor's assessment. Whatever his thoughts, he was not prepared to take the very drastic step of ordering Westmoreland to dismantle Khe Sanh. He genuinely liked Westmoreland, and was not about to embarrass or humiliate him. Nonetheless, Taylor had frightened him enough so that he likewise was not prepared to accept at face value Westmoreland's contention that Khe Sanh was in no danger of being overrun. He wanted as much reassurance as he could get, and he especially wanted to be reassured by the JCS. "I don't want no damned Dinbinfoo [*sic*]," he told Wheeler in a private meeting, then demanded of the general that he and the rest of the Joint Chiefs sign a written statement pledging their complete confidence in Westmoreland's ability to hold Khe Sanh.

While the Chiefs were signing this "oath in blood," as it came to be called, in Saigon Westmoreland was attempting to make sense of a number of recent events. On the twenty-fourth, the National Security Agency (NSA) notified him that from radio intercepts they had determined that enemy units were going to attack urban areas in both I and II Corps, and the attacks were imminent. A few hours later, he received a report from ARVN intelligence containing the news that the VC were moving large amounts of weapons and ammunition into Saigon. The next day, NSA sent him a second report. Based on an "almost unprecedented volume of urgent messages . . . passing among major enemy commands," NSA had now concluded that the enemy planned on launching major attacks not only in I and II Corps but throughout all of South Vietnam. NSA continued to believe, however, that the main brunt of the enemy offensive would be in I Corps. The most startling report Westmoreland received came from the ARVN military police. It detailed their capture on January 27 of eleven VC cadremen in Qui Nhon. On the men, they found two tapes that were to be played over captured radio stations. The tapes announced that "the forces struggling for peace and sovereignty" had occupied Saigon, Hue, and Da Nang and that the South Vietnamese people should join the revolutionary forces and topple the government.

On the same day those tapes were captured, during a Saturday morning strategy and intelligence conference, Davidson announced that he was now certain that the enemy was preparing to launch a nationwide attack. Two towns certain to be hit were Pleiku and Kontum. As Westmoreland notes, Davidson "ventured no starting date and pinpointed no cities and towns." Westmoreland tended to agree with Davidson's report. Neither man, however, gave much credence to the captured tapes. As a precaution, Westmoreland did move a squadron of the 4th Armored Cavalry to the outskirts of Tan Son Nhut, but like his intelligence chief, he rejected as unbelievable the idea that the Communists would launch a major assault against Saigon and the other major cities. Such a move simply did not make sense to Westmoreland.

What made sense was I Corps and Khe Sanh. That was where

Giap was strong, and that was where it made sense for him to strike. And when he did strike, Westmoreland would be ready for him. In spite of the major shortcomings he saw in many of their senior commanders, he had enormous faith in the fighting ability of the individual Marine rifleman. Backed by Niagara, he was certain they could do what the French had tried and failed to do at Dien Bien Phu, which was to lure Giap's crack legions into a prepared killing ground and then crush them.

As confident as he was that Giap could be decisively defeated at Khe Sanh, Westmoreland was still leaving nothing to chance. While it angered him that Taylor was creating doubts in Johnson's mind, he knew Taylor had been correct when he said that a determined commander could take any fortified position if he was willing to pay the price in casualties. Like Johnson, he would have been unable to accept the ignominy that would have been heaped on him should Khe Sanh fall. And so he had decided that regardless of how many troops Giap committed to the Khe Sanh battle, he was going to do everything in his power to make sure the base didn't fall, and this included using tactical nuclear weapons if necessary. Unknown to most of his MACV staff, he had secretly assembled a small group of men at MACV headquarters and sequestered them in a small private office. There they were now studying the most detailed terrain maps of the area around Khe Sanh, comparing different wind patterns in the area, and in map overlays computing the blast patterns and radiation yields of various types of bombs.

Westmoreland did not look at their work as an academic exercise or even as a remote contingency plan. He was prepared to use nuclear weapons at Khe Sanh, prepared as he put it later, "to send a message to Hanoi." Two atomic bombs had sent a very clear message to the Japanese during World War II, and Eisenhower's threat to use nuclear weapons in Korea had motivated the North Koreans to begin meaningful negotiations. Maybe using a few nuclear weapons—or even threatening to use them—could bring a premature end to the Vietnam War. As far as he was concerned it was worth a try. All he needed now was the President's approval.

CHAPTER TWENTY-THREE

Tet

The most famous photograph of the First Indochina War shows Ho Chi Minh and two other members of the Political Bureau of the Vietnam Workers Party Central Committee sitting around a table at the mouth of a cave and watching intently while Giap, pointer in hand, explains his plan for attacking Dien Bien Phu. Although difficult to tell from the photo, the cave was a deep, spacious one, and from his command post there, Giap directly controlled the nearly fifty thousand Vietminh troops laying siege to the French camp. In late January 1968, an NSA radio intercept station, using directional equipment, began intercepting an unusually large volume of radio traffic coming from what they thought was a similar cave just across the Laotian border from Khe Sanh. After further analyzing a number of radio intercepts from the cave, MACV intelligence concluded that the transmissions were coming from a major North Vietnamese headquarters, perhaps the controlling headquarters for the coming attack on Khe Sanh. A number of other radio intercepts seemed to indicate that Giap himself had left his headquarters north of the demilitarized zone and moved to this new headquarters to take personal command of the Khe Sanh front. This, of course, could not be determined with complete accuracy, but Westmoreland was not willing to wait while his analyst filtered through more intelligence data. The time to strike was now. If there was even the slightest chance of destroying the headquarters for the Khe Sanh front, while bagging Giap in the process, it was worth the effort. On January 29, he ordered the cave bombed, and bombed like no target this small had ever been bombed in the history of aerial warfare.

Westmoreland ordered his B-52s to do the job. At MACV headquarters, in a room next to his own conference room, a special staff of Air Force officers made up a list of possible targets for the raid. The list included the cave and every possible target in the immediate vicinity. Even stretching the target list, they could only use half the forty-five B-52s on the available list. Westmoreland wanted them all used, however, and in addition wanted a second raid. The Air Force balked at what they considered clear overkill, but Westmoreland was adamant. He wanted the cave and everything around it hit with everything available, and he wanted it hit twice.

He got what he wanted. And so on the morning of January 29, thirty-six B-52s bombed the target area with just over twenty-two hundred 750-pound bombs. In the second raid later that day, another nine of the heavy bombers dropped an additional six hundred 750s. Together, both raids put over two million pounds of high explosives on the target area.

Needless to say, after the first raid, all radio traffic from the cave stopped and never resumed. Whatever headquarters Hanoi maintained there disappeared in a cataclysmic explosion, along with all the personnel manning it. It was assumed that a number of high-ranking North Vietnamese officers perished in the bombing. Giap, it turned out, was not among them. At the moment the bombs were falling, he was visiting his headquarters in Hanoi, overseeing the final preparations for the Tet Offensive.

Military historians have yet to determine exactly what was in that cave, but it was likely something very important. A number of NVA officers captured during the Khe Sanh battle told their interrogators that the bombing attack threw their chain of command in I and II Corps into confusion, triggering the premature Tet attacks and possibly forcing the cancellation of a massive ground assault on Khe Sanh scheduled either before, during, or after Tet.

Whether by design or by accident, the Communists launched a series of attacks in I and II Corps during the early morning hours of

January 30. The first attack came at the highland town of Ban Me Thuot. There, at 1:35 A.M. two thousand enemy soldiers stormed the town behind a mortar barrage. At 2:00 A.M., Kontum, another highland town, was attacked by three other enemy battalions. Two battalions smashed into Hoi An at 3:00 A.M. Finally, between three and five, another twenty enemy battalions attacked Da Nang, Qui Nhon, Pleiku, Nha Trang, and Kontum. Vietcong units were used in all the assaults, and all the assaults were, in turn, directed at ARVN units and installations.

To the considerable surprise of the attacking forces, the ARVN units not only held the line, but quickly launched counterattacks. Except at Ban Me Thout, where some VC diehards held out for six days in one section of town, most of the attackers were either killed or driven off within twenty-four hours. Vietcong losses were a staggering 5,405 killed and 704 captured. Allied losses, most of which were ARVN, stood at 427 killed and three times that number wounded.

Westmoreland was at his villa when the attacks started, but had himself immediately driven to MACV headquarters. There he was met by his intelligence chief, Phillip Davidson, who had plotted all the attacks on a map and come to what he thought was an important conclusion. "This is going to happen in the rest of the country tonight or tomorrow night," he told Westmoreland. Westmoreland claims he agreed with Davidson. In spite of his agreement, he did not attempt to redeploy any of the considerable forces he had in I Corps back to the cities. He still felt that any attacks against the cities would be secondary to the main attack in I Corps.

He did, however, contact President Thieu and General Vien and after considerable wrangling convinced them to cancel the rest of the cease-fire. Thieu was not particularly alarmed. Rather than returning to his command post in Saigon, he instead flew back to My Tho to rejoin his wife's family and participate in another day of Tet celebrations. The ARVN commanders were also not particularly alarmed. While some of them tightened security at their installations and made a concerted effort to call back all their soldiers on leave, others continued celebrating and made little effort to find their men. The ARVN problems were compounded when thousands of South Vietnamese soldiers chose to ignore the order to return to their units. Like Thieu, they all wanted to enjoy another day of celebration.

Following his talk with Thieu and Vien, Westmoreland placed a conference call to all his senior commanders and according to his own account warned them of "the likelihood of immediate widespread attacks . . ." It is obvious from what followed that while his warning seems clear enough, he failed to fully communicate to them the gravity of the situation. One reason he failed was that during the last six months, he had had his forces on maximum alert 50 percent of the time. By now, many of his commanders and troops were becoming immune to maximum alerts. Many officers took the warning so lightly, in fact, that they did not even bother protecting themselves personally against the threat of an enemy attack. On the evening of January 30, for instance, two hundred colonels, all ironically on Davidson's staff, attended a pool party at bachelor officers quarters in the heart of Saigon. One of the colonels was James Meecham, an analyst at the Combined Intelligence Center (CICV), where, among many things, analyses of enemy intentions and capabilities were produced. "Maybe Westy knew about Tet," Meecham said after the war, "but not the people down below. I had no conception Tet was coming, absolutely zero. I'm categorically sure of that. Of the 200-odd colonels, not one I talked to knew Tet was coming, without exception."

Westmoreland also failed to communicate fully the gravity of the situation to President Johnson and his senior advisers. As a result, they were completely unprepared for the emotional shock of the attacks. Both Westmoreland and Admiral Sharp claim otherwise, that the numerous cables both men sent to Washington between January 25 and 30 warning of "widespread" attacks should have been enough to prepare Washington for what followed. Their argument, of course, is a weak one. By "widespread" they meant ten, possibly fifteen attacks, numbers Johnson and his senior advisers were emotionally prepared to deal with. They were, however, in no way prepared to deal with fifteen times that number of attacks. Like a lot of military men in South Vietnam, Johnson and his senior advisers were expecting some enemy attacks during or after Tet. No one—either in Vietnam or Washington—was expecting what happened, which was a simultaneous attack by a mostly Vietcong force of eighty-four thousand against 36 of South Vietnam's provincial capitals, 5 of its 6 autonomous cities, 64 of its 242 district capitals, and 50 of its hamlets.

The attacks began at three in the morning of January 31. Westmoreland was sleeping soundly at his villa when they started, but was quickly awakened by his current aide, Marine Major Charles Sampson. After dressing, he took a call from the combat operations center at MACV headquarters. He listened calmly as the officer read him a litany of the attacks.

• In I Corps, enemy battalions were attacking Quang Tri City, Tam Ky, Hue, and the United States military installations at Phu Bai and Chu Lai.

• In II Corps, the site of the eight abortive attacks the night before, the enemy had launched new attacks against the towns of Thuy Hoa and Phan Thiet and against United States bases at Bong Son and An Khe.

• In IV Corps, more enemy battalions were attacking the towns of Vinh Long, Can Tho, and Ben Tre.

• In the area around Saigon, major attacks were either under way or building against the big United States and Vietnamese base at Long Binh and against the big air bases at Bien Hoa and Tan Son Nhut. The Tan Son Nhut attack seemed to be the most serious at the moment. There five VC battalions were attacking from the west, north, and east, and threatening the MACV compound.

• In the central part of Saigon, sapper and infantry attacks had been launched against the Presidential Palace, the Vietnamese Navy Headquarters, the National Radio Stations, the United States embassy and twenty other government installations.

Although hardly the most important attack militarily, the attack on the United States embassy quickly became the focus of much of Westmoreland's attention. There, at 2:45, a twenty-man Vietcong sapper platoon blew a hole in the concrete wall surrounding the embassy, then with automatic rifles blazing charged into the compound. In the shootout that followed, the sappers killed five American MPs, but lost two of their own men, one of whom was the platoon leader. Leaderless, the eighteen remaining men tried to blow down the heavy wooden door of the chancery with rocket grenades. When unsuccessful, they took cover on the grounds and began shooting back at a number of Americans who were now firing down on them from rooftops overlooking the compound.

At 4:20, Westmoreland got a call from the political counselor at the embassy, John Calhoun, asking for an American reaction force and some medical evacuation helicopters. Westmoreland, in turn, ordered the 716th Military Police Battalion to clear the embassy ground as a "first priority effort." He also ordered a platoon from the 101st Airborne Division to land on the roof of the embassy and take control of it.

At 9:30 A.M., Westmoreland had himself driven to the embassy. He arrived just minutes after a group of Marines and MPs had battered down the main gate to the embassy with a jeep and gone in shooting. Clean-shaven and wearing a pressed uniform, Westmoreland stolidly walked into the compound and inspected the damage. There was much to inspect. The lawn was blood-splattered and in places churned into a muddy stew from explosions. Everywhere there were unexploded rocket grenades and satchel charges, broken rifles, bandoliers of ammunition, and bloody clothing and bandages. The bodies of two United States MPs, nineteen VC sappers, and four South Vietnamese embassy employees still lay where they had fallen. A group of American MPs, all wearing protective vests and carrying M-16s, were holding a vigil over their fallen friends. Two of the MPs were crying while a half-dozen photographers and TV cameramen photographed and filmed them. Many more press people were scattered all over the compound. One in particular was Kate Webb, a UPI feature writer. In a memorable piece published the next day, she described the scene around her as looking "like a butcher shop in Eden."

After walking through the center of this "butcher shop," Westmoreland paused for a long moment to inspect the damage to the chancery's front door, then stepped inside. There he placed a call to Washington and spoke briefly with Phillip Habib, the deputy assistant secretary of state, telling him that the situation was under control at the embassy and would soon be under control in the rest of Saigon. At the invitation of Barry Zorthian, the public relations director for the United States embassy, he then went out to address the press and give them what Zorthian called a "balanced perspective" on the embassy attack.

As one of Kate Webb's colleagues, Don Oberdorfer, noted, the "normally garrulous" reporters were not as quick to pressure Westmoreland with questions as they ordinarily would have been.

> The six-and-a-half-hour Viet Cong occupation seemed to many of them the most embarrassing defeat the United States had suffered in Vietnam. Even though the scale was small, this was a big story, very big. It seemed to give a lie to the rosy pictures and victory claims that Westmoreland and others had been dishing out. For once the reporters felt sorry for Westmoreland. What could he possibly say of this disaster?

Westmoreland gave the group a strictly military view of the situation. "The enemy has very deceitfully taken advantage of the Tet truce," he said. In spite of that fact, his "well-laid plans went afoul. Some superficial damage was done to the building. All of the enemy who entered the compound so far as I can determine were killed. Nineteen bodies have been found on the premises—enemy bodies." He assured them, however, that contrary to reports floating about, not one of those enemy soldiers had entered the chancery itself.

As to the reason for the attacks, Westmoreland surmised that they had been calculated to create maximum consternation in Vietnam and that they were "diversionary" to the main effort still to come at Khe Sanh and the northern part of the country. Until those attacks developed, he was more than happy to take advantage of the opportunity the Communists had presented him by coming into the open and exposing themselves to his firepower. Finally he assured them that the enemy offensive would eventually end in failure.

As Don Oberdorfer also wrote, most of the reporters there could hardly believe their ears. There was Westmoreland "standing in the ruins saying everything was great." Many of those same reporters were equally incredulous over the general's contention that the Tet attacks were a diversion. Summing up the feeling of many of his colleagues there, *Washington Post* reporter Peter Braestrup asked, "How could any effort against Saigon, especially downtown Saigon, be a diversion?"

Events would prove Westmoreland's optimistic appraisal to be correct. He had made himself look foolish, however, contending that the Tet attacks were a diversion. His obsession with Khe Sanh and I Corps had completely blinded him to the fact that 155 attacks launched by eighty-four thousand troops cannot be a diversion.

The reporters were right to be incredulous. Unfortunately, many carried their incredulity to an extreme. A number took note of Westmoreland's statement that no enemy had penetrated the chancery. One man in particular questioned him about the statement, then added that according to his own sources—which it turned out was the word of a single MP—the VC had actually gotten into the chancery.

Westmoreland bristled, furious that the reporter had dared question his truthfulness. "Was the word of a professional military man," he later wrote, "who bore over-all military responsibility for the war in South Vietnam and also had personally gone through the Embassy building to have no precedence over rumors? Had the level of credibility and the art of reporting sunk so low?"

Apparently it had. In spite of Westmoreland's statement, few reporters bothered to investigate the embassy story any further. Most assumed, as Associated Press repoter Peter Arnett put it, that West-moreland was lying. "We had little faith in what General Westmore-land said," Arnett told a journalist after the war. Arnett proved that with a report written two hours after the embassy was secured. For it, he gave Westmoreland's version of the incident, but added that "dozens of persons on the scene" claimed the VC had entered the chancery. Other AP reporters expanded on Arnett's version. In Edwin Q. White's account, based, he claimed, on the word of an American captain, "a Viet Cong suicide squad had blasted its way into the U.S. embassy compound" and seized the first floor. According to White, it had then taken MPs and paratroopers over seven hours to blast the VC out of the chancery. Both Arnett's and White's stories were widely printed in newspapers across the country.

Two of the national television networks, NBC and ABC, also chose to disbelieve Westmoreland. NBC's Chet Huntley not only had Viet-cong inside the chancery, but "on buildings and rooftops near the embassy," from which they were "firing down on American personnel in the compound." These false reports not only stunned the American public but editors, reporters, and feature writers as well. As Peter Braestrup notes, many of these media people read the reports from the embassy in total shock and concluded that "the roof had fallen in on Vietnam. . . . The Viet Cong had even taken over the Embassy."

That shock was quickly reflected in the news stories they wrote. In a special television report, CBS new correspondent Mike Wallace said that the raid had "demolished the myth" that the Allies controlled South Vietnam, even that they controlled Saigon. During a Wash-ington, D.C., news program, *Capital Tieline*, Sarah McClendon won-dered aloud just how it was possible when the Allies knew an offensive was coming that the Vietcong had been able to penetrate the embassy. If we could not keep the VC out of our embassy, then we obviously could not keep them out of any city or town. A *New York Times* editorial on February 1 contended that the raid had completely "un-dermined" the optimism of President Johnson and General West-moreland.

The shock experienced by the news media was nothing compared with that which hit President Johnson. He was, as Westmoreland put it, in a "state of great consternation." Only a few days before, the North Koreans had seized an American electronic surveillance vessel, the U.S.S. *Pueblo,* and coming on the heels of that considerable crisis, the Tet Offensive was almost more than the weary President could bear.

In an attempt to provide the President with more accurate information on the attacks, Westmoreland had himself driven from the embassy straight to his headquarters at Tan Son Nhut. The air base had been attacked from three directions during the night by three VC battalions. They had been threatening to overrun the giant base when an armored cavalry troop from the 25th Infantry Division arrived in the nick of time and hit them from the rear. Two of the VC battalions had then retreated to the giant Vinatexco cotton mill across the road from Tan Son Nhut. When Westmoreland arrived at his headquarters, dive bombers were plastering the cotton mill with napalm and high-explosive bombs and gunships were attacking it with rockets and mini-gun fire. The two thousand to three thousand VC in the mill were firing back with heavy machine guns and rocket grenades, and a lot of the enemy fire was striking MACV headquarters itself.

Westmoreland wrote after the war that when he gave his optimistic appraisal at the embassy, he had not known if it would stand up to the light of day. He had had faith that the Allies would quickly turn back the enemy offensive, but he had no hard facts to back up that faith. At his headquarters, with the sound of exploding bombs and the crackle of rifle and machine-gun fire ringing in his ears, he began accumulating the facts he needed. Before the end of the day, he discovered that his optimistic appraisal had been on the mark. By noon, air strikes had leveled the textile mill, killing 162 of the Vietcong inside. The rest had fled. More good news followed from other parts of Saigon. A little after noon, he learned that the thirteen VC sappers who had attacked Independence Palace during the night had all been killed. A similar-size force that had attacked the Vietnamese Navy headquarters had all died in the first few minutes of their assault.

Westmoreland was also happy to discover that owing to confusion and incompetence, the enemy had bungled many of their attacks. Carrying the tapes of a liberation broadcast, two platoons of Vietcong had fought their way into the South Vietnamese government radio station only to discover that someone had cut off all power to the building. A Vietcong battalion tasked with the mission of liberating five thousand prisoners in the Saigon jail got lost in a Saigon cemetery. Before they could find their way out, they were brought under fire by an ARVN infantry company and routed. Two other VC companies in the same area experienced an equal amount of confusion. After suffering terrible casualties overrunning the ARVN Armored and Artillery Command, they discovered that the tanks they were after had been moved and that their assault had been for nothing.

The enemy had had some successes, however. A number of VC battalions had succeeded in establishing footholds in the northern suburbs, in Cholon, and at the Phu Tho racetrack, but Westmoreland was assured by commanders on the scene that it was only a matter of time before the enemy was driven from all three areas.

The news was as encouraging from the rest of the country. Although the enemy was still holding positions in Quang Tri City, Hue, Da Nang, Nha Trang, Qui Nhon, Kontum City, Ban Me Thout, Dalat, Phan Thiet, My Tho, Can Tho, and Ben Tre, nearly 90 percent of the 155 attacks he had launched had already been turned back. The ARVN, who had been the primary target of most of the offensive, had stopped some of the enemy attacks in less than an hour.

In response to a request from President Johnson for an update on the situation, Westmoreland relayed to him through Wheeler much of the same information he had just collected from his field commanders. He made a special effort to let the President know that the enemy, who had suffered over five thousand killed in just the first day of fighting, did not control a single town in South Vietnam. He had "some degree of control in several towns," but, Westmoreland assured Johnson, he would not have it for long.

Johnson was heartened by the news and requested that Westmoreland "make a brief personal comment to the press each day . . . to convey to the American public your confidence in our capability to blunt these enemy moves." As instructed, Westmoreland held a press conference later in the day at the Joint United States Public Affairs Office (JUSPAO). The auditorium was packed with newsmen, and as he stepped up to the podium, cameras flashed from every part of the room.

"Gentlemen, I thought I would try and put into perspective the events of the last several months and those of the last several days in particular," he said. These recent attacks, he reported, were part of a three-phase campaign plan that had recently been drafted in Hanoi. During phase one, the enemy had launched attacks at Dak To and other border areas in order to force the Allies to divert troops from the urban areas. These recent attacks had been part of phase two. Phase three, the main effort, was still to come at Khe Sanh and northern I Corps. It would be more violent than the phase two attacks and longer-lasting since the enemy had an extensive logistics network already in place in the North.

Westmoreland then read off a list of the cities that had already been attacked and gave a short summary of the situation at each.

During those attacks, he announced, the enemy had suffered over 5,000 killed, compared with only 530 Allied troops. If he continued his attacks, his losses would be staggering, so staggering that it would take the units committed to the attack many months to rebuild their strength. "In summary, gentlemen, this second phase of the campaign was a bold one. It was characterized by treachery and deceitfulness. It showed a callous disregard for human life."

It was the kind of news Washington wanted to hear. A few hours later, Wheeler held his own news conference at the Pentagon and repeated much of what Westmoreland had said. He concluded his remarks by announcing that the enemy had suffered so many casualties that the Tet Offensive had to be considered a total failure.

The press was not buying it. Except for a few diehard administration supporters like Joseph Alsop, the majority of correspondents and editorial writers generally saw the statements of Westmoreland and Wheeler as blatant lies. *The New York Times*, in fact, two full days after the embassy attack, still refused to accept Westmoreland's version of it. Based on unnamed witnesses, correspondent Tom Buckley insisted that not only had guerrillas penetrated the chancery but they had held it for seven hours. An editorial writer in the same edition of the paper lambasted Westmoreland for initially calling the attack a "diversion." Far from being a diversion, the writer asserted, the attacks had been a serious setback for the United States, throwing into doubt official claims of progress and raising serious questions about the competence of the South Vietnamese leadership and their military. A *Christian Science Monitor* reporter, Beverly Deepe, leveled an even harsher attack. Following a lengthy diatribe against the entire United States policy in Vietnam, Deepe took a giant leap in logic, concluding that the United States for the first time in the war faced the possibility of military defeat.

On instruction from President Johnson, Westmoreland began making daily statements to the press, statements Johnson hoped "would reassure the public here that you have the situation under control." Johnson's was a false hope. Westmoreland's daily statements might have relieved his personal anxiety over the situation in Vietnam, but they did little for the American public. As Don Oberdorfer, a *Washington Post* correspondent at the time, notes, while Johnson and his senior advisers "were receiving, reading, and disseminating after-the-fact official summaries of what had happened, the public was experiencing the worst of the bloodshed through the new technology of television." Westmoreland could talk about how the enemy was being defeated, he could reel off impressive statistics of enemy killed and captured, but his words could not compete with television images of burning houses and streets strewn with bodies and debris. To Westmoreland the attack on the embassy was a "piddling platoon action," but to a television viewer in America, it looked like a full-scale battle. To Westmoreland ten or fifteen Vietcong under siege in a pagoda hardly warranted his attention, but the television image of that siege made Americans think they were viewing street fighting as bad as anything in World War II.

Damage to most cities that came under attack was extremely light by the standards of a World War II urban battle. But as the military historian Charles McDonald notes, "television cameras focusing on one badly damaged block could give the impression of an entire city in ruins." Saigon, for instance, suffered only light damage, but after a few days of watching the fighting there on TV, American audiences became convinced that the city had been reduced to a smoldering ruin. In reality, only 10 percent of Saigon's city dwellers were directly affected by the fighting there, and that statistic was generally true for all other cities the enemy attacked.

With their commentaries, television commentators added to the misperception Americans got from their TV screens. In grim, depressing language, those commentators served up for their viewers what Peter Braestrup, another *Washington Post* reporter, called "the disaster image." Like Job, one after another they stood in the rubble of bombed buildings and cried out to the heavens. How could this have happened? How could an enemy Westmoreland had claimed was being systematically defeated have caused all this destruction and chaos?

Those same commentators simultaneously ignored facts that did not fit into the "disaster image." Although most of their units were only at 50 percent strength, both South Vietnamese militiamen and regulars performed professionally and courageously throughout the offensive. Their performance, however, was given scant coverage by the press. Part of this was because few Americans in the Saigon press corps ever covered ARVN units in combat, and that did not change during Tet, in spite of the ARVN bearing the brunt of the fighting. Part of it was also due to many commentators not wanting to tamper with an image firmly established in the public's mind, an image of the ARVN as conniving, treacherous, and most of all, cowardly. One scene that did receive wide and repeated television play was of four or five ARVN soldiers gleefully looting the bodies of some VC sappers who had been killed assaulting the National Radio Station.

On the other hand, commentators frequently made reference in their broadcasts to the VC and NVA, and when they did it was often with a sense of awe. In contrast to our "unworthy allies," the enemy soldiers were praised for their intelligence, bravery, tenaciousness, boldness, careful planning, skill of execution, and willingness to die for a cause. Nothing was said, however, of the dozens of enemy units that quickly retreated when brought under fire, got lost on the way to their staging areas or assault positions, or worse, attacked the wrong installations.

Westmoreland himself was another major omission from Tet coverage. As Braestrup further notes, neither his failures nor successes as a commander during Tet were examined by commentators. Such major stories as his redeployment of United States troops to help ARVN units in the cities, his orchestration of B-52 raids around Khe Sanh, and his personal involvement in the battle for Hue, received no mention. And they did not, according to Braestrup, because neither the TV commentators nor their bosses in New York thought it interesting or important. Their interest instead was in "action and drama," in strafing jets, devastated neighborhoods, crying women, and orphaned children.

These same commentators also paid scant attention to Westmoreland's daily press reports, the reports Johnson had hoped would bolster the morale of the American people. Such appearances by the general lacked the visual impact and shock value that were a staple of Tet coverage. In addition, like Arnett, many commentators questioned the veracity of such reports. They were generally seen as feeble attempts on Westmoreland's part to try to put a good face on a very bad situation.

TV commentators, and the press in general, were much kinder to Giap. The North Vietnamese general was frequently tagged with adjectives like wily, bold, crafty, and brilliant, and just as frequently referred to as a master planner, brilliant tactician, or tactical genius. No mention was made of the fact that the Tet attacks, while certainly "bold," were also as *Newsweek* alone put it, "plagued by confusion" from start to finish. Commentators made much of the tactical surprise Giap achieved with Tet, but failed to see that after gaining that surprise, he neglected to exploit it, "committing just enough troops (an estimated 84,000) to make good targets for allied firepower—and far more than enough to make headlines—but not enough in any one place at any one time to score decisively on the ground."

Giap's attacks may not have scored decisively on the ground, but they continued to score spectacularly in the United States. Though most supporters of the war were generally silent during the initial stages of the offensive, critics spoke up with a vengeance. Some of the loudest voices came out of the Congress. For many congressmen, the offensive was concrete evidence to back up what they had been saying all along, that the war was a monumental error.

From the Senate floor, Senator Edward Kennedy claimed that the success of the Tet attacks was a result of the "deadly apathy" of the South Vietnamese people. He was followed by Senator Mansfield, who said that the attacks proved that no place in South Vietnam was secure, and there "was not the beginning of a stable political situation" in Vietnam. On the floor the next day, Senator Jacob Javits claimed that Westmoreland's statements in November about the declining fortunes of the enemy had been wrong. Javits was seconded by Senator Eugene McCarthy. Westmoreland and Johnson, said McCarthy, had been deceiving the American people and deceiving themselves.

The attacks had a much more profound effect on former supporters of administration policy, and especially among the vocal elites from education, religion, and the media. Most in this group had long had doubts about the war, but had been unwilling to express them and break with the administration. Foremost among these new doubters was Walter Cronkite, CBS's venerable newscaster. On seeing early wire reports indicating that the VC had occupied the embassy chancery, he snapped at an associate, "What the hell is going on? I thought we were winning this war!" After a quick trip to Vietnam to get a close-up look at the damage, he went on the air and told the nearly twenty million viewers of his evening news program that it seemed "more certain than ever that the bloody experience of Vietnam is to end in a stalemate."

Cronkite's statement shocked and depressed President Johnson. After the broadcast, he turned to his press secretary, George Mc-Christian, and said dejectedly, "If we've lost Cronkite, we've lost middle America." Westmoreland was furious when he heard Cronkite's words. He felt it was not the job of the media to attempt to formulate public policy, but only to report events accurately. Unfortunately, Cronkite was such a powerful man in America that Westmoreland feared the commentator's words might become a self-fulfilling prophecy.

From Wheeler, Westmoreland learned that even White House insiders were affected by the Tet attacks. In early February, General Wheeler cabled him with the news that there was nothing but doom and gloom on the Potomac. It reminded him of the historical descriptions of Washington following the Union debacle at the First

Battle of Bull Run, Wheeler said, "when all seemed lost and recriminations filled the air."

Though he did not mention it to Westmoreland, Wheeler himself was deeply depressed over the Tet attacks. He had tried to remain upbeat as he read Westmoreland's cables, but the sight of the war on TV had demoralized him.

Harry McPherson, a White House insider and a confidant of the President, claims he had a similar reaction watching Tet reports on TV. "I watched the invasion of the American embassy compound and the terrible sight of General Loan killing the Vietcong captive . . . and got a sense of the awfulness, the endlessness of the war . . . I put aside the confidential cables. I was more persuaded by the tube and by the newspapers."

While the furor over the significance of Tet raged back in the United States, in South Vietnam the offensive was in its final death throes. On February 2, Westmoreland began taking the first steps toward putting his forces back on an offensive footing. Though major fighting was still continuing in Hue, Pleiku, Phu Loc, My Tho, Dalat, Ben Tre, and some areas of Saigon, Westmoreland ordered his field force commanders to begin pursuing the enemy forces fleeing from the battlefield. To accelerate the mop-up, he also ordered United States troops into Kontum City, Phu Loc, My Tho, and Ben Tre. Then he turned his full attention on Hue.

Of all the Tet attacks, the one against Hue was the most intense. In the early morning hours of January 31, under the cover of a thick fog, sixteen battalions of NVA and Vietcong had infiltrated Hue and quickly taken control of most of the city on the south bank of the Perfume River and the bulk of the northern half, including the Imperial Citadel. In some of the hardest fighting of the war, U.S. Marines and various ARVN units had managed to drive the enemy out of most of the south bank area in the first week, but their attack against the citadel had stalled.

Frustrated by the lack of progress in Hue, Westmoreland had flown up to Phu Bai for a council of war with General Abrams. Both were very dissatisfied with the way Lieutenant General Cushman, the commander of the III MAF, was handling the retaking of Hue. They thought the assault was going too slowly and that Cushman was not properly using the resources at his disposal. The commander of the 1st ARVN Division, which was leading the assault on the citadel, complained that the Marines were not supplying his units properly or providing them with proper air support.

Westmoreland and Abrams changed all that. Working together,

they quickly hammered out a plan to retake the citadel. The plan called for the introduction of the Army's 1st Cavalry Division and 101st Airborne Division into the battle. The 1st was tasked with pressing the enemy in Hue from the northwest, and the 101st with blocking enemy avenues of escape to the south and southwest. At the same time, the ARVN were to attack from the west and clear the southwestern wall of the citadel, and from the south toward the imperial palace. The Marines were to continue their attack along the southwestern wall of the citadel. Abrams's final instructions to Cushman were quite specific, reflecting, as Lewis Sorley writes, "a very high degree of dissatisfaction with the way Cushman had been running the operation." Cushman, Abrams's orders read, was to make sure all the forces attacking the citadel had plenty of ammunition and first priority on artillery and air support.

Cushman has left no record of how he reacted to this second considerable blow to his ego. Whatever his reaction, the attack on the citadel quickly took on a renewed momentum. Behind naval gunfire, tactical air strikes and heavy artillery, the Marine, Army and ARVN troops began the final assault. A week later, enemy troops began abandoning the city. Finally on February 24, South Vietnamese troops overran the imperial palace, tore down the National Liberation Front flag, and flew in its place the flag of the Republic of Vietnam. The twenty-five-day battle was over.

Hue was a shattered, stinking ruin, its narrow streets clogged with hundreds of rotting bodies and debris. The battle had been costly for both sides, but most of all for the North Vietnamese and Vietcong. During the twenty-five-day siege, they had lost between 4,000 and 5,000 men killed and had double that number of wounded. American and South Vietnamese units together had over 500 killed and 3,000 wounded. Civilian casualties were also serious. Around 4,000 had been killed in the crossfire and another 100,000 made homeless. As Allied soldiers began mopping up, they discovered another 3,000 Hue residents buried in mass graves in and around the city, the victims of a systematic enemy reign of terror. Another 2,000 Hue citizens remained unaccounted for, but they were presumed murdered also. Most of the victims had been teachers, priests, intellectuals, political leaders, and others the Communists considered "social negatives." Many of the dead had been buried alive, others clubbed to death or strangled.

The recapture of Hue sounded the death knell for the Tet Offensive. Evaluated in strictly military terms, the offensive had been a complete failure. Westmoreland claimed the Communists had lost over 37,000 killed and 5,800 captured—close to half the number of troops committed to the actual assaults. While the press disputed that number, after the war, Truong Nhu Tang, a founder of the National Liberation Front, corroborated Westmoreland's figures. According to Tang, the Communists lost over half their forces during Tet. "Our losses were so immense that we were simply unable to replace them with new recruits." To make up for those losses, the leadership in Hanoi began to move unprecedented numbers of troops into the South. They brought in so many troops, in fact, that by May 1968, only two months after the end of Tet, over 70 percent of all Communist soldiers in the South were northerners. After Tet, the Vietcong was no longer a viable fighting force. The arrival of so many northerners bred widespread discontent in the ranks of the Vietcong. Many felt that Hanoi had cynically used them to fight a battle that was doomed from the start.

Tet also destroyed the esprit and elan of many surviving Vietcong. Until Tet, many in the ranks had fought with the sure conviction that the South Vietnamese people saw them as patriots and liberators. They had truly believed their political officers when told that the Tet attacks would trigger a general uprising among the "downtrodden urban masses," and that the "puppet" ARVN troops would either throw down their weapons and run or join them to fight the Americans. Neither had happened. The urban masses had wanted nothing to do with the liberation being offered them, and most ARVN troops, to the surprise of just about everyone, fought tenaciously, and many with exceptional bravery. Official reports sent back to Hanoi after Tet described many of the survivors of the offensive as having "lost confidence" in the leadership in Hanoi and having given up on the idea that the war could be won.

Tet had a completely opposite impact on the South Vietnamese people. The audacity and violence of the attacks frightened and outraged hundreds of thousands of people and forced them out of their lethargy and into a more active support of the government. Out of fear that the Communists might strike again, thousands demanded that the government arm them. Saigon was happy to oblige. Having seen how vehemently many average citizens had rejected Communist exhortation during Tet, for the first time in the war the government felt confident enough to arm almost the entire countryside. They also felt confident enough to pass a full Mobilization Decree in the National Assembly, a decree that had failed to pass only five months before because of strong political opposition. This new decree called for the drafting of all eighteen- and nineteen-year-olds. By the end of 1968, South Vietnam's overall military strength would rise to over nine hundred thousand. As Maxwell Taylor noted, the days after Tet were South Vietnam's finest hour.

The reaction of the American people to Tet was much more complicated than that of either the Vietcong or South Vietnamese. They were neither demoralized nor galvanized by the attacks, but left somewhat confused as to the true meaning of them. Most wondered if Tet was a defeat for the United States, proof, as some critics of the war claimed, that all the United States effort in Vietnam had been for naught, that after committing billions of dollars and thousands of lives the United States had achieved little but a stalemate. Or was Tet, as Westmoreland claimed, merely a desperation attack like the 1944 German offensive in the Ardennes Forest, an attack that had proved nothing except that an enemy willing to throw away thirty thousand lives can cause havoc for a few days?

During a number of vituperative tirades after the war, Westmoreland claimed that distorted and biased newspaper and television reports of the Tet attacks had transformed a devastating Communist military defeat into a "psychological victory" for the enemy. That "psychological victory," he further claimed, had caused many thousands of average Americans to suffer a loss of morale and to quit supporting the war. And that loss of support, in turn, led to the United States' precipitous withdrawal from Vietnam and the loss of the war. Westmoreland's sentiment was shared by a large percentage of the Vietnam-era military men. One of the most prominent and outspoken of those men was Westmoreland's intelligence chief during Tet, Phillip Davidson. In his history of the war, he claimed that Tet reporting had "shattered public morale and destroyed support of the war in the United States." General Taylor, while he certainly did not agree with many of Westmoreland's tactical decisions in Vietnam, agreed with his view of the press. Distorted reporting, he wrote in his reminiscences, *Swords and Plowshares*, had "contributed to mass pessimism in the United States, a pessimism that had broken the will of the American people to support the war."

Ironically, Westmoreland got additional support for his view from an unlikely source, members of the news media itself. In March 1968, Howard K. Smith, the eminent commentator, resigned his position at ABC in part because of the press's muddled handling of Tet. "Vietcong casualties were one hundred times ours," he angrily told an interviewer. "But we never told the public that. We just showed pictures day after day of Americans getting the hell kicked out of them. That was enough to break America apart." Robert Elegant, a correspondent in Vietnam, was even more hostile, writing that "never before Vietnam had the collective policy of the media—no less stringent term will serve—sought by graphic and unremitting distortion the victory of the enemies of the correspondent's own side." The coup de grace against the press's reporting of Tet, however, was delivered by former *Washington Post* correspondent, Peter Braestrup. In *Big Story*, his exhaustive two-volume study of Tet and the media's response to it, Braestrup harshly concluded that "rarely had contemporary crisis-journalism turned out, in retrospect, to have veered so widely from reality. . . . To have portrayed such a setback for one side as a defeat for the other . . . cannot be counted as a triumph for American journalism."

That the media was hostile to the Vietnam War is now a well-accepted fact among many historians. That its reporting of the war, and especially of the Tet Offensive, was widely biased and distorted is likewise accepted. That this bias and distortion led, as Westmoreland bitterly complained, to the loss of the war is not so well accepted, however. And it is not widely accepted because it is a view, as recent scholarship has shown, that is not firmly founded in fact.

As the historian William M. Hammond notes in his *The Military and the Media*, a book published by the U.S. Army's Center for Military History, the polls after Tet

> indicated that far from suffering a loss of morale or fighting spirit, the majority of Americans had rallied aggressively to the side of the President. Whereas in January 1968, 56 percent of those polled by the Gallup organization had considered themselves hawks on the war and 27 percent doves, with 17 percent voicing no opinion, by early February at the height of the offensive, 61 percent considered themselves hawks and 23 percent doves. In the same way, the number of Americans who expressed confidence in U.S. military policy in South Vietnam rose from 61 percent in December 1967 to 74 percent in February 1968.

The loss of morale that Westmoreland claims afflicted the American people after Tet is certainly not reflected in these statistics. To the contrary, despite the obvious pessimism and bias of the press, Tet, if anything, made Americans more hawkish on the war, made them more willing than ever before to back Johnson should he decide to take more aggressive actions against North Vietnam.

But Johnson was not willing to take such actions, was not willing to invade Cambodia, Laos, or North Vietnam itself or to escalate the bombing of North Vietnam. Johnson was not even willing to appear publicly and talk frankly with the American people about Tet. He left that job to his aides in Washington and to Westmoreland and his staff in Saigon. As Hammond also notes, "The lack of any effort by Johnson to marshall public opinion in his favor also affected the American mood of aggressiveness." And like the sands of an hourglass, that collective aggressiveness began slowly draining away. By the end of February, the percentage of Americans disapproving of Johnson's handling of the war rose sharply from 47 to 63. The average American had not become demoralized by the press coverage of the war, as Westmoreland so passionately maintained, but by the realization after Tet that the President had no winning strategy, that the American war effort was like a giant rudderless ship drifting aimlessly across the endless green sea of Indochina jungle.

End of the Line

A month after the last shot of the Tet Offensive was fired, members of President Johnson's Foreign Intelligence Advisory Board visited South Vietnam to investigate the charge that Allied forces had been caught by surprise at Tet. After two weeks of asking questions and poring over documents, they concluded that Tet had not been a complete surprise as was generally thought. Westmoreland and his staff, they noted in their report to the President, had been expecting some kind of attack during the Vietnamese holiday. They had not, however, been expecting one of such "intensity, coordination, and timing . . ."

A year after the PFIAB report, some instructors of military science at West Point collaborated on a military history textbook to be used by cadets studying the Vietnam War. The section in the book on the Tet Offensive was written by one of Westmoreland's former aides, Major David R. Palmer. In spite of his long and intimate association with Westmoreland, Palmer's conclusion was merciless. "The first thing to say about Giap's Tet Offensive," Palmer wrote, "is that it was an allied intelligence failure ranking with Pearl Harbor in 1941 or the Ardennes Offensive in 1944. The North Vietnamese gained complete surprise." It can be argued whether Palmer's conclusion is exaggerated, but it cannot be argued that the Tet Offensive did a great deal of damage to Westmoreland's reputation. Unlike Rear Admiral Husband E. Kimmel or Major General Walter C. Short, the respective Navy and Army commanders at Pearl Harbor, he did not have to suffer the humiliation of being disciplined and denied further command, but his reputation suffered grievously nonetheless. Many people then and now felt he was somehow at fault for the embarrassment the United States military and government suffered because of Tet, and there was no shortage of those people willing to step forward and say so.

The greatest amount of criticism came from those who felt Westmoreland had misled the country with what many called his "rosy and optimistic" statements, especially those he made during his April and November trips home. Leading a particularly virulent attack on Westmoreland in the Senate was Stephen Young of Ohio. During a thirty-minute diatribe, he said that "Westmoreland's optimistic statements of victory . . . have proved fraudulent and wrong. . . . The attacks clearly revealed that he grossly misjudged the character of the war and the basic untenability of the American military position." Young's charge was echoed in the House by Congresswoman Margaret Heckler of Massachusetts, who claimed that Westmoreland "was engaged in the vain art of self-delusion, and is certainly deluding himself." The delusional theme was given a more lengthy and more humorous treatment by Art Buchwald in his syndicated column of February 6. There he portrayed an arrogant General George Armstrong Custer bragging to a correspondent at the height of the Battle of the Little Bighorn that the battle "had just turned the corner," the Sioux were "on the run," and he could now "see the light at the end of the tunnel."

A large amount of criticism was also directed at Westmoreland by those who thought his strategy for fighting the war was flawed and his skills as a general wanting. Some of the most virulent attacks again came in the Congress. From the Senate floor, Senator Richard Russell of Georgia said that Westmoreland had adopted a strategy similar to the one the French had used, and like the French commanders, he had been "outgeneralled and outwitted by North Vietnam's Minister of Defense Giap." During his own Senate speech, Senator Robert Kennedy of New York bluntly told his colleagues that "half a million American soldiers, with 700,000 Vietnamese allies, with a total command of the air and total command of the sea, backed by huge resources and the most modern weapons, are unable to secure even a single city from the attacks of an enemy whose total strength is about 250,000."

Some indictments of Westmoreland's strategy and generalship by the press were equally blunt. In _Newsweek_, an unnamed staff writer claimed that Westmoreland's strategy in Vietnam "had run into a dead end," and that only the "deluded can console themselves with the comforting feeling that suddenly the war will turn the corner." Keyes Beech, a _New York Post_ correspondent and old Vietnam hand, claimed that Westmoreland had been "humiliated" by Giap during Tet. In a single blow, the North Vietnamese "demolished Westmoreland's optimism" and destroyed "his reputation." The bluntest indictment was delivered by the Pulitzer Prize-winning historian Arthur M. Schlesinger. "Westmoreland," he wrote, "may go down in history as our most disastrous general since Custer."

As the criticism of Westmoreland began accumulating, so too did cries for his removal. Writing in _The Washington Post_, another Pulitzer Prize-winning historian, Marquis Childs, suggested that since Lincoln had not hesitated to fire a number of generals until he found Ulysses S. Grant nor President Truman to relieve MacArthur, then President Johnson ought to have the guts to cashier Westmoreland. In a _Washington Star_ editorial, Clayton Fitchey agreed. Westmoreland, he wrote, "seems to have no idea how to win the war" and needed to be replaced by someone who did.

It is difficult to determine who started the rumor, but in early February, one began circulating in Washington claiming that Westmoreland was about to be relieved. The rumor was fueled during a Senate Armed Forces Committee meeting when several senators pointedly asked General Wheeler if the White House was thinking of removing Westmoreland. Wheeler told them no, but when that did not squelch the rumor, McNamara held a press conference and asserted that "it is quite unreasonable" to think Westmoreland would soon be removed from command. To ease Westmoreland's mind, President Johnson had Wheeler add a personal message from him to the end of a routine cable. "As a personal matter," Wheeler wrote, "you should know that all of us, including the Commander-in-Chief, repose compete confidence in your judgment, your capacity of careful prudent planning, and your ability to cope with the enemy in all circumstances. I say this because I do not want you to be misled and upset by untrue news media comments."

Johnson backed up his words by telling Wheeler to provide West-moreland with whatever support he needed. Wheeler passed this second message on in a February 4 cable, quoting the President as asking, ". . . is there any reinforcements or help we can give you?"

Westmoreland chose not to respond to this direct question. In his return cable, he instead gave a detailed and very optimistic appraisal of the situation in all four corps areas. He made no mention of needing additional troops.

That same evening, sensors north of Khe Sanh started broadcasting urgent signals. A large body of enemy troops, estimated at between 400 and 1,000, were closing in on Hill 881 from the west. Fire control specialists at Khe Sanh plotted the movement of the enemy formation and sent five hundred high-explosive artillery rounds crashing into the jungle. Enemy gunners responded by hitting Khe Sanh and three of the hill positions with a five-hundred-round barrage of their own. At 3:00 A.M., enemy sappers blew holes in the wire around Hill 881, then charged the Marine bunkers. Enemy infantry followed behind them. In the initial shooting, they overran a dozen bunkers, killing 7 Marines and wounding 30. The enemy troops were consolidating their gains when the Marines launched a spontaneous and wild coun-terattack. Using knives, bayonets, machetes, and their rifle butts, they drove the enemy troops out of the bunkers and back down the hill. The next morning, Marines policing the hill counted 109 enemy bodies. Their own losses were 10 killed and 32 wounded.

Westmoreland believed the attack on Hill 881 was likely a prelude to something bigger. His belief was confirmed after midnight on the morning of February 7 when a North Vietnamese infantry regiment spearheaded by nine Soviet-built PT-76 tanks attacked the Lang Vei Special Forces camp, which was located a mere five miles southwest of Khe Sanh. The attacking force quickly overran part of the camp and were threatening to overrun the rest.

Under established plans, the Marines had direct jurisdiction over the camp and its 500 defenders, which included 12 American Army Special Forces troops, and were supposed to come to the camp's aid in the event of an attack. Fearing that a relief force sent overland would surely be ambushed and that a helicopter assault in the face of tanks would be suicidal, the Marine commander at Khe Sanh, Colonel Lownds, had decided against any kind of rescue attempt. After listening to the desperation radio calls from his men inside the camp, Colonel Jonathan Ladd, the Special Forces commander in Vietnam, had called Westmoreland's villa directly and demanded to

be put through to him. Ladd pleaded with Westmoreland to intervene, to overrule Lownds and order the Marines to send a relief force
in, regardless of the cost. They just could not leave those men to a
certain death, he told Westmoreland. Westmoreland, as he himself
put it, "declined to intervene," feeling that he had no choice but to
"honor the prerogative of the field commander on the scene."

It was not a decision Westmoreland made easily, however. According to Marine Brigadier General Edwin H. Simmons, Westmoreland was left in a "cold fury" by the fact that the Marines were
not making any attempt to either reinforce Lang Vei or rescue its
defenders. After mulling the entire situation over, he decided to
personally intervene. Since Abrams was not officially tasked to take
over as commander of MACV Forward until February 13, he would
have to go up to Da Nang himself. He arrived there at noon and
immediately went into a closed session with all the senior Marine
and Army commanders operating in I Corps.

At the opening of the meeting, Colonel Ladd took center stage
and briefed the group on the present situation at Lang Vei. Although
the press had reported the fall of the camp, in reality ten Americans
and forty civilian irregulars were still holding out in a large bunker
at one corner of the camp while continuous volleys of Marine artillery
from Khe Sanh kept the NVA infantry at bay. When Ladd finished
his briefing, Colonel Daniel L. Baldwin III, senior MACV SOG commander, stood up and said that if the Marines would give him the
helicopters, he would personally lead a rescue attempt. An argument
ensued over the advisability of air assault into an area where enemy
tanks were roaming.

"Give him the helicopters," Ladd begged.

"Well, I can't do that," a Marine air officer replied. "We may
need them for our own evacuation."

At that point, Westmoreland abruptly stood up. "You need helicopters, Baldwin?"

"Yes, sir."

"Then give him the helicopters," he snapped, turning directly to
General Chapman. "Assault the camp, extract the survivors, use
CBUs [cluster bombs]—let's go!"

Ladd and the SOG commander then left the meeting with the
Marine air officer to begin organizing the rescue attempt, an attempt
that was ultimately successful in bringing out ten Americans and over
two hundred civilian irregulars.

Westmoreland decided then to turn the focus of the meeting to a broader issue. The meeting so far, as he noted in his diary, had "confirmed concerns that for some time had been troubling" him. His primary concern was with someone countering Cushman, who had shown a clear "absence of initiative . . . dealing forcefully" not only with Lang Vei, but with all of I Corps. "I found Cushman and all his subordinates in shock from the Tet Offensive," he said later. "No one was doing anything." And yet, there was plenty to be done. Besides the enemy threat to Khe Sanh, five enemy divisions were loose in I Corps. Although he had reinforced the Marines in I Corps with the Americal Division, two brigades of the 1st Cavalry Division, a Korean Marine brigade, and a brigade from the 101st Airborne Division, Cushman "appeared complacent, seemingly reluctant to use the Army forces" at his disposal.

Westmoreland ordered each commander present to make a detailed report of the situation in his area of operation. As he listened, he "was shocked at things that virtually begged to be done, yet remained undone." Since so many "local decisions were urgently needed," after listening to all the reports Westmoreland took the almost unprecedented step of giving a direct order to Cushman's subordinate units. Concerned that an NVA division near Da Nang might attack the Marine air base there, he suggested to the Marines present that they consider using a brigade from Major General Samuel Koster's Americal Division to protect Da Nang. When the discussion seemed to be going nowhere, an exasperated Westmoreland ordered Koster and the commander of the 1st Marine Division, Major General Donn G. Robinson, to "leave the room and return only when they had worked out a viable plan for closely coordinated offensive action against the enemy threatening the airfield." Then according to the director of MACV's combat operations center, Brigadier General John Chaisson, Westmoreland went at the rest of the commanders, all one- and two-star generals, snapping out orders to them as if they were a group of green second lieutenants: "You've got to get those roads open, and you've got to do it now. Time is of the essence. . . . The Qua Viet River must be kept open; this is a must. . . . Get troops between the enemy and Da Nang; this is also a must. . . . We've got to take some risk; time is of the essence; let's go!"

In his pocket diary, Chaisson wrote: "One of Westy's best days."

Back in Saigon the next day, Westmoreland began worrying about the future. To help stop any further attacks in I Corps, he decided to transfer a brigade of the 101st Airborne Division from the Saigon area to northern I Corps. The withdrawal of the unit from Saigon upset General Wheeler. He felt that Westmoreland was taking a serious risk weakening the defenses of Saigon and told him so in a February 8 cable. Westmoreland, on the other hand, thought the risk slight. He was confident the situation in Saigon would soon be completely under control and did not greatly fear another enemy attack there.

In spite of Westmoreland's optimism, Wheeler continued to fret and agonize. Like President Johnson, he was still badly shaken by the Tet attacks and worried that the enemy was preparing to launch another wave of attacks against South Vietnam's cities, especially Saigon. Wheeler's major worry, however, other than the United States suffering an embarrassing setback in Vietnam, was the deplorable state of United States forces worldwide. Out of fear of the political backlash it would cause, the President had been unwilling to call up the Reserves. Because of that, American forces and resources worldwide were stretched to the breaking point. The Marine Corps was only just barely able to maintain its commitment in Vietnam, and the Army was not in much better shape. In order to maintain its troop level in Vietnam, the Army had been forced to cannibalize its units in Germany and other areas. At the moment, the only combat-ready division in the United States was the 82nd Airborne Division, and two of its brigades had been stripped to fill the ranks of its third brigade, which was preparing for deployment to Vietnam.

In Wheeler's considered judgment, the manpower problems facing the military were compounded further by the present ominous state of affairs worldwide. In North Korea, Kim El Sung was rattling his sword again and making threats against the United States, and in Berlin and the Middle East there were also indications of potential trouble. Wheeler quite rightly feared that if trouble broke out anywhere else in the world, trouble that required military intervention, the United States would be unable to act.

Given all this, Wheeler had become convinced that national security demanded that the United States call up the Reserves. With the strategic reserve filled to capacity, he would be able to deal with a military emergency anywhere in the world. He would also have the troops available, if the President could be persuaded, to expand the war in Vietnam, to invade Cambodia and Laos and possibly even North Vietnam itself.

Wheeler realized, however, that given Johnson's continued reluctance to expand the ground war into Laos, Cambodia, and North Vietnam, he could not request a Reserve call-up to provide troops for an expanded war. Johnson simply would not buy it. To get the call-up, and to get an expanded war in the process, Wheeler concocted an elaborate scheme, a scheme that would require him to dupe both Westmoreland and the President, while simultaneously playing them off against each other. It would be Machiavellian politics at its best. And though Wheeler began with the best of intentions, when his scheme had run its course, Westmoreland's reputation would be even more tattered than it had been after Tet, and the White House would be faced with another public relations disaster. Ironically, Wheeler, the instigator of the scheme, would walk away almost completely unscathed, prompting White House insider Morton Halperin to dub him "the evil genius of the war."

Wheeler began his scheme on February 8 with a cable to Westmoreland in which he popped the startling question:

> Do you need reinforcements? Our capabilities are limited. We can provide the 82d Airborne Division and about one-half of a Marine division, both loaded with Vietnam vets. . . . If you consider reinforcements imperative you should not be bound by an earlier agreement. . . . The United States government is not prepared to accept a defeat in Vietnam.

Westmoreland was a bit startled by the question. He had not been expecting such a query at that time. Given the strategic guideline he was operating under at the moment, reinforcements simply were not needed. In his return cable, he told Wheeler that since "it was only prudent to plan for the worst contingency," he could use the troops mentioned. He thought they might be perfect for an April amphibious landing behind enemy lines in northern I Corps that he had been planning for some time.

Wheeler was as shocked by Westmoreland's reply as Westmoreland had been by Wheeler's question. Wheeler thought the troops were needed now, not in April. He responded in his second cable by playing down his anxieties. "Please understand," he stated, "that I am not trying to sell you in the deployment of additional forces, which in any event I cannot guarantee. . . . However, my sensing is that the critical phase of the war is upon us, and I do not believe that you should refrain from asking for what you believe is required under the circumstances."

By now, Westmoreland realized Wheeler's game, realized that his boss was telling him in the most certain terms to request more troops. And so did, telling Wheeler in his second cable that he could use "immediately a Marine regiment package and a brigade package of the 82d Airborne Division." He tried to make it clear, however, that he did not need them because he feared defeat, but because they would enable him to take advantage of the heavy losses the enemy had suffered during Tet. He wanted to capitalize on those losses by "seizing the initiative in other areas. Exploiting this opportunity could materially shorten the war."

The next day, Wheeler presented Westmoreland's proposal to the President, who immediately called a meeting with Secretaries McNamara and Rusk; Generals Taylor and Wheeler; the head of the CIA, Richard Helms; and the man soon to replace McNamara, Clark Clifford. After the meeting, Wheeler cabled Westmoreland and told him the conferees were not quite sure of a paragraph in his (West-moreland's) last cable and wanted a clarification. "Specifically your message is interpreted here as expressing the following: You could use additional U.S. troops, but you are not expressing a firm demand for them. In sum, you do not fear defeat if you are not reinforced."

"I am expressing a firm request for additional troops," West-moreland responded, "not because I fear defeat if I am not reinforced, but because I do not feel that I can fully grasp the initiative from the recently reinforced enemy without them."

While Westmoreland's troop request was being mulled over at the White House, the Joint Chiefs met at the Pentagon and did something they had never done before: They refused to support a Westmoreland troop request, a troop request ironically that Wheeler had coaxed out of him. In a memo to the President, they argued that sending Westmoreland the forces he had requested without a si-multaneous call-up of nearly 120,000 Army and Marine Corps Re-serves would seriously drain the available manpower pool. To prod the President into approving both Westmoreland's troop request and the Reserve call-up, they tried to frighten him a bit, to play on his anxieties. "It is not clear at this time," they warned, "whether the enemy will be able to mount and sustain a second series of major attacks throughout the country. It is equally unclear as to how well the Vietnamese Armed forces would be able to stand up to such a series of attacks if they were to occur."

Though the Joint Chiefs' words did heighten the President's anx-ieties, Johnson was not prepared at this point to call up the Reserves. Nonetheless, he did approve the reinforcements Westmoreland had requested. As to the Reserve call-up, he told Wheeler and McNamara to study the problem further.

The Joint Chiefs approved the deployment almost immediately. The Army brigade had an approximate strength of 4,000; the Marine regiment around thirty-six hundred. Logistical troops brought the total deployment up to ten thousand. When President Johnson was notified the troops would begin flying out of the United States on February 17, he decided to visit them and bid them a personal farewell. He flew first to Fort Bragg to see off the Army paratroopers, then on to El Toro, California, to see off the Marines. He then spent the night on the carrier *Constellation,* which had just returned from a tour of duty off the Vietnam coast. It was an emotional journey for the President. Many of the men were being sent off for their second and third tour to Vietnam, and Johnson was visibly anguished as he shook hands with the men as they boarded their planes. Before returning to Washington, Johnson decided to make a final stop at the winter home of former President Eisenhower at Palm Desert, California. In Eisenhower's living room, Walt Rostow and Marine General Lewis Walt briefed him on the Tet Offensive. Eisenhower proceeded to question both men on the present military situation in South Vietnam. Even though Johnson specifically requested it, Eisenhower refused to give military advice. He told Johnson that he simply did not believe in second-guessing a commander in the field. Then in an aside, he said that Westmoreland had "the greatest responsibility of any general I have ever known in history."

Johnson was shocked by the statement. In dismay, he asked Eisenhower pointedly if he actually thought Westmoreland's responsibility for a half-million American men in Vietnam was greater than his own responsibility for five million men and an invasion of Nazi-controlled Europe.

Yes, Eisenhower answered, he did think that. "Westmoreland's job is tougher. I always knew where the enemy was."

Both Westmoreland and Wheeler were happy to see reinforcements on their way to Vietnam. Wheeler, however, was not happy to have his Reserve call-up denied. Undaunted, he began trying to work his scheme again. He made his first move this time with a February 12 cable to Westmoreland, containing some news he was certain the general would be pleased with. During a meeting at the White House, he told Westmoreland, there had been a lengthy discussion about the abrupt change in enemy strategy and "the question arose as to whether or not we should not change our strategy." Wheeler's statement was like a hook, and Westmoreland gladly took it. As Davidson notes, it "kindled Westmoreland's long-held hope and growing belief that the administration was about to adopt a more offensive strategy." Admiral Sharp helped kindle that hope even more with the announcement in a February 17 cable to Westmoreland that with the changed situation in Vietnam, he did not think the 525,000 troop-ceiling could possibly stand any longer. Around this time, Westmoreland also learned that South Carolina Congressman Mendel Rivers, the chairman of the House Armed Services Committee and a strong Westmoreland backer, had begun publicly calling for a "reserve call-up and more offensive strategy."

In the days following Wheeler's cable, Westmoreland and his staff began dusting off various plans for offensive operations aimed at Laos, Cambodia, and North Vietnam. In a cable on February 20, Wheeler warned him against submitting any more long-range troop requests because, as he put it, the White House "can handle only one major problem at a time." Two days later, Westmoreland learned why Wheeler wanted the delay. In a lengthy cable, Wheeler informed him that at the President's request he was going to fly to Saigon for a firsthand evaluation and to work with Westmoreland at "coming up with a broad estimate of what we can expect in the future. By this I mean what strategies will be open to the enemy, what forces will be available, what opportunities have been opened to us, what problems we must be prepared to face." The President, Wheeler said, was awaiting his return before making "some hard decisions on how best to build up the strategic reserve and what reinforcements to send to Vietnam."

Wheeler arrived in Saigon on February 23, accompanied by Major General William DePuy, now a special assistant to the Joint Chiefs for counterinsurgency. Westmoreland, in his own words, found Wheeler a "tired man, seemingly near the point of exhaustion." Instead of the stately, erect, handsome soldier he remembered from his last trip home, he found a haggard, overweight, thick-jowled, gouty old man. Although DePuy—the same DePuy who while commander of the 1st Infantry Division had fired a dozen senior officers for lack of aggressiveness—had not physically deteriorated, like Wheeler he "mirrored the gloom that pervaded official circles in Washington, a reflection of the doomsday reporting by press and television."

If Wheeler was indeed in a fit of depression, as Westmoreland claims, that depression only deepened his first night in Saigon. As Wheeler slept in Abrams's former house, a rocket landed nearby, shaking the house and bouncing Wheeler awake. Wheeler was so unnerved that he told a colleague that he was certain enemy gunners had specifically targeted the house. Given the inaccuracy of enemy rockets, it was a preposterous idea, yet Wheeler persisted in believing it. The next morning, Westmoreland convinced Wheeler to move into a heavily sandbagged room at MACV headquarters. In a conference room nearby, the two men and their staffs began a series of lengthy meetings. During the first meeting, Westmoreland briefed everyone present, giving them a quick overview of the situation countrywide. His message was a simple, upbeat one: The enemy had been soundly defeated during Tet and was now on the run. Westmoreland's message did not please the dour Wheeler, nor DePuy. Both repeatedly questioned Westmoreland about the enemy's capability to launch another round of Tetlike attacks. Westmoreland tried to downplay the possibility, reiterating his contention that the enemy had "shot his wad" at Tet, but neither Wheeler nor DePuy was buying it. Both remained convinced that South Vietnam was still in grave danger.

Wheeler was not dour about everything. He was genuinely happy that in only eight days the hawkish Clark Clifford would be replacing Robert McNamara, a man he and the other Chiefs had come to detest. With Clifford at the reins at Defense, he was convinced the military might finally get permission to expand the war, maybe even permission to go for a knockout blow against North Vietnam. Westmoreland was also elated over McNamara's replacement, and in anticipation of Clifford's arrival, he and Wheeler began hammering out various force requirements for Vietnam to meet a wide spectrum of possible situations. They hoped the situation would be one in which Clifford talked Johnson into expanding the war, but both also prepared contingency plans for a number of worst-case scenarios, such as the collapse of the South Vietnamese Army or government, or a major conventional invasion of South Vietnam by North Vietnam. Working together, the two arrived at a list of reinforcements totaling approximately 206,000 men. According to Westmoreland, there was a "clear understanding" between them that only 108,000 men of the 206,000 were actually earmarked for Vietnam, and then only if the President decided to widen the war. The rest of the troops were meant only to pump up the strategic reserve in the United States.

The report that Wheeler delivered to the President and his advisers at the White House, however, said nothing about a new strategy or that the troop package was merely to back up various contingency plans. Instead, he painted a grim picture of the situation in South

Vietnam at the moment, a picture that clearly contradicted the one
Westmoreland had painted for him. Wheeler told the President that
the enemy attacks "had nearly succeeded in a dozen places, and defeat
in those places was only averted by the timely reaction of U.S. forces.
In short it was a very near thing." In addition, he pointed out, the
enemy offensive had not yet run its course. With the enemy preparing
fresh attacks against Khe Sanh, Hue, Quang Tri, the Central Highlands, and even Saigon, and with half the American maneuver battalions deployed to I Corps, "MACV will be hard pressed to meet
adequately all threats. Under these circumstances, we must be prepared to accept some reverses."

As Wheeler was only too aware, the President was not prepared
to accept any reverses, and he continued his briefing with that fact
uppermost in his mind. To avoid any reverses, Wheeler argued that
the United States had "first, to counter the enemy offensive and to
destroy or eject the NVA invasion force in the north. Second, to
restore security in the cities and towns. Third, to restore security in
the heavily populated areas of the countryside. Fourth, to regain the
initiative through offensive operations."

But to accomplish all those tasks, Wheeler finally pointed out, it
would take large numbers of troops: 108,000 for deployment to Vietnam and approximately 100,000 more to rebuild the strategic reserve.
Without those reinforcements, he warned, Westmoreland's forces
would be too badly stretched to react to every enemy threat everywhere. Westmoreland might even be forced to "give up the two
northern provinces."

On that final grim note, Wheeler finished his briefing. As Herbert
Y. Schandler notes in his *The Unmaking of the President*, a study of
the political impact of Tet, "the Chairman of the Joint Chiefs, in
stressing the negative aspects of the situation in Vietnam, again saw
Tet and the reaction to it as an opportunity, perhaps the last opportunity, to convince the administration to call up the reserves forces"
and expand the war.

Following the briefing, the President ordered Clifford to head a
task force to study the troop request, with the instructions, "Give me
the lesser of evils." The task force was immediately divided down the
middle about the troop request, with some members—Maxwell Taylor, Walt Rostow, and Wheeler—arguing that the Tet Offensive had
provided the United States with the opportunity to smash the enemy
in Vietnam, rebuild the strategic reserve, and mobilize the American
people. Opposing the troop request were Deputy Secretary of De-

fense Paul Nitze, Assistant Secretary of Defense Paul Warnke, and Assistant Secretary for Public Affairs Paul Goulding. All three argued that the war was a stalemate, that it had been too costly and too divisive, and it was time for the United States to begin looking for a way out of Vietnam. During the meeting, Clifford was increasingly troubled by what he heard from the dissenters on the task force. He was also troubled by what he had heard from a number of senior members of Congress, whom he had discreetly queried at the President's request to get their opinions on national mobilization. Not only were most opposed to the idea, but a number were extremely critical of Westmoreland's generalship and the tactics he was using in Vietnam.

It is not known just how seriously the President was considering mobilization at the time, but if he was, he must have had second thoughts when he read his March 7 *New York Times.* On page two of the paper was an article by Gene Roberts quoting a senior military spokeman in Saigon as saying that he did not think the "enemy has any great capacity to assume any general offensive in the near future. He has been hurt and hurt badly. He is tired." Westmoreland received no response from the President, but he did from Wheeler. In a short cable, he instructed Westmoreland that when speaking to the press, he should not "denigrate the enemy or make predictions of victory." He should, however, "express the view that there is tough fighting ahead and that the enemy has residual capabilities not yet committed."

Westmoreland, still unaware of Wheeler's elaborate scheme, responded that he "would do his best to comply, consistent with intellectual honesty."

Clifford, in the meantime, had filed his final report on the deliberations of his task force. It represented a compromise between those who wanted to escalate the war and those wanted to deescalate. It recommended that the President immediately authorize the deployment of 22,000 new troops and issue a call-up of 245,000 reservists. Clifford later wrote that although the military perceived him as a hawk, he had concluded during the task force deliberations that it was time to start scaling the war down. He felt, however, that at the moment Johnson would not have been able to accept the implied assumption that the American strategy in Vietnam had failed. Rather than being immediately frank with Johnson, he decided instead to gradually prepare him to face that grim fact.

Though pressured by Rostow to make a quick decision on the troop request, Johnson chose to wait. Frightened of the political turmoil a massive call-up of the Reserves would cause in the country, he decided to discuss the troop request further with his advisers.

He was in the middle of one of these discussions when on the morning of March 10, two investigative reporters, Hedrick Smith and Neil Sheehan, revealed in a front-page article in *The New York Times* that Westmoreland had requested 206,000 more troops. The request, they wrote, "has touched off a divisive internal debate within high levels of the Johnson administration." The article made no mention of the fact that the troop request was based on a contingency plan. To the contrary, Westmoreland was portrayed in the article as having requested the troops as an emergency request so he could "regain the initiative and to continue toward our objective."

When Westmoreland first read the article, he did not at first understand what he was reading. A 206,000-troop request? What request? It was a long moment before he made the connection, before he realized that the contingency plan he had hammered out with Wheeler—a plan he had felt only had a fair chance of being accepted—was being portrayed by Smith and Sheehan as a near desperation request on his part. As this realization hit him, so did an overwhelming feeling of shock.

As he feared would happen, the Smith-Sheehan story startled the nation. For those already shaken by Tet, the 206,000-troop request was like the proverbial straw that broke the camel's back. If, as Westmoreland claimed, Tet had been a great United States victory, people across the country asked, then why did he now need 206,000 additional troops; what guarantee was there that he would not ask for another 206,000, maybe even a third; was Vietnam really unwinnable? Was it really just a bottomless pit? For many Americans, the troop request was conclusive proof that it was.

While many millions of average Americans pondered these questions, Westmoreland's critics, now even more emboldened than they had been after Tet, quickly sharpened their knives and went on the attack. On the same day the Smith-Sheehan article appeared, NBC correspondent Frank McGee, already on record for strongly opposing the war, hosted a special program on Vietnam and announced that Westmoreland's troop request was evidence that the United States was losing the war. McGee's views were soon reflected in dozens of newspapers and magazine editorials. A *Newsweek* editorial was typical of many of them. It referred to Westmoreland's troop request as proof that, short of using nuclear weapons, the United States had no way to "achieve decisive military superiority in Vietnam."

The troop request provoked the stormiest reaction in Congress, something that had been just the opposite after Tet. There on March 12, Senators Robert Kennedy, Clifford Chase, Mike Mansfield, and Frank Church denounced the war variously as "a mistake," "unwinnable," "divisive," and "criminal." Their voices were quickly joined by a chorus of other voices, most of whom spoke out against the war for the first time. *Newsweek*'s chief correspondent, Samuel Shaffer, noted that Westmoreland's troop request had brought Congress close to mutiny. "Hawks are being converted overnight into doves," he wrote, "and House members in particular are falling over each other to get resolutions in the hopper demanding that no more troops be sent." One resolution, backed by 139 members, called for a full review of American policy in Vietnam.

Westmoreland was dumbfounded by all the frenetic activity. He was further dumbfounded by a cable he got from Wheeler on March 12. "I was directed to keep you informed of the status of our forces," Wheeler wrote, "so that you will not in the future be placed in the position of asking for something that does not exist or is not available." Having worked with Wheeler to put together a trooop package that was based only on a contingency plan, Westmoreland could not understand why Wheeler was now berating him for requesting troops that "did not exist or were not available." It was an incredible cable.

What followed during the next week was even more incredible. Treasury Secretary Henry Fowler warned Johnson that an approval of the troop request could set off a severe monetary crisis. Following Fowler's warning, stock prices, which had fallen sharply after Tet, fell yet again. Then on March 12 came the real shocker. Senator Eugene McCarthy, who opposed the war, came within 330 votes of beating the President in the New Hampshire Democratic primary. Four days later, sensing an easy kill, Senator Robert Kennedy announced that he would oppose the President in the remaining Democratic primaries. In the matter of a week, Johnson's political consensus had evaporated. Although support for the war continued to remain steady (for many Americans support meant support for the boys fighting the war), approval of Johnson's handling of it plummeted to an all-time low of 26 percent.

But Johnson was not quite ready to give up. On March 15, he sought guidance from Dean Acheson, the former secretary of state under Truman. Acheson was a longtime supporter of the war, but during the last six months he had had a change of heart. He was unusually blunt with Johnson, telling him that the war in Vietnam was hopeless, that the United States had neither the time nor the resources to achieve its military objectives in Vietnam. Johnson heard much the same message from United Nations Ambassador Arthur Goldberg. The war was a stalemate, Goldberg told him, and as a goodwill gesture, the United States should stop the bombing of North Vietnam.

Johnson was reaching the end of his tether. On March 23, he took the first step toward putting the country on a new course when he announced at a White House news conference that he was bringing Westmoreland home in early July to replace General Johnson as Army Chief of Staff. He emphasized, however, that "strategy and tactical operations have nothing to do with the appointment as such."

Three days later, Johnson got an even greater shock than the one Acheson and Goldberg had given him when he met with the so-called Wise Men, a group of distinguished former Cabinet secretaries, ambassadors, and generals that he had consulted on several previous occasions. The group had unanimously endorsed his policy in Vietnam as recently as November, but Tet and the fallout over the troop request had drastically changed the way most of them viewed the war. Speaking for the majority, McGeorge Bundy told the President that they felt the United States was no longer capable of doing the job it had set out to do in Vietnam, and "we must now begin to take steps to disengage."

For Johnson it was over for good now. He had had enough. Acheson and Goldberg had staggered him and the Wise Men had knocked him down. Still stinging from their report, on March 31, in a nationwide telecast, he announced to the world a number of major decisions he had just made. While he had decided to send Westmoreland an additional 13,500 troops, he told his audience, he had also decided to limit the bombing of North Vietnam to the area just above the demilitarized zone. He announced that he had named Averell Harriman as his personal representative, and that the United States was ready to talk peace at any time.

Then Johnson dropped a bomb. ". . . I have concluded," he said, "that I should not permit the Presidency to become involved in the partisan divisions that are developing in this political year. . . . Accordingly, I shall not seek, and I will not accept, the nomination of my Party for another term as your President." These final words sent a shock wave through the country and the world. Even though Johnson had told a number of close friends and associates, Westmoreland included, that he was not going to run, few had believed him.

With Westmoreland's transfer and Johnson's decision not to run, editorial writers around the country sharpened their pencils once again. Most were in agreement when it came to Johnson—the war had exhausted him physically and emotionally, and he had lost his political consensus. Another term, most correctly concluded, would have only been divisive, would have divided the country even more than it already was.

These same editorial writers were not so certain what Westmoreland's transfer meant. Had he been "kicked upstairs," as many Saigon newspapers claimed, or had he merely completed his four-year term in Vietnam and been promoted, as the White House claimed? The *Buffalo Evening News, Salt Lake City Tribune, Denver Post, Wall Street Journal, St. Louis Post Dispatch,* and *Christian Science Monitor* claimed the former, that the move was in some way or another a result of the White House's unhappiness with the way Westmoreland was running the war. A number of other newspapers, however— the most prominent among them being the *Washington Post, New York Times,* and *Chicago Tribune*—thought the entire issue of Westmoreland's transfer too cloudy to speculate about. Owing to a lack of documents on the incident, and President Johnson's so carefully guarding his motives for the move, the issue is still cloudy today.

Westmoreland himself naturally claims that his move to Army Chief was a promotion. To back up that claim, he has on a number of occasions produced for historians a letter from Wheeler to him dated December 22, 1967. In the letter, Wheeler tells him that he was "the obvious candidate for Chief of Staff Army (CSA)," and that he would become Chief either in mid-1968 if General Johnson retired, or a year or two later, if Johnson chose to remain. In his lengthy history of the Vietnam wars, *Vietnam at War,* Phillip Davidson vehemently defends Westmoreland's claim. As a basis for his defense, he also points to the Wheeler letter, which for him at least, offers conclusive proof that the President had selected Westmoreland to be Army Chief forty days before Tet.

Clark Clifford supports Westmoreland's and Davidson's version. He claims that McNamara had recommended Westmoreland's transfer prior to Tet. Unfortunately, says Clifford, "the delay in announcement left the inevitable impression that Westmoreland had been relieved because of Tet." Clifford does not explain why McNamara wanted Westmoreland transferred, whether he was unhappy with the way Westmoreland was running the war, or if it was merely routine, as McNamara himself claims. Clifford likewise is unable to provide us with Johnson's thoughts about the issue in November 1967.

A prominent foreign correspondent in the 1960s, Henry Brandon, feels the decision to transfer Westmoreland was far from being finalized in late 1967. According to Brandon, the question of what to do about Westmoreland was still troubling the President on February 18 when he visited ex-President Eisenhower at his Desert Springs home. Alone with Eisenhower, Johnson unburdened himself, says Brandon, asking the general pointedly how long a President should back a military commander. According to Brandon, Eisenhower replied that a President must back his general as long as he has confidence in him. If he has lost his confidence, he should replace him. Although Brandon does not provide documentation for the account, it seems very plausible that Johnson would ask Eisenhower such a question.

If the account is true and Johnson was still uncertain what to do with Westmoreland in late February, then it might very well be that Johnson tranferred Westmoreland because of the problems the 206,000-troop request caused him. Wheeler had presented the request in such a way as to back Johnson into a corner. Besides repeatedly painting the troop package as an absolute necessity if Westmoreland was to avoid a major setback in Vietnam, Wheeler also on a number of occasions made it clear "that the full 206,000 men were needed, and to provide less would be taken by Westmoreland as a vote of no confidence." Wheeler was lying. Westmoreland had never said anything like that, nor did he think he was in danger of suffering a major setback on the battlefield. Unfortunately for Westmoreland, Johnson did not know any of this. He took Wheeler at his words, and they were words that he might have thought left him but two options. Either give Westmoreland the troops and a "vote of confidence," or replace him.

That the troop request likely had something to do with Westmoreland's transfer became obvious on March 26 when Johnson ordered Abrams back to Washington for consultation. One of the first questions Johnson asked Abrams was whether more troops were needed in Vietnam. Unaware of the troop request, Abrams responded, "Oh, no, sir, Mr. President, we've got plenty of troops." Abrams's statement likely gave the President great comfort, but it did little to relieve the considerable guilt he felt having to end Westmoreland's tenure in Vietnam under such suspicious circumstances. In an effort to relieve some of that guilt, he sent Wheeler to meet Westmoreland in the Philippines. There in a private conversation, Wheeler tried to ease Westmoreland's pain somewhat. He did not succeed. Wheeler, as he told President Johnson afterward, found Westmoreland "bitter" that "he didn't get the support in Washington" he wanted and upset that he "has now been made the goat for the war."

Westmoreland felt he had a right to be bitter. He felt that at the moment he had in Vietnam "the finest military force ever assembled." If the President had only intensified the bombing of the North, mined Haiphong Harbor, and given him permission to expand the war, he was certain the North Vietnamese could be broken. After the war, in speech and in his writing, he frequently liked to compare the situation in Vietnam to a boxing match. "It was like two boxers in a ring," he was fond of telling people, "one having the other on the ropes, close to a knock-out, when the apparent winner's second inexplicably throws in the towel."

Westmoreland might have been right. An expanded intensified war might well have broken North Vietnam's will to continue. He was wrong, however, in thinking that it was possible at that time. It certainly would have been possible in 1965, and it most likely would have been possible in 1966 and even in 1967. It was not, however, possible in March 1968. Westmoreland indeed might have had the finest military force ever assembled, and there can be no doubt he had the finest machines of war ever assembled, but he lacked one important asset—time. Ambassador Bunker says he tried to tell Westmoreland just that in late March, that the United States had run out of time in Vietnam, that it was now too late to mobilize the Reserves and expand the war, that, in effect, the United States was going to have to accept a stalemate in Vietnam. But, according to Bunker, Westmoreland was not interested in hearing what he had to say. He still wanted to win the war or at least to badly smash North Vietnam so that they would call it quits, and he did not give a damn about the political situation in the United States.

Army Chief

On the day President Johnson announced Westmoreland's transfer, Giap decided to add insult to injury by ordering his gunners around Khe Sanh to give the Marine base an unusually hard shelling. They responded by firing 1,307 rounds into the base, a record number of incoming rounds for a single day. If Westmoreland was aware of Giap's slight, he did not mention it. Besides, Giap's shelling was piddling compared with what Westmoreland was preparing to unleash. Westmoreland was on his way out as a commander, but he intended to go out in a big way. And on his way out, he intended to prove what he had been saying for the last months, that the Tet attacks had hurt the enemy badly and left him very vulnerable to a counterattack.

In early April, he put in motion that counterattack. Officially designated the Counteroffensive, it was designed to sweep away any remnants of enemy units still near the populated coastal lowlands and then attack the last of the big enemy sanctuaries near the border.

In Saigon, Westmoreland massed fifty thousand United States and ARVN troops, then ordered them to fan out into the six provinces surrounding the capital and begin rooting out the remnants of three enemy divisions still lurking in the area. In over twenty sharp battles that followed, Allied forces killed over twenty-six hundred enemy soldiers and drove the rest out of the area. In a follow-up operation, one hundred thousand Allied troops invaded Gia Dinh Province and killed another seventy-six hundred enemy soldiers. Farther north, American airborne troopers swept away the last of enemy survivors from the area around Hue.

Simultaneous with these attacks, other Allied units smashed into a dozen enemy base areas. In the Mekong Delta, United States and ARVN units set up blocking positions around the U Minh Forest, a formidable Communist bastion deep in the Mekong Delta. Taking advantage of a long dry spell, United States jets set the fifteen hundred square miles of jungle on fire with napalm and phosphorus while United States Navy cruisers in the Gulf of Thailand plastered enemy positions with thousands of rockets and high-explosive shells. Fierce winds quickly turned the isolated fires into a huge firestorm, which swept through the Minh, setting off thousands of tons of explosives that the enemy had stored there. A week after the bombing and shelling started, the U Minh had been reduced to a smoldering ruin.

Westmoreland ordered an equally strong attack against the A Shau, a long, narrow valley near the Laotian border that the NVA had used as a staging area for their attack on Hue. From his intelligence staff, Westmoreland had learned that there were as many as ten thousand NVA regulars in the valley at the moment, either guarding the numerous supply depots there or preparing for further attacks against the coast.

Beginning in early April and for the next six days and nights, Westmoreland sent wave after wave of B-52s against enemy gun positions, bivouacs, and supply depots scattered from one end of the valley floor to the other. He followed this massive prep with an equally massive assault. Behind a rain of artillery fire and more prep fire from fleets of jet fighters and helicopter gunships, battalions from the 101st Airborne Division, the 1st Cavalry Division, the ARVN 327th Infantry Brigade, and 6th Airborne Division were airlifted into the valley from five different directions. Once on the ground, these forces began attacking overland, again with massive support from jet fighters and helicopter gunships. In the sharp fighting that followed, the United States lost over sixty helicopters to ground fire and suffered 139 killed and wounded. They, in turn, killed over 1,000 enemy soldiers and sent the remaining into hiding. A sweep of the valley floor uncovered a cornucopia of supplies, including 2,200 tons of explosives, 135,000 rounds of small arms ammunition, 5,000 rockets, 75 trucks, 3 tracked vehicles, and a single tank.

Westmoreland was pleased with the attack on the A Shau, but in early April, he had his mind on something much bigger—Khe Sanh. Since Tet, the Marine base had been out of the spotlight, but never for a moment out of Westmoreland's thoughts. Now, with his Counteroffensive in full gear and enemy forces on the run all across South Vietnam, he could turn his full attention to it once again. It was time, he decided, to lift the siege of Khe Sanh. To avoid controversy in the press, however, and to avoid further bruising of Marine egos, he was careful to point out in public statements that it would "not be a relief in the sense of a rescue . . . but relief in the sense of opening ground contact and eliminating the enemy with mobile operations." According to his plan, which was code-named Pegasus, the Army and Marines were to coordinate two separate ground attacks and then link up together outside Khe Sanh's wire. Leading the Army attack was the 1st Cavalry Division. Tasked with reopening Highway 9 and eliminating any enemy troops along the way, the 1st began their attack with an air assault east of Khe Sanh on April 1. They expected stiff resistance, but discovered instead that enemy troops around Khe Sanh, on direct orders from Giap, were abandoning their bunkers and trench lines and fleeing from the area. The 1st did discover just how successful Westmoreland's Operation Niagara had been four months before. "The place was absolutely denuded," the commander of the 1st Cavalry Division, Major General Rathvon McC. Tompkins, wrote later. "The trees were gone . . . everything was gone. Pockmarked and ruined and burnt . . . like the surface of the moon. Scattered around the apocalyptic landscape, 1st Cavalry troopers found hundreds of enemy corpses. Some lay where they had fallen. Others were buried in shallow, hastily-dug graves." Leading the Marine attack from Ca Lu, the 1st Marine Regiment encountered much the same scene as the 1st Cavalry Division: denuded terrain and piles of enemy corpses. They likewise met only sporadic enemy resistance.

The battle for Khe Sanh was over. It ended with a wh′ rather than with the bang Westmoreland had hoped for. watching his forces around Khe Sanh being obliterated by ′ and torrents of artillery fire, Giap had decided to call

On April 6, Westmoreland, at the request of t′ flew home to consult with the President. By now Wes.

the complete story of Wheeler's machinations and realized that those machinations, at least indirectly, had caused him great harm. He expressed no anger toward Wheeler when they met at the Pentagon, however, nor at any time thereafter. To the contrary, after the war when journalists and historians asked him, as they frequently did, for his feeling about Wheeler and his scheme, Westmoreland always spoke with kindness of the general. Wheeler had had a terribly unpleasant job to do, he would say. That job had been to convince the President to do something that was best for the country. When one of these interviewers once asked him pointedly if he thought he had been "conned" by Wheeler, Westmoreland quickly and politely changed the subject.

A few hours after arriving in Washington, Westmoreland went to the White House, where the President, Clark Clifford, Averell Harriman, and a number of key presidential advisers were waiting for him. At the opening of the meeting, the President asked him to comment on the military situation in Vietnam at the moment and to make any suggestions he thought important to Harriman, who was preparing for his upcoming negotiations with the Communists. In spite of being personally bitter, Westmoreland's presentation was upbeat. He told the assembled men that since Tet, the enemy had lost sixty thousand men killed and eighteen thousand weapons, losses he could not easily replace. While the North Vietnamese had 20,000 men moving down the trail at the moment, they needed over 40,000 to refill their depleted ranks. Harriman should keep all this in mind when negotiating, he pointed out. Keep in mind that he would be negotiating from a position of strength.

Westmoreland then turned to Khe Sanh. There the North Vietnamese had lost between 10,000 and 15,000 men killed, he said. "I know there was great concern back here over Khe Sanh, but it was a great victory. They gave us the best targets we have had in the war. From January until just a few days ago, we had over 6,000 secondary explosions and 1,300 bodies seen on the ground, 900 bunkers destroyed and 300 gun positions. The NVA are not ten feet tall as the press reports them. The Dien Bien Phu veterans are old and gray now."

The assembled men were not particularly interested in Westmoreland's recitations of statistics, especially statistics they were already familiar with. They were more interested in getting his response a complete bombing halt. Westmoreland told them that he was only opposed to one, but thought that the United States should instead escalate the bombing of North Vietnam and begin bombing Cambodia.

"They would impeach me if I did," the President said.

"Under what conditions would a cease-fire be acceptable?" Clifford asked.

"I don't see the acceptability of that," Westmoreland responded. "We would like the North Vietnamese to go home and turn in their weapons."

Westmoreland's intransigence was out of place at the meeting. Clifford had decided a month earlier that the war had to be brought to a swift conclusion, and Harriman, who had always had serious doubts about the possibility of any military solution in Vietnam, believed the U.S. should unilaterally stop all bombing. Both men were looking for ways to deescalate the war, not escalate. Following a quick press conference at the White House, where he announced that the U.S. was "on top again in Vietnam," Westmoreland flew back to Vietnam. Three days later, the President announced that Westmoreland's successor had finally been picked. As everyone had expected, it was General Creighton W. Abrams.

Back in Vietnam, Westmoreland performed his last duties as a battlefield commander, helping to oversee the Allied response to another round of enemy attacks—119 in all—that came to be called Mini-Tet. Most of the attacks were limited to mortar and rocket fire, and were designed only for psychological impact. A number of enemy battalions did manage to penetrate the suburbs of Saigon, however, where they wreaked considerable havoc until driven out.

Westmoreland dismissed the Communists attacks as insignificant. "Every enemy battalion that made contact in the Saigon area," he told reporters, "has been hurt to the point that most can no longer be considered combat effective. The quality of the enemy's battlefield performance is—well, it approached the pathetic in some cases." When asked whether the United States could win the war, Westmoreland was less self-assured, admitting that the war couldn't "be won in the classic sense." Still, when questioned further, he flatly rejected the idea that the war was a stalemate.

When the last shot of Mini-Tet was fired in late May, Westmoreland began putting his affairs in order in Saigon and preparing to depart. He spent his last few days in country on a farewell tour, flying from one end of the country to the other, visiting dozens of base camps and installations. Everywhere he went, he was greeted by hundreds of camera-toting soldiers and sailors, who swarmed about him without regard to military decorum. Always ramrod straight, Westmoreland gave each group much the same speech, telling them that they had served their country well and should be proud of what they had helped achieve in Vietnam.

On June 9, again ramrod straight, Westmoreland said farewell to the six hundred members of his staff at a ceremony on the MACV parade grounds. Following his address, Abrams took the podium and praised Westmoreland as the skilled architect "who had forged into an effective military force" the American, South Vietnamese, and Allied units fighting in Vietnam. In spite of his kind word, Abrams had decided against having a formal change of command ceremony. It was the first indication he gave that he was going to do things differently than Westmoreland. The second came a few minutes after Westmoreland's plane lifted off from Ton Son Nhut Airport. Sitting in his new office at MACV headquarters, Abrams pressed the inter-com connecting him to his chief of staff, Major General Walter T. Kerwin. It was time to start working at closing Khe Sanh, he told Kerwin.

In June 1945, General George Patton left Europe and returned to the United States for his triumphal tour. His first stop was Boston. From Bedford Airport, he stood in the backseat of a convertible the entire twenty-five miles into the city, acknowledging with salutes and waves the wild cheers of the more than one million people who lined the entire route. The next stop was Denver, where he addressed a wildly enthusiastic audience of over fifty thousand. Then it was on to Los Angeles, where one hundred thousand flag-waving Patton lovers packed the Coliseum, screaming themselves hoarse at the sight of the pistol-packing legend.

For Westmoreland, there was no triumphal return, no parades down streets packed ten deep for miles, no speeches to thousands of screaming patriotic fans. Given the temper of the times, any kind of conspicuous return on his part through a major city like Boston, Denver, New York, or Los Angeles was simply inconceivable. Instead of a triumphal return, Westmoreland had a slow, inconspicuous one. From Tan Son Nhut, he flew directly to the Philippines to pick up Kitsy and Margaret. There the three boarded the U.S. *Wilson* for a leisurely cruise to Hawaii. After a stop in Japan and another at Hong Kong, they landed in Honolulu on June 26. Waiting there for them was Rip, who had just completed his sophomore year of high school at a private school on the main island. From Honolulu, they all flew directly to Washington and another reunion with Stevie, who had just graduated from Bradford Junior College in Massachusetts and was preparing to start Pitzer College in California in the fall. The next three months would be the first time the family had all been together since 1964.

On July 3, a week after his return, Westmoreland was sworn in as Army Chief of Staff during a ceremony at the Pentagon. A surprise visitor at the ceremony was President Johnson. He gave Kitsy a kiss on the cheek and Westmoreland a Texas handshake. Afterward everyone was photographed together, and there were smiles all around.

Only Westmoreland was not smiling. He was not because he knew something that no one else there knew. Only a few hours earlier, he had received a cable from Abrams notifying him that Lieutenant Colonel Frederick F. Van Deusen—Kitsy's brother—had been killed in action while commanding the battalion with the 9th Division. According to Abrams's cable, the helicopter Van Deusen was riding in was shot down by enemy ground fire and crashed in the center of the Mekong River. Westmoreland had decided against telling Kitsy until after the ceremony.

Because it took considerable time to bring the helicopter up from the bottom of the river, it took nearly a week before the body was returned to Fayetteville, North Carolina, for the funeral. Fred had been the baby of the Van Duesen family, a happy-go-lucky child whom Kitsy had doted on and cared for like a mother. She was grief-stricken by his death. Westmoreland had also come to care deeply for Fred, attracted to him in part by his outgoing, easy temperament. They had frequently played golf together and much more frequently gone jogging together. For him, Fred's death became the proverbial straw that broke the camel's back. Already suffering under the stress of being the point man for an unpopular war and the further stress of having to return to the Pentagon and take up a new job, Fred's death was almost more than he could handle at the moment. After returning to Washington, all the stress suddenly overwhelmed him and he came down with a serious case of pneumonia. Before he could even get settled into Quarters One, the Chief of Staff's residence at Fort Myer, Westmoreland had to check into Walter Reed Army Medical Center. There, weak and emotionally drained, he spent the next week.

When Westmoreland reported to his new job as Army Chief in late July, he apparently did not report a happy man. Though Westmoreland vehemently denies it, according to a retired JCS staff officer, Westmoreland was so uncomfortable with his new job that he sat through his first JCS meeting without uttering a a single word, forcing Wheeler, Admiral Thomas Moorer, and Air Force General John P. McConnell to carry the entire discussion without him. His muteness during this meeting was somehow leaked to the press, and a few days later *The Washington Press* ran an article on page three with the heading WESTY SULKS.

Realizing that Westmoreland, because of his continued worries about the Vietnam War and his role in it, could not give the Army the strong hand it needed at the moment, Wheeler had to pressure him to appoint Bruce Palmer as his vice chief. Westmoreland resented Wheeler's pressure, and only did so reluctantly. According to another former JCS officer, Westmoreland had wanted his own man for the job, and Palmer was not that man. Palmer was simply too ambitious for Westmoreland's tastes. Like Westmoreland, he had been on Eisenhower's "rocket list" back in the 1950s, and since that time he had been bucking for the Army's top job. Palmer wanted the vice chief's job, says this former JCS officer, because he figured that a new administration would force Westmoreland out and make him, Palmer, Chief. Westmoreland, of course, knew Palmer wanted his job and did not want him to have it. As Palmer himself tells it, Westmoreland tried to get Palmer out of Washington by reassigning him to other commands. He first tried to make him commander of the Continental Army Command, and later tried to make him commander of the U.S. Army, Europe. The secretary of the Army, Stanley Resor, however, blocked both moves. Resor thought Palmer was indispensable as vice chief and told Westmoreland that under no circumstances would he let Palmer go.

Used to having his way in Vietnam, Westmoreland smarted from suddenly having his power curtailed by Wheeler and Resor. There were worse blows to his ego to come. In Saigon on June 17, Abrams gave the Marines the order to close Khe Sanh. In interviews, Westmoreland has said that he concurred with the decision to close the base, since the main reason for holding it—namely as a staging area for attacks on the Ho Chi Minh Trail—"appeared no longer valid." A cable exchange between Westmoreland and Abrams in early July tells a different story, however. From those cables, we learn that Westmoreland was surprised by Abrams's decision to close the base. Some military historians believe that if Westmoreland had been given a choice he would have kept the Marine base at Khe Sanh indefinitely, regardless of the pressure on him from men like Taylor to close it. Abrams, on the other hand, had never liked the base where it was.

During his March 26 visit to Washington, speculation has it, he had spoken privately with the President and Taylor and the two had told him in the most certain terms that they wanted Khe Sanh closed. Abrams did not need to be told.

The closing of Khe Sanh set off another round of public questioning and criticism of Westmoreland. If the base was as critical as Westmoreland said it was, editorial writers across the country asked, then why was it now being closed? Most thought they knew the answer. The base, they wrote, had merely been a reflection of Westmoreland's ego, a manifestation of his desire to best Giap in a showdown battle.

During a news conference at the Pentagon, Westmoreland claimed that he did not know much about the closing, and that the decision had been made by Abrams, not by him. He did not mention anything about being surprised by the closing. The decision to close the base was the first hint that Abrams was going to make changes in Vietnam. Other changes were to follow in quick succession. Just how revolutionary those changes were and what they accomplished remains a serious point of contention with military historians.

Abrams partisans—and there are many—claim the changes were significant. The most significant change Abrams made, they say, was in the way the war was being fought at the tactical level. According to them, Abrams had little enthusiasm for Westmoreland's large search-and-destroy operations. In place of them, he sent out hundreds of small-unit patrols not to find the enemy so much as to find his base camps and supply caches. With those patrols, Abrams was able to prevent enemy forces from preparing the battlefield in advance. Without supplies and ammunition, the enemy supposedly could not mount his attacks. They claim Abrams also changed the main focus of the war. Whereas Westmoreland's main focus had been on attacking the enemy's big units along the border, Abrams concentrated his operations in the populated lowlands, convinced that pacification was more important than smashing enemy battalions and regiments and running up big body counts. Finally, they claim that Abrams made drastic changes in the way firepower was used in populated areas by making it clear to his subordinate commanders that its indiscriminate use would no longer be tolerated. Such use of firepower, Abrams claimed, not only "endangered lives and property, but destroyed any allegiance people had to their government.'

A number of former military men, government officials, and analysts, however, take issue with the notion that Abrams brought revolutionary tactical changes in Vietnam. Robert Komer, who served as Westmoreland's pacification chief for two years and Abrams's for one, says there was no difference between the way each of his bosses operated. "I was there when Gen. Abrams took over," Komer says, "and there was no change in strategy whatsoever. The myth of a change in strategy is a figment of the media's imagination." Lieutenant General Davidson, who was Westmoreland's intelligence chief for two years and Abrams's for one, agrees with Komer. Abrams, he said, "never spoke of any new strategy nor ever expressed any dissatisfaction with large search and destroy operations." Westmoreland himself, while admitting that Abrams used more small-unit tactics, claims that he was only able to do so because of the bad beating the enemy had received at Tet. After Tet, Westmoreland says, the enemy, short of manpower, had no choice but to revert to small-unit tactics, which allowed Abrams to do the same. General David Palmer—the same Palmer who helped write the portion of the West Point textbook dealing with the Allied intelligence failure at Tet—agrees with Westmoreland's assessment. The Allied military victory at Tet, he felt, had given South Vietnam a year's breathing spell, which allowed the South Vietnamese Army to rebuild and allowed Abrams the opportunity to experiment with tactics.

There are many, however, who think that all talk of Abrams's new tactics was merely an exercise in semantics, that while Abrams may have experimented with small-unit tactics, he still more or less continued Westmoreland's search-and-destroy strategy. If Abrams was so certain pacification was the key to South Vietnam's survival, they ask, why did he so vehemently push to get ground invasions of both Cambodia and Laos approved?

In the end, it apparently did not matter whether Abrams's method of operation in Vietnam was new and innovative, for statistically nothing changed. While much has been made of Abrams's small-unit tactics, they certainly did not make matters any less bloody for those who carried them out. Nearly the same number of Americans were killed in Vietnam in 1969, the first full year Abrams commanded in Vietnam, as were killed in 1967, the last full year Westmoreland commanded. And while much has likewise been made of Abrams's campaign to lessen civilian casualties, it apparently brought no results. Approximately the same number of civilians were killed and wounded in 1969 as had been in 1967.

Unfortunately for Westmoreland, the press did not see any of this, nor care to. To them, Abrams was a breath of fresh air blowing into a war that had become stale and tedious, and they welcomed his arrival with open arms. Abrams was everything a dull war needed. While Westmoreland tended to be reserved and proper, Abrams was outgoing and gregarious, a man who with a cigar always in his mouth liked to belly up to a bar, slug down three or four drinks, all the while cussing and trading war stories with those around him. While Westmoreland had always tried to project a positive image and a positive attitude toward the war, Abrams was noted for joking about military absurdities and for disregarding rules and traditions. And while Westmoreland had always assiduously tried to cultivate a relationship with the press, Abrams let it be known that he had nothing but contempt for most reporters and would seldom allow himself to be interviewed. The press ironically found Abrams's abrasive, contemptuous behavior endearing and treated him far better than they had treated Westmoreland. After Abrams took over as COMUSMACV, a series of flattering portraits of him began appearing in newspapers and magazines. In a lengthy piece in *The New York Times*—"General Abrams Deserves a Better War"—Kevin P. Buckley praised the general for changing the whole course of the war through the use of more innovative, flexible tactics. Because of those tactics, Buckley wrote, the war has "been brought under control to a degree it never was before." Writing in *Time*, a staff writer claimed in " The General vs. 'The System' " that Abrams had introduced numerous innovative tactics since taking over, including long-range patrols, reinforcing battles with helicopters, and overlapping artillery support from firebases.

According to one source, Westmoreland became so distraught as he read such articles that he wanted to hold a press conference and speak out publicly, explaining to a gullible public that the gains Abrams was being credited with had been achieved during his tour and that the tactics Abrams was using had been developed in 1965. Westmoreland's friends, however, pulled him aside and convinced him that speaking out in public would only damage the Army and give the impression that he and Abrams were feuding.

If Westmoreland could not reply publicly, some of his close friends and associates could for him. One friend who did was Charles McDonald, the noted military historian, who at the time held a position in the U.S. Army's Center for Military History. Always a strong supporter of Westmoreland and his strategy in Vietnam, McDonald bristled when he saw the *Time* article and immediately penned a response. In it, he pointed out that everything Abrams was presently doing in Vietnam had originated with Westmoreland, including the use of long-range patrols, overlapping artillery fire, and the use of helicopters to reinforce battles. As far as Abrams's extensive use of small-unit tactics was concerned, McDonald argued that the only reason he could use them was because the enemy had been so badly battered at Tet. Owing to that battering, the enemy had been forced to reduce the size of his operations and the forces employed. The only reason Abrams could operate with squads and platoons, McDonald pointed out, was that the enemy was operating with squads and platoons. If the enemy had been roaming the jungle in battalion, brigade, and division strength, then Abrams would have had to operate similarly, or else face the piecemeal destruction of his forces.

Also responding in Westmoreland's behalf was his chief of information, Major General Winant Sidle. He addressed his response directly to Hedley Donovan, *Time*'s illustrious editor. *Time*'s article, he told Donovan, was completely "inaccurate and misleading. . . . Such a naive analysis has no place in a respected news magazine like Time. The record needs to be set straight."

It was not going to be, however, for *Time* refused to print a retraction. In a reply to McDonald, Barbara Stofer, the head of *Time*'s editorial office, wrote that upon looking McDonald's argument over carefully, *Time* was not "entirely convinced" but "was partially" convinced it had some merit. "The men do however operate in different ways," she went on. "Westmoreland was much more committed to massive attacks, Abrams had attempted to fit standard warfare to guerrilla tactics in pinpointing his attacks and retaliations and finding specific objectives for every action—the known supply depots, etc."

Stofer's reply apparently angered McDonald as much as the original article, for he made a copy of the letter and sent it directly to Westmoreland. On the bottom of her letter, McDonald wrote in longhand, "Have you ever read such unadulterated crap?"

If Westmoreland was disgruntled over the press treatment of Abrams, his spirit was shortly raised by the election of Richard M. Nixon as President in November 1968. Nixon was on record for saying he had a "secret plan to end the war," and all the members of the JCS hoped that "secret plan" was a military solution to the war, not a diplomatic one. Either way, the Joint Chiefs knew that Nixon, an old anti-Communist hard-liner was sure to prosecute the war more aggressively than Johnson had.

Nixon certainly gave early indications that he would. A few days after officially assuming the presidency, he called General Wheeler into his office to discuss Wheeler's impending retirement. Though

Wheeler was exhausted and demoralized, Nixon convinced him to stay on for another year with the implicit promise that the war could be and would be won. "The moment of decision" had not yet passed in Vietnam, he told the general, contrary to what men like Clark Clifford thought, men for whom, Nixon also made it clear, he had nothing but contempt.

Nixon, as we know now, did not really have a plan to end the Vietnam War. If the hopes of Wheeler, Westmoreland, and the rest of the Joint Chiefs were buoyed for a brief moment, they were just as quickly deflated. Though Nixon initially gave the impression that he wanted a military decision in Vietnam, it was soon obvious that he was unwilling to take the radical steps, such as permanently cutting the Ho Chi Minh Trail and invading North Vietnam, that the Chiefs felt were necessary to win the war. Instead of an outright victory in Vietnam, Nixon, with the help of his national security adviser, Henry Kissinger, developed a plan designed only to get North Vietnam to agree to a "fair" settlement. That plan called for the use of a combination of great-power diplomacy with China and Russia and punishing military blows against North Vietnam. A fourth-rate military power like North Vietnam "must have a breaking point," Kissinger said, and he and Nixon were prepared to find that point, even if it meant threatening North Vietnam with total destruction. Nixon hoped to play on his image as a hard-liner to make that threat real. "They'll believe any threat of force Nixon makes because it's Nixon," he told an adviser. "We'll just let slip the word to them that 'for God's sake, you know, Nixon's obsessed about communism . . . and he has his hand on the nuclear button.' "

With what one historian called the "sublime self-confidence among men new to power," Nixon and Kissinger set out to end the war. To show Hanoi they meant business, they ordered intensive B-52 strikes against Communist base areas in neutral Cambodia and greatly intensified the bombing of North Vietnam, moves that Westmoreland and the other Chiefs had repeatedly tried to get Johnson to make. To appease critics of the war and many political moderates in Congress, Nixon and Kissinger began even more vigorously Vietnamizing the war, and laid out a rough schedule for the gradual withdrawal of all United States troops from Vietnam.

Westmoreland supported Nixon's Vietnamization plan, which called for the accelerated modernization of South Vietnam's armed forces. Like the rest of the Chiefs, he did not fully support the withdrawal plan, which he felt was based more on political necessity than on the reality of the situation in South Vietnam. It was the view of all the Chiefs that it would take as long as a decade to make Vietnamization work properly, and would, as in Korea, require the permanent presence of American troops on South Vietnamese soil. Melvin Laird, Nixon's secretary of defense, did not subscribe to that view. He believed Nixon's goodwill on Capitol Hill would run thin if he did not set a specific timetable and begin aggressively withdrawing all American troops. Laird's insistence on troop withdrawals disturbed Westmoreland, who felt the South Vietnamese could not go it alone without some strong United States military presence in South Vietnam, and unnerved Kissinger, who thought the withdrawals would undermine his negotiating position in the upcoming talks in Paris.

Neither Nixon nor Kissinger, however, was particularly interested in Westmoreland's opinion. Nixon looked upon the general as a political liability, someone who had become too closely associated in the public mind with the Johnson administration and had therefore outlived his usefulness. Kissinger, on the other hand, had little respect for Westmoreland as a strategist and tactician. He felt Westmoreland's search-and-destroy strategy had been an exercise in futility, and that while it had produced numerous battlefield victories, those victories "could not be translated into permanent political advantage." In addition, Kissinger felt that Westmoreland, like the rest of the generals and admirals who had been running the war, had no one to blame but themselves for the failure in Vietnam. They had "brought on some of their own troubles," he told an associate in late 1968, and they had done so primarily by permitting "themselves to be coopted" by the Johnson White House, permitting themselves to go along with a policy that, as he put it, they "inwardly resented."

It is unclear just how much Nixon and Kissinger's treatment of Westmoreland influenced his subsequent decisions, but it seems it must have had some effect. Palmer, for one, says that it had a significant effect, that, stung by the indifferent treatment accorded him by the two, Westmoreland decided to do a lot of traveling and to stay out of Washington as much as possible. Whatever the case, in early 1969 Westmoreland announced that he was going on an extended speaking tour, in order, as he explained later, to give the country "the facts of life with respect to the military and some appreciation of the role of the military" in a democracy. In doing so, he hoped additionally to counter the "adverse propaganda" generated by the antiwar movement. Although he was severely criticized in some corners for leaving his post as Army Chief, he felt there was an important job to do in helping to rebuild the Army's tarnished image and that he was the only one who could do that job. Who else could tell the Army's side of the story? he asked an interviewer in 1982. "Who else would they listen to? They were not going to listen to a secretary whose name they had never heard of or to some general they had never heard of."

A speech he gave at the Lincoln Academy in Springfield, Illinois, set the tone for more than two hundred speeches to follow. In that speech, he praised the armed forces and begged his audience to give it the respect he felt it deserved. "The armed forces of the United States," he said, "had never failed our country on the field of battle. Starting with our own revolution, we have never lost a war. I ask you in all humility, and yet with a deep sense of pride, What more could you ask of your soldiers?"

But instead of the respect the armed forces deserved, he went on, they were being heaped with scorn and derision. "The picture of the American fighting man as the hero of World War Two has decomposed into the hired killer of Vietnam in the eyes of some whose emotions cloud good judgment." This false picture unfortunately was doing terrible damage to the morale of the men still in Vietnam and to the "more than two million who have served with distinction and selfless devotion in Vietnam."

Westmoreland received a warm reception from the more than five hundred people gathered at the Lincoln Academy that day, and he would receive an equally warm reception during most of his other appearances. Not everyone, however, was eager to hear Westmoreland speak. In spite of his no longer being the commander in Vietnam, the antiwar movement still perceived him as the primary symbol of the war. To them he was Mr. Body-Count, Mr. Search and Destroy, and when they thought of television images of the war—images of smashed burning villages and wounded villagers—they simultaneously thought of him. It was still his war, even if he was no longer directly involved in it.

As a result, at nearly half the towns and cities where Westmoreland spoke, he was met by organized demonstrations. While he was speaking at the Nashville Civic Center, a group of youths interrupted his speech with heckles and taunts. While in Worcester, Massachusetts, to speak at a hospital fund-raiser, he had to pass through a gauntlet of fifty demonstrators as he entered the auditorium. In Lincoln, Nebraska, the hall where he was speaking was surrounded by over five hundred chanting demonstrators from the University of Nebraska carrying signs that read, WESTMORELAND—WAR CRIMINAL and WESTMORELAND—AMERICA'S EICHMANN. At the University of Cincinnati to speak to a Boy Scout convention, several hundred students greeted his arrival by knocking out thirty windows in the ROTC building. At Penn State, a bus he was riding in was stoned by demonstrators. In Portland, Oregon, one hundred demonstrators stood outside the hall where he was speaking, shouting over and over again, "Ho, Ho, Ho Chi Minh; NLF is gonna win." At Ohio State to address an ROTC graduating class, his car was surrounded by fifty protesters carrying Vietcong flags and signs that read, WAR IS BIG BUSINESS. All during the ceremony, a girl stood outside the door to the auditorium reading the names of Americans killed in Vietnam.

The worst incident took place at Yale University. There Westmoreland was slated to address members of the university's Political Union. Before he entered the hall, however, an angry crowd of three hundred, carrying Vietcong flags and placards labelling him a WAR CRIMINAL, shoved their way through a cordon of Yale security police and seized the hall. Realizing he would likely be physically assaulted if he entered the hall, Westmoreland canceled the speech and decided to return to Washington. Before leaving, he scribbled a short note to the head of the Political Union expressing his regret. When the note was read to the protesters, two of them seized it, tore it into pieces, then stomped on the pieces, all the while shouting, "Victory to the NLF."

Problems, Problems, Problems

W**hile Westmoreland was travel-
ing around the country trying to rebuild the Army's image, sometime
in early May 1969 a former Vietnam veteran named Ron Ridenhour was sitting down at his desk and penning a letter that would
undo much of the general's work. While serving with the Americal
Division in Quang Ngai Province in 1968, Ridenhour had listened to
a man describe how in mid-1968 a platoon from Charlie Company of
the 1st Battalion, 20th Infantry, Americal Division, had massacred
over three hundred men, women, and children at a village called My
Lai. Ridenhour had at first been skeptical of the man's story but after
talking to numerous others who had either heard of My Lai or admitted to actually participating in the massacre, he became convinced
the story was true. By the time of his discharge from the Army,
Ridenhour had decided that the story of My Lai needed to be told,
that the massacre committed there had been so horrendous that it
cried out for justice. And so in early April, he penned a three-page
letter describing in detail what he called the "dark and bloody" deeds
committed there by the platoon from Charlie Company.

Ridenhour posted his letter on April 2 to thirty prominent men in Washington, including Morris Udall, Richard Nixon, Melvin Laird, General Wheeler, Edward Kennedy, and Barry Goldwater. Upon getting his letter, Wheeler forwarded it to Westmoreland, who, as he noted in his memoirs, read it with great incredulity, finding it "beyond belief that American soldiers could engage in mass murder of unarmed South Vietnamese civilians." In spite of his disbelief, Westmoreland ordered an immediate check with MACV headquartersto see if there was even the vaguest possibility that something out of the ordinary had taken place at My Lai. When the MACV inspector general reported back that something unusual just might have taken place there, Westmoreland ordered Major General William E. Enemark, the inspector general of the Army, to begin an immediate investigation. After traveling over ten thousand miles, during which he interviewed fourteen former members of Charlie Company, one of Enemark's investigators, a Colonel William Wilson, reported to Westmoreland that there had indeed been a massacre at My Lai and it had been a massive one. Wilson's report gave Westmoreland another considerable shock, for he realized, as did most senior officers privy to information about My Lai, that the Army was about to suffer a grievous blow to its image. Nevertheless in mid-July, he ordered the Army Criminal Investigation Division to do even more lengthy interviews with the men Wilson had interviewed and to interview additional men. When the CID report was completed in early September, the Army formally charged the leader of Charlie Company's 3rd Platoon, Lieutenant William C. Calley, with the murder of "109 Oriental human beings." Murder charges were subsequently brought against ten other members of Charlie Company, including the company commander, Captain Ernest Medina.

Westmoreland was troubled by the enormity of the crimes committed at My Lai, but he was just as troubled by the fact that not a single officer in the chain of command above Medina had filed a report on the massacre, which was specifically mandated by MACV guidelines. It became obvious to him that some type of cover-up had taken place at My Lai and that that cover-up might well reach all the way to the top of the Americal Division, all the way up to its commander at the time, Major General Samuel W. Koster, a man who at the moment was the superintendent of the U.S. Military Academy at West Point. After consulting with Stanley Resor, the secretary of the Army, Westmoreland decided to appoint a board to investigate the possibility of a cover-up. Before he could choose a board, however, he learned "that some members of the Nixon administration wanted to whitewash any possible negligence within the chain of command." When those same men began exerting what Westmoreland felt was undue pressure on him to drop the inquiry, he called in Al Haig, now a brigadier general serving as Henry Kissinger's military adviser. He told Haig to go back to the White House and tell those exerting the pressure that if they did not stop immediately, he would exercise his "prerogative as a member of the Joint Chiefs of Staff to go personally to the President and object." Westmoreland, of course, did not know at the time that one of those who wanted the whitewash was Nixon himself. In fact, shortly after hearing of My Lai, Nixon had snapped to a staff member that "it's the dirty rotten Jews from New York who are behind it." Regardless, Westmoreland's talk with Haig "squelched any further pressure for a white-wash."

Westmoreland at first considered picking a civilian board to head the inquiry, in order, as he put it, "to enhance the credibility of the finding." On further thought, though, he decided that the military situation in Vietnam was simply too complicated for civilians to understand. He decided instead to head the board with a military man. Westmoreland eventually chose Lieutenant General William R. Peers. Peers had been the I Field Force commander in Vietnam, and was known throughout the Army for his fairness and objectivity. At least as far as this particular investigation was concerned, an equally important attribute of Peers's was that he had not attended West Point, but was instead an ROTC graduate from the University of California. By choosing Peers, Westmoreland felt he would be able to avoid being accused of creating another cover-up through the machinations of what critics of the Army called the WPPA, short for West Point Protection Association. According to these critics, the WPPA maintained strong but invisible bonds among all West Point graduates. Because of those bonds, academy graduates would supposedly do anything, including lying and cheating, to protect one another. Westmoreland felt the whole idea of a WPPA was "bunk," but he did not want even a hint of scandal hovering over the head of the board of inquiry. To further invest the board with credibility, he appointed two distinguished New York attorneys, Robert MacCrate and Jerome K. Walsh, Jr., to assist Peers. Like Peers, both believed that truth was an absolute and that they had to discover that absolute no matter what it took or whose reputation was damaged in the process.

And damage reputations they did. On March 17, following a four-month-long investigation, Peers announced the findings of his board of inquiry. They were explosive. Based on those findings, he accused two generals, four full colonels, four lieutenant colonels, four majors, six captains, and eight lieutenants of a total of 224 serious military offenses and recommended that all be formally charged. Those offenses ranged from participating in war crimes or failing to report them, to attempting to suppress information and giving false testimony. Koster's name was prominently displayed on the top of Peers's list. Although he and Peers were longtime personal friends, Koster stood accused of four different offenses.

Westmoreland had been shocked by the IG and CID reports; he was devastated by Peers's report. It was one thing to have a lieutenant accused of murder and quite another to have an entire chain of command in an infantry division, including the commander, accused of a cover-up. A few days after getting the report, he ordered Major General Walter T. Kerwin, his personal chief, to go up to West Point and formally relieve Koster of command.

After being relieved, Koster summoned the entire corps of cadets to the dining hall and then addressed them from the balcony above. He made no mention of the fact that he had been relieved, but instead told the cadets that he was requesting reassignment to save the academy from further embarrassment. After speaking for a few minutes about his deep love for West Point, Koster ended his speech by defiantly snapping, "Don't let the bastards get you down." Koster never revealed who the "bastards" were, whether he was referring to Westmoreland or to the media, but it was the impression of most of the cadets that their superintendent was taking the blame for others. To show their feelings for Koster, the entire cadet corps organized a final parade in his honor and silently marched by his home. Unfortunately for Koster, the cadets had no say in the matter of his guilt or innocence, and formal charges were soon brought against him and thirteen other officers for dereliction of duty, suppressing information, and failure to obey lawful regulations.

Westmoreland has never revealed what type of punishment he felt Koster and the other charged officers deserved. Peers did. He thought they were all guilty and felt they all deserved to be severely punished. In spite of Peers's strong feelings, only one man, a colonel, was ever tried by a court-martial, and he was found innocent. Charges were dropped against all the other officers by Lieutenant General Jonathan O. Seaman, the commanding general of First Army and the person with jurisdiction over the cases. Because of Army regulations,

Westmoreland had no control over Seaman's decision not to prosecute Koster and the others. To avoid the possibility of command influence, he was not even allowed to talk with Seaman about any matter that dealt with My Lai. Nevertheless, following Seaman's decision to drop the charges, it was assumed by many that Westmoreland had done just that, that he had somehow communicated with Seaman and convinced him to let the officers off.

One of the first to level that charge was Congressman Samuel S. Stratton, a Democrat from New York. On February 4, 1971, he argued in Congress that the decision not to prosecute the officers was a blatant miscarriage of justice and implied that Westmoreland and Resor had had a direct hand in it. "I just cannot honestly believe," he shouted during a thirty-minute harangue, "that General Seaman made the decision to drop the charges against General Koster on his own and without any reference to the Pentagon. . . . It hardly makes sense to suppose that the Army hierarchy, the Secretary and the Chief of Staff would have been so deeply concerned about My Lai and a My Lai coverup in November 1969 . . . and then a year later allow one obscure officer . . . to blow the whole case on his own say so."

Stratton's feelings were shared by editorial writers around the country, who saw the entire incident as a cover-up of a cover-up. Seaman himself claimed he dropped the charges because there simply was not enough evidence to support a conviction. This, of course, was a self-serving statement, for there was more than enough evidence to convict at least half the officers and possibly all of them. Peers certainly thought so. In his book about the investigation, *The My Lai Inquiry*, he unabashedly called Seaman's dismissal of charges a "travesty of justice." He nevertheless never, even in retirement, even vaguely hinted that Westmoreland was in any way in complicity with Seaman. As for Seaman himself, he has never spoken frankly about his decision. Some historians believe he was merely trying to protect the image of the Army; others that he was only trying to save Koster's career.

If so, he was not completely successful. A short time after Seaman dropped the charges against the officers, Westmoreland had a talk with Resor and recommended that he take administrative action against Koster and Brigadier General George Young, who had been the assistant commander of the Americal Division at the time of the massacre. Westmoreland recommended specifically that Koster be demoted from two stars to one star and that both he and Young be stripped of their Distinguished Service Medals and have a letter of censure placed in their personnel records. Resor agreed. It is unclear if Westmoreland and Resor took the action because they felt it was the right thing to do or because they were bowing to criticism, but the action set off another storm of protest. Congressman Stratton criticized it as a "slap on the wrist." Koster called it "unfair and unjust" and based on "faulty conclusions," while Young claimed that he had been made a "scapegoat" to satisfy Stratton.

Westmoreland, as one of his aides noted, endured this new controversy "stoically." His stoicism, however, was about to be put to another severe test. Major General Edwin Connor, the commanding general of the third Army at Fort McPherson, Georgia, and the man with jurisdiction over nine of the men charged with murder at My Lai, dropped charges against seven of the men, saying there was a lack of evidence to get a conviction. The two remaining men were tried and found not guilty at Fort Hood, Texas. Two other men accused of murder at My Lai—Captain Medina and Sergeant David Mitchell—were likewise found not guilty following similar trials.

Cries of "whitewash" once more rang out in the press, and Westmoreland was again charged with using his office to influence the actions of Connor and the different court-martial juries. Westmoreland was attempting to deal with this second round of controversy when on March 31, 1971, a jury of six officers at Fort Benning, Georgia, found Lieutenant Calley guilty of the "murder of twenty-two Oriental human beings." The judge sentenced Calley to life in prison.

The conviction set off a firestorm of protest around the country. Minutes after the conviction was announced, the White House received over five thousand telegrams, with a ratio of 100 to 1 in favor of clemency. Congressman Dan Fuqua, speaking for many of his colleagues, introduced a resolution calling for an invitation to Calley to address a joint session of Congress. At Fort Benning, Georgia, the American Legion post announced plans to raise $100,000 for Calley's expected appeal. In Georgia, Governor Jimmy Carter proclaimed March 31 the American Fighting Man's Day. In Jackson, Mississippi, Governor John Bill spoke from the capitol steps to a rally of nearly four thousand Calley supporters. In Arkansas and Kansas, the legislatures passed resolutions urging President Nixon to pardon Calley. Similar resolutions were quickly adopted in a dozen more states. Hundreds of draft boards from Maine to California wired the White House and announced that they would not draft more young men for Vietnam until Calley was released. In Nashville, Tennessee, a recording company reported that it had sold 202,000 copies of a record titled "The Battle Hymn of Lieutenant Calley" in a week, and in Miami, a man hijacked an airliner to Cuba and announced that he was doing it to protest the Calley conviction. Editorial writers—the majority of them in the South and Midwest—quickly jumped into the fray, charging with passionate rhetoric that Calley was a "scapegoat," a hopeless soul thrown to the wolves to protect higher-ups, who were equally guilty. Others charged that numerous other My Lais had taken place and it was wrong now to charge Calley with something that hundreds of others were guilty of.

In Houston to give a speech, Westmoreland told reporters that he was "surprised at the outcry following the conviction of First Lieutenant William L. Calley." When asked by a reporter if he, as some were maintaining, should likewise share the guilt for My Lai, he snapped, "No, I feel no guilt, not in the least. It is an absurd allegation. My orders were that all atrocities would be reported and investigated according to the rules of the Geneva Convention and it is our obligation to follow through and punish these atrocities."

In order to stem the tide of public opinion running against the Calley conviction, Westmoreland and Resor issued a comprehensive report on My Lai. In it, they pointed out that the United States was obliged under the Geneva Convention on the rules of war to try Calley and the others. They termed the notion that Calley was a scapegoat ridiculous.

The report generated little interest and even less acceptance, and did little to dispel the widely held notion that Calley was a scapegoat. To the contrary, that idea was given new vigor in the days that followed, and not by the political Right, which had raised the initial outcry over the verdict, but by the Left. It was one of the few times in American history that the Right and the Left passionately agreed on an issue. The only difference between their positions was that the Left was not content to merely label Calley a scapegoat or to intimate that Westmoreland might share some responsibility for My Lai. To the Left, Westmoreland shared complete responsibility for My Lai and for the entire war.

This view was most vocally expressed at a conference in Washington sponsored by the National Committee for a Citizens Commission of Inquiry on United States War Crimes in Vietnam, an antiwar group with a New Left political orientation that was seeking a national inquest into the war crimes question. During the three-day conference, forty Vietnam veterans appeared to talk about war crimes they had either participated in or had firsthand knowledge of. To a man, they felt, as one vet put it, that the responsibility for these crimes rested not with the soldiers who had actually committed them, but "at the highest levels" of command. None of the men, however, would be specific as to what units they had served with and where and on what specific dates these war crimes took place.

At a similar conference in Detroit sponsored by the Vietnam Veterans Against the War, a group financed largely by the actress Jane Fonda, another parade of vets with stories of war crimes—although again with few specifics—took their turn at the microphone and unburdened themselves. The purpose of the conference, according to Jan Crum, the founder of the group, was "to show that atrocities were not isolated incidents, but permeated the war and so could not be the fault of individual soldiers or junior officers." All these war crimes, said Crum, were instead the fault of "the leadership of the Army." They were the real "war criminals," not men like Calley.

Similar statements were expressed at a number of strictly academic conferences around the country in 1970 and 1971. At a conference held in New York City in late 1970 to discuss war crimes in Vietnam, Gabriel Kolko, a left-wing history professor at the University of New York at Buffalo, likewise absolved individual soldiers of any guilt for war crimes in Vietnam. All the guilt lay at the top, he said. The soldiers who had participated in the My Lai massacre and other slaughters had all merely been expressing "the axiom of fire and terror" that their superiors had devised. At the same conference, Edward M. Opton, a senior research psychologist at the University of California at Berkeley, likened My Lai to the lynching of blacks in the South during the 1930s. Those lynchings had only been possible because community leaders had approved of them, Opton told the conference, and My Lai had only been possible because top Army leaders approved of it. Those leaders were ultimately responsible for My Lai, not the soldiers who actually did the killing.

The most extensive indictment of Westmoreland as a war criminal was leveled by a third academic, and an eminently more important one, Telford Taylor, a man who during World War II had been the chief United States prosecutor at the Nuremberg war crimes trials and who now taught law at Columbia University. In *Nuremberg and Vietnam*, a book published in early 1971, Taylor argued that Westmoreland might be convicted as a war criminal if war crimes standards established during World War II were applied to his conduct of the war in Vietnam. They were hard words, and especially so given Taylor's background. Needless to say, the book became an instant cause célèbre, and Taylor was soon making the same accusations on the radio and TV talk-show circuit. On *The Dick Cavett Show*, he startled millions of Americans by suggesting that Westmoreland might well be as guilty of war crimes as General Yamashita, the Japanese general hanged for such crimes after World War II.

Westmoreland had made but the briefest comments in response to the attacks from the Right. He responded vigorously to the charges of the Left, however. Owing to his efforts and the efforts of the Navy, both the Army's and Navy's investigative services launched an immediate investigation into the charges leveled at the Detroit conference. Both groups ran into immediate difficulty. The leadership of the Vietnam Veterans Against the War instructed its entire membership not to cooperate with the investigators in any way. Even when offered immunity from prosecution, most men refused to talk. In spite of VVAW stonewalling, investigators did discover that one black soldier had not committed the war crimes he claimed to have committed. His testimony instead had been provided to him by a member of the Nation of Islam. Investigators also discovered that several veterans listed as having testified at Detroit had in reality never been anywhere near the conference. Men using their names obviously had, though the investigator could not discover who the men were.

The Detroit hearings lost more credibility in late December 1971 when *New York Times* investigative reporter Neil Sheehan reviewed *Conversations with Americans*, a book written by Mark Lane, one of the key organizers of the Detroit conference. Because of a best-seller he had written attacking the Warren Commission's probe of the Kennedy assassination, Lane had great credibility in some antiwar circles. His new book purported to show, through numerous eyewitness accounts of atrocities in Vietnam, that such crimes were not only widespread there but part of official United States policy. He claimed, in fact, that Westmoreland operated in Vietnam much as Hitler's SS had operated in Europe, Eastern Europe, and Russia. Sheehan destroyed much of Lane's credibility in his two-page book review. With hard facts, he proved conclusively that many of Lane's witnesses to war crimes in Vietnam had never even served there, and that others, while they had been in Vietnam, had not been in the areas where the atrocities they claimed to have witnessed took place. Taking his key from Sheehan, James Reston also reviewed Lane's book in the *Saturday Review*. Reston came to a similar conclusion. Lane, he wrote, suffered from an apparent inability to discriminate between the truth and "a soldier's talent for embellishment."

Neither review apparently fazed Lane, for he continued holding war crimes hearings, during which veterans confessed to having participated in an endless string of massacres and atrocities, while he himself lashed out at Westmoreland for being on a par with the worst war criminals of the twentieth century. Lane finally got to confront Westmoreland personally in late August 1971 when both men found themselves in Boise, Idaho, on the same day: Westmoreland to deliver a speech to the local chamber of commerce in the banquet hall of a hotel, and Lane to give a teach-in at a local antiwar coffee shop. On hearing that Westmoreland was in town, Lane led fifty demonstrators to the hotel. While they paraded and chanted just outside the banquet hall, Lane rushed about handing out pamphlets that called for Westmoreland's trial as a war criminal and likened him to General Yamashita and Hitler.

While Lane's accusations seemed ludicrous to moderates like Sheehan—a man who had come to know the war intimately as a battlefield reporter and who thought that those who opposed the war should oppose it with the truth and not with wild accusations and concocted accounts—many hundreds of thousands of Americans, both in the antiwar movement and out of it, were ready to believe anything written about the war and about Westmoreland, be it written by a pure sensationalist like Lane or an established academic like Taylor.

Realizing this, Westmoreland concluded that he could not expect to counter the charges of the antiwar movement with mere denials. What he needed to counter them with was facts. And so a few weeks after the Calley conviction, he and Resor commissioned the Army's judge advocate general to compile a detailed report on United States personnel in Vietnam who had been prosecuted and convicted of crimes against the Vietnamese, be they villagers, Saigon bar girls, or Vietcong captives. The report was completed in May 1971 and immediately released to the press. It showed, as Westmoreland hoped it would, that crimes against the Vietnamese people, rather than being part of a deliberate genocidal policy, were routinely investigated and the perpetrators of these crimes just as routinely prosecuted, convicted, and punished. According to the report, between January 1964 and January 1971 nearly 180 Army personnel were convicted of serious crimes against the Vietnamese. Those crimes included murder, rape, mutilation of a corpse, and negligent homicide. Of the 180, 25 were convicted of war crimes and received sentences ranging from ten years to life. Of 77 Marines convicted of serious offenses, 27 convictions were for murder, with sentences again ranging from ten years to life.

Along with statistics, the JAG office also included in their report what they felt was a detailed refutation of the charge that Westmoreland was responsible for extensive war crimes in Vietnam. Unlike General Yamashita, JAG argued, Westmoreland as a commander had established specific procedures for the proper treatment of civilians and POWs and laid out guidelines that put restraints on the use of United States air support in populated areas. And he had backed up those procedures and guidelines, JAG went on, by holding frequent conferences with his senior commanders, during which he had hammered home "the absolute necessity of proper treatment of South Vietnamese civilians." In response to commentators who claimed that United States personnel were not severely punished for killing Vietnamese people because they were thought to be racially inferior, JAG presented the case of a Sergeant Condron, a career NCO who had been court-martialed and sentenced to life in prison for killing two Vietnamese children. And the Condron case, JAG pointed out, was only one of many.

Westmoreland and Resor had great expectations for the JAG report. It ran to nearly one hundred pages and was carefully documented with 169 footnotes. They hoped it would open a reasonable public debate on the issue of war crimes in Vietnam, during which the Army's point of view would get a fair hearing. Their hope was ill founded. The report got only the briefest mention in the press, and was completely ignored by the antiwar movement, which was only interested in ending the war, not in carrying on a rational discourse with Westmoreland.

On the same day—May 15, 1971—Peers submitted the report on his official investigation of the My Lai massacre, he also handed Westmoreland a secret memo. "That memo," according to Major General Franklin M. Davis, "shook Westy to the core." In the memo, Peers pointed out that after interviewing over three hundred officers in connection with his investigation, he had concluded that there was something deeply and basically wrong with "the moral and ethical standards" of the Army officers corps. Peers then read off a litany of those qualities that he thought essential to the makeup of a good Army officer, with the clear implication that all of those qualities had been in short supply among the officers in the Americal Division's chain of command. A good officer, Peers wrote, should first of all be willing to take responsibility for the actions and the welfare of the men under him. He must, second, show a complete dedication to the truth, and should never vacillate, no matter what the circumstances or pressures, from that dedication. Third, he must be willing to take "corrective actions on the spot" when he sees that something is wrong. And if that means taking actions against a fellow officer—no matter what his rank—then he must do so. Fourth, he must exert leadership on a face-to-face basis, not by a telephone or through junior officers. And finally, he must always remember that his "highest loyalty is to the Army and the nation" and to a higher moral code. It is his job, therefore, to ensure that all his men understand and put into practice

> the principles of discriminate and tightly controlled applications of firepower; genuine and practical concern for private property no matter how valueless or insignificant it may appear; humane treatment and care of refugees, noncombatants, and wounded (whether friendly or enemy); and the judicious safeguarding and processing of suspects and prisoners of war. . . . The combat commander at any level who fails to keep these considerations uppermost in his mind and in the minds of the men who serve under him, invites disaster.

And that is exactly what happened at My Lai, he concluded.

Although Peers did not actually state it in writing, it was obvious enough from the moral indignation in his report that he wanted Westmoreland to take some type of further action. Westmoreland at first was not certain what to do, and for a month he pondered the question. He eventually commissioned the Army War College at Carlisle Barracks, Pennsylvania, to conduct a study of the leadership and professional attitudes of Army officers and to measure the moral climate of the entire officers corps. Westmoreland made it plain, however, that while "several unfavorable events" had been of "grave concern" to him, by "no means" did he "believe that the Army as an institution is in moral crisis."

The Army War College completed their study in June 1970. Westmoreland called it a "masterpiece," but he was obviously not completely comfortable with all their conclusions, for he had it classified.

Like Peers's secret memo, the report came to some damning conclusions about the state of the Army officers corps, some conclusions that Westmoreland did not want in the hands of the press. Based on a questionnaire filled out by 420 officers, the report concluded that there was a massive gap between the ideals the Army set forth and the way things were actually done. Those 420 officers, as one internal Army memorandum on the report noted, "saw a system that rewarded selfishness, incompetence and dishonesty. Commanders sought transitory ephemeral gains at the expense of enduring benefits and replaced substance with statistics. Furthermore, senior commanders, as a result of their isolation (sometimes self-imposed) and absence of communication with subordinates, lacked any solid foundation with which to initiate necessary corrective actions." In addition, the study pointed out that "careerism" was out of control in the Army and that most Army officers were only interested in "ticket-punching," that is, in advancing their careers from one rung of the ladder to the other, and not with actually performing their duties, caring for their men, and advancing the best interests of the Army.

In spite of the fact that he did not think the officers corps was in as bad shape as both Peers and the Army War College thought it was, Westmoreland moved immediately to begin prescribing some new moral guidelines for officers while at the same time instituting some substantial changes in the way an officer advanced in the Army. He began by sending a letter to each Army officer, be he a mere second lieutenant or a lieutenant general, on the meaning of integrity. "I want to make it clear beyond any question," he wrote, "that absolute integrity of an officer's word, deed, and signature is a matter that permits no compromise." He repeated the gist of this message in a number of speeches he gave to various groups of officers. "Integrity of character," he told a group of newly minted brigadier generals, "is fundamental to the character of an officer."

Westmoreland also ordered his personnel chief to create a program to redress the rampant "careerism" in the Army by revising the service school curricula and establishing a leadership board to conduct leadership seminars throughout the Army. He himself personally ordered the noted military historian and journalist, Brigadier General S. L. A. Marshall to tour a number of Army bases, critically examine the professionalism of the officers corps, and suggest any reforms needed. Westmoreland's reforms did much to alter for the better the professional and moral standards of the officers corps. Unfortunately, as he discovered, he could not do the same for the Army as a whole, at least not quickly enough that it mattered.

That Army, as Westmoreland himself liked to brag, that had arrived in Vietnam was probably the best the country had ever produced. The average soldier in those early years was better educated, better trained, and better motivated than his counterparts from either World War II or Korea. And so too were his officers and NCOs. Together they had formed companies, battalions, brigades, and divisions that had been unbeatable. In battle after battle, these units had decisively defeated Vietcong and North Vietnamese units of equivalent size or larger and had done so with an enthusiasm that had made their commanders proud.

But that had been in the early years. Beginning in early 1969, the stresses and strains of a long war began taking the same toll on the U.S. Army that it was taking on the body politic in the United States. Those stresses and strains were especially evident in the individual soldiers, who as the war ground on became more and more embittered as they were being asked to risk their lives in a war from which their country was withdrawing. Their bitterness was increased by what they saw back home. There the antiwar movement was telling them in the clearest of terms that the war was immoral and that they were fools for taking part in it, fools for risking life and limb when hundreds of thousands of youths their own age, many of whom were their friends and relatives, were getting deferments, leaving for Canada, or manipulating the system in other ways to get out of the draft.

During the early days of the war, it had been common for soldiers to admit to reporters that they were willing to give their life if necessary to stop communism in Vietnam. Such sentiment became rare after 1969. More and more from 1969 on, the great majority of soldiers came to accept the antiwar contention that the war was not worth even one more American life. "Why be the last man killed in Vietnam," soldiers all across Vietnam cynically asked each other when avoiding combat. They mouthed the words not as a question that required an answer, but as a mere statement of fact, a fact that they all agreed on.

"Field refusals"—that is, refusing to advance against an enemy position or even refusing to board a helicopter headed for the field—was one immediate result of this new cynicism among soldiers. Such refusals became so common by late 1970 that many division commanders set up special companies in rear areas to hold men who would not go to the field. One of the most notorious refusals came in 1969 when an entire infantry company from the 196th Light Infantry Brigade refused to attack an enemy-held hill. An equally notorious incident took place six months later when another company—this one from the once vaunted 1st Cavalry Division—refused to advance down a jungle road for fear of being ambushed. To the Army's great embarrassment, a CBS television reporter, John Laurence, filmed the entire incident.

With unit discipline breaking down in Vietnam, so also did the bonds between the races, bonds that before had been held together by the shared experience of combat. Racial disturbances were one immediate result of this breakdown. In one incident, black and white soldiers faced off with rifles and machine guns following an argument. Only the timely intervention of their commander stopped them from opening fire on each other. In Da Nang, following an argument over a juke box selection, a black soldier threw a grenade in an enlisted men's club, killing one man and wounding forty others. Such incidents were so common in Saigon that blacks established a black-only off-duty area there, an area white MPs refused to enter for fear of being attacked.

Dedicated officers and NCOs who tried to enforce discipline in Vietnam soon found that they were themselves targets. Such killings were called "fraggings" after the weapons most frequently used in such attacks: the fragmentation grenade. In 1970, pressure from Senator Mike Mansfield forced the Army to reveal that there had been 207 "fraggings" that year, double the number for 1969. In one incident, a young captain from Mansfield's home state, Montana, was blown up in his sleep by men angry at him for ordering them to go on dangerous patrols. In another incident, a young lieutenant suffered a similar fate for threatening to court-martial four men for continually shirking combat. Grenades were not the only weapon used, however. In one incident that sent a shock wave through senior command circles, a private walked boldly into an officers club with an M-16, pumped two shots into his company commander, then walked back out to the cheers of his friends. It was not an unusual occurrence. Word of the death of some officer often brought cheers from men gathered in a bivouac or attending an outdoor movie.

Given this breakdown in discipline and increased lawlessness, many soldiers eventually turned to drugs as a way of escape, a way to block out a reality that had become grim and meaningless. In the early years of the war, drug use was almost unheard of, but by 1968 nearly 20 percent of GIs in Vietnam were smoking marijuana. That figure climbed to 50 percent in 1969. In 1971, the Army embarrassingly revealed that from 10 to 15 percent of GIs there were using heroin. The army had to also reveal that the problems in Vietnam had spread to other Army posts. Racial incidents, insubordination, and drug use were soon common in places like Fort Ord, California, and Fort Leonard Wood, Missouri.

The Army experienced some of its worst trouble, however, in Germany, where three hundred thousand Americans of the Seventh Army were supposed to be holding the line against the armies of the Warsaw Pact. Headlines in the German press told a different story. AMERICAN TERROR AS NEVER BEFORE, screamed a headline in the *Neve Revue*. VIETNAM HAS POISONED THE U.S. ARMY IN EUROPE, cried out the *Berlin Tagesspiegel*. Daily in Germany, soldiers committed crimes against each other and against the German people. In the town of Neu Ulm, a gang of GIs kidnapped a sixteen-year-old German girl and raped her repeatedly. In Stuttgart, eighty drunken GIs, armed with knives and clubs, fought the police for four hours. In Berlin, dozens of whites and blacks fought a running battle with stones and clubs. In Hohenfels, a hand grenade was thrown through a mess hall window, seriously wounding ten men. And in Munich and Nuremberg, gangs of whites and blacks roamed the streets, smashing store windows and attacking German citizens on sight.

All these problems the Army faced were compounded in October 1970 when President Nixon notified Westmoreland that he wanted the Army to become a completely volunteer force by 1973. To Westmoreland, Nixon's order was somewhat of a shock. He had always been vehemently opposed to ending the draft and creating a volunteer force. He did not philosophically believe in the idea of a volunteer force, feeling it was every American's duty to serve in the military. But just as important, he did not believe it was possible to create such a force, that the quality manpower simply would not be available. In spite of his personal feeling, he assured Nixon that he would do everything in his power to create what came to be known as the Modern Volunteer Army (MVA).

Before laying the groundwork for the MVA, Westmoreland first had to begin dealing with the many problems plaguing the Army at the moment. One of the most serious problems was, of course, racism, an institutionalized racism that blacks were reacting to with increasing militancy. To begin bringing that problem into focus, he scheduled a series of racial seminars on posts throughout the United States. The purpose of these seminars was to "seek out, identify, and eliminate racial tension in the Army," as he himself put it, and to develop ways by which equal opportunity in the Army could be assured. At these seminars, which were frequently moderated by a colonel, blacks were encouraged to speak out, to air their grievances, and seek redress for them.

To deal with the enormous problems facing the Seventh Army in Germany, Westmoreland sent Lieutenant General Michael S. Davison there to take over from the retiring Lieutenant General James H. Polk. Although Polk was retiring on schedule, he was doing so under a dark cloud, having recently been accused by a black military judge, Captain Curtis Smothers, with "dereliction of duty" for failing to combat housing discrimination against black soldiers by German landlords. Polk had also been accused by Congressman William L. Clay of Missouri of "being a bigot" who should be "thrown out of the Army rather than retired." Further aggravating the situation in Germany was Brigadier General George S. Young, a division commander under Polk. In spite of Smothers's vehement objections, Young had persisted in using the word "negra" in his presence.

Needless to say, Davison arrived at Seventh Army at a most critical time. With a mandate from Westmoreland to take drastic steps, he did just that. With an abruptness that shocked many officers in the Seventh Army, he immediately ordered all German landlords to integrate their housing. Those who did not comply were denied the right to rent to any Army personnel. He did the same to German businesses that catered to GIs. Those that refused service to blacks were blacklisted and put off limits to all GIs. Davison was as abrupt with the officers in Seventh Army. Those who did not show a full commitment to ending racism in their commands were relieved of command and shipped home. And so too were troublemakers in the ranks, be they black or white. They likewise were rounded up and shipped home, often with bad conduct discharges. To deal with the growing drug problem, he conducted frequent searches of barracks and forced suspected users to take urine tests. Violators were put into drug programs; repeated violators were discharged.

Abrams also initiated a number of reforms in Vietnam. They were not, however, as draconian as Davison's. Abrams was more concerned with getting his army out of Vietnam than in reforming it. Reforms in Vietnam were likewise not a big preoccupation with Westmoreland. Though disheartened that his once crack army had been reduced to the state it was in, he was a realist who realized that there was not that much he could do. His main preoccupation from 1970 on was with changing the Army as an institution. And that he did and with an apparent enthusiasm for change that angered many in the Army.

To make the Army more palatable to a new generation of youth, he abolished reveille, put beer on the evening mess, allowed soldiers to grow sideburns and longer hair, abolished the traditional pass policies, increased the distances soldiers could travel on leave, and established an open door policy whereby an enlisted man could complain directly to his commanding officer at any time. Finally, he created a task force under Lieutenant General George Forsythe, for the express purpose of suggesting other reforms and experimenting with them on selected posts.

Westmoreland's reforms ran into immediate, and at times hostile, resistance. Despite recruiting posters, approved by Forsythe's office, showing soldiers with longer hair, many base commanders refused to allow soldiers in their command to wear their hair similarly. One soldier, in fact, was court-martialed at Fort Meade, Maryland, for wearing his hair just like the soldiers on the posters, which brought a howl of protest from the syndicated columnist, Jack Anderson. At other bases, commanders forced soldiers to take down posters and pinups in their rooms, despite a new program allowing such personal freedoms. There was also a concerted outcry from senior officers and NCOs at a series of recruiting posters, capped with the slogan, TODAY'S ARMY WANTS TO JOIN YOU. Senior military men bristled as they read the line, for to them it implied that the Army was there to accommodate and cater to the new enlistee, and they would be damned if they did that. Their blood collectively boiled at the thought. Their feelings about the slogan soon found expression in a nationally syndicated Oliphant political cartoon that showed a new recruit waking up one morning in his own private room, which is furnished with a TV and beer cooler and the walls of which are plastered with nude pinups. Holding a cup of coffee and the morning's newspaper, a first sergeant is standing over the soldier's bed. "General Westmoreland's compliments, Private," the sergeant is saying. "And after coffee would you kindly join us at the ten-thirty reveille gathering." A short time after the Oliphant cartoon ran, the *Army Times* ran their own cartoon satirizing Westmoreland's reforms. It showed a slightly deranged looking American soldier with his shirt open, a peace symbol around his neck, and a can of beer in his hand. The caption read, "The Modern Volunteer Army."

Westmoreland was not pleased with either the resistance his reforms were generating from senior officers and NCOs or with the pokings he was taking in the press. As Lieutenant General George Rogers notes, although Westmoreland believed the Army needed to be both reformed and modernized, he did not want to be the man to do it. He thought of himself as a field soldier, says Rogers, and found going head-to-head with the Army establishment distasteful, and being lampooned in the press degrading. Do I really need all this grief? he frequently asked Rogers. Rogers assured him that his work would eventually be appreciated, and Westmoreland swallowed his distaste for the role of reformer and continued with his work. No matter what they might think of it, he told numerous gatherings of Army officers and NCOs, both retired and active duty, the Army was now committed to being an all-volunteer force and to basic reforms. And to make both work, they, the commanders and leaders, had to begin making the Army more attractive to the new citizen-soldier. In a series of memos to post commanders, he urged them to root out all vestiges of racism from their commands, to eliminate "lock-step training," and improve communications with all soldiers, regardless of their rank. Those officers not comfortable with these changes should be removed from positions of command, he added. In a series of letters specifically addressed to senior officers, he urged them to put "first things first," to stop holding inspections merely to harass troops, and to eliminate irritants like "make work" and meaningless rituals.

Westmoreland was forced, however, to back down on some reforms. Though Secretary Resor himself thought soldiers should be allowed to wear longer hair, Westmoreland ran into such stiff resistance from army traditionalists that he had to compromise, allowing a style which was much longer than the traditional burr haircut but shorter than the three inches on top that he had originally approved.

All in all, Westmoreland's reform had a significant impact on the way the Army would look in the future. Irritants such as reveille, KP, bed checks, and Saturday inspections were abolished, and such enticements as beer in the barracks and a five-day work week added. Though many in the military believed it impossible to abolish the draft and have a completely volunteer military, that, in fact, became a reality in 1973 when Congress doubled the pay of enlisted men. The reforms plus higher pay encouraged the needed enlistments, so that on January 27, 1973, Nixon was able to safely abolish the draft.

Many traditionalists refused to accept the changes taking place in the Army, and many were extremely bitter at what they saw as a degradation of their beloved institution. That bitterness many times turned into vindictiveness, as many officers associated with Westmoreland's volunteer Army task force discovered. Forsythe, who ran the task force and who was personally responsible for a number of reforms, retired in frustration in mid-1972, tired of all the hostility he was getting from traditionalists. So also did his deputy, Brigadier General Robert Montague. Throughout his career, Montague had been considered one of the Army's rising stars. Following his association with the task force, he was twice passed over for promotion to major general. A third to feel the traditionalist backlash was Colonel David R. Hughes. Although he had held only a minor position under Forsythe, it was enough, he felt, to get him passed over for promotion to brigadier general.

Westmoreland personally did not suffer anything from the backlash. He did nonetheless incur the eternal enmity of many Army traditionalists who felt that for the sake of political expediency he had wrecked the Army. They were wrong, of course. The Army not only survived, but became better because of his reforms. While the quality of the first enlistees in the volunteer Army was low, continued reforms and pay increases eventually brought in better and better people. It was generally agreed that by the late 1970s, the Army was once again a professional force.

Bitter Fruit

While Westmoreland was preoc-
cupied reforming, modernizing, and defending the Army, the Vietnam War—a war in which he was now but a bit player—continued
on for three more years. Nixon, as he had promised, began his presidency by aggressively Vietnamizing the war. The South Vietnamese
armed forces was increased from 685,000 to 850,000, training programs were improved, and ARVN units were equipped with the finest
arms and equipment available. Also, as he had promised, Nixon began
rapidly withdrawing U.S. troops. Nearly 100,000 were pulled out in
1969 and 150,000 in 1970. Continued withdrawals through 1971
brought the number of American servicemen down to 140,000 by
year's end.

Westmoreland and the other Chiefs were completely opposed to
these massive withdrawals. In a classified study, NSSM 1, they
warned the President that at the present rate of progress in South
Vietnam, the country could not be expected to be pacified for another
eight years. And theirs was an optimistic assessment. The CIA thought
it would take another ten years. Until the country was pacified, the

Chiefs warned, the ARVN simply could not take over the burden of fighting alone. As the historian Mark Perry notes, the study's conclusions "would have been enough to paralyze the Johnson administration, but for Nixon they were only proof that the United States had to design a policy that would short-circuit the pessimists' predictions, a policy that linked pressure on Hanoi" with negotiations and diplomacy.

Nixon showed just how much "pressure" he was willing to apply to North Vietnam in mid-March 1969 when he gave the military permission to launch a series of massive B-52 strikes against enemy base camps and sanctuaries in Cambodia. Whereas President Johnson, in spite of Westmoreland's repeated entreaties, had shuddered at the idea of bombing Cambodia, Nixon did not hesitate okaying the raids.

A year later in April 1970, Nixon applied even more pressure to the North when he okayed Abrams's request to invade Cambodia with United States and ARVN troops. As noted earlier, throughout his tenure as COMUSMACV, Westmoreland had lobbied Johnson for just such an invasion, but Johnson had never given this second option serious consideration either. In April 1970, however, Abrams had little trouble convincing Nixon. Nixon was eager to punish the North Vietnamese, eager to let them know that they were now dealing with a determined adversary, who was not about to be the first President to lose a war. In addition, Nixon hoped the invasion would break the stalemate at the negotiating table in Paris.

While the invasion did not do that, it did nonetheless seriously damage North Vietnam's war-making capability. The invading force of twenty-three thousand American and ARVN troops utterly smashed a dozen enemy sanctuaries and overran countless arms caches. Enough weapons were discovered in those caches to equip eighty North Vietnamese battalions and enough food to feed every Communist soldier in South Vietnam for six months. Denied these captured arms, the Communists could no longer launch their customary spring offensive in the South.

While the Allies could see an immediate benefit from the Cambodian invasion, it meant nothing to the hundreds of thousands of men and women in the antiwar movement. To them, the invasion was a clear sign Nixon was expanding the war, and they reacted immediately. Overnight, demonstrations and rioting broke out on college campuses across the country. On May 4, 1970, four days after the start of the invasion, national guardsmen opened fire on a group of rock-throwing students at Kent State University in Ohio, killing two protesters and two bystanders. The killings provoked even more demonstrations and rioting, and within a week 448 colleges and universities were forced to close down.

President Johnson would have been devastated by such a response. It only angered Nixon. He was determined to stay the course in Vietnam, regardless of what his critics thought of him. And to stay the course, he felt he had to continue delivering punishing blows against North Vietnam. With that thought in mind, he turned his attention to Laos. Deprived of his sanctuaries in Cambodia by the Allied invasion, Giap had begun to reinforce his units operating from base areas in Laos and to stockpile an unusually large amount of equipment and supplies near the Laotian town of Tchepone, a major transshipment point on the Ho Chi Minh Trail. With those supplies, Nixon feared, with good reason, that the North Vietnamese might be planning a major Tetlike assault against South Vietnam's two northern provinces. After consulting with Abrams about the situation there, Nixon ordered him to put together a plan of attack and invade Laos as soon as possible. Both men were enthused about the invasion, in spite of some obvious problems facing it. The most obvious was the Cooper-Church amendment, which an angry Congress had passed after the Cambodian invasion. The amendment specifically prohibited American troops from entering into either Cambodia or Laos. The ARVN would have the benefit of American air support, including helicopters, but not even the American advisers to ARVN units would be allowed to enter Laos.

Though Westmoreland had worked up numerous plans for an Allied invasion of Laos, Nixon, as Kissinger notes in his memoirs, did not bother seeking the general's advice before arriving at a decision. Nor did Nixon, as Kissinger also notes, ask Westmoreland's opinion of Abrams's plan of attack when it was submitted. When Kissinger revealed the plan to Westmoreland and asked his frank opinion of it, the national security adviser was quite shocked by the response he got. For a start, Westmoreland said, he did not think Abrams had allocated enough troops to make the invasion a success. Abrams had earmarked only two ARVN divisions to attack and hold Tchepone, whereas he had always felt it would take at least four American divisions to hold the town and deal with the large enemy attempt to retake it that could be expected. Westmoreland's implication was obvious: How could two ARVN divisions be expected to do the job of four United States divisions? Westmoreland also told Kissinger that he did not feel a frontal assault was the best way to attack the Ho Chi Minh Trail at this point in time. Westmoreland did not say so specifically, but again the implication was obvious. American troops could successfully invade Laos, but the ARVN was still not competent enough to handle it alone. Instead of a conventional invasion with tanks and armored personnel carriers, Westmoreland recommended that the ARVN reopen Khe Sanh, then use it as a base from which to launch a series of hit-and-run raids by airmobile units against the Ho Chi Minh Trail and the area around Tchepone.

In spite of Kissinger's great disdain for the way Westmoreland had run the war, in his memoir he grudgingly admits that the general's ideas made a "great deal of sense." Unfortunately, Westmoreland's ideas did not make as much sense to Secretary Laird or to the new Chairman of the Joint Chiefs of Staff, Admiral Thomas Moorer. But even if they had, it apparently would not have made any difference. Both told Kissinger that they did not think it best to hold further meetings to discuss Westmoreland's objections in more detail. As Kissinger put it, both were "convinced Abrams would resent being second-guessed by his predecessor."

Both men would soon wish they had allowed some second-guessing. Code-named Lam Son 719, the invasion of Laos kicked off on January 30, 1971, and ran into immediate problems. Forewarned of the attack by spies in ARVN headquarters, Giap met the three attacking ARVN divisions with six divisions of his own. He also moved up two hundred heavy antiaircraft guns, numerous long-range artillery batteries, and two hundred tanks. What followed was a gigantic World War II-like land battle that ebbed and flowed along a twenty-mile by five-mile swath of land from the border to Tchepone. Hundreds of American and ARVN fighter-bombers swarmed over the battlefield, blasting Giap's force with hundreds of tons of bombs and rockets. As always, Giap was not afraid of suffering casualties. He had the ARVN units outnumbered two to one, and he threw his troops against them with abandon, determined to hurt and embarrass them, determined to show that Vietnamization was a hoax. Giap lost thousands of men in these assaults, but he badly hurt the ARVN units in the process, chewing them up with furious tank and infantry assaults. Though the ARVN fought well, they were too outnumbered to hold out against Giap's determined assaults and after forty days of constant fighting began giving way. They were also hampered by confusion among their senior commanders. To compound the problem, a number of severe disagreements had developed between President Thieu and Abrams. Each had different ideas about how the attack should proceed, and that difference created confusion. In frustration the ARVN high command finally ordered their forces to withdraw from Laos. In some places, that withdrawal turned into a panicked retreat.

The final tally for Lam Son 719, although somewhat obscured by the confusion surrounding the battle, was staggering. Nearly 20,000 NVA soldiers were killed in the fighting. Enemy losses in equipment were also heavy: 2,000 trucks, 106 tanks, 13 artillery pieces, 170,346 tons of ammunition and 1,250 tons of rice. South Vietnamese casualties were not as heavy, but serious nonetheless. They had 3,800 dead and 9,775 wounded, and left destroyed or abandoned in Laos 211 trucks, 87 combat vehicles, 54 tanks, and 96 artillery pieces. American losses alone could have told the true scope and ferocity of the fighting in Laos, however. Giap's antiaircraft guns brought down 108 helicopters and damaged another 600. These same guns also took an awful toll on their pilots and crews. Of the 201 American killed and the 1,200 wounded during Lam Son, the great majority were either helicopter pilots or crewmen.

The results of the Laotian invasion, according to Westmoreland's deputy, Bruce Palmer, "caused much pain and anxiety at the White House." Following a few heated arguments and a few recriminations, Al Haig, Kissinger's military adviser, was sent to Vietnam for a first-hand assessment of the situation. In his report to Nixon and Kissinger, Haig concluded that Abrams's plan was not only ill conceived, but that the MACV commander had failed to provide the kind of leadership necessary once the attack ran into difficulty. After the war, Abrams's deputy, Fred Weyand, made a similar accusation, and frankly revealed that the plan and execution of the Laotian invasion had badly undermined his faith in Abrams's tactical and strategic abilities.

The press, however, was not aware of the Haig report, and Abrams was able to avoid the kind of pillorying that Westmoreland got after Tet. The press ascribed complete blame for Lam Son to ARVN incompetence and cowardice.

In spite of Lam Son 719, Nixon continued his troop withdrawals. Early in 1972, the last United States maneuver battalion left Vietnam. All that remained were 90,000 troops who provided advice and support to ARVN units. With the departure of this last battalion, American participation in the ground war in Vietnam ended. In the seven years since the Marines splashed ashore at Da Nang, 57,000 Americans and 224,000 ARVN had been killed in Vietnam, either from wounds or accidents, and another 304,000 and 571,000 respectively had been wounded or injured. The North Vietnamese and Vietcong suffered the worst, with over 660,000 KIAs and four to five times that number of wounded.

By any standard, the war was a bloody stalemate, with neither side through force of arms able to convince the other to withdraw. Both continued to try, however. Nixon continued his B-52 strikes against Cambodia and drastically escalated the tonnage of bombs dropped on conventional targets in North Vietnam. Having dealt firsthand now for three years with North Vietnamese intransigence, neither he nor Kissinger was as arrogant as he had been in early 1969 upon coming to power. Nonetheless, both still believed that they could use force to pressure North Vietnam into signing a peace agreement. The North Vietnamese, on the other hand, were not interested in signing anything at the moment. To the contrary, in early 1972, they were in the last stages of preparations for the biggest offensive of the war so far, an offensive that would be larger than the Tet Offensive by three times and would pack ten times as much punch. To spearhead what would become known as the Easter Offensive, Giap had assembled twenty main-force infantry divisions—two hundred thousand men in all—and to give them the maximum striking power put in their support one thousand tanks, four hundred antiaircraft guns, and hundreds of long-range artillery pieces. As Davidson notes, it was a larger force than Patton had commanded in World War II.

On January 25, 1972, while the enemy was in the final stage of preparation for their offensive, Westmoreland flew to Indochina for a visit. After stops in Cambodia and Thailand, his trip ended in Saigon. There, during a news conference at MACV headquarters, he announced that he expected the Communists to soon launch a major drive against the South, with the fighting centered largely in the northernmost provinces and the Central Highlands. He predicted that because of North Vietnam's limited logistical capability, the "staying power of the enemy is not great" and that any attack would likely fade "in a matter of days." Westmoreland was wrong. In a conventional infantry assault, such as the one they launched at Tet, the North Vietnamese forces would have had little staying power. But the addition of hundreds of tanks to the battle would give the attack enough initial shock to compensate for logistical problems. The Allies were not aware of these tanks, unfortunately, for none of their intelligence units had detected them.

The North Vietnamese struck on March 31, 1972, with a three-pronged assault. In the northern province, spearheaded by large tank formations, NVA divisions overran Quang Tri City and were quickly rolling south toward Hue. In the highlands, again behind tanks, NVA forces seized part of Kontum City, and in the far south, they captured Loc Ninh and prepared to move against An Loc.

A day after the start of the attacks, Nixon, for the first time in the war, ordered his B-52s to begin launching massive strikes against targets in North Vietnam. For Westmoreland and the other Chiefs, the attacks were not massive enough. In early May, they held a series of meetings and agreed that now was the time to mine Haiphong and every other port and to deal North Vietnam a truly punishing air attack. They feared, however, that Nixon would not react strongly enough, that he would instead let the Communists off the hook. They were so convinced that mining North Vietnam's harbors would cripple the enemy offensive that, according to Admiral Moorer, they were "ready to walk out the door unless Nixon did it." "I'm telling you plain," Moorer told an interviewer in 1977. "We thought we had a real chance to break their backs—we weren't going to throw it away the way Johnson did [during Tet]."

It is unknown just how many Chiefs were prepared to walk out with Moorer. Westmoreland attended a number of meetings during this period, but claims he was not at the meeting where the Chiefs considered resigning. He claims additionally that he would have never gone along with something like that.

Whatever the truth, Moorer did tell Nixon how strongly the Chiefs felt and with the kind of language he knew would appeal to him. "We've got to make those bastards pay for the American blood they've spilled," he shouted. Moorer discovered that he was preaching to the choir. Nixon was as angry as the Chiefs over the enemy's offensive, and he was eager and willing to deal them a hard counterblow. "The bastards have never been bombed like they're going to be bombed this time," he said, matching the intensity of Moorer's rhetoric.

Following his invective, Nixon stepped aside and turned the entire bombing campaign over to the Joint Chiefs, a gesture that gladdened their hearts. For the first time in the war, they, and not the President and the secretary of defense, would pick the targets and manage the air attack. The Chiefs took on their new responsibility with a vengeance. Navy jets were soon in the air and within hours laid hundreds of mines in Haiphong and every other major port in the North, completely closing them to any further shipping. Other Navy jets cut the rail lines to China and knocked down two critical bridges near the Chinese border. For the first time in the war, B-52s attacked Hanoi and Haiphong, destroying dozens of military installations and massive stockpiles of ammunition and fuel that had been off limits during the Johnson years. All that materiel and fuel was destined for the South, and as it went up in smoke so did Giap's chances of initiating a second phase of attacks. Without the needed fuel and ammunition, many of his tanks soon ground to a halt. To further hamper the enemy attack, elite ARVN airborne battalions were flown by helicopter behind enemy lines, where they ran wild destroying fuel depots, ammunition dumps, and terrorizing rear-echelon troops.

Having played havoc in North Vietnam, the B-52s were now shifted to the South to be used against the attacking forces themselves. Behind B-52 strikes in the Central Highlands and in Quang Tri Province, ARVN troops, led by their own tanks, began a grinding counterattack. Initially stunned by the NVA tanks, ARVN soldiers, using wire-guided rockets hurriedly flown in from the States, were soon knocking them out with ease. Other enemy tanks were hunted down and destroyed by helicopter gunships.

By early June, the North Vietnamese were in full retreat, pulling back across the demilitarized zone in the north and in the south heading for their border sanctuaries. While they did manage to remain in control of some mountainous areas of South Vietnam, that was all they had to show for their efforts. Their casualties were staggering. Nearly half the two hundred thousand men Giap committed to the offensive were dead, and over half the one thousand tanks reduced to scrap metal. The South Vietnamese also suffered terrible casualties, with nearly twenty-five thousand dead—more dead than the United States had suffered in all of 1968—and one hundred thousand wounded. In spite of these terrible casualties, they were able to take heart from the attack. While they were still no match for the North Vietnamese without American air support, their units had fought well overall and many times with exceptional courage. As the military historian, David Richard Palmer notes, if the ARVN response proved nothing else, it proved that "Vietnamization was a fact."

Westmoreland and the other Chiefs were elated by the collapse of the enemy offensive. And just as they had done to Johnson after Tet, they began prodding Nixon to take even more aggressive actions against the North, to really hit them while they were staggering and on the run. Instead of escalating the attack, Nixon stunned the Chiefs by suddenly offering the North Vietnamese a new peace proposal, one that called for a cease-fire in place. In addition, he proposed that the Vietcong be allowed a role in any postwar government in South Vietnam.

The Joint Chiefs were, of course, vehemently opposed to the proposal and told Nixon so. They wanted the North Vietnamese to pull up stakes in the South and head home. Only then, they said, should Nixon sign a peace proposal. Kissinger, however, convinced Nixon that the Chiefs' demand could not be met. Since a complete withdrawal of North Vietnamese troops from the South had been "unobtainable through ten years of war," he argued, how could it possibly be made a "condition for a final settlement"? Kissinger wanted a settlement with the Communists as quickly as possible, regardless of what the Chiefs or anyone else thought of it. He felt it was time to compromise, even if the United States didn't get all the terms it wanted. The United States could not "stay there [in Vietnam] forever," he angrily told an aide who argued with the Chiefs.

If Nixon and Kissinger were ready to compromise, so too were the Communists. They had been disappointed with the results of their offensive, and with a presidential election only five months away—an election it seemed clear Nixon would win in a landslide—they realized that now was the time to compromise. After the election, they feared Nixon might revert to a hard-line position. And so in late summer, the two nations began carefully laying the groundwork for a settlement.

Still unhappy with the terms Nixon was offering the North Vietnamese, Westmoreland retired on June 30, 1972, and was replaced by Abrams. In a formal ceremony at Fort Myer, Virginia, he was officially praised by Secretary of Defense Melvin Laird. "In the Second World War, in Korea, and in Vietnam," Laird said, "General Westmoreland commanded American fighting men with boldness, valor, and quiet professional skill. In Vietnam, he led our forces in one of their most difficult challenges. He has served his country well."

His critics were not so kind. They saw his retirement as an opportunity to criticize once more his handling of the war, and they did so with great enthusiasm. One of Westmoreland's most prominent critics was Colonel David H. Hackworth, a highly decorated combat officer in Vietnam. While being interviewed on TV by ABC's Howard Tuckner, Hackworth denounced the war effort and the Army's senior leadership. The colonel then retired and entered the civilian world as a cause célèbre. In an editorial in *The Washington Post* he denigrated Westmoreland's leadership abilities and claimed that the United States could have won the war in Vietnam if Westmoreland had tailored his American forces to guerrilla warfare rather than pummeling Vietnam with firepower.

Needless to say, the press found a hot story in Hackworth, and before long they were touting him as an honest, decent man who had willingly destroyed his career in order to speak out against the way Westmoreland had run the war. Members of the press apparently were not aware of the fact that while in Vietnam Hackworth had smoked marijuana with his troops and been involved in currency violations, gambling, theft of government vehicles and equipment, and other acts that were clear violations of Army regulations. Nor were they apparently aware that the Army Criminal Investigation Division had compiled a report in excess of four thousand pages on these activities and that the Army had considered putting him on trial. Indeed, some senior officers speculated that Hackworth retired because he recognized that, as a result of his irregular activities, he had no future left in the Army. Members of the press were not aware of any of these things and Hackworth did not tell them, maintaining that he retired because of his disgust with the war.*

Eventually Hackworth emigrated to Australia, but he left behind his views on the war. To many Americans, not a few of whom were professional military men and veterans, Hackworth's contention that Westmoreland had mishandled the war was an attractive one, and they eagerly embraced it, finding in it a ready, simple explanation for what went wrong in Vietnam.

In the years after the war, the Army would likewise ask itself what went wrong in Vietnam, and attempt to come up with an answer. Was defeat there inevitable? Or was there a tactic or strategy that would have brought us victory?

In the late 1970s, the Army's Command and General Staff College at Forth Leavenworth, Kansas, commissioned a group of young bright Army officers at the school—many of whom were Vietnam veterans— to attempt to come up with some solid answers. In their final report,

---

*Hackworth finally revealed these activities in his 1989 best-selling autobiography, *About Face*, likely surmising that to have someone expose them would have damaged his book's credibility. I wanted to compare his version of these activities with the Army Criminal Investigation Division's (CID) version. Because of the Privacy Act, I needed Hackworth's permission to view the CID's file on him. I sent him a registered letter requesting permission. He wrote back wishing me luck with my book, but didn't respond to my request.

they carefully analyzed Hackworth's views and concluded that there was no evidence to suggest that guerrilla tactics "would have been any more successful than the semi-conventional tactics employed against the enemy." On the other hand, they did feel that guerrilla tactics would most certainly have "resulted in vastly increased casualties, and in an increasingly unpopular war, such losses would obviously have been unacceptable."

These young officers concluded that "given the strategic limitations of the war"—limitations that denied the Army the right to permanently cut the Ho Chi Minh Trail and mine North Vietnam's harbors—"improved tactical methods probably would not have changed the final outcome of the war."

In his now classic study of the Vietnam War, *On Strategy*, Colonel Harry G. Summers, Jr., an instructor at the Army War College at Carlisle, Pennsylvania, came to a similar conclusion. Different tactics simply would not have affected the final outcome of the war, Summers maintains, for North Vietnam was the real opponent in Vietnam, not the Vietcong. Hanoi carefully hid its involvement in the war behind a smokescreen of guerrillas, Summers argued. Consequently, the United States got carried away by the mystique of fighting a guerrilla war against the Vietcong, when, in fact, the real enemy was North Vietnam. Summers further maintains that the war was winnable and that if Westmoreland's plan to permanently cut the Ho Chi Minh Trail had been coupled with a naval blockade of the North, the United States could have achieved the same results in Vietnam it achieved in Korea.

In some of his other conclusions, Summers was not as kind to Westmoreland or to the Joint Chiefs. He asserts that they should have actually done what the Chiefs contemplated doing on two separate occasions. It was their duty as military men, Summers says, to warn President Johnson "of the likely consequences of his actions, to recommend alternatives," and, as Napoleon put it, "to tender their resignations rather than be the instruments of their Army's downfall."

In his own defense, Westmoreland claims that he never imagined that the Vietnam War would end the way it did, that he honestly believed that the ARVN, with continuing American support would be able to hold the line in Vietnam. "I suffered my problems in Vietnam," he says, "because I believed that success eventually would be ours despite them."

Despite the forcefulness of Summers's indictment of Westmoreland and the Joint Chiefs, there is no consensus among Vietnam historians about what went wrong in Vietnam nor what anyone could have done to change it. It is doubtful that a mass resignation of senior military men during the war would have convinced Johnson to expand the war, for Johnson feared losing the war much less than he did a wider war with China. While permanently cutting the Ho Chi Minh Trail and blockading North Vietnam might well have produced a result similar to the one achieved in Korea, it might also have drawn the Chinese into the war, with consequences far worse than what actually happened. Many Vietnam historians think, and the noted Indochina expert Doug Pike includes himself in that group, that short of nuclear war there was no guaranteed way for the United States to win in Vietnam. No one can say with certainty, Pike says, whether the use of a different strategy might have produced a victory there. There is simply no way of knowing for sure. "Even occupation of the North," Pike and Benjamin Ward wrote in a recent essay on the subject, "could not have succeeded in suppressing guerrilla activity entirely; hence some level of fighting might have continued almost indefinitely in Indochina."

In the end, instead of an easy answer to what went wrong in Vietnam, we might have to accept the words of Robert Shaplen, a man who spent years in Indochina as a *New York Times* correspondent. "Vietnam, Vietnam," he lamented, "there are no sure answers."

A few months after Westmoreland's retirement, President Johnson invited him and Kitsy down to his Texas ranch for a few days. Westmoreland gladly accepted. He had paid a short visit to the former President in 1969, but this was the first time since the war that he would spend any time with Johnson. One of the most striking stories of the Vietnam War was the deep, enduring loyalty that developed between Westmoreland and President Johnson. It developed in spite of their dissimilar backgrounds and temperaments, and throughout the war was impervious to the shocks and traumas that they endured together. Whereas the Korean War turned MacArthur and Truman into the most bitter of enemies, Vietnam only increased the mutual respect Westmoreland and Johnson felt for each other. As Blair Clark notes, "If Johnson had wanted to," he could have easily made "Westmoreland the scapegoat for the failure of his policy in Vietnam." Scapegoating Westmoreland, however, apparently never entered Johnson's mind. It was the same with Westmoreland. Although sorely used by Johnson, the general never expressed any bitterness over it. He felt Johnson was primarily responsible for what happened in Vietnam, but never said so until after Johnson's death. Westmoreland refrained from any harsh criticism of him, just as he had refrained from criticizing Wheeler for his machinations after Tet.

Although not a well man, Johnson was visibly happy to see Westmoreland, and eager to show him how much he enjoyed his new life as a rancher. A short time after they arrived, Johnson and Lady Bird took him and Kitsy for a tour of their twelve-thousand-acre ranch in their Lincoln convertible. Johnson was in an expansive mood. At the sight of three young black boys playing in front of a tenant house, he stopped the car and called out, "Come on, boys, give the President a kiss." When each had, he drove on, stopping again a mile or so down the road at another tenant house. On his car phone, he called the kitchen back at the main house and told the cook to bring out some sausage and biscuits. When they arrived, the four of them sat on the front porch, eating the sandwiches and sipping mixed drinks prepared by a group of secret service agents.

When they finished the first drink, Johnson said, "Let's have another drink. As the old Mexican says, 'It'll make us feel smart and rich.' " They had that second drink, and were soon, according to Westmoreland, reminiscing, sharing memories "of what was, of what might have been and a certain sadness, a certain frustration that for all our efforts we had been unable to shape events full in the mold that we deemed was right. We also shared pride in having fallen heir to a part of history, however minor that part might turn out to be."

Later that evening after dinner, Westmoreland and Johnson sat down over drinks again and discussed the war. Johnson praised Nixon for the aggressive actions he had taken against the North so far. He regretted that he had not done a number of things differently in Vietnam. If he had it to do over again, he said, he would have fired all the holdovers from the Kennedy administration, except Dean Rusk, and would have imposed press censorship early in the war. He was certain that because of the press the message of United States resolve never got through to Hanoi. The next morning at breakfast, Johnson told Westmoreland in confidence that with his heart condition, he knew his days were numbered. Johnson apparently knew his body well for he died two months later on January 23, 1973.

A few days after his visit with Johnson, Westmoreland received a call from Nixon requesting that he immediately fly to Washington to give his opinion of a peace agreement that Nixon was thinking of signing. Among other things, the agreement called for a return of all American POWs in exchange for allowing North Vietnamese troops in the South to remain there. Westmoreland arrived in Washington on October 2 and a short time later met with Alexander Haig, who had recently resigned from the Army and was now Nixon's personal chief of staff. Haig was upset over the agreement and complained to Westmoreland that "Mel Laird had turned 'dove,' " and that he was one of the few advising the President to take a tough stand with the North Vietnamese.

Westmoreland agreed completely with Haig's sentiments. When he met with Nixon later in the day, he told him he thought he should "delay action on the new agreement and to hold out for better terms." He felt that for South Vietnam to survive, North Vietnamese troops had to be compelled to completely withdraw from the South. To ensure that they did, he advised Nixon to continue the bombing, upgrade United States economic and military support for South Vietnam, and build up the South Vietnamese Air Force. He assumed, he told Nixon, that whatever agreement was signed, American air power would still be available outside South Vietnam to punish the North should they attack again. Nixon assured Westmoreland that he completely agreed with his views, but Westmoreland feared that "the President was determined to reach an agreement soon, regardless of the long-term consequences for South Vietnam."

Westmoreland was right. On January 27, 1973, an agreement that was supposed to end the war in Vietnam was signed by Kissinger in Paris. It called for a complete cease-fire in Vietnam, the return of all POWs, withdrawal of United States and Allied forces from South Vietnam in sixty days, and recognition of the PRG, the political arm of the Vietcong. As Westmoreland had feared, the agreement also allowed over 100,000 North Vietnamese troops to remain in the South.

Nixon and Kissinger crowed over the agreement. Westmoreland, on the other hand, felt it was tantamount to a surrender, in spite of Nixon's contention that he could enforce the agreement with air power. Whatever the truth, it soon did not matter. In July 1973, to show their disgust with the war, Congress passed a bill that prohibited United States combat over, on, or near Cambodia, Laos, and both Vietnams. Two months later, they passed another bill, the War Powers Resolution, requiring the President to consult with Congress before committing military forces anywhere in the world. Any commitment that was made could not continue for over ninety days without congressional approval. Hamstrung by the Watergate investigation, Nixon could do little to stop either bill.

To further show its disgust with the war, in early 1973 Congress cut the bill containing military aid to South Vietnam from the requested $1.6 billion to $1.1 billion, then a year later cut it again to $700 million. When shipping expenses were deducted and inflation factored in, South Vietnam received only about 20 percent of the aid in 1974 that it had in 1972. These cuts severely curtailed South Vietnam's ability to fight the war. To conserve what supplies they did have, the ARVN high command instituted strict rationing, allowing the average soldier only one grenade and eighty-five bullets per month, and howitzer batteries only four rounds per day. The ARVN, in short, was now fighting what the Communists themselves recognized as a "poor man's war." These shortages forced ARVN units to halt any further deep-penetration helicopter and tank assaults. Instead they had to dig in in static defensive positions and wait for the Communists to attack them. These cuts also eroded the will of the average soldier, demoralized him at a most critical point in the war. Like his leaders, he might have been able to accept the congressional cuts if he had believed them necessary. But he knew otherwise. He knew Congress could have easily doubled and tripled the aid to them, but chose not to. And it chose not to, the ARVN knew, because it no longer cared whether South Vietnam survived. The Congress was sick of the war, and it was washing its hands of it.

While the ARVN was rationing bullets in the South, in the North, the Communists, with their ports cleared of mines, were the beneficiaries of a cornucopia of new tanks, artillery pieces, antiaircraft guns, and missiles pouring in from the factories of China, the Soviet Union, and Eastern Europe. And as they poured in, the North Vietnamese hurriedly rushed them south down the Ho Chi Minh Trail and into stockpiles all along the Laotian and Cambodian borders, all in preparation for yet another offensive—the final one, they hoped. To lead this new offensive, they equipped and trained thousands of new troops, so many new troops, in fact, that by 1974 they were able to field twenty infantry divisions to South Vietnam's thirteen.

With the Communist forces continuing to grow stronger, another chain of events began that sealed South Vietnam's fate. Facing a possible impeachment, on August 8, 1974, Richard Nixon resigned the presidency. The next day, Gerald Ford was sworn in as the thirty-eighth President. Ford immediately appealed to Congress to restore the deep cut made in aid to South Vietnam. Congress, however, rebuffed him. A majority there were not only opposed to further aid to South Vietnam, but some of their number wanted to cut off all aid. The rebuff sent a clear message to Ford, which was that he would be unable to intervene militarily in Vietnam, even if he wanted to. Some in Congress did not think he wanted to. They believed that if the truth were known, he also had lost his stomach for the war, that he likewise was weary of the whole thing.

None of this was lost on the North Vietnamese, who throughout 1974 continued their buildup. In the midst of that buildup—sometime in the summer of 1974—Hanoi decided that the time had arrived to launch the final offensive, the *Götterdämmerung* of the Second Indochina War.

Hanoi opened the offensive with a three-division assault against Phuoc Long Province on December 26, 1974. Though the ARVN defenders there fought well, they were greatly outnumbered and outgunned and after five days of vicious fighting gave way. Unable to pay the price in men and materiel that would be required to take back the province, Thieu wrote it off. That pleased Hanoi, but what pleased it even more was that the United States, in the face of a massive violation of the Paris agreement, did not intervene militarily. To Hanoi, this was the green light, a clear signal that they could launch their offensive without having to contend with the dreaded B-52s.

They opened the second round of their offensive on March 10, with large-scale attacks in I Corps, the Central Highlands, and in the area along the Cambodian border northwest of Saigon. In I Corps, three NVA divisions overran Quang Tri and were soon headed south toward Da Nang; in the Central Highlands, two NVA divisions, attacking behind tanks, overran Ban Me Thuot; and along the border southwest of Saigon, a single NVA division, also attacking behind tanks, overran the district town of Tri Tam.

Four days after the offensive began, Westmoreland flew to Washington to pay what he told the press was a "courtesy call" on President Ford. In reality, he had come to try to pressure Ford into mining Haiphong and turning the B-52s loose against the North. He made a passionate request. The present situation, he told Ford, was "reminiscent of the early days of the German military threat. The North Vietnamese are the Prussians of the Orient."

"That's my impression, Westy."

"There's only one language that Hanoi understands, and that's force. If we'd just send our B-52s in there to bomb the supply trails and mine Haiphong harbor for a month, the whole atmosphere would change."

"Unfortunately the law says we can't do that, Westy."

Westmoreland's conversation with Ford ended there. He continued his railings in the press, however, both against North Vietnam for being an aggressive nation and against Congress for refusing to allow the United States to reenter the war. His railings accomplished nothing. The Congress not only refused to allow American military intervention, but even voted down supplementary aid to the South Vietnamese military requested by Kissinger.

Kissinger persisted in seeking additional funds, but his requests soon became meaningless. In the South, although it looked like the ARVN had regrouped after the shock of the initial attacks, things suddenly went into a tailspin. Realizing that he was facing a much stronger force in the Central Highlands than he could contend with, President Thieu decided to abandon the area and pull his troops back into an enclave around Saigon. Thieu meant the withdrawal to be orderly, but a series of confused orders panicked a large portion of the highlands population into fleeing for the coast. In a matter of a few hours, all the roads to Saigon were clogged with soldiers and civilians, trampling each other to avoid the Communist forces nipping at their heels. Rumors of the highlands debacle triggered another frantic retreat in the northern provinces, where in a matter of days Quang Tri, Hue, and Da Nang fell like a house of cards. Hanoi had figured that it would take until 1976 to conquer the South. To its surprise, its tanks were in Saigon on April 30, 1975.

Like most Americans, Westmoreland watched the fall of Saigon on television. He watched with a sick feeling in his stomach as the last chopper carrying the last Americans lifted off from the roof of the United States embassy, and then, with an even sicker feeling, as the ARVN pilots ditched their helicopters in the South China Sea and then swam to the safety of waiting American ships. The preceding two months had left him emotionally drained, but this was by far the worst thing he had had to endure. Everything he had worked so hard for for so many years was gone. What had taken years to build had disappeared in less than a month.

To make him feel even worse, he received a phone call a short time after the fall of Saigon from Tran Kim Phuong, South Vietnam's ambassador to the United States. Phuong was near tears. "General, you spent so much time with us," he said, his voice breaking with anguish. "You worked so hard trying to save us. I'm turning to you. What can we do? We have no arms, no reinforcements. We've got about 10 million dollars worth of gold that we were able to get out. Do you think it will be possible for us to go into the international arms markets and get arms that could help us?" Westmoreland listened in silence, as anguished as Phuong. He wished there was something he could do, he finally said. But there was not. It was too late to do anything. It was over.

The emotional shock Westmoreland endured during the final days of the Republic of Vietnam soon gave way to anger, an anger that was unbridled at times. For a man who had spent his entire military career containing himself, it was very uncharacteristic. He told a *Time* magazine correspondent that the fall of Saigon was a "sad day in the glorious history of our country. But elements of this country have been working for this end. We failed. We let an ally down. But it was inevitable after Congress pulled the rug out from under the President with the War Powers Act. Hanoi was home free at that moment, for our only trump card was gone. Other countries in Southeast Asia must be lonely and frightened. People who dismiss the domino theory are all wet."

A few days later during an AP interview, Westmoreland lashed out even harder at Congress, saying that the War Powers Act was "tantamount to surrender . . . it made us look like damned fools in the international arena. Maybe we in this country can understand the conflict between the legislative and executive branches. But can anybody else? To them it must look as if we had two governments." They were harsh words, but they brought no response from Congress. There were few there who were particularly interested in what Westmoreland had to say anymore. Most there just wanted to forget the war and him with it.

Politician Westmoreland

General MacArthur's haunting refrain—"Old soldiers never die; they just fade away"—touched the hearts of millions of his countrymen when he uttered it on the eve of his retirement. They were fine, stirring words, but unfortunately, they were not true. In the real world, old soldiers do not fade away— they fade into the military-industrial complex. A short time after delivering his "Old soldiers" speech to Congress, MacArthur became the chairman of the board of the Sperry Rand Corporation. Of the noted World War II commanders, he was hardly alone in making the switch. Upon retirement, General George C. Marshall became a consultant to Pan American Airways; General Omar Bradley, chairman of the Bullova Research and Development Corporation; Lieutenant General James Doolittle, the vice president of Shell Oil Company of California; and Lieutenant General Joseph T. McNarney, the president of the Corvair Division of General Dynamics, to name but a few.

Such switches were so common after World War II that in 1959, Senator Paul Douglas of Illinois shocked the Congress and the country by revealing that 495 retired colonels and Navy captains, and 226 retired generals and admirals were working for the top one hundred defense contractors. In spite of attempts at reform and the passage of various conflict-of-interest laws, by the time of the Vietnam War that number had tripled to over three thousand and was growing daily.

Following the end of that war, one who particularly benefited making the switch was General Alexander Haig. Upon leaving the Nixon administration, he spent a year as president of United Technologies at a salary of over $800,000 a year. After a short stint as President Ronald Reagan's Secretary of State, Haig went into the consulting business. In that capacity, he picked up another $2.5 million from companies like Sperry Electronic Systems, United Technologies, Boeing, and ISC Technologies.

It is not known just how handsomely Westmoreland could have cashed in with the military-industrial complex, for he made it clear before retiring that as a matter of principle he did not intend to promote any product sold through a defense contractor. Nor did he intend to do any consulting work for such companies. He did, however, join the boards of Aladdin Industries, the United Life Insurance Company, the Pantasote Company, and Tyco Laboratories. His pay for each board job was around $1,000 a month, easy money for the amount of work required, but a paltry sum compared with what he could have commanded as president of United Technologies, Bell Aircraft, or Boeing.

Still he was hardly destitute. When his board salaries were added to the inheritance he had received from his father, and that to his military retirement pay of $30,000 a year, he had enough to live very comfortably.

Westmoreland's income got a further boost in late 1972 when John West, the Democratic governor of South Carolina, offered him a part-time job as head of a trade development task force at a salary of $25,000 a year. Westmoreland had turned down a half-dozen similar offers, but he quickly jumped at the chance to return, possibly permanently, to his home state. Kitsy was a North Carolina girl, but on visiting Charleston, she quickly fell in love with the majestic old seaport. The two were soon combing the city's neighborhoods looking for a place to live. After a month-long search, they finally purchased a lot on Tradd Street, a narrow, tree-lined lane only a few hundred feet from Charleston's historic Battery. For Charlestonians, the Battery was a general term used to describe a long curving seawall, fronted by the Atlantic Ocean and backed by rows of palm trees and gracious three-story homes. In the seventeenth and eighteenth centuries, pirates and criminals were hanged there to the delight of hundreds of Charlestonians. On April 12, 1861, hundreds more gathered there to cheer as cannons and mortars on the Charleston shore bombarded Fort Sumter, setting off the Civil War. The Battery was now a social center for the town, a promenade where lovers came to walk and talk or sit idly on park benches staring out at the Atlantic Ocean, where the elderly gathered to chat with friends under the palm trees, and where artists sketched and painted the many lovely scenes around them. The Westmorelands thought they had found the perfect place to live.

A short time after buying their lot, the Westmorelands hired a contractor to begin construction of what would be their first home after twenty-six years of marriage. Like many other homes on Tradd Street, it was to be built in the Colonial style, with white stucco walls, shutters, simple cornices, sloping hip-roofs of tin, with the front door on the side. Already on the rear of the lot was a two-story stucco carriage house, dating from the nineteenth century. While the foundation was being laid for the house, carpenters began remodeling and restoring this carriage house, turning the upstairs into a small guest apartment and the downstairs into an office for the general, an office that would soon be crammed with his private papers, books, photos, and various mementos of his long Army career. Visiting journalists liked to refer to this room as the general's new command post, and in a sense it was. From there Westmoreland would fight the postwar battle over how the war was interpreted and what his place and the places of the millions of men who had served under him would be. He would discover that the ideological battle over the interpretation of the war would be just as hard fought as the actual shooting war.

But for now, his command post was only a shell, and while carpenters and plumbers worked to make it habitable, in early 1973 he and Kitsy rented another carriage house on nearby Price Alley, and moved there with their daughter, Margaret, now a student at Charleston's prestigious private academy, Ashley Hall. Rip had been living with them, but he was now enrolled as a freshman at St. Lawrence University in upstate New York and on his way to a law degree. Katherine was likewise gone. She had graduated with a B.A. degree from Pitzer College in 1970 and married a year later. With her schoolteacher husband, Blair Weymouth, she was now living in Rindge, New Hampshire and teaching exceptional children at a local school.

The family, however, frequently got together on holidays, either in Charleston or at a condominium the Westmorelands later purchased in North Carolina's Blue Ridge Mountains.

On Price Alley, the Westmorelands settled into the routine of being Charlestonians. To become better acquainted with her neighbors, Kitsy got a part-time job at a fashionable dress store nearby, and was soon riding her bike back and forth there every day. Westmoreland, of course, did not need to get acquainted with anyone. Everyone in South Carolina knew who he was, and when he walked to the post office in the morning or over to Tradd Street to see how construction was going on their home, he was frequently stopped by people who wanted to shake his hand and chat with him for a second. No matter who stopped him he was always friendly. He went out of his way, however, to be friendly with veterans. Once when he ran into three Charleston college students all wearing Army fatigue jackets, he became, according to a local reporter, positively animated.

"Where did you young men serve?" he asked.

" 'Nam, sir," one boy answered.

"All of you?"

"Yes, sir," they all answered.

"What units were you with?"

"Big Red One, sir."

"First Cav, sir."

"First Cav also, sir."

According to the *Charleston News and Courier* reporter present, Westmoreland spent the next ten minutes with the men talking about the war and about their units before going on his way.

Two days a week, Westmoreland's duties as head of Governor West's economic task force took him on the road. With his aide and driver, retired Army Colonel William Ballou, he journeyed all over South Carolina, visiting factories, speaking to civic groups, meeting with schoolteachers and principals, and conferring with South Carolina bankers and foreign businessmen.

A good number of South Carolinians concluded that Westmoreland was promoting more than economic development as head of the task force. Newspapers around the state were soon speculating that West was either grooming Westmoreland to become chairman of the powerful State Development Board or, better yet, to become governor once his own term expired.

Not all state Democrats were happy to have him suddenly appear on the scene—appear, as one prominent Democrat put it, "like a king waiting to be coronated." After Westmoreland had been at his new job for about six months, a member of the State Development Board, speaking in anonymity, lashed out at him during an interview with a Columbia newsman. The former general, he said, was "arrogant and ignorant of South Carolina's real development needs. I told him I didn't want him around us again." Another board member, Peter J. Stathakis, was equally hard on Westmoreland. In an interview with the *Charleston News and Courier*, he claimed that Westmoreland, for all the "hullabaloo" over his hiring, in six months on the job had not "contributed one iota toward economic growth or foreign trade." Stathakis also did not like Westmoreland's administrative style. "The general has got to learn that he cannot run us like a bunch of privates and get cooperation."

Westmoreland received the most severe criticism from Robert Liming, the governmental affairs reporter from *The State*, Columbia's daily newspaper. Liming did not like Westmoreland, and in one of his columns made that fact very clear. He accused Westmoreland of spending extravagantly, of misusing state aircraft, and of being overpaid. He even appeared to contest Governor West's statement that Westmoreland was the most outstanding military figure that South Carolina had ever produced. "Some palmetto state historians might differ with that assessment," wrote Liming.

According to someone on the task force staff, Westmoreland was stung by all the criticism, and especially by the Liming piece. The vindictiveness of the attack caused him to wonder if the reporter had some ulterior motive, maybe a hidden ideological agenda. Liming never explained his motives, but Westmoreland was discovering that the press could be just as rough on him at the state level as they had at the national level. As a number of those close to him noted, this fact surprised him. He had assumed that most in the state would welcome him back with open arms, grateful that he was lending his name and clout to South Carolina's economic development. He discovered instead that wherever he went, he was treading on turf other people had already staked out, and these people were willing to fight to hold on to it. South Carolina was a new battlefield, and he was going to have to learn a new set of rules to play it. Unfortunately for his political career, he did not learn these rules fast enough.

In spite of the attacks on Westmoreland, he was still enormously popular with the average South Carolinian. South Carolina was a fiercely patriotic state, and to a large portion of its population, he was a living embodiment of patriotism—basic, old-fashioned, flag-waving patriotism. Given this fact, as 1974 opened and the November elections began looming on the horizon, both parties began actively courting him to enter the race for governor.

Most political observers were convinced that if Westmoreland decided to run for governor, he would run as a Democrat. His father had been a lifelong Democrat, they pointed out, and the general's career had benefited greatly from his close association with two Democratic Presidents. Even if Westmoreland was not a Democrat, these same observers felt, he would still have to run as one. South Carolina was a Democratic-controlled state, and had been since Reconstruction. There had never been a Republican governor in the state's history, and Senator Strom Thurmond, a former Democrat, was the only consistent Republican winner there.

These political observers were wrong. After lengthy discussion with President Ford and Thurmond, and after Lee Atwater, who would later chair the Republican party through the 1980s, organized a Draft Westmoreland campaign and collected forty-two hundred signatures on a petition, Westmoreland quit his task force job and announced his candidacy for governor on the Republican ticket. He told a disappointed Governor West that he had decided to run as a Republican because he thought it would be good for the political health of the state to have strong two-party government. Many suspected, however, that he had swung to the GOP because of his deep discontent with the Democratic party. Since 1968, that party had been gradually drifting to the left, an ideological position he obviously found disconcerting, and it had been the Democrats who were primarily responsible for passing the War Powers Act and cutting military aid to South Vietnam. If Westmoreland had ever been a Democrat in his heart, he could not be one any longer.

Westmoreland's decision to run as a Republican brought no public response from West, even though privately he was very disappointed. Nonetheless, it brought a howl of protest from other Democrats. The strongest came from Democratic State Chairman Donald Fowler, a political science professor at the College of Charleston. Fowler had made every effort to convince Westmoreland to run as a Democrat, and he now referred to the general as a "crass opportunist." Nothing in Westmoreland's thirty-six-year military career qualified him to be South Carolina's governor, Fowler declared, and that was most evident from some of his public statements, which showed he knew nothing about the state or the critical issues facing it. Finally, Fowler accused Westmoreland of being guilty of a "significant lack of loyalty" to the party that had made his career.

Fowler was right about one thing: Westmoreland indeed did not know much about his home state or the critical issues facing it. That was evident as soon as he hit the campaign trail. During an appearance in Greenville early in the campaign, when asked by a reporter what the campaign issues would be, Westmoreland answered that he did not know yet. During a press conference in Columbia, Westmoreland, according to a reporter from *The State*, "stammered confused responses in a losing effort to explain his thinking and his campaign plan."

If Westmoreland did not know the campaign issues, he also did not know how to campaign, did not have what politicians call the aptitude for the campaign trail. He was a man who had spent most of his adult life having his every wish attended to by subordinates who treated him with imperial respect. But they were now gone. The campaign trail was pure democracy. It meant making endless small talk, which Westmoreland was not good at; it meant equally endless handshaking and backslapping, which he was very uncomfortable with; and even worse, it meant asking for campaign contributions, which he found degrading.

The people Westmoreland encountered on the campaign trail were often as uncomfortable in his presence as he was shaking their hands and mouthing the line "Hi, I'm William Westmoreland. I'm running for governor and I'd appreciate your vote in November." To many South Carolinians, and especially those who had served in the military, Westmoreland would always be General Westmoreland. He might be wearing a sport shirt and a pair of summer slacks, but in their mind's eye, they saw him in full dress uniform, bedecked in battle ribbons, four stars gleaming on his shoulders. Frequently when he burst into a country store or restaurant, one or two men inevitably snapped to attention. Occasionally, some, in a reflex action, even lifted their right hand in a salute, then stood there looking foolish waiting for him to return it.

His real problem from the beginning was money and staff, which he had thought the Republican party would somehow provide once he decided to run. He had thought the state GOP executive director, Gay Suber, was going to serve as his campaign manager, but Suber inexplicably backed out. He had also thought that Columbia millionaire, J. Drake Edens, Jr., was going to head his finance committee, but Edens also bowed out. Westmoreland did manage to eventually get people to run his campaign, but the effort was confused, a fact the press reminded him of daily.

In spite of the confusion, however, early polls put Westmoreland as a 3 to 1 favorite over any "potential" Republican opposition. "Potential" is, of course, a vague word. It certainly did not take into account James Edwards, a Charleston oral surgeon and state senator who entered the Republican primary in late March. Unlike Westmoreland, Edwards knew the issues and knew where he stood on them. An ultraconservative, Edwards identified with such old-line Republicans as Senator Barry Goldwater of Arizona and California Governor Ronald Reagan. Also unlike Westmoreland, Edwards was a real politician with a natural, jocular speaking style and a warm, gregarious personality, who looked at home shaking hands and kissing babies.

But Edwards was more than a glad-hander. He was also a tough political infighter, who was passionately committed to the bedrock conservatism he espoused and was willing to fight tenaciously to see it prevail in South Carolina. He did not believe Westmoreland was a true conservative, and with a hard-hitting campaign intended to prove that to South Carolina's very conservative Republican minority. When early in the campaign he discovered that Westmoreland had never voted in a presidential election, he seized on the issue and blitzed the state with campaign literature and radio announcements asking the voters a simple question: Can you afford to cast your vote for a man who has never voted himself? He did not mention that as an officer Westmoreland had had to avoid any political connections or even a hint of partisanship, and few voters bothered to ask. Putting a spin on that same issue, Edwards frequently reminded voters that he had been in the trenches for the last fifteen years fighting for the Republican party, trying to make it once again a viable entity in South Carolina. Was it fair now, he asked them, to pass him over and vote for someone who arrives in the state one day and wants to be governor the next?

Edwards delivered his most telling blow against Westmoreland's candidacy in purely ideological terms, and it was a blow that galvanized the Far Right in the state. Upon likewise discovering that Westmoreland briefly in 1964 had been a member of the Council on Foreign Relations, Edwards found the best issue of the campaign. The CFR is a private nonpartisan membership organization that, since 1921, has functioned as an interest group and think tank for the United States foreign policy establishment. Membership in the council is by invitation only, and invitations are only tendered to the movers and shakers in American foreign policy, be they Democrats or Republicans. To moderates, the CFR has never been anything but a high-level clearing house for ideas, ideas put on display five times a year in their prestigious periodical, *Foreign Affairs*, wherein authoritative contributors publish probing analyses of political, economic, and social developments in the world scene. It was in *Foreign Affairs*, in fact, that Henry Kissinger—a CFR member—first criticized Westmoreland's Vietnam strategy and proposed his own plan to end the war. To some on the Far Right, however, the CFR has a much more nefarious purpose, namely to bypass the United States Congress and set up a socialist one-world government. Because of Westmoreland's association with the CFR, Edwards's backers began accusing the general of being somewhere on the political spectrum between "liberal" and "ultraleftist."

Although Westmoreland thought the charge absurd, many South Carolinians, especially in superconservative Charleston County, took it very seriously. It is difficult to tell how many voters decided to support Edwards based on this single issue, but on July 16, primary day, thousands who had started the campaign supporting Westmoreland voted for Edwards. The state senator ended up with 57 percent of the vote, and went on to win the general election, becoming the first Republican in history to win the governorship.

Coming on the heels of Vietnam, many thought Westmoreland would take the defeat badly. His supporters, however, suffered more than he did. He was, in fact, relieved the election was over and equally relieved that he had not won the primary. Shocking his supporters, he admitted to reporters after the election that he was an "inept candidate. I'm accustomed to a more structured organization. Something like this is so nebulous." Later in Charleston he was even franker with another group of reporters, telling them that he was a poor campaigner, poor politician, and would have made a poor governor. "I'm glad now I didn't win."

Another Soldier Reports

Following his defeat, Westmoreland and Kitsy retreated to their condominium at Grandfather Mountain near Linville, North Carolina. Westmoreland had been working on his memoirs since 1973, but because of his task force job and the primary campaign he had been unable to devote much time to them. With the help of an old friend, the noted military historian Charles McDonald, Westmoreland now began working on the book full time. The book was based heavily on the detailed diaries Westmoreland kept in Vietnam and took a little less than a year to complete. Doubleday published *A Soldier Reports* in January 1976 with a moderate publicity campaign that emphasized the point that the country was finally going to get to hear Westmoreland's perspective on the war, a perspective free of political constraints.

Westmoreland's main thesis in the book was that the war was winnable, but was lost because Washington lacked the will to win. He vehemently defended his search-and-destroy strategy, his decision to hold Khe Sanh, and the conduct of the American soldier during the war. He just as vehemently criticized President Johnson for allowing public opinion to dictate his actions, McNamara and the other presidential advisers for giving undue counsel to their fears, and Nixon and Kissinger for agreeing to a cease-fire in January 1973 and abandoning the South Vietnamese regime. Westmoreland was especially critical of the press, contending that they exaggerated American and South Vietnamese failures and poisoned the public-opinion well in the United States with defeatist accounts of the war.

Considering that Westmoreland was the most prominent American military figure since the Korean War, the book was not widely reviewed, and the reviews it did get were divided along partisan lines, with those who had supported the war loving it, and those who had opposed it, hating it.

Reviewing in the *Los Angeles Times*, Westmoreland's friend and associate, Brigadier General S.L.A. Marshall praised the book for being a moderate account of the war and commiserated with Westmoreland for having stayed the course in Vietnam, in spite of having his hands tied behind his back by the "coteries of crisis managers" and "naysayers" in the White House. Writing in *The Wall Street Journal*, another former military man, Burke Wilkinson, called *A Soldier Reports* "an absorbing and important book." In the *National Review*, Norman Hannah confessed that after reading the book he better understood Westmoreland and the problems he had endured in Vietnam. Professor P. J. Honey, a noted orientalist at the University of London, gave the book its best endorsement. *A Soldier Reports*, he wrote in the *London Times*, "will outlast the mountain of ephemeral trash which has been published on the Vietnam War and I shall be most surprised if, in years to come, it is not regarded as a standard historical work."

Slightly better than half the people who reviewed the book did not share Honey's high regard for it. To this other half, Westmoreland deserved not sympathy for what he had endured in Vietnam, but condemnation for his handling of the war. In *The New York Times*, Ward Just, a journalist and novelist who had written extensively about the war, called the book "a sad and defensive memoir" filled with an "air of confusion, bewilderment, and pain." From the evidence presented in the book, Just wrote, it was obvious that Westmoreland did not "understand that the war was essentially a political struggle" or what America's role should have been in such a struggle. Just ripped into Westmoreland's defense of his search-and-destroy tactics, claiming that that defense was "as chaotic as the strategy and tactics themselves." He concluded his review by taking Westmoreland to task for his criticism of the press. That criticism, he contended, was simply "cockeyed." Herbert Mitgang was another *New York Times* reviewer who took umbrage with Westmoreland's diatribe against the press. Mitgang called it a "fantasyland explanation" for what went wrong in Vietnam. George C. Wilson, the military affairs writer for *The Washington Post*, also thought Westmoreland wrong for blaming the press for what happened in Vietnam. Such an explanation was simply too simplistic, he wrote. He likewise wondered why when passing out the blame for the war, Westmoreland was not willing to accept some of it himself. Why, asked Wilson, did not the general "take on such fundamental questions as whether American policy makers committed a monstrous mistake at the outset of our involvement by embracing the South Vietnamese stooges left over from the French colonial days."

In spite of the small number of reviews and the negative tone of so many of them, Westmoreland had high hopes for *A Soldier Reports*. Given the public response to the memoirs of other prominent United States military men, such hopes seemed logical. In the annals of publishing history, soldier memoirs were routinely best-sellers, and many dominated the best-seller lists for months at a time. Grant's memoirs, published in 1885, sold over 300,000 copies the first year and earned him $450,000 in royalties, a princely sum at that time. General "Black Jack" Pershing's rambling narrative of his experiences as commander of the American Expeditionary Force during World War I earned him a long ride at the top of the best-seller list, wide syndication, and a Pulitzer Prize. After World War II, a number of prominent military men penned memoirs and found a public eager to read them. As could be expected, the most notable of those first-time authors were Generals Eisenhower and MacArthur. MacArthur received over $900,000 from Time, Inc., just for the serial rights to his memoirs, *MacArthur Reminisces*. The hardcover dominated *The New York Times* best-seller list for six months and earned the general over one million more. Eisenhower did not make as much money for his own story, *At Ease*, but only because he foolishly signed a contract with Doubleday for a one-time payment of $635,000. *At Ease* sold by the millions, was translated into twenty-two foreign languages, and reprinted in dozens of different editions.

Westmoreland obviously did not think his book would do as well as Eisenhower's and MacArthur's books, but he did think the public would respond in a big way to it. He was so confident they would, in fact, that in July 1976, after being interviewed by the writer Joe

McGinnis, Westmoreland suddenly announced that he thought *A Soldier Reports* would make a great movie. For that reason, he went on, he had made sure to maintain the book's movie rights. . . .

McGinnis was incredulous. "Movie rights?"

"Yes, I think quite a movie could be made from my experiences," Westmoreland went on. "Especially my experiences in Vietnam. I'm just throwing this out, you understand. I'm not looking for any commitment. But the way I would want to do it, I thought it might appeal to you. Because of your book about television and Nixon and image and all that."

"Yes."

"You see, I think the movie should focus on the Vietnam portion of my career. And the point would be about the difference between the image and the reality of what went on in Vietnam. About how the people at home were so misinformed about the war through the television coverage and things like that, which gave a false image, while I, who had all the facts, couldn't get my message across. Does that make sense?"

"Yes, yes, that makes sense."

"I think the movie should be called 'Vietnam—the TV War.' "

" 'The TV War'?"

"That's right. And I was wondering—now you understand this is just something I thought I'd throw out, and I'm not looking for a definite answer this morning either way, and as a matter of fact, I've still got a lot of thinking to do about it myself—but do you think you might be interested in, possibly, writing the script?"

McGinnis says he did not know quite how to respond, but finally said, "I don't know, General, I've never written a movie script."

"That's all right," Westmoreland said, laughing. "You can practice on me."

"I don't know, General. I'm not sure the time is right for a movie about Vietnam in which you, ah, would be played by John Wayne."

"Oh, no, no," Westmoreland said, laughing again. "I wasn't thinking of the John Wayne kind of thing at all."

McGinnis, of course, was being kind. He did not believe there was even a vague possibility of *A Soldier Reports* being made into a movie. People were sick of the Vietnam War. They were sick of reading about it and just as sick of watching it on TV. They certainly were not interested in seeing a movie about the war. He could see that, but Westmoreland obviously could not.

A Soldier Reports did manage to sell over thirty thousand copies in hardcover, a respectable number for a first author, but minuscule compared with the sales racked up by other eminent United States military men. As McGinnis had foreseen, Hollywood did not come calling.

If Westmoreland was bothered by the fact that *A Soldier Reports* was not a publishing sensation, he did not mention it to anyone. He had decided early in his retirement to dedicate himself to changing perceptions about the war, and the book was but one way he planned to do it. He had given a number of speeches about the war since retirement, but his primary run and the work on the book had considerably curtailed his ability to travel, especially in 1975. With both behind him now, he decided to devote more of his time to speaking and traveling. Eager to reach as wide an audience as possible with his views, he agreed to talk to any group that would have him.

He especially liked talking to groups of Vietnam veterans. He felt more comfortable with them—they were, as he liked to say, "my boys"—but more important, he felt he had a duty to talk with them, almost a moral obligation. Throughout the war, he had watched in horror the plight of returning veterans, watched them degraded by some in the antiwar movement, shunned and ignored by the society at large, watched them depicted as weirdos and psychotics in television shows and in the movies. It was a sad spectacle, and he had decided after the war to begin doing something to help these men.

"I said to myself," he told a journalist in 1984, "who had more experience in the arena than I? Abrams, maybe, but Abrams was dead . . . Who can speak in behalf of those who gave the Vietnam War their best, particularly the enlisted men? Who was in a better position to try and straighten out the record? Me. Who else? McNamara could have done it, but McNamara chose not to."

Westmoreland delivered much the same message to every group of Vietnam veterans he spoke to. Ironically, it was a message quite similar to the one his Civil War ancestors had listened to at the numerous Confederate Veterans reunions they had attended. In it, there were clear echoes of the "lost cause." They had fought well and bravely, Westmoreland told them all, and they had nothing to be ashamed of. The war had not been lost through any fault of their own, but because Washington had been unwilling to go all out and win it. They were heroes whether the country recognized them as such or not.

To men who felt defiled by the war, to men who had been denied the ritualistic welcome-home parades through the center of their hometowns, to men who had had no monuments erected to their ordeal, no statues unveiled to their honor, no plaques listing and commemorating their fallen comrades, Westmoreland's words were a balm for their bruised egos. Westmoreland was heavily criticized for such speeches. Many claimed he gave them strictly for selfish reasons. They claimed he was merely trying to improve his image with his men, trying to rewrite a sad chapter in America's history and in so doing to put himself in a better light. His former troops, however, appreciated his appearances. He was the only one who seemed to give a damn about them, and whatever they might have thought about him during the war, they loved him now.

Westmoreland only delivered about half his speeches to veterans groups or other sympathetic audiences. He delivered the others on college campuses, where the audiences were usually contentious and many times openly hostile. As the writer Don Kowet notes, "his friends regarded these forays into the enemy camp as reckless. They advised him to devote his retirement years to his wife, Kitsy, and their three children. They advised him to cultivate a low profile and leave the defense of his reputation in the hands of historians."

Westmoreland ignored their advice. He felt he had an important message to deliver, and on one college campus after another, he delivered it. During many of these speeches the scenario was much the same. He would be introduced, oftentimes to scattered boos, then take the podium, again often to scattered boos. He would begin his speech over the boos, only to be interrupted by hecklers, shouting that he was a "liar" or a "baby killer" or a "war criminal." While the shouting went on he would stand there impassively, though obviously angry inside. If it died down for a moment, he would start his speech again, but inevitably be interrupted again. Often a professor or student, thrown into a proxysm of righteous anger at finally confronting someone they had passionately hated for years, would actually leap onto the stage and begin delivering his or her own speech, shouting to the audience that Westmoreland was a "fascist" or a "war criminal" and that what he did in Vietnam was a "war crime." Westmoreland always let them finish their diatribe, then continued with his speech once again, determined that the audience was going to hear every word of it. Without apology, he told his audiences that Vietnam had been a just cause, and the South Vietnamese a just people yearning for democracy. Our abandonment of them had been shameful, and blame for what happened there lay with the press and Congress. He also told them that contrary to what they had read in the press, most

United States soldiers in Vietnam had fought bravely and with honor, and My Lai was not the norm but an aberration. Often to get back at his hecklers, he reminded his audiences that hundreds of thousands of people had fled Vietnam since the fall of Saigon, and millions more would get out if they could. If the government in Hanoi was the legitimate one, he asked, why were so many people trying to get out? He hoped this last argument would convert many in his audience to his way of viewing the war, and possibly it did, but those who opposed him only jeered the louder.

As the years passed, the jeering grew less and less frequent, and eventually stopped altogether. It was not his arguments, however, that stopped it, but the times. Vietnam had still been a lively topic on college campuses after the war, but as the 1970s began drawing to a close and a new sense of complacency became the norm there, interest in the war began waning. To many of the new students flooding the campuses in the late 1970s—students who had not had to confront the draft or the possibility of being sent to Vietnam— Vietnam was no longer an issue of any importance. It was now a part of history, with no more relevance to their lives than World War II or the Korean War.

This fact was never more evident than on October 20, 1981, when Westmoreland returned to New Haven, Connecticut, to deliver a speech at Southern Connecticut State College. The school is but a few miles from Yale, where only nine years before he had attempted to deliver a speech at the university's Political Union, only to be denied entrance by hundreds of antiwar demonstrators. Instead of a mob this time, Westmoreland spoke to a nearly empty hall. The sixty students who did attend were described by a staff reporter from the New Haven Register as polite and mild-mannered. When the writer questioned students outside the hall to see if they recognized the name, Westmoreland, he discovered that only a few knew who the general was.

They all soon would, however, for in only three days, Westmoreland's name and face would once again dominate headlines and television screens across the country.

CHAPTER THIRTY

"Rattlesnaked"

I f not for the Lindbergh and Scopes trials, the CBS libel trial might very well be listed in histories of United States jurisprudence as the trial of the century. While the general public was never as enthralled with it as they were with its two better-known predecessors, to those with an active interest in the Vietnam War—be they veterans, former antiwar activists, members of the media, or ideologues of various persuasions—it was a cultural-ideological event of the first rank and as controversial and divisive as the war itself. Like the war, there is still a lot of confusion surrounding it, confusion that will likely never be resolved. Although the majority of those with a passing knowledge of the trial think CBS won the case, the network nevertheless suffered grievous damage in the process. The trial badly tarnished the reputation of a CBS producer, drove one of the nation's most respected broadcast journalists to attempt suicide, and brought a wide harsh public scrutiny of CBS's once inviolate journalistic standards. Westmoreland, on the other hand, the one perceived by most as having lost the trial, came out of it more popular and respected than he had ever been.

The beginning of this strange chain of events can be traced to two large Allied search-and-destroy operations, Cedar Falls and Junction City, targeted in early 1967 against enemy base areas in the Iron Triangle and War Zone C. Both operations were massive, and both uncovered thousands of tons of enemy supplies, ammunition, and weapons. Also uncovered, to the joy of Allied commanders, were over a million pages of enemy documents, which were hurriedly flown to CIA headquarters in Langley, Virginia, to be analyzed. It is not known what the CIA hoped to find in the documents, but one analyst there, Samuel Adams, felt he discovered in them facts that conclusively proved that Westmoreland had been consistently falsifying the enemy strength figures and deliberately lying to the President, the Joint Chiefs, and Congress. The present MACV figure for Vietcong in the South was 270,000, but Adams now believed that if the "irregulars" were counted, something Westmoreland was not doing, the real enemy strength figure would be close to 600,000.

Adams proceeded to put this new figure and his rationale for it in a short memo, which was then circulated around the CIA and in selected military circles. One copy of the memo eventually ended up in the hands of Westmoreland's order of battle (OB) chief at MACV, Colonel Gains Hawkins. After a long perusal of the memo, Hawkins concluded that Adams was correct. He told Westmoreland so during a meeting a few days later. According to Hawkins's later testimony, Westmoreland appeared stunned by the OB chief's announcement and stammered, "What am I going to tell Congress? What am I going to tell the President?" Hawkins assumed Westmoreland would have to tell them the truth, which was that the United States was losing the war of attrition.

Hawkins's immediate boss, Major General Joseph McChristian, MACV's intelligence chief at the time, also believed the new figures to be accurate and likewise told Westmoreland so. McChristian also told him that, like Hawkins, he thought these new figures should be included in the new OB data sent to Washington. According to McChristian's later testimony, Westmoreland responded by saying, "If I send that cable to Washington, it will create a political bombshell."

Westmoreland's version of what was said at both meetings was considerably different from that of either man. He claims he told both of them that according to the Geneva Convention, these Vietcong "irregulars"—old men and women, children, and their mothers—simply could not be included in the OB. The only ones who could be included were those men and women who actually carried weapons and actively participated in the war. He considered it both improper and dangerous to include civilians in the OB, even if they supported the VC, for to do so would be to make them legitimate Allied targets. If the Geneva Convention said these people could not be counted as enemy soldiers, he reasoned, then he could not do so.

"Joe, we're not fighting these people," Westmoreland says he told McChristian during their meeting. "They're civilians. They don't belong in the numerical strength of the enemy."

The CIA, however, thought that these "irregulars" needed to be counted. "They were the ones that ambushed our forces when they would enter a VC-held area," said George Allen, the agency's deputy assistant director for Vietnamese affairs. "They were the ones who booby trapped."

Westmoreland challenged Allen's view. In a MACV memo, he referred to these forces as "essentially low-level fifth columnists, used for information collection. Although they cause some casualties and some damage, they do not form a valid part of the enemy force."

When Westmoreland and the CIA were unable to resolve their differences, a conference was held in Saigon to discuss the problem further and attempt a resolution. There, after much further haggling, a compromise was struck. The CIA dropped its insistence that the irregular forces be included in the OB, and Westmoreland agreed to add an addendum to the OB, listing the number of those forces and their capabilities.

Few were completely happy with the agreement. One man, Samuel Adams, was particularly unhappy with it. He was still so convinced that Westmoreland had gotten away with something that he began proselytizing inside the CIA trying to make converts to his position. When no one joined him, Adams retired from the agency in disgust, determined to dedicate his retirement years to exposing Westmoreland.

In May 1975, based in part on two boxes of classified material he had stolen from CIA files, Adams published an article in *Harper's* magazine detailing his allegations about the manipulation of enemy troop figures.

Five years later, a former *Harper's* editor, now a CBS producer, George Crile, visited Adams at his farmhouse in Virginia, curious to see if Adams had done any more work on his conspiracy theory. Adams had. He told Crile that, based on his most recent research, he had concluded that Westmoreland had lied not only about the OB figures but also about the number of North Vietnamese regulars who had infiltrated South Vietnam via the Ho Chi Minh Trail prior to Tet.

Crile was excited about what he had heard, and a few days later delivered a proposal for a documentary based on Adams's revelations to the CBS Reports documentary department. The proposal outlined how the documentary would show "how the U.S. military commanders in Vietnam entered into an elaborate conspiracy to deceive Washington and the American public as to the nature and size of the enemy we were fighting." As a result of that conspiracy, the country was "robbed of the ability to make critical judgments about its most vital security interest during a time of war." The words "conspiracy" or "conspirator" appeared in the rest of the proposal twenty-four more times.

After a six-month deliberation, in April of 1981 Howard Stringer, the executive producer of CBS Reports, approved the documentary. With that approval in hand, Crile convinced Mike Wallace to join the program as its chief correspondent. Samuel Adams also signed on as a paid consultant, and the three were soon filming interviews with nearly a dozen men who had intimate knowledge of the OB debate. Prominent among those men were Harkins and McChristian, both long retired from the Army.

On May 7, Mike Wallace telephoned Westmoreland at his home in Charleston. After a brief discussion of the topic, Westmoreland agreed to be interviewed. Wallace did not mention that Adams was now a paid consultant with the project, for he suspected what was, in fact, true, that had Westmoreland known he would have refused to be interviewed. Crile likewise telephoned Westmoreland a few days later in order to give him a basic idea what the documentary was going to be about. Crile also sent the general a short letter, which also supposedly explained the purpose of the documentary. Both Crile's explanation and the letter were vague. "Using the Tet offensive as a jumping-off point," the letter read, "we plan to explore the role of intelligence in the Vietnam War: How well did we identify and report the intention and capabilities of the enemy we were fighting . . ." Crile likewise did not mention that Adams was now a paid consultant with the project. He did not even hint at the fact that the documentary would be accusing Westmoreland of participating in a "conspiracy."

The actual interview took place on Saturday morning, May 16, at a Manhattan hotel, in a room CBS had rented. In his book, *A Matter of Honor*, Don Kowet called what happened next "vigilante journalism" at its best. Not knowing exactly what the interview was to be about, Westmoreland was woefully unprepared for it. Wallace was prepared, however, and pounded away at Westmoreland, firing questions at him like staccato bursts of machine-gun fire.

WALLACE You say that thirty-five thousand of them were killed, of the VC, North Vietnamese, were killed in the first few weeks of the Tet offensive.

WESTMORELAND Yes, in accordance with—

WALLACE And how many wounded?

WESTMORELAND Well—we have no way of knowing that. But usually the ratio is about three to one: three wounded for every one that is killed.

WALLACE So you have thirty-five, forty [thousand] killed, then conceivably you would have as many as a hundred thousand more wounded.

WESTMORELAND Well conceivably, but I—I think that's probably an overstatement. Probably an overstatement.

WALLACE At three-to-one, it's an understatement.

WESTMORELAND Well, the three-to-one is not a precise calculation, and you cannot extrapolate that the way you have.

Both Wallace and Crile knew that the real ratio of enemy wounded to dead was 1.5 to 1. They knew that from reading official military documents. That fact was also to be found in *A Soldier Reports,* a book Crile had read exhaustively. The reason neither Wallace nor Crile corrected Westmoreland was that having the general mouth the 3 to 1 figure better fit the purposes of the documentary. The 3 to 1 figure would be used to make Westmoreland look foolish, for if it were true, every single Vietcong in South Vietnam would have had to be either killed or wounded during Tet.

Wallace was just as merciless and manipulative when grilling Westmoreland on his decision to eliminate the "irregulars" from the OB.

WALLACE Isn't it a possibility that the real reason for suddenly deciding in the summer of 1967 to remove an entire category of the enemy from the Order of Battle, a category that had been in the Order of Battle since 1961, was based on political considerations.

WESTMORELAND No decidedly not. That—that—

WALLACE Didn't you make it clear in your August 20th cable?

WESTMORELAND No, no. Yeah. No.

WALLACE I have a copy of your August 20th cable—

WESTMORELAND Well, sure. Okay, okay. All right, all right.

WALLACE —spelling out the command position on the self-defense controversy.

WESTMORELAND Yeah.

WALLACE As you put it in your cable, you say the principal reason why the self-defense militia must go, quote, was "press reaction."

WESTMORELAND Well, sure. They would have drawn an erroneous conclusion because it was a non-issue. It was a false issue.

Crile and Wallace did not mention in the documentary that they had failed to provide Westmoreland with a copy of the fifteen-year-old cable, and that he was confused because he was suddenly being confronted with material that he had not seen in years. Viewers instead watched a red-faced, stuttering Westmoreland and concluded that he was lying. During a break in the filming, Westmoreland rose from his chair and, red with rage, stepped across the room and thrust his face into Crile's. "You rattlesnaked me," he hissed.

Crile did not respond, and fifteen minutes later the interview continued. During this second round, Wallace honed in on the Adams accusation that there had been nearly 600,000 Vietcong in the South, 350,000 more than Westmoreland had claimed.

For a brief moment, Westmoreland came out on top, throwing out an argument that Wallace was not prepared for. If there were indeed 600,000 enemy soldiers in the South, as Adams claimed, he asked, where were they during the Tet Offensive? All intelligence estimates after Tet concluded that the enemy had thrown everything they had into the attack, that in some instances they had literally scraped the bottom of the barrel to field units for the attack. In doing so, they had been able to put together an attacking force of around 100,000. That force suffered so many casualties during Tet that afterward the Vietcong was never again a viable fighting force. After Tet, NVA forces took over the brunt of the fighting. If indeed VC forces in the South numbered 600,000, Westmoreland argued, they would have been capable of sustaining the Tet attacks much longer and of launching another wave of attacks. "The proof of the pudding is in the eating," he said. "After the Tet Offensive was over, and we assessed the—the number of Viet Cong indigenous combatants that were involved, and this was an all-out effort, go for broke, it proved to be less than our estimate, considerably less. Less by a—order of magnitude of ten percent."

It was an argument both Crile and Wallace had heard before. The Defense Intelligence Agency, which at first had believed the CIA's contention that there were over 500,000 VC in the South, had later rejected that figure once the dust settled from Tet. Wallace, however, did not bring up the DIA's conclusion. Instead, finding Westmoreland's argument at odds with the documentary thesis, he quickly moved the interview on to a new subject, the dispute over the number of North Vietnamese regulars who had infiltrated into the South prior to the Tet Offensive. Adams's second accusation against Westmoreland was that he knew the NVA had stepped up this infiltration prior to Tet from 6,000 to 20,000 a month, but in order to continue to show progress in the war he had not sent this critical information to President Johnson. Because Johnson was not aware of this fact, Adams's theory went, he was not prepared for the shock of Tet, a fact that had grave political repercussions. As the facts would later show, Adams's argument was a foolish one. Johnson had access to many more intelligence sources than MACV, and even if Westmoreland had wanted to he could not have fooled the President. The argument was not foolish to Wallace, however. He believed it, and he hammered an unprepared Westmoreland with it.

WALLACE Didn't anyone feel the need—well obviously, no one did feel the need to alert the President of the fact that there was—the enemy had a considerably greater capability than was imagined. Shouldn't someone from MACV have told the President—

WESTMORELAND But—

WALLACE —that not only were the VC planning a massive attack, but that they were flooding the South with North Vietnamese regulars.

WESTMORELAND Well, sure. That—that—that—that was known, that was known.

WALLACE The President knew?

WESTMORELAND I—I have no idea if the President knew or not.

Wallace's interview ended late in the afternoon. As one columnist noted after viewing the documentary, Wallace's inquisitorial style had made Westmoreland look like the "village idiot." Westmoreland apparently knew he had been made to look bad. His face and neck still flushed red with rage, he got up from his chair slowly and glared at Wallace. Wallace turned away, unwilling to face the anger. Crile asked Westmoreland if he needed a ride anywhere, but Westmoreland ignored the question and strode purposefully from the room.

Later that afternoon, Westmoreland returned to Charleston. There he began going through his personal files, reviewing his figures on enemy infiltration during the fall of 1967, something he should have been forewarned to do before the interview. When he noticed numerous discrepancies between what he had told Wallace and what he discovered in his files, he wrote Crile and Wallace a latter and asked them to include these corrections in the documentary. To back up his statements, he included copies of official documents. That done, Westmoreland went back to his life on Tradd Street, still unaware that Crile and Wallace were going to accuse him of leading a "conspiracy" against the U.S. government.

He got his first inkling of what the documentary was going to be about seven months later on Thursday morning, January 21, 1982. On this particular morning, as he did religiously nearly every morning, he was starting his day in the den with a bowl of cereal. He was about five minutes into his cereal and the CBS news program *Morning with Charles Kuralt and Diane Sawyer*, when Sawyer suddenly appeared alone on the screen with an announcement for an upcoming CBS documentary. He was preparing to put a spoonful of cereal in his mouth when Sawyer's words froze his arms and the spoon in midair.

"It is an axiom of war," said Sawyer, "that, above all, one must know the enemy. On Saturday night the CBS News broadcast CBS Reports will show that the American government in Washington was deceived about the enemy in Vietnam—specifically in 1966 and 1967, deceived about how vast their numbers were. The broadcast is called *The Uncounted Enemy: A Vietnam Deception*, reported by Mike Wallace and producer-writer George Crile, who found at the heart of the deception not the hand of the enemy but the American military command." Sawyer proceeded to introduce Wallace and Crile, then cut to a sequence from Westmoreland's interview, where he is explaining his rationale for not accepting the McChristian-Hawkins OB statistics for the Vietcong. Westmoreland's explanation was cut in such a way that it appeared that the only reason he had reduced the OB figure was because "the people in Washington were not sophisticated enough to understand and evaluate this thing. And neither were the media."

Other sequences followed. All seemed to prove conclusively that Westmoreland, in order to show progress with the war, had duped the Joint Chiefs, the Congress, the President, and the American people as to the size of the enemy forces the U.S. military was facing prior to the Tet Offensive. As a result of this deception, United States troops were not prepared for the size and scope of the enemy's Tet attacks.

When the promotional ad finally ended, Westmoreland looked down to discover that the spoonful of cereal was still frozen in midair and that his hand was shaking uncontrollably. He dropped the spoon, picked up the phone, and called Dave Henderson, a partner of a prominent Washington, D.C., public relations firm with whom he frequently went hunting. As Henderson explained later, Westmoreland was very disturbed, but uncertain what to do. He was thinking of writing an article to rebut the broadcast, but Henderson told him such an act would have little impact in countering the enormous influence of a CBS documentary. Henderson recommended instead that he hold a news conference on Tuesday at the Army-Navy Club in Washington, D.C. There with other high-level officials from the war years, he could systematically respond to the CBS charges. Westmoreland said that he did not have the "means" to put on a press conference but Henderson replied that he would put one on *pro bono*. Westmoreland then spent the rest of the day on the phone convincing five of his former officers to appear with him on the podium at the Army-Navy Club.

The next day, a full-page ad alerting readers to the documentary appeared in *The New York Times* and *The Washington Post*. The ad had a sinister quality about it. It showed eight darkened figures, their faces hidden in shadows, huddling over a small rectangular table. Emblazoned in white across the dark table was the single word CONSPIRACY.

Below the table was the message:

CBS Reports reveals the shocking decision made at the highest level of military intelligence to suppress and alter critical information on the number and placement of enemy troops in Vietnam. A deliberate plot to fool the American public, the Congress, and perhaps the White House into believing we were winning a war that in fact we were losing. Who lied to us? Why did they do it? What did they hope to gain? How did they succeed so long? And what were the tragic consequences of their deception? Tomorrow night the incredible answers to these questions. At last.

"The Uncounted Enemy" aired on Saturday night January 23, to an audience of nine million Americans. It argued four main points: first, that because of growing antiwar pressure back home and the need to show progress in the war, Westmoreland's command had kept enemy troop strength figures below 300,000, even though evidence indicated that the figure should have been at least twice as high; second, that Westmoreland had suppressed information about the vastly increased numbers of North Vietnamese regulars coming down the Ho Chi Minh Trail prior to Tet (because of this deception, neither the U.S. troops in Vietnam nor the White House was prepared for the scope and savagery of the attacks); third, that Westmoreland had delayed a cable to Washington containing higher enemy-strength figures because, according to Lieutenant General George Mc-Christian, the author of the cable and MACV's intelligence chief, it would be a "political bombshell"; and finally, that Brigadier General Daniel Graham, the head of MACV's Current Estimates and Intelligence Division in 1967 and 1968, erased computer tapes after Tet in order to hide Westmoreland's deception.

The day after the broadcast, the press responded. To a person, commentators accepted the show's premise and reacted with righteous indignation. Writing in *The Wall Street Journal*, Hodding Carter declared that CBS Reports had "rendered an important service the other night with 'The Uncounted Enemy,' . . . [which] detailed the appalling lies which were fed to upper reaches of the government and to the American people." In *The New York Times*, an unknown editorial writer opined that the documentary had conclusively shown how Lyndon Johnson was "victimized by mendacious intelligence." Even the conservative columnist William F. Buckley accepted the validity of the "The Uncounted Enemy." Also writing in *The Washington Post*, he called it a "truly extraordinary" achievement, which "absolutely established that Gen. William Westmoreland, for political reasons, withheld from the president, probably from the Joint Chiefs, from Congress, and from the American people information about the enemy that was vital."

As scheduled, Westmoreland held his news conference on January 26, at the Army-Navy Club. He was joined by what *The Washington Post* called "all the old Vietnam hands." The most prominent among those who gathered were the former ambassador to South Vietnam, Ellsworth Bunker; former CIA Director Richard Helms; the CIA's former special assistant for Vietnamese affairs, Richard Carver; Lieutenant General Phillip Davidson, Westmoreland's former intelligence chief; and Brigadier General Daniel Graham, the former chief of MACV estimates.

Westmoreland was the first to take the podium. ". . . Last week," he said, his voice choked with emotion, "my wife urged me to attend a movie which was my first in five years. The name of that movie was *Absence of Malice*. Although I did not take the movie literally, it did show an innocent man whose life and many others were ruined by the unscrupulous use of the media. Little did I know that within a week a real life, notorious reporter, Mike Wallace, would try to prosecute me in a star-chamber procedure with distorted, false, and specious information, plain lies, derived by sinister deception—and attempt to execute me on the guillotine of public opinion. It was all there, the arrogance, the color, the drama, the contrived plot, the close shots—everything but the truth." Westmoreland then proceeded to detail how CBS had made him look so confused during his interview. He told them that he had not learned about Sam Adams's involvement with the project until the interview was already under way and that he had not been forewarned what the documentary was charging him with. Since he had not been forewarned, he said, he had been unable to refresh his fourteen-year-old memories, which explained why he looked so befuddled during the interview. Finally, he revealed that after the interview, he had checked his personal files, and, upon discovering that he had made a number of inaccurate statements during his interview, had sent a list of corrections to Crile and Wallace. The two unfortunately had not used this new material.

During his conclusion, Westmoreland explained again his decision not to include the "irregulars" in the order of battle. To do so, he said, would have been "to introduce a substantial jump in enemy strength when in fact there was no increase in combat strength." Westmoreland assured the assembled throng of newsmen that everyone from the Commander in Chief, Pacific, to the President was familiar with all the OB figures.

He was followed to the podium by Daniel Graham, who assured the newsmen that "all evidence collected by military intelligence was reported back to Washington. It was also reported back through State and CIA channels as Mr. Bunker and Mr. Carver will attest."

Davidson was next. He reiterated what Graham had just said, then went on to defend Westmoreland's decision not to add the figure for the "irregulars" to the regular OB. Given the press's great "itch for simplification," Davidson said, they simply would not have given the issue the kind of complex explanation it needed.

Finally, Carver took the podium. He discussed the conference during which MACV and the CIA hammered out a compromise and denied categorically that the CIA had caved in to pressure from Westmoreland, as the documentary charged. It was he, not Westmoreland, Carver said, who made the decision to drop the "irregulars" from the OB and include them in an addendum.

Although this last revelation of Carver's was somewhat of a bombshell, it did not succeed in changing the minds of anyone in the press. Nearly every major newspaper in the country did a story on the press conference, and all three network anchormen mentioned it during their evening news broadcast. Not one from either group came to Westmoreland's defense. While Westmoreland's presentation had been a passionate one, it had not caused anyone in the media to change their mind. Nor, as Westmoreland had hoped, had it brought an apology from CBS.

Westmoreland's news conference had accomplished one thing, however. It had caught the interest of Sally Bedell and Don Kowet, two feature writers from *TV Guide*. They were the only ones among the dozens of newsmen covering it who were troubled by what they heard, and in early 1982 they started what would turn out to be a five-month investigation of the making of "The Uncounted Enemy."

In the meantime, Westmoreland had to endure one of the darkest periods of his life. Over thirty million people had viewed the documentary, and many of them were enraged at the CBS charges. A few days after the documentary aired, Westmoreland received a flood of rancorous letters from people all over the country. He was particularly hurt by a letter he received from a Houston woman named Linda Shelton. She wrote:

Your interview with Mike Wallace, Saturday, January 23, 1982, and what I saw on Vietnam appalled me.

For years the American public resented, even hated Lyndon Johnson for the mismanagement of the war when in reality so much of it was your lack of leadership and lies.

You ordered our sons, husbands, brothers, fathers, and friends to fight a hopeless battle against insurmountable odds. How could you have such little regard for our young Americans? You knew that these boys were going to their death and so they did.

You played God with those lives and to this day American parents are still grieving. If anyone ever deserved to be stripped of their so-called honors it is you. You lied to President Johnson and to Congress hoping to buy time and come out a hero. You made the statement that we won the war over there, but lost it at home. We lost the war . . . period!

After seeing that show on TV, I hope the American people never give you another moment's peace. You needed a lot of help in making decisions but refused to listen to the advice of those around you. The aftermath now lies on your shoulders.

Letters like Linda Shelton's were difficult for Westmoreland to take. Even more difficult, however, was the response he got from the veterans community. A front-page editorial in one national veterans paper demanded that charges be brought against him. A veterans organization in Pittsburgh sent him an ultimatum, demanding that he explain his action or they were going to go to Congress and demand that he "be condemned."

Although Walt Rostow, Maxwell Taylor, and others wrote lengthy pieces for *The New York Times* and *The Washington Post* in defense of Westmoreland, the press and the public did not take them any more seriously than they had the men who had testified at the news conference. By late April 1982, three months after the broadcast, the court of public opinion had met and declared Westmoreland guilty of all the CBS charges.

It was a verdict that might have stuck if not for Sally Bedell and Don Kowet. When everything was at its darkest for Westmoreland, they published the findings of their five-month investigation in the May 29, 1982, issue of *TV Guide* and instantly retrieved Westmoreland's reputation from history's junkyard. Titled "Anatomy of a Smear: How CBS Broke the Rules and 'Got' Gen. Westmoreland," the article found at least two dozen flaws in the documentary. Among the most serious were: (1) Crile began the project already convinced that a conspiracy had taken place and turned a deaf ear to evidence that suggested otherwise. (2) CBS paid $25,000 to their consultant, Sam Adams, without adequately investigating his conspiracy theory. (3) CBS violated its own guidelines by rehearsing Sam Adams before he went on camera. (4) In order to encourage a witness to give a more sympathetic testimony, CBS screened for him the testimony of others. (5) CBS asked sympathetic witnesses soft questions while unmercifully grilling unsympathetic ones. (6) CBS misrepresented the testimony of some witnesses and ignored the testimony of witnesses who would have challenged the documentary's premise. (7) CBS pulled quotes out of context to imply that Westmoreland was familiar with a crucial meeting. Bedell and Smith did not reveal that the main source for much of their investigation was Ira Klein, the editor of "The Uncounted Enemy." They nonetheless did reveal that Sam Adams himself now doubted the documentary's premise of a Westmoreland-led conspiracy.

"Anatomy of a Smear" hit CBS like a bomb. The day the article first appeared, most CBS executives were in San Francisco attending their annual convention. There they went into a huddle in an attempt to respond. They couldn't, however, for they lacked enough information. Instead, Van Gordon Sauter, the news division president, ordered Burton Benjamin, an experienced documentary maker, to investigate the charges.

Like every executive at CBS, Sauter hoped Benjamin's investigation would completely absolve their documentary. Unfortunately for them, after a two-month investigation Benjamin came to basically the same conclusion as Bedell and Kowet—the documentary was riddled with flaws and inaccuracies. He also noted that a "conspiracy," given the accepted definition of the word, was not proved, nor was it provable. In spite of all the flaws, Benjamin felt the documentary had some merit. "To get a group of high-ranking military men and former Central Intelligence Agents to say that this is what happened was an achievement of no small dimension. They were not fringe people but prototypical Americans."

CBS refused to release the Benjamin Report to the public. Van Gordon Sauter did write an eight-page memo for press release. Supposedly a distillation of the Benjamin Report, the memo affirmed CBS's support for the "substance of the documentary." While admitting the word "conspiracy" was inappropriate to describe Westmoreland's action and that some of the interviewing techniques were improper, Sauter nonetheless made it clear that CBS stood behind the central premise of the show. There was to be no apology.

Witnesses for Westmoreland

Westmoreland had been considering a lawsuit against CBS from the moment their documentary aired. Several prominent lawyers had told him, however, that it was a waste of time, that the libel law strongly favored the defendant, and it would almost be impossible for a public figure like himself to win a judgment. The *TV Guide* article increased his chances of winning tenfold. A few days after its appearance, Peter Grace of W. R. Grace and Company called Westmoreland and suggested that he talk with Godfrey Schmidt of Schmidt, Aghayan and Associates. After reading the *TV Guide* article, Schmidt felt the general just might have a chance of winning.

Westmoreland was shopping around for funding and a lawyer when his friend Dave Henderson suggested another possibility, that he contact Dan Burt, the head of Capital Legal, a conservative public-interest law firm, and see if he would be interested in taking the case. Burt was not only interested, he was champing at the bit to take on CBS. A former street tough, he had worked his way through Yale Law School, then made a small fortune doing international tax work.

Although he had never done trial work before, he was eager to cut his teeth on CBS.

During his first meeting with Westmoreland he immediately showed the rough side of his character. "General," he said, "let's get this straight. I want you to think very carefully. Have you ever done anything that you should be ashamed of—have you ever done anything wrong that I should know about?"

"No, absolutely not," Westmoreland said.

"General, I am the toughest son of a bitch who ever lived. If you're lying to me there will be nothing I can do to save you from utter ruin."

"I understand that."

Before launching a lawsuit, Burt thought it best to give CBS a quick, easy way out. On August 10, 1982, he helped Westmoreland compose a letter to network president Thomas Wyman in which they laid out their grievances against the documentary and demanded of the network "a complete apology, approved in advance by me, in the same manner and in the same media in which you advertised the program." Westmoreland also asked for monetary compensation for the harm he had suffered and "a full retraction, of not less than forty-five minutes' duration."

Sauter rejected the demands outright, but did offer Westmoreland an invitation to appear on a televised round-table discussion, during which he and other experts on the war could discuss in detail the program and the various issues surrounding it. Westmoreland, in turn, rejected Sauter's offer. CBS quickly sent Westmoreland a second proposal. This time they offered to allow him fifteen minutes of air time to explain his case. Westmoreland also rejected this second offer, calling it too little, too late. Six days after CBS's second offer, lawyers from the Capital Legal Foundation, on Westmoreland's behalf, filed a $120 million libel suit in the U.S. District Court in Greenville, South Carolina. Besides CBS, the suit named as defendants Sam Adams, George Crile, Mike Wallace, and Van Gordon Sauter.

At the same time this suit was being filed in Greenville, Westmoreland held a second press conference at the Army-Navy Club. Westmoreland was not as emotional this time, was not as obviously wounded as he had been during his first press conference.

"I am an old soldier who loves his country and have had enough of war," he said calmly. "It was my fate to serve for over four years as senior American commander in the most unpopular war this country ever fought. I have been reviled, burned in effigy, spat upon. Neither I nor my wife nor my family want me to go to battle once again.

"But all my life I have valued 'duty, honor, country' above all else. Even as my friends and family urged me to ignore CBS and leave the field, I reflected on those Americans who had died in service in Vietnam. Even as I considered the enormous wealth and power that make CBS so formidable an adversary, I thought too of the troops I had commanded and sent to battle, and those who never returned.

"Finally I have dwelled at length upon the tremendous bulwark of liberty and freedom that is the First Amendment to the Constitution of the United States. I now fear that public reaction to CBS as the truth came out might lead to weakening of that bulwark through legislated codes of conduct or other attempts to restrain the media."

Westmoreland said he had so feared a backlash against the press that he had at first asked for nothing from CBS but a simple apology, ample air time to explain his side of the story, a full retraction, and some monetary compensation. CBS, he said, had offered him only fifteen minutes of air time, which was hardly enough to undo the damage. As a result, he had had no choice but to file a lawsuit. He ended his speech by making it clear that he was not interested in either vengeance or money, and that he intended to donate any monetary award he received to charity.

Following his speech, the battle between him and CBS was officially joined. CBS reacted swiftly, hiring Craveth, Swaine and Moore, one of the best law firms in the country, to represent them. Led by their chief lawyer and a partner in the firm, David Boies, the firm launched an immediate counterattack. On November 1, Boise argued before Judge G. Ross Anderson, Jr., in the federal district court in Greenville that given Westmoreland's popularity in South Carolina, CBS could not get a fair trial there. Anderson agreed and shifted the site of the lawsuit to the Southern District of New York, New York City. The move was a grievous blow to Westmoreland's case, for CBS was as at home in New York as he was in South Carolina.

Two months later, Westmoreland got some breaks to make up for this setback. Burt petitioned Pierre Leval, the judge now handling the case, to force CBS to release the Benjamin Report. Disregarding CBS's fierce resistance, Leval ordered the network to turn a copy of the report over to Capital Legal.

On January 25, 1983, CBS delivered a counterstroke, something they hoped would compensate for the damage the Benjamin Report was going to do to their case. In an address to the Society of Professional Journalists meeting in Philadelphia, Van Gordon Sauter, the executive producer of the documentary and now one of the four defendants, accused Westmoreland of being the "pointman for right-wing forces in their search and destroy mission against the media."

The charge, of course, was not true, and no one knew that more than Sauter. Westmoreland was no ideologue. He had never lent his voice or name to any cause on the right and was not about to now. He had filed the lawsuit because of the harm the documentary had done to his reputation, and that was the only reason. He was simply not the kind of person to get involved in a cause or ideological vendetta. While he had accepted $2 million to cover legal expenses from the conservative Richard Mellon Scaife, he had likewise refused a contribution from Accuracy in the Media (AIM), a far-right media watchdog group that made no pretense of its hatred of all three national television networks.

Sauter's charge seemed potentially damaging at first, and many in the press believed it. Many more, however, saw it as a desperate attempt on CBS's part to undermine Westmoreland's credibility. On March 8, 1983, the Society of Professional Journalists flew right in the face of CBS and announced the winner of its 1982 Distinguished Service Award. Honored in the category of magazine reporting were the authors of *TV Guide*'s "Anatomy of a Smear." Sauter vehemently protested the award, charging that "Anatomy" was riddled with errors, but the SPJ ignored his protest. Adding insult to CBS's injury, Hodding Carter, who had praised "The Uncounted Enemy" when it first aired, suddenly reversed himself. During the April 21 edition of his PBS show *Inside Story*, he challenged the documentary's thesis. "CBS is entitled to its opinions," he said. "But we're entitled to a more balanced presentation . . . There's a vast difference between a fair trial and a lynching." CBS responded by claiming that Carter had it all wrong, that it was they, not Westmoreland, who were being lynched. Still portraying themselves as the ones being victimized, a week later they petitioned Judge Leval to dismiss the suit. Leval denied their petition and set a trial date for October 9, 1984.

In a pretrial session with Leval, Burt announced that he had decided to drop a large portion of his case. He no longer intended to contest the CBS premise that Westmoreland had deceived the press, the Congress, and the public about enemy troop strengths in Vietnam. Instead, Burt said, he intended to narrow the focus of his charge, arguing only that CBS had defamed Westmoreland by ac-

cusing him of lying to the Joint Chiefs and the President. Leval was
not particularly happy with the change. To him it implied that Westmoreland might have misled the public and Congress, but had told
the truth to the JCS and the President. Realizing he would have an
easier time having to prove only that Westmoreland had not misled
the President and the JCS, Burt insisted on the change. Leval reluctantly allowed him to make it.

The trial opened as scheduled on October 9. Westmoreland and
Kitsy had rented a hotel room on Manhattan's Upper East Side, but
they rode the subway from the hotel to Foley Square. On the train,
a number of people greeted them and wished them well. One of them
was a well-known TV commentator, who told them, "I'm for you."
During the walk from Foley Square to the federal courthouse, drivers
of trucks and taxis leaned out of their windows and shouted their
support. "Give 'em hell, Westy," one taxi driver yelled. In the hallway
of the courthouse, a porter mopping the floor stopped Westmoreland
in his tracks and began talking about his Vietnam experiences. Farther
down the hallway, a federal parole officer, who had also served in
Vietnam, stopped Westmoreland again to ask for an autograph and
to voice his support.

Not everyone was supportive, though. As the Westmorelands
were preparing to enter the courtroom, they were suddenly confronted by Daniel Ellsberg, the man who had leaked the Pentagon
Papers to the press in 1971. In a loud voice, Ellsberg accused Westmoreland of deceiving the public, then shouted, "You should have
known better at the time and should not have done this." When
reporters rushed up and asked Westmoreland what the former antiwar
activist had said, Westmoreland answered, "He said something to me
but I didn't answer."

Inside the courtroom, Westmoreland took a seat to the left of the
judge's raised desk, next to Burt and his assistant, attorney David
Dorsen. Kitsy thought she would be allowed to sit next to Wes, as
she referred to her husband, with reporters. She was shocked to find
herself being seated instead in the third row—right in the midst of
a group of Cravath paralegals. She had been violently opposed to the
lawsuit, which was stressful enough, but being seated in the heart of
the enemy camp almost caused her to lose her composure. "I was so
alone," she revealed later, "—the press was in front of me, and I
didn't know anyone. I've never prayed so hard in my life. I asked,
what would my mother do in a situation like this? And I thought,
she'd smile and say good morning. So I did."

During the next two days, the jury was picked. Jury selection in a federal trial is left up to the judge, and Leval, a man noted for his fairness and common sense, picked what one commentator called the "seemingly perfect panel." Of the twelve jurors and six alternates, not one knew anything substantial about the war. When asked, not one, in fact, recognized the name Robert McNamara.

On October 11, Judge Leval gave his instruction to the jury, spelling out the criteria they would have to follow when trying to decide if Westmoreland had indeed been libeled. They were rigorous criteria, and they favored the defendant, CBS. To prove libel, he said, Burt and Dorsen would have to prove that CBS in preparing the broadcast "made defamatory statements about General Westmoreland; whether the defamatory statements, if they were defamatory, were false; if they were false, whether they were made with knowledge of falsity, whether the statements were made with reckless disregard of the truth or falsity; and whether the plaintiff suffered damage or injury as a result of these statements."

As Westmoreland would soon discover, proving he had been injured by the CBS documentary would be easy. Proving wrong many of the statements in the documentary, including portions of its main premise, would also be easy. Proving Crile had shown a "reckless disregard" for the truth when making "The Uncounted Enemy" would be far more difficult. To prove it, Burt and Dorsen would have to convince a jury not only that CBS had made defamatory statements about Westmoreland, but that they had made them knowing they were false. The burden of proof lay in Westmoreland's corner, and in libel trials it was a very heavy burden.

When Leval finished giving his instructions to the jury, Burt took center stage for his opening statement. Standing behind a lectern, he told the jury that the "issue here is very specific and very limited. It is, did General Westmoreland lie to his superiors? Did he order his troops to hide evidence of the enemy strength from our government?"

He went on to say that he would prove that Westmoreland had not, as the documentary claimed, attempted to fool either the Joint Chiefs or the President. To prove Westmoreland innocent, he would show how Crile, with cuts and splices, had manipulated the truth in order to get the "sensational story" he wanted. "George Crile needed a big story," Burt said. "He was ambitious to become a famous correspondent like Mike Wallace" and was willing to do anything to become one. "We will show you how he did it, show you the statements taken out of context, half quotes, misattributions, hypothetical questions paired with lead-ins to make it appear that answers were being given to questions that were never asked, and collapsing multiple events to create events which never existed."

Burt next revealed what he hoped would be a bombshell to the jury, that these were not his perceptions alone. They were shared by Ira Klein, the film editor of "The Uncounted Enemy." Klein had worked closely with Crile during the documentary's production, and he also knew that it had been made with "reckless disregard for the truth."

With the help of an engineer and a TV monitor, Burt then proceeded to go through the documentary scene by scene in the hope of convincing the jurors that Crile had systematically twisted the truth. Although the engineer had difficulty operating the machine, the presentation was damaging to Crile. At one point during it, Boies objected, saying that Burt's "use and misuse of evidence goes beyond anything that is permissible in an opening statement to a jury." Leval overruled him.

Boies was up next. In his opening, he attacked Burt's presentation and criticized his editing, claiming he was doing the same thing he accused CBS of doing, that is, editing out words, lines and scenes that did not fit into his argument. He then proceeded to replay every scene of tape Burt had played and to counter it with scenes of his own.

This completed, he turned the focus of his discussion on Mike Wallace and begged the jury to ask themselves some simple questions: What did Mike Wallace—a man at the pinnacle of his career, a man who had received every broadcasting award given, a man who had received ten Emmys—have to gain by "fabricating" a documentary? Did they think Wallace was the kind of man willing to risk his considerable reputation to help produce a documentary that he knew was false?

With this small seed of doubt planted in the minds of the jurors, Boies went on to announce that he would now show them that the broadcast was true. To buttress his argument, he briefly introduced sworn statements from former military men and CIA officials. All attested to the fact that there had been a deliberate effort by Westmoreland to juggle enemy strength figures and they had unwillingly taken part in it. To give the statements of these men more import, Boies had them printed in large letters on a chart, which he now put on display for the jury.

Commentators watching the trial had difficulty deciding who had won the first round. With his opening statement, Burt had certainly struck a hard blow against Crile's credibility, but Boise with his defense of Mike Wallace and with his chart had come back with a solid counterblow. Many thought this opening round was a draw.

On October 15, the following day, Walt Rostow, the first of the witnesses for Westmoreland, took the stand. As one of President Johnson's closest advisers, he told the jury, he had been there at the center of power all through the war. He could say confidently therefore that CBS was wrong in maintaining that Westmoreland fed Johnson "mostly good news" about the war, leaving him unprepared for the shock of the Tet Offensive. He also denied that Johnson pressured Westmoreland to keep the numbers down in order to generate public support. Under cross-examination, Rostow was not so confident. With relentless grilling, Boies forced him to admit that his knowledge of the numbers controversy was sketchy and his memory of key meetings incomplete.

Next was Robert Komer, the man who because of the aggressive style he used to run the pacification program in Vietnam was nicknamed the Blow Torch. Komer proved a stronger, more knowledgeable witness than Rostow, and for good reason. As pacification chief, he had gained a more intimate knowledge of the Vietcong than anyone in Vietnam. On the basis of that knowledge, he said, he had concluded that the "irregulars" were not any kind of military threat. Most of the booby-trap casualties were not caused by these "irregulars," he maintained, but by trained Vietcong and sapper units.

Komer then proceeded to attack Adams's theory that there were 500,000 to 600,000 VC in South Vietnam, twice the number Westmoreland claimed. That higher figure, he said, was based primarily on Adams's interpretation of captured enemy documents. Unfortunately, such documents "represented the view of higher VC headquarters" and were no more reliable than similar documents produced by the ARVN. Like their ARVN counterparts, VC headquarters units inflated their strength figures to make themselves look stronger than they really were. The Tet attacks, he continued, also proved Adams's figure for enemy troop strength to be wrong. As pacification chief, he had toured the major scenes of fighting during Tet, and "if it had been an attack with 500,000 troops, it would have been one hell of a lot more attack than what we were enduring at the time."

In his cross-examination, Boies tried to get Komer to contradict himself, but without success. Komer ended up being one of the strongest witnesses for Westmoreland.

The next witness, retired Air Force Colonel Edward Caton, was as weak as Komer had been strong. Under examination by Burt's assistant, David Dorsen, Caton won some points criticizing one of CBS's key witnesses in the documentary, retired Army Colonel Gains Hawkins. Caton said Hawkins was a minor player in MACV intelligence and had no real understanding of order-of-battle figures. Under cross-examination, however, Caton committed a major blunder when he blurted out that the "irregular" forces were capable of using passive devices like "booby traps and satchel charges" to inflict U.S. casualties.

Burt next put retired Army Lieutenant General Phillip Davidson, Jr., on the stand, hoping to undo the damage Caton had caused. Davidson, who had been the head of military intelligence in South Vietnam in 1967 and 1968, proved a strong witness under Burt's examination. Replying directly to the CBS charges raised in the documentary, he denied there was an arbitrary ceiling on enemy troop strength and said that the self-defense and secret self-defense troops had been dropped from the OB because they were no real threat, not as the documentary claimed because Westmoreland feared press reaction. Under cross-examination, however, the three-star general was unable to provide what solid evidence he had used to conclude that the self-defense and secret self-defense forces were not a military threat. He was likewise unable to provide the names of other intelligence officers who had convinced him that these forces posed no threat.

Davidson was followed to the stand by retired Brigadier General George Godding. In 1967, when only a colonel, Godding had been MACV's chief negotiator at the conference held at CIA headquarters to iron out the OB differences between the military and the CIA. In spite of his considerable knowledge of the issue, he fared no better as a witness than had Davidson. Under questioning from Burt, he said he had been under no pressure from Westmoreland to defend an enemy troop strength estimate of 297,000. Under cross-examination, however, Boies made him look foolish when he held up a deposition Godding had given to the court in which he claimed the contrary, namely that Westmoreland had instructed him not to agree to an enemy strength figure over 300,000. Boies forced Godding to admit that he was contradicting himself.

"Those damn depositions," a reporter heard Kitsy Westmoreland murmur to a friend as an embarrassed Godding left the stand.

Kitsy was happier with the performance of the next witness, Brigadier General Daniel Graham, the present head of the government's "Star Wars" program. In the CBS documentary, Graham, then the chief of MACV's Current Intelligence and Estimates Division, was portrayed as one of the key conspirators. That portrayal was based primarily on interviews with Commander James Meecham and Colonel Russel Cooley, two former subordinates of Graham's. In the documentary, they are shown telling Wallace that Graham had ordered them to alter MACV records in order to maintain an artificial level for enemy troop strength. In Vietnam, Graham was noted for his combative personality. On the stand, he showed that he had not softened it a bit in the last eighteen years. When asked by Burt to comment on Sam Adams's theory, Graham snapped contemptuously that Adams had been involved "in a pedantic exercise that bore little connection to reality." It was simply impossible to determine which Communists were members of the self-defense forces, the secret self-defense forces, or main-force units and which were military-political cadre or mere supporters, he said. He also snapped that it was ridiculous to think Westmoreland would ask him to erase data on a computer. Later during his cross-examination when asked by Boies why the "irregulars" were not included in the OB, Graham contemptuously said because "politicians are not normally arranged in battalions, companies, and platoons."

Robert S. McNamara followed Graham on the stand. He had not spoken publicly about the war since February 1968, when during a farewell ceremony at the White House, he became so choked up that he could not speak. Although he was not happy to once again be thrown into the spotlight, he felt it was his duty, nonetheless, to come to Westmoreland's defense. The two had had radically different views of the war, but, as he told Burt, he had nothing but respect for the general. Westmoreland, he said, "was a person of great integrity who could never have lied to his superiors." He added that he had told Crile that off the record.

When questioned by Boies about Westmoreland's estimates of enemy troop strength, he replied that while he differed with Westmoreland (he thought the estimate should have been higher), it was an honest difference of opinion. He felt, though, that ultimately such disagreements did not matter, for enemy troop strength figures were unreliable and unimportant.

Boies tried to discredit McNamara by contrasting pessimistic statements the former secretary had made during the war in private with his public pronouncements, which were positive. McNamara answered that while he had been pessimistic about the possibility of the United States winning the war, he had always held out hope for a political solution.

Westmoreland was scheduled to take the stand next. On Friday, the last day of McNamara's testimony, he ducked out of the trial early and with Kitsy flew to Washington, D.C., where thousands of Vietnam veterans were gathering to take part in the dedication of a new statue at the Vietnam Memorial.

Upon arriving in Washington, the two started making the round of the hotels where most of the vets were staying. Originally angry with Westmoreland over the accusations leveled at him in the documentary, most vets had changed their attitude toward him following the appearance of the *TV Guide* article. The majority now viewed the documentary as an unjustified attack on both Westmoreland and themselves. Because of this change in attitude in the vet community, wherever Westmoreland appeared, he was greeted with cheers and shouts from throngs of approving vets. On Saturday night when he and Kitsy entered the lobby of the Washington Hotel, a mob of veterans—bedecked in camouflage fatigues, jungle boots, and bush hats—swarmed around them, all it seemed eager to either shake the general's hand, get his autograph, shout encouragement, or tell him what units they had served with in Vietnam.

In the basement of the hotel, Westmoreland greeted another group of vets operating a "Veterans for Westmoreland" table to raise money for his legal costs. Vets who gave money were issued a brightly colored badge with large blue letters reading WESTY'S WARRIORS. In the last six months, the group had raised nearly $80,000 and planned to double that amount before the trial ended. One piece of public relations literature on the table read: "General Westmoreland had no choice but to sue for libel. His fight is for more than his own honor. It is for all of us—for every veteran and for the military as an institution." A letter prominently displayed on the same table was from a disabled Vietnam vet. He wrote that because of his injuries he could afford to only send $1, but he wanted it used to "beat those anti-veteran scribes. . . . I believe in you and what you stand for and will fight anyone who says different. . . . U.S. paratroopers stick together. Geronimo on your way to victory." Westmoreland began shaking hands with the men around the table, but was soon interrupted by a reporter who had tracked him down. What did he think of the fund-raising drive? the man asked.

"I was amazed by it," he answered. "I did not initiate it, I did not endorse it, but I told them that if that's what they wanted to do I would not reject it. I was touched by it."

The next morning, Westmoreland attended an early-morning ceremony at Arlington National Cemetery, where the Secretary of Defense, Caspar Weinberger, laid a wreath at the Tomb of the Unknowns. After the ceremony, Weinberger gave a speech to the more than five thousand Vietnam veterans in the cemetery amphitheater. After the speech, he briefly introduced a number of politicians and military men seated behind the podium. The veterans applauded politely each introduction until Westmoreland was introduced. At the sound of his name, the applause was thunderous. In unison, the vets were soon shouting, "Speech! Speech!" over and over again. When the shout continued, Weinberger nodded for Westmoreland to take the stand. Westmoreland only had a few words to say—"You did the job your country asked of you. You did it magnificently and nobody could have done it better."—but they brought another thunderous round of applause and hundreds of shouts of support for him in his battle against CBS.

On this high note, Westmoreland returned to New York. As one commentator noted, the general "needed the psychological boost he received that weekend. Just a month into the trial, Burt's case against CBS appeared less solid than it had in the month before the trial." Although Burt had come to the trial arrogant and self-assured, the fact that he had had no previous trial experience was becoming evident to most observers. Boies, on the other hand, had come to the trial with a reputation as a skilled litigator and was proving that reputation well-deserved. Burt had not prepared his witnesses for the hard questions they might face in a cross-examination, and time after time Boies had made them contradict themselves and look foolish. Legal experts viewing the trial agreed that Westmoreland needed to make a good showing if he was going to salvage his case. Few thought he would, however. Most thought he would look as bumbling and confused on the stand as he had in the documentary.

They were wrong. Westmoreland was surprisingly an effective witness. After giving the jury a short biographical sketch of himself, with Burt's guidance, he began a detailed discussion of CBS's accusation that he had suppressed a cable drawn up by his intelligence chief, Lieutenant General McChristian, showing a considerably larger enemy force in Vietnam than formerly reported. Westmoreland denied that McChristian had disagreed with him when the lower figure was sent and denied additionally that he had had McChristian transferred back to the States as a punishment for taking a different position on the OB controversy.

"Well, McChristian, he wanted a command," he explained. "He was an armored officer and we had no armored divisions in Vietnam. And I corresponded with Army Chief of Staff General Johnson and asked if he would put General McChristian in command of an armored division, and I did receive notice that he would be reassigned to Fort Hood, Texas and given command of an armored division." All this happened, he went on, in April 1967, a full month before McChristian wrote his cable containing a higher enemy strength figure.

When Burt next asked Westmoreland why the "inflated" irregular force figure was not included in the OB, Westmoreland seemed eager to answer. To begin with, he said, these irregular forces were made up primarily of "old men, women, and young boys . . . who were not a military threat." Another reason they were excluded was because the press was sure to draw an "erroneous and gloomy conclusion as to the meaning of this increase."

Why did he believe this? Burt asked.

Westmoreland thought for a moment, then launched a vehement condemnation of the press in Vietnam and an equally vehement defense of his men in Vietnam. Because of the unique nature of the Vietnam War, he said, it was the first one America ever fought in which there was no press censorship. Although some in Washington had wanted some kind of censorship, he had always been opposed to it. At the height of the war, there were over five hundred reporters accredited to his headquarters, and while most wrote accurately about the war, a number did not. Bad, slanted reporting, he said, was hard on his troops. "They got clippings from home and when they didn't get credit, it was detrimental to their morale."

"Were you sensitive to press reactions?" Burt asked.

"Sure we were sensitive to press reaction. We would have been dumb oxes if we weren't. I felt an obligation to my troops that what they were doing be given the credit they deserved and to come out publicly with a statement they were fighting over 100,000 more people than we said we were fighting, which was a distortion—the additional people were not fighters, they were not fighters we wanted to do battle with, they were not people we wanted to kill, they were basically civilians—and to come out with a hard figure that was brought about by virtue of adding these people would have been terribly detrimental to the morale of my troops . . . who were already distressed by the negative clips they received from home about the war."

Having dealt with the media in Vietnam, Westmoreland moved on to the documentary itself and the way Crile and Wallace bushwhacked him in the process of making it. He began at the beginning, with the first call he got from Wallace. Wallace wanted to know, he said, if he would be interested in helping them with a program they were doing about Vietnam. "Is this going to be a 60 Minutes type program?" he said he asked Wallace, to which Wallace replied, "Oh no, this is going to be an educational and objective type of program."

The courtroom audience roared with laughter, and just the hint of a smile crossed Westmoreland's face. When the laughter stopped Westmoreland began describing the interview itself. "I realized that I was not participating in a rational interview, that this was an inquisition, and I also realized that I was participating in my own lynching . . . I realized that he and Mr. Crile had orchestrated a scenario so that they would go for the kill. They wanted to go for my jugular . . . I realized that I was ambushed."

Burt let the full import of Westmoreland's words sink in with the jury, then turned the discussion to another emotional issue: The harm the documentary had personally caused Westmoreland. Over Boies's objection, he introduced a number of hostile letters Westmoreland had gotten and some cartoons that held the general up to ridicule. To give the jury some idea of the hostility in the letters, Burt read out loud the letter from Linda Shelton that had caused Westmoreland so much anguish.

Burt then handed Westmoreland a syndicated cartoon that had appeared in newspapers shortly after the documentary. The cartoon showed a caricature of Westmoreland standing over three dead bodies that were labeled with the West Point motto of HONOR, DUTY, COUNTRY. Burt described the cartoon to the jury, then asked Westmoreland what he had felt when he first saw it.

"It was a most humiliating experience," he answered.

"How long have you been in the Army, General Westmoreland?"

"Forty years."

"And while you were in the service, did you ever lie to a superior officer?"

"Never," Westmoreland answered, snapping out the single word like a sharp salute.

The direct examination over, Westmoreland rose from his chair and stepped to the center of the aisle and joined Kitsy, who was crying. Arm in arm, they left the courtroom.

Witnesses for CBS

Westmoreland's testimony and his highly dramatic exit from the courtroom had a tremendous impact on the jury and spectators alike. As Connie Bruck, a legal expert and journalist, noted, "until Westmoreland took the stand, his case had not looked like a winner. . . . During his testimony, however, Westmoreland—by sheer force of personality—breathed new life into his case."

Boies was not happy with this unexpected turn of events. When he began his cross-examination, he felt that if he did not break Westmoreland, he might lose the case. He managed to score some early points when he showed that a report issued in February 1967 by Westmoreland's intelligence chief—a report showing a sharp increase in the number of irregulars to be carried in the order of battle—had not been shown to the President when Westmoreland met him in Honolulu two months later. Westmoreland claimed he could only vaguely remember the details of both meetings, an answer Boies was unwilling to accept. He implied instead that the general had only conveniently had a loss of memory and that in reality he had hid the higher enemy strength figure from the President.

Boies then turned the discussion to one of the pivotal events portrayed in the documentary, the meeting between Westmoreland and McChristian to discuss a cable containing a higher enemy strength figure that McChristian wanted to send back to Washington. As Connie Bruck noted, "Boies set out to shake Westmoreland's story. But Westmoreland dug in his heels, rattling Boies by resisting his characterization of McChristian's briefing as a report on "enemy strength." Westmoreland instead asserted that McChristian's briefing had actually been about "enemy organization" and nothing else. Boies also tried to shake Westmoreland's contention that the irregulars had no military capability, but failed there also.

According to Bruck, Boies's inability to crack Westmoreland infuriated the Cravath attorney. That fury quickly turned to nasty sarcasm.

"When you say the so-called order of battle," Boies sneered, "it was so called by MACV, correct, sir?"

"It was called that at the time," Westmoreland answered matter-of-factly.

"And you were the commander of MACV, correct, sir?"

"Mr. Boies, you know that," a peeved Westmoreland answered.

"Yes, I do know that," Boies said, nearly shouting. "What I am wondering is whether you forgot it, sir?"

"Mr. Boies, Mr. Boies, Mr. Boies," Leval shouted, in a tone that clearly indicated that Boies was out of line.

Boies quickly turned the discussion to McChristian's claim in the documentary that he had told Westmoreland that the self-defense and secret self-defense forces should remain in the order of battle. Did not he remember McChristian telling him that? he asked.

"I don't remember whether he did or not," Westmoreland said, giving Boies a quick study in command presence. "But that's totally immaterial. What he believed is one thing, what I believed was another. And I happened to have the responsibility. I was the commander. I had the responsibility to make judgments. I made those judgments."

As a number of observers noted after the cross-examination, Boies looked exhausted by his encounter with Westmoreland. He had thought the general would come apart on the stand as quickly and easily as had some of the other witnesses for the plaintiff and was shocked when he did not. Unfortunately for Boies, he had an even greater shock awaiting him in the hallway outside the courtroom.

There a reporter handed him a story that had just come in over the wire. In stunned silence, Boies read that Ed Joyce, the CBS News president, had announced to reporters that he expected CBS to lose the libel trial before the jury, but eventually to win the case on appeal.

Following a short break, Boies returned to the courtroom and introduced into evidence a pile of newspaper and magazine articles. All, he told Leval, were critical of Westmoreland's handling of the war. By introducing them into evidence, he intended to show that CBS was not alone in criticizing Westmoreland, a fact that he felt should diminish any damages Westmoreland might get should he win the trial. Four of the articles were critical of Westmoreland's handling of the OB statistics. Two others detailed Telford Taylor's charge that "Westmoreland could be found guilty of Vietnam war crimes if he were to be tried by the same standards under which the U.S. hanged Japanese General Tomayuki Yamashita." The most damning piece of evidence Boies introduced was a quote from a book by former South Vietnamese Premier Nguyen Cao Ky. "Westmoreland must have known all about the impending Tet attacks," wrote Ky. "I am convinced that the White House did not. American leaders in Saigon deliberately issued a string of lies to the White House, in an effort to maintain the impression that the Americans were getting on top of the Vietcong."

Burt countered Boies with some evidence of his own. To prove that Westmoreland had not attempted to hide the real enemy strength figures from his military superiors, as the documentary claimed, Burt introduced into evidence a May 17, 1967, memo describing in detail a Command Information and Intelligence Conference held at MACV headquarters. The memo established that there had been a briefing at the conference on the higher guerrilla-strength figures that Admiral Ulysses Grant Sharp, the CINCPAC commander and Westmoreland's superior, had been there to hear it. Since Sharp had been at the conference, Burt argued, Westmoreland could not have conspired to deceive his superiors, as CBS claimed.

Boies had never seen the memo before and was upset that it had suddenly been introduced. He immediately contested its authenticity, forcing Leval to call the Army's archives to have it authenticated. When it was, Boies was forced to back down.

A smiling Burt had copies of the memo made, then personally passed them out to the jury. Then to hammer home the importance of the memo, he put Westmoreland back on the stand.

"Did Admiral Sharp give this briefing aloud?" he asked. "Was it spoken?"

A grinning Westmoreland answered, "Oh, yes. In English." At which the courtroom broke into laughter.

Savoring his victory, Burt called Crile to the stand to testify as a "hostile witness." As a number of legal observers noted, during his examination of Crile, Burt showed his shortcomings as a litigator, and they were considerable. Crile was the weakest link in CBS's case, and a skilled trial attorney would have taken him apart on the stand. Burt was not that attorney. Burt attempted to skewer Crile with quick attacks on the producer's credibility, but Crile blunted those attacks with what one observer called a "cotton batting of verbosity." No matter what question Burt asked, no matter how simple or direct, Crile answered it with a torrent of words designed to skirt the issue. Leval repeatedly broke in to reprimand Crile, telling him on one occasion that he was "to answer the question that is put to you." These reprimands accomplished little, for Crile continued his verbal meanderings. Lacking the skills to pin Crile down on certain points, Burt eventually became confused, a fact that was evident in his questions, which lacked any kind of coherent focus. "I have found this examination very confusing." Leval told Burt at one point. "I really am at a loss as to what the facts are that you are trying to bring out."

Whatever Burt was trying to bring out, apparently only he knew. Even David Dorsen, an outside lawyer brought in to help the Capital Legal Team, was confused by Burt's intent. "I don't know what the hell he had in mind," he said of Burt after the trial. Dorsen, of course, knew that there were some mitigating circumstances behind Burt's muddled handling of Crile, besides the most obvious fact that Burt simply was not an experienced trial attorney. The most mitigating circumstance was the fact that Burt's marriage was troubled. The time Burt should have spent preparing himself for the rigorous examinations and cross-examinations, he instead spent on the phone trying to resolve problems with his wife, a doctoral candidate at Harvard.

Burt was not the only one, however, whose personal life was suffering because of the ordeal and stress of the trial. Someone suffering even more than Burt was one of his main adversaries, Mike Wallace. As one of Wallace's colleagues noted later, Wallace was particularly aggrieved by the trial and what it was doing to his reputation. Wallace, he said, felt he was innocent and was traumatized coming into the courtroom every day to hear himself being called a liar and deceitful. He was equally traumatized at the thought of eventually having to take the stand. He felt, said his friend, that he was one of the premier TV journalists of his time and did not relish the idea of being on the other side of a public grilling, or of having a jury pass judgment on his career.

On a Saturday night in late December, Wallace apparently decided he could not take all the pressure any longer. After retiring to his New York apartment with his girlfriend, he went into his bedroom and collapsed unconscious on the floor. When his girlfriend could not revive him, she summoned an ambulance. At the hospital he was revived, but a rumor was soon circulating that he had attempted suicide by taking an overdose of drugs. CBS denied that the rumor had any validity, but Burt told one reporter that the rumor was indeed true. Westmoreland claims the information came from a clerk at the hospital, who in an effort to hurt CBS had purloined a copy of Wallace's admission records and offered it to the Westmoreland camp. Westmoreland wanted no part of such skullduggery, however. "There is no way I would stoop so low as to accept such material," he said later. "I wouldn't have accepted it even if I was sure it would have helped me win the trial. I'm certain, though, that if the situation had been reversed, CBS would not have hesitated to use that material against me."

In spite of that certainty, Westmoreland's harsh feelings for Wallace had been softened by the trial. As soon as he and Kitsy learned of Wallace's misfortune, they sent a bunch of flowers and a get-well card to his hospital room. Wallace spent the next twelve days in the hospital resting. His collapse, while it certainly put a pall over the CBS camp, did not slow down the trial.

It did, however, give new momentum to the Westmoreland camp. Hoping to keep that momentum going, on January 8, 1985, Burt put Ira Klein on the stand. Klein was the film editor of "The Uncounted Enemy." While working on it, he had become very unhappy with Crile and his method of editing. When *TV Guide* began their investigation of the documentary, Klein decided to open up and tell them everything he knew. His revelations to Bedell and Kowet provided them with 80 percent of the material for their "Anatomy of a Smear."

Klein now rehashed most of those revelations for the jury. He told them bluntly that while working on the documentary, he had come to dislike Crile and for good reason. Crile, he said, had deliberately avoided interviewing witnesses who contradicted the documentary's point of view. To avoid interviewing Lieutenant General Davidson, a man who did not accept the documentary's thesis, Crile had even gone so far as to tell CBS that Davidson was too ill to be interviewed when he knew quite well the general was quite healthy. For the sake of fairness and truth, Klein added, he had urged Crile to give Westmoreland more time in the documentary in order to fully explain his point of view, but Crile had answered that as producer he would decide what was true and what was not.

Klein also testified that Crile had used blatantly dishonest interviewing and editing techniques and, to hide his dishonesty, frequently lied to his CBS bosses. Klein's most damning revelation was that after Westmoreland's press conference, a panicked Sam Adams had entered the editing room and told Crile, "We have to come clean, we have to make a statement, the premise of the show is inaccurate."

In his cross-examination, Boies tried to portray Klein as an embittered employee who had a grudge against a number of people at CBS other than Crile. He also tried to impeach Klein's credibility by bringing out the fact that Klein did not know much about the Vietnam War, news reporting, or documentary production. In spite of Boies' cross-examination, Klein's testimony ended up being a plus for the Westmoreland camp.

Klein was the last witness for the plaintiff and the last chance for Burt to present direct evidence to support Westmoreland's contention that he had been libeled and the libel had been committed with malice. Now it was Boies' turn to present witnesses who would testify to the contrary.

Boies called as his first witness, Sam Adams, the disgruntled CIA intelligence analyst whose initial doubts about MACV's OB statistics had led to the trial. In the three years since "The Uncounted Enemy" first aired, Adams had come to personally believe that Westmoreland had not lied to his military superiors or to the President, as the documentary claimed. He still believed nonetheless that Westmoreland, in complicity with the JCS and the President, had lied to the American people.

With Adams on the stand, Boies decided to play the entire ninety minutes of the documentary for the jury, stopping periodically at different scenes so Adams could comment on them. As Bob Brewin and Sydney Shaw note in their book *Vietnam on Trial*, it was a difficult moment for both Westmorelands, but most particularly for Kitsy. She, they wrote, "had never seen the complete show and she didn't want to see it this time, either. Each time Boies started up the videotape, she attacked her needlepoint feverishly, scowling in mock concentration and yanking haphazardly at gold- and pewter-colored threads until she could no longer ignore the monitors. When she did glance up, it was only for a moment. She deliberately avoided looking at her husband, who shifted uncomfortably in his seat, occasionally clenching his fists. "It was all I could do to keep from running up and grabbing George Crile and saying, 'You son of a bitch,' " she confided to Brewin and Shaw after the trial.

Dorsen handled the cross-examination of Adams. Taking a page from Boies's book, he immediately set out to show that Adams over the years had made a number of contradictory statements. Dorsen began by pointing out that during his testimony in the Pentagon Papers trial in 1973, Adams had said that when trying to come up with an enemy OB, "it is very difficult to decide who to count. The problem always was in Vietnam to sort out who was a soldier and who wasn't. A person that lays a grenade on a path with a trip wire . . . Now whether you consider this man a military man or a civilian, I couldn't say." This statement of Adams's, Dorsen pointed out to the jury, was just the opposite of later statements he made about the enemy OB.

To show further inconsistent and sloppy thinking on Adams's part, Dorsen produced a copy of an article on the OB controversy that Adams had written for *Harper's* in 1975. Dorsen then read a passage from the article in which Adams claimed that ten thousand American soldiers had been killed during the Tet Offensive. How had he managed to come up with a figure that was ten times higher than the official count? Dorsen asked Adams. Adams replied, "That number was too high. I flipped out that one by mistake."

Dorsen next moved to analyze a long-held Adams belief, which became one of the four major premises of the documentary, that 150,000 NVA troops had moved down the Ho Chi Minh Trail prior to Tet and that Westmoreland had kept this fact hidden from Washington. In his cross-examination, he asked Adams how it was that the National Security Agency, which was completely independent of MACV, had electronically monitored the Ho Chi Minh Trail all through the war and had not detected these 150,000 troops? "All these people coming up with studies, all these 100,000 to 150,000 unreported infiltrators, as you say, and it took fifteen years before this information came to light?"

"That's the long and the short of it," Adams answered.

And how had he determined that these large numbers of troops had entered South Vietnam prior to Tet? Dorsen asked next.

Those estimates, Adams answered, were based on "guesses by

various military sources." Pressed as to what he meant by "guesses," Adams said that "in intelligence it is almost impossible to do anything but guess. . . . You never have firm and solid information. We didn't have any clicker counting off troops coming down the Ho Chi Minh Trail." Pressed further as to what documents these "guesses" were based on, Adams had to admit that they were not based on any documents but on the estimates of several former military intelligence officers. Asked to name those officers, Adams said that the 150,000 figure was "confirmed" by a former intelligence officer named Michael Hankins, who held a lieutenant's rank in 1967.

Dorsen then reminded Adams that another former intelligence officer, Bernard Gattozzi, had told George Crile in 1981 that he thought 70,000 NVA troops a month had come down the Ho Chi Minh Trail prior to Tet, for a total pre-Tet infiltration of over 350,000. Why had he, Adams, decided to go with Hankins's figure instead of Gattozzi's? Dorsen asked.

"We went with the lower figure," Adams responded, "because we did not believe Mr. Gattozzi meant to say that the 70,000 figure was the rate each month."

"Did it occur to you," Dorsen continued, "that these gentlemen might be mistaken?"

Adams replied that it might have occurred to him, but after talking to the officer "my doubts went away."

Adams's testimony had not been persuasive, but before leaving the stand he predicted that the witnesses scheduled to follow him would destroy Westmoreland's case. "Westy is wrong and he's going to lose," he said with great passion. "When he filed the lawsuit my jaw just dropped to the floor. . . . He's just going to back into a twirling fan. And he's doing it and the chunks are going to start flying in the next six weeks."

The first witness earmarked to knock chunks out of Westmoreland's case was George W. Allen, the former chief of Vietnam affairs for the CIA. Asked by Boies to describe his feelings about the order-of-battle compromise MACV and the CIA had come to in 1967, Allen replied that it was "disgraceful," that the CIA had "sold out" to MACV. As a result of that sell-out, he went on, President Johnson had ended up with an enemy troop estimate that was "essentially a dishonest piece of paper, a dishonest document." His own research, Allen said, "supported a force of half a million being the organized communist forces facing us in Vietnam," not the 250,000 figure MACV carried on their books.

Asked why the CIA had gone along with this dishonest estimate, Allen unabashedly replied that they had done it because of "political expediency."

How was he certain there were twice as many enemy troops in South Vietnam as MACV claimed? Boies asked.

Allen said he thought the higher enemy strength figure was proven true by the Tet attacks. "Given the strength of the attack," he said, "the enemy force conducting them had to total at least 400,000."

In his cross-examination, Dorsen suggested that Allen was only testifying to help a beleaguered former CIA colleague, Sam Adams. Allen, however, aggressively denied the charge. Dorsen nonetheless got Allen to admit that he had written a draft statement in 1975 for a House committee, in which he denied that the CIA, as Adams claimed, had caved in to pressure from Westmoreland and modified their enemy OB figures. But, said Allen, he had been pressured to make that statement by William Colby, the director of the CIA.

When Dorsen finished his cross-examination of Allen, Boies changed the entire focus of the trial. Until now, the witnesses for both sides were former bureaucrats, military men, CIA officials, and diplomats. All had spoken of the war in a kind of formal official jargon that had left many of the jurors either bored or confused or both. With his next two witnesses—two ex-infantrymen—Boies brought the war down to ground level and gave it an immediacy that perked every sagging eyelid in the courtroom.

Boies put former Specialist 4 Daniel Friedman on the stand first, then asked him if these irregular, these self-defense forces and secret self-defense forces, had posed any threat to the men in his unit? Those "self-defense forces," Friedman said, "were an integral part of the irregulars of the Vietcong, and were responsible for many terrorist acts against us." Boies put the same question to former Captain Howard Embree, the other ex-infantryman. He got much the same answer. While "guerrillas" were more active than the self-defense forces, Embree said, the latter were still dangerous and were responsible for much of the "mining, booby-trapping, and sniping in the proximity" of their villages.

To give more impact to Embree's testimony, Boies asked the former captain to show the jury how a booby trap was set using a defused grenade and a trip wire. Dorsen strenuously objected to the demonstration, calling it inflammatory. He was overruled, however, and had to sit back in frustration as Embree showed an enthralled jury how to build a simple booby trap.

The demonstration was an emotional coup for CBS. Boies followed it with his strongest witness of the trial, Westmoreland's former intelligence chief, George McChristian. Westmoreland had been wounded by McChristian's appearance in the documentary and had hoped, as was rumored, that he would decide not to testify at the trial.

It was an ill-founded rumor, for on February 6, 1985, the man capable of damaging Westmoreland's case the most took the stand. Although obviously hurt, Westmoreland showed no emotion at the sight of McChristian directly across from him.

After giving a short biography of himself, McChristian with Boies's guidance began a detailed discussion of the irregulars and their importance to the enemy. He said that it was his "strong conviction from the beginning" that these units should have been included in the OB. While he admitted they had no offensive capability, "that wasn't their job. Their job was to carry out these roles, these missions down within the hamlets and the villages, and they were looked upon as a training base and mobilization base to upgrade the local and main Vietcong units."

Boies next moved the discussion to that day in mid-March 1967 when McChristian brought the cable to Westmoreland containing the higher enemy strength figures. "And what was Westmoreland's response when you showed him the cable?" Boies asked.

"He read it. He looked up at me and said, 'If I send this cable to Washington, it will create a political bombshell.' "

McChristian said that he told Westmoreland that he did not know why the cable should cause problems. "Send me back and I'll explain to anyone who wants to know what we've been doing to collect this information," McChristian claimed he told Westmoreland. But Westmoreland wanted nothing to do with such an arrangement, he said, and told him to instead leave the cable with him.

"At any prior time in your military service," Boies asked, "had you ever had a superior officer discuss with you the political implications of an enemy strength estimate?"

"No, sir."

"Did you believe it was improper for General Westmoreland to hold your cable?"

"I think that for a military man to withhold a report based upon political considerations would be improper."

In his cross-examination, Dorsen set out to show that McChristian had made a number of contradictory statements since first being interviewed by CBS three years before and that it was difficult to figure out which statement was to be believed.

He began by asking the general if he believed Westmoreland had actually attempted to "suppress" the higher enemy strength figure. "This was the only time he exercised any control over my reporting," McChristian answered. "And he asked to hold it up based on political considerations."

Dorsen then handed McChristian the transcript of a conversation the general had had in 1982 with Don Kowet, the coauthor of "Anatomy of a Smear." Dorsen pointed out to McChristian that when Kowet asked him whether he believed Westmoreland had asked him to suppress enemy strength information in 1967, he, McChristian, had answered, "Absolutely not."

A flustered McChristian replied that "there is a difference between talking under oath and talking to journalists over the phone."

Dorsen let the general's answer stand, quickly changing the subject.

"Now you testified, I believe," Dorsen went on, "that the words 'political bombshell' are burned in your mind, in your memory, is that correct?"

"Yes, sir, that's correct."

"Didn't you tell George Crile, when you were being videotaped, that you didn't recall the precise words that General Westmoreland used?"

"I would like to see that in context," a confused McChristian said. "I don't believe I said that."

Without a word Dorsen handed the general a transcript of the Crile interview with the damning words underlined. McChristian said nothing.

Dorsen likely gained points with the jury with his cross-examination of McChristian. If nothing else, it brought into question McChristian's contention that Westmoreland had used the words "political bombshell." During his redirect examination of McChristian, however, Boies gained some of those points back when he got McChristian to admit something he had been reluctant to talk about before, which was that Westmoreland had asked him not to cooperate with CBS.

"Did there come a time," Boies asked, "when General Westmoreland called you on the telephone and told you in words or substance that he thought the conversation that he had with you in May of 1967 was a private conversation between West Pointers?"

"Yes, sir."

Boies then handed McChristian notes the general had made of that phone conversation with Westmoreland and asked him to read them. "He thought our conversation was private and official between West Pointers," McChristian said. "I replied that I spoke the truth. . . . He said that he stood up and took the brunt of Vietnam for all of us. He as much as accused me of being the one mainly responsible for his integrity being impugned by [CBS]."

Westmoreland frowned as he listened to McChristian. He had found it difficult throughout the trial having to sit quietly and listen to the witnesses for CBS say things that he felt were wrong. Listening to McChristian, however, was the most difficult. He wanted to get up and tell the jury that McChristian was either lying or confused. Then he wanted to tell them what had actually been said during their phone conversation. As he did eventually tell a reporter after the trial, he wanted to tell the jury that he had called McChristian "as an old friend and former colleague and expressed my surprise that he would go on national TV without the courtesy of informing me. I told him in essence that it was an unusual performance and alluded to the confidence that had traditionally prevailed between West Point graduates. I added that I was disappointed to have him add to the burden I already carried for those of us who fought an unpopular war." Westmoreland, of course, didn't get a chance to give his version of the conversation. Instead, as he told the same reporter, he had to sit silently and "work to keep myself in check."

Westmoreland had to exert his self-control once again for the man who followed McChristian to the stand. Former Colonel Gains Hawkins had been his order-of-battle chief in 1967. Now he was a witness for CBS, come, like McChristian, to call the man who had once been his boss, a liar. With Boies's prodding, Hawkins began his testimony by repeating for the jury what he had already told CBS cameras, that during a briefing Hawkins had given Westmoreland on May 26, 1967, Westmoreland refused for "political" reasons to accept an increased estimate for the enemy irregular forces in South Vietnam.

Asked by Boies what precisely Westmoreland said when presented with the higher figure, Hawkins replied, "The substance of General Westmoreland's statement was that these figures were politically unacceptable. The substance of his statement included statements like: What will I tell the President? What will I tell Congress? What will be the reaction of the press to these higher figures?" Hawkins proceeded to reveal that Davidson, once he had replaced McChristian as intelligence chief, also became involved with Westmoreland in defending the lower enemy strength figure, or as Hawkins termed it, the "command position."

"And what was Gen. Davidson's personal response to the higher enemy troop strength estimate?" Boies asked.

Hawkins said that Davidson replied that the higher estimate was "unacceptable." And it was unacceptable, Hawkins went on, not because Davidson disagreed with "our methodology," but only because the figure was "politically" unacceptable.

As a great number of legal experts observing the trial noted, Hawkins seemed a strong witness for CBS under direct examination. Few in the courtroom were not impressed by his ability to recall Westmoreland and Davidson's exact words. During his cross-examination by Dorsen, however, Hawkins's memory suddenly failed him, and much of his testimony was muddled and contradictory. One of the major premises of the CBS documentary—a premise based on interviews with both McChristian and Hawkins—was that Westmoreland had transferred McChristian out of Vietnam because of their disagreement over enemy strength figures. In his first move as cross-examiner, Dorsen presented into evidence a letter from Hawkins to his wife dated a full two months before Westmoreland and McChristian locked horns over the enemy OB. Dorsen read out loud the paragraph in the letter where Hawkins notified his wife that McChristian was leaving Vietnam in June. "He gets the 2nd Armored Div. at Ft. Hood, Texas, I think. Glad he got his command. He wants the third star and the fourth."

After reading the paragraph, Dorsen had Hawkins read the portion of his deposition in which he had accused Westmoreland of shipping McChristian out because of their disagreement over enemy strength figures. When Hawkins finished, Dorsen then got him to admit that CBS had had a copy of the damning letter before they made the documentary.

How did he account for all these discrepancies? Dorsen asked.

". . . I made a mistake," Hawkins answered.

Dorsen next produced the draft of an article Hawkins had written, in which he described his former boss, McChristian, as "relentless ambitious man," who would do anything to keep advancing in rank.

Which was the real McChristian, Dorsen asked. The relentlessly ambitious man in the draft article or the McChristian Hawkins had lavished praise on while being examined by Boies? Hawkins, however, so resisted answering the question directly that Dorsen was finally forced to let it stand unanswered and move the discussion on.

For his third point of contention, Dorsen produced a 1967 document detailing a mission a Colonel Barrie Williams had taken to Vietnam in March and April of that year as a representative of the Defense Intelligence Agency. The document, Dorsen pointed out, flew in the face of the notion that Westmoreland had tried to hide the higher enemy strength figure, for in the document Williams detailed how during a briefing at MACV he was given precise information on the enemy irregular strength. That information, Dorsen explained, was included in Williams's report to the DIA. The DIA, in turn, passed it on to the White House.

During questioning, Hawkins admitted to vaguely remembering coming in contact with Williams while the DIA official was in Saigon, but could not recall attending the briefing where the irregular strength figure was discussed.

Under further questioning, Hawkins likewise could not recall a briefing he had given Admiral Sharp on these same enemy strength figures in May of 1967. During that briefing, Dorsen was careful to tell the jury, Hawkins had provided Sharp with the same material the documentary claimed was suppressed.

As Brewin and Shaw point out, "When Hawkins stepped down from the stand that Friday, February 13, with a few days remaining for the attorneys to make their case, he left many questions unanswered. Why was his memory so selective? Why could he recite conversations with Westmoreland for the CBS cameras—and for Boies—almost verbatim, but could not recall things he had written to his wife?" They were big questions, important questions, and Dorsen intended to take them up again on Monday morning when he resumed his cross-examination of Hawkins. Then he planned on finishing off the colonel's credibility and with it, he hoped, any chance CBS had of winning the trial.

Westy's Revenge

Dorsen would never get his chance to finish off Hawkins. Following the colonel's testimony Friday afternoon, Judge Leval called Dan Burt and David Boies into his chamber for a private conference. With the trial winding down, Leval had drawn up a draft of his instructions to the jury and he wanted the two opposing attorneys to look it over before he made a final decision on it.

As he told reporters later, Burt was overcome with anguish as he read the draft. Both he and Westmoreland had hoped that Leval's instruction would ask the jury to render a single verdict. A single verdict would have allowed the Westmoreland camp to claim, if they lost that verdict, that the documentary was false, but that the requirements to prove malice were simply too difficult to satisfy. Leval instead was thinking of having the jury judge each issue—truth, injury, state of mind, libel, and defamation—separately. Even worse from Burt's point of view was the fact that Leval was thinking of instructing the jury that in order to find the documentary false, they would have to do so by "clear and convincing evidence," rather than by a "preponderance of evidence," which was a much less demanding standard.

As Burt and Boies were occupied reading the draft, Leval told them that after they had both had a chance to go over it more carefully at their leisure, he welcomed any comments they might have about it. Burt told Leval that he had already read the part of the draft that most concerned him, that about the burden of proof, and he felt it was too heavy a burden for Westmoreland to carry. "If he loses in truth, it will kill the old man."

Leval said in response that his decision on burden of proof was tentative, and that before giving his final instructions to the jury, he was still willing to consider any objection to the draft either man had. After his conference with Leval, Burt called Westmoreland and they sat down to discuss what their next move should be. Burt said he was thinking of reaching a deal with CBS, and wanted to get the general's reaction.

Westmoreland had been hesitant at first to even discuss the possibility of a settlement, but his camp was now so overwhelmed with problems, that to continue with the trial would be self-destructive. To begin with, there was the problem of Dan Burt himself. Burt's marriage was still under a lot of strain, and the continued physical separation from his wife and baby daughter was moving it closer and closer to the breaking point. In an attempt to ease some of the pain of separation, Burt had moved his baby daughter into his hotel room. The move seemed to help his marriage, but it robbed him of the time he needed to apply to the trial. Burt's marital difficulties had, in turn, created a serious problem for the Capital Legal Foundation. In late January, the foundation ran out of money. Some of Capital's conservative backers, and most especially Richard Mellon Scaife, the millionaire who had picked up the lion's share of Westmoreland's three-million-dollar legal tab, were so unhappy with Burt's handling of the trial that they were hesitant to send in any more money. To continue the trial not only threatened to compromise the Westmoreland case but to destroy Capital Legal in the process. To compound Capital Legal's financial problem was the absolute certainty that should CBS lose the trial, network lawyers would launch a lengthy appeal. If Capital Legal was not already bankrupt after the trial, it certainly would become so trying to fight an appeal against one of the richest corporations in America.

After mulling over all these factors, Westmoreland agreed with Burt that it might be time to settle. Westmoreland said he realized that the odds of him now winning, given the severe burden of proof laid down by Leval, "were no better than the flip of a coin. And that was not good enough."

During the next two days, Burt negotiated a settlement with CBS general counsel George Vrandenburg. Late Sunday afternoon, February 17, Westmoreland signed it.

Burt did not notify anyone on his legal team that he was negotiating a settlement, a fact that upset a number of people on the team. David Dorsen, Burt's cocounsel, was the most upset. He had worked all day Sunday honing the questions he intended to ask Hawkins on Monday morning, only to discover Sunday evening from a reporter that Burt came to an agreement with CBS. "At first I didn't believe it," he said. "Then I was outraged at not having been consulted."

Someone equally upset was Kitsy Westmoreland. Although she had vehemently opposed the lawsuit, once the trial began she thought it should have been fought to the bitter end. She was so upset, in fact, that Sunday evening she instructed the switchboard at their hotel not to let any calls through to their room. She was simply too angry to talk with reporters. Kitsy was still upset late Monday morning when she and her husband arrived at the lobby of the Harley Hotel, where over 250 members of the media had gathered to hear the general make the formal announcement of his withdrawal from the trial. Awaiting her were morning newspapers from every major daily on the East Coast. Some of the morning headlines, like that in *The Washington Post*—WESTMORELAND TO DROP SUIT—merely stated the obvious. Others like that in the *New York Post*—WESTY RAISES WHITE FLAG—she found painful to look at.

If Westmoreland was in any pain, he did not show it as he stepped up onto the podium. Although weary, he hid his weariness behind what a close friend of his called the "classic visage of the stoic." There was no anger in his face, no sadness, no confusion. Fate had once again disappointed him, but he did not intend to show it.

In a deliberate voice, he began reading the joint statement. "CBS respects General Westmoreland's long and faithful service to his country and never intended to assert, and does not believe, that General Westmoreland was unpatriotic or disloyal in performing his duties as he saw fit."

Westmoreland paused for a moment, gripped the podium with both hands and leaned toward the crowd. "If that statement had been made after the CBS broadcast, it would have satisfied me. After my press conference in Washington three days after the broadcast, it would have satisfied me. After the publication of the *TV Guide* article, it would have satisfied me. If made after the publication of the book *A Matter of Honor,* it would have satisfied me. If made during the first days in federal court, it would have ended the episode.

"I got all that I wanted," he continued after another short pause, then added that as far as he was concerned, CBS's statement was much the same as a formal apology.

CBS did not see it as an apology. As Brewin and Shaw note, "There would be no monetary reward, no jury verdict, and no retraction. There would not even be the free TV air time to rebut the CBS show, as the network had offered before the suit was filed. On the surface, the settlement looked like much less than the general could have commanded before the trial. Nevertheless, he was claiming victory."

One who refused to concede that victory was Mike Wallace. Later that afternoon while Westmoreland was waiting in ABC's Green Room to go on the network's nightly news, he spotted Wallace on the screen defending "The Uncounted Enemy." Wallace said he still believed, as the documentary contended, that there had been a "conspiracy" to supress enemy troop data during the Vietnam War.

"What a bunch of baloney," a suddenly combative Westmoreland told some reporters in the room. When he went on camera himself, Westmoreland was just as combative answering a series of questions about some of the main players in the trial.

On the former Army and CIA officials who testified for CBS: "they sat there regurgitating rumors and suppositions and myths and barracks gossip."

On General McChristian: "I never had any indication that he had a vendetta against me. This totally perplexes me. It is perplexing to me, and it is also disillusioning to me. You know, loyalty is a trait of the military. I was certainly loyal to him."

On Colonel Hawkins: "He was a big boy. He had been in the service a number of years and there was no indication he had been disgruntled until Sam Adams made 10 trips down to Mississippi to talk to him. Then he suddenly develops this posture. All on his own."

Westmoreland also defended his removal of the "irregulars" from the OB, repeating yet again his belief that "they were merely children, women and the elderly." To include them in the OB, he went on, would have given American troops "a license to kill," creating the possibility of many more My Lais. "In effect you would have told your troops that they would have the right to go into villages and kill almost anybody they wanted."

The next morning, Judge Leval signed the papers that formally ended the trial. He then dismissed the jurors, most of whom were unhappy that they were not going to be able to render a verdict. He told them, however, that it was probably best that the trial ended without a verdict. "Judgments of history," he said, "are too subtle and too complex to be resolved satisfactorily with the simplicity of a jury verdict. I think it is safe to say that no verdict of judgment that either you or I would have been able to render in the case could have escaped widespread disagreement. So I suggest to you that it may be for the best that the verdict will be left to history."

In spite of Leval's pronouncement, all twelve of the jurors were fairly certain how they intended to vote. Three of them said that without reservation they felt the documentary was true. "I would like to shake Sam Adams's hand," said Phillip Chase, one of the three.

Most of the rest of the jurors said that despite the contradictory testimony, enough evidence had been presented to discount the notion that the documentary had been made with "reckless disregard" for the truth. Most of these same men and women, however, felt Westmoreland had presented a compelling case and that CBS had, as juror Randy Front put it, "blown the conspiracy question all out of proportion." Michael Sussman, another juror from this latter group, had even harsher things to say about CBS. He told a *Washington Post* reporter that he felt Crile and Wallace had tricked Westmoreland into appearing guilty on camera. Sussman then added, "If I were a soldier, I'd like him to be my general."

The nation's newspapers and magazines also chose to ignore Leval's pronouncement. Most had staked out strong positions during the trial and, with its end, were eager to make some kind of final statement. For many that statement was a neutral one. Writing for *The Washington Post*, Jody Powell, former President Jimmy Carter's press secretary, admitted that after closely following the trial, he had been unable to decide who was right and who wrong. "The truth is probably unknowable," he wrote. "There are good arguments and an ample quantity of evidence on both sides." In the same issue of the *Post*, Edwin M. Yoder, Jr., also admitted being unable to make up his mind. In the end, he felt that Judge Leval's contention that "questions of history were not suited to judicial determination" was probably a wise one.

The best-selling author and social commentator, Renata Adler, saw things quite differently. After covering the trial for *The New Yorker*, she concluded that CBS was clearly in the wrong. In a lengthy polemic in that magazine, which was later published in book form as

Reckless Disregard, she referred to the CBS documentary variously as "ridiculous," "pernicious," and "contrived," and accused Crile and Wallace of ignoring the most basic journalistic ethics while making it. The two, she wrote, "took a thesis; found witnesses more or less to support it; interviewed those witnesses, and cut those parts of the interview that did not support the thesis . . . rehearsed and re-interviewed some friendly witnesses; and found reason not to interview other witnesses who had information that would undermine the thesis." In short, she wrote, "they were acting not as press but as producers and directors casting for a piece of theatre."

CBS was upset having someone of Adler's literary reputation attack them so unmercifully, but they were able to take comfort from the fact that a great many more writers and journalists sided with them. In this group were the great majority of editorial cartoonists, who seemed of one mind when it came to imputing meaning to Westmoreland's sudden withdrawal. As Brewin and Shaw noted, they "favored the image of the evacuation helicopter." In the *Boston Globe,* cartoonist Paul Szep drew a frazzled, hollow-eyed Westmoreland desperately clinging to a rope ladder beneath a helicopter, which is hurriedly lifting off from the roof of the federal courthouse. "The Fall of Westmoreland," read the caption. In his version of the evacuation, Doug Marlette of the *Los Angeles Times* depicted Westmoreland hanging from the skids of a helicopter, which is also lifting off from the roof of the federal courthouse. The caption this time read, "Westmoreland declares victory over CBS and pulls out."

A number of editorial writers were just as strong in their support for CBS. To Frank Lombardi of the *New York Daily News,* the meaning of Westmoreland's sudden withdrawal was obvious: "All the face-saving stipulations, statements, comments, and rationales offered by Westmoreland and his lawyer do not, and will not, stand up against the cold reality that the other side wasn't the one that blinked first and asked to have the heavy shelling come to an end." An editorial in *Newsday* agreed. Westmoreland's withdrawal, it bluntly stated, was proof that his "case had fallen apart." An editor from the *Baltimore Sun,* however, had the harshest words for the general. Westmoreland, he said, lost the trial, "no matter what face he put on it and he deserved to lose."

A number of editors and commentators also sought to gauge just what this defeat meant to Westmoreland's reputation. Not a few thought the defeat had damaged it even more than it had been damaged by the Vietnam War. One who certainly thought so was John

R. MacArthur, the publisher of *Harper's*, the magazine that in 1975 first published Samuel Adams's accusations against Westmoreland. MacArthur claimed the trial had been a "crude attempt by ideologues to rewrite the history of the Vietnam War" and that they had sorely used Westmoreland in the process. When those ideologues realized they were not going to be able to achieve this goal, MacArthur contended, they abandoned the lawsuit and Westmoreland with it, unbothered by the fact that they had helped humiliate the general and ruin his reputation. "What of General Westmoreland's honor now?" MacArthur asked. "Was it served in any way by this wasteful lawsuit? Was the principle of fairness, which most Americans believe in, advanced to any degree? Of course not. General Westmoreland will be remembered bravely insisting, in his hotel room, that defeat was victory and that CBS had apologized." The only apology, however, said MacArthur, should come from Westmoreland's financial backers. They should apologize to him for destroying his reputation.

In an article in the prestigious *New York Law Journal*, James D. Zirin, a former assistant United States attorney for the Southern District of New York, expressed similar sentiments. While he did not blame Westmoreland's financial backers for the trial's untimely end, he nonetheless felt Westmoreland would have been better off if he had "stayed home." Because of the trial, Zirin wrote, Westmoreland's "reputation as a warrior is in worse shape than it was before he filed suit. The charges against him, long since forgotten or dismissed by many, have been resurrected with a born-again vitality that sully the record of a career committed to duty, honor, and country."

If Westmoreland felt humiliated by the trial's end, it was a short-lived humiliation. On February 18, he gave his last press interview before departing New York. He told reporters that he was returning to Charleston in the morning, where he intended spending the next few days resting and "trying to get the media exposure behind me . . . Then like a good general, I'll just fade away." Westmoreland did not fade away for long. A few days after his return home, he got a call from the National Press Club requesting that he be their keynote speaker at their annual meeting in Washington, D.C., on March 15, 1985. Even though he worried about how he would be accepted by the NPC members, he nonetheless accepted the invitation.

He had last spoken before the National Press Club in late November 1967, at the height of the war. The majority of the men and women who comprised the audience then had either opposed the war or had great misgivings about it. As the most visible symbol of the war, the reception he had received then had been little more than attentive and polite. The mood this time was lighter, and the reception quite different. Polite clapping had followed his introduction in 1967. This time he was greeted by thunderous applause.

Warmed by the applause, Westmoreland stepped up to the podium and smiled. "I feel somewhat like Daniel as he was about to be thrown into the lion's den. Daniel was asked if he was scared. 'No,' he said, 'only curious.' Then Daniel asked, 'Are those lions hungry?' 'No,' replied the innkeeper, 'but they are armed to the teeth.' When I told my wife that I had accepted your invitation to the den, she replied, 'We must inscribe that act of bravery on your tombstone.'" Laughter rippled through the audience, but quickly turned to long applause. The audience interrupted his ten-minute speech eight more times. When he ended it, they stood in unison and applauded for over a minute. Seated now, a pleased Westmoreland nodded his head to the audience, like an actor responding to a second curtain call.

A week later, Westmoreland got another warm reception at the Gridiron dinner, a yearly gathering of Washington's most prominent government and business leaders. Although he did not speak this time, when he was introduced to the audience, he got an even greater applause than his old nemesis Walter Cronkite, a fact that immensely pleased Westmoreland and surely rankled Cronkite.

Westmoreland's warm receptions at the National Press Club meeting and Gridiron dinner were but hints of things to come. Within a week, as Fred Barnes noted in the *New Republic*, he was one of the most sought after men in America, invited to lead parades, speak at conventions and seminars, and asked by the leading magazines and newspapers in the country to give his opinion on a wide variety of issues and topics. Ironically, a documentary that had been made in part to discredit him, had made him more credible than he had ever been.

Westmoreland's greatest honor came over a year after the trial when he was asked to be the grand marshal of the Chicago Vietnam Veterans Parade scheduled for June 1, 1986. He would not, however, realize how significant an honor it was until the day of the parade.

The parade was the idea of a group of Chicago veterans who felt that both the city and the country were ready to pay tribute to Vietnam vets on a grand scale. They felt the public's perception of Vietnam vets and the vets' self-perception had been undergoing a radical change in the past three or four years, and they expected the Chicago parade to be the crescendo of that change, the high point of a struggle for respect and recognition that Vietnam vets had been crying out for since the war's end. To make the parade a reality, those vets had labored for over a year raising the $700,000 needed to cover the necessary expenses.

Many officials with the city of Chicago thought they had wasted their time. They did not think enough veterans would show up to keep the parade from being an embarrassment, or that the people of Chicago were ready to celebrate veterans from a war that had been so indecisive. When Tom Stack, a Vietnam vet who headed the parade committee publicly announced that he felt that one hundred thousand vets would show up to march, these same city officials shook their heads in disbelief. "I think they thought I was sniffing airplane glue," Stack said later.

These officials soon became believers, however. Beginning a week before the parade, vets from every state in the union, and even from Australia, began pouring into Chicago. They came first by the hundreds, then by the thousands, and in the last few days before the parade by the tens of thousands. By June 12, their number had grown to over two hundred thousand, prompting one Chicago official to remark to Stark, "My God, it's going to be what you guys said it would be."

On the morning of June 13, most of those two hundred thousand gathered along Navy Pier in a long column. They came dressed in an assortment of clothing. Some wore business suits and neatly polished wing-tip shoes; others were dressed casually in shorts or slacks and sport shirts. By far the majority arrived in bits and pieces of old uniforms and jungle fatigues, their middle-aged stomachs bulging against pants and shirts now two and three sizes too small. Regardless of how they dressed, most were in a festive mood, and a carnivallike atmosphere reigned up and down Navy Pier as many greeted buddies from Vietnam they had not seen since the war, then as often as not toasted them and their memories with a can of beer or bottle of whiskey. Many of the vets had brought along their wives and children to march beside them, and the children were likewise in a festive mood. Many were dressed like their fathers in bits and pieces of uniforms and jungle fatigues, and a number carried small American or POW-MIA flags, which they waved with abandon.

Westmoreland arrived at Navy Pier at 9:00 A.M., accompanied by two men who were going to help him lead the parade, Tom Stack, the head of the parade committee, and Jim Patridge, a wheelchair-bound vet who had lost both legs to a land mine in Vietnam. Both

Stack and Patridge were dressed casually, but Westmoreland had worn his full-dress uniform, which he had bedecked with all his medals and campaign ribbons. He had told a friend earlier that although he had seldom worn his uniform for public appearances since retirement, he intended to wear it today because "somehow today it just feels right."

The uniform was a wise choice. Those few men near the front of the column who could see Westmoreland responded to the sight of their former commander in full-dress uniform with wild shouts of "Westy!" He had wanted to mingle with the men for a while, but the parade organizers told him that because of the unusually large crowd, they had to start the parade an hour early or face the possibility of not having it completed before Chicago's late afternoon rush-hour traffic.

And so at approximately nine-thirty, the three men left the entrance to Navy Pier, passed through Olive Park, and started west down Grand Avenue. They had not gone twenty-five yards, however, before something happened that would set the emotional tone for the entire day. At that moment a car pulled up blocking their path. Out of the passenger's side of the car leaped Bob Wieland, a legless vet. Wieland had fitted the bottom of his torso with specially designed pads so he could pull himself along on his hands. With a rapidity that surprised everyone, he moved quickly across the ground and told Westmoreland that he wanted to march with him at the front of the parade. Would that be okay?

Of course, it would be, Westmoreland said. Then, with eyes now filled with tears, Westmoreland turned to a friend behind him and choked out, "My God, what guts. What guts!"

With Wieland now in the lead, the column lurched forward again and began moving at a rapid clip. There were few spectators along Grand Street, and that fact gave the leaders of the parade a moment of pause. Would anyone bother to turn out to see them? Or would they be shunned as they had been after the war? And if spectators did turn out, would they be friendly? Or would there instead be ugly incidents, protesters calling them baby killers or disgruntled World War II vets calling them crybabies or losers or drug fiends? No one knew for sure what they could expect, and many feared the worst.

Their fears were quickly proved unfounded. As Stack had hoped, Chicagoans were not going to fail them. Although the crowds were sparse along Grand, as the parade approached the Michigan Street bridge, the first of nearly five hundred thousand spectators turned out. Construction workers from a dozen buildings under construction greeted them with wild shouts of encouragement. Motormen slowed their elevated trains and blew their whistles in salute. All the while, thousands of employees from banks, commodity exchanges, and department stores filled the windows of all the surrounding buildings or flooded into the street. In a matter of minutes, spectators were eight and ten deep along Michigan Avenue. All of them were clapping and hundreds were shouting over and over again, "Welcome home!" and "We love you!" Young women in business suits, their eyes brimming with tears, rushed out to hug veterans, and young men—stockbrokers, bankers, and businessmen—rushed out to shake their hands. One young woman admitted later that she cried from the beginning of the parade until the end.

The vets responded with equal enthusiasm. "Thank you, Chicago," they shouted back. "Thank you. Thank you." As William Mullen noted in the *Chicago Tribune*, "tears began to streak the battered faces of veterans who looked so hardened that they would rather die than show emotion. Arms began to entwine in the ranks, to drape and hug shoulders. Wives marching with their men leaned into them, kissed them, adored them, while their children seemed bedazzled by it all."

All the while the two-mile-long column continued moving forward. As it moved up State Street, then south across the Chicago River to Wacker Drive, the crowds continued to grow. It seemed every window in every building was filled with spectators now, and the crowds along the street were so thick at points that many of the spectators were within inches of the marchers.

The high point of the parade, however, awaited the marchers along LaSalle Street in the heart of Chicago's financial district. As Westmoreland, Stack, Patridge, and Wieland turned the corner of LaSalle and Wacker, they stepped into a blizzard of confetti being tossed from the windows of the surrounding twenty- and thirty-story office buildings by hundreds of secretaries and stockbrokers. The wind off Lake Michigan kept the confetti swirling upward, and for a time it was so thick that the front of the parade was lost to sight.

Near the corner of Washington and LaSalle, Westmoreland slipped out of the parade and joined Illinois Governor Jim Thompson and Chicago Mayor Harold Washington on the reviewing stand. For the organizers of the parade, it was another tense, anxious moment. Many veterans, and most especially those who had helped raise money to pay Westmoreland's legal bills during the CBS libel trial, had been upset with the general for pulling out of the trial. They thought he should have fought CBS to the bitter end, and there was some concern among the parade organizers that some of these vets might express their feelings once they saw Westmoreland face-to-face. The parade organizers were equally concerned that vets who disagreed sharply with Westmoreland's handling of the war might likewise express their feelings once they confronted the general. Not a few vets had bought into the Hackworth thesis, namely that Westmoreland's search-and-destroy strategy had been the wrong strategy in Vietnam, and that Westmoreland, if not completely, was at least partially responsible for what happened in Vietnam. If only a few dozen out of the two hundred thousand marching decided to get nasty, it could cast a pall over the entire event.

Fortunately for the organizers, none did. If any of the marchers held any rancor toward Westmoreland, they did not intend to display it today. To the contrary, the marchers' response to the sight of Westmoreland was overwhelmingly positive.

"Hey! Westy's here," men cried out excitedly at the first sight of him. "Look, it's Westy! The old man came!"

Men who had cameras took them out and began snapping pictures of Westmoreland. Others lifted their small children up over the press of bodies. Some just stopped momentarily to salute him. Within seconds, the parade slowed to a crawl, forcing the public address announcer to repeatedly ask the groups and clusters of men and their family members to please keep moving.

Fortunately for the public address announcer, a large number of the men marching today had decided to do so in organized groups under the banners and flag of old units. These groups marched crisply by the reviewing stand, often identifying their units for Westmoreland with nicknames and slogans. A group from the 1st Cavalry Division shouted out their division's nickname, "First Team," over and over again as they marched by. A second group of men—this one from the 173rd Airborne Brigade—growled out their nickname, "the Herd," as they passed by. A third group, representing a battalion from the 25th Infantry Division nicknamed the Wolfhounds in Vietnam, made repeated "woofing" sounds for Westmoreland's benefit. Westmoreland smiled broadly, loving the camaraderie and unit pride his former troops were displaying.

The groups marching under banners were followed by groups representing more traditional veterans' groups—groups like the American Legion, the Veterans of Foreign Wars, and the Disabled

American Veterans. Many of these marchers were clearly disabled and they pulled themselves along in wheelchairs or limped forward on artificial legs. The crowds became particularly animated at the sight of these men, and a number of men and women near the reviewing stand rushed out to hug them, to shake their hands, and thank them for their sacrifices. Many of the disabled men stopped to salute Westmoreland, and he, with tears in his eyes, saluted them back.

These traditional groups were followed by more groups marching under banners and flags, then by a bevy of bands and marching groups, then by more large groups of vets marching with their wives and children. On and on they came for the next five hours, in groups of twenty and fifty and one hundred. Through it all, Westmoreland stayed glued to his spot on the reviewing stand, despite the temperature, which hit ninety at noon and kept climbing. Drenched in perspiration, his arms stiff from the hundreds of thumbs-up signals he had flashed, from all the waving and salutes, he stood there until the last groups passed by the reviewing stand at three in the afternoon. This was his and their finest moment, and he wanted to savor every last minute of it.

In that last group was a thirty-six-year-old veteran from Milwaukee, who had walked the entire distance hand-in-hand with his ten-year-old daughter. Both were thoroughly exhausted, worn ragged by the heat and the crush of people. Directly across from the reviewing stand, the father told his daughter that he could not walk any farther, that he had to sit down and rest for a minute. With that, he pulled a cold beer from a small cooler he was carrying, opened it, and took a long sip, then with a sigh dropped to the curb. His daughter dropped down beside him and curled against his chest.

"It was a long parade, Daddy," she said quietly.

"It was a long war, honey," he answered.

NOTES

Prologue: April 28, 1967

Westmoreland's speech to Congress is based on articles from *Newsweek, Time, The Nation, The New York Times,* and *The Washington Post.* Invaluable was a video of an NBC special report on the speech available at the LBJ Library.

Speeches of other military men before Congress: Office File of Cecil Ballinger, Westmoreland Trip Home, LBJ Library.

Response of southern senators: "The Westmoreland Caper," p. 221.

Chapter One: Lost Causes

The Westmoreland family history from their earliest years in America through the Revolutionary War is based on a large box of miscellaneous family records, letters and personal accounts, provided to me by Edna Westmoreland of Woodruff, South Carolina. Particularly valuable were an eight-page family history written by James White Westmoreland in 1932 and a forty-page history authored by Olin Vennis Mapes in the late 1960s.

The books I relied heavily on were Landrum's *Colonial and Revolution History of Upper South Carolina* and Hewell's *The Pedens of America.*

The section detailing the impact of the Civil War on the Westmoreland family is based on "Gone to Rest," a eulogy on Squire Jim written by H. P. Griffith, and on "A Pair of Noble Brothers," a newspaper article Griffith wrote for the *Spartanburg Daily Herald.* In the article, Griffith details his lifelong friendship and business association with Squire Jim and Dr. D. D. Westmoreland. Very useful were two articles that reporters from the *Herald* wrote about James White Westmoreland in 1940 and 1941. Both provided specific information about Squire Jim and his two sons' experiences during the war.

Books that were helpful in re-creating this period are Caldwell's *The History of a Brigade of South Carolinians;* Edward's *Condensed History of the Seventeenth Regiments;* Tompkins's *Company K, 14th South Carolina Volunteers;* Owen's *Camp-Fire Stories and Reminiscences;* and Brown's *A Colonel at Gettysburg and Spotsylvania.*

Chapter Two: Rip's Son

The story of the Westmoreland family following the Civil War is based on some of the same sources cited earlier, especially James White's short history and Griffith's eulogy and newspaper article. Edna Westmoreland filled in the gaps.

To reconstruct the life of James "Rip" Westmoreland, I utilized a multitude of sources, many of which are stored in the Citadel's archives.

17 Description of Rip Westmoreland: Lanford, p. 132.
17 Rip's ambition: *The Sphinx,* pp. 38, 45, 46, 73, 186, 194.
17 The Citadel riot: Moore, "The Riot at the Citadel"; "There Was Nothing Else to Do," p. 8; Marshall, "The Class That Did Not Graduate."
18 Rip's early business experiences are reconstructed from biographies of him found in a number of histories of South Carolina and in biographical dictionaries of prominent South Carolinians. I found valuable information about Rip's financial dealings in the South Carolina Archives.
18 Relationship of Rip and Eugenia Talley: Furgurson, pp. 34–34.
19 Description of Pacolet and Victor Park: Kirby, interview with the author.
20 The lives of millworkers: Ibid.; Carlton, pp. 8–11, 168–211.
20 Coleman, Blease: Ibid., pp. 246–49; Kirby, interview with the author.
20 "Mimi wasn't about": Edna Westmoreland, interview with the author.
21 Westmoreland's love of uniforms: Margaret Westmoreland, interview with the author.
21 "You'd think the boy": Monts, p. 1B.

21 "He was so committed": Margaret Westmoreland, interview with the author.

21 Rip's influence on his son: Westmoreland, interview with the author.

22 Early scouting experience: Hammond, interview with the author; Monts, p. 1B; Furgurson, p. 40.

22 Trip to Europe: Westmoreland, *Soldier*, pp. 10, 20; Furgurson, pp. 42–44; "Westmoreland Goes to World Scout Jamboree," p. 3.

24 Last two years in high school: Author interviews with Kirby, Jones, Blackwell, Jackson, and Hammond; Furgurson, pp. 45–49.

Chapter Three: Cadet Westmoreland

28 "a philosophical city-state" Dodson, p. 12.

30 Westmoreland at the Citadel: Author interviews with Glover, Marchant, and Earle.

32 Appointment to West Point: *Soldier*, p. 10; Furgurson, p. 57.

35 Heintges's impressions of Westmoreland: Heintges, interview by Pellici, p. 32.

35 Clifton and Westmoreland talk: Halberstam, p. 548; Mylander, p. 119.

35 MacArthur's speech: Westmoreland, *Soldier*, p. 11.

36 Encounter with Bradley: Westmoreland, interview by Ganderson, pp. 16–19; Westmoreland, *Soldier*, p. 167.

38 Reunion of the "Big Twelve": Jackson, interview with the author.

38 Practices parade commands: Furgurson, p. 62.

38 Visits James White: Westmoreland, *Soldier*, p. 12.

40 Tenure as First Captain: Furgurson, pp. 65–74; Westmoreland, interview with the author.

42 Receives Pershing Sword: "Gravity Register," p. 15; Westmoreland, *Soldier*, pp. 12–13.

Chapter Four: "Sir, that man's going to be Chief of Staff someday."

43 The Army in 1936: For good descriptions of the Army during this period, see Vogel's *Soldiers of the Old Army;* and Weigley's "The Interwar Army, 1919–1941," in Hagan's *Against All Enemies.* The best description can be found in James Jones's classic novel, *From Here to Eternity.*

44 "Lieutenant, I think": Furgurson, pp. 77–78.

46 Fox hunting: Davis, interview by Fullerton, p. 39; Westmoreland, interview by McDonald, March 19, 1973.

46 Meets Kitsy: Furgurson, pp. 79–80; Westmoreland, interview by McDonald, March 19, 1973; Westmoreland, *Soldier*, p. 17.

47 Mitchell's description of Hawaii: Gauvreau, pp. 173–75.

47 Officers not aware of impending danger: Dupuy, p. 42.

47 "in the idyllic setting": Westmoreland, *Soldier*, p. 17.

48 Social life at Schofield Barracks: Westmoreland, *Soldier*, p. 19; Furgurson, pp. 81–83.
49 Develops new firing data: Furgurson, p. 84.
50 "war was now knocking": Mittelman, p. 25.
51 Takes command of the 34th: Letters from Connolly and Birum to the author.
54 "sir, that man": Just, p. 134.

Chapter Five: Hotshot

56 Trains his troops: Letter from Connolly to the author.
56 The author relied heavily on a number of books about World War II in order to create the following section. A few of the most important are Mittelman, *Eight Stars to Victory;* Garland and Smith, *Sicily and the Surrender of Italy;* Howe, *Northwest Africa: Seizing the Initiative in the West;* Harrison, *Cross-Channel Attack;* Blumenson, *Breakout and Pursuit, Patton,* and *Kasserine Pass;* McDonald, *The Siegfried Line Campaign;* Bradley, *A Soldier's Story;* and Heckler, *The Bridge at Remagen.*
57 "When you fellows came": Furgurson, p. 107.
57 789-mile journey: Letters from Connolly and Birum to the author.
58 Westmoreland at Thala: Furgurson, pp. 110–13; Letter from Connolly to the author.
61 "That Westmoreland is a real hotshot": Halberstam, p. 555.
62 Taylor impressed with Westmoreland: Furgurson, p. 125.
63 "with lines of succession": Mylander, p. 148.
63 Wins Legion of Merit: Furgurson, p. 130.
64 Refuses to clean up bivouack: Letter from Birum to the author.
70 Takes charge of the Remagen bridgehead: Furgurson, pp. 160–64; Heckler, p. 165.
71 Talks to Sylvan: Westmoreland, interview with McDonald, February 11, 1973; Westmoreland, *Soldier*, p. 22.
71 Millikin's relief: Bradley, p. 408.
71 "I have some bad news": Sylvan, p. 215.
73 Patton's advice: Westmoreland, *Soldier*, p. 22.
73 Takes command of the 60th: Westmoreland, *Soldier*, p. 23; Westmoreland, interview with author.

Chapter Six: The Rocket List

75 Returns home: Margaret Clarkson, interview with the author.
76 "How would you like": Furgurson, p. 182.
76 Wood's version: Wood, interview by Narus, p. 19.
77 "are we fighting the Russians?": Westmoreland, *Soldier*, p. 23.
77 Rocket list: Davidson, *Vietnam*, pp. 333–34.

78 Gets reacquainted with Kitsy: Westmoreland, interview by McDonald, March 19–20, 1973. Westmoreland, *Soldier*, p. 24.
78 Description of Kitsy: Davidson, *Vietnam*, p. 341.
79 "crusty bachelor": Westmoreland, *Soldier*, p. 23.
79 "Don't worry": Furgurson, p. 197.
80 "Westmoreland had never read the book": Davidson, *Vietnam*, p. 335.
80 "The Uses of Mother's Milk": Furgurson, p. 84.
82 Description of Barriger: Barthomees, interview with the author.
82 Disagreement with Barriger: Flannagan, Crittenberger, and Barthomees, interview with the author.
83 "Westmoreland had a lot of power": Two-star general, interview with the author.

Chapter Seven: Protégé

84 "to impress congressmen": Davidson, *Vietnam*, p. 335.
85 "doom-and-gloom": Wilson, p. 12.
85 Ridgway's presentation: Halberstam, *Best*, pp. 143–44; Perret, p. 490.
86 "There would be no U.S. Cavalry": Perret, p. 490.
86 "distrust and disdain": Davidson, *Vietnam*, p. 336. See also Halberstam, *Best*, p. 679.
87 "away from the ethos of combat": Baritz, pp. 159–60; see also Halberstam, *Best*, p. 560.
87 Westmoreland as SGS: Furgurson, pp. 332–36; Davidson, *Vietnam*, p. 336.
88 "The 1.4 million-man Army": Taylor, *General Maxwell Taylor*, p. 193.
88 "garrison state": Perry, p. 82.
88 Policy of massive retaliation: Taylor, *General Maxwell Taylor*, pp. 204–5; Perret, p. 473; Clark, "General Maxwell Taylor and His Successful Campaign Against the Strategy of Massive Retaliation," pp. 6–7.
89 Radford's hatred of the Army: Palmer, interview by Bradshaw, p. 374.
89 "Just enough troops" Forsythe, interview by Henry, p. 316.
89 Ridgway argues with Eisenhower: Perry, p. 55.
89 "tiny army": Ibid., p. 58.
89 "departure was a clear signal": Perret, p. 474.
90 "had a determined reluctance": Geelhoed, p. 136.
90 "without Taylor's supervision": Ibid.
90 Newspaper headlines: Quoted in Halberstam, *Best*, p. 476.
91 Actions taken against the colonels: Ibid.
91 Westmoreland's account of the revolt: Westmoreland, interview by Ganderson, p. 71.
91 "initiating firm, if brief, contacts": Perry, p. 70.
92 "the United States was willing to share": Taylor, *Uncertain*, p. 153.

Chapter Eight: The Job of a Lifetime

93 The story of White Cloud: Singlaub, pp. 245–46.

94 "People in the airborne had style": Just, p. 135.

95 "the airborne concept had barely proven itself": Ibid.

95 "prima facie evidence": Ibid., p. 130.

95 "a soldier's soldier": Atkinson, p. 65.

96 Prepares cadets for counterinsurgency warfare: Wilson, p. 13; Westmoreland, interview by Miles, p. 3.

96 Rostow's speech: Atkinson, p. 66.

96 Johnson's speech: Westmoreland, *Soldier*, p. 33.

97 MacArthur's speech: Ibid., pp. 34–35.

97 Kennedy's speech: Ibid., pp. 38–39. Text of speech in *New York Times*, June 7, 1962, p. 26.

97 Westmoreland arranges Kennedy's schedule: Halberstam, *Best*, p. 559.

97 Denies trying to impress Kennedy: Westmoreland, interview with the author.

98 Kennedy impressed with Westmoreland: Halberstam, *Best*, p. 559.

98 "entirely too unorthodox": Perry, p. 136.

98 "a military careerist rejects promotion": Davidson, *Vietnam*, p. 338.

100 "wish to stimulate": Gravel, II, p. 257.

100 "leaped to his feet": Taylor, *Swords*, p. 301.

100 Vietnam great foreign policy failure: Schlesinger, *One Thousand Days*, pp. 997–98; Herring, p. 107.

101 "skeptical of the extent of our involvement": Sorensen, p. 639.

101 Kennedy was simply going to weather it": Ibid., p. 661.

101 "supporting a non-communist Vietnam": Bassett and Pelz, p. 252.

101 "failure of his counterinsurgency effort": Ibid. See also Gelb and Betts, p. 196.

101 McNamara's trip to Saigon: Karnow, p. 325; Herring, p. 110.

102 Harkins's relief: Krepinevich, p. 94.

102 McNamara to Harkins: Msg., OSD to CINCPAC and COMUSMACV, January 10, 1964.

102 "lack of political tact or grace": Halberstam, *Best*, p. 559.

103 On Palmer: Ibid.

103 On Abrams: Ibid.

103 Decision to pick Westmoreland: Furgurson, p. 285; Perry, p. 136; Halberstam, p. 669.

104 View of Janowitz: Janowitz, p. xxxix.

104 "I hope you don't": Westmoreland, *Soldier*, p. 159.

104 Meeting with Wheeler: Westmoreland, interview by Miles.

105 Meeting with MacArthur: Ibid.

106 Speech at West Point: Halberstam, *Best*, pp. 560–61; Furgurson, pp. 287–92.

107 "books to friends": Halberstam, *Best*, p. 562.

Chapter Nine: Decisions

108 North Vietnam's decision to send cadremen south: Davidson, *Vietnam*, pp. 271–74; Herring, pp. 66–67; Duiker, p. 226.

110 "Westmoreland in all his conventionality": Clark, "Westmoreland Appraised," p. 101.
111 "overoptimism and self-delusion": Halberstam, *Best*, p. 562.
111 "he wanted to learn the full story": Furgurson, p. 297.
111 "high sounding declarations": Westmoreland, *Soldier*, p. 58.
112 "built his career": Karnow, p. 335.
112 "amazed and depressed": Perret, p. 497.
112 "there is no military solution": Clark, "Westmoreland Appraised," p. 96.
112 "optimistic to the point of fault": Westmoreland, *Soldier*, p. 66.
112 Conversation with Lodge: Westmoreland, interview by Miles, pp. 19–20.
113 Harkins, Westmoreland meets with McNamara: Ibid., pp. 3–4.
114 Westmoreland meets with McNamara: Ibid., p. 11; Westmoreland, interview by Ganderson; Wilson, p. 14; Westmoreland, interview by McDonald, March 12, 1973; Westmoreland, interview by Miles.
115 McNamara memo to Johnson: Gravel, III, p. 501; Davidson, *Vietnam*, pp. 282–83.
115 Honolulu meeting: Westmoreland, *Soldier*, pp. 70–71; Westmoreland, interview by McDonald, May 14, 1973; Sharp, *Strategy*, pp. 77–80.
116 North Vietnam's decision to send troops south: Duiker, p. 226.
117 Eisenhower's mission directive contrasted with Westmoreland's: Clark, "Westmoreland Appraised," p. 97.
118 Picking Throckmorton: See the cable traffic between Westmoreland and Wheeler from June 21 to July 17, 1964. For Wheeler's feeling about Abrams, see Perry, p. 138.
120 "full responsibility for the effort": Johnson to Taylor, July 2, 1964, quoted in Taylor, *General Maxwell Taylor*, p. 299.
120 "entire philosophy": Ibid., p. 300.
122 "indicate to the North": Herring, p. 122.
122 Meeting with Khanh: Msg., Westmoreland to CINCPAC, August 5, 1964.
123 Responds to Binh Gia: Westmoreland, *Soldier*, p. 126; Sharp, *Report*, p. 95.
124 "hinge events": Davidson, *Vietnam*, p. 291.
124 "tit-for-tat": Karnow, p. 402.
125 Rip's letter: Westmoreland, *Soldier*, p. 89.
125 Scene at the Brink's Hotel: Westmoreland, interview by McDonald, March 12, 1972.
125 Johnson cable: Westmoreland, *Soldier*, p. 113.
126 "stung": Ibid.
126 Reply to Johnson: Ibid., p. 114.
126 "personal challenge of Ho Chi Minh": Stoessinger, p. 185. See also Berman, *Planning*, p. 6.
127 "If I left the woman I really loved": Kearns, p. 251.
128 Gets permission to begin joint planning: Westmoreland, *Soldier*, p. 114.

128 Bundy's visit: Ibid., pp. 114–16.
129 "continued acts of aggression": Gravel, III, p. 271.
129 "measured and limited": Ibid., p. 305.
129 "It is not": Maitland, p. 170.
130 For a detailed description of the debate between the JCS and McNamara over strategy, see James Bond Stockdale's speech, "The Total Vietnam War Story Needs to Be Told," in the June 15, 1989 edition of *Vital Speeches.*

Chapter Ten: Fire Brigade

132 "long-standing policy": Gravel, III, p. 418.
132 "mobile counter-VC operation": Ibid.
133 Gets dressed down by Taylor: Westmoreland, *Soldier,* p. 125.
133 "isolated phenomenon": Gravel, III, p. 243.
133 "saw it as the first step": Ibid.
133 "that regardless of your actions": Msg., Wheeler to Westmoreland, March 4, 1965.
133 "massive and rapid": Msg., Westmoreland to Wheeler, March 5, 1965.
135 "seemed to all of us the bottom of the barrel": Bundy, *Oral History.*
135 "coup shit": Karnow, p. 412.
135 Johnson meets with Johnson: Perry, p. 148; Karnow, p. 417.
136 "assume no limitation of funds", Karnow, p. 417.
137 "intrinsic": Ibid.
137 Chiefs attack enclave strategy: Davidson, *Vietnam,* p. 311.
138 "interim measure": Westmoreland, *Soldier,* p. 132.
138 Compromise strategy: Halberstam, *Best,* pp. 576–77.
139 "to break the will of the DRV/VC": Gravel, III, p. 410.
139 "perhaps a year or two": Halberstam, *Best,* p. 577.
139 "I can't get out": Franklin, p. 644.
140 Response to Ba Gia: Gravel, III, p. 440.
141 "stop-gap": Ibid.
141 "indirection and dissimulation": Herring, p. 134.
141 "stirred up a veritable hornet's nest": Gravel, III, p. 462.
142 Rusk, Taylor, and the CIA respond to troop request: Karnow, p. 423.
142 Sharp, JCS, and McNamara support troop request: Ibid., p. 424.
143 Considers committing 173rd: Msg., Westmoreland to Sharp, June 13, 1965; Msg., Sharp to Westmoreland, June 13, 1965.
143 "commit U.S. troops to combat": Gravel, III, p. 461.
144 "overcome by events": Ibid.
144 Unveils campaign plan for McNamara: Westmoreland, *Soldier,* pp. 142–43.
145 "it was not very inspired deception": Gelb, p. 132.

145 Taylor's removal: Karnow, p. 378.

Chapter Eleven: Light at the End of the Tunnel

148 Operation Starlite: See Lynn, "Ordeal on the Van Tuong."
149 Sharp fears U.S. Army not ready to face NVA: Duiker, p. 239.
149 Westmoreland feels he must accept enemy challenge: Ibid.
151 There are numerous excellent accounts of the Ia Drang battle. Some of the best are Summer, "Bitter Triumph of the Ia Drang"; Gwin, "Ambush at Albany"; Triplett, "Ia Drang"; Kinnard, "Victory in the Ia Drang"; and Galloway, "Fatal Victory."
152 Fear of another Little Bighorn: Davidson, *Vietnam*, p. 324.
153 "into the delusion": Summers, "Bitter Triumph," p. 58.
153 "provided a valuable lesson": Ibid.
153 "social programs": Ibid.
154 "If the Ia Drang was a milestone": Galloway, p. 32.
154 North Vietnam's leaders debate strategy after Ia Drang: Duiker, pp. 240–41.
155 Cable to McNamara: Gravel, IV, pp. 403–20.
156 Wheeler tells what it will take to win in Vietnam: Halberstam, *Best*, p. 596.
156 Signa I: Karnow, p. 399.
156 "it will be a long war": Sheehan, *Pentagon Papers*, p. 466.
156 "will not guarantee success": Ibid.
157 "no sudden revelation": Davidson, *Vietnam*, p. 352.
157 Gelb's view of the quagmire theory: Gelb, pp. 131–33.

Chapter Twelve: Search and Destroy

159 Honolulu conference: Westmoreland, *Soldier*, pp. 131–32.
160 Memo mandating attritional warfare: Thompson, p. 10; Davidson, *Vietnam*, pp. 358–60.
161 "that they cannot win": Msg., Wheeler to Westmoreland, June 29, 1965.
161 "breaking the will of the DRV/VC": Quoted in Sharp, *Strategy*, p. 79.
162 The roots of the search-and-destroy strategy: Doughty, p. 31.
164 Johnson on removing Seaman: Msg., Johnson to Westmoreland, August 14, 1965.
168 Marine reluctance to go north: Chaisson, interview by Frank, pp. 294, 370–76. General Krulak details the difference he had with Westmoreland over strategy in his book, *First to Fight*, pp. 195–204.
169 "they sortie out": Doyle, p. 65.
169 "every man we put into hunting": Ibid.
169 Sheehan criticism: Sheehan, *Bright*, pp. 346–47, 629–33.
170 Criticism of Marine strategy: Doyles, p. 65; Doughty, pp. 38–40.

Chapter Thirteen: The Same Old Message

171 Political turmoil in I Corps: Karnow, pp. 445–50; Westmoreland, *Soldier*, pp. 168–76.
171 "What are we doing here": Karnow, p. 446.
171 "foolishness": Westmoreland, *Soldier*, p. 170.
173 Walt doubts NVA will invade I Corps: Shulimson, *U.S. Marines in Vietnam—1966*, p. 140.
173 A good account of Operation Hastings can be found in Wharton's "Invasion Repelled," pp. 159–76.
174 Krulak cable: Msg., Krulak to Westmoreland, July 22, 1966, quoted in Shulimson's *U.S. Marines in Vietnam—1966*, p. 177.
174 Westmoreland's reply: Ibid.
174 Marines mock Westmoreland: Ibid.
175 For a detailed account of McNamara's plans for a barrier across the DMZ see Hemingway's "The McNamara Line."
175 McNamara's trip to Vietnam: Westmoreland, *Soldier*, p. 154; Westmoreland, "Diary," October 10, 1966, pp. 2–12.
177 McNamara's memo: Memo, McNamara to Johnson, October 14, 1966, quoted in Gravel, IV, pp. 348–54.
178 "lot of shit": Halberstam, *Best*, p. 645.
178 JCS reaction to memo: Gravel, IV, pp. 356–61.
178 "I'm not gonna spit in China's face": Karnow, p. 318.
178 "chasing deer": Westmoreland, *Soldier*, p. 189.
178 Manila Conference: Ibid., p. 122.

Chapter Fourteen: Attacking the Base Areas

180 "any commander-in-chief who undertakes": Westmoreland, *Soldier*, p. 261.
182 Antiwar attack on his family: Ibid., p. 264.
182 Old-fashioned patriot: Davidson, *Vietnam*, p. 342.
183 "The antiwar movement was alien to him": Two-star general, interview with the author.
183 "might as well be considered part of North Vietnam": Msg., Westmoreland to Sharp and Wheeler, February 14, 1967.
184 Combined Campaign Plan for 1967: Sharp, *Report*, pp. 131–33.
187 "was a serious defeat": Hammond, p. 220.
189 "adverse military tide had been reversed": Msg., Wheeler to Westmoreland, March 9, 1967.
189 "I can only interpret the new figures to mean": Msg., Wheeler to Westmoreland, March 11, 1967.
190 "far from reflecting any inclination": Msg., Westmoreland to Wheeler, March 12, 1967.
190 "disputed issues": Msg., Westmoreland to Sharp, March 22, 1967.

190 "There is an amazing lack of boldness": Westmoreland, "Diary," January 29, 1967, p. 24.
191 Guam meeting: Westmoreland, *Soldier*, pp. 213–14.
191 Rostow accuses Westmoreland of exaggerating: Memo, Rostow to the president, March 22, 1967, quoted in Berman, *Lyndon*, pp. 33–34.
191 "tactical initiative": Msg., Westmoreland to JCS, March 28, 1967. See also Westmoreland, *Soldier*, p. 227.
191 Chiefs call for McNamara to mobilize the Reserves: Memo, JCS to McNamara, April 20, 1967.
192 "Before I came out here a year ago": Karnow, p. 512.
192 Rostow's public relations campaign: Hammond, pp. 338–40.
192 "battle-scarred soldiers": Karnow, p. 513.
193 Johnson orders Westmoreland to give speech: Hammond, pp. 287–88. Westmoreland, *Soldier*, p. 224.
193 "the American people informed": Westmoreland, *Soldier*, p. 224.

Chapter Fifteen: Public Relations Duty

194 Burned in effigy: Westmoreland, *Soldier*, p. 225.
194 AP speech: Ibid., p. 225; Kihss, p. 1; "Text of Westmoreland's Address at A.P. Meeting," p. 14.
195 Congressional response to speech: Herbers, p. 1; "Excerpts From Senate Exchange on Vietnam War Speech," p. 14; 1967 *Facts on File*, p. 146; Kenworthy, p. 1.
196 Editorial criticism: Hammond, p. 289.
196 Westmoreland defenders: "The War," p. 17.
196 Arrives in Columbia: "Westmoreland Visits Family in Columbia," p. 1.
197 Praises Negro servicemen: *Congressional Record*, April 26, 1967, p. A2046; Nicely, pp. 1–2; Prossner, pp. 1–2; Westmoreland, interview by Miles, pp. 19–21; Westmoreland, "Diary," April 26, 1967, pp. 13–14.
197 King and Carmichael criticism: 1967 *Facts on File*, pp. 138–39.
197 Billy Graham's support: "Graham Denounces Dissenters," p. 645.
198 Meeting with Johnson: Gravel, IV, pp. 151–53; meeting notes transcript, April 27, 1967, LBJ Library; Westmoreland, *Soldier*, pp. 227–28; Berman, *Lyndon*, pp. 34–36; Westmoreland, "Diary," April 27, 1967, pp. 14–17.
200 Hawks praise speech: CBS New Special Report, "Westmoreland: Senate Reaction," April 28, 1967, CBS Archives.
201 Doves praise speech: Ibid.
201 American people support speech: WHCF Name File, LBJ Library.
201 "overwhelmed": Westmoreland, *Soldier*, p. 229.
201 Credibility damaged by trip: Hammond, pp. 289–90.

Chapter Sixteen: Khe Sanh

202 Visit with Eisenhower: Westmoreland, *Soldier*, pp. 229–30; Westmoreland, "Diary," April 29, 1967, pp. 19–20.
204 Plan to invade Laos: Westmoreland, *Soldier*, pp. 271–72.
205 Krulak's feelings about Khe Sanh: Sheehan, *Bright*, p. 646.
206 "When you're at the Khe Sanh": Dougan, p. 42.

Chapter Seventeen: Abrams and Komer Arrive

207 McNamara attempts to convince Johnson not to okay troop request: Memo, McNamara to the President, May 19, 1967, quoted in Berman, *Lyndon*, pp. 46–48.
208 JCS react to memo: Memo, Wheeler to the President, May 20, 1967, quoted in Berman, *Lyndon*, pp. 46–47.
209 "simply not going to be provided": Msg., Sharp to Westmoreland, June 13, 1967.
210 General Johnson's dislike of Westmoreland's handling of the war: Perry, p. 174.
210 Abrams does not want job: Kanamine, interview by Lightner, p. 5.
210 Abrams heir apparent: Chaisson, interview by Frank, p. 56.
210 Relationship between Westmoreland and Abrams: Kerwin, interview by Bradshaw, p. 351.
210 "I'm here to help Westy": Cochran, p. 25.
210 Westmoreland's respect for Abrams: Ibid., pp. 25–26.
211 "to give his field and staff advisory effort": Clarke, p. 506.
211 For a good description of the one-war concept see Davidson, *Vietnam*, p. 411.
215 "though the enemy is tough": Msg., Westmoreland to his senior commander, quoted in Hammond, p. 385.
215 Meets with McNamara: Meeting notes, July 7, 1967, quoted in Berman, *Lyndon*, p. 54; Westmoreland, "Diary," July 7–9, 1967, pp. 1–2. Included in the diary is a copy of a Westmoreland briefing, titled, "Assessment of Alternatives."

Chapter Eighteen: Revolt of the Generals

216 McNamara's sudden optimism: Meeting notes, July 7, 1967, quoted in Berman, *Lyndon*, p. 55.
216 "We've begun to turn defeat into victory": Notes of meeting with Peter Lisagor of *Chicago Daily News*, quoted in Berman, *Lyndon*, p. 55.
217 "escalating military stalemate": Sheehan, *Pentagon Papers*, p. 472.
217 Press conference: Berman, *Lyndon*, p. 55.
218 Chiefs contemplate resigning: Perry, pp. 62–66.
219 "I was not about to go to the commander in chief": Perret, p. 497.

220 "I suffered my problems in Vietnam": Westmoreland, *Soldier*, p. 262.
220 "warn him of the likely consequences": Summers, pp. 167–68.

Chapter Nineteen: A Day in the Life

Much of this chapter is based on a lengthy interview I did with Major General Larry Budge, who was Westmoreland's aide in 1967. Also useful were Reedy, "A Typical Day in the Life of General Westmoreland"; Mulligan, "A Day with Westmoreland Keeps You Running"; Hughes, "The General Inspects the Vietnam War"; Hubbell and Reed, "The Man for the Job in Vietnam." The discussion about how World War II generals would have fared in Vietnam is from Furgurson, pp. 312–13. Westmoreland's sensitivity to the media was explored in Bergen's interview of Neel. For Westmoreland's transfer of DeSaussure, I relied on "Changing an Army," an oral history of General DePuy, which is available at the U.S. Military History Institute. Also helpful were two personal letters written to me by Major General Guy S. Meloy, who was a battalion commander during Operation Attleboro and very familiar with the DeSaussure "transfer."

Blair Clark's appraisal of Westmoreland in the November 1970 *Harper's* provided me with the most thorough and insightful delineation of Westmoreland's character and personality that I have read. Westmoreland discussed his signing of next-of-kin letters during an interview he gave to Laura Palmer, which she published as "The General at Ease." Westmoreland discussed his obsession with the Groupement Mobile debacle in his *A Soldier Reports*.

Chapter Twenty: Border Battles

230 "those who trembled": Thies, p. 336.
231 Ho, Thanh, and Giap: Pike, p. 349.
231 Momyer on COSVN: Momyer, pp. 296–97.
231 Thanh's death: Palmer, *Summons*, p. 121; Maitland, p. 99.
232 Politburo meets: Wirtz, p. 53; Duiker, pp. 261–65; Davidson, interview by Gittinger, pp. 36–41; Chaisson, interview by Frank, p. 207.
232 "taut as a bowstring": Duiker, p. 261.
234 Tet plan of attack: Pike, interview with the author; Davidson, interview by Gittinger, pp. 50–52.
235 Khe Sanh as phase three: Pike, interview with the author.
235 "no general uses 40,000 men": Davidson, interview by Gittinger, p. 51.
235 "logical conclusion": Pike, interview with author.
237 Operation Neutralize: Maitland, pp. 164–65.
237 "a Dienbienphu in reverse": Westmoreland, *Soldier*, p. 204.
238 Cancels news conference: Clarke, p. 331.
239 "Every minute hundreds of thousands of people die": Davidson, *Vietnam*, p. 12.

240 "It's been debated": Maitland, p. 183.
241 Editorial writers respond to Dak To: Hammond, p. 333.
241 "distorted": Ibid., p. 332.
241 "refutation": Ibid.
241 Opposed to graphic depictions of battles: Ibid., p. 213.
241 Tried to get censorship: Ibid.
242 "couldn't control": Neel, interview by Bergen.

Chapter Twenty-One: Switching on the Light

243 "court": Westmoreland, interview by McDonald, November 13–29, 1967.
243 Kraft, Reston criticize trip home: Hammond, pp. 334–36.
244 Drew Pearson column: Quoted in a memo from Walt Rostow to James R. Jones, November 14, 1967, LBJ Library.
244 "Westmoreland wasn't McNamara's golden boy": News conference at the White House with George McChristian, November 24, 1967. White House Press Office File, Press Secretaries News Conference, LBJ Library.
244 "to prevail": Westmoreland, *Soldier*, p. 276.
244 "The allegation that there is disillusionment": Statement by Secretary of Defense Robert S. McNamara, White House Press Conference File, Press Secretaries News Conference, November 14, 1967, LBJ Library.
245 Interview at Andrews AFB: Westmoreland, "Diary," November 15, 1967, p. 2. Transcript included in diary.
245 Briefs House Armed Services Committee: Westmoreland, *Soldier*, p. 231.
245 National Press Club speech: Westmoreland, "Diary," November 21, 1967, p. 7. Transcript of speech attached to diary. See also Oberdorfer, p. 105.
246 "Westmoreland had switched on the light": Oberdorfer, p. 105.
247 Private conversation with Johnson: Westmoreland, interview by Miles; Westmoreland, *Soldier*, p. 233.
248 "Probably no field commander in our history": Clark, "Westmoreland Appraised," p. 98.
248 "All I know": Westmoreland, "Diary," November 29–December 16, 1967, p. 1. Transcript attached.
248 Westmoreland's hopes for a new administration: Westmoreland, *Soldier*, p. 448.
249 "As you know": Msg., Westmoreland to Sharp, January 8, 1968.
249 "major NVA force": Msg., Sharp to Westmoreland, January 25, 1968.
249 Westmoreland continues pushing for invasion of Laos: Msg., Westmoreland to Sharp, January 29, 1967.

Chapter Twenty-Two: Battling the Marines

259 "If we'd gotten the whole battle plan": Oberdorfer, p. 121.
260 Signals of impending attack: Wirtz, pp. 202–203; Dougan, pp. 10–11.

261 "The enemy has decided": Msg., Westmoreland to Wheeler, December 20, 1967.
262 Wheeler's speech: Hammond, p. 342.
262 Johnson's speech: Ibid.
263 Weyand's warning: Oberdorfer, pp. 137–38.
264 Argument with the Marines over the single-management concept: Davidson, p. 501; Pisor, pp. 126–27, 243; Westmoreland, interview by Ganderson, p. 181; Chaisson, interview by Frank, p. 236. The cable exchange between Westmoreland, Cushman, and Sharp can be found in Nalty, pp. 68–70.
265 Cushman pleads with JCS: Westmoreland, *Soldier*, pp. 343–44.
266 Considers resigning: Ibid., p. 344.
266 Explains case to Wheeler: Davidson, *Vietnam*, p. 501.
266 "dog's breakfast": Westmoreland, *Soldier*, p. 343.
267 "narrow and parochial": Westmoreland, interview with author.
267 Sends Davidson to Khe Sanh: Wirtz, p. 204; Prados, p. 228–29; Davidson, *Vietnam*, pp. 497–98.
267 Davidson briefs Westmoreland: Davidson, *Vietnam*, pp. 498–99.
267 "Abe, you're going to have to go up there": Davidson, *Vietnam*, p. 556.
268 "The military professionalism of the Marines": Msg., Westmoreland to Wheeler, January 22, 1968.
268 "a slap in the face": Tompkins, interviewed by Frank, p. 82.
268 "fire Lownds on the spot": Palmer, interview with author.
268 Tonc surrenders: Dougan, p. 44.
269 "the enemy will soon seek victories": Msg., Westmoreland to Wheeler and Sharp, January 20, 1968.
270 Operation Niagara is well described in "How the Battle of Khe Sanh Was Won." See also Nalty, p. 82; and Pearson, p. 76.
271 Meeting with Bunker: Msg., Westmoreland to Sharp and Wheeler, January 24, 1968.
272 Wants to attack enemy forces along the DMZ: Msg., Westmoreland to Sharp, January 24, 1968.
272 Johnson's obsession with Khe Sanh: Kearns, p. 271; Berman, *Lyndon*, pp. 141–44.
273 "We should not seek battle": Prados, p. 357.
273 Rationale for Khe Sanh: Msg., Westmoreland to Wheeler and Sharp, January 12, 1968.
273 Tries to calm Johnson's fears: Pisor, pp. 134–35.
274 Taylor makes independent assessment of Khe Sanh: Schandler, p. 88; Nalty, p. 17; Pisor, p. 118 (paper).
275 "I don't want no damn Dinbinfoo [*sic*]": Pisor, p. 118.
275 "oath in blood": Ibid.
275 Warning from NSA: Wirtz, p. 214.
275 "almost unprecedented volume": Ibid., p. 215.
275 "the forces struggling for peace": Ibid., p. 217.

275 "ventured no starting date": Westmoreland, *Soldier*, pp. 320–21; Wirtz, p. 216.
276 Prepares to use nuclear weapons: Schandler, p. 88.

Chapter Twenty-Three: Tet

277 Bombing the cave: Prados, pp. 298–99; Dougan, p. 46.
278 Bombing prematurely triggers Tet attacks: Dougan, p. 46.
278 The best description of the Tet attacks can be found in Oberdorfer, *Tet*.
279 "This is going to happen": Dougan, p. 12; Oberdorfer, pp. 132–32; Davidson, interview by Gittinger, p. 53.
280 "the likelihood of immediate widespread attacks": Westmoreland, *Soldier*, p. 323.
280 Reason warnings not taken seriously: Wirtz, pp. 221–22.
280 Westmoreland, Sharp claim they gave Washington ample warning: Wirtz, p. 234; Sharp, *Strategy*, p. 215.
281 "first priority effort": Oberdorfer, p. 23.
282 "like a butcher shop in Eden": Ibid., p. 33.
282 "balanced perspective": Ibid.
282 "normally garrulous": Ibid.
282 Speech to reporters: Ibid., p. 34.
283 "standing in the ruins": Ibid.
283 "How could any effort against Saigon": Braestrup, p. 108.
283 "Was the word of a professional military man": Westmoreland, *Soldier*, p. 325.
284 "We had little faith in what General Westmoreland said": Braestrup, p. 85.
284 "dozens of persons on the scene": Ibid.
284 "a Viet Cong suicide squad": Ibid.
284 "on buildings and rooftops": Ibid., pp. 116–17.
284 "roof had fallen in in Vietnam": Ibid., p. 110.
284 "demolished the myth": Hammond, p. 344.
284 McClendon quote: Ibid.
284 "undermined": Ibid.
284 "state of great consternation": Westmoreland, interview with the author.
286 "some degree of control": Msg., Westmoreland to Wheeler, February 1, 1968.
286 "make a brief personal comment to the press": Hammond, p. 347.
286 Speech at JUSPAO: Ibid. See also Oberdorfer, p. 165.
287 Wheeler's news conference: Hammond, p. 347.
287 Press response to news conference: Ibid.
287 "would reassure the public": Karnow, p. 547.
287 "were receiving, reading, and disseminating": Oberdorfer, p. 159.
288 "television cameras": McDonald, "Communist thrust—the Tet Offensive of 1968," p. 152.
288 "the disaster image": Braestrup, p. 509.

289 "unworthy allies": Ibid., p. 144.
289 Westmoreland's actions ignored by press: Ibid., p. 254.
289 The press's handling of Giap: Ibid., p. 145.
290 Senators comment on Tet attacks: Ibid., p. 473.
290 "What the hell is going on?" Oberdorfer, p. 158.
291 "when all seemed lost": Ibid., p. 186.
291 "I watched the invasion": Karnow, p. 548.
292 "a very high degree of dissatisfaction": Sorley, p. 216. See also Perry, p. 183.
293 "Our losses were so immense": Dougan, p. 145.
293 "lost confidence": Karnow, p. 544.
294 "psychological victory": Ibid., p. 145.
294 "shattered public morale": Davidson, *Vietnam*, p. 438.
294 "contributed to mass pessimism": Taylor, *Swords*, p. 384.
294 "Vietcong casualties": Davidson, *Vietnam*, p. 436.
295 "never before Vietnam": Elegant, p. 89.
295 "rarely had contemporary crisis journalism": Braestrup, p. 508.
295 Media hostility to war: Herring, p. 200.
295 "indicated that far from suffering": Hammond, pp. 370–71.
296 "the lack of any effort by Johnson": Ibid., p. 373.

Chapter Twenty-Four: End of the Line

297 "intensity, coordination, and timing": President's Foreign Intelligence Advisory Board, p. 4.
297 "The first thing to say about Giap's Tet Offensive": Palmer, *Summons*, p. 179.
298 "Westmoreland's optimistic statements of victory": *Congressional Record*, February 16, 1968, p. 3085.
298 "was engaged in the vain art of self-delusion": "Westmoreland Criticized for Deluding Congress," p. 2.
298 "had just turned the corner": Buchwald, p. A15.
298 "half a million American soldiers": Schlesinger, *Robert Kennedy*, Vol. II, p. 879.
299 "had run into a dead end": "More of the Same Won't Do," p. 28.
299 "humiliated": Beech, p. 6.
299 "Westmoreland may go down in history": Purcell, p. 6.
299 Childs's criticism: Quoted in *The Congressional Record*, February 7, 1968, pp. 3086–87.
299 "seems to have no idea": Ibid.
299 Wheeler, McNamara respond to rumor Westmoreland will be relieved: "General Westmoreland Shift Held Unlikely," p. 4.
299 "As a personal matter": Msg., Wheeler to Westmoreland, February 4, 1968; Westmoreland, *Soldier*, p. 336.
300 "is there any reinforcements or help": Msg., Wheeler to Westmoreland, February 4, 1968.

300 Gives optimistic appraisal of situation: Msg., Westmoreland to Wheeler, February 4, 1968.

300 The entire story of Lang Vei is well told in Albright's *Seven Firefights in Vietnam.*

301 Ladd pleads with Westmoreland to intervene: Prados, pp. 332–33; Westmoreland, *Soldier,* pp. 340–41; Oberdorfer, p. 189.

301 "cold fury": Simmons, p. 101.

301 Da Nang meeting: Prados, pp. 332–33; Oberdorfer, pp. 189–90; Davidson, p. 443.

302 "One of Westy's best days": Oberdorfer, p. 190.

303 For the full story of Wheeler's machinations and the 206,000-troop request, see Schandler's *The Unmaking of the President.*

303 Problems facing Wheeler: Schandler, p. 109.

304 "the evil genius of the war": Willenson, p. 97.

304 "Do you need reinforcements?": Msg., Wheeler to Westmoreland, February 8, 1968.

304 "it was only prudent to plan": Msg., Westmoreland to Sharp and Wheeler, February 8, 1969.

304 "Please understand": Msg., Wheeler to Westmoreland, February 9, 1968.

305 "immediately a marine regiment": Westmoreland, *Soldier,* p. 352.

305 "Specifically your message is interpreted here": Msg., Wheeler to Westmoreland, February 12, 1968.

305 "I am expressing a firm request": Msg., Westmoreland to Wheeler, February 12, 1968.

305 "It is not clear at this time": *Report of the Chairman, JCS,* February 27, 1968, quoted in Schandler, pp. 110–14.

306 Johnson visits Eisenhower: Tom Johnson's Notes of Meetings, February 12, 1968, LBJ Library; Oberdorfer, p. 195.

306 "the question arose": Msg., Wheeler to Westmoreland, February 12, 1968.

307 "kindled General Westmoreland's long-held hope": Davidson, *Vietnam,* p. 354.

307 Sharp doesn't think troop ceiling can stand: Msg., Sharp to Westmoreland, February 15, 1968.

307 "reserve call-up": Westmoreland, *Soldier,* p. 354.

307 "Can handle only one major problem at a time": Msg., Wheeler to Westmoreland, February 9, 1968; Westmoreland, *Soldier,* p. 353.

307 "tired": Westmoreland, *Soldier,* p. 54.

307 "mirrored the gloom": Ibid.

307 Wheeler unnerved by rocket: Schandler, p. 108.

308 Briefs Wheeler: Ibid., pp. 107–08.

308 "clear understanding": Westmoreland, interview with the author.

308 Wheeler's pessimistic briefing: Schandler, p. 115.

309 "the Chairman of the Joint Chiefs": Ibid., p. 115.

309 Clifford chairs task force: Oberdorfer, pp. 286–88.

310 "enemy has any great capacity": Ibid., p. 290.
310 "denigrate the enemy": Msg., Wheeler to Westmoreland, March 8, 1968.
310 "would do his best to comply": Msg., Westmoreland to Wheeler, March 8, 1968.
310 Clifford's final report: Oberdorfer, p. 289.
311 "has touched off" Sheehan, "Westmoreland Requests 206,000 More Men," p. 1.
311 Westmoreland's shock: Schandler, p. 203; Westmoreland, *Soldier*, p. 358.
311 McGee's special report: Oberdorfer, p. 273.
311 Congressional reaction: Hammond, p. 382.
312 "I was directed to keep you informed": Msg., Wheeler to Westmoreland, March 12, 1968.
312 Responds to Wheeler's cable: Msg., Westmoreland to Wheeler, March 16, 1968, quoted in Schandler, p. 231.
312 Johnson's political consensus evaporates: Herring, p. 199.
312 Johnson meets with Acheson, Goldberg: Oberdorfer, p. 294.
313 Johnson announced Westmoreland's appointment as Army Chief: *1968 Facts on File*, p. 116.
313 Wise men level with Johnson: Berman, *Lyndon*, pp. 195–99.
313 Johnson speech: Ibid., pp. 200–201.
313 Editorial writers respond to transfer: Editorials from the *Buffalo Evening News, Chicago Tribune, New York Times,* and *Washington Post* were excerpted in the March 26, 1968 edition of the *Honolulu Advertiser.* The rest are: *Denver Post,* March 26, 1968, p. 22; *Wall Street Journal,* March 25, 1968, p. 2; *St. Louis Post Dispatch,* March 24, 1968, p. 18.
314 Wheeler's letter: Davidson, *Vietnam,* p. 480.
314 "the delay in announcement": Clifford, p. 511.
315 Brandon's account of meeting: Brandon, p. 130.
315 "that the full 206,000 men were needed": Sorley, p. 221.
315 "Oh, no, sir, Mr. President": Sorley, p. 222; Starry, interview by Bergen, p. 32.
316 "bitter": George McChristian's Notes of Meeting, April 8, 1968, LBJ Library.
316 "It was like two boxers": Westmoreland, *Soldier,* p. 410.
316 Bunker tells Westmoreland is it too late to expand war: Sheehan, *Bright,* p. 720.

Chapter Twenty-Five: Army Chief

319 "not to be a relief": Dougan, p. 51.
319 "The place was absolutely denuded": Tompkins, interview by Frank, p. 48.
320 "conned": Davidson, *Vietnam,* p. 456.

320 White House Meeting: Tom Johnson's Notes of Meeting, April 6, 1968, LBJ Library.
321 Westmoreland downgrades impact of Mini-Tet: Hammond, p. 290.
322 Westmoreland speech: Sorley, p. 229.
322 Abrams calls Kerwin: Ibid.
323 Fred's death: Palmer, "The General at Ease," p. 32.
324 WESTY SULKS: Perry, p. 197.
324 Wheeler pressures Westmoreland to appoint Palmer: Ibid.
324 Westmoreland wants his own man: Two-star general, interview with the author.
324 Tries to reassign Palmer: Palmer, interview by Shelton, pp. 415–17.
324 "appeared no longer valid": Westmoreland, interview with the author.
324 Abrams never liked Khe Sanh: Cochran, p. 27.
325 Abrams and Johnson discuss Khe Sanh: Sorley, pp. 225–26; Prados, p. 448.
325 Abrams's supposed tactical changes: Sorley, pp. 228–42.
326 Vietnam casualties: See Lewy, *America in Vietnam.*
326 Komer, Davidson claim Abrams made no changes: Davidson, *Vietnam,* p. 512.
326 Palmer agrees with Westmoreland: Palmer, *Summons,* pp. 223–25.
327 *New York Times, Time* praise Abrams: Buckley, "General Abrams Deserves a Better War," p. 36; "The General vs. 'The System,' " pp. 26–27.
327 Westmoreland distraught over article praising Abrams: Halberstam, *Best,* pp. 548–49.
327 McDonald, Sidle defend Westmoreland: Letter from Charles McDonald to Jonathan Larsen, Time-Life News Service, Saigon, March 17, 1971; Letter from Lieutenant General Winant Sidle to Hedley Donovan, March 18, 1971. Both letters located in Westmoreland History Notes, Box 22, Military History Institute.
328 *Time's* response: Letter from Barbara Stofer to Charles McDonald, March 30, 1971. Ibid.
328 "Have you ever read such unadulterated crap": Ibid.
329 "The moment of decision": Perry, p. 202.
329 "must have a breaking point": Morris, p. 165.
329 "They'll believe any threat of force": Haldeman, p. 83.
329 "sublime self-confidence": Herring, p. 221.
330 Upset with Laird's impatience: Davidson, *Vietnam,* p. 547.
330 Nixon sees Westmoreland as political liability: Palmer, interview by Shelton, p. 413.
330 Kissinger on Westmoreland as strategist: Kissinger, "The Vietnam Negotiations," p. 229.
330 "brought on some of their own troubles": Perry, p. 203.
330 Decides to travel: Palmer, interview by Shelton, p. 413.
330 "the facts of life": Westmoreland, interview by Ganderson, p. 49.
331 Speeches. Springfield: Just, pp. 186–87; Estill, p. 1. Nashville: "Command Marks General's Presence," p. 7. Worcester: Agnew, p. 17. Lin-

coln: Eutzy, p. 1. Penn State: Westmoreland, *Soldier,* p. 365. Portland: Homer, p. 5. Ohio State: Fenton, p. 1. U of C: "Westmoreland Addresses Court of Honor at UC," p. 1. Yale: O'Gara, p. 1.

Chapter Twenty-Six: Problems, Problems, Problems

334 "beyond belief": Westmoreland, *Soldier,* p. 375.
335 "that some members of the Nixon administration": Ibid.
335 "it's the dirty rotten Jews": Hersh, p. 135.
335 Picks Peers to lead investigation and MacCrate and Walsh to assist: Bilton, p. 292; Westmoreland, *Soldier,* p. 376.
336 Shocked by report: Wilton, p. 233.
336 Koster relieved: Kerwin, interview with the author.
336 "Don't let the bastards get you down": "U.S. Generals Charged Over My Lai," p. 8.
337 Stratton accusation: *Congressional Record,* February 4, 1971, pp. 1725–26.
337 "travesty of justice": Peers, p. xii.
337 Seaman action analyzed: Bilton, p. 328.
337 Actions taken against Koster and Young: Ibid., p. 326.
338 Stratton, Koster, Young criticize actions: Beecher, p. 1.
339 "surprised at the outcry": "Westmoreland Says He Harbors No Guilt," p. 1.
339 Westmoreland-Resor report: *Facts on File. South Vietnam–U.S.–Communist Confrontation in Southeast Asia, 1971,* Vol. 5, p. 203.
339 Citizens Commission of Inquiry: Sheehan, "Five Officers Say They Seek Formal War Crimes Inquiry," p. 7.
339 Vets Against the War Conference: Flint, p. 17.
340 New York City conference: Knoll, pp. 6, 113.
340 Taylor appears on *Cavett Show:* Sheehan, "Taylor Says By Yamashita Ruling Westmoreland May Be Guilty," p. 3.
341 Military investigates war crimes: Lewy, p. 317.
341 Sheehan review: Sheehan, "Conversations with Americans," Sec. 7, p. 5.
341 Reston review quoted in Lewy, p. 16.
342 Lane confronts Westmoreland: "Deputies Arrest 11 Anti-War Demonstrators," p. 1.
342 Judge Advocate General report: "Final Report of the Research Project: Conduct of the War in Vietnam, May 1971," Box 15, Westmoreland Papers, Military History Institute.
343 "That memo shook Westy to the core": Loory, p. 28.
343 Peers memo: Cincinnatus, pp. 206–10.
344 Commission study: "The Study on Military Professionalism," p. 53.
344 "masterpiece": Mylander, p. 301.
344 "saw a system": Fulghum, p. 43.

345 "I want to make it clear": Loory, p. 90.

345 "careerism": Mylander, p. 311.

346 For the most graphic account of the problems the military faced during this period, see Heinl's "The Collapse of the Armed Forces."

347 Problems in Germany: Atkinson, pp. 365–69.

348 Racial seminars: Mylander, p. 311.

349 Smothers's charge: Loory, p. 159.

349 Clay charge: *Congressional Record*, March 25, 1971, p. 82,310.

349 "negra": Prugh, interview by Badman, p. 40.

349 Davison reforms: Atkinson, p. 374.

349 "a state approaching collapse": Heinl, p. 30.

349 Changes Westmoreland made in the Army: *1970 Facts on File*, December 17, 1970, p. 22.

350 Oliphant cartoon: *Washington Post*, December 12, 1970, p. A22.

350 The *Army Times* cartoon is described in Henry's interview of Forsythe, p. 25.

350 Rogers comments: Mylander, p. 311.

350 Memos and letter: Ibid., p. 312.

351 Traditionalist "backlash": Ibid., p. 313.

Chapter Twenty-Seven: Bitter Fruit

355 NSSMI: Perry, p. 219.

355 Kissinger reveals plan to Westmoreland: Kissinger, *White House Years*, p. 1005.

356 "convinced Abrams would resent": Ibid.

357 "caused much pain and anxiety": Palmer, *25-Year War*, p. 115.

357 Haig report: Ibid.

357 Weyand accusation: Sorley, p. 314.

358 Giap's forces: Davidson, *Vietnam*, p. 605.

358 "staying power of the enemy": "Extracts from Press Conferences," January 31, 1972, Box 7, Westmoreland Papers, Military History Institute.

359 "ready to walk out the door": Perry, p. 237.

359 Claims he would not have resigned: Westmoreland, interview with the author.

359 "We've got to make the bastards pay": Perry, p. 237.

359 "The bastards have never been bombed": Palmer, *Summons*, p. 252.

360 "Vietnamization was a fact": Ibid., p. 324.

361 "unobtainable": Karnow, p. 648.

361 "stay there [in Vietnam] forever": Ibid.

361 Retirement ceremony: Cordry, p. 5.

361 Hackworth's illegal activities: Hackworth, pp. 38–40.

362 "Report commissioned: see Doughty, *Leaveworth Papers*.

363 "Would have been any more successful": Ibid., p. 39.

363 North Vietnam as real enemy: Summers, p. 88.

363 "of the likely consequences": Ibid., p. 168.

363 "I suffered my problems in Vietnam": Westmoreland, *Soldier*, pp. 261–62.

364 "there is no plausible way": Pike, interview with the author.

364 "Vietnam, Vietnam": Shaplen, p. 228.

364 Relationship between Johnson and Westmoreland: Clark, "Westmoreland Appraised," p. 98.

364 Trip to the ranch: Westmoreland, *Soldier*, p. 385–86; Alston, p. 5.

366 "Mel Laird had turned 'dove' ": Hersh, p. 597.

366 Meets with Nixon: Westmoreland, *Soldier*, p. 394.

367 "poor man's war": Van Tien Dung, p. 17.

368 Visit with Ford: Hersey, Sec. VI, pp. 102–103.

369 Call from Phuong: Wilson, pp. 20–21.

370 "sad day": "After the Fall," p. 20.

370 "tantamount to surrender": "Westy: U.S. Looks 'Like Damned Fool,' " p. 1.

Chapter Twenty-Eight: Politician Westmoreland

371 Jobs for retired general and admirals: Mylander, p. 280.

371 Douglas shocks Congress: Ibid., p. 281.

372 Haig after retirement: Babcock, p. A3.

372 Task force: McGinnis, "Winning Hearts and Minds in South Carolina," pp. 65–72; Page, "Westmoreland Named to Head Trade Effort," p. 1.

374 Talks with veterans: Page, "Westy: Prestige Not Consideration," p. 3.

374 "like a king waiting to be coronated," Ibid., p. 4.

375 "arrogant and ignorant": Ibid.

375 "hullabaloo": "Civilian Westmoreland," p. 2.

375 Liming criticism: Liming, "Special Report," p. 6.

376 "crass opportunist": Gibson, p. 6.

377 Westmoreland campaigning: See Gibson, "Finding Staff Westmoreland's Problem"; Woods, "Westy: Call Me Childs"; Arnett, "Governor's Race Puts New Light on General's Life"; Furgurson, "Westmoreland the Candidate"; and Liming, "Westmoreland—an Efficiency Report."

378 Edwards's campaign is thoroughly chronicled in Shirley, *Uncommon Victory*.

379 Accused of being too liberal: Bandy, p. 1; Shirley, p. 65.

379 Relieved he lost: "Westy Glad He Didn't Win," p. 1B; Hamrick, pp. 30–32.

Chapter Twenty-Nine: Another Soldier Reports

Reviews of *A Soldier Reports: Los Angeles Times*, January 22, 1976, Book Sec., p. 1; *Wall Street Jurnal*, February 24, 1976, p. 18; *National Review*, June 11, 1976, pp. 612–16; *London Times*, May 10, 1976, p. 5; *New York Times*, February 1, 1976, p. 5; *New York Times*, February 18, 1976, p. 5; *Washington Post*, January 25, 1976, Sec. G, p. 13.

382 Grant's memoirs: Woodward, *Meet General Grant*, pp. 494–95; Pershing's: Vandiver, p. 1086; Eisenhower's: Ambrose, pp. 474–75, 560; MacArthur's: Clayton, pp. 683–85.
382 Conversation with McGinnis: McGinnis, p. 14.
384 "I said to myself": Brewin, p. 42.
385 Criticized for giving speeches: Ibid., p. 43.
385 "his friends regarded these forays": Kowet, p. 68.
385 Hostile audiences: Wilson, p. 20.
386 Speeches in the late 1970s: Kowet, p. 68.
386 Speech at Southern Connecticut State: Beach, p. 5.

Chapter Thirty: "Rattlesnaked"

Readers wanting a fuller treatment of the CBS libel trial and the events that led up to it should read Don Kowet's *A Matter of Honor* and Bob Brewin and Sydney Shaw's *Vietnam on Trial*. Kowet's book covers the period from the airing of the CBS documentary to Westmoreland's decision to file suit. Brewin and Shaw cover the same ground as Kowet, but end with the trial and its aftermath. Kowet is a conservative, and his book is a blistering attack on the CBS documentary and on the men who made it. Brewin and Shaw, on the other hand, are liberals. They, however, take a middle point in their book, giving each side of the controversy equal coverage. I relied heavily on both books. I also found helpful a series of articles about the trial written by Connie Bruck for *The American Lawyer*. Bruck, who seemed to favor CBS, provided some brilliant insights into the character of the Westmoreland camp's chief litigator, Dan Burt. A fourth source for the chapter was Renata Adler. Adler wrote two lengthy pieces on the trial for *The New Yorker*, which were subsequently published as *Reckless Disregard*. Although left leaning, Adler surprised not a few people by concluding that CBS had shown a "reckless disregard" for the truth while producing their documentary and in the process had done grievous harm to Westmoreland's reputation and to journalistic standards. A final source that I relied on heavily was *Westmoreland v. CBS*, which consists of two drawers of microfilm, on which is stored most of the more than eighty thousand pages of documents generated by the trial. Included are copies of the depositions, exhibits, the trial transcript, and a multitude of other items. A printed guide allows easy access to the microfilm. Copies of the collection can be found in a dozen libraries around the country.

Documents captured during Operations Cedar Falls and Junction City: Dougan, p. 22. For a more comprehensive account of Adams's analyses of these captured documents see *Vietnam on Trial*.
388 "What am I going to tell Congress?": Brewin, p. 329.
388 "If I send that cable": Ibid., p. 322.
389 "Joe, we're not fighting these people.": Ibid., p. 265.
389 "They were the ones": Dougan, p. 23.
389 "essentially low-level fifth columnists": Ibid.

389 OB conference: Ibid.

390 Adams-Crile proposal: Brewin, pp. 26–27.

390 Westmoreland is interviewed: transcript of CBS Reports, pp. 12–23, CBS Archives; Kowet, pp. 61–66.

393 "village idiot": Davidson, *Vietnam*, p. 343.

394 Sawyer announces documentary: Kowet, p. 159.

395 Full-page ad: *New York Times*, January 22, 1982, p. A32.

396 "rendered an important service": Carter, p. 27.

396 "victimized by mendacious intelligence": "War, Intelligence and Truth," p. 18E.

396 "truly extraordinary": Buckley, "The Uncounted Enemy," p. A15.

396 News conference: Kaiser, p. A3; Kowet, pp. 165–69.

398 Shelton letter: Schneir, card 871.

399 Negative response from vets: Ibid., card 872.

400 Benjamin Report: Kowet, pp. 270–71.

400 Sauter memo: Ibid., pp. 221–22.

Chapter Thirty-One: Witnesses for Westmoreland

402 "General, let's get this straight.": Ibid., p. 225.

402 "a complete apology": Ibid., p. 226.

402 Second press conference: Ibid., pp. 229–31.

403 Accused of being point man for right wing forces: Brewin, p. 92.

404 "Anatomy" honored: Ibid.

404 Carter reverses himself: Ibid., p. 183.

405 Greeting from supporters: Ibid., p. 213.

405 Confrontation with Ellsburg: "Jury Picked in CBS Case," p. 6.

405 "I was so alone": Brewin, p. 213.

406 Leval's instructions to the jury: Brewin, p. 216.

406 Burt's opening statement: Schneir, cards 888–898.

407 Boies's opening statement: Ibid., cards 889–90.

408 Komer testimony: Ibid., cards 894–96.

409 Caton testimony: Ibid., cards 896–97.

409 Davidson testimony: Ibid., cards 899–902.

409 Godding testimony: Ibid., cards 904–906.

409 "those damn depositions": Bruck, "Westmoreland Case Gets Off to a Rocky Start," p. 33.

410 Graham testimony: Schneir, cards 907–11.

410 McNamara testimony: Ibid., cards 947–48.

411 Flies to Washington for dedication of statue: Brewin, p. 259–60.

412 Ceremony at Arlington: Brisbane, pp. A1, A14.

412 "needed the psychological boost": Brewin, p. 260.

412 Westmoreland testimony: Schneir, cards 926–46.

Chapter Thirty-Two: Witnesses for CBS

415 "until Westmoreland took the stand": Bruck, "The Soldier Takes the Stand," p. 115.
417 Joyce expects CBS to lose: Ibid., p. 117.
418 Crile testimony: Brewin, pp. 282–84.
418 "cotton batting of verbosity": Ibid., p. 283.
418 "I don't know what the hell": Ibid., p. 285.
418 Wallace traumatized: Shales, pp. D1, D4.
419 Wallace breakdown: Boyer, pp. 193–94; Brewin, p. 289.
419 Refuses to take advantage of Wallace: Westmoreland, interview with the author.
419 Send flowers: Brewin, p. 289.
419 Klein testimony: Schneir, cards 966–67.
420 Adams testimony: Ibid., cards 972–82.
420 "had never seen the complete show": Brewin, p. 301.
422 Allen testimony: Schneir, cards 982–86.
423 Friedman testimony: Ibid., cards 995–96.
423 Embree testimony: Ibid., card 996.
424 McChristian testimony: Ibid., cards 999–1000.
424 Westmoreland keeps self in check: Brewin, p. 315.
426 Hawkins testimony: Schneir, cards 10,007–09.
428 "When Hawkins stepped down": Brewin, p. 343.

Chapter Thirty-Three: Westy's Revenge

430 "If he loses in truth": Brewin, p. 354.
430 Burt's personal problems: Brewin, p. 365; Davidson, *Secrets*, p. 89.
430 Scaife unhappy with Burt: Brewin, pp. 365–66.
431 "were no better than the flip of a coin": Ibid., p. 354; Davidson, *Secrets*, p. 89.
431 "At first I didn't believe it.": Ibid., p. 350.
431 Reads statement at Harley Hotel: Henry, pp. 70–71; Brewin, p. 344.
431 "classic visage": Neel, interview by Bergen, p. 182.
432 Wallace refuses to concede: Randolph, "General, CBS End their War, Still Quarrel," p. A1.
432 "What a bunch of baloney": Ibid.
432 statements on camera: Ibid., p. A12.
433 Leval's statement: Brewin, pp. 356–57.
433 How jurors intended to vote: Randolph, "Judge Excuses Jury in General's Suit Against CBS," pp. A1, A6; Brewin, pp. 356–57.
433 ". . . the truth is probably unknowable": Powell, p. C8.
433 "questions of history": Ibid.
434 "took a thesis": Adler, p. 66.
434 "They favored the image": Brewin, p. 355.

434 Cartoons: *Boston Globe*, February 21, 1985; *Los Angeles Times*, February 20, 1985.
434 "All the face-saving stipulations": Lombardi editorial quoted in Brewin, p. 354.
434 "his case had fallen apart": Ibid.
434 "no matter what face he put on": Ibid., p. 355.
435 "crude attempt by ideologues": MacArthur, "A Plaintiff Ill-Used," p. E9.
435 "stayed home": Zirin, pp. 3, 4.
435 "trying to get the media exposure": Randolph, "General, CBS End Their War, Still Quarrel," p. A12.
435 Addresses National Press Club: Transcript of Speech, National Press Club Archives; Brewin, pp. 360–63.
436 Westmoreland's new popularity: Barnes, p. 21; Brewin, p. 364.

Much of the section dealing with the parade is based on William Mullen's "After 11 Years an Emotional Parade," which appeared in the *Sunday Magazine* section of the *Chicago Tribune* on August 17, 1986, and on a WBBM video of the parade, which I viewed at the Museum of Broadcast Journalism in Chicago. I also utilized numerous other articles written for the *Tribune* by Anne Keegan, Wes Smith, Robert Davis, and Patrick Reardon.

INTERVIEWS

Location abbreviations

AC—Author's collection.

HMD—History and Museums Division, Headquarters, U.S. Marine Corp, Washington Navy Yard, Washington, D.C.

LBJ—Lyndon Baines Johnson Library, Austin, Texas.

MHI—Military History Institute, Carlisle, Pennsylvania.

Almquist, Lt. Gen. Elmer H. Interviewed by Lt. Col. Steve C. Glick, April 1976. MHI.

Bartholomees, Col. James D. (Ret). Interviewed by the author, January 21, 1992. AC.

Berger, Ambassador Samuel. Interviewed by James B. Bergen and Col. John M. Callison, May 17, 1977. MHI.

Blackwell, Elizabeth Lyles. Interviewed by the author, November 18, 1991. AC.

Brown, Maj. Gen. Charles P. Interviewed by Col. John C. Burlingame, January 31, 1983. MHI.

Budge, Maj. Gen. Larry (Ret.). Interviewed by the author, June 13, 1992 and August 2, 1992. AC.

Chaisson, Lt. Gen. John A. Interviewed by Benis M. Frank, 1974. HMD.

Clarkson, Margaret Westmoreland. Interviewed by the author. November 29, 1991. AC.

Corcoran, Lt. Gen. Charles A. Interviewed by Lt. Col. Joseph A. Langer, Jr., 1975. MHI.

Cowles, Lt. Gen. Donald A. Interviewed by Lt. Col. Alvin G. Wheeler and Lt. Col. Ronald E. Craven, December 20, 1975. MHI.

Critternberger, Maj. Gen. Willis D. (Ret.). Interviewed by the author, February 21, 1992.

Davidson, Lt. Gen. Phillip (Ret.). Interviewed by Ted Gittinger, March 30, 1982. LBJ.

Davis, Lt. Gen. John J. Interviewed by Lt. Col. Robert J. Fullerton, 1986. MHI.

Davison, Gen. Michael S. Interviewed by Col. Douglas H. Farmer and Lt. Col. Dale K. Brudwig, February 22, 1976. MHI.

Earle, Col. Wilton (Ret.). Interviewed by the author, November 17, 1991. AC.

Ewell, Lt. Gen. Julian J. Interviewed by Robert Crowley and Lt. Col. Norman M. Bissell, nd. MHI.

Flanagan, Lt. Gen. Edward (Ret.). Interviewed by the author, February 2, 1991. AC.

Forrester, Gen. Eugene P. Interviewed by Lt. Col. Raymond K. Bluhm, 1985. MHI.

Forsythe, Gen. Eugene P. Interviewed by Lt. Col. Frank L. Henry, 1974. MHI.

Glover, Hayne. Interviewed by the author, November 17, 1991. AC.

Goodpaster, Gen. Andrew J. Interviewed by Col. William D. Johnson and Lt. Col. James C. Ferguson, 1976. MHI.

Hammond, Wardlaw. Interviewed by the author, November 20, 1991. AC.

Harkins, Gen. Paul D. Interviewed by Maj. Jacob B. Couch, Jr., April 28, 1974. MHI.

Heintges, Lt. Gen. John A. Interviewed by Jack A. Pellicci, 1974, MHI.

Hodson, Maj. Gen. Kenneth J. Interviewed by Lt. Col. Robert E. Boyer, August 27, 1976.

Ignatius, Honorable Paul R. Interviewed by Lt. Col. James P. Bergen and Col. John Collison, March 11, 1977. MHI.

Jackson, Elizabeth Jennings. Interviewed by the author, November 20, 1991. AC.

Jones. Lt. Gen. William K. Interviewed by Benis M. Frank, April 13, 1973. HMD.

Kanamine, Col. Ted. Interviewed by Lt. Col. Tom Lightner and Lt. Col. Steve Glik, 1976. MHI.

Kerwin, Gen. Walter T. Interviewed by the author, December 8, 1992. AC.

Kerwin, Gen. Walter T. Interviewed by Lt. Col. Jack Bradshaw and Lt. Col. Bill Sweet, 1974. MHI.

Kerwin, Gen. Walter T. Interviewed by Lt. Col. Doehle, 1980. MHI.

Kerwin, Gen. Walter T. Interviewed by Lt. Col. Albin G. Wheeler and Lt. Col. Ronald D. Craven, April 9, 1976. MHI.

Kinnard, Lt. Gen. Harry W. O. Interviewed by Lt. Col. Jacob B. Couch, Jr., June 20, 1983. MHI.

Kirby, Leo. Interviewed by the author. November 19, 1991. AC.

Kroesen, Gen. Frederick J. Interviewed by Lt. Col. Jerry D. Front, 1987. MHI.

Krulak, Lt. Gen. Victor H. Interviewed by Benis M. Frank, 1970. HMD.

Ladd, Col. Jonathan F. Interviewed by Lt. Col. James P. Bergen and Lt. Col. William M. Burleson, February 26, 1977. MHI.

Lemley, Lt. Gen. Harry. Interviewed by Lt. Col. Jerry D. Frost, 1987. MHI.

McGarrigle, Col. George (Ret.). Interviewed by the author, February 10, 1993. AC.

Marchant, Luther. Interviewed by the author, November 17, 1991. AC.

Marshall, Brig. Gen. S.L.A. Interviewed by Lt. Col. George J. Stapleton, 1974. MHI.

Mildren, Gen. Frank T. Interviewed by Lt. Col. Steve Glick and Tom Lightner, February 24, 1976. MHI.

Neel, Maj. Gen. Spurgeon H. Interviewed by Lt. Col. James P. Bergen and Lt. Col. Angelo de Guttadauro, March 18, 1977. MHI.

Palmer, Gen. Bruce, Jr. (Ret.). Interviewed by Col. Rick Bradshaw, May 29, 1975. MHI.

Palmer, Gen. Bruce, Jr. Interviewed by Lt. Col. James Shelton and Lt. Col. Edward Smith, December 5, 1975. MHI.

Peers, Lt. Gen. William P. Interviewed by Lt. Col. Breen and Lt. Col. Moore, June 27, 1977. MHI.

Person, Maj. Gen. Wilton B. Interviewed by Lt. Col. Herbert J. Green and Col. Thomas M. Crean, 1985. MHI.

Pike, Douglas. Interviewed by the author, June 13, 1992 and September 8, 1992. AC.

Polk, Gen. James H. Interviewed by Lt. Col. Roland D. Taush, May 15, 1972. MHI.

Prugh, Gen. James H. Interviewed by Maj. James A. Badami. Col. Thomas D. Andrews and Col. Patrick A. Tocher, July 11, 1975. MHI.

Rich, Lt. Gen. Charles W. Interviewed by Lt. Col. Steve Glick and Lt. Col. Thomas Lightner, February 25, 1976. MHI.

Rosson, Gen. William B. Interviewed by Lt. Col. Douglas R. Burgess, 1981. MHI.

Starry, Gen. Donn. Interviewed by Lt. Col. Kim Bergen and Lt. Col. Bill Burleson, December 14, 1976. MHI.

Sutherland, Gen. James W. Interviewed by Col. Steve Glick and Lt. Col. Tom Lightner, 1976. MHI.

Taylor, Gen. Maxwell D. Interviewed by Col. Richard A. Manion, October 19, 1972. MHI.

Tompkins, Maj. Gen. Rathvon McClure. Interviewed by Benis M. Frank, 1973. HMD.

Walt, Gen. Lewis W. Interviewed by Paige E. Mulhollan, June 24, 1969. LBJ.

Warner, Gen. Volney F. Interviewed by Col. Dean W. Owen, February 2, 1983. MHI.

Westmoreland, Edna. Interviewed by the author, February 10, 1991. AC.

Westmoreland, Gen. William C. Interviewed by Lt. Col. Marvin Ganderson, 1982. MHI.

Westmoreland, Gen. William C. Interviewed by Maj. Paul L. Miles, Jr., October 10, 1970. MHI.

Westmoreland, Gen. William C. Interviewed by Dorothy Pierce McSweeny, February 8, 1969. LBJ.

Westmoreland, William C. Interviewed by the author, 1991–1993. AC.

Wetzel, Gen. Robert L. (Ret.). Interviewed by the author, November 23, 1991. AC.

Wheeler, Gen. Earle G. Interviewed by Dorothy Pierce McSweeny, August 21, 1968. LBJ.

Wood, Gen. Robert J. Interviewed by Lt. Col. William E. Narus, Jr., 1973. MHI.

Zais, Gen. Melvin. Interviewed by Lt. Col. William Golden and Col. Richard C. Rice, 1977. MHI.

BIBLIOGRAPHY

Adams, Sam. "Vietnam Cover-up: Playing with Numbers—a CIA Conspiracy Against Its Own Intelligence." *Harper's*, May 1975.

Adler, Renata. "Annals of Law, Two Trials II." *New Yorker*, June 23, 1986.

"After the Fall: Reactions and Rationales." *Time*, May 12, 1975.

Agnew, John C. "Project Concern Project Praised by Westmoreland." *The Gazette*, April 14, 1969.

Albright, John, John A. Cash, and Allan W. Sandstrum. *Seven Firefights in Vietnam*. Washington, D.C.: U.S. Government Printing Office, 1970.

Alston, John A. "General Says LBJ Knew Death Near." *Charleston News and Courier*, January 24, 1975.

Ambrose, Stephen. *Eisenhower: Soldier, General of the Army, President-Elect*. New York: Simon and Schuster, 1983.

Arnett, Peter. "Governor's Race Puts New Light on General's Life." *Charleston News and Courier*, June 14, 1974.

Atkinson, Rick. *The Long Gray Line*. Boston: Houghton Mifflin, 1989.

Babcock, Charles R. "Haig Discloses Earning of $3 Million in 2 Years." *Washington Post*, May 25, 1987.

Bandy, Lee. "Westmoreland: Cards Stacked Against Me." *The State*, August 5, 1974.

Baritz, Loren. *Backfire*. New York: William Morrow, 1985.

Barnes, Fred. "Westy's Revenge." *New Republic*, April 6, 1987.

Basset, Lawrence, and Stephen E. Pelz. "The Failed Search for Victory: Vietnam and the Politics of War." In *Kennedy's Quest for Victory*, ed. Thomas G. Patterson. Oxford, U.K. Oxford University Press, 1989.

Beach, Randall. "Draft, Military Buildup Urged." New Haven, Conn.: *Register*, October 21, 1981.

Beech, Keyes. "Westmoreland Image Tarnished by Red Drive." *New York Post*, March 9, 1968.

Beecher, William. "General Demoted over My Lai Case." *New York Times*, May 20, 1971.

Berman, Larry. *Lyndon Johnson's War*. New York: Norton, 1989.

———. *Planning a Tragedy: The Americanization of the War in Vietnam*. New York: Norton, 1982.

Bilton, Michael, and Kevin Sim. *Four Hands in My Lai*. New York: Viking, 1992.

Blumenson, Martin. *Breakout and Pursuit*. United States Army in World War II. Washington, D.C.: U.S. Government Printing Office. 1961.

———. *Kasserine Pass*. New York: Houghton Mifflin, 1966.

———. *Patton*. New York: William Morrow, 1985.

Boettcher, Thomas D. *Vietnam, the Valor and the Sorrow*. Boston: Little, Brown, 1985.

Boyer, Peters J. *Who Killed CBS*. New York: Random House, 1988.

Braestrup, Peter. *Big Story*. New Haven, Conn.: Yale University Press, 1983.

Bradley, Omar. *A Soldier's Story*. New York: Henry Holt, 1951.

Brandon, Henry. *Anatomy of Error: The Secret History of the Vietnam War*. London: Andre Deutsch, 1970.

Brewin, Bob, and Sydney Shaw. *Vietnam on Trial*. New York: Atheneum, 1987.

Brisbane, Arthur S. "Reconciliation Theme Voiced in Mall Ceremony." *Washington Post*, November 12, 1984.

Brown, Varina D. *A Colonel at Gettysburg and Spotsylvania*. Columbia, S.C.: The State Company, 1931.

Bruck, Connie. "The Soldier Takes the Stand." *American Lawyer*, January/February, 1985.

————. "Westmoreland's Case Gets Off to a Rocky Start." *American Lawyer*, December 1984.

Buchwald, Art. " 'We Have Enemy on the Run' Says Gen. Custer at Big Horn." *New York Times*, February 6, 1968.

Buckley, Kevin P. "General Abrams Deserves a Better War." *New York Times Magazine*, October 5, 1969.

Buckley, William F. "The Untouched Enemy." *Washington Post*, February 2, 1982.

Caldwell, J.F.J. *The History of a Brigade of South Carolinians*. Dayton, Ohio: Morningside Press, 1984.

Carlton, David L. *Mill and Town in South Carolina, 1880–1920*. Baton Rouge, La.: Louisiana State University Press, 1982.

Carter, Hodding. "Time to Trust the Government Again, Right?" *Wall Street Journal*, January 28, 1982.

CBS Reports transcript. "The Uncounted Enemy: A Vietnam Deception," January 23, 1982.

Childs, Marquis. "On Westmoreland, Generals and War," *Washington Post*, February 7, 1968.

Cincinnatus. *Self-Destruction*. New York: Norton, 1987.

"Civilian Westmoreland." *Time*, January 21, 1975.

Clark, Blair. "Westmoreland Appraised: Questions and Answers," *Harper's*, November 1970.

Clark, Mark Edmond. "General Maxwell Taylor and His Successful Campaign Against the Strategy of Massive Retaliation." *Army History*, Fall 1990.

Clarke, Jeffrey J. *Advise and Support: The Final Years, 1965–1973*. Washington, D.C.: U.S. Army Center of Military History/Government Printing Office, 1988.

Clayton, James D. *The Years of MacArthur*, Vol. III, *Triumph and Disaster*. Boston: Houghton Mifflin, 1985.

Clifford, Clark, with Richard Holbrooke. *Counsel to the President*. New York: Random House, 1991.

Cochran, Alexander S. "The Tragic Commander." *Vietnam Magazine*, December 1989.

"Command Marks General's Presence." *The Banner*, February 14, 1968.

Conroy, Pat. *The Boo*. Verona, Va.: McClure Press, 1970.

Cordry, Charles W. "Westmoreland Gets Full-Dress Army Farewell." *Baltimore Sun*, July 1, 1972.

Davidson, Phillip. *Secrets of the Vietnam War*. Novato, Calif.: Presidio Press, 1990.

————. *Vietnam at War*. Novato, Calif.: Presidio Press, 1988.

"Deputies Arrest 11 Anti-War Demonstrators, Including Mark Lane, at Westmoreland Talk." *The Idaho Statesman*, August 21, 1971.

Dodson, James. "Neither Athens nor Sparta." *Atlanta Weekly*, January 9, 1983.

Dougan, Clark, and Stephen Weiss. *The Vietnam Experience: Nineteen Sixty-Eight*. Boston: Boston Publishing Co., 1983.

Doughty, Robert A. *Leavenworth Papers. Volume I: The Evolution of U.S. Army Tactical Doctrine, 1946–76*. Fort Levenworth, Kan.: Combat Studies Institute (U.S. Army Command and General Staff College), 1979.

Doyle, Edward, and Samuel Lipsman. *The Vietnam Experience: America Takes Over, 1965–67*. Boston: Boston Publishing Co., 1982.

Duiker, William J. *The Communist Road to Power in Vietnam*. Boulder, Colo.: Westview Press, 1981.

Dunlop, William S. *Lee's Sharpshooters; Or, the Forefront of Battle*. Little Rock, Ark.: Tunnah and Pittard, 1899.

Dupuy, R. Ernest. "Pass in Review." Army Combat Journal, October 5, 1954.

————. "The Wheel of Time." In *Army Combat Forces Journal 5*, October 1954.

Elegant, Robert. "Looking back at Vietnam: How to Lose a War." *Encounter*, August 1981.

Estill, Bob. "Westmoreland Defends Servicemen in Vietnam." *The State Journal and Register*, February 1, 1970.

Eutzy, Bill. "Chanting Anti-War Protesters Greet Westmoreland." *Lincoln Journal*, September 26, 1970.

"Excerpts from Senate Exchange on Vietnam War Speech." *New York Times*, April 26, 1967.

Facts on File. Volume 5: South Vietnam-U.S.-Communist Confrontation in Southeast Asia. New York: Facts on File, Inc., 1971.

————. Facts on File. New York: Facts on File, Inc., 1968.

Fenton, Charles. "Viet Protesters Greet Westy." *Columbus Journal*, June 7, 1969.

Fitchey, Clayton. "Westmoreland's Vietnam Strategy." *Washington Star*, February 9, 1968.

Fleming, Thomas J. *West Point*. New York: William Morrow, 1969.

Fleming, Willie. *The History of Pacolet*. Publisher unknown, 1983.

Flint, Jerry M. "Veterans Assess Atrocity Blame." *New York Times*, February 7, 1971.

Fulghum, David, and Terrance Maitland. *The Vietnam Experience: South Vietnam on Trial.* Boston: Boston Publishing Co., 1984.

Furgurson, Ernest B. *Westmoreland.* Boston: Little, Brown, 1968.

———. "Westmoreland the Candidate." *The State,* March 27, 1974.

Gabriel, Richard A., and Paul L. Savage. *Crisis in Command.* New York: Hill and Wang, 1978.

Galloway, Joseph L. "Fatal Victory," *U.S. News and World Report,* October 29, 1990.

———. "Vietnam Story." *U.S. News and World Report,* October 29, 1990.

Garland, Albert, and Howard M. Smyth. *Sicily and the Surrender of Italy. U.S. Army in World War II.* Washington, D.C.: U.S. Government Printing Office, 1965.

Gauvreau, Emile, and Lester Cohen. *Billy Mitchell.* New York: E. P. Dutton, 1942.

Geelhoed, E. Bruce. *Charles E. Wilson and Controversy at the Pentagon, 1953 to 1957.* Detroit: Wayne State University Press, 1979.

Gelb, Leslie, and Richard K. Betts. *The Irony of Vietnam: The System Worked.* Washington: Brookings Institution, 1979.

"The General v. 'The System.' " *Time,* February 15, 1971.

"General Westmoreland Shift Held Unlikely." *Washington Post,* February 6, 1968.

Gibson, Hugh E. "Funding Stuff Westmoreland's Problem." *Charleston News and Courier,* March 30, 1974.

———. "Fowler Pins 'Opportunist' Label on Westmoreland." *The State,* March 13, 1974.

"Graham Denounces Dissenters." *Christian Century,* May 17, 1967.

Gravel, Mike, ed. *The Pentagon Papers,* 5 vols. Boston: Beacon Press, 1971.

"Gravity Register." *Newsview,* June 13, 1936.

Griffith, H. P. "Gone to Rest," eulogy, no date.

———. "A Pair of Noble Brothers." eulogy, September 9, 1907.

Gwin, S. Lawrence, Jr. "Ambush at Albany." *Vietnam Magazine,* October 1990.

Hackworth, David. *About Face.* New York: Simon and Schuster, 1989.

Hagan, Kenneth J., and William R. Roberts, eds., *Against All Enemies.* New York: Greenwood Press, 1986.

Halberstam, David. *The Best and the Brightest.* New York: Random House, 1972.

Haldeman, H. R. *End of Power.* New York: *New York Times,* 1978.

Homer, John, "PCS Student Protest Irks Rotary Clubbers." *Oregon Journal*, January 29, 1969.

Hammond, William M. *Public Affairs: The Military and the Media*. Washington, D.C.: U.S. Army Center for Military History/U.S. Government Printing Office, 1988.

Hamrick, Tom. "An Old Soldier Speaks Out." *Charleston Magazine*, March 1977.

Hannah, Norman. "Vietnam: Now We Know." *National Review*, June 11, 1976.

Harrison, Gordon A. *Cross-Channel Attack. U.S. Army in World War II*. Washington, D.C.: U.S. Government Printing Office, 1951.

Hechler, Ken. *The Bridge at Remagen*. New York: Ballantine Books, 1957.

Heinl, Robert D. "The Collapse of the Armed Forces." *Armed Forces Journal*, June 7, 1971.

Hemingway, Albert, and Charles N. Pallesen. "The McNamara Line." *Vietnam Magazine*, October 1990.

Henry, William A., III. "It Was the Best I Could Get." *Time*, March 4, 1985.

Herbers, John. "Morton Accuses Johnson of Stifling Debate." *New York Times*, April 28, 1967.

Hermes, Walter G. *Truce Tent and Fighting Front. U.S. Army in the Korean War*. Washington, D.C.: Office of the Chief of Military History/U.S. Government Printing Office, 1966.

Herring, George C. *America's Longest War*. New York: Knopf, 1979.

Hersey, John. "The President." *New York Times*, April 20, 1975.

Hersh, Seymour M. *The Price of Power*. New York: Summit Books, 1983.

Hewell, Eleanor M. *The Pedens of America*. Columbia, S.C.: State Printing Company, 1961.

History and Museum Division. *The Marines in Vietnam, 1954–1974*, 2nd ed. Washington, D.C.: History and Museums Division, Headquarters, U.S. Marine Corps/U.S. Government Printing Office, 1985.

Howe, George F. *Northwest Africa: Seizing the Initiative in the West*. Washington, D.C.: Center of Military History/U.S. Government Printing Office, 1957.

"How the Battle for Khe Sanh Was Won." *Time*, April 19, 1968.

Hubbell, John G., and David Reed. "The Man for the Job in Vietnam." *Reader's Digest*, January 1966.

Hughes, Emmet John. "The General Inspects the Vietnam War." *Washington Post*, April 17, 1966.

Janowitz, Morris. *The Professional Soldier.* New York: The Free Press, 1971.

Jones, James. *From Here to Eternity.* New York: Scribner's, 1951.

Just, Ward. *Military Men.* New York: Knopf, 1970.

———. "A Soldier Reports." *New York Times Book Review,* February 1, 1976.

"Jury Picked in CBS Case." *New Haven Register,* October 10, 1984.

Kaiser, Robert G. "Westmoreland Denounces TV Program Accusing Him of Cover-up." *Washington Post,* January 27, 1982.

Karnow, Stanley. *Vietnam: A History.* New York: Viking Press, 1983.

Kearns, Doris. *Lyndon Johnson and the American Dream.* New York: Harper and Row, 1976.

Kenworth, E. W. "McGovern Leads Democratic Attack in Senate on Escalation." *New York Times,* April 26, 1967.

Kihss, Peter. "Westmoreland Decries Protest." *New York Times,* April 25, 1967.

Kinnard, Douglas. *The War Managers.* Hanover, N.H.: University of Vermont/University Press of New England, 1977.

Kinnard, Harry W. O. "Victory in the Ia Drang: The Triumph of a Concept." *Army,* September 1967.

Kissinger, Henry. "The Vietnam Negotiations." *Foreign Affairs,* January 1969.

Knoll, Edwin, and Judith Nies McFadden. *War Crimes and the American Conscience.* New York: Holt, 1970.

Kowet, Don. *A Matter of Honor.* New York: Macmillan, 1985.

Krepinevich, Andrew F., Jr. *The Army and Vietnam.* Baltimore: Johns Hopkins, 1986.

Krulak, Victor. *First to Fight.* Annapolis, Md.: U.S. Naval Institute Press, 1984.

Landrum, J.B.O. *Colonial and Revolutionary History of Upper South Carolina.* Greenville, S.C.: Shannon & Co., 1897.

———. *History of Spartanburg County.* Atlanta: The Franklin Printing and Publishing Co., 1900.

Lanford, Helen W. *Miss Minnie.* Copyright 1970 by Mr. and Mrs. B. M. Lanford.

Liming, Robert G. "The State, Special Report." *The State,* January 3, 1973.

———. "Westmoreland—An Efficiency Report." *The State,* May 26, 1974.

Loory, Stuart H. *Defeated: Inside America's Military Machine.* New York: Random House, 1973.

Lynn, Robert A., and Albert Hemingway. "Ordeal on the Van Tuong." *Vietnam Magazine,* October 1989.

MacArthur, John R. "A Plaintiff Ill-Used." *New York Times,* February 24, 1985.

MacDonald, Charles B. "Communist Thrust—the Tet Offensive of 1968." In *The Vietnam War,* ed. Ray Bonds. New York: Crown, 1979.

———. *The Siegfried Line Campaign. U.S. Army in World War II.* Washington, D.C.: U.S. Government Printing Office, 1963.

McGinnis, Joe. "At Ease with Yesterday's Warriors." *Chicago Tribune,* July 25, 1976.

———. "Winning Hearts and Minds in South Carolina." *Harper's,* April 1974.

Maitland, Terrence, and Peter McInerney. *The Vietnam Experience: A Contagion of War.* Boston: Boston Publishing Co., 1983.

Maitland, Terrence, and Stephen Weiss. *The Vietnam Experience: Raising the Stakes.* Boston: Boston Publishing Co., 1982.

Manchester, William. *American Caesar.* Boston: Little, Brown, 1978.

Mapes, Olin. "Westmoreland Ancestry." Unpublished paper, no date.

Marshall, H. L. "The Class That Did Not Graduate." *The Shako,* 1966.

Marshall, S.L.A. *Bringing Up the Rear.* San Rafael, Calif.: Presidio Press, 1979.

———. "Communiqué from a Half-Forgotten Front." *Los Angeles Times,* February 22, 1976.

Miroff, Bruce. *Pragmatic Illusions.* New York: David McKay, 1976.

Mitgang, Herbert. "Notes from a Foreign Land." *New York Times,* February 18, 1976.

Mittelman, Joseph B. *Eight Stars to Victory.* Columbus, Ga.: F.J. Heer Printing Co., 1948.

Momyer, William. *Air Power in three Wars.* Washington, D.C.: U.S. Government Printing Office, 1978.

Monts, Vivian. "Mother Recalls General's Boyhood." *The State,* January 9, 1966.

Moore, John W. "The Riot at the Citadel." Unpublished account, no date.

"More of the Same Won't Do." *Newsweek,* March 18, 1968.

Morris, Roger. *Uncertain Greatness: Henry Kissinger and American Foreign Policy.* New York: Harper and Row, 1977.

Mulligan, Hugh G. "A Day with Westmoreland Keeps You Running." *The State,* April 23, 1967.

Mylander, Maureen. *The Generals.* New York: Dial Press, 1974.

Nalty, Bernard C. *Air Power and the Fight for Khe Sanh.* Washington, D.C.: Office of Air Force History, 1973.

Nelson, Daniel J. *A History of U.S. Military Forces in Germany.* Boulder, Colo.: Westview Press, 1987.

Nicely, Margaret. "Westmoreland Lauds Negroes' War work." *Columbia Record,* April 27, 1967.

Oberdorfer, Don. *Tet!* Garden City, N.Y.: Doubleday, 1971.

O'Gara, Sheila. "Westmoreland Talk Blocked by Pickets." *New Haven Register Journal Courier,* April 5, 1972.

Olson, James S. *Dictionary of the Vietnam War.* New York: Peter Bedrick Books, 1987.

Page, Levon. "Westmoreland Named to Head Trade Effort." *The State,* October 3, 1972.

———. "Westy: Prestige Not Consideration." *The State,* January 21, 1974.

Palmer, David Richard. *Summons of the Trumpet.* San Raphael, Calif.: Presidio Press, 1978.

Palmer, Laura. "The General at Ease." *Military History Quarterly,* August 1988.

Paterson, Thomas G., ed. *Kennedy's Quest for Victory.* New York: Oxford University Press, 1989.

Peace, Roger. "Vet, 93, Recalls War Days; Hiked Home from Virginia." *Spartanburg Daily Herald,* April 5, 1940.

Pearson, Willard. *The War in the Northern Provinces, 1966–68.* Washington, D.C.: Department of the Army, 1975.

Peers, William R. *The My Lai Inquiry.* New York: Norton, 1979.

Perret, Geoffrey. *A Country Made by War.* New York: Random House, 1989.

Perry, Mark. *Four Stars.* Boston: Houghton Mifflin, 1989.

Pike, Douglas, and Benjamin Ward. "Losing and Winning Abroad, Korea and Vietnam as Successes." *Current,* May 1988.

———. *PAVN: People's Army of Vietnam.* Novato, Calif.: Presidio Press, 1986.

Pisor, Robert. *The End of the Line.* New York: Norton, 1982.

Potwin, Marjorie. *Cotton Mill People of the Piedmont.* New York: AMS Press, 1968.

Powe, Lucas A., Jr., *The Fourth Estate.* Berkeley, Calif.: University of California Press, 1991.

Powell, Jody. "The 'Truth' Other Media Should Have Looked For." *Washington Post,* January 24, 1985.

Prados, John, and Roy S. Stubble. *Valley of Decision.* New York: Houghton Mifflin, 1991.

President's Foreign Intelligence Advisory Board. "Intelligence Warning of the Tet Offensive in South Vietnam." Washington, D.C., April 1968.

Prossner, Leverne. "U.S. Presence in Vietnam Is Defended." *Charleston News and Courier,* April 27, 1967.

Purcell, Jean. "Schlesinger Scores General." *New York Times,* March 22, 1968.

Randolph, Eleanor. "General, CBS End Their War, Still Quarrel." *Washington Post,* February 18, 1985.

Reedy, Thomas A. "A Typical Day in the Life of General Westmoreland." *Washington Star,* February 13, 1966.

Schlesinger, Arthur. *One Thousand Days.* New York: Houghton Mifflin, 1965.

———. *Robert Kennedy and His Times.* Boston: Houghton Mifflin, 1978.

Schneir, Walter, ed. *Westmoreland v. CBS.* New York: Clearwater Publishing Co., 1987.

Shandler, Herbert. *The Unmaking of the President.* Princeton, N.J.: Princeton University Press, 1977.

Shaplen, Robert. *The Road from War.* New York: Harper and Row, 1970.

Sharp, U.S.G., and William C. Westmoreland. *Report on the War in Vietnam.* Washington, D.C.: U.S. Government Printing Office, 1968.

———. *Strategy for Defeat.* Novato, Calif.: Presidio Press, 1978.

Sheehan, Neil. *A Bright Shining Lie.* New York: Random House, 1988.

———. "Conversations with Americans," *New York Times Book Review,* December 27, 1970.

———. "Five Officers Say They Seek Formal War Crimes Inquiry." *New York Times,* January 13, 1971.

———. "Taylor Says by Yamashita Ruling Westmoreland May Be Guilty." *New York Times,* January 9, 1971.

———, and Hedrick Smith, E.W. Kenworthy, and Fox Butterfield. *The Pentagon Papers.* New York: New York Times/Bantam Book, 1971.

Shirley, J. Clyde. *Uncommon Victory.* Columbia, S.C.: R.L. Bryan Co., 1978.

Shulminson, Jack, and Major Charles M. Johnson. *U.S. Marines in Vietnam, 1965; The Landing and the Buildup.* Washington, D.C.: History and Museum Division, Headquarters, U.S. Marine Corps, 1978.

————. *U.S. Marines in Vietnam, 1966; An Expanding War*. Washington, D.C.: History and Museums Division, Headquarters, U.S. Marine Corps, 1982.

Simmons, Edwin H. *Marines: The Illustrated History of the War*. New York: Bantam Books, 1987.

Singlaub, John K. *Hazardous Duty*. New York: Summit Books, 1991.

Sorensen, Theodore. *Kennedy*. New York: Harper and Row, 1965.

Sorley, Lewis. *Thunderbolt*. New York: Simon and Schuster, 1993.

The Sphinx. 1900 edition of the Citadel's yearbook.

Stanton, Shelby. *Green Berets at War*. Novato, Calif.: Presidio Press, 1985.

Stockdale, James Bond. "The Total Vietnam War Story Needs to Be Told." *Vital Speeches*, June 15, 1989.

Stoessinger, John. *Crusaders and Pragmatists*. New York: W. W. Norton, 1979.

"The Study on Military Professionalism." Carlisle Barracks: U.S. Army War College, 30 June 1970.

Summers, Harry. "Bitter Triumph at the Ia Drang." *American Heritage*, February/March 1984.

————. *On Strategy*. Novato, Calif.: Presidio Press, 1982.

Sylvan, Bill. "Personal Diary." Military History Institute.

Taylor, John M. *General Maxwell Taylor*. Garden City, N.Y.: Doubleday, 1989.

Taylor, Maxwell. *Swords and Plowshares*. New York: Norton, 1972.

————. *The Uncertain Trumpet*. New York: Harper and Row, 1960.

Telfer, Gary L., Lane Rogers, and V. Keith Fleming, Jr. *U.S. Marines in Vietnam, 1967; Fighting the North Vietnamese*. Washington, D.C.: History and Museums Division, Headquarters, U.S. Marine Corps, 1984.

"Text of Westmoreland's Address at A.P. Meeting." *New York Times*, April 24, 1967.

"There Was Nothing Else to Do." *Charleston News and Courier*, April 9, 1898.

Thies, Wallace J. *When Governments Collide*. Berkeley, Calif.: University of California Press, 1980.

Thompson, W. Scott, and Donaldson D. Frizzel. *The Lessons of Vietnam*. New York: Crane, Russak, & Co., 1977.

Tompkins, D. *Company K. Fourteenth South Carolina Volunteers, Charlotte* (N.C.) *Observer*, 1897.

Triplett, William. "Ia Drang." *VVA Veteran*, October 1986.

Truscott, Lucian K., Jr. *The Twilight of the U.S. Cavalry: Life in the Old Army, 1917–1942*. Lawrence, Kans.: University of Kansas Press, 1989.

Tuchman, Barbara W. *Stillwell and the American Experience in China*. New York: Macmillan, 1970.

"U.S. General Charged over My Lai." *London Times*, March 18, 1970.

Vandiver, Frank E. *Black Jack*, Vol. II. College Station, Tex.: Texas A&M University Press, 1977.

Van Tien Dung. *Great Spring Victory*. Foreign Broadcast Information Service Daily Report: Asia and Pacific, Vol. 4, No. 110, Supplement 38, June 7, 1976.

Vogel, Victor. *Soldiers of the Old Army*. College Station, Tex.: Texas A&M Press, 1990.

Walton, George. *The Tarnished Shield*. New York: Dodd, Mead, 1973.

"The War." *Time*, May 5, 1967.

Weigley, Russell. "The Interwar Army, 1919–1941." In *Against All Odds*, ed. Kenneth J. Hagan and William K. Roberts. New York: Greenwood, 1986.

"Westmoreland Addresses Court of Honor at UC." *UC News Record*, February 23, 1971.

"Westmoreland Criticized for 'Deluding' Congress." *New York Times*, February 12, 1969.

"Westmoreland Funeral Is Today." *Spartanburg Daily Herald*, January 18, 1941.

"Westmoreland Goes to World Scout Jamboree." *Spartanburg Herald*, May 30, 1929.

Westmoreland, James White. "History of the Westmoreland Families in South Carolina." Unpublished paper written in 1932.

"Westmoreland Says He Harbors No Guilt." *New York Times*, April 3, 1970.

"Westmoreland Visits Family in Columbia." *Charleston Evening Post*, April 25, 1967.

Westmoreland, William. *A Soldier Reports*. Garden City, N.Y.: Doubleday, 1976.

"Westy Glad He Didn't Win." *The State*, March 14, 1977.

"Westy: U.S. Looks 'Like Damned Fool.' " *The State*. May 7, 1975.

Wharton, Donald. "Invasion Repelled." *Vietnam Magazine*, December 1989.

Willenson, Kim. *The Bad War*. New York: New American Library, 1987.

Wilkenson, Burke. "Westmoreland Shares Sound of the Drum He Marched To." *Wall Street Journal*, February 24, 1976.

Wilson, George C. "The End of the Tunnel," *Washington Post*, January 25, 1976.

Wilson, James. *Landing Zone*. Durham, N.C.: Duke University Press, 1990.

Wirtz, James J. *The Tet Offensive*. Ithaca, N.Y.: Cornell University Press, 1991.

"War, Intelligence and Truth." *New York Times*, January 24, 1982.

Woodward, William E. *Meet General Grant*. New York: Liveright, 1946.

Woods, Rob. "Westy: Call Me Childs." *The State*, June 16, 1974.

Yoder, Edwin M. "History by Lawsuit." *Washington Post*, January 24, 1985.

Zirin, James D. "Westmoreland's Capitulation—A Trial Lawyer's Perspective." *New York Law Journal*, February 26, 1985.

INDEX

and search-and-destroy strategy, 169
Tet Offensive and, 280
Westmoreland's manpower requests
  and, 142, 209
and Westmoreland's statistics on
  enemy-initiated actions, 190
and Westmoreland's suit against
  CBS, 417–418, 428
Shaw, Sydney, 420–421, 428, 432, 434
Shea, Leonard, 45
Sheehan, Neil, 169, 311, 341–342
Shelton, Linda, 398–399, 413
Sherman, William Tecumseh, 33, 38
Short, Walter C., 298
Sicily, Allied invasion of, 52, 61–64, 76
Sidle, Winant, 201, 328
Siegfried Line, 67
Sigma I war game, 156
Simmons, Edwin H., 301
Singlaub, John, 94
60th Infantry Regiment, U.S., 73–74
Smith, Augustus W., Jr., 18
Smith, Hedrick, 311
Smith, Howard K., 294–295
Smothers, Curtis, 349
Society of Professional Journalists, 404
Soldier Reports, A (Westmoreland),
  380–384, 391
Song Be, 140, 238, 240
Sorensen, Ted, 101
Sorley, Lewis, 292
South Carolina, 372–380
  General Assembly of, 196–197, 244
  Revolutionary War in, 10–11
  State Development Board of, 374–
    375
  Westmoreland's government job in,
    372, 374–376
  Westmoreland's gubernatorial cam-
    paign in, 376–380
  Westmorelands in, 8–12, 14–20, 22–
    25
  Westmoreland's popularity in, 375–
    376
  and Westmoreland's suit against
    CBS, 402–403
Soviet Union:
  threat posed by, 88–89, 91–92
  Vietnam War and, 130, 217, 221,
    329, 367
Strok Dong, battle of, 166
Stack, Tom, 437–439
Stanton, Shelby, 187
Starlite, Operation, 148
Stathakis, Peter J., 375

Stegmann, Rudolf, 65
Stennis, John, 200
Stoessinger, John, 126
Stofer, Barbara, 328
Stratton, Samuel S., 337–338
Stringer, Howard, 390
Suber, Gay, 377
Sullivan, William, 120
Summerall, Charles Pelot, 31
Summers, Harry G., Jr., 153, 220,
  363–364
Sung, Kim Il, 303
Sussman, Michael, 433
Sylvan, Billy, 71
Szep, Paul, 434

Tang, Truong Nhu, 293
Taylor, Maxwell D., 79, 91–95, 117–
  121, 144–146, 148–149, 220
  and allegations of Westmoreland's
    falsifying enemy strength, 399
  and assassination of Diem, 100
  and bombing of North Vietnam, 124–
    126, 128–130
  Da Nang and, 132–133
  defense policy and, 89–92
  enclave strategy of, 137–140, 142,
    144, 149
  and invasion of Europe, 64
  and invasion of Sicily, 62–63
  Kennedy's relationship with, 91–
    92
  Khe Sanh and, 273–274, 276, 324–
    325
  Korean War and, 81, 83
  Ky-Thieu government and, 135
  reserve call-up and, 309
  and Revolt of the Colonels, 90–91
  Tet Offensive and, 294
  Vietnam ambassadorship of, 119–
    121, 133, 145
  Vietnam policy and, 100, 102–104,
    113–115, 120–121, 124–129
  Westmoreland's manpower requests
    and, 132–133, 137–139, 142,
    145, 155, 305
  Westmoreland's relationship with,
    63–64, 87, 90–91, 93–95, 97–
    98, 120, 130, 133, 145
  Westmoreland's USMACV command
    and, 117–119
Taylor, Telford, 340–342, 417
Tay Ninh Province, attack in, 123
Tet Offensive, 5, 246–247, 259–264,
  272, 275, 278–299, 302–307,